Management of Freshwater Biodiversity

Crayfish as Bioindicators

Integrating research into freshwater biodiversity and the role of keystone species, this fascinating book presents freshwater crayfish as representatives of human-exacerbated threats to biodiversity and conservation. It uses examples from these and other large decapod invertebrates to explore how communities function and are controlled, alongside the implications of human demands and conflicts over limited resources, notably the severe impacts on biodiversity.

The discussion is structured around three key topics – the present situation of crayfish in world freshwater ecosystems, the application of science to conservation management, and knowledge transfer for successful crayfish management. It outlines the historic exploitation of crayfish, addressing the problems caused by invasive alien forms and explaining the importance of correct identification when dealing with conservation issues. Offering a global perspective on freshwater systems, the book ultimately highlights how the conservation of such large and long-lived species will help protect ecosystem quality in the future.

Julian Reynolds is Emeritus Fellow of Trinity College Dublin, Ireland and former Head of its Department of Zoology. He is a freshwater ecologist with particular interests in crustaceans and in small, extreme or ephemeral habitats (fens, bog pools and turloughs). He has extensive experience consulting on environmental pollution and crayfish management.

Catherine Souty-Grosset is a research scientist and head of the Populations and Communities group of the 'Ecology, Evolution, Symbiosis' Laboratory at the University of Poitiers, France. Her research focuses on both population biology of isopods and conservation biology of indigenous European crayfish, including the control of invasive crayfish species.

Management of Freshwater Biodiversity

Crayfish as Bioindicators

JULIAN REYNOLDS

Trinity College Dublin, Ireland

CATHERINE SOUTY-GROSSET

University of Poitiers, France

With contributions from Keith Crandall, Alastair Richardson and Francesca Gherardi

CAMBRIDGE
UNIVERSITY PRESS

CAMBRIDGE UNIVERSITY PRESS
Cambridge, New York, Melbourne, Madrid, Cape Town,
Singapore, São Paulo, Delhi, Tokyo, Mexico City

Cambridge University Press
The Edinburgh Building, Cambridge CB2 8RU, UK

Published in the United States of America by Cambridge University Press, New York

www.cambridge.org
Information on this title: www.cambridge.org/9780521514002

First published 2012

Printed in the United Kingdom at the University Press, Cambridge

A catalogue record for this publication is available from the British Library

Library of Congress Cataloguing in Publication data
Reynolds, J. D. (Julian D.)
  Management of freshwater biodiversity : crayfish as bioindicators / Julian Reynolds,
  Catherine Souty-Grosset ; with contributions from Keith Crandall, Alastair Richardson,
  and Francesca Gherardi.
    p.   cm.
  Includes bibliographical references and index.
  ISBN 978-0-521-51400-2 (hardback)
  1. Crayfish–Ecology.   2. Freshwater biodiversity conservation.   3. Indicators (Biology)
  I. Souty-Grosset, Catherine.   II. Title.
  QL444.M33R49 2012
  595.3′84–dc23
  2011031541

ISBN 978-0-521-51400-2 Hardback

Contents

          The colour plates will be found between pages 146 and 147

Preface

This book is not just about freshwater crayfish – it is about the plight of biodiversity in a world of growing demands on resources. Freshwater crayfish are widespread, often dominant, members of many aquatic habitats, and excite interest because of their size and edible nature, but freshwater resources are under heavy and increasing pressure.

Over the past 50 years, humans have altered ecosystems more rapidly and extensively than in any comparable period of time in human history. Introductions of non-native species have been made with the intention of improving our quality of life, but largely in ignorance of ecological consequences. Development of genetically engineered organisms adds a new dimension to the question of introduced species and the threat to biodiversity. The increasing globalization of the economy, with extensive travel and shipment of goods between continents, brings increasing numbers of unintended new invasions.

In addition, the projected rate of global climate change in the coming century is more rapid than any such change that has occurred in the last 10 000 years. According to the International Union for Conservation of Nature (IUCN), some species will be more vulnerable because of climate change, and even where they are able to tolerate changes, they will have to deal with a variety of new competitors, predators, diseases, and alien species for which they have no natural defences.

Many countries have put in place a monitoring framework to assess the extent of freshwater deterioration and to suggest remedial action. In Europe this has been stimulated by the Water Framework Directive (WFD). Internationally, studies are most complete on larger lakes and rivers, but are still poor for other ponds and lakes, which may also have high biodiversity. Thus there are still gaps in our understanding of biodiversity in fresh waters, with uneven geographical and taxonomic coverage. We also need a better understanding of the link between species diversity and ecosystem functioning, particularly the roles of natural communities in recycling nutrients and providing other services.

There is now increasing interest in freshwater decapods, particularly crayfish, both from producing and consuming countries and from those who simply value these large invertebrates for their own sake. Various management, conservation and protective measures have been put in place. All these initiatives are good for preventing further declines in native stocks, but the spread of alien crayfish species remains the paramount problem in most areas, and the extent of their impacts is only now being realized.

There are already several books about freshwater crayfish, from the magisterial volume on a global scale edited by Holdich (2002a) and the one concentrating on the European situation (Gherardi & Holdich, 1999), to several books on a regional scale (e.g. Füreder, 2009). To these we must add the four edited volumes on *European Crayfish* (Vigneux, 1997, 2000, 2001; Souty-Grosset & Grandjean, 2002) and four further volumes from the European network CRAYNET ('European crayfish as keystone species – linking science, management and economics with sustainable environmental quality') in 2003, 2004, 2005 and 2006, all published as Special Issues of *Bulletin Français de la Pêche et de la Pisciculture* (now *Knowledge and Management of Aquatic Ecosystems*), culminating in the *Atlas of Crayfish in Europe* (ed. Souty-Grosset *et al.*, 2006).

The present book does not seek to cover the same ground; instead it uses examples from freshwater decapods, notably the many species of crayfish, to focus on current ideas about how freshwater communities function and are controlled, and on the implications of human demands and conflicts over the limited freshwater resource, including severe impacts on freshwater biodiversity. The failure of the International Year of Biodiversity (2010) to meet its targets proved that we need to try harder to understand and rectify biodiversity loss, and to project the conservation message – and we hope that this book will help towards this important aim.

Acknowledgements

A great many people have helped us in the preparation of this book, and we would like to thank them all. In particular, we owe a great debt of gratitude to the three people who co-wrote several chapters with us; Keith Crandall (Brigham Young University, Utah, USA) for crayfish phylogeny (Chapter 1), Alastair Richardson (University of Tasmania, Australia) for the ecological material (Chapters 2 and 3), and Francesca Gherardi (University of Firenze, Italy) for Chapters 4 and 8, dealing with alien crayfish and their impacts.

We thank Sylvia Reynolds for critically reading the entire manuscript, Leo Füreder and David Holdich for their advice in many areas, and Bernard Grosset for much practical assistance throughout. Many others responded generously to requests for information on specific topics, particularly about distributions or regarding legislation relating to crayfish in their countries, and we would like to thank the following:

Introduction (Freshwater biodiversity and the role of crayfish): inputs from Peter Bliss (Germany), Nadia Richman (UK) and Russell Poole (Ireland).

Chapter 1 (Decapod phylogeny and crayfish distribution): main contributor Keith Crandall (USA); inputs from Robert DiStefano (USA), Premek Hamr (Canada), Julia Jones (Madagascar), James Furse and John J.S. Bunn (Australia), Mauricio Almerão and Paulo Alves (Brazil), Thomas Stucki (Switzerland) and Tadashi Kawai (Japan).

Chapter 2 (Crayfish biology): main contributor Alastair Richardson (Australia); inputs from Alexandre O. de Almeida and Mauricio Almerão (Brazil).

Chapter 3 (Ecology): main contributor Alastair Richardson (Australia); inputs from Stephanie Peay (UK), Andréanne Demers (Canada) and Milton Matthews (Ireland).

Chapter 4 (Threats to survival): main contributor Francesca Gherardi (Italy); inputs from Tadashi Kawai (Japan), Javier Diéguez-Uribeondo (Spain) and Garth Foster (UK).

Chapter 5 (Exploitation): inputs from Javier Diéguez-Uribeondo and A.P. Gaudé (Spain), John Lucey and Ciaran O'Keeffe (Ireland), Japo Jussila (Finland), Lennart Edsman (Sweden), Jose Carral (Spain), Tomas Policar (Czech Republic) and Jay Huner (USA).

Chapter 6 (Managing biodiversity): input from Leopold Füreder (Austria).

Chapter 7 (Monitoring ICS): input from Alastair Richardson (Australia).

Chapter 8 (Control and management of aliens): main contributor Francesca Gherardi (Italy); with inputs from Trond Taugbøl (Norway), Javier Diéguez-Uribeondo (Spain) and Stephanie Peay (UK).

Chapter 9 (Reintroductions): inputs from Lennart Edsman and Jenny Zimmermann (Sweden), Eric R. Larson and Robert DiStefano (USA) and Kenneth Whelan (Ireland).

Chapter 10 (Legislation and education): inputs from Roger Cammaerts (Belgium), Leopold Füreder (Austria), Bram Koese (Netherlands), Ralf Schulz and Holger Schulz (Germany), David Holdich (UK), Pavel Kozák (Czech Republic), Nadia Richman (UK), Manfred Pöckl (Austria), Lennart Edsman (Sweden), Antonio Garza de Yta, Chris Taylor and Robert DiStefano (USA), Erich H. Rudolph (Chile), Mauricio Almerão (Brazil), Nisikawa Usio (Japan), Patrick Haffner (France), Julia Bywater (UK), Premek Hamr (Canada), Alastair Richardson (Australia), Miklos Puky (Hungary) and Fernando Alonso (Spain).

Chapter 11 (Synthesis of management strategies): inputs from Nadia Richman and John Foster (UK) and Lennart Edsman (Sweden).

We thank James W. Fetzner Jr (Pittsburgh, USA) for valued help with mapping and other items, and the following for allowing us to use their pictures: Chris Lukhaup (Germany), Tomas Policar (Czech Republic), Wray R. McClain (USA), Robert P. Romaire (USA) and Elinor Wiltshire (UK).

Finally, we want to acknowledge the support and interest of very many colleagues (including our European research colleagues from the European network CRAYNET 'European crayfish as keystone species – linking science, management and economics with sustainable environmental quality' and other projects) and students throughout our careers, who contributed greatly to our knowledge and understanding of freshwater systems and crustacean biology and so enhanced this book.

Introduction: Biodiversity in freshwater systems, and the key roles played by crayfish

More than 20 years ago, the term 'biodiversity' was coined, deriving its name from the concept of 'biological diversity', at a time when the ecological importance of the various components in communities was becoming generally evident (Wilson, 1988). Several authors, such as Gaston & Spicer (1998), have since emphasized the multiplicity and range of meanings associated with the term. Biodiversity, the variety of life and its processes, includes not just the panoply of living organisms (species diversity) and the genetic differences between them, but the communities and ecosystems, including landscapes (habitat diversity), in which they occur, and the ecological and evolutionary processes through which they function, change and adapt. The pool of living diversity is dynamic, with changes in genetic variation, structure and function. However, the biodiversity of an area cannot be simply represented as the number of taxa present; thus, introducing a species to a community does not necessarily increase its biodiversity, and may in fact deplete it. Nonetheless, as we shall see, focusing on individual species is a valuable means of monitoring and protecting biodiversity.

Freshwater communities: structure and function

Fresh waters are an essential component of landscapes in most of the world, and are often critically linked to the welfare of terrestrial and marine ecosystems. Freshwater availability or flow is the dominant variable in freshwater ecosystem functioning, so it is vitally important to maintain and secure water supply to streams and wetlands. Indicators of functioning, or their measurable surrogates, have been suggested for some freshwater ecosystems: these include litter breakdown rates, benthic metabolism, and functional feeding groups. Among the most important members of any community are 'keystone species', defined as those that control communities by reason of their size, abundance, feeding patterns or dominance in interactions, and which thereby affect ecosystem functioning. Numerous fish and crayfish species are excellent examples of keystone species in freshwater communities, and the latter are the main focus of this book.

Many ideas current in freshwater ecological thinking have been derived from terrestrial systems. However, participation at multiple trophic levels is common in freshwater organisms, more so than in terrestrial ones. Freshwater systems are often complex, interacting mosaics with important boundary properties, and there is a contemporary focus on habitat spatial heterogeneity and patch connectivity. Functional linkages include exchanges of materials and nutrients between water and landscape, and trophic fluxes, with overall a net transfer of aquatic-derived energy into riparian food webs. How might the diversity of aquatic and terrestrial communities affect the amount and direction of transfer? Aquatic insects may spend only short periods of time in the terrestrial phase, but life history events such as mating and egg-laying may be restricted to the terrestrial 'airscape', leading to system nutrient losses or gains. Some crustaceans – crayfish, crabs and amphipods – are amphibious or will forage on land. However, exclusively aquatic (homotopic) crustaceans or molluscs must chiefly be transferred through the aquatic food web, or to terrestrial systems through amphibious predators such as newts, otters and herons. Detailed measurement is lacking for such land–aquatic interactions.

Freshwater species richness

At the global level, species richness increases strongly towards the equator. This is true for freshwater fishes in general, although certain well-studied groups such as freshwater crayfish are much less diverse in the tropics than in temperate regions. The overall number of freshwater species (species richness, a major component of biodiversity) is low compared with either marine or terrestrial systems. However, species richness in fresh waters is enormous in relation to the tiny global extent of surface water habitats (0.3% by area). Among the diverse and species-rich animal groups in freshwater habitats are fishes, decapod crustaceans, bivalve molluscs, dragonflies and water beetles; for example, over 40% of the 28 000 known fish species are freshwater forms and, given the distribution of water on the Earth's surface, this is equivalent to one fish species for every 15 km^3 of fresh waters, compared to one for every 100 000 km^3 of seawater. This richness is often associated with the linear or fragmented, 'island' nature of catchments and waterbodies, with high border to area ratios. While much catchment diversity often resides outside the main channel, in marshes and ditches, individual small lakes and ponds may also develop high biodiversity. Ecological corridors are vital to link such sites both in floodplains and upper catchments, and such ecosystem connectivity enhances biodiversity. Diversity 'hot-spots' for several freshwater groups, including crayfish, occur where there has been a mixture of isolation and climatic stability; particularly rich areas are in the south-eastern USA, Southeast Asia and western Australia.

However, biological diversity is not just concerned with species richness – a list of species observed over several visits and with standardized methodology; it also involves species evenness, dominance, rarity and indicator status, and the recognition of naturally fluctuating species. Susceptibility to invasions of alien species is also important, including the question of whether high biodiversity affords better protection against invasion by an alien species, or whether species richness is irrelevant in this context. Other knowledge gaps include demonstrating a fundamental relationship between biodiversity and the maintenance of important ecosystem processes in fresh

Table 1. Comparison of bird and amphibian species in the 2008 IUCN Red List, assessed for climate-change susceptibility. Categories: RED: threatened and climate-change-susceptible; ORANGE: threatened but not climate-change-susceptible; YELLOW: not threatened but climate-change-susceptible; and GREEN: not threatened and not climate-change-susceptible (after Foden *et al.*, 2009).

		Birds			Amphibians		
Threatened?		Yes	No	Totals	Yes	No	Totals
Climate-change-susceptible?	Yes	978 (10%) [RED]	2452 (25%) [YELLOW]	35%	1488 (24%) [RED]	1729 (28%) [YELLOW]	52%
	No	248 (2%) [ORANGE]	6172 (67%) [GREEN]	65%	503 (8%) [ORANGE]	2502 (40%) [GREEN]	48%
	Total	12%	88%	9856	32%	68%	6222

waters, and determining whether there are any intrinsic relationships between freshwater biodiversity and the health of humans and wild organisms.

Among freshwater organisms, some crustaceans are characteristic of wetlands and marshes, while others are restricted to rivers, streams and small lakes. Freshwater crayfish living in shallow water are important components of each of these systems, and may be indicators of water quality or habitat. Crayfish ecology is discussed in Chapters 3 and 6. The impacts of invasive non-indigenous crayfish species (NICS) on indigenous crayfish species (ICS) and their habitats are introduced below, further examined in Chapter 4, and their control through management in order to protect ICS discussed in Chapter 8.

Drivers of freshwater biodiversity

By their nature, freshwater systems are often fragmented (patchy) or linear in structure. Freshwater ecosystems and communities occupy a wide variety of waterbody types both above and below ground, large and small, temporary and permanent, stationary and flowing, intermittent and continuous. They range from springs and headwaters to rivers, lakes and wetlands; they also include transitional systems such as marshes, karstic temporary ponds or turloughs, and estuaries that link freshwater systems with terrestrial and marine environments. Small systems are intrinsically vulnerable to disturbance and stresses. In addition, freshwater systems necessarily lie at the lowest points in the landscape, where they collect and integrate multiple inputs and influences from the entire catchment. These systems are also often highly dynamic, with rapid changes in both space and time in their biological, hydrological, chemical and physical properties. All these features contribute to their vulnerability to disturbance. Table 1 illustrates this, contrasting data for birds and for amphibians (representing wetlands) derived from the 2008 IUCN Red List (after Foden *et al.*, 2009).

In most countries today there are marked gradients in species distribution and richness. Such gradients often indicate a decline in diversity. The situation is most evident in fresh waters, but there may be many different causes. Dudgeon *et al.* (2006) explored the special features of freshwater habitats and the communities they support that make them especially vulnerable to human activities. They documented threats to global freshwater biodiversity under five headings: overexploitation, water pollution, flow modification, destruction or degradation of habitat, and invasion by exotic species. Their combined and interacting influences have resulted in population declines and range reductions of freshwater biodiversity worldwide (Dudgeon *et al.*, 2006). The drivers of biodiversity in fresh waters are both natural and anthropogenic and, while the former are fairly well understood, there is immediate need for the latter to be quantified and communicated to decision makers if effective management is envisaged.

Across the globe, natural drivers have produced gradients in species distribution and richness. Natural drivers include evolutionary pressures and hot-spots, affecting biodiversity through habitat restriction, isolation, change over time associated with mountain building, infilling of lakes, and climatic change. However, observed gradients in biodiversity in fresh waters are frequently due to human intervention, where a gradient may indicate a loss of biodiversity. Climate change and anthropogenic drivers are discussed below.

Climate change

Climate change, by encouraging migrations and leading to extinctions and new evolutionary situations, can influence biodiversity in fresh waters. A drying climate – or its anthropogenic analogue, increased abstraction – will reduce both perennial flows and seasonal supplies to off-river habitats and could depress gene flow. Species characteristics which increase susceptibility to climate change impacts have been described by Foden *et al.* (2009) and are summarized in Table 2. This is further developed with reference to crayfish in Chapter 6.

Recent research has addressed the reductions in freshwater biodiversity under plausible scenarios of climate change and water consumption. About half of the world's investigated rivers may experience reduced water availability due to both global warming and the withdrawal of water for human needs. By 2070, in these drying rivers, the loss of local fish species is suggested to range from less than 4% to more than 22%, with up to 75% loss predicted in the most severely affected rivers.

In 1990, for the first time, a team of international experts responded to this problem, using two climate change scenarios from the Intergovernmental Panel on Climate Change (IPCC) to cover a large range of possible outcomes. They combined these scenarios with a global hydrological model to estimate possible losses in river water availability due to climate change and trends in water consumption. Linking the obtained results to known relationships between fish species and changes in water availability, they investigated future trends in riverine fish richness for over 300 of the world's river basins (Tockner & Stanford, 2002; Xenopoulos *et al.* (2005).

In both scenarios, their calculations showed that, by 2070, water availability would decrease up to 80% in more than 130 investigated rivers with available fish data. About half of these rivers were predicted to lose more than 10% of their fish species when

Table 2. Species characteristics which make them susceptible to climate change (after Foden *et al.*, 2009). Species phenotypic plasticity and genetic diversity will determine the likelihood of adaptation.

A. Specialized habitat or microhabitat requirements, especially where opportunities for dispersal are restricted.

B. Narrow environmental tolerances or thresholds, occurring at any stage in the life cycle, likely to be exceeded due to climate change (e.g. temperature, pH, rainfall, flooding).

C. Dependence on specific environmental triggers likely to be disrupted by climate change; e.g., for migration, onset of breeding, egg-laying, hibernation or emergence; climate change may lead to uncoupling of such activities from necessary resources.

D. Dependence on interspecific interactions that are likely to be disrupted by climate change (e.g. interactions with prey, competitors or symbionts).

E. Poor or restricted ability to disperse or colonize a more suitable range as the 'bioclimatic envelope' shifts polewards or to higher altitudes.

climate change and water consumption impacts were considered, and a maximum of 75% of local fish losses was calculated for several rivers. The effect of climate change was by far the most important factor contributing to freshwater fish loss under the scenarios, with anthropogenic water withdrawal contributing much less to species loss (an additional 0–5%). However, in regions where substantial irrigation has occurred in the past and is expected to increase (e.g. southern Asia and the Middle East), water consumption is particularly important for fish biodiversity decline. These forecasts are probably underestimates of fish losses, because many other important drivers (e.g. introduced species, reductions in channel–floodplain connectivity) were not included in the calculations.

Most catchments thus have multiple stressors. In a well-studied example, the North American Great Lakes ecosystem, containing some 18% of the planet's supply of fresh water, lies in a basin that is home to 25% of Canadian agricultural production and 7% of that of the USA, and that provides drinking water for 40 million people, as well as 210 million m³ daily for municipal, agricultural and industrial use. The implications of climate change (lower lake levels, extreme swings) on major catchments and large lake ecosystems are profound. Point source pollution regulation has dramatically improved water quality since the 1980s (helped by the filtering activities of invasive zebra mussels).

Anthropogenic drivers

Twenty-five years ago, economists estimated that organic material equivalent to about 40% of the present net primary production (photosynthesis) in terrestrial ecosystems is being co-opted by human beings each year, and concluded that the diversion and destruction of these terrestrial resources clearly contributes to human-caused extinctions of species and to genetically distinct populations (Vitousek *et al.*, 1986). Today, the situation is even more extreme, because of rising populations and increasing consumer demands. We now know that the Earth's hydrological regimes are being fundamentally altered to meet the needs of rapidly expanding societies (Vörösmarty *et al.*, 2004), despite our incomplete knowledge and understanding of either the diverse species present or the larger-scale consequences.

Many human activities lead to increases in highly managed, species-poor freshwater habitats (e.g. canalized rivers, drainage ditches, eutrophic ponds, and reservoirs) and promote deterioration and fragmentation, increasing the patchiness of natural and often species-rich habitats such as river floodplains. However, some species can have their movement restricted by something as apparently trivial as a road though otherwise pristine habitat (Trombulak & Frissell, 2000). Short-term monitoring measurements, e.g. of dissolved oxygen, bacteria or water chemistry, may not indicate longer-term impacts, but biological water quality, measured universally by the range of macroinvertebrates present, inevitably falls. Residual small and isolated populations tend to be more sensitive than larger ones to both demographic and environmental factors such as the spread of disease or changes in food supply. To other human impacts are added the effects of many introduced species, and we need a better understanding of how these affect biodiversity.

Rivers, lakes, wetlands and connecting groundwaters are the lowest points, the 'sinks' into which landscapes drain, and freshwater ecosystems are greatly influenced by human modifications of such landscapes as well as to the waters (Baron *et al.*, 2003). However, knowledge about the resistance of our biosphere to human-caused changes in biodiversity is still lacking. Monitoring the impact of anthropogenic drivers of biodiversity is often unfeasibly complex. We need a better understanding of the effects of introduced species. More knowledge is also needed about natural ecological processes in the face of increasing use of artificial pesticides, fertilizers, and pharmaceutical and veterinary drugs. Pollution and pesticides can lower habitat quality, reduce species breeding and survival rates, and even cause local species extinction.

Three global anthropogenic drivers of aquatic ecosystems are nutrient enrichment from agriculture and/or organic pollution, physical disturbance (alterations in hydrology), and toxicity (trace metals, pesticides, acidification). Up to half of all nutrient loads in large lowland rivers originate from agriculture, because of inadequate controls – much more than from industry. Agriculture has a major impact on fresh waters through land-use change and increasing production intensity, and through its impacts on stream boundaries. Crops, both edible and for biomass, may require increased water abstraction at sensitive times, while intensive dairying and fish farming may cause other environmental stresses through the concentration of silage and other feedstuffs, and disposal of wastes. There is a continuing need for applied agro-ecological research into the roles of natural communities in recycling nutrients and animal wastes. Other impacts come from soil erosion and the destruction of floodplains. Further research is also needed on the detrimental impacts of land drainage in environmentally fragile landscapes. The Organisation for Economic Cooperation and Development (OECD) in 2001 recommended taking a holistic view of agricultural impacts on biodiversity rather than focusing exclusively on threatened species and habitats (see www.oecd.org) – but this approach has obvious limitations and dangers.

Invasive species

Biological invasions are considered to be one of the main issues in conservation biology worldwide (e.g. Mack *et al.*, 2000; Sala *et al.*, 2000), and their success is acknowledged to be supported by climate change processes. The global homogenization of biota is under way, through the worldwide introduction and establishment of non-indigenous (exotic) species (Lodge *et al.*, 1998). This is particularly true for freshwater ecosystems because of their greater vulnerability than terrestrial biomes to biological invasions (Rodrigues *et al.*, 2006). The rate of colonization has gone up many times in recent years but it is not clear whether these aliens, including crayfish, may find impacted systems easier to infiltrate than intact ones.

Major differences between the impacts of invasive alien species (biological pollution) and of chemical pollution include the fact that ecosystem recovery from chemical pollution typically begins once the stress has been removed, and engineering solutions can often be highly successful. However, invasive species, like extinctions, are typically permanent and their impacts are irreversible. Prevention is thus the preferred option, although this is very difficult.

Invasive alien species are now a global problem, reflecting world trade, and exacerbated by free trade conventions and agreements. Well-known aquatic examples from the last 100 years are the impacts of North American waterweeds (*Elodea* spp.) in Europe, the invasion of lampreys into the North American Great Lakes, the recent spread of Ponto-Caspian amphipods from the Black Sea across Europe, and the worldwide movements of zebra mussels (*Dreissena* spp.). There are at least 162 exotic invasive species that have modified Great Lakes habitats, reduced native biodiversity and altered food webs; they include zebra and quagga mussels, sea lamprey, predatory zooplankton and amphipods. Human translocations of crayfish, an important focus of this book, have been a major problem for over a century.

Invasive species ecology has obvious synergies with anthropogenic threats to aquatic biodiversity and ecosystem functioning. While some positive impacts of species introductions have been mooted (e.g. American crayfish in East Africa and in lagoons of southern Spain, providing a novel food source for declining native predators such as otters and field-feeding storks and cranes), human-mediated invasives usually result in community change; by being dominant competitors or effective predators, they can drive many native species to low densities or extinction, thus reducing biodiversity (Reid & Miller, 1989; Holdich & Pöckl, 2007).

Key principles in the management of aquatic invasive species include detailed risk assessments of known potential invaders to prevent future problems, assessment of the potential impacts of climate change, and studies on distribution, ecology and genetics. Management involves controlling external sources, taking early action on new outbreaks, providing long-term funding, involving stakeholders and invoking their responsibilities, while developing good monitoring systems. In the context of this book, we are primarily concerned about direct invasions by exotic crayfish, and their food, predators and parasites. The invasion of a number of North American crayfish species into other continents is discussed in Chapter 4, and attempts at their management and control in Chapter 8.

Threats to biodiversity and ecosystem functioning

Worldwide, it is clear that – on average – freshwater biodiversity is more threatened than terrestrial biodiversity (Allan & Flecker, 1993; Williams *et al.*, 1993; McAllister *et al.*, 1997; Ricciardi & Rasmussen, 1999). Freshwater organisms are severely threatened globally because bodies of fresh water are at the heart of social and economic sustainability, and demands for water are steadily expanding. However, freshwater biodiversity underpins many processes, e.g. self-purification and protein production, and is important for sustaining goods and services for humans. From those species considered in the 1996 IUCN Red List, Abell *et al.* (2002) concluded that some 20% of reptiles, 25% of amphibians, and 34% of fishes (mostly freshwater species) were threatened (crayfish had not then been evaluated). At a regional scale, the projected mean future extinction rate for North American freshwater fauna was considered to be about five times greater than that for terrestrial fauna. There is no evidence that this number is too high for Europe, with its millennia of land development and wetland alteration.

The implications of this worldwide decline in freshwater biodiversity are potentially serious. Baron *et al.* (2003) noted that human societies extract increasingly vast quantities of water to supply their various requirements, while overlooking the equally vital benefits of water remaining instream that provide economically valuable commodities and ecosystem services. These include flood control, fish and other foods, and marketable goods. Intact systems are more likely to sustain production of these goods and services in the face of future environmental disruptions such as climate change.

Ecological services are defined as the conditions and processes through which natural ecosystems, and the species that make them up, sustain human life. They are costly or impossible to replace when systems are degraded. One salient example is flooding, a natural function of every river. Small streams and wetlands normally absorb significant amounts of rainwater, run-off and snowmelt before flooding occurs. They also slow flow rates through irregular beds, trap sediment, and their natural cleansing ability improves water quality and stores nutrients, recycling them instream and sustaining downstream ecosystems. Stream modifications by humans or by landscape changes include more incised channels and a smoother bed that harbours fewer organisms and allows water to run faster, eroding more strongly and flooding earlier. Even if the headwaters maintain the biological diversity that underpins ecosystem services, this biodiversity is easily threatened because of the small size of these habitats.

Decline in freshwater habitat quality and species populations is evident worldwide, and at present poor water quality is increasingly the norm. Many human activities promote the fragmentation of natural and often species-rich habitats (e.g. river floodplains) and the increase in highly managed habitats that may be species-poor. Many freshwater ecosystems are now disconnected from each other, rendering each system more vulnerable to degradation. Small, isolated populations tend to be more sensitive than larger ones, because of demographic factors, random events affecting the survival and reproduction of individuals, or environmental factors such as the spread of pollutants or disease, or a reduction in food supply. Other external pressures such as overexploitation or introduced predators may also threaten the survival of small or isolated populations of a species.

In summary, the chief threats to freshwater biodiversity include biological invasions, organic and chemical pollution, and climate change, arguably all caused by increasing demands from burgeoning human populations. Environmental changes occurring at the global scale, such as nitrogen deposition, warming, and shifts in precipitation and run-off patterns, are superimposed upon all of these threat categories (Dudgeon *et al.*, 2006). The biodiversity loss in fresh waters is even greater and more rapid than in terrestrial systems. Freshwater ecosystem functioning is a critical component of almost all human activities, but is also strongly impacted by these activities as they modify water flow or use the systems for waste disposal.

Key indicators of biodiversity

Monitoring for management

Biodiversity in fresh waters is thus subject to multiple stressors and drivers. Because of its complexity, a good way to understand and manage biodiversity is by identifying and studying representative key functional species. These indicators of biodiversity can be the focus of local-scale monitoring for biodiversity drivers (Kapoor-Vijay & Usher, 1993). Other types of indicator, e.g. impact indicators for such parameters as the degree of habitat fragmentation, are also important in systems management for conservation. Indicators of habitat quality are different from those that measure biodiversity, but there has been insufficient research into selecting those indicators whose abundance and distribution reflect general trends in biodiversity, disagreement as to which bioindicators are best (Andersen, 1999), and indeed, whether there are useful synergies between bioindicators of species richness or biodiversity, and other social or economic indicators.

Conventions on biological diversity and landscape strategy all stress the importance of biodiversity indicators, but there have been few attempts to develop technical lists of biodiversity indicators (e.g. Reid *et al.*, 1993). However, this has since been streamlined by the International Convention on Biological Diversity (CBD) in 2002 (at COP-VI), which supported the initiative to stop biodiversity loss by 2010 – the International Year of Biodiversity. Some observers feel that indicators should be confined to ecologically important components of a community, but others believe that threatened species can also provide useful indicators for monitoring biodiversity. Biodiversity indicators should be suitable at different scales. Stakeholders and policy makers demand regional and national-scale data, but ecological meaning is first studied and understood at a local scale. If losses in biodiversity are detected, experimentation is needed to see how these trends can be reduced or reversed through sustainable development management. Finally,

Table 3. Life history traits of surrogate, umbrella and flagship species (after Caro & O'Doherty, 1999).

Indicator type	Body size	Generation time	Sensitive to human disturbance
Health indicator	Small	Short	Yes
Population indicator	Irrelevant	Short	Yes
Biodiversity indicator	Irrelevant	Irrelevant	Irrelevant
Umbrella species	Large	Long	Not necessarily
Flagship species	Large	Long	Yes

can threatened indicator species be adequately monitored without risk to their status? All these problems are relevant to freshwater indicator organisms such as crayfish.

The choice of indicators may also have consequences for conservation policy. If indicators focus on habitat quality rather than biodiversity, then legislation will do likewise. Legislation rewards management practices that result in good-quality habitats, including the presence or absence of specific indicator species. This also affects the type and timing of monitoring. If monitoring for habitat quality, indicators can be selected to assess the capacity of ecological corridors. In some cases, a suite of rare species, as developed in the IUCN Red Lists, might provide a better estimate of habitat quality than common species. However, some indicator lists may be politically developed, rather than being a useful monitoring tool. Table 3 (after Caro & O'Doherty, 1999) summarizes the ecological attributes of indicator species.

The 2008 update of the IUCN Red List includes conservation assessments for nearly 45 000 species (Vié *et al.*, 2008), dominated by an evaluation of all the described mammals and birds. However, these represent a tiny fraction of the world's known biodiversity (fewer than 300 000 out of 1.8 million species) and many other groups are hardly considered. Again, it appears that freshwater groups are most at risk, including 37% of fishes and 30% of amphibians. There is also recent information for dragonflies and damselflies (Odonata) and for freshwater crabs (16% threatened). For such threatened invertebrates, the species most at risk are those with very restricted ranges. There are centres of threat in Southeast Asia, in Sri Lanka, and in Colombia and Mexico, related directly or indirectly to human population pressures. The level of threat for freshwater crayfish has recently been assessed (Nadia Richman, personal communication, 2010) and the IUCN approval process is now under way (see Chapter 12). However, although human pressures on freshwater resources remain the root cause, the threat pattern for crayfish, as elaborated in this book, appears different from that for other evaluated invertebrates.

Species indicators for communities and habitats

Heritage or flagship species are iconic species used in conservation to attract the attention of the public; the panda and polar bear are prime examples. In freshwater habitats, iconic species need to be of interest to human observers and also ecologically significant organisms that can carry the flag for other aquatic denizens. However, not all have equal weight as bioindicators of water or habitat quality, or are at present exploited as such.

There are a number of well-known examples of aquatic heritage and flagship species, including birds such as storks, kingfishers and waterfowl. Mammals with a flagship role include otters; after serious declines from hunting for their pelts, and indirectly from pesticides, these are currently recovering through management in many parts of the world (e.g. Prigioni *et al.*, 2007). Flagship reptiles and amphibians include certain turtles, crocodiles, frogs and salamanders. Amphibians with a large variety of lifestyles, especially in warm temperate and tropical regions, are often used as indicators. Fish species, both widespread and relict, may be monitored as flagship species – the Nile perch in Africa or the Amazon's arapaima are good examples. Cool-temperate salmonids are widely used as bioindicators of good water quality in the northern hemisphere (Roussel *et al.*, 1999), for instance in the determination of European 'salmonid waters' status, and – like crayfish – their cultural or heritage value is enhanced by their economic desirability. The disappearance of 'heritage' salmonid and coregonid fishes from eutrophic waters is keenly felt, particularly by anglers, but how this happens is still not perfectly understood (Russell Poole, personal communication, 2010).

Invertebrates are widely featured as indicator species of water quality, although, apart from a few dragonflies, water beetles and large freshwater mussels, few have been proposed as heritage species. Freshwater crayfish are prime candidates for indicator status among invertebrates because of their large size, longevity and reliance on aquatic systems throughout their life, and some also become flagship species because of these qualities, almost unique among invertebrates, and also their accessibility and tolerance of handling. Being edible, many crayfish also have a strong cultural and economic value. The value of crayfish as functional key indicator species, useful for conservation purposes, is developed further in Chapter 3. We later expand on the usefulness of crayfish in freshwater management in Part II (Chapters 6–9).

There are other types of biodiversity indicator. In conservation biology, one or a number of species are often used as surrogate species to portray conservation problems (Caro & O'Doherty, 1999). They may be selected and used in various ways, e.g. to indicate the extent of various types of anthropogenic impact (health indicator species), to track population changes of other species (population indicator species), to identify areas of high biodiversity (biodiversity indicator species), to act as 'umbrellas' for the requirements of sympatric species (umbrella species), or to attract the attention of the public (flagship species). Surrogate species may be assigned either as representative indicators for a suite of less accessible species in the aquatic community, or as typifying environmental features (water quality, habitat quality). In one example, Wenger (2008) used a widespread darter (*Percina*) species as a surrogate for a related but rarer fish species, to predict its response to stressors in the environment. Habitat quality is widely used for conservation site selection (Southwood, 1977), but is often ill-defined. Burrowing vertebrates and invertebrates, including crayfish, function as biodiversity drivers and might be excellent indicators for habitat quality assessment (Meadows & Meadows, 1991).

Table 4. Measurement attributes of surrogate species (after Caro & O'Doherty, 1999).

Type of surrogate	Represents other species	Biology well known	Accessible breeding, easily sampled site
Health indicator	Not necessarily	Yes	Probably
Population indicator	Yes	Yes	Possibly
Biodiversity indicator (guild)	Yes	Yes	No
Umbrella species	Yes	Yes	No
Flagship species	Usually	Not necessarily	No

In complex systems, appropriate surrogate species are needed to answer many relevant questions. Table 4 shows the measurement attributes of surrogate species (after Caro & O'Doherty, 1999). Freshwater crayfish fulfil most of the prerequisites stated above, and can provide useful surrogates for the communities in a range of biotopes. In many countries, conservation programmes have been initiated, utilizing the paradigm of surrogate species to consolidate and improve the situation of the native freshwater crayfish and to further public awareness.

The best universal indicator of biodiversity should be based on species richness and habitat complexity. Our understanding of invertebrates, fungi and microorganisms is still poor for many habitats, so we rely on focal or umbrella indicator species whose presence and relatively high numbers indicate high quality or high biodiversity of a site. The indicator should be capable of being used to compare habitats across a broad region, even a continent, but also to value different habitats. The protection afforded to an umbrella species also confers protection on a wide range of coexisting species in the same habitat, which may otherwise be poorly known and difficult to protect. However, we need to use both species-based and habitat-based approaches in biodiversity conservation. Species responses to habitat management by humans are not linear and deterministic, nor are they independent of the current species mix, state of the environment, or preceding historic events. In this respect, freshwater crayfish are ideal umbrella species; they may be used to specify the size and type of habitat to be protected, rather than just its location. However, Caro & O'Doherty (1999) warn that no studies have demonstrated the effectiveness of umbrella species in protecting other species.

Particular threats to freshwater biodiversity

A number of conclusions relevant to this book are apparent from the analysis of IUCN Red List data by Darwall *et al.* (2009).

• Freshwater biodiversity is extremely threatened, and probably more so than in other ecosystems. This appears to be largely a result of the high degree of connectivity within freshwater systems, such that threats such as pollution and invasive alien species can – and do – spread more rapidly and easily than in terrestrial ecosystems; and the rapidly increasing human use and development of fresh waters, to the detriment of the freshwater-dependent species sharing the resource.

- The level of threat to freshwater biodiversity is extremely high, yet public awareness of this situation remains woefully low (Darwall *et al.*, 2009). Freshwater species, largely unseen by the general public, are not often considered charismatic and their value to people is not well recognized. Conservation of freshwater species needs to be treated on a par with other more visible and charismatic species groups, such as birds and large mammals. This means that freshwater species need to be treated as being worthy of conservation in their own right, not simply as exploitable resources for human consumption. This book is an attempt to do this for freshwater crayfish.
- The high value of freshwater species to people's livelihoods is not fully appreciated, and is rarely considered when decisions are taken on the potential development of wetland resources for alternative uses. For example, a single freshwater bivalve may filter litres of water a day, maintaining the quality of water in river systems.
- Most existing protected areas are not designed to protect freshwater species. Protected areas for freshwater species need to employ the principles of catchment protection.
- Increased support is needed for *in situ* conservation initiatives. This includes support for conservation education programmes aimed at increasing local awareness and developing practical solutions (see Chapter 10).
- Many freshwater species remain 'Data Deficient' (DD) in IUCN terminology, in particular due to lack of taxonomic expertise and the absence of information on species distributions. This situation appears to be getting worse; for example, an estimated 35% of the world's dragonflies that have been assessed are classified as Data Deficient, and there is currently little opportunity to obtain better information on these species. The same situation is true for freshwater crayfish, recently evaluated, and for water beetles, a group not yet tackled by the IUCN.

The key roles played by crayfish

Because crayfish are often important components of the communities that develop in and characterize different freshwater habitats, we have tried to indicate the various roles they play. This book concentrates on crayfish as indicators for biodiversity, on their threats and losses, and on management to restore them. Part I (Chapters 1–5) outlines the present state of knowledge of freshwater crayfish lineage. Their diversity – with hot-spots in south-eastern North America and south-western Australia – is examined in Chapter 1. Other relevant aspects of their biology are teased out in Chapter 2 and, as crayfish are both components of – and often controllers of – freshwater biodiversity, relevant areas of their ecology are discussed in Chapter 3. Some freshwater crayfish are characteristic of marshy or impermanent wetlands, while others are restricted to rivers, streams and small lakes, particularly those stable enough to accommodate their often long life spans and large size. However, where species are translocated, they may take on new roles in the alien environment (Chapter 4). The exploitation of crayfish, both native stocks and translocated aliens, is discussed in Chapter 5.

Part II (Chapters 6–9) introduces management options for crayfish and their habitats, and Part III (Chapters 10–12) looks at conservation, assisted by legislation and education. The book ends with an assessment of the future for freshwater crayfish and possible options to maintain biological diversity as well as human values.

Part I

The present situation of crayfish in world freshwater ecosystems

1 Crayfish in the decapod lineage, their natural distribution and their threatened status

(with Keith Crandall)

1.1 The place of crayfish among decapod crustaceans

Arthropods are undeniably the most successful animal group on Earth. When only terrestrial arthropods are considered, insects, spiders, mites and myriapods are almost ubiquitous, but in fact crustaceans are the most widely distributed group among the arthropods. They are at home in the sea, in fresh waters and in moist areas on land (notably crabs, isopod woodlice and some amphipods), limited only by their requirements for gas exchange, excretion and osmoregulation. No other group of animals or plants on the planet exhibits the range of morphological diversity seen among the extant Crustacea (Martin & Davis, 2001), of which there are an estimated 50 000–67 000 species. The group also includes the largest of the mobile invertebrates – some crabs, clawed and spiny lobsters, and freshwater crayfish may reach several kilograms in weight, and some stone crabs have leg spans of more than two metres. At the other end of the spectrum are parasitic barnacles and copepods and tiny parthenogenic cladocerans less than one millimetre in total length. Such diversity also has its parallel in the range of habitats exploited, making the Crustacea ideal for any study of biodiversity.

Class Malacostraca

Class Malacostraca, the largest and most advanced group (containing more than 23 000 species), includes almost all large and edible crustaceans, also the smaller but very abundant Peracarida (Isopoda, Amphipoda) and mysids as well as stomatopods (mantis shrimps) and euphausiids (krill).

Crustacean, and apparently malacostracan, fossils date back to the Cambrian, 540 million years ago (MYA), possibly an ancient paraphyletic assemblage emerging from the Precambrian/early Cambrian radiation, and perhaps spinning off related groups such as the trilobites and the cheliceriform eurypterids.

Within the Crustacea, the Malacostraca are apparently monophyletic, with a standard segmented body plan of 20 segments. There is a head and thorax (6 + 8 segments), often fused into a cephalothorax (sometimes covered dorsally with a carapace) and a six-segmented abdomen. This *bauplan* is sometimes called the 'caridoid facies' (Calman, 1904, 1909), and is shown well by shrimps, lobsters and crayfish. The main modifications are to the abdomen, either elongated for swimming (although the heavier forms chiefly crawl) or reduced for more agile walking, as in the crabs.

Table 1.1. Classification overview (selected taxa) and numbers of species of Decapoda (after De Grave *et al.*, 2009).

Taxon	Extant species	Extinct species	Total species
Order Decapoda Latreille 1802	14 656	2 979	17 635
2 Suborders, including			
SubO Pleocyemata Burkenroad 1963	14 116	2 862	16 978
10 Infraorders, including			
InfraO Caridea Dana 1852	3 268	57	3 325
InfraO Brachyura Linnaeus 1758 (crabs)	6 835	1 781	8 616
InfraO Astacidea Latreille 1802	658	124	782
5 Superfamilies, including			
Supfam Nephropoidea Dana 1852 (clawed lobsters)	53	106	159
Supfam Astacoidea Latreille 1802 (N crayfish)	428	9	437
Supfam Parastacoidea Huxley 1879 (S crayfish)	165	3	168

Order Decapoda

Decapods – including crabs, shrimps, lobsters and crayfish – are among the most species-rich groups of malacostracan crustaceans, with about 17 635 described species in some 233 families (De Grave *et al.*, 2009). They are economically of great importance, clawed lobsters alone bringing in billions of dollars each year to world fisheries, while crabs comprise 20% of all marine crustaceans caught or farmed; 1.5 million tons being caught and eaten annually. On a lesser scale, freshwater crayfish have stimulated much interest and economic activity, and are the subject of many books and thousands of research articles. *Procambarus clarkii* (the red swamp crayfish or Louisiana crayfish) is Louisiana's 'state crustacean', while *Astacus astacus* (the noble crayfish) underpins large-scale summer festivities in Scandinavian countries.

Decapods (meaning 'ten legs') have eight pairs of thoracic limbs, but only five pairs are ambulatory (pereiopods), giving the group its name. The head has paired compound eyes, usually stalked, two pairs of sensory antennae, and three pairs of mouthparts. A further three pairs of thoracic limbs (the maxillipeds) are incorporated into the mouthparts. The six abdominal segments each have a pair of swimming limbs, the last pair (the uropods) expanded into a tail fan in crawling and swimming forms. However, in the crabs or Brachyura, the last abdominal segment and telson are reduced.

An overview of decapod classification, concentrating on groups with freshwater members, is given in Table 1.1.

1.2   Decapod origins and evolution

Phylogenetic relationships among decapods remain unsettled at many taxonomic levels. One problem is the length of time, estimated at 437 million years, since their origins (Porter *et al.*, 2005), coupled with the group's morphological diversity and complexity. The difficulty of inferring phylogenetic relationships across such a broad timescale and species-rich group has resulted in many conflicting ideas of how decapods evolved.

A recent survey of the evolution of decapods, including both crayfish and crabs, has been provided by Bracken *et al.* (2009), based upon a set of genetic molecular markers (three nuclear and one mitochondrial genes) that have long been applied to decapod crustaceans. The Decapod Tree of Life project (see http://decapoda.nhm.org/) is an ongoing compilation of these genetic findings (Bracken *et al.*, 2009).

Early classifications divided the decapods into swimming (Natantia) and walking (Reptantia) lineages (Boas, 1880). However, later findings based largely on gill morphology and reproductive biology proposed a new classification for the Decapoda and rendered the Natantia paraphyletic (Burkenroad, 1963, 1981). Today, there is little debate over the monophyly of the major decapod suborders Dendrobranchiata and Pleocyemata. Likewise, the basal position of the informal 'natant' groups (Caridea, Penaeoidea and Stenopodidea) is generally accepted, and many studies have also supported as a monophyletic clade the traditional 'reptant' groups Brachyura, Anomura, Thalassinidea, Astacidea and Palinura (Crandall *et al.*, 2000a, 2006b; Schram, 2001; Ahyong & O'Meally, 2004; Porter *et al.*, 2005; Tsang *et al.*, 2008; Robles *et al.*, 2009; Toon *et al.*, 2009). However, the internal relationships are not yet fixed or agreed by all researchers. The lack of agreement may stem from a shortage of phylogenetically informative molecular markers (Bracken *et al.*, 2009).

Morphological and molecular studies of the Decapoda have given rise to conflicting hypotheses (see Figure 1.1) (Burkenroad, 1963, 1981; Abele & Felgenhauer, 1986; Christoffersen, 1988; Scholtz & Richter, 1995; Dixon *et al.*, 2003; Ahyong & O'Meally, 2004; Porter *et al.*, 2005; Tsang *et al.*, 2008; Toon *et al.*, 2009). The group is morphologically diverse, leading to difficulties in coming up with a suite of phylogenetically informative characters applicable across the whole group. Different and conflicting phylogenies have been suggested by different combinations of molecular markers, both mitochondrial and nuclear (Bracken *et al.*, 2009).

The most recent catalogue of crustaceans (De Grave *et al.*, 2009), up to the end of July 2009, includes a large literature of over 400 papers on decapod fossils. Cenozoic decapods closely resembling modern extant species are easily classified, but many ancient decapods are morphologically quite dissimilar from known modern decapods, and therefore pose special problems in classification (De Grave *et al.*, 2009). One such fossil, a petrified specimen found in the Jurassic limestone of Solnhofen, Bavaria, from the same place where *Archaeopteryx* was found, is dated to 135–145 MYA and has been assigned to one of the species *Aeger tippularius* (Schlothuis 1822), *A. bronni* (Oppel 1862) or *A. antumpsos speciosus* (Münster 1839). A specimen of this fossil is used as the insignia of the current President of the International Association of Astacology (IAA).

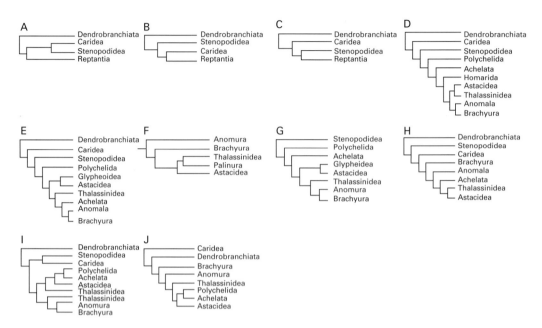

Figure 1.1. Hypotheses of higher-level decapod relationships based on morphological similarity (A–C); morphological cladistic analyses (D, E); and molecular phylogenetic analyses (F–J). (A) Burkenroad 1963, 1981; (B) Christoffersen 1988; (C) Abele & Felgenhauer 1986; (D) Scholtz & Richter 1995; (E) Dixon *et al*. 2003; (F) Crandall *et al*. 2000a, 2006b; (G) Ahyong & O'Meally 2004; (H) Porter *et al*. 2005; (I) Tsang *et al*. 2008; (J) Toon *et al*. 2009.

Bracken *et al*. (2009) present a molecular phylogeny for the order Decapoda, combining nuclear and mitochondrial sequences to investigate the relationships among nine pleocyemate infraorders. With the origin of the Decapoda estimated at 437 MYA, two mitochondrial genes (12S, 16S) and three nuclear genes (18S, 28S, H3) were selected as markers known to resolve phylogenetic relationships across a broad time scale (Spears *et al*., 1992, 1994; Giribet *et al*., 1996; Schubart *et al*., 2000; Stillman & Reeb, 2001; Tudge & Cunningham, 2002; Porter *et al*., 2005; Mantelatto *et al*., 2006, 2007; Robles *et al*., 2007, Bracken *et al*., 2009).

Within the Astacidea, the higher-level relationships are well understood (Crandall *et al*., 2000a, 2000b; Rode & Babcock, 2003). The astacideans form three strongly supported subclades: two of crayfish corresponding to the superfamilies Astacoidea and Parastacoidea, and the marine Nephropoidea (clawed lobsters). The Nephropoidea are thus close relatives of the freshwater crayfish (Crandall *et al*., 2000a, 2000b).

The more than 650 species of freshwater crayfish are monophyletic and composed of two superfamilies, Astacoidea and Parastacoidea, with centres of diversification within the northern and southern hemisphere, respectively. At the family level, findings suggest polyphyly within several families (Bracken *et al*., 2009). The northern-hemisphere crayfish families Cambaridae and Astacidae form the sister clade to the southern-hemisphere crayfish family Parastacidae. As shown by Braband *et al*. (2006), the family Cambaridae is paraphyletic, with the East Asian genus *Cambaroides* being a sister group to the family Astacidae (Figure 1.2).

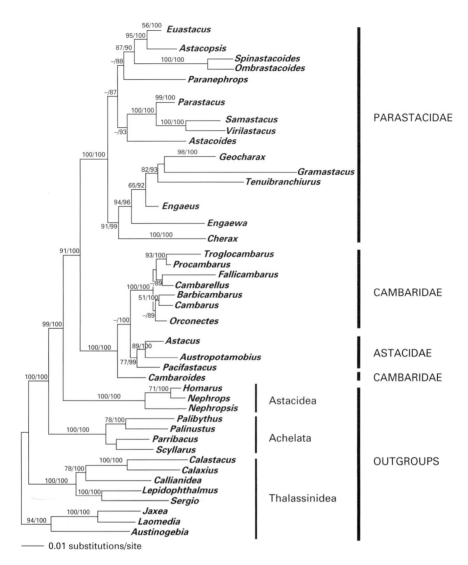

Figure 1.2.   Phylogenetic relationships among the freshwater crayfish with their closely related decapod outgroups estimated using a Bayesian approach with maximum likelihood bootstrap values/ posterior probabilities shown on well-supported nodes. The phylogeny was estimated using five genes (12S, 16S, 18S, 28S, H3) with a total of 3694 base pairs of nucleotide sequence data. (Phylogeny courtesy of Heather Bracken-Grissom and Keith Crandall.)

1.3   Crayfish radiation

Crayfish are ancient creatures. Permian trace fossils from nearly 300 million years ago have been found in Antarctica, although these have been disputed. Evidence suggests that, despite the marine origin of the Astacida, the common ancestor of crayfish already lived in fresh water, and dating of molecular divergences indicates that the timing of range fragmentation is consistent with the break-up of Pangea into a northern and a southern continent, Laurasia and Gondwana, respectively, during the Jurassic period

(200–140 MYA) (Scholtz, 2002). After this break-up, the differences are believed to have evolved between the northern-hemisphere Astacoidea and the southern-hemisphere Parastacoidea. The monophyly of the two crayfish superfamilies Parastacoidea (southern hemisphere) and Astacoidea (northern hemisphere) (Crandall *et al.*, 2000a, 2000b) is consistent with the break-up of Pangea. Subsequently the Parastacidae have radiated in Australasia, New Zealand, South America and Madagascar. Molecular genetics studies support the monophyly of the continental subgroups (Sinclair *et al.*, 2004), but the relationships between them remain unresolved. However, Riek (1972) suggested that *Astacoides* of Madagascar appears closer to *Astacopsis* of Tasmania than to South American species.

The fossil record appears older for Astacoidea than for Parastacoidea (Scholtz, 2002) and is supported by fossil evidence of burrows. The centre of origin of the Astacoidea is suggested to be eastern Asia, from where the cambarid ancestors could have migrated via the Bering land bridge to eastern North America, while most of the Astacidae dispersed westwards into Europe, the oldest known *Austropotamobius* appearing there in the early Cretaceous (Souty-Grosset *et al.*, 2006) (see Table 1.2). American astacids of the genus *Pacifastacus* must have dispersed eastward after the cambarids; they are considered to be the most primitive of this family (Scholtz, 2002). Ice Ages following the break-up of Pangea would have extinguished crayfish from Siberia and central Asia, although this does not explain their absence from Africa and India. Either they never got there, or they were eliminated by some process: competitive exclusion by freshwater crabs has been postulated. However, elsewhere, representatives of these two groups coexist today in southern Europe, Turkey, Madagascar, Australia and New Guinea (Scholtz, 2002).

Finally, there is still some debate about the classification and relationships of crayfish at the genus and species level (Starobogatov, 1995; Crandall *et al.*, 2000a, 2000b; Braband *et al.*, 2006; Buhay & Crandall, 2008; Bracken *et al.*, 2009). In particular, Hansen & Richardson (2006) have revised the parastacid genus *Parastacoides* Clark 1936, and created two new genera, *Spinastacoides* Hansen & Richardson 2006, and *Ombrastacoides* Hansen & Richardson 2006, with 3 and 11 species, respectively (De Grave *et al.*, 2009).

Anomura and Brachyura: hermit crabs and crabs

A brief examination of the position of related decapod groups is of interest. That Anomura and Brachyura form a clade has been supported by numerous morphological and molecular analyses (Ahyong & O'Meally, 2004; Miller & Austin, 2006; Carapelli *et al.*, 2007; Tsang *et al.*, 2008). Representing almost two-thirds of all decapods, with over 9300 species, the anomurans, including hermit crabs, king crabs, squat lobsters and porcelain crabs, represent a very diverse array of body forms and functions, while the asymmetrical abdomen in the spiny crabs suggests a relationship between these two groups, most of which are marine.

Crabs show carcinization, with the development of an increasingly boxy cephalothorax and reduced abdomen. The brachyurans, or true crabs, are the second-largest

Table 1.2. Geological time periods and crayfish events (Souty-Grosset *et al.*, 2006).

Era	Period	Epoch (million years)	Major crayfish events
'Quaternary'		Littorina period (*c.* 3000–1000 yrs BC)	
		Holocene (0.01)	Post-glacial colonizations
		Pleistocene (1.8)	'Actual' subspecies differentiations?
	Neogene	Pliocene (5)	'Actual' species differentiations?
CENEZOIC 'Tertiary'		Miocene (23)	Messinian crisis (*c.* 5.5 MYA)
	Paleogene	Oligocene (33.9)	
		Eocene (55.8)	
		Paleocene (65.5)	
	Cretaceous	(145)	Oldest known *Austropotamobius*
MESOZOIC 'Secondary'	Jurassic	(200)	Oldest known Astacidae
	Triassic	(251)	Differentiation Astacoids / Parastacoids
PALAEOZOIC 'Primary'	Permian	(299)	From seawater to freshwater 'crayfish' Nephropoid ancestors in Antarctica

group among decapod crustaceans, with almost 7000 species in about 100 families (Ng *et al.*, 2008); their monophyly is indicated by molecular findings (Bracken *et al.*, 2009). Brachyuran crabs are traditionally divided into two major groups, the Eubrachyura or 'advanced crabs' and Podotremata or 'primitive crabs', united by the presence of gonopores on the coxae of the pereiopods. Podotreme crabs now appear to be paraphyletic (Ahyong & O'Meally, 2004; Ahyong *et al.*, 2007; Scholtz & McLay, 2009), and De Grave *et al.* (2009) have recognized this reality. There is, however, strong evidence to suggest that Eubrachyura are monophyletic, with a clade uniting Potamidae, Ocypodidae and Grapsidae (Bracken *et al.*, 2009).

Crab fossils are known since the Jurassic, possibly even the Carboniferous. A major radiation occurred in the Jurassic, in varied habitats – linked possibly to the break-up of Gondwana, or to the concurrent radiation of bony fishes, including crab predators. Today more than 1200 crab species are freshwater or semi-terrestrial, with distinct old-world and new-world lineages.

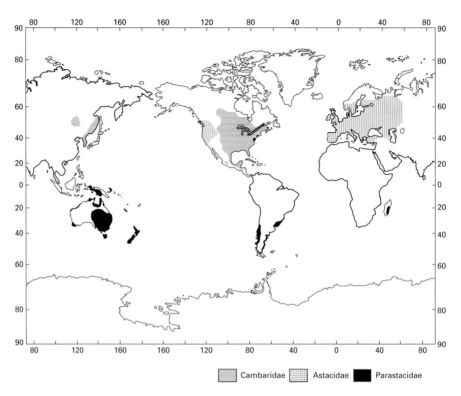

Figure 1.3.   Indigenous distribution of crayfish in the world. Cambaridae, Astacidae, Parastacidae. (Map courtesy of, and created by, James W. Fetzner Jr.)

1.4   Crayfish natural distribution and translocation events

Freshwater crayfish occur naturally on all the continents except most of Africa. We have seen that they are taxonomically arranged into two superfamilies: on one hand the Astacoidea (northern-hemisphere crayfish), with two families, Astacidae and Cambaridae; on the other hand Parastacoidea (southern-hemisphere crayfish), with one family, Parastacidae (Figure 1.3). There are two centres of species diversity for freshwater crayfish. The first is located in the south-eastern USA, where some 80% of the cambarid species can be found. In this region, the diversity of habitats, warm climate and geological stability, along with an escape from glaciation during the last Ice Age, have favoured the evolution of a diverse community of freshwater animals, including crayfish. The second centre of diversity is in Victoria, Australia, housing a large proportion of the parastacid species.

The natural distribution of crayfish is somewhat disjunct (Figure 1.3). The Astacidae (6 genera, 39 species) are distributed west of the Rocky Mountains in the north-west of the USA into British Columbia, and in Europe. The Cambaridae are distributed in North America east of the Rocky Mountains, north into southern Canada and south through Mexico, and in eastern Asia. The largest number of species of freshwater crayfish occurs in this family, with over 440 described species among 12 genera. The superfamily Parastacoidea contains a single family, Parastacidae, with 14 genera and around 180 species. Nine out of 14 genera are found in Australia and New Guinea. Three genera are distributed in southern South America, while New Zealand and Madagascar each contain an endemic genus belonging to this family.

1.4.1   Europe

The recent *Atlas of Crayfish in Europe* (Souty-Grosset *et al.*, 2006) shows that only five crayfish species, all Astacidae, are native to Europe, according to the taxonomy adopted by Holdich (2002a), with three from the genus *Astacus* and two from *Austropotamobius*. These are the noble crayfish *Astacus astacus*, thin-clawed crayfish *A. leptodactylus* and thick-clawed crayfish *A. pachypus*, and the white-clawed crayfish *Austropotamobius pallipes* and stone crayfish *A. torrentium*. Their present distribution is the result of both natural events that occurred from the Pleistocene until recent historical times, and translocations attributable to human activities.

In the genus *Astacus*, the noble crayfish *Astacus astacus* (Linnaeus 1758), is widely distributed in Europe, from France in the south-west to Russia in the east, and from Italy, Albania and Greece in the south to Scandinavia in the north (Cukerzis, 1988; Skurdal & Taugbøl, 2002) and has been stocked into numerous new localities, especially in marginal areas, so that this crayfish now has a wider distribution than the original. The thin-clawed crayfish, *Astacus leptodactylus* Eschscholtz 1823, has a south-eastern European range and is indigenous to Russia and the Ponto-Caspian area. It was originally distributed over an area corresponding more or less to Turkey, the Ukraine, Turkmen and south-western Russia, but also in Iran, Kazakstan, Georgia, Belarus, Bulgaria, Romania, Hungary and Slovakia. The Caspian Sea, the Black Sea and the lower and middle Danube are in its original distribution area, along with the lower reaches of the rivers Don, Dniester and Volga and their tributaries (Köksal, 1988; Holdich, 2002a). However, this crayfish has been widely introduced into many countries to replace noble crayfish populations lost from crayfish plague. The thick-clawed crayfish, *Astacus pachypus* Rathke 1837, occurs in the Caspian Sea and in the brackish waters of the estuaries of the Dniester and the Bug, and is recorded from two European countries, as well as some western Asian countries.

Among the European crayfish, the genus *Austropotamobius* Skorikov 1907, is widely distributed throughout west and central Europe, from the Iberian Peninsula in the west and the British Isles in the north to Italy and the Balkan Peninsula in the south and east (Holdich, 2002a). It comprises two species, the circum-alpine stone crayfish *Austropotamobius torrentium* (Schrank 1803) and the white-clawed crayfish *Austropotamobius pallipes* (Lereboullet 1858). There is a wide genetic diversity within the second taxon, so that some authors have suggested dividing it into two phylogenetic species: *Austropotamobius pallipes* and *A. italicus* (Grandjean *et al.*, 2000; Zaccara *et al.*, 2004; Fratini *et al.*, 2005). In northern Europe these two species are clear at a molecular level, but further south several subspecies have been recognized. Allopatric speciation of the two taxa led to *A. pallipes* being distributed in west-central Europe

(France, Great Britain and northern Italy) and *A. italicus* in Switzerland, Austria, Italy, the Balkans and Spain (Grandjean *et al.*, 2002a, 2002b). Phylogeographical studies confirmed the presence in Italy of both *A. pallipes*, confined to north-western Italy, and *A. italicus*, distributed across the peninsula (Fratini *et al.*, 2005). However, research is still in a state of flux, so that the general consensus is to define the taxon as a species complex, with a number of distinct genetic strands related to their recent history, but which are not distinguishable morphologically (Souty-Grosset *et al.*, 2006). The same is also true for the thin-clawed crayfish *Astacus leptodactylus* of eastern Europe; and no doubt similar complex population structuring will be found when crayfish elsewhere are examined in more detail. Molecular methods have been applied widely to the phylogenetics and systematics of crayfish, so that the status of perhaps the majority of species has been established with some confidence, although the phylogenetic relationships, particularly of the North American radiation, require further elucidation (Crandall & Buhay, 2008).

1.4.2   North and Central America

Taylor *et al.* (2007) provided a list of all crayfish (families Astacidae and Cambaridae) in the USA and Canada. The two families, Astacidae and Cambaridae, occur natively in North America and it is here that crayfish reach their highest level of diversity. Reasons for the high level of biodiversity include isolation from glacial advances and geological diversity. Approximately 77% (405 species and subspecies) of the world's known crayfish occur in North America (Taylor, 2002), with the overwhelming majority of that continent's crayfish fauna (99%) assigned to the family Cambaridae. With over two-thirds of its species endemic to the south-eastern USA, the distribution of crayfish diversity in North America closely follows those observed in other freshwater aquatic taxa such as fishes (Warren & Burr, 1994) and mussels (Williams *et al.*, 1993).

With about 63 species belonging to 6 genera, Mississippi has one of the most diverse crayfish faunas in the world and is home to at least 17 endemic species. However, many species are under threat, and Mississippi's Comprehensive Wildlife Conservation Strategy deems 18 species in need of immediate conservation action or research. In Missouri, the longpincered crayfish *Orconectes longidigitus*, native to the White River drainage, is among the largest in North America. A recreational fishery is becoming increasingly popular (Robert DiStefano, personal communication, 2008). *Orconectes meeki* is found in the upper White River drainage of Missouri and Arkansas. It is listed as critically imperilled and is among the rarest crayfish in the state. The state of Alabama in south-eastern USA probably harbours the greatest diversity of crayfish in the world for an area of its size. At least 85 species of crayfish are reported for this state, of which only the virile crayfish *Orconectes virilis* is non-native. The geographical distribution of crayfish strongly favours upland drainages in the northern and central portions of the state, particularly the Tennessee River drainage (Schuster *et al.*, 2008).

Further north, the number of crayfish species declines; for example, in Canada only 11 species were recognized by Hamr (Premek Hamr, personal communication, 2008), of which eight are native, two introduced and one undetermined. Most (nine crayfish species) are known from Ontario, made up of five species of *Orconectes*, two of *Cambarus* and one of *Fallicambarus*, plus the northern clearwater crayfish *Orconectes propinquus* spreading up to the St Lawrence River from Quebec.

In Central America, Mexico is a hot-spot, with about 49 cambarid species, whereas only four have been described in Guatemala, two from Belize to the Dominican Republic, one in Costa Rica (probably introduced) and four in Cuba. Several recent attempts have been made, not only by Mexican scientists but by many other organizations, to identify all the Mexican species. For example, *Procambarus regiomontanus* was only found in the state of Nuevo Leon and this endemic species is endangered because of the introduced crayfish *Procambarus clarkii*. There have also been introductions of the parastacid *Cherax quadricarinatus*, but mainly in areas where native crayfish were not believed present (e.g. in man-made dams). There have not been many reports of introduced crayfish outside those areas. *Procambarus clarkii* is the prime example of an introduced species from North America; the species is encountered in all the countries of Central America and is the only species found in Ecuador and Venezuela. The state of knowledge about the distribution of crayfish in Central America is summarized in Table 1.3.

1.4.3   South America

Crayfish species found in South America (11 species known, specifically in southeastern Brazil, Uruguay, central-southern Chile and southern Argentina) are parastacids mostly from the genera *Parastacus* and *Samastacus*. It seems that the world-invader *Procambarus clarkii* is only recorded from Ecuador and Brazil.

In Chile, only six native species have been described, particularly the burrowing crayfishes *Parastacus nicoleti* – considered as a unique model with both male and female gonopores – and *Samastacus spinifrons* located on the western side of the Andes. New species have recently been discovered, including *Virilastacus rucapihuelensis*, named after the locality Rucapihuel (Rudolph & Crandall, 2005) and *Virilastacus retamali* (Rudolph & Crandall, 2007). Other species may still remain to be discovered. In Brazil, three species have been studied, particularly in terms of their reproduction: *Parastacus brasiliensis* (hermaphrodism; Almeida & Buckup, 2000; Horn *et al.*, 2008), *P. defossus* (Noro *et al.*, 2008) and *P. varicosus* (Da Silva-Castiglioni *et al.*, 2008). *P. saffordi* is mostly encountered in Uruguay.

Some species in South America have very recently been classed as Vulnerable (VU) or Endangered (EN) (Rudolph & Crandall, 2007; Mauricio Almerão, personal communication, 2008) but no species from either Central or South America have yet been listed by IUCN (see Table 1.4 and conservation status in Part II).

1.4.4   Japan and Southeast Asia

The taxonomy of the Asian cambarid genus *Cambaroides*, known from Russia, Mongolia, South and North Korea, China and Japan, remains unresolved. The taxa are considered endangered in Mongolia, Russia and Japan (Tadashi Kawai, personal communication, 2010).

Table 1.3. Crayfish distribution in Central America.

Species	Mexico	Guatemala	Belize El Salvador Nicaragua Dominican Republic	Costa Rica	Cuba	Brazil	Uruguay	Chile	Argentina	Ecuador Venezuela
Cambarellus alvazeri	+									
Cambarellus aerolatus	+									
Cambarellus chapalanus	+									
Cambarellus chihuahuae	+									
Cambarellus montezumae	+									
Cambarellus occidentalis	+									
Cambarellus patzcuarensis	+									
Cambarellus prolixus	+									
Cambarellus zempoalensis	+									
Orconectes virilis	+									
Procambarus acanthophorus	+									
Procambarus acutus cuevachichae	+									
Procambarus atkinsoni					+					
Procambarus bouvieri	+									
Procambarus caballeroi	+									
Procambarus citlaltepeti	+									
Procambarus clarkii	+	+	+	+		+				+
Procambarus contrerasi	+									
Procambarus cubensis cubensis					+					
Procambarus cubensis rivalis					+					

Species			
Procambarus cuetzalanae	+		
Procambarus digueti	+		
Procambarus erichsoni	+		
Procambarus gonopodocristatus	+		
Procambarus hoffmanni	+		
Procambarus hortonhobbsi	+	+	
Procambarus llmasi	+		
Procambarus mexicanus	+		
Procambarus mirandai	+		
Procambarus niveus	+	+	
Procambarus oaxacae oaxacae	+		
Procambarus oaxacae redelli	+		
Procambarus olmecorum	+		
Procambarus ortmanni	+		
Procambarus paradoxus	+		
Procambarus pilosimanus	+	+	+
Procambarus regiomontanus	+		
Procambarus riojai	+		
Procambarus roberti	+		
Procambarus rodriguezi	+		
Procambarus ruthveni	+		
Procambarus sbordoni	+		
Procambarus strenthi	+		
Procambarus teziutlanensis	+		
Procambarus tiapacoyanensis	+		
Procambarus toltecae	+		

Table 1.3. (cont.)

Species	Mexico	Guatemala	Belize El Salvador Nicaragua Dominican Republic	Costa Rica	Cuba	Brazil	Uruguay	Chile	Argentina	Ecuador Venezuela
Procambarus vazquezae	+									
Procambarus veracruzanus	+									
Procambarus villalobosi	+									
Procambarus xilitiae	+									
Procambarus xochitianae	+									
Procambarus zapoapensis	+									
Procambarus zihuateutlensis	+									
Procambarus williamsoni		+								

Table 1.4. Crayfish distribution in South America.

Species	Brazil	Uruguay	Chile	Argentina	Status
Parastacus brasiliensis	+				DD
Parastacus defossus	+	+			DD
Parastacus laevigatus	+				DD
Parastacus pilimanus	+	+			DD
Parastacus varicosus	+	+			DD
Parastacus nicoleti			+		**VU**
Parastacus pugnax			+		**VU**
Parastacus saffordi	+	+			DD **VU**
Parastacus spinifrons			+	+	**VU**
Parastacus araucanus			+		
Parastacus rucapihuelensis			+		**EN** (Rudolph & Crandall, 2005)
Parastacus retanali			+		**EN** (Rudolph & Crandall, 2007)

Cambaroides japonicus is the only crayfish native to Japan and is restricted to Hokkaido (Kawai, 1996). The invaders *Procambarus clarkii* and *Pacifastacus leniusculus* are now also present. The same native genus is encountered in Korea, with the named species *Cambaroides similis* and *C. wladiwostokensis*, and in central China, with the species *Cambaroides koshevonikowi*. Here again, *P. clarkii* is present, and farmed on a large scale (production exceeding 100 000 tonnes per year).

1.4.5   Madagascar

Freshwater crayfish of the genus *Astacoides* are endemic to the highlands of eastern Madagascar, with six uniquely tropical species: *Astacoides madagascariensis*, *A. caldwelli*, *A. betsileoensis*, *A. granulimanus*, *A. crosnieri* and *A. petiti*. Growth rates for *Astacoides granulimanus* and *A. crosnieri* are among the slowest known in any crayfish. Madagascar's freshwater habitats have great significance for global biodiversity, yet conservation efforts, as in so much of the world, have focused on terrestrial ecosystems.

Jones *et al*. (2007) call for more attention to be paid to Madagascar's exceptional – yet understudied – freshwater biodiversity, which is now coming under increasing threat.

1.4.6   Australia

Australia, including Tasmania, is home to the world's largest crayfish species, which include good examples of flagship species in conservation terms (see below and Chapter 6). The largest, the Tasmanian giant freshwater crayfish *Astacopsis gouldi*, is found in the rivers of northern Tasmania. Others include the genus *Cherax*, with the marron (*C. tenuimanus*), the redclaw crayfish (*C. quadricarinatus*), the yabby (*C. destructor*) and the western yabby (*C. preissii*).

In New South Wales, the Murray River crayfish *Euastacus armatus* (Parastacidae) is the most commonly known species, and is the world's second-largest freshwater crayfish, endemic to the streams and tributaries of the Murray–Darling catchment, where it plays a vital role in ecosystem processes and is an important tourist attraction. However, population numbers have been declining due to habitat modification and overfishing (Natalie Alves, personal communication, 2008). In north-eastern New South Wales, two endemic species of *Cherax*, *C. cuspidatus* and *C. leckii*, were recently discovered (Coughran, 2006, 2008). In Western Australia, the hairy marron, *C. tenuimanus*, is endemic to the Margaret River and under threat of extinction due to its rapid replacement following the introduction of the widespread smooth marron, *C. cainii* (John J.S. Bunn, personal communication, 2008). *C. tenuimanus* is indigenous to the south-west of Western Australia between Harvey and Albany (Kent River) and is considered to be a good biological indicator of the quality of the south-western rivers in Western Australia. Also in south-west Australia, the burrowing freshwater crayfish genus *Engaewa* is a Gondwanan relict restricted to the high-rainfall zone. Of five species of *Engaewa* recognized within the genus, three are of conservation concern. In Victoria, the Grampians National Park is a hot-spot for crayfish diversity, with seven species from six genera (*Euastacus bispinosus*, *Cherax destructor*, *Geocharax falcata*, *Gramastacus insolitus* (the smallest) and *Engaeus lyelli*) occurring in sympatry. In Queensland, the crayfish *Euastacus sulcatus* is abundant; it is a keystone species functioning as an ecosystem engineer (James Furse, personal communication, 2008).

The yabby, *Cherax destructor*, is native to the eastern states of Australia and is considered invasive in Western Australia, where it competes with native marron (*C. tenuimanus*). *C. destructor* is of special interest because the species is the most widespread and abundant of all Australian freshwater crayfish, with a natural distribution covering over 2 million square kilometres, from South Australia and the southern Northern Territory in central Australia, to the Great Dividing Range in the east (Nguyen *et al*., 2004). *Cherax quadricarinatus* is indigenous to the rivers of north-western Queensland and the Northern Territory in tropical Australia, and also extends into the catchments of south-eastern Papua New Guinea. Tasmania has a rich freshwater crayfish fauna, with about 37 species from 4 genera; relatively high in the context of the total Australian fauna (Whiting *et al*., 2000). They range from the world's largest crayfish *Astacopsis gouldi* – found throughout the country – to the tiny burrowing crayfish of the *Engaeus* genus mainly found in the west and north of the island. Within *Engaeus* there are 15 known species, 13 occurring only in Tasmania and 2 shared with Victoria in mainland Australia. Areas of high diversity are in the north-east (*Engaeus* spp.) and the central west (*Engaeus* and *Parastacoides* spp.) (Richardson *et al.*, 2006).

In New Zealand, the family Parastacidae is also present, with just two endemic species of *Paranephrops* in the main islands and no introduced species.

The global crayfish distribution, presented above, reveals a great variety of available information for different native crayfish species, ranging from the well-studied high diversity of the USA and Australia and the few species of Europe to the still incomplete knowledge of the crayfish fauna of Mexico and South America. The following section looks at the relationships between the diversity of crayfish species, current knowledge about the species, and the need to assess these in terms of conservation requirements.

1. 5   Conservation status of crayfish

The threatened species categories used in Red Data Books and Red Lists have been in place, with some modification, for almost 30 years. Since their introduction, these categories have become widely recognized internationally, and they are now used in a whole range of publications and listings produced by IUCN, as well as by numerous governmental and non-governmental organizations. The Red Data Book categories provide an easy and widely understood method for highlighting those species under higher extinction risk, so as to focus attention on conservation measures designed to protect them. The several threatened species categories form a part of the overall scheme. The broad category 'Vulnerable' includes the more threatened groups 'Endangered' and 'Critically Endangered'. It should be possible to place all taxa into one of the following categories recorded by IUCN (see Box 1.1).

The IUCN recently released its 2008 total *Red List of Threatened Species* (Vié *et al.*, 2009). The Red List now includes 16 928 animal species that are threatened with extinction. Of these, 3246 are Critically Endangered (the highest category of threat), 4770 are Endangered, and 8912 are Vulnerable to extinction. Table 1.5 shows the number of recognized threatened crustacean species, compared from 1996 to 2008.

Only two species were added to the crustacean list between 1998 and 2003, and 51 between 2003 and 2006, whereas 146 were added from 2007 to 2008, suggesting both an appreciation of increasing threats and an urgent desire to protect crustaceans and particularly crayfish, because many of these were among the evaluated species.

While it is difficult to portray population trends for some aquatic plants and invertebrates, the available data give an insight into the condition of freshwater ecosystems and species. In terms of aquatic plants, Revenga & Kura (2003) noted that most macrophytic species are probably not threatened at global or continental scales, but many bryophytes with restricted distributions are rare and threatened. In the USA, one of the few countries to assess more comprehensively the conservation status of freshwater crustaceans and molluscs, one-half of the known crayfish species and two-thirds of freshwater molluscs

---

Box 1.1 IUCN definitions of categories

EXTINCT (EX) – A taxon is Extinct when there is no reasonable doubt that the last individual has died.

EXTINCT IN THE WILD (EW) – A taxon is Extinct in the Wild when it is known only to survive in cultivation, in captivity, or as a naturalized population (or populations) well outside the past range. A taxon is presumed Extinct in the Wild when exhaustive surveys in known and/or expected habitat, at appropriate times (diurnal, seasonal, annual), throughout its historical range have failed to record an individual. Surveys should be over a time frame appropriate to the taxon's life cycle and life form.

CRITICALLY ENDANGERED (CR) – A taxon is Critically Endangered when it is facing an extremely high risk of extinction in the wild in the immediate future, as defined by any of the criteria (A–E) below.

ENDANGERED (EN) – A taxon is Endangered when it is not Critically Endangered but is facing a very high risk of extinction in the wild in the near future, as defined by any of the criteria (A–E) below.

VULNERABLE (VU) – A taxon is Vulnerable when it is not Critically Endangered or Endangered but is facing a high risk of extinction in the wild in the medium-term future, as defined by any of the criteria (A–E) below.

The IUCN criteria, derived from broad review and developed through wide consultation, may be summarized as follows:
A: population size reductions; **B**: geographical range fluctuating, declining or small; **C**: <250 mature individuals and declining population or poor population structure; **D**: <50 mature individuals; **E**: high probability of extinction within 10 years or 3 generations, based on quantitative analysis.

LOWER RISK (LR) – A taxon is Lower Risk when it has been evaluated, but does not satisfy the criteria for any of the categories Critically Endangered, Endangered or Vulnerable. Taxa included in the Lower Risk category can be separated into three subcategories:

1. **Conservation Dependent** (cd). Taxa which are the focus of a continuing taxon-specific or habitat-specific conservation programme targeted towards the taxon in question, the cessation of which would result in the taxon qualifying for one of the threatened categories above within a period of 5 years.
2. **Near Threatened** (nt). Taxa which do not qualify for Conservation Dependent, but which are close to qualifying for Vulnerable.
3. **Least Concern** (lc). Taxa which do not qualify for Conservation Dependent or Near Threatened.

DATA DEFICIENT (DD) – A taxon is Data Deficient when there is inadequate information to make a direct, or indirect, assessment of its risk of extinction based on its distribution and/or population status. A taxon in this category may be well studied, and its biology well known, but appropriate data on abundance and/or distribution are lacking. Data Deficient is therefore not a category of threat or risk. Listing of taxa in this category indicates that more information is required and acknowledges the possibility that future research will show that threatened classification is appropriate. In many cases, great care should be exercised in choosing between DD and threatened status. If the range of a taxon is suspected to be relatively circumscribed, and if a considerable period of time has elapsed since the last record of the taxon, threatened status may well be justified.

NOT EVALUATED (NE) – A taxon is Not Evaluated when it is has not yet been assessed against the criteria.

(also with a Missouri hot-spot) are at risk of extinction (Master *et al.*, 1998), with severe declines in their populations in recent years. Furthermore, at least 1 in 10 of the freshwater molluscs are likely to have already become extinct (Master *et al.*, 1998).

In the 2008 Red List category summary for Crustacea, among 1735 species considered, 663 species were classed as Data Deficient, including 638 Decapoda with 3 crayfish species. Others for which data were adequate were classified as in Table 1.6.

1.6   Status of crayfish throughout the world

In the IUCN 2007 analysis, if we consider the status recorded in each country (Appendix 1.1), the 151 crayfish species listed correspond to around 23% of the total 650 species of crayfish (Table 1.7).

The second list (Table 1.8) shows that the genera *Cambarus* and *Procambarus* in the eastern USA and Southeast Asia and the genus *Euastacus* in the southern hemisphere have the most listed species in terms of conservation issues.

1.6.1   Some examples of threatened status

Astacidae in Europe

Astacus astacus was classified in 2006 as 'Vulnerable' in the international Red List, lying in the range from 'Declining, Care Demanding' to 'Endangered' in different national Red Lists (Souty-Grosset *et al.*, 2006). It is included in the Bern Convention and in Annex V of the EU Habitat Directive, permitting its exploitation only when stocks are of favourable status. The main aims of the legislation in most countries or regions containing *A. astacus* are to protect and conserve the species, and where possible to reintroduce it, e.g. in Greece. Restrictions differ greatly, depending upon whether or not there are harvestable populations and an existing tradition of eating crayfish. In some countries no harvest of *A. astacus* is permitted, while the opposite is true in others; for instance, in the Nordic countries it is recognized that exploitation is a prerequisite for conservation of the species. As the situation is very complex and differs between countries, it is neither possible nor desirable to fully harmonize regulations within Europe. *Austropotamobius pallipes* is protected under international and

Table 1.5. Number of threatened crustacean species evaluated by IUCN from 1996 to 2008.

Estimated number of described species	Number of species evaluated by 2008	Number of threatened species in 1996/8	Number of threatened species in 2000	Number of threatened species in 2002	Number of threatened species in 2003	Number of threatened species in 2004	Number of threatened species in 2006	Number of threatened species in 2007	Number of threatened species in 2008	Number of threatened species in 2008 as % of species described	Number of threatened species in 2008 as % of species evaluated
40 000	1735	437	407	408	409	429	459	460	606	1.5%	35%

Table 1.6. Red List category summary for evaluated crustaceans (crustaceans: 1735 species; decapods: 1450 species; crayfish: 650 species).

	EX	EW	Threatened			Lower Risk		
			CR	EN	VU	cd	nt	lc
Crustaceans	7	1	84	127	395	9	19	430
Decapods	1	0	52	102	211	0	18	428
Crayfish			14	41	93			

Table 1.7. According to the IUCN 2007 analysis per country, the 151 species listed correspond to around 23% of the 650 species of crayfish.

IUCN 2007	CR	EN	VU	DD	Total
Madagascar				1	1
Tasmania		1			1
Australia		24	17	2	43
USA	14	16	73		103
Europe			3		3
Total	14	41	93	3	151
Total number listed	650				
%	23				

national legislation, and is no longer legally exploited. Many countries in Europe have active programmes for the conservation of *A. pallipes* and some also have reintroduction programmes. However, none currently show 'favourable status' for this species.

In several European countries, *Austropotamobius torrentium* has been declared a threatened species, e.g. it is listed in the German Red List (RL3, Appendix I) of endangered species, and in Austria as a highly endangered species. *A. torrentium* is considered critically endangered in the Czech Republic and Hungary. It was recently added to Annex II of the EU Habitats Directive, as a species requiring special conservation measures. Existing Member States do not have to suggest new areas of protection, but they must include the species in already existing Natura 2000 areas. However, new Member States (central and eastern European countries) must, as well as considering this species when they set up protected areas, define protected areas where this species occurs. *A. torrentium* is not subject to much harvesting, but in a few territories there is an open season for male specimens with a total body length of approximately 10–12 cm (e.g. Fisheries Acts of some states in Austria).

USA and Canada

Taylor *et al.* (2007) provide a list of all crayfish (families Astacidae and Cambaridae) in the USA and Canada, which includes state and provincial distributions, a comprehensive review of the conservation status of all taxa, and references on biology, conservation and distribution. The list includes 363 native crayfish, of which 189 (52.1%) are

Table 1.8. The IUCN list expressed by genus and biogeographical region (*N* = number of species for each genus).

IUCN 2007 (genus)	N	CR	EN	VU	DD	Total at risk	%
Eastern North America							
Southeast Asia							
Cambarellus	17		1	2		3	
Cambarus	98	2	8	24		34	
Distocambarus	5			2		2	
Fallicambarus	18	1	2	5		8	
Faxonella	4						
Hobbseus	7			6		6	
Orconectes	92	2		19		21	
Procambarus	175	7	7	21		35	
Cambaroides	7						
TOTAL	**423**	**12**	**18**	**79**		**109**	
Europe and western Asia							
Western North America							
Astacus	3			1		1	
Austropotamobius	7			2		2	
Pacifastacus	8	2				2	
TOTAL	**18**	**2**		**3**		**5**	
Southern hemisphere							
Astacoides	7				1	1	
Astacopsis	3		1			1	
Cherax	45			3	2	5	
Engaeus	35		12	1		13	
Engaewa	4		1			1	
Euastacus	48		9	7		16	
Geocharax	2						
Gramastacus	1						
Ombrastacoides	11						
Paranephrops	2						
Parastacus	8						
Samastacus	1						
Spinastacoides	3						
Tenuibranchiurus	1						
Virilastacus	2						
Parastacoides	3						
TOTAL	**176**		**23**	**11**	**3**	**37**	
Total	**617**	**14**	**41**	**93**	**3**	**151**	24%

Currently Stable. Two taxa (< 1%) are listed as Endangered, Possibly Extinct, 66 (18.2%) are Endangered, 52 (14.3%) are Threatened and 54 (14.9%) are Vulnerable – a percentage well below the global average for threatened crayfish species of 23%. Limited natural range continues to be the primary factor responsible for the recognized imperilment of crayfish; other threats include the introduction of non-indigenous crayfish and habitat alteration. While progress has been made in recognizing the plight of crayfish in individual states, much work is still needed.

Japan

While *Cambaroides japonicus* is the only crayfish species native to Japan, it has been designated an endangered species (Vulnerable) in central Hokkaido streams by the Ministry of the Environment of Japan (Usio *et al.*, 2007). To date, however, the species has not been listed as Vulnerable under the IUCN because of a lack of data.

Tasmania

Of the 15 confirmed species of burrowing crayfish found in Tasmania, 13 are endemic and 5 species of the genus *Engaeus* are considered as threatened. Of these, three species are Endangered (*E. spinicaudatus, E. martigener, E. granulatus*) and two are Vulnerable (*E. orramakunna, E. yabbimunna*). These burrowing species with a limited range are especially impacted by human activities.

1.7   Threatened crayfish and IUCN assessments

During this last decade, significant advances have been made on the taxonomy and evolution of crayfish. Breinholt *et al.* (2009) dwell on the interest in freshwater crayfish as model organisms for diverse disciplines, from neurology to toxicology, and how they have been the focus of many physiological, ecological and molecular-based studies. Although much of the recent work has dealt with the evolutionary history, phylogeography and conservation biology of freshwater crayfish, estimations of their divergence times and radiations have never been made. Recently, divergence time estimations for decapods have provided the first proposed molecular-timing hypothesis involving freshwater crayfish. These authors have increased the accuracy and provided divergence estimations specific to freshwater crayfish. The molecular time estimation supports a late Permian to early Triassic divergence from Nephropoidea, with radiation and dispersal before the break-up of Pangea, as well as subsequent speciation and radiation prior to, or directly associated with, the disassembly of Gondwana and Laurasia. The splitting of Gondwana and Laurasia resulted in the separation of Parastacoidea and Astacoidea during the Jurassic. The hypothesized divergence and radiation of these two superfamilies are also supported by molecular time estimations. For the three families of crayfish, Breinholt *et al.* (2009) estimated the diversification of Parastacidae at about 161 MYA, the radiation of Astacidae at about 153 MYA and the Cambaridae radiation at about 90 MYA.

   Toon *et al.* (2009) present the most up-to-date phylogeny for parastacid crayfish inclusive of all genera and representative of their Gondwanan distribution. Robust empirical evolutionary studies rely on a combination of geological hypotheses, molecular, morphological and biological data, as well as the fossil record to uncover the history of the taxa of interest. Parastacidae have a Gondwanan distribution, show deep divergences based on combined fossil and molecular data consistent with estimates of continental drift, and have the biology expected of an organism that would be restricted by oceanic dispersal. The most basal split in the parastacid crayfish separates South American crayfish from all others, even though geological data suggest that a land bridge allowed dispersal of organisms between eastern and western Gondwana until 52–35 MYA. Although the sequential break-up of Gondwana may underlie the overall biogeographical pattern seen in parastacids, an important factor is also likely to be the historical isolation of river systems and the sheer magnitude of distances across the Gondwana supercontinent. All extant southern-hemisphere crayfish are distributed on land-masses that were separated from each other by Antarctica early in the break-up of Gondwana. This separation by a continent that eventually lost all its endemic crayfish is likely to affect the phylogenetic tree that we are able to build from the available extant taxa, and needs to be taken into account when considering the evolution of this group.

However, at the same time as our evolutionary knowledge is increasing, recent Red List conservation assessments indicate that significant numbers of species around the world are threatened with extinction through the destruction of freshwater habitats, overuse of water, pollution and diversion of drainages, and overharvesting for human consumption. It has been estimated that between one-third and one-half of the world's crayfish species are threatened with population decline or extinction (Taylor, 2002). Since 2009, the IUCN has completed assessments of many crayfish species, published in mid-2010 (IUCN, 2010). The list of all the assessed species (provided by Nadia Richman, SRLI Freshwater Invertebrate Coordinator) shows a major effort, involving the examination of 585 species including about 398 Cambaridae, 175 Parastacidae and 12 Astacidae. Among Cambaridae, the genera *Procambarus* (164 species), *Cambarus* (99) and *Orconectes* (85) have been most thoroughly investigated, while the Parastacidae genera *Euastacus* (49 species) and *Cherax* (44) are also well analysed. The threat situation is becoming increasingly dramatic because eight species are now labelled extinct, for example *Pacifastacus nigrescens*, classified as CR (Critically Endangered) as recently as 2007 (see Box 1.1). In Europe, *A. astacus* and *A. pallipes* are clearly assessed as Endangered. There are now 48 species classified as CR, 63 as EN, 48 as VU (CR, EN and VU together representing about 27% of the total) and 50 as NT (around 8.5%). If we consider CR-classed Cambaridae and Parastacidae separately, those with a classification of EN and VU correspond to about 21.3% and 30.5%, respectively. Actions to save freshwater crayfish must thus become an urgent priority and have the potential to limit the loss of an important part of the biodiversity in the freshwater realm worldwide.

Results from the recent 2010 update to the *IUCN Red List of Threatened Species* (Richman *et al.*, 2010) indicate that crayfish are one of the most threatened freshwater taxa yet to be assessed. Hot-spots of high extinction risk are located in the south-eastern USA, where future projected extinction rates for freshwater taxa (freshwater fish, molluscs, crayfish and amphibians) are 4% per decade (Ricciardi & Rasmussen, 1999), and south-east Australia, where water shortages are significantly reducing habitat availability for freshwater species.

Appendix 1.1

Change in conservation status of crayfish in 2007 by comparison with previous years (data compiled from the literature). Bold indicates status change

Southern hemisphere

Species	Country	LIT	2007
Astacoides madagascariensis	Madagascar		DD
Astacopsis franklinii	Tasmania	**HCS**	
Astacopsis gouldi	**Tasmania**	VU	**EN**
Astacopsis tricornis	Tasmania	**HCS**	—
Cherax destructor	Australia	VU	VU
Cherax nucifraga	Australia		DD
Cherax parvus	Australia		DD
Cherax quadricarinatrus	Australia		VU
Cherax tenuimanus	Australia	VU	VU
Engaeus australis	Australia	EN	EN
Engaeus curvisuturus	Australia	EN	EN
Engaeus disjuncticus	Tasmania		EN
Engaeus granulatus	Tasmania		EN
Engaeus mallacoota	**Australia**	VU	**EN**
Engaeus martigener	Tasmania		EN
Engaeus nulloporius	Tasmania		EN
Engaeus orramakunna	**Tasmania**	VU	**EN**
Engaeus phyllocercus	Australia	VU	VU
Engaeus rostrogaleatus	Australia	EN	EN

Eastern USA & Southeast Asia

Species	Country	LIT	2007 specs
Cambarellus blacki	USA	EN	EN
Cambarellus diminutus	USA	T	VU
Cambarellus lesliei	USA	T	VU
Cambarus howardi	USA	**CS**	VU
Cambarus catagius	USA	VU	VU
Cambarus cymatilis	USA	**CS**	VU
Cambarus deweesae	USA	**CS**	EN
Cambarus halli	USA	**CS (VU)**	
Cambarus harti	USA	EN	EN
Cambarus strigosus	USA	T	EN
Cambarus truncatus	USA	T	EN
Cambarus williami	USA	EN	EN
Cambarus coosawattae	USA	EN	VU
Cambarus elkensis	USA	T	VU
Cambarus fasciatus	USA	T	VU
Cambarus speciosus	USA	EN	VU
Cambarus aculabrum	USA	EN	EN
Cambarus batchi	USA	VU	VU
Cambarus bouchardi	USA	EN	VU
Cambarus cryptodytes	USA	T	VU
Cambarus obeyensis	USA	EN	VU
Cambarus subterraneus	USA	EN	EN

Species	Country	LIT	2007
Orconectes bisectus	USA	EN	VU
Orconectes jeffersoni	USA	EN	VU
Orconectes marchandi	USA	T	VU
Orconectes shoupi	USA	EN	**CR**
Orconectes stannardi	USA	VU	VU
Orconectes wrighti	USA	EN	VU
Orconectes jonesi	USA	VU	VU
Orconectes blacki	USA	T	VU
Orconectes deanae	USA	**CS**	VU
Orconectes hartfieldi	USA	T	VU
Orconectes maletae	USA	T	VU
Orconectes incomptus	USA	EN	VU
Orconectes menae	USA	T	VU
Orconectes peruncus	USA	T	VU
Orconectes quadruncus	USA	T	VU
Orconectes saxatilis	USA	EN	**CR**
Orconectes kentuckiensis	USA	**CS**	VU
Orconectes sloanii	USA	VU	VU
Orconectes cooperi	USA	EN	VU
Orconectes holti	USA	VU	VU
Orconectes mississippiensis	USA	VU	VU
Procambarus brazoriensis	USA	EN	VU

Appendix 1.1 (cont.)

Species	Country	LIT	2007
Engaeus spinicaudatus	Tasmania	VU	EN
Engaeus sternalis	Australia	EN	EN
Engaeus urostrichus	Australia	EN	EN
Engaeus yabbimunna	Tasmania	VU	
Engaewa similis	Australia		EN
Engaewa subcoerulea	Australia	EN	
Euastacus armatus	Australia	VU	VU
Euastacus bispinosus	Australia	VU	VU
Euastacus crassus	Australia	EN	EN
Euastacus diversus	Australia	EN	EN
Euastacus eungella	Australia	VU	VU
Euastacus fleckeri	Australia	VU	VU
Euastacus hystricosus	Australia	VU	VU
Euastacus jagara	Australia	EN	EN
Euastacus maidae	Australia	EN	EN
Euastacus monteithorum	Australia	EN	EN
Euastacus neodiversus	Australia	VU	VU
Euastacus robertsi	Australia	EN	EN
Euastacus setosus	Australia	VU	VU
Euastacus urospinosus	Australia	EN	EN
Euastacus yigara	Australia	EN	EN
Euastacus bindal	Australia		EN

Species	Country	LIT	2007 specs
Cambarus tartarus	USA	EN	CR
Cambarus unestami	USA	T	VU
Cambarus zophonastes	USA	EN	CR
Cambarus miltus	USA	T	VU
Cambarus chaugaensis	USA	T	VU
Cambarus extraneus	USA	T	VU
Cambarus georgiae	USA	VU	VU
Cambarus hiwasseensis	USA	VU	VU
Cambarus nerterius	USA	EN	VU
Cambarus parrishi	USA	EN	VU
Cambarus reburrus	USA	CS	VU
Cambarus pyronotus	USA	EN	EN
Cambarus scotti	USA	T	VU
Cambarus spicatus	USA	VU	VU
Cambarus veteranus	USA	T	VU
Cambarus pristinus	USA	EN	VU
Distocambarus devexus	USA	T	VU
Distocambarus youngineri	USA	EN	VU
Fallicambarus burrisi	USA	T	VU
Fallicambarus danielae	USA	T	VU
Fallicambarus gilpini	USA	EN	VU
Fallicambarus gordoni	USA	T	VU
Fallicambarus hortoni	USA	EN	EN

Species	Country	LIT	2007
Procambarus barbiger	USA	VU	VU
Procambarus cometes	USA	EN	VU
Procambarus connus	USA	EN	VU
Procambarus nigrocinctus	USA	EN	VU
Procambarus pogum	USA	EN	VU
Procambarus reimeri	USA	EN	VU
Procambarus steigmani	USA	EN	CR
Procambarus apachicolae	USA	T	VU
Procambarus econfinae	USA	EN	EN
Procambarus escambiensis	USA	EN	VU
Procambarus latipleurum	USA	EN	VU
Procambarus milleri	USA	EN	EN
Procambarus rathbunae	USA	T	VU
Procambarus acherontis	USA	EN	EN
Procambarus morrisi	USA	EN	CR
Procambarus angustatus	USA	EN	CR
Procambarus attiguus	USA	EN	CR
Procambarus delicatus	USA	EN	CR
Procambarus franzi	USA	EN	EN
Procambarus horsti	USA	EN	EN
Procambarus leitheuseri	USA	EN	VU
Procambarus nechesae	USA	T	VU
Procambarus nueces	USA	EN	CR
Procambarus orcinus	USA	T	VU
Procambarus pictus	USA	T	VU

Species	Region		
Gramastacus insolitus	Australia	VU	
Europe and western USA			
Astacus astacus	Europe	EN	VU
Austropotamobius pallipes	Europe	EN	VU
Austropotamobius torrentium	Europe	EN	VU
Pacifastacus fortis	USA	EN	CR
Pacifastacus nigrescens	USA	**CR**	**CR**

Species	Region		
Fallicambarus harpi	USA	VU	EN
Fallicambarus petilicarpus	USA	EN	**CR**
Fallicambarus strawni	USA	T	VU
Hobbseus attenuatus	USA	EN	VU
Hobbseus cristatus	USA	T	VU
Hobbseus orconectoides	USA	T	VU
Hobbseus petilus	USA	T	VU
Hobbseus valleculus	USA	T	VU
Hobbseus valobushensis	USA	T	VU

Species	Region	**CS**	
Procambarus plumimanus	USA	**CS**	VU
Procambarus texanus	USA	EN	**CR**
Procambarus echinatus	USA	VU	VU
Procambarus gibbus	USA	T	VU
Procambarus lagniappe	USA	T	VU
Procambarus pecki	USA	EN	VU
Procambarus erythrops	USA	EN	EN
Procambarus fitzpatricki	USA	T	VU
Procambarus ferugineus	USA	NL	EN

NL Not listed

LIT Literature

EN Endangered

VU Vulnerable

T Threatened

CS Currently Stable

CR Critically Endangered

HCS High Conservation Significance (Tasmania)

2   Why are crayfish, among freshwater decapods, considered pivotal in freshwater ecosystems?

(with Alastair Richardson)

2.1   The roles of crayfish, crabs and other decapods in fresh waters

In contrast to sea shores, freshwater habitats often seem to lack excitement and interest, although both may be biodiverse. Most freshwater invertebrates are small or cryptic, and usually only discovered by sweep-netting. The largest aquatic insects, including some water beetles, belostomatid bugs, water-measurers and odonates, nearly all have a winged adult phase, for survival or dispersal. In contrast, many freshwater decapod crustaceans – the lobster-like freshwater crayfish, brachyuran freshwater crabs and various 'shrimps' – are sharply different, and more like denizens of marine rock pools. All stages are homotopic, aquatic or semi-aquatic, and most adults are larger – often much larger – than insects or other crustaceans. Unlike their decapod relatives the primarily tropical freshwater crabs, crayfish are predominantly temperate, only extending into the tropics in North and Central America, in Madagascar and in Australasia, where they tend to live at higher altitudes than in the temperate zone (Hobbs, 1987). In addition to their large size, crayfish are often long-lived compared with other invertebrates, enhancing their significance in many freshwater systems.

The number of freshwater crayfish species is more than 650, but the exact total is as yet undetermined. There are twice as many species of freshwater crab (Cumberlidge *et al.*, 2009), reflecting their high levels of endemism in the tropics. Crayfish make an especially impressive contribution to freshwater ecosystems in two regions of the world because of their diversity, size, longevity and varied ecology; a point that will be developed in the next chapter. More than 400 cambarid species occur in North America in a wide variety of habitats, many tolerating broad temperature ranges, e.g. *Orconectes rusticus* (2.5°–33°C) and *Procambarus clarkii* (up to 35°C), and the continent also supports a few cool-water indigenous astacid species, again with broad temperature tolerances (see Table 2.1). Australia has upwards of 100 parastacids of hugely varying sizes and ecological specializations, extending from cool temperate to tropical latitudes, and including burrowing forms that live far from open water. South America and Madagascar also have suites of parastacids that use a range of habitats, from cool forest streams to warm swamps. In contrast, Europe has only five indigenous species (Souty-Grosset *et al.*, 2006), all Astacidae, all living in streams, ponds and lakes, and all with relatively similar life histories.

Table 2.1. Comparative tolerances of crayfish (adapted from Nyström, 2002).

Species	Temperature range (°C)	Minimum oxygen (mg L^{-1})	Salinity range (ppt)
Astacidae			
Astacus astacus	1–28	3.2	0
A. leptodactylus	4–32	4	0–14
Austropotamobius pallipes	1–28	2.7	0
Pacifastacus leniusculus	1–33	–	0–21
Parastacidae			
Cherax destructor	1–35	1.0	0–12
C. tenuimanus	4–28	3.7	0.3–12
C. quadricarinatus	10–30	0.5	0–12
Cambaridae			
Orconectes rusticus	2.5–33		
Procambarus clarkii	<35	0.4	0–12

In some parts of the world, particularly where crabs and crayfish are lacking from fresh waters, other large freshwater crustaceans may take their place. In South American and West African rivers, heavily built shrimps (family Atyidae) occur in areas of rapid flow, where they are primarily algal feeders (Obande & Kusemiju, 2008). Fossils found in Brazil show that these crayfish analogues have been in fresh waters since at least the Cretaceous. They had a Caribbean focus of radiation in the Miocene or Pliocene, where some forms have adopted a lentic habit (Page *et al.*, 2007) and also extend across the Indo-Pacific.

Another shrimp genus, *Macrobrachium*, males of which can attain a large size (32 cm total length for *M. rosenbergii*), is found in lowland tropical waters around the world. However, these need connections to the sea for reproduction. Gravid females make their way downstream to estuaries, where the eggs hatch, releasing planktonic larvae. Only at the juvenile stage will these make their way upriver again. Species of *Macrobrachium* are now widely farmed in the tropics, with a production of over 200 000 t per year.

Their large size and bizarre body form mean that freshwater decapods, principally crabs and crayfish, often attract the attention of the curious public (thus they may be valuable in public education about human pressures on finite freshwater resources; see Chapter 11). For centuries at least, large crayfish and crabs have been a valuable addition to the human diet and, in the course of their exploitation, some crayfish stocks have been overfished and others moved around for aquaculture – both processes causing damage to the habitats and communities in which they live.

Crabs represent an alternative body form and architecture to crayfish and shrimps. The elongate abdomen is reduced, tucked under the thorax, and locomotion is typically sideways, allowing rapid movement and manoeuvrability out of the water. Freshwater crabs, with 1280 species, represent one-fifth of all the world's brachyurans, but are often quite restricted in distribution. The highest species numbers are found in China, India, Thailand, Malaysia, Indonesia and the Philippines (Cumberlidge *et al.*, 2009), with other foci of endemicity in Colombia and Mexico. Many or most tropical crabs live in high-quality waters – streams, wetlands and caves – unlike many tropical crayfish. They tend to be restricted to headwater systems, where there has been much speciation and endemism; for example, 41 species are recognized in the Philippines and 148 species in Penghu Islands off Taiwan. In Sri Lanka, where all but one of the 50 crab species are endemic, their distribution is often very restricted within the rainforest, and half of the species are currently threatened, chiefly by habitat alteration. This can be contrasted with Madagascar, where there are 12 endemic species of freshwater crabs, mostly very restricted (Cumberlidge & Sternberg, 2002) and six endemic crayfish species spanning 700 km of mountainous terrain, and a wide range of habitats from forested streams to floodplain swamps. These crayfish are chiefly vulnerable to human overharvesting, habitat alteration, and introduced alien species.

Freshwater crabs are locally important in human diets in Bangladesh and elsewhere in Southeast Asia, and there are also small-scale fisheries in Lakes Nyasa and Tanganyika in Africa. Crabs are important intermediate hosts for the human lung fluke, *Paragonimus*, with some 20 million human infections worldwide; a role that has been taken over in some regions by the red swamp crayfish *Procambarus clarkii*, wherever it has been introduced in the tropics. The fluke is transmitted when crabs or crayfish are eaten raw or when they are prepared for cooking on the same chopping block as that used for vegetables. Crabs may have been translocated to some degree in prehistoric times, but because they lack the muscular abdomen so prized as food in crayfish, they have not been moved around by developed nations in the same way as crayfish have, for food or for aquaculture.

In southern Europe, where there are three native species, freshwater crabs are only significant in Italy, where they may interact with crayfish (Barbaresi & Gherardi, 1997) they also extend into southernmost France and more eastern Mediterranean lands. In addition, the catadromous Chinese mitten crab (*Eriocheir sinensis*) of estuaries and the lower courses of rivers is becoming economically important on several continents. Crab aquaculture (chiefly saltwater – swimming crabs and mud crabs) has emerged as a new industry in recent decades, driven by increasing market demands and the collapse of crab stocks and fisheries worldwide. China is undoubtedly the biggest farmed-crab producer in the world, with annual aquaculture production of various crab species approaching 700 000 tonnes, and substantial crab restocking programmes have also been under way for some time.

The Chinese mitten crab has a long history of invasion in Europe, and is now expanding northwards and inland as far as the upper Danube in Austria. Based on ecological niche modelling of suitable habitats, further expansion is predicted. Heborg *et al.* (2007) used a model based on the ecological features of 42 sites inhabited by mitten crabs in its native Asia as a basis for predicting the potential European distribution. Climatic variables such as air temperature and amount of precipitation contributed significantly to predictions of native distribution limits. The mitten crab's extensive distribution in Europe allowed independent validation of the predictions, with 84% of nearly 500 occurrences predicted to be suitable by >80% of the models. The model also identified large areas of Europe, particularly along the Mediterranean coast, as being vulnerable to future invasion. In eastern North America, the mitten crab invader has recently arrived at Chesapeake Bay, Delaware, and the Hudson River, threatening the renowned native blue crab fisheries there.

Like *Macrobrachium*, but unlike true freshwater crabs and crayfish, mitten crabs require a breeding connection with the sea. In their fourth or fifth year, they move down to the estuaries where they mature and breed. The females then migrate seawards into deeper waters, returning to the estuaries in spring, where the eggs hatch and the larvae settle, metamorphose into juvenile crabs, and gradually move upriver and even overland. Here they may take keystone roles equivalent to crayfish, burrowing into banks and feeding voraciously.

Factors which contribute to the success of both crabs and crayfish in fresh waters include their amphibious potential and their ability to survive shorter or longer periods out of water. The differences between these two freshwater decapod groups, especially when they come into contact with one another, are of significance in their ecology and, more generally, in understanding their importance in communities. Their different geographical distributions (freshwater crabs being primarily tropical, crayfish primarily temperate) has to do with their evolutionary lineage and the time and place of their first colonization of fresh waters. As we have seen in Chapter 1, freshwater crayfish are an extremely old group of organisms with the last common ancestor existing prior to the break-up of the supercontinent Pangea during the Triassic (245–200 MYA). This hypothesis is strongly supported by paleontological data (Hasiotis & Mitchell, 1989; Hasiotis, 1999). Molecular methods have been applied widely to the phylogenetics and systematics of crayfish (see Chapter 1) so that the status of perhaps the majority of species has been established with some confidence, although the phylogenetic relationships, particularly of the North American radiation, require further elucidation (Crandall & Buhay, 2008).

The history of crabs in fresh waters is more complex. The systematics of freshwater crabs is not yet fully understood, but several families are involved and the group is not monophyletic. The freshwater families with marine affinities probably fall into two groups: the Tridactylidae (close to Portunidae) and the rest (close to Grapsidae and Ocypodidae), representing two or more invasions of fresh waters. New- and old-world freshwater crabs represent two independent clades: Potamoidea (old world) versus Geocarcinucoidea (India, Australasia) and Pseudothelphusoidea (new world) (Martin & Davis, 2001), with the latter also occurring in Australasia. Apart from Australasia, crabs have not generally come into contact with crayfish, except recently in Madagascar, and also in Italy and the Adriatic as a result of the global invasive spread of alien crayfish, enthusiastically mediated by humans.

The ecological roles of crabs in freshwater communities are also less well studied than those of crayfish (see Chapter 3), perhaps because most crab species are tropical and often isolated in headwaters. Out of water, crabs are generally more agile than crayfish, which affects their ecology, but some crabs – like crayfish – have important or even keystone functions: they affect many other organisms and hence may control biodiversity through a cascading effect on the rest of the ecosystem. For example, a species of shore crab in the tropical dry forest of Costa Rica feeds primarily on tree saplings (Brook *et al.*, 2009). The saplings that are distasteful to crabs grow into mature trees and eventually dominate the landscape. The environment provided by a forest of these trees is relatively open, attracting particular animal species that prefer open forests, such as howler monkeys, coatis and tapirs. If the crab colony were to suddenly become extinct, the forest would recover its dense heterogeneous character because the saplings of invasive trees would no longer be cut back. Those animals that depend on the open forest ecosystem would languish, and could undergo local extinctions.

Crabs such as the fiddler crab *Uca lactea* are keystone species in mangrove ecosystems, where they can reach high densities. Their presence in the community makes it possible for many other species to live there. The crabs undergo their larval development in the water beneath the mangroves. When they have metamorphosed, they crawl up on the mangroves and feed on leaves. They are crucial in the processing of leaf litter. Burrowing activities (as discussed in the following chapter) also take place (Katz, 1980; Montague, 1982). The microtopography of the bottom will be modified and the soil will be aerated. This decreases sulphide levels in the soil and positively influences tree productivity. Two of the most important functions are stimulating the transfer of mangrove leaves to the rest of the food web and aeration of the flooded soils. While shredding and eating the mangrove leaf litter, they break it into smaller particles, which are more readily colonized by bacteria and fungi. Some crabs, such as the mangrove tree crab, reside in the canopy, feeding primarily on red mangrove leaves, while others live in the mud flats eating dead leaves. Crabs burrowing in the mud flats allow oxygenated water to reach deeper sediments. This helps the flooded soils to breathe and reduces the build-up of toxic chemicals such as hydrogen sulphide and ammonium.

About one-sixth of all freshwater crab species are now under imminent threat, due to deterioration of their habitat. The majority of threatened species are semi-terrestrial endemics with restricted ranges living in habitats subjected to deforestation, alteration of drainage patterns, and pollution. A parallel group might be the diverse but restricted burrowing crayfish of south-eastern Australia (Horwitz, 1995; Richardson *et al.*, 1999). Endemic crabs are as yet little monitored, and are especially vulnerable to sudden disruption from local events such as habitat fragmentation, pollution, and invasive species. In most countries with threatened species of freshwater crabs, anthropogenic disturbance associated with development is increasing. Many lowland disturbed habitats in Asia which are now plantations or rice fields have been recolonized by some of the more adaptable species of geocarcinid crab, or by the invasive crayfish *Procambarus clarkii*, but potamid crabs with more specialized habitat requirements may not be able to adapt to such a degree of change. The freshwater crabs that live in the major rivers of the Amazon Basin have the lowest proportion of threatened species. However, even widely distributed species with an apparent tolerance of land-use change could suffer catastrophic declines as a result of changes in land developments, hydrology or pesticide use (Cumberlidge *et al.*, 2009). Acidification of waters is also a major threat to freshwater decapods, both crabs and crayfish. Many species of freshwater crabs are under threat, although as yet none have been confirmed extinct. In view of increasingly pressing human needs for water and farmland, together with climate change and environmental degradation, the challenges on a global scale are very severe, particularly in the developing world, where most freshwater crab species are found (Cumberlidge *et al.*, 2009).

2.2 Aspects of crayfish biology that make them prime players in freshwater ecosystems

We have seen that many crayfish are long-lived and may attain a large size, in contrast to most other benthic freshwater invertebrates. For centuries at least, large crayfish have been a valued addition to the human diet and, in pursuit of their exploitation, some crayfish stocks have been overfished and others moved around for aquaculture, both processes causing damage to habitats and communities in which indigenous crayfish species (ICS) live. Through these and other pressures on their environment, indigenous crayfish are often very threatened. The same cannot be said about invasive, non-indigenous crayfish species (NICS). There is currently much concern about invasive species, including crayfish, especially in fresh waters.

Many aspects of crayfish biology have been discussed in detail in recent edited works such as Holdich (2002a) and Souty-Grosset *et al.* (2006). Crayfish biology has also been described in the 17 volumes of *Freshwater Crayfish* and, although with a European emphasis, in the four special volumes on crayfish in the *Bulletin Français de la Pêche et de la Pisciculture* (Vigneux, 1997, 2000, 2001; Souty-Grosset & Grandjean, 2002) and those edited by the European research network CRAYNET (Reynolds & Souty-Grosset, 2003b; Taugbøl & Souty-Grosset, 2004; Füreder & Souty-Grosset, 2005; Gherardi & Souty-Grosset, 2006). The ecology of crayfish species also appears more individualistic than that of most other invertebrates (partly because their larger size allows us to perceive the subtleties of their ecology better) and may be more akin to that of cold-blooded vertebrates. The general ecology of crayfish is fairly well covered elsewhere, and has, for instance, been comprehensively reviewed by Nyström (2002). This chapter provides a brief overview of crayfish morphology, physiology, growth and reproduction, while Chapter 3 concentrates on specific aspects of crayfish ecology in relation to biodiversity, such as life-history strategies as they relate to habitat and roles in the ecosystem.

2.2.1 Morphology and functional anatomy

Crayfish show a consistently repeated decapod *bauplan* based on the malacostracan 'caridoid facies', first defined and described by Calman in 1904, and a characteristic structure (Figure 2.1), well described by Holdich (2002b). The body of 20 segments is covered by a protective exoskeleton, forming a rigid dorsal carapace over the anterior part, the thorax. Ventrally, however, the segmentation can be seen, each segment with a pair of limbs appropriately modified for its sensory, feeding, walking or swimming

Figure 2.1.   (a) The large stream-dwelling crayfish *Astacopsis gouldi*; (b) a burrowing crayfish, *Engaeus orramakunna*. See also colour plate section (photos courtesy of Neil Doran).

function, as recognized by Huxley (1880) well over a century ago. The well-developed musculature of the chelae (first pair of walking limbs) and abdomen are the main parts that are eaten; in some large Australian crayfish these edible parts may constitute some 60% of body weight.

The 'caridoid facies' is shared by most other decapods in fresh waters. However, in crabs, while the segmental limbs are somewhat similar, the abdomen is greatly reduced and folded beneath the inflated, box-shaped carapace. As it is not used in locomotion, only in egg incubation, musculature is also reduced and a tail fan with uropods is usually absent. Finally, there is often asymmetry between the chelae in crabs, something more rarely seen in crayfish and not in *Macrobrachium*.

While the crayfish body plan is remarkably uniform, some modifications are evident in relation to habitat. Cave-dwelling crayfish may be blind, colourless and have elongated sensory appendages. In the strongly terrestrial burrowing crayfish, the abdomen has been reduced relative to the cephalothorax. Other morphological adaptations of strongly burrowing crayfish include vaulting of the carapace to increase the volume of the gill chamber, relative enlargement (for digging) and vertical orientation of the claws (for easier passage), and reduction of the eyes. These species do not employ the typical crayfish tail flip as an escape mechanism, and the main function of the abdomen appears to be the protection of eggs and juveniles during incubation.

The degree of spination of the carapace and other body parts varies extensively among crayfish. In general, open-water species are more spinose than burrowers, and those from running waters, for example *Astacoides betsileoensis* from Madagascar and *Euastacus armatus* from south-eastern Australia, are spinier than species from lentic habitats. The most glabrous species are usually swamp dwellers, such as the yabby, *Cherax destructor*, whereas in strongly burrowing species the chelae often carry numerous sensory setae (e.g. in *Engaeus cisternarius* and other strongly burrowing *Engaeus* species). Terminal spination of the tail fan (i.e. the telson plus the rami of the uropods) is apparently unknown in astacuran decapods, but a small number of parastacids and cambarids develop either terminal or lateral spines on the uropods, which may assist in locomotion in their burrows (Richardson & Swain, 2002)

Claw morphology varies somewhat with species (see colour plate section). Except for strongly burrowing crayfish, where the claws are modified for digging, the claws of adult crayfish play a primarily reproductive and signalling function as well as defence.

In general, the fecundity of burrowing crayfish seems to be lower than that of open-water species (Lowery, 1988), perhaps as a response to a stressful environment, or reflecting an improved probability of survivorship in a burrow. The reduction in abdomen size is weakly associated with a reduction in brood size; however, there is no apparent compensation in egg size in Australian *Engaeus* species (Richardson, 2007). In South America, the burrower *Parastacus defossus* has abdominal somites shorter than in the lotic species *P. brasiliensis*. In *P. defossus* there are also differences between the sexes, with females having larger abdominal somites than males (Almeida & Buckup, 1999, 2000; Alexandre Almeida, personal communication, 2009).

2.2.2   Physiological adaptations

As a group, crayfish have defined physiological adaptations to life in fresh water and, with their gills enclosed in a carapace, can tolerate periods of exposure to moist air (McMahon, 2002). Many crayfish need to survive periods of drought, which they do by constructing burrows, in which the air remains moist. Oxygen uptake can occur even when dissolved oxygen is depleted, but since the gills are protected by the carapace and do not collapse out of water, most crayfish can switch from water to air as an oxygen source (McMahon, 2002), and will sometimes come to the surface or even climb out of waterbodies whose oxygen levels have become depleted. Burrowing crayfish are best adapted to these circumstances (e.g. McMahon & Hankinson, 1993), and air breathing may even be their primary mode of obtaining oxygen.

In general, the most widespread species have broad tolerances to ranges or extremes of temperature, dissolved oxygen and salinity (Table 2.1). However, fresh waters can be extremely variable, and different crayfish species have developed physiological adaptations to their specific habitat, which may restrict their spread. Species adapted to western Australia (e.g. the smooth marron, *Cherax cainii*), where the predominant ions are sodium and chloride, or those adapted to the deltas of the Black and Caspian seas (e.g. *Astacus pachypus*) may be more tolerant to dilute seawater than are stocks elsewhere. Brackish water conditions are also tolerated by the signal crayfish *Pacifastacus leniusculus* in California and the thin-clawed crayfish *Astacus leptodactylus* in Turkey (Holdich *et al.*, 1997).

Warm temperate or subtropical crayfish species are more tolerant to poor or stressful oxygen–temperature combinations than those from cooler latitudes and, if burrowers, can survive out of water for long periods. These features not only allow them to be concentrated in commercial rearing ponds, but also facilitate their spread as

NICS. The species currently most evident in its global spread is the red swamp crayfish *Procambarus clarkii*, originally from the swamps and ponds of Louisiana but now widespread in both tropical and warm temperate areas (Huner, 2002).

2.2.3 Age and growth

Like other arthropods, crayfish possess a hard exoskeleton, and must shed it periodically in order to grow. Moult increments are usually around 15% of body length. Juveniles moult many times at first, larger forms only once or twice a year in temperate regions (Reynolds, 2002). The moult, or *ecdysis*, poses a particular danger to the individual, and indeed, in any captive batch of juveniles, the largest – moulting before the rest – are usually cannibalized (Reynolds, 1989). Large crayfish can usually find some form of retreat in which to hide until the new, larger exoskeleton has hardened. Depending on the environment and species, crayfish may live for one or many years. Crayfish age and growth patterns are not fixed, but relate to the environment. Thus, in Europe, the invasive alien signal crayfish *Pacifastacus leniusculus* may reach 95 mm carapace length – some 15 mm larger than recorded in its native range (Holdich, 2002b), while the red swamp crayfish *Procambarus clarkii* is known to live for up to 4 years, which is longer than in its native range in Louisiana. Freshwater crabs are generally short-lived.

Male crayfish may grow larger than females, as the latter are constrained from moulting while incubating eggs or young. Growth does not stop at sexual maturity, but males and females approaching maturity may grow differently. In this sex-specific allometric growth, the claws of male crayfish become larger than those of comparably sized females, while females develop broader abdomens (Reynolds, 2002). The chelae of decapods often make up 33–50% of total dry body weight. In most crayfish species, male chelae are longer and heavier than those in females; thus, allometric growth is selected for, especially in males (Stein, 1976).

Chela function may include (1) the capture and manipulation of prey, (2) defence against fish predators, (3) inter- and intraspecific interactions, and (4) reproductive activities. In laboratory tests, males of *Orconectes propinquus* selected similar-sized females to mate with. Males with large chelae were more likely to survive predation, occupy dominant positions in the group, and copulate with females, than males with small chelae. Non-mating cambarid males show a summer reduction in chelae, indicating that chelae are most important for male–male interactions and sexual bouts with females, but less so for prey manipulation and defence and not necessarily required for these functions (Stein, 1976). Chela dimorphism in males of *Orconectes virilis* has been remarked on for at least half a century (Williams & Leonard, 1952). Measurements showed that all three adult forms had recognizably different shapes, characterized by different ratios of length to width: 'Form I' males had chelae 19% longer and 12% wider than those of 'Form II' males, and 24% longer and 16% wider than those of females (Weagle & Ozburn, 1970). However, Buřič *et al.* (2008) have recently shown that female cambarid crayfish also moult between Form I and Form II. This is thought to conserve energy for egg production and growth.

2.2.4   Reproductive biology

In most decapods there is a post-naupliar larval stage, usually marine or estuarine, which metamorphoses into a juvenile. Freshwater shrimps, and also land crabs, retain this breeding link with the oceans. Crayfish and 'true' freshwater crabs, however, share a distinct adaptive feature: the females incubate the fertilized eggs (fewer than ten up to several hundred) through direct development to a juvenile stage, and are independent of seawater.

In crabs and crayfish the sexes are separate, and normally show an equal sex ratio, with the exception of some burrowing crayfish described below, and the parthenogenetic marbled crayfish or 'marmorkrebs' (*Procambarus fallax f. virginalis*), an all-female stock that has arisen in captivity (Scholtz *et al.*, 2003). Vogt (2008) has investigated the early post-embryonic life of marmorkrebs.

The crayfish families show some distinct differences in sexual morphology and function. Cambarid females store sperm in a ventral structure, the *annulus ventralis*, not present in the Astacidae, whose spermatophores are deposited on the underside of the female thorax, close to the oviduct openings. Deposition of the spermatophore is by the modified first pair of pleopods in astacoids, but in the Parastacoidea there is no such specialization of the pleopods and the spermatophore is deposited from the male gonopore directly onto the lateral processes of the sternal keel. In most parastacids there is little sexual differentiation, though Horwitz (1988) notes the development of lateral breeding flaps on the second abdominal segment of female *Engaeus* spp. that may have a role in protecting the eggs.

Animals showing both male and female gonopores are common in some parastacid species, particularly in burrowing forms of *Parastacus* and *Samastacus* from South America, while among the Australian genera *Engaeus*, *Engaewa*, *Cherax* and *Euastacus* there are species with supernumerary gonopores. Such 'intersex' animals may make up the majority of the populations of some Australian burrowing species; in his review of the genus, Horwitz (1990a) found that in nine (*Engaeus quadrimanus*, *E. sericatus*, *E. karnanga*, *E. merosetosus*, *E. hemicirratulus*, *E. australis*, *E. mallacoota*, *E. martigener* and *E. tayatea*) out of 34 species, all – or virtually all – the specimens examined were intersex, though in some cases it was possible to determine the functional sex by dissection. In South America, intersexuality is also known among burrowing parastacid crayfish (Rudolph *et al.*, 2001; Rudolph, 2002). The burrowing Chilean species *Parastacus nicoleti*, which spends its entire life underground, has both male and female gonopores, as do all six Brazilian species of the genus. Rudolph (2002) has described five different forms or reproductive variants of the Chilean burrowing crayfish *P. nicoleti*: individuals with both male and female openings, others with male gonopores in addition to a pair of primordial female gonopores, those with female genital openings only, those with a pair of female primordial gonopores only, or those with one male gonopore and a pair of female primordial gonopores. While hermaphroditism is probably indicated, the evidence is not sufficient to confirm this (Rudolph, 1990) nor to explain the functional basis of such variation. River populations of the burrowing crayfish *Samastacus spinifrons* had a small percentage (up to 12.5%) of intersex individuals with masculine-type abdomens, but also had several different gonopore patterns corresponding to the gonad. Ovotestes were found in 17% of 41 Chilean *S. spinifrons* with both male and female gonopores (Rudolph, 2002).

Breeding biology is well studied in species subject to exploitation (see Reynolds *et al.*, 1992). In temperate crayfish, breeding is usually iteroparous and seasonal but may be semelparous; however, it may be more prolonged or even continuous in the tropics and in cave-dwelling forms. Hamr & Richardson (1994) present strong evidence for biennial breeding in some *Parastacoides* (now *Ombrastacoides*) species in Tasmania; approximately half the females in a population mate in late autumn and carry their eggs through winter, the young hatching in early summer. The hatchlings are carried by the female into the following summer, and remain in the female's burrow over winter; she does not mate again until the following year. This breeding pattern is interpreted as a response to the difficulty of accumulating the reserves necessary to create a set of eggs in nutrient-poor sedgeland peats. A comparable biennial pattern has been suggested for northern European astacids in oligotrophic waters.

Breeding behaviour is complex and prolonged, and the different approaches between the sexes and the act of copulation itself have aroused interest and been described for over a century. Andrews (1907) recognized 17 stages in the copulation of *Orconectes limosus*, taking 9 hours, while Ingle & Thomas (1974) give a detailed review of mating behaviour in crayfish and describe seven stages in *Austropotamobius pallipes*, taking place over 10–15 minutes.

Patterns differ somewhat between the families (reviewed in Gherardi, 2002). Pheromones are always involved. Cambarid adults can tell the sex of another crayfish, and whether it is in Form I or Form II, by the use of a polysaccharide hormone (Ameyaw-Akumfi & Hazlett, 1975). Hypogean cambarids have less defined seasonality of breeding than epigean species, and Form I males may be found throughout the year.

Apart from biennial breeders, almost all female crayfish participate in mating, sometimes more than once, but not all mature males may have the opportunity. As in most decapods, there is pheromone-based mate attraction and males may also use their conspicuous chelae for signalling, for driving off competitors, and to hold the female while mating. In general, the pair may come to lie together in a complex mating ritual, with the male on top or (less usually) side by side, for periods from minutes to many hours. Female crayfish then go through a further behavioural sequence culminating in oviposition of large eggs, up to several hundred depending on the species. These are then fertilized by sperm stored in the *annulus ventralis* or in attached spermatophores before being glued to the hairs of the abdominal pleopods by the hardening of a sticky secretion called 'glair'. Depending on species and type of life history, incubation may last weeks or months, during which time there is a degree of parental care (see Richardson, 2007). Mason (1970) has described egg grooming and maternal–offspring behaviour, now used in crayfish hatcheries. Brooding females do not feed, thus brooding female ecology and behaviour is distinct from that of males or non-incubating females. Also, ovigerous females cannot moult, often leading to a slight size disparity between the sexes.

Hatchling astacid crayfish cling to the maternal pleopods with their chelae, and parastacids use specialized hooks on their pereiopods. Once free-living after two or three moults, they will at first return to the mother for predator protection. This phase has been much studied and has also been shown to be mediated by pheromones. In addition, Little (1979) showed that in the cambarids *Orconectes sanbornii*, *Cambarus virilis* and *Procambarus clarkii*, brooding females emit a pheromone which enables the young to identify and home in on them. Cambarid juveniles start to forage away from females at stage 3 but will return to a brooding female, and disperse at stage 4. Non-brooding females will eat them, but the juveniles can distinguish between non-brooding and brooding females, although not between different brooding females. Brooding cambarid females, if disturbed, signal to the young by posture and frequent beats of the pleopods (Ameyaw-Akumfi, 1976). In species inhabiting lakes and rivers, once the juveniles become free-living the female's appetite returns (as suggested by Little (1976), related to the loss of weight on her pleopods), and the young must scatter in order not to become prey. However, in primary burrowers living in habitats that prohibit easy dispersal, the juveniles may live with their mother for a year or more, often coexisting with subsequent broods (Horwitz *et al.*, 1984).

Eggs of astacid crayfish take 6–9 months to hatching, which is longer than most other crayfish. In captivity, eggs of the cave species *Orconectes pellucidus* hatched in 1 month. Forty days after hatching, young were moving about the aquarium and were being eaten by the female (Bechler, 1981); they would presumably disperse in nature. In most other crayfish, the same fate befalls juveniles in captivity, but in the wild surviving juveniles live away from the adults in vegetation, litter or gravel, usually in shallower, warmer water, and grow relatively rapidly through many moults. This ontogenetic shift in habitat use has been described, for instance, for *Orconectes propinquus* in Augusta Creek, Michigan (Creed, 1994), and allows adults and juveniles to affect biodiversity in different compartments of the aquatic ecosystem. Crayfish juveniles will reach sexual maturity after a number of weeks to several years, according to species.

2.2.5   Relations with the environment: diet

The ecological importance of crayfish in freshwater communities has already been mentioned and will be examined in detail in Chapter 3. Here we touch on one aspect of crayfish community ecology – that of trophic relations.

Some kinds of crayfish are predominantly carnivorous, detritivorous or vegetation-feeding, but most are omnivores. The same is also true for tropical freshwater crabs (Cumberlidge *et al.*, 2009). The broadly omnivorous diet allows certain species to be more abundant in a habitat than would be the case with more specialized feeders. By cropping stands of aquatic vegetation such as *Chara*, crayfish may control the levels of plant-living invertebrates, and by shedding leaf litter they make particulate matter available to collector species. There may also be ontogenetic shifts in food preferences, by which the food resource can be partitioned (Reynolds & O'Keeffe, 2005).

Most studies have been made on crayfish in littoral areas of ponds and in streams, but their effects in large rivers are not as well known. One study on a large river eco-system showed that two species of crayfish, *Orconectes cristavarius* and *Cambarus chasmodactylus*, coexist in the South Fork of the New River in western North Carolina. Crayfish guts contained mostly sediment and vegetative detritus, but those of *C. chasmodactylus* contained significantly more detritus and animal matter and less sediment than those of *O. cristavarius*. Nonetheless, despite a measurable impact on sediment accumulation, these crayfish did not significantly affect the density of any invertebrate group, suggesting that these two crayfish species may be functionally redundant in this river community, despite detectable differences in their diets (Helms & Creed, 2005).

Most studies, however, show a clear impact by feeding crayfish on vegetation, invertebrates, or both. Juveniles and adults may have different impacts. While juvenile *Austropotamobius pallipes* eat mostly animal food, large adults are predominantly vegetation feeders, although they will occasionally capture small fish (Reynolds & O'Keeffe, 2005). The chelae may be used to catch or collect food items, but these are transferred to the mouth by the pereiopods. Most crayfish forage cautiously, starting at dusk and feeding for up to an hour at a time in a relatively small area, in contrast to the behaviour of river crabs in the same environment (Gherardi *et al.*, 1989). As already described, the chelae of male crayfish become larger than those of comparably sized females, but the impacts of chela size on crayfish feeding ecology are so far unquantified.

Few data are available on the diet of burrowing crayfish, but they are probably also omnivorous. The Tasmanian burrowers *Engaeus cisternarius* and *E. fossor* both had predominantly vegetable material in their guts (Suter & Richardson, 1977). In the sedgeland-dwelling *Parastacoides tasmanicus* (now *Ombrastacoides huonensis*), Growns & Richardson (1988) found that the adults mainly consumed the roots and leaves of sedges (possibly gathering some material from the surface), while juveniles had a significantly greater animal component in their diet.

2.3 Conclusions: importance of crayfish

In this chapter we have concentrated on the morphology and biology of freshwater decapods, and especially crayfish, particularly those aspects that make them prime players in many freshwater ecosystems. Habitat heterogeneity – hides for juveniles and burrows for refuge – is important for the successful survival of all life stages of these long-lived and eventually large invertebrates, which usually lack the possibility of moving to an alternative habitat for their adult stage, as many insects are able to do. The claws of decapods are seen to have a number of roles – defence, digging, signalling – while pheromones control both breeding behaviour and parental care of offspring. Crayfish are widespread, not just in well-oxygenated surface waters. Some crayfish tolerate low levels of dissolved oxygen, breathing moist air; a few occur in brackish conditions. Finally, their frequently omnivorous diet allows greater dominance of their habitat and the invertebrate community.

We will be returning to look at their ecology in greater detail in Chapter 3, including threats to their well-being, one aspect of which – competition – is developed in Chapter 4. Their ecology relates to economic aspects of their population biology and abundance, discussed in Chapter 5. Crayfish may act as umbrella species for the conservation of complex communities (Chapter 6). Their body form and large size also attract the attention of members of the public, and this allows them be considered as useful flagship species for public education programmes (Chapters 5, 6 and 10).

3   Crayfish as prime players in ecosystems: life-history strategies

(with Alastair Richardson)

3.1   Overview of life-history studies

In the previous chapter we saw that many crayfish are both long-lived and attain a very large size compared with other benthic freshwater invertebrates. Crayfish ecology is also individualistic – to some extent more like that of cold-blooded vertebrates than of most invertebrates. As the general ecology of crayfish has recently been comprehensively reviewed (Nyström, 2002), this chapter concentrates on those aspects of crayfish ecology with a direct bearing on management and conservation of biodiversity, such as life-history strategies as they relate to habitat, and roles in the community and ecosystem. The particular impacts of crayfish translocation and of the spread of non-indigenous crayfish species (NICS) into new habitats and their effects on indigenous crayfish species (ICS) are discussed in Chapter 4, and their economic importance through exploitation of both ICS and NICS in Chapter 5.

Most crayfish of streams and ponds are shallow-water dwellers, but juveniles and adults may play different roles in the littoral benthic community. By virtue of their size and cryptic nature, the ecological roles of juvenile crayfish resemble those of other benthic crustaceans, or of some insect larvae. However, adults of the larger species have more in common with benthic fish or reptiles than with other invertebrates, in their longevity and dominance over a patch of stream or wetland substrate.

Crayfish densities in natural systems vary markedly, from less than 1 per m^2 to 70 or more (Nyström, 2002). An interesting comparison is that of *Pacifastacus leniusculus* in its native range (recorded densities of 0.25–1.8 per m^2) and in introduced situations in Europe (0.4–34 per m^2) (Nyström, 2002). Other invasive NICS in Europe reach similarly high densities. Such high densities have the ability to greatly affect their environment. Thus, particularly in smaller lakes where the bentho-littoral system is more important than the pelagic, crayfish may attain considerable importance, both in numbers and in their dominance of the community. Similarly, burrowing crayfish may also reach densities that give them a significant role in their communities. The relationships between biodiversity and abundance of ICS and NICS are complex, and the implications of environmental dominance will be taken up again later in this chapter.

3.1.1   Life history patterns

In decapods such as crayfish, complex behaviour patterns determine many of their interactions with the environment. As outlined in Chapter 2, in most crayfish the sexes are separate and approximately equal in numbers. Female crayfish incubate the eggs for weeks or months, during which time there is a degree of parental care; then follows a prolonged juvenile period, usually in areas away from the adults.

In primary burrowers living in habitats that prohibit easy dispersal, the juveniles may live with their mother for one or more years, often coexisting with subsequent broods (Horwitz *et al.*, 1984). In most other crayfish, maternal care ceases soon after the juveniles become free-living, so there is a danger of cannibalism of the young by the mother. Surviving juveniles live away from the adults, in vegetation, litter or gravel, growing relatively rapidly through many moults. They reach sexual maturity after a number of weeks to several years, according to species. Adult life may extend for one (semelparous) or several breeding periods (iteroparous) which may be annual or seasonal. Growth continues after maturity and some parts show allometric growth, as described in Chapter 2; for example, the claws of male crayfish become larger than those of comparably sized females. Some freshwater crayfish can grow remarkably large, the biggest being Australian forms such as the Murray River crayfish *Euastacus armatus* from the Murray–Darling system, and the Tasmanian giant freshwater crayfish (also known as the 'Tasmanian freshwater lobster') *Astacopsis gouldi* from forested northern Tasmanian catchments, which may reach several kilograms in weight. Interestingly, fossil crayfish burrows from the Cretaceous in Victoria also suggest similarly large dimensions.

Across each of the major crayfish families there are several different life-history patterns. Where resources are abundant, the cost of reproduction is low, apart from the risks involved over the long brooding period, when the female cannot feed and must hide from predators. Here, early breeding is favoured. In a less benign environment, crayfish may benefit by delaying reproduction until they reach a size when adverse factors are least harmful; thus longevity, age at maturity, and egg number and size all come into play. The concept of r and K selection (the letters relating to the parameters of the logistic equation) was originally propounded by MacArthur & Wilson (1967) to explain which kinds of colonists would do best if arriving at an uninhabited island, and developed more generally by Pianka (1970). In r-selected organisms, the ability to reproduce rapidly is favoured; they should have a relatively small size, early maturity, possibly semelparity, a large reproductive allocation, and produce more and smaller offspring. Such species are most likely to colonize the island situation, where copious reproduction is of greater value than individual survivorship in the often unpredictable habitats they may encounter.

By contrast, K-selected organisms are favoured for their ability to make a relatively large contribution to a population that remains at its carrying capacity (K), which is more or less the situation in many fairly stable or predictable environments. This implies a relatively large size, delayed and usually iteroparous reproduction, a lower reproductive allocation, and fewer, larger offspring, often with some parental care. However, adult and offspring habitats need not be linked in this way, and other more complex mortality or competition factors may drive life histories to an r or K pattern.

Whilst a dichotomy between *r*- and *K*-selected organisms is an oversimplification, the environments in which organisms live, and their incurred costs and available resources, tend to drive life-history strategies towards one or other extreme. Southwood (1972) was among the first to recognize such a 'chasm' or dichotomy operating in the *r* and *K* continuum. Good examples of *r* and *K* selection can be seen among crayfish: *r*-selected crayfish are typified by the red swamp crayfish *Procambarus clarkii* from Louisiana, and *K*-selected crayfish are exemplified by the European white-clawed crayfish *Austropotamobius pallipes*. However, many or most crayfish, including the large *Astacopsis gouldi* of Tasmania, exhibit trends at different points along the *r*/*K* continuum. Thus, in North America, *Cambarus robustus* has fewer, larger eggs, and perhaps lower juvenile mortality rates than *Orconectes rusticus*, making the former more *K*-selected (Corey, 1987). The latter, however, living for up to 4 years in large rivers and lakes would be more *K*-selected than many other cambarid crayfish, such as *Procambarus clarkii*, whose life span is a little over one year, during which it may produce 600 eggs. In Europe, the long-lived noble crayfish *Astacus astacus* breeds late and iteroparously, producing relatively fewer eggs each year than the faster-growing, earlier-maturing, thin-clawed crayfish *A. leptodactylus*. The latter species is also more tolerant of warm, moderately poor-quality waters and has been translocated across the continent, beyond its original range. In comparison, another astacid species, the signal crayfish *Pacifastastus leniusculus*, which is a non-indigenous crayfish species (NICS) in Europe, would be considered more *r*-selected than indigenous astacids, while another NICS in Europe, the cambarid red swamp crayfish *Procambarus clarkii*, lies still further along the *r*-selected scale. This probably helps to account for their very successful colonization and spread (see Chapter 4). Interestingly, the life history of *P. clarkii* as a NICS in Europe shows differences from that in its native range, especially in cool-water habitats (Gherardi *et al.*, 2000c; Gherardi, 2006). This aspect of its biology must then be considered plastic, an indication that its life span, realized niche and range in North America are probably defined by competition and other biotic interactions rather than by its biology.

Table 3.1 (after Füreder & Pöckl, 2007) shows an analysis of *r* and *K* traits for stocks of European crayfish.

3.1.2 Competition

Competition between crayfish species has long been recognized as an important factor explaining their distribution and coexistence. Eberly (1960) hypothesized on the effects of competition on the past and future evolution of *Orconectes pellucidus* and *Cambarus bartonii laevis* in Indiana caves. Penn & Fitzpatrick (1963), studying interspecific encounters with *Cambarellus shufeldti* and *C. puer* in laboratory conditions, found that the former won out in most agonistic interactions, explaining its increasing expansion and displacement of *C. puer* in the wild. However, both laboratory and field studies showed that other behavioural differences were as important as interspecies aggression in the dominance of *Orconectes virilis* over *O. immunis* in Iowa (Bovbjerg, 1961).

Competition for optimal habitat is important. *Cambarus bartonii* and *Orconectes rusticus* are fairly streamlined and able to hold their position in fast flows, which goes some

Table 3.1. Classification of crayfish species from Brittany (France) according to the two strategies *r* and *K* in relation to their life history characteristics (after Füreder & Pöckl, 2007).

	AUP	ASA	ASL	PAL	ORL	PRC
r-selected						
Early sexual maturity			*		***	***
High fecundity				*	**	***
Small egg size				*	***	***
Rapid egg development					**	***
Long egg-laying duration						***
Short hatching duration						***
Fast growth 1st summer			***		***	*
Fast growth 2nd summer		**	***	*	**	***
Small body 2nd summer	**			*	***	
Variable size 1st summer			*	*	*	***
Short life span					**	***
Resistant to plague				***	***	***
Total score	**2**	**2**	**8**	**8**	**24**	**31**
K-selected						
Extended sexual maturity	***	**		**		
Low fecundity	***	***	**			
Large egg size	***	**	*			
Slow egg development	***	**	*	*		
Short egg-laying duration	***	*	*	***	***	
Short hatching duration	***	*	*	***	***	
Slow growth 1st summer	***					
Slow growth 2nd summer	***					
Larger size 2nd summer		**	***	**		***
Uniform size 1st summer	***	***	*			
Long life span	**	***	***	*		
Susceptible to plague	***	***	***			
Total score	**32**	**22**	**16**	**12**	**6**	**3**

***: strong test; **: medium test; * low test; total score: sum of stars from each species

(AUP *Austropotamobius pallipes*, ASA *Astacus astacus*, ASL *Astacus leptodactylus*; PAL *Pacifastacus leniusculus*, ORL *Orconectes limosus*, PRC *Procambarus clarkii*).

way to explain the superiority of these species over *C. fodiens, O. obscurus, O. virilis* and *O. immunis*, all of which prefer a muddy substrate (Mande & Williams, 1963). It also helps to explain the expansion of *O. rusticus* in Ontario and elsewhere since its introduction. Competitive interactions are often complex; Hill & Lodge (1999) examined the relative importance of intra- and interspecific competition, and susceptibility to predation, in the interactions between the invasive rusty crayfish (*O. rusticus*), an earlier invader (*O. propinquus*), and *O. virilis*, which is native to the region (northern Wisconsin). Rusty crayfish not only outcompeted the other species in direct interactions, but also suffered less direct mortality from a fish predator, and their growth was less inhibited by the presence of the predator. This competition–predation mechanism has merited considerable study, well summarized in a recent review by Olden *et al*. (2006).

There are few reports of competitive exclusion between parastacid crayfish in Australia. However, there has been widespread translocation of several commercial species. In Western Australia, with its noted endemic fauna, exotic species of *Cherax* have been introduced, as well as translocations of indigenous species within the state. Lynas *et al*. (2007) have examined the introduction and spread of several commercially important *Cherax* species (*C. destructor* – yabby, *C. cainii* – smooth marron, and *C. quadricarinatus* – redclaw), and their potential to displace indigenous species. Redclaw are endemic to ephemeral ponds and wetlands of northern Australia but have been widely translocated, including into western Australia. The yabby of east-central Australia is now also widespread in western Australia and in Tasmania. In trials, yabby used their size advantage in agonistic encounters to exclude both marron and gilgie (*C. quinquecarinatus*) native to western Australia.

3.2   Contrasting life-history strategies

Among freshwater wetland organisms the primary division by habitat tends to be made between still-water and running-water species. Turbulent river flows incorporate dissolved oxygen, and provide some dilution and removal of intermittent pollutants and a different range of physical habitats than are encountered in ponds. As a result, many invertebrates tend to be restricted to either running or still waters. Their environmental needs, including habitat type and oxygen requirements, determine whether they can survive in still waters or must live in running-water habitats, where they generally have to possess some kind of adaptation to water movement, ranging from streamlining and adhesion structures to behavioural responses. Many stonefly and mayfly nymphs are restricted to running waters, while most water beetles are still-water dwellers, with a few specialized exceptions. Most freshwater crabs are stream-dwelling. In contrast, however, many crayfish species are equally at home in ponds and in slower-moving stretches of streams and rivers, and can tolerate a moderate flow by virtue of their large size and weight. The five species of European crayfish, all of which are found in both still and flowing water, well exemplify this breadth of habitat acceptance (Table 3.2).

Most freshwater crayfish show one of four main habitat preferences:

* More than half of all species of astacids and cambarids, but fewer parastacids, require cool-water, good-quality streams and lakes, where they take shelter under stones or create shallow burrows, emerging to forage by night.
* Some 20% of the overall total, representing all three families, live among weeds and roots in warm-water ponds and ditches; in particular, many cambarids (chiefly in south-eastern North America) and some parastacids.

Table 3.2. Crayfish habitat preferences in Europe (after Füreder *et al.*, (2006, in Souty-Grosset *et al.*, 2006).

Species	Freshwater /brackish	Water quality	Habitat quality
Astacus astacus	fresh	high	varied
Astacus leptodactylus	fresh, brackish	moderate	moderate
Astacus pachypus	fresh, brackish	high	moderate
Austropotamobius pallipes	fresh	moderate	moderate
Austropotamobius torrentium	fresh	high	high

Table 3.3. Overview of crayfish wetland habitat templets or preferences.

Habitat type	Examples
Cool high-quality water	*Pacifastacus leniusculus*
	Astacus astacus
	Astacopsis gouldi
Warm high-quality water	*Astacus leptodactylus*
	Cherax tenuimanus
Warm lower-quality water	*Cherax quadricarinatus*
	Cherax destructor
	Procambarus clarkii
Warm to cool temperate wetlands (semi-terrestrial, burrowing)	*Fallicambarus* spp.
	Engaeus spp.

- All crayfish have some propensity to burrow (Berrill & Chenoweth, 1982), but this habit becomes obligate in another 20% – cambarids and parastacids living in swampy or seasonally wet ground.
- Finally, some crayfish in each family (8% of the total, chiefly cambarids; very few Australian parastacids) are cave-dwelling.

Here, we look at crayfish from the viewpoint of preferences for temperature and water quality (Table 3.3). This table presents a useful oversimplification because it is often not possible in practice to draw rigid boundaries between the four habitat templet types listed. For example, the difference between cool- and warm-water high-quality sites is clear in some restricted situations, related to insularity or altitude, but one type may often merge into the other.

3.2.1   Cool-water, high-quality habitats

Crayfish in this group are typically long-lived and *K*-selected, achieving relatively large maximum sizes. Astacids are generally longer-lived than cambarids, but both may reach high population densities in suitable habitats, and so may be attractive for exploitation. However, their longevity and slow recruitment give them a long environmental memory, so even a rare incidence of pollution, disease or natural catastrophic event can affect stocks adversely over many years. The European members, at least, are known to be very susceptible to the causative pathogen of crayfish plague *Aphanomyces astaci*, and extinctions or large fluctuations have been noted in most exploited stocks. However, this is probably true of all crayfish with these preferences, except for the North American species.

Crayfish in this group are more important in streams and shallow ponds than in deep water of large lakes, although *Pacifastacus leniusculus* from Oregon has been introduced to the littoral of the large, ultra-oligotrophic Lake Tahoe, where it is now the dominant benthic invertebrate, occurring down to a depth in excess of 100 m (Goldman & Rundquist, 1977). In Europe, large stocks of *Astacus astacus* occur in Scandinavian lakes, while *Austropotamobius pallipes*, now in decline, still occurs in parts of the littoral of large Irish lakes and was formerly sparsely scattered in Lake Geneva, in both cases particularly near influents.

Signal crayfish (*Pacifastacus leniusculus*), among the largest of North American species and one of a few closely related Astacidae in the Pacific Northwest, have been widely introduced as NICS in Europe, where most interest surrounds their commerciality and negative ecological impacts (Souty-Grosset *et al.*, 2006). Like other astacids, the species is relatively long-lived and slow-growing, reaching maturity at between 6 and 9 cm total length (TL) when they are 1–3 years old, and living for at least 16 years (Belchier *et al.*, 1998; Lewis, 2002). However, in their native range centred on the Columbia River basin in Oregon and Washington (reviewed by Miller & Van Hyning, 1970), signal crayfish have been commercially fished since the 1890s, with fluctuating yields averaging 50 t annually. The signal crayfish fishery (discussed in Chapter 5) was actively regulated in Oregon, with close seasons and restricted areas, designed principally to protect egg-bearing females. Despite such closely monitored regulatory controls, however, the fishery tended to collapse at times, perhaps owing to a combination of harsh winters and overfishing leading to poor reproductive success. This indicates the importance of the influence of a sometimes unpredictable environment, when *K*-selected attributes are not always useful and hence populations may periodically fall a long way below their carrying capacity.

The native European astacids – noble (*Astacus astacus*) and white-clawed (*Austropotamobius pallipes*) crayfish – are typical members of this ecological grouping, albeit with somewhat lower temperature tolerances. Both are slow-growing and long-lived, and are very sensitive to plague. Noble crayfish (*A. astacus*) occur in northern lakes and rivers, chiefly around the Baltic Sea, but have been badly affected by plague outbreaks. Depending on latitude, they may take several years to mature at up to 10 cm TL and reach a final size of more than 15 cm TL. Stocks are highly valued and are regulated by fishing. Throughout the twentieth century it was clear that disease (later identified as 'crayfish plague', see Chapter 4) was perhaps the principal cause of stock declines, and in the 1950s a new remedy for declining stocks was advocated, the introduction of an 'ecological homologue' species. The species chosen was the signal crayfish from western North America; at the time it was not realized that it was a carrier of plague and so would further decimate native stocks. As a result, in northern Europe, noble crayfish are in continuing decline and signals have largely replaced nobles in crayfish catches in Finland and southern Sweden.

White-clawed crayfish (*A. pallipes*) occur in streams and lakes across western Europe from Ireland to Spain and Italy, and eastward to Switzerland, Austria and Dalmatia as far south as Montenegro. They tolerate some deterioration in water quality, sometimes occurring in muddy habitats (Holdich *et al.*, 2006; Peay *et al.*, 2006b), but in conditions of moderate pollution may rapidly decline and disappear (e.g. Lyons & Kelly-Quinn, 2003). Lake stocks are especially vulnerable to eutrophication and plague from the introduction of exotic species, and today lake stocks of white-clawed crayfish are mostly confined to Ireland, where frequent cool winds keep the lake water circulating and the sedimentary film oxidized (Reynolds, 1998). Members of this species complex mature at around 3 years old, at just 5 cm TL, and their maximum size of 10–12 cm TL is reached only slowly.

Other good examples of cool-water crayfish in North America include a group of cambarids such as the virile crayfish *Orconectes virilis* and the big water crayfish *Cambarus robustus*. These species occur in northern American rivers and lakes and can be exposed to a wide range of water temperatures. They typically reach maturity in 1–2 years, with a life span of up to 4 years; in some studied cases they are semelparous, dying after breeding once. One cambarid in this cool-water group, widespread across North America and favouring cool gravelly creeks, is the common or eastern crayfish *Cambarus bartonii*. Several other larger (generally reaching 10–12 cm TL) cambarid crayfish in North America also require cool to warm, good-quality water; these include the virile (*Orconectes virilis*), spiny-cheek (*O. limosus*), rusty (*O. rusticus*) and big water crayfish (*Cambarus robustus*) (Guiaşu, 2002; Hamr, 2002). While all burrow to some extent into banks and substrates, virile crayfish (*O. virilis*) burrows are known to sometimes lead to subsidence and dam failure. Richards *et al.* (1996) contrasted lake and stream catches of *Orconectes*, lakes containing *O. virilis*, and streams with *O. propinquus*. Spiny-cheek crayfish (*O. limosus*) are now widespread in larger rivers, ponds and wetlands across much of Europe, where they are still spreading eastwards (Souty-Grosset *et al.*, 2006).

Among the southern-hemisphere parastacids, species in the genera *Astacopsis* and *Euastacus* (Australia), *Paranephrops* (New Zealand), *Parastacus* (South America) and *Astacoides* (Madagascar) could be considered members of this group. Many species in these genera are found in upland streams, where waters are cool and dilute, although the largest species, such as *A. gouldi* and *E. armatus* in Australia, may extend their range into lowland rivers where water temperatures sometimes exceed 20°C. *Astacopsis gouldi* from Tasmania is the world's largest freshwater crayfish, exceeding 25 cm carapace length (CL) and 5 kg in weight. Sexual maturity is not reached until age 9 in males or 14 in females, and its life span probably exceeds 30 years (Hamr, 1997). Juveniles are found in small perennial headwater streams fed by springs, while adults prefer shaded stream pools with decaying wood. Clearing and desnagging streams, and siltation resulting from forestry practices are the main threats, along with illegal fishing. *Astacopsis tricornis* from western Tasmania also grows to quite a large size (more than 1 kg) and is often found in oligotrophic mountain lakes as well as lowland rivers.

In South America the Osorno River crayfish *Samastacus spinifrons* lives in rivers with vegetated margins and muddy bottoms with vegetable detritus, at low temperatures up to 15.5°C. It reaches a maximum length of 60 mm CL, and only 11% of females studied had eggs (Bocic *et al.*, 1988).

Lodge & Hill (1994) surveyed the literature to indicate what factors may govern species composition, population size and productivity of cool-water astacid and cambarid crayfish. The abiotic factors temperature, calcium, pH, dissolved oxygen, salinity and substratum may all be important in limiting population size. Among biotic factors, competition for refuges, thermal habitat and food, and predation by both invertebrates and vertebrates may often be important. Anecdotal evidence from Scandinavia suggests that increased human harvesting of mature crayfish may often result in increased crayfish yield (see also Momot, 1993), while – as shown above – population densities may be higher among invasive stocks than in their native habitats.

There is now much evidence that cool-water crayfish may control the abundance of macrophytes and their associated invertebrates (e.g. Peters *et al.*, 2008), with the result of increasing habitat biodiversity by controlling the commoner species (they are thus functioning as 'keystone species'). Fish populations may also be affected by predation or by competition with crayfish (Guan & Wiles, 1997); non-indigenous signal crayfish may eat salmonid eggs in streams (Stephanie Peay, personal communication, 2009). However, at the densities shown by native European crayfish stocks, there is no evidence of negative impacts from crayfish on eggs or juveniles of cohabiting fishes (Reynolds & O'Keeffe, 2005), and experimental Swedish data showed that neither *Astacus astacus* nor *Pacifastacus leniusculus* necessarily affect stream fish populations, nor was there an observed effect in the longer term (Degerman *et al.*, 2006).

3.2.2   Warm-water, high-quality habitats

Although crayfish in this group may tolerate low winter temperatures (0°–4°C), when they tend to be quiescent, they require warmer temperatures than those described in the previous section for optimum growth. Among examples are the large thin-clawed or Turkish crayfish *Astacus leptodactylus* of eastern Europe, the less well-known thick-clawed crayfish *A. pachypus* from the Black and Caspian seas, and the marron *Cherax tenuimanus* of south-western Australia. Some *Cambarus* species of central North America and *Orconectes rusticus* in its original distribution in the Ohio River drainage may also be examples of this group. Rusty crayfish *O. rusticus* have expanded their range into Canada and were also listed in the first group, bearing out their environmental plasticity and the suggestion that some species may form a continuum between the two groups in moderately good-quality waters.

Mundahl & Benton (1990) obtained experimental evidence of the thermal tolerances of free-living juveniles and adults of *O. rusticus* in south-western Ohio. Experiments predicted maximum growth rates of *O. rusticus* juveniles at water temperatures between 26° and 28°C, but greatest survival was between 20° and 22°C. Critical thermal maxima and minima of juveniles were 0.5°–2.6°C higher than those of adults throughout the summer, suggesting that juveniles were exposed to warmer water than adults were. As in most other crayfish, juvenile and adult *O. rusticus* are not usually found together in the same habitat; adults apparently displace the juveniles into warmer habitats. Warmer temperatures can decrease the survival of juveniles but improve their growth rates, leading to enhanced fecundity and competitive ability (Mundahl & Benton, 1990). This strategy is also found in other crayfish, with *A. pallipes* juveniles often congregating in very shallow weedy gravels (Demers *et al.*, 2003).

Astacus leptodactylus may inhabit brackish waters (lagoons, estuaries), as well as rivers, canals and lakes. For example, adults can survive near-seawater salinities of 28 parts per thousand (ppt) over a 9-week period (Yildiz *et al.*, 2004). This species is relatively tolerant to low oxygen content, low water transparency and temperature changes, and is a popular farmed crayfish in some regions. It also does well in newly established waterbodies such as water-filled gravel pits and quarries and even park ponds (e.g. Wiltshire & Reynolds, 2006).

The marron, the name generally given to *Cherax tenuimanus* (Smith), though more strictly *C. cainii* (see Austin & Ryan, 2002) is a large *K*-selected species with a limited natural range in rivers of the south-western corner of Western Australia, where it can also tolerate brackish conditions. It has relatively slow growth in its first year, reaching 30–50 g at 1 year old, and breeds in the spring of years 2 or 3. Unlike the hardier yabby, *Cherax destructor*, the marron needs good oxygen conditions and dense vegetation. In the wild, the young live away from the adults in masses of trailing weed; hence flowing water is essential, because the survival and growth of juveniles is related to cover and to density (Morrissy, 2002).

Very large marron specimens are up to 2 kg and probably at least 14 years old. There was early concern for the conservation of these large crayfish, and so marron were protected from commercial fishing in the south-western rivers of Western Australia from 1955 under state legislation (Molony *et al.*, 2002; Wingfield, 2002). In unexploited wild stocks, female marron spawn well below the legal size limit of 76 mm carapace length (CL), but in many exploited stocks they are fast-growing and mature close to the legal limit. Growth may reach 100 g in the first year, 300 g in the second, but the highest growth rates occur only at low densities, 0.1 per m², when biomass can reach 1000 kg per hectare. Thus, both growth and production of this clearly *K*-selected species are regulated by density. The favourable temperature range is 13°–30°C, with maximum growth at 24°C. Morrissy (1990) reports water temperature extremes of 8° and 26°C in the central part of the marron's natural distribution, where its abundance is highest. However, marron can survive for short periods at temperatures as low as 4°C.

Marron are sensitive to low oxygen and high salinity, so both eutrophication and salinization are threats in the wild and in culture. However, as discussed in Chapter 2, marron appear to tolerate low levels of salinity better than the other Australian crayfish. This may be due to western Australia's comparatively high natural (background) salinity concentrations. Their endemic home range occurs within flowing water habitats, with typically higher oxygen levels, which may explain their intolerance to low dissolved oxygen concentrations. Like species of *Euastacus* and indeed many astacid crayfish, marron have been observed to avoid unfavourable conditions by physically removing themselves from the water (Morrissy, 1978).

3.2.3 Warm-water, lower-quality wetland habitats

Crayfish in this group prefer vegetated mesotrophic to eutrophic ponds, wetlands and ditches, and include the red swamp crayfish (*Procambarus clarkii*), Gulf white river (*P. zonangulus*), calico (*Orconectes immunis*) and other cambarid crayfish, the Australian yabby (*Cherax destructor*) and redclaw (*C. quadricarinatus*), and also some South American *Parastacus* species.

The red swamp crayfish *Procambarus clarkii* is a cambarid species native to north-eastern Mexico and south-central USA (Huner, 2002). It has been introduced widely into Europe, Africa and Asia, often with its congener *P. zonangulus*, although the latter is a poorer colonist (Souty-Grosset *et al.*, 2006). Unlike astacid crayfish in North America or Europe, *P. clarkii* is able to tolerate dry periods of up to 4 months; thus it has also been listed in the fourth habitat group. Because of this ability, it can occupy a wide variety of habitats, including subterranean situations, wet meadows, seasonally flooded swamps and marshes, and permanent lakes and streams. It thrives in warm, shallow wetland ecosystems such as natural swamps and agricultural areas (rice-fields) throughout south-central Europe, where it has been introduced (Henttonen & Huner, 1999). It is also one of rather few crayfish species with some tolerance of saline waters.

Red swamp crayfish are short-lived, rarely exceeding 12–18 months in their natural range, where they may mature at between 45 and 125 mm total length (TL). They are adapted to life in seasonally flooded wetlands, feeding on plants, detritus and animal food, and retreating into burrows during periods of low water. Throughout the year some individuals are reproductive, allowing a quick colonization of reflooded habitats. Females lay up to 600 eggs which hatch in 2–3 weeks at 22°C, when the female is in her burrow. In their native range, numbers are checked by a wide range of predators, from mink and otter to many birds and reptiles and a variety of carnivorous arthropods. These checks are less evident in introduced habitats, although otters and herons have benefited from increasing crayfish populations in Spain.

Calico crayfish (*Orconectes immunis*) live in shallow ditches and vegetated river backwaters. They are also burrowers, and tolerate low oxygen and fairly high temperatures. These relatively small crayfish are, like other *Orconectes* species, short-lived. They become reproductive in 6 months to a year, and may live for two or three years to reach a maximum total length of 10 cm.

The yabby *Cherax destructor* of eastern and central Australia occupies a varied range of habitats, occurring in springs, rivers, ephemeral lakes and swamps. Unlike *P. clarkii*, yabby make shallow burrows that are not very destructive to banks and impoundments. They live for at least 3 years, maturing early at about 20 g weight and under 1 year old. Females spawn an average of 350 eggs, from early spring to summer, when the water temperature is above 15°C, and usually again in late summer, incubation lasting 3–6 weeks. Yabby grow best at 28°C and do not grow below 15°C, although they tolerate temperatures as low as 1°C. In contrast, redclaw crayfish (*Cherax quadricarinatus*), endemic to tropical areas of northern Queensland and the north of the Northern Territory (Jones, 1990), require higher water temperatures and do not survive long periods below 10°C in their native range. Redclaw mature at around 7 months and 120 g, and will breed at temperatures over 23°C, but can tolerate lower oxygen levels. In the dry season, unlike most crayfish, they may become gregarious in caves and residual water holes.

In summary, some crayfish of warm-water wetlands may also live a semi-terrestrial existence, forming a continuum with species of the fourth group, described next.

3.2.4   Semi-terrestrial burrowers in swamps, temporary wetlands and forests

While almost all crayfish burrow to some extent (Berrill & Chenoweth, 1982), a number of species in the American and Australian faunas have developed this habit to the extent that they have become independent of surface waters (Horwitz & Richardson, 1986; Welch & Eversole, 2006). This lifestyle no doubt originated in swamps and temporary wetlands as an adaptation to dewatering of the habitat, but it has led to the evolution of several highly terrestrial species in the genera *Engaeus* (Australia), *Parastacus* (South America) and *Distocambarus* (Georgia/ North Carolina). Primary burrowing crayfish (see below) are found mainly in south-eastern North America, southern South America and south-western Australia, in the families Cambaridae and Parastacidae. Primary burrowers do not appear to have evolved in the Astacidae, and so they are absent from western Eurasia (Hortwitz & Richardson, 1986).

Crayfish can be classified on their degree of dependence on a burrow (Hobbs, 1942). Primary burrowers are restricted to their burrows for the majority of their lives; secondary burrowers leave their burrows to wander in open water during the rainy season when the ground is flooded; while tertiary burrowers live primarily in open water, retreating to a burrow for shelter when moulting or breeding. Further, the burrows constructed by crayfish can be simply classified (Horwitz & Richardson, 1986) into those that are associated with lotic or lentic surface waterbodies (type 1), those that do not contact surface waters but penetrate down to the water table (type 2), and those that neither contact surface waters nor the water table but obtain their water from surface run-off or percolation and store that water in chambers perched above the water table (type 3). Table 3.4 shows the ecological, morphological and reproductive correlates of crayfish that construct these burrow types. Welch & Eversole (2006) bring these two classifications together, recognizing 'classes' of burrowers, following Hobbs (1942), and subdividing these into 'types', based on the burrow's relationship to the water table, citing examples from the North American fauna of both primary and secondary burrowers that retain water in their burrows, independent of the water table.

In contrast to open-water crayfish, primary burrowers use their burrows not only for shelter but to provide much of their food supply. Their morphological adaptations to burrow life include a tendency to hold the claws in the vertical plane to facilitate movement in the burrow, reduction of the eyes but increased setation of the claws for sensory purposes, a vaulted carapace with an enlarged gill chamber to improve gas exchange, and a reduced abdomen, reflecting the disuse of the aquatic tail-flip escape response. These trends are seen most strongly in *Engaeus* species from south-eastern Australia and in primary burrowers such as *Fallicambarus devastator* from Texas.

Table 3.4. Burrow classification of Horwitz & Richardson (1986), with ecological, morphological and reproductive correlates.

Burrow type	Water source	Burrow development	Range & typical genera	Burrow occupation	Burrow function	Typical crayfish morphology	Brood size[a]	Duration of mother–offspring association	Dispersal of young
1a	Open water	Simple, usually short & unbranching, under rock or log; all entrances under water	All continents: *Orconectes, Austropotamobius, Pacifastacus*	Temporary	Breeding, predator refuge	Body & claws spiny; claws held horizontally, usually isomorphic	90–1000	Weeks	Open water
1b	Open water	Simple, openings under water & on land	All continents: *Euastacus, Cherax*	Temporary	Breeding, predator refuge	Body & claws spiny; claws held horizontally, usually isomorphic	36–126	Weeks	Open water
2	Water table	Simple to complex; several openings; sometimes with ramifying subsurface tunnels; depth may be >4 m	N & S America, Australia: *Cambarus, Procambarus, Fallicambarus, Engaeus, Cherax, Parastacoides*	Permanent; sometimes surface excursions to forage & find mates	Desiccation, predator refuge; food source	Body & claws smooth; claws held at 45°, dimorphic or isomorphic; tail fan sometimes terminally spiny	22–108	<1 year	Overland in wet season (annual)?

Table 3.4. (cont.)

Burrow type	Water source	Burrow development	Range & typical genera	Burrow occupation	Burrow function	Typical crayfish morphology	Brood size[a]	Duration of mother–offspring association	Dispersal of young
3	Surface run-off	Complex; sometimes with ramifying subsurface tunnels; one to several water storage chambers	SE Australia (and SE USA?) only: *Engaeus*, *Distocambarus*?	Permanent; sometimes surface excursions to forage & find mates	Desiccation, predator refuge, food source	Body & claws smooth; eyes small; claws carry sensory setae; claws held vertically, dimorphic or isomorphic; abdomen reduced	13–61	<3 years	Overland, following infrequent (>1 year) rainfall events?

[a] Brood size: the range of egg numbers is given for Australian species only.

In the temperate rainforests of north-western Tasmania, where annual rainfall exceeds 1000 mm per annum, *Engaeus cisternarius* is a primary burrower living in type-3 burrows. The burrows ramify extensively beneath the surface of the clay soils, descending occasionally to chambers that store water less than a metre below the surface. They may have many openings, each marked by a chimney of excavated pellets, and the openings are often associated with fallen logs (Suter & Richardson, 1977). Females carry 45–75 eggs in the austral summer (October–April), incubating them for about 4 months; adults probably moult twice a year and may live for at least 4 years (Suter, 1977).

More than one generation of crayfish share these extensive burrows, as in other *Engaeus* spp. from type-3 burrows (Horwitz *et al.*, 1984). Burrow-sharing is not uncommon in primary burrowers, particularly between mother and offspring (Williams *et al.*, 1974; Huner & Barr, 1991; Hamr & Richardson, 1994), but also between adults, especially during drought (Horwitz & Knott, 1983; Norrocky, 1991). Evidence suggests that levels of aggression between individuals of burrowing crayfish are much reduced compared with those of open-water species (Guiaşu *et al.*, 2005).

As an example of primary burrowers in type-2 burrows, we can take any of several species of *Ombrastacoides* from the sedgelands of western Tasmania. The soils in this region are peats overlying glacial tills and very old quartzite rocks, so they are acidic and nutrient-poor. However, they support large numbers of burrowing crayfish, from valley floors to ridge tops at over 1000 m, unlike acid peatlands in most regions elsewhere, perhaps because the average temperature is high enough to prevent ground-freezing frosts (Brown *et al.*, 1993). The density of burrows, and hence adult crayfish, can exceed 1 per m², and their depths range from >1.5 m on valley floors to <0.5 m on slopes where the soils are very shallow. Because the peats are highly coherent, these burrows outlive their occupants, and the construction of fresh burrows seems to be rare (Richardson & Swain, 1990). A positive relationship between burrow volume and the size of the occupying crayfish suggests that there is competition for the largest burrows, with animals moving into larger quarters as they grow, rather like the shell-swapping of hermit crabs (Growns & Richardson, 1988). These burrows are in contact with the water table for most of the year, but may lack free water for a week or two in summer. Some species respond to this by closing the burrow entrance, while others push debris away from the burrow entrances to construct catchment areas around the entrances, apparently to maximize the capture of rainfall and direct it into the burrow. Adult *O. huonensis* feed almost entirely on vegetable material, both the roots and leaves of sedges, apparently gathering the latter from the surface, a habit also recorded in some North American crayfish such as *Cambarus dubius* (Taylor & Schuster, 2004).

Significant numbers of *Ombrastacoides huonensis* can be caught in pitfall traps in burrowed areas, and carapaces of predated animals are frequently seen, suggesting that excursions from the burrow are quite common in these Tasmanian crayfish. Surface activity of primary burrowing crayfish is commonly recorded in North American species. Norrocky (1991) trapped and marked over 200 individuals of *Fallicambarus fodiens* in roadside ditches and residential lawns in north-central Ohio; he found that surface activity followed rain or snow melt, mostly in spring and autumn. Well over half the marked crayfish changed location between captures, moving as far as 66 m from the last site of capture. Burrow-sharing between sexes, reproductive forms and even between *F. fodiens* and *Cambarus diogenes* was quite common. Punzalan *et al.* (2001) showed that juvenile *F. fodiens*, using chemical cues, could distinguish between chimneys made by conspecifics and artificial ones constructed by the researchers. Since the animals were attracted to the burrows of conspecifics, this may explain why burrowing crayfish tend to occur in colonies within more extensive areas of suitable habitat.

Similar patterns of habitat use occur among parastacid crayfish in Chile and Brazil, some burrowing in swampy ground away from open water, others in the muddy banks of rivers. Both Chilean species of *Parastacus* (*P. pugnax* and *P. nicoleti*) are good examples of primary burrowing species, as are *P. defossus* from Brazil, Uruguay and Argentina, and *Virilastacus araucanius* and *V. rucapihuelensis* from southern Chile (Rudolph & Crandall, 2007; Alexandre Almeida, personal communication, 2009).

The parastacid crayfish of Madagascar are largely secondary or tertiary burrowers, but *Astacoides crosnieri* is a primary burrower, building complex burrows up to 1.5 m deep that seldom make contact with open water (Jones *et al.*, 2007).

A few burrowing crayfish have been elevated to the status of significant pests, either as a result of their foraging or their burrowing. In Australia, 'land crabs' (i.e. burrowing crayfish of the genus *Engaeus*) have been blamed for damaging fruit trees through their extensive underground chambers and posing a risk to cows and horses (Clark, 1936). The prairie crayfish *Procambarus hagenianus* is the only North American crayfish listed as a significant crop pest, although others, such as *Fallicambarus devastator*, may cause damage through their burrows (Hobbs & Whiteman, 1991). *P. hagenianus* is particularly devastating when the animals emerge on rainy spring nights to feed on the seedlings of corn and cotton. Numbers may reach 12 000–37 000 burrows per hectare (Fitzpatrick, 1975). They generally occupy somewhat raised ground, remote from watercourses, in central and eastern Mississippi and western Alabama.

The large Lamington spiny crayfish, *Euastacus sulcatus*, which lives in subtropical rain forests in Queensland, Australia, has taken a different route towards terrestriality. Although it constructs only simple type-1 burrows at the edges of streams, it behaves in some ways like a land crab, making extensive excursions on land through the forest to forage, and returning to its home burrow (Furse & Wild, 2002).

3.2.5   Cave dwellers

While cave populations of crayfish are rare in most parts of the world, they occur in many caves in the southern states of the USA. Despite restrictions in food type and availability, caves may host an astonishingly rich fauna, which has been well studied. Interestingly, the main cave crayfish species also have specific host–commensal relationships with ostracods. There are, for example, some 1 400 caves in two major karst areas in southern Indiana. Some of these contain the blind, colourless troglobite *Orconectes inermis*, first reported by Cope in 1872, and the eyed troglophile *C. laevis* (the commonest cave crayfish) (Hobbs, 1974). *C. laevis* constructs simple burrows which open below the water surface. This species also has surface (epigean) populations, which exchange genes with hypogean ones. Finally, there are also some accidental cave dwellers, particularly *O. immunis*, *O. propinquus* and *O. sloanii* (Hobbs, 1974).

The biodiverse Shelta cave in Alabama, extending for almost 800 m, including an underground lake of nearly 3 ha, contains at least three *Orconectes* species including *O. australis* and O. *sheltae*; their genetic identity has been elucidated by Buhay & Crandall (2008). Population estimates for *O. australis* were around 1000 individuals over the cave area, and they are apparently very long-lived; two different growth rate calculations gave estimates of age between 37 and 176 years to reach a maximum carapace length of 47 mm (Cooper, 1975). Females are sexually mature at 38 mm but first reproduce successfully at 45–47 mm (at an estimated age of 16–35 years), making them highly *K*-selected.

3.3   Crayfish key ecosystem roles and attributes

Much of the interest in crayfish centres on their roles in wetland communities, and so relates to biodiversity in these communities. Any assessment of biodiversity involves much more than just a species list for each habitat; it also includes rarity and indicator status, and must also take on board the apparent differences in community impact between rare and common species, large and small, or predators and detritivores. However, we still have many knowledge gaps in freshwater biodiversity, and both geographical and taxonomic coverage is uneven. Freshwater crayfish diversity – with its hot-spots in the south-east of North America and south-western Australia – was examined in Chapter 1. In Chapter 2 we introduced the concept that crayfish are not only components of community biodiversity, but also often controllers of it; here we discuss further these important aspects of their community ecology.

Much catchment diversity resides outside the main channel, in marshes and ditches. For both invertebrates and vertebrates, a freshwater site's physical qualities (temperature, flow, substrate, etc.) are often as important as its vegetational components. We have seen that while some crayfish have a broad habitat range, others are characteristic of wetlands outside the main drainages, while more are restricted to rivers, streams and small lakes. However, where crayfish species have been translocated, they may survive in unexpected habitats and take on new roles in the alien environment, suggesting a degree of plasticity in habitat selection not seen in their native ranges (see Chapters 4 and 8).

Because the freshwater environment is often linear or fragmented, the boundaries between land and water, and hence the functional linkages between the terrestrial and aquatic environments, are often significant. There are both nutrient and geomorphological links, as well as biotic, between a stream channel and its floodplain. Trophic fluxes are important among such functional linkages, with overall a net transfer of aquatic-derived energy to or from riparian food webs. Insect larvae living an aquatic existence often breed terrestrially or aerially, while the energy and nutrients of homotopic aquatic crustaceans must chiefly be transferred through the aquatic food web, or through amphibious predators such as newts, otters and herons. Many crayfish, furthermore, feed on terrestrial material such as fallen leaves or woody debris from

Table 3.5. Some of the indicator designations applied to crayfish.

Indicator role	Crayfish examples
'Charismatic' or 'iconic' species	
Umbrella species, Heritage / Flagship species	Noble *Astacus astacus,* Marron *Cherax cainii/tenuimanus*
Surrogate species	Various
Key roles in environment:	
Keystone (trophic) regulators	Red swamp *Procambarus clarkii*
Ecological engineers	Eastern *Cambarus bartonii,* Southeastern Prairie *C. hagenianus*
Indicators or Surrogates for water quality	Marron *Cherax cainii/tenuimanus,* Stone *Austropotamobius torrentium*
Biodiversity indicators	White-clawed *Austropotamobius pallipes*

riparian woodlands. Ecosystem connectivity thus affects biodiversity, and more study on the role of crayfish in terrestrial–aquatic interactions is needed.

Key functional species such as freshwater crayfish have been identified as useful community indicators for conservation purposes. The usefulness and range of types of indicator species has already been outlined in the Introduction. Some workers feel that indicators should be confined to ecologically important components of a community, but others believe that threatened species can also provide useful indicators for monitoring biodiversity. However, it may be difficult to adequately monitor threatened indicator species without risk to their status, and their very rarity compounds the monitoring problem. Such difficulties are relevant to studies of freshwater crayfish.

3.3.1   Crayfish species as bioindicators for communities or habitats

Species that fascinate or attract the interest of humans as well as being ecologically significant are sometimes called charismatic or iconic species; these can include some crayfish. If protected or the object of conservation interest, they may be useful umbrella species; this refers to the protection of a selected wide-ranging species that also confers protection on other species in the same habitat, including those more cryptic or less well known. The concept was first developed by Wilcox (1984), and revisited and redefined by, among others, Caro & O'Doherty (1999). Even if not specifically protected, they may be designated as heritage or flagship species. These are species of particular importance or interest to the general public, which may provide a rationale for their protection and conservation and also for their habitat and associated species. Some designations applied to crayfish are listed in Table 3.5.

The terms 'charismatic species' or 'iconic species' mean approximately the same thing. However, 'heritage species' often has a historical or cultural connotation; these are more usually rare or restricted in their distribution, while 'flagship species' may well be widespread and come to typify the entire landscape unit to be conserved. In this context, a flagship or heritage species is acting as an umbrella to conserve the associated species in the environment. In northern waters, while certain fish species such as the Atlantic salmon may be considered heritage species, all salmonids may act as flagship and umbrella species, as may the crayfish of moderately good-quality cool waters. Being suitable for the communication of conservation concerns, they are often important in conservation monitoring and guiding the management of fresh waters for the preservation of optimum biodiversity.

Invertebrates increasingly feature as indicator species, although rather few are flashy enough to capture the interest of the public and be considered true flagship species. Freshwater crayfish are prime players among invertebrates because of their size, longevity and reliance on aquatic systems throughout life. Some also become flagship species because of their edibility, accessibility and tolerance of handling. However, not all have equal weight as bioindicators of water or habitat quality, and only a few are at present exploited as food, which tends to be the prime focus of human interest. For example, in western Australia the marron is recognized as a flagship species for river conservation, with emphasis on endemic communities.

There are other types of biodiversity indicator. Surrogate species, typifying environmental features such as water or habitat quality, may be assigned as representative indicators for a suite of less accessible species in the aquatic community. Surrogate indicators of various ecosystem functions have been suggested for aquatic systems, including for litter breakdown rates or benthic metabolism. In conservation biology, often one or a small number of species are used as surrogate species (*sensu* Caro & O'Doherty, 1999) to illustrate conservation problems. They may be used in various ways, e.g. to indicate the extent of various types of anthropogenic impacts (health indicator species), to track population changes of other species (population indicator species), to locate key areas of high biodiversity (biodiversity indicator species), to act as 'umbrellas' for the requirements of sympatric species (umbrella species), or to attract the attention of the public (flagship species). Due to their attributes and peculiarities, freshwater crayfish may be useful surrogate and umbrella species, fulfilling most of the above prerequisites in a range of biotopes. They may also be used to specify the size and type of habitat to be protected as well as just its location.

The brief discussion of ecological requirements presented above and summarized in Table 3.3 underlines the diversity of habitats occupied by crayfish. While most crayfish are aquatic, we have seen that some burrowing crayfish live essentially terrestrially, and their ecological roles relate to terrestrial ecosystems. An important part of crayfish ecology is their role and impact within the aquatic or terrestrial community or ecosystem. This may lead to the identification of attributes that define them as keystone species, as surrogate species for water quality, as bioindicators, or as flagship species, in some cases with important socio-economic values. These are described below.

3.3.2   Key roles in trophic webs

Crayfish feeding is an important aspect of their synecology. They may be predominantly carnivorous, omnivorous and scavenging, or vegetation and/or detritus feeders. For example, Haertel-Borer *et al.* (2005) described the complexity of ecological roles of the spiny-cheek crayfish *Orconectes limosus* introduced to a small north German lake, while Reynolds & O'Keeffe (2005) showed that different year-classes of white-clawed crayfish *Austropotamobius pallipes* had different feeding patterns in an Irish lake and stream. The broad diet in both these species (which may be atypical of second-level consumers) showed ontogenetic shifts, with juveniles eating more invertebrates than adults do. The large chelae of adult males are less effective at trapping live prey than might at first be expected, but in both these studies adult crayfish were shown to be more important carnivores than previously thought.

One study of cambarid crayfish has shown few impacts on a river ecosystem, leading to the conclusion that these crayfish were functionally redundant in large rivers, as opposed to streams (Helms & Creed, 2005). Crayfish guts contained mostly sediment and vegetative detritus, and field experiments showed some effect on sediment accumulation. However, crayfish did not significantly affect the density of any invertebrate group.

While Helms & Creed (2005) found that some river crayfish do not seem to exert pronounced effects on their communities or habitats, the majority of studies have indicated the extent to which crayfish populations may alter their littoral aquatic or semi-terrestrial surroundings by selective feeding. This is usually most clearly seen when a species alters its density, expands or contracts its range, or is transferred to a new location (translocation). In such situations, the crayfish may reach densities far greater than those seen in natural habitats within their native range. For example, the structure and functioning of freshwater marsh habitats in the Doñana National Park, Spain, were significantly altered as a result of the introduction of the red swamp crayfish *Procambarus clarkii* from Louisiana in 1973 and its trophic interactions with existing food webs (Gutiérrez-Yurrita *et al.*, 1998). These crayfish are polytrophic, most frequently eating non-green plant litter (occurring in 80% of the population), followed by *Scirpus* rhizomes (50%), green plants (37%) and organic sediment (occurring in 30%). Animal food items comprised mostly insects (25% occurrence), cladocerans (16%) and mosquito fish (14%). Young crayfish contained a higher proportion of animal food than did adults. Not surprisingly, given the rapid growth and early breeding of *P. clarkii*, several components of the Doñana marsh community were severely affected (Delibes & Adrian, 1987).

Within North America, some cambarid crayfish have extended their range, also bringing with them drastic changes to the new habitat. Perhaps best known is the situation with the rusty crayfish (*Orconectes rusticus*), mentioned in Section 3.1.2.

3.3.3 Crayfish as keystone species

Organisms that dominate energy flow and thus, or otherwise, affect ecosystem structure or function are called 'keystone species' in the ecosystem. This much-debated concept was originally proposed by Paine (1969) as typifying a species of 'high trophic status' whose activities exert a disproportionate influence on the pattern of species diversity in a community. Many scientists have further developed the concept – see, for example, the review by Mills *et al.* (1993) – and the redefinition by, among others,

Davic (2003). Indeed, some ecologists have broadened the definitions of keystone species to include other disproportionate but non-trophic impacts on communities (see Section 3.3.4 – Crayfish as ecological engineers).

For several decades, researchers have considered certain crayfish to have keystone roles or attributes, controlling energy flow and producing important changes in ecosystem structure and function (e.g. Hall *et al.*, 1970; Momot *et al.*, 1978; Holdich, 1987; Matthews & Reynolds, 1992; Momot, 1995). Modifications of existing food chains by crayfish were predicted by Lodge *et al.* (1985), Feminella & Resh (1989) and Hanson *et al.* (1990). Indeed, the European research network CRAYNET is subtitled 'European crayfish as keystone species – linking science, management and economics with sustainable environmental quality' to particularly emphasize this aspect of their ecology (Reynolds & Souty-Grosset, 2003a). Large invertebrates such as crayfish can have very important influences on stream or pond community structure.

There is much evidence of the controlling nature of crayfish on their aquatic ecosystems, with significant implications for ecosystem biodiversity. The impact of crayfish on the structure of food webs has been reviewed by Nyström (2002), dealing separately with their impacts on primary producers, macroinvertebrates and vertebrates. In North America, Creed (1994) demonstrated the dramatic impacts of the northern clearwater crayfish *Orconectes propinquus* in Michigan streams on the abundance of a dominant filamentous alga (*Cladophora glomerata*). By reducing the abundance of this coarse blanketing alga, these crayfish indirectly facilitated the growth of smaller benthic algae (e.g. diatoms) and the invertebrates that feed on them, thereby increasing stream biodiversity. In this stream, crayfish were acting as keystone species. There is equivalent evidence for Astacidae; for example, the control of aquatic plants by signal crayfish *Pacifastacus leniusculus* in North America, e.g. in Lake Tahoe (Goldman, 1973), and of some aquatic submerged macrophytes in European lakes by noble crayfish *Astacus astacus* (Abrahamsson, 1973) although not of *Elodea* in Lake Steinsfjorden (Skurdal *et al.*, 2002). The impacts of white-clawed crayfish *Austropotamobius pallipes* on charophytes and benthic macrofauna of lakes have also been described (e.g. Matthews *et al.*, 1993).

As we have seen, ponds, swamps and marshes, including seasonally flooded wetlands (short-hydroperiod ecosystems), often contain crayfish functioning as keystone species. In warm-water wetlands, red swamp crayfish *Procambarus clarkii* may be keystone aquatic invertebrates, consuming large quantities of animal prey and plant forages, while Australian crayfish such as the smooth marron, *Cherax cainii*, can survive for long periods by consuming decomposing plant material and digesting its living cover of microbes (O'Brien, 1998).

As well as dominating the flora and invertebrate fauna in the hierarchy of the wetland environment, crayfish are also an important resource for many other animals, serving as conduits of energy to larger predatory animals – fish, amphibians, reptiles, birds and mammals – and hence directly affecting species diversity and abundance, thus underlining their role as keystone species within the community. Introduced or spreading crayfish stocks are now known to affect food webs and be responsible for a rapid decrease in aquatic community biodiversity, through their direct consumption of macrophytes and huge releases of nutrients. While the ecosystem role of crayfish may be deduced from observation, and tested by experiment, invasive exotic crayfish provide good natural experiments to investigate the ecological roles of crayfish in ecosystems. This will be developed in more detail in Chapter 4.

A related but different concept is that of 'keystone structures' in the sense of Tews *et al.* (2004). These authors conclude from a selective review of the literature that for some species a habitat structure with a disproportionate impact on the community (such as a tree in the savanna, or a temporary field pond in agricultural land) may contribute to biodiversity, and conversely, its removal would have a profound effect on biodiversity. This concept has been justified for large mobile animals in terrestrial systems, but its emphasis on habitat heterogeneity would appear also to be relevant to crayfish and, for example, submerged plant beds, although its usefulness has yet to be established.

3.3.4   Crayfish as ecological engineers

Research conducted in experimental streams demonstrated that when crayfish accelerate leaf decomposition rates they may affect sediment accumulation in streams (Jones *et al.*, 1994). The impact of large *Cambarus bartonii* on leaf packs and their associated fauna was tested in an experimental stream (Creed & Reed, 2004). Leaf pack breakdown was significantly faster in the presence of crayfish, which changed the abundance of fine particulate matter and associated chironomid larvae and harpacticoid copepods. However, heptageniid mayfly larvae were found only where crayfish had reduced the fine particulate organic matter (FPOM). In these streams, crayfish were acting as ecosystem engineers, i.e. by their activities they were influencing habitat quality and resource abundance (availability of fine particles of detritus) for coexisting taxa. These results demonstrate that crayfish can shape community biodiversity in forested, headwater streams through their influence on detrital processing rates and the distribution of FPOM.

Other crayfish elsewhere have also been shown experimentally to be ecosystem engineers, modifying resources for other organisms (Momot, 1995), and as geomorphic agents, affecting the degree of erosion and base flow in experimental streams (Statzner *et al.*, 2000, 2003; Moore, 2006). The different abilities of fish and crayfish in disturbing stream gravels are assessed by Statzner & Sagnes (2008). Apart from such instream effects, burrowing crayfish can produce prodigious tunnel systems that have a significant impact on the surrounding ecosystem. Fitzpatrick (1975) records burrows of the prairie crayfish *Cambarus hagenianus* extending 4 m below the surface (although 1–2 m is more typical of burrowing crayfish) and it is common to find at least one crayfish burrow system per square metre in suitable habitats. Crayfish burrows act as conduits for water and gases through what are often saturated and poorly oxygenated soils (see, e.g. Richardson, 1983, 2007), ameliorating soil conditions and probably enhancing plant growth (Richardson & Wong, 1995). The burrows also act as important refuges or habitat for other species (Lake, 1977; Horwitz & Knott, 1991). All these activities qualify burrowing crayfish for the role of ecological engineers (*sensu* Jones *et al.*, 1994), and in this they may be recognized as keystone species in some ecosystems (Richardson & Doran, 2008).

3.3.5 Crayfish as indicators or surrogates for water quality

Due to their homotopic (solely aquatic or semi-aquatic) and benthic nature, many crayfish are necessarily dependent throughout their life on specific features of the aquatic ecosystem, including habitat heterogeneity, water quality and a lack of pollutants (Füreder & Reynolds, 2003). As many long-lived crayfish occur in good-quality habitats, they have been considered as indicators of such conditions, and thus are assigned a high score in various biological water quality indices such as the BMWP and its derivative the ASPT (UK), IBGN (France), Q index (Ireland), and the AUSRIVAS of Australia. There is also a range of water quality indexes for the USA, some including crayfish. The confusing influence of other species should not be overlooked. In France the white-clawed crayfish *Austropotamobius pallipes* is often considered a surrogate bioindicator for excellent water quality (e.g. Grandjean *et al.*, 2004; Trouilhé *et al.*, 2004; Renai *et al.*, 2006; Brusconi *et al.*, 2008). However, the high indicator value attributed to this cray-fish is probably related to its current restriction in the main to isolated spring-fed headwater habitats, brought about through the ravages of crayfish plague carried by invasive American crayfish species moving up rivers. Many French populations are now largely restricted to headwaters (Changeux, 2003; Collas *et al.*, 2007). In contrast, in Ireland, where (uniquely in Europe) alien crayfish have not been introduced, the same species *A. pallipes* occurs in streams, rivers and lakes that may be slightly or even moderately polluted by organic waste, down to an ASPT value of 4 or a Q value of 3 (Demers & Reynolds, 2003; Gallagher *et al.*, 2006). In the UK, white-clawed crayfish may also occur in poor-quality habitats with extensive mudbanks (Holdich *et al.*, 2006; Peay *et al.*, 2006b). It can be concluded that, in general, *A. pallipes* would be better designated a 'flagship species' than a 'bioindicator' – one whose high visibility is a potential source of pride and concern, not least because of its cultural heritage value.

Noble and signal crayfish are also capable of withstanding a degree of adverse water quality although, given their commercial value, the importance of good-quality, unpolluted water is often promoted. A sample of adult signal crayfish from a Swedish pond with a hepatotoxic bloom of the benthic cyanobacterium *Oscillatoria sancta* was found not to show ill-effects (Liras *et al.*, 2002), although cyanobacteria were found in the stomachs of almost all the crayfish examined. Following feeding trials using hepatotoxic cyanophytes, high performance liquid chromatography (HPLC) showed that microcystins (the toxins of *Planktothrix agardhii*) had accumulated in the hepato-pancreas of 50% of the animals in the toxic treatment, but there were no apparent ill-effects; all the crayfish survived, remained motile and ate throughout the experiment. This and other evidence indicates that crayfish in Category 1 (cool-water, high-quality) are, at best, indicators for a moderate level of water quality.

Among other crayfish that demand relatively high water quality, smooth marron (*Cherax cainii*) evolved in Australian waters (which are unusual compared with fresh waters in other parts of the world in that the dissolved salts are mainly sodium chloride) and can live without any reduction in growth rates in water from 170 to 2500 ppm salinity. The optimum temperature for growth of this warm-water crayfish is 24°C and for good growth marron need dissolved oxygen levels in the water to be above 8 ppm at all times. Thus they would be among the better indicators of high environmental quality.

New Zealand koura act as an umbrella indicator species of good-quality habitats for a range of organisms in that habitat (Parkyn *et al.*, 2002; Kusabs & Quinn, 2009). Koura hide during the day, moving around at night to scavenge old leaves and small insects that float by in the water; they also filter fine sediments. Scientists can therefore monitor koura populations in order to determine the overall health of a lake or river system.

3.4   The roles of crayfish in wetland systems

We have shown that crayfish dominate many aquatic and semi-terrestrial ecosystems, from cool temperate to subtropical fresh waters, and within those systems they may control biodiversity through their activities. However, over the last century there has also been much translocation of crayfish, both within and even between continents. Invasive exotic crayfish provide good natural experiments to investigate the ecological roles of crayfish in ecosystems. This will be developed in more detail in Chapter 4.

While crayfish as a group show a mix of lifestyles, some species show unexpected plasticity in their ecologies. One of the best-studied examples is the warm-water American red swamp crayfish *Procambarus clarkii*, which shows cold-hardiness in Europe (Gherardi *et al.*, 2000b; Gherardi, 2006; Souty-Grosset *et al.*, 2006) and has proven itself able to live in very different habitats from its core native range of semi-terrestrial, warm ponds or rivers. *P. clarkii* is also a resistant carrier of plague, and so can be considered a superecological strategist.

Cool-water heritage species (ICS) are increasingly threatened by invading non-indigenous crayfish species (NICS) in Europe and East Asia. These NICS are generally warmer-water species, and their expansion is favoured by climate change, as discussed in Chapter 4. Exploitation opportunities and economic dictates of such changes are discussed in Chapter 5. Not all perceived economic benefits have proved sound, as in the case of signal crayfish in the UK, which are now considered to have cost the host country more than any profits derived from their introduction (Stephanie Peay, personal communication, 2009).

There are also some more subtle range extensions and invasions taking place within continents, such as in North America, with rusty crayfish *Orconectes rusticus* moving into virile crayfish (*O. virilis*) territory, or in Australia, with the widespread translocation of the smooth marron *Cherax cainii* or the hardier yabby *C. destructor*. Something similar may have occurred in central and eastern Europe with the spread of the thin-clawed crayfish *Astacus leptodactylus* into the native range of the noble crayfish *A. astacus*. In each case the invading species is tolerant of higher temperatures and more variable dissolved oxygen. It is thus competitively superior to the indigenous species, and replacement or range restriction may occur. Biodiversity management may be necessary, and this idea is developed in Chapter 6.

4 Human-mediated threats to crayfish survival: environmental degradation, climate change and translocations

(with Francesca Gherardi)

We have seen how crayfish are important elements in many different kinds of freshwater ecosystem, often acting as keystone species and enhancing biodiversity through controlling the abundance of many other organisms in the community. However, the all-pervading handiwork of humans has threatened their existence in many ways. In this chapter we look at the negative impacts of environmental deterioration and the introduction of alien species and, in the next, at exploitation.

The Millennium Ecosystem Assessment (MEA; proposed in 2000 and initiated in 2001) noted that different environmental pressures were important on each continent. Among regions containing crayfish, water quality was especially poor in Europe (Füreder *et al.*, 2006), whereas on other continents water shortages, wetland conversion, droughts and fire were among the significant pressures affecting crayfish. In Europe, the few crayfish species were formerly distributed more widely, and were found in many lakes, rivers and brooks until the beginning of the twentieth century, but their distribution has shrunk and become fragmented. The threats considered most important to indigenous European crayfish are crayfish plague, the continued spread of non-indigenous signal, red swamp and spiny-cheek crayfish (Holdich, 2003), and the illegal exploitation and trading of crayfish. Threats considered of lower or local importance include habitat management-related parameters such as predators and habitat alterations, and watercourse alteration – damming, abstraction and the drying out of habitats through drainage (Füreder *et al.*, 2006).

4.1 Threats to survival

Crayfish have evolved physiological adaptations to survive in changeable environments, explaining their current distribution. However, several abiotic and biotic factors, including water temperature, water quality, habitat structure, physical disturbance, diseases, competition and predation, may all affect these patterns. Crayfish face many human-induced threats to their survival, including overfishing, degradation of habitat and water quality, land-use activities and discharge of toxic substances, climate change effects such as droughts and raised temperatures, and the impacts of biotic competition with non-indigenous species (Füreder *et al.*, 2006).

Given the key ecological roles played by many crayfish in various freshwater ecosystems and their large size and longevity, a mass mortality of crayfish will have marked impacts on the freshwater community and its environment, ranging from changes in abundance of other invertebrates to overgrowth of vegetation, with knock-on effects on vertebrates from fishes and amphibians to water birds. This aspect of the ecology of crayfish was explored in Chapter 3.

4.1.1   Environmental threats

Habitat degradation and declining water quality

Human activities have also affected the physical habitat for crayfish; for example, the channelization of streams, silt deposition and sawmill operations have all been reported to be directly responsible for the permanent loss of crayfish populations (Füreder *et al.*, 2006).

As crayfish are primarily nocturnally active, their chief requirement is for hiding places during the daytime. Because of their great increase in size over their long life span, most crayfish species require a complex aquatic habitat. Juvenile hides may be vegetation, rootlets or plant debris; adults hide in most cases under stones or in burrows. Juveniles generally avoid the preferred habitats of adults except in burrowing forms where, as we have seen, they may have to share a confined space for extended periods.

Where loss of hides occurs, e.g. through bank reconstruction or siltation from natural causes or human activity, the habitat's carrying capacity for crayfish diminishes. In some species such as *Astacopsis gouldi*, whose diet is chiefly decaying woody matter, the clearance of snags from a stream is deleterious to their survival through the loss of a food source as well as shelter.

The survival of indigenous crayfish species (ICS) is usually more threatened by habitat deterioration than the survival of non-indigenous crayfish species (NICS) is. Apart from the direct effect of refuge loss on ICS, the spread of NICS is favoured because of their superior ability to live in modified and lower-quality habitats.

Water quality and pollution

Though many crayfish species are considered to be denizens of good-quality water, they may persist where there are mild or even moderate levels of organic pollution, with lowered oxygen levels (Demers & Reynolds, 2003; Demers *et al.*, 2006). Among five native species of crayfish in Europe occupying the same range of biotopes, the stone crayfish *Austropotamobius torrentium* is the most sensitive to lowered water quality, and the thin-clawed crayfish *Astacus leptodactylus* is the least sensitive (see Table 3.2).

Crayfish may be exposed to inorganic pollutants such as sulphur dioxide (causing acid rain), fertilizers (eutrophication) and heavy metals (Kouba *et al.*, 2010), but also to artificial organic pollutants. The effect of acidification on the distribution of crayfish is well studied because of widespread lake acidification. Noble crayfish rarely occur in lakes with a pH below 6, and the percentage of Swedish lakes with noble crayfish has declined with decreasing pH. Adult crayfish have a substantial reservoir of calcium (gastrolith) in their carapaces, but acidification is likely to have severe impacts on moulting and reproduction, with egg production declining because of incomplete hardening of the capsule and death of the embryo (France, 1993). Most crayfish species are negatively affected by acid water at a pH below 5.5, but there are differences in sensitivity. For example, the Tasmanian species *Parastacoides tasmanicus*, which occurs in naturally acidic waters around pH 4.5, was found to survive experimental acid conditions of pH 2.75 indefinitely (Newcombe, 1975), while the parastacid *Cherax destructor* has a less alkaline haemolymph, at pH 7.6, than do northern-hemisphere astacid and cambarid crayfish, at around pH 7.9 (Ellis & Morris, 1995). This is probably a pre-adaptation to the more dilute ionic conditions, particularly of calcium and bicarbonates, in Australian fresh waters.

Toxic materials in water may have catastrophic effects. Aquatic habitats may receive inputs of toxic chemicals, either inorganic (e.g. nutrients, metals) or organic (e.g. pharmaceutical residues, pesticides, polycyclic aromatic hydrocarbons PAHs, polychlorinated biphenyls PCBs). These may accumulate within the aquatic food web, but many studies have shown that they may also directly affect freshwater crayfish, causing damage at the cellular and organism level or even mortalities (e.g. Hobbs & Hall, 1975; Schulz, 2004; Füreder *et al.*, 2006). This is an active area of research, and susceptibility levels are now known to differ between cambarid, parastacid and astacid crayfish, and even within a single genus. Gherardi *et al.* (2002b) studied the concentrations of Cd, Cu, Fe, Mg, Mn, Ni, Pb and Zn in three freshwater macro-decapods from Tuscany, Italy: the ICS *Austropotamobius pallipes* (the white-clawed crayfish) and *Potamon fluviatile* (the river crab), and the NICS *Procambarus clarkii* (red swamp crayfish) after analysis of trace metals to evaluate the degree of contamination of the habitats. *P. clarkii* showed a significantly higher accumulation of most of the metals analysed, including the non-essential cadmium, nickel and lead. Interspecific differences were not related to exposure to higher concentrations of metals, but indigenous and alien macro-decapods possibly differ in their physiological requirements for essential trace metals and/or in their rates of essential and non-essential metal uptake, accumulation, detoxification and excretion. A number of studies, reviewed in Füreder *et al.* (2006), have looked at the effects of chemicals, including pyrethroid and other insecticides, on crayfish under controlled laboratory conditions. In an evaluation of 183 acute toxicity tests for almost 100 chemicals with *Procambarus* or *Orconectes* species, it was found that insecticides were the most toxic group of chemicals (Eversole & Seller, 1996), with implications for their use in the control of unwanted or invasive crayfish species. Control of non-indigenous crayfish is discussed further in Chapter 8.

Although caution is needed in the transfer of laboratory toxicity data to field conditions, some field studies have associated chemical contamination with effects on crayfish species. For example, exposure to the metals copper and nickel in lakes of northern Ontario (Canada) was linked with their bioaccumulation in tissues of *Cambarus bartonii* (Alikhan *et al.*, 1990), and this is now used as a reliable bioindicator of heavy-metal contamination near Sudbury, Ontario. Copper is chiefly found in hepatopancreas tissues, cadmium in hepato-pancreas and gut, iron and manganese in the gut, and magnesium in the exoskeleton (Alikhan *et al.*, 1990). A cocktail of chemical pollutants in the River Meuse in the Netherlands has also been associated with their presence in the non-indigenous crayfish *Orconectes limosus* (Schilderman *et al.*, 1999).

Other complex organic compounds from industry may have damaging effects on crayfish stocks (see Holdich, 2002a), and recent work has shown the importance of complex organic compounds. In western France, following habitat degradation and particularly the presence of cattle, organic compounds are suspected to be responsible for crayfish loss despite apparently good water quality parameters such as pH and dissolved oxygen (Trouilhé *et al.*, 2008). However, in Tuscany, Italy, where habitats are more pristine and cattle not common, it is primarily the water quality parameters that determine the presence or absence of crayfish (Brusconi *et al.*, 2008).

4.1.2 Susceptibility to climate change

Crayfish which are widespread have more opportunities to change their preferred locations, but endemic or restricted species are more vulnerable to environmental deterioration. With their limited capacity for dispersal, burrowing crayfish that are restricted to small ranges at the edge of suitable climatic zones, or at high altitudes, are particularly at risk from climate change (Box 4.1). For example, *Engaeus martigener* is restricted to a few wet gullies near the tops of the mountains of the Furneaux group of islands in Bass Strait, between Tasmania and the mainland of Australia. Further drying of the climate would eliminate the wet gullies and hence the crayfish (Doran & Richards, 1996). However, in other cases, crayfish may be enabled to expand their natural ranges northwards or to higher altitudes.

Box 4.1 **Which traits or characteristics make species susceptible to climate change?**

In 2007, Imperial College London, IUCN and the Zoological Society of London hosted a four-day workshop to identify the traits associated with elevated extinction risk, particularly due to climate change. Thirty-one biologists refined traits forming the basis of IUCN's ongoing assessment of species susceptibility to climate change. The traits fall into five trait groups:

A. **Specialized habitat and/or microhabitat requirements**. Species with specialized habitat requirements are less likely to be able to tolerate a level of climatic and ecosystem change than unspecialized species. Where such species can disperse to new climatically suitable areas, the chances of fulfilling all their habitat requirements are low. Susceptibility is exacerbated where a species has several life stages, each with different habitat or microhabitat requirements, or when the habitat or microhabitat to which the species is specialized is particularly vulnerable to climate change impacts.

B. **Narrow environmental tolerances or thresholds that are likely to be exceeded due to climate change at any stage in the life cycle**. The physiology and ecology of many species is tightly coupled to very specific ranges of climatic variables such as temperature, precipitation and pH and oxygen levels, and those with narrow tolerance ranges are particularly vulnerable to climate change. Even species with broad environmental tolerances and unspecialized habitat requirements may already be close to thresholds beyond which ecological or physiological function quickly breaks down (e.g. protein and enzyme function in animals).

C. **Dependence on specific environmental cues likely to be disrupted by climate change**. Many species rely on environmental triggers or cues for migration, breeding, egg-laying, and a range of other essential processes. While some cues such as day length and lunar cycles will be unaffected by climate change, others such as rainfall and temperature (including their interacting and cumulative effects) will be heavily impacted upon by climate change. Species become vulnerable to changes in the magnitude and timing of these cues when they lead to an uncoupling with resources or other essential ecological processes; e.g. early spring warming causes the emergence of a species before their food sources are available. Climate change susceptibility is compounded when different stages of a species' life history or different sexes rely on different cues.

D. **Dependence on interspecific interactions that are likely to be disrupted by climate change**. Many species' interactions with prey, hosts, symbionts, pathogens and competitors will be affected by climate change, due to either the decline or loss of these resource species from the dependent species' ranges or loss of synchronization in phenology. Species dependent on interactions with other species that are susceptible to disruption by climate change are at risk of extinction, particularly where they have a high degree of specialization for the particular resource species and are unlikely to be able to switch to or substitute other species.

E. **Poor ability to disperse to or to colonize a new or more suitable habitat**. In general, the particular set of environmental conditions to which each species is adapted (its 'bioclimatic envelope') will shift polewards and to increasing altitudes in response to climate change. Species with low rates or short distances of dispersal are unlikely to migrate fast enough to keep up with these shifting climatic envelopes and will face increasing extinction risk as their habitats become exposed to progressively greater climatic changes. Even where species could disperse to newly suitable bioclimatic areas, several other factors may affect colonization success. Species' phenotypic plasticity and genetic diversity will determine the likelihood of adaptation over different timescales. Where they exist, direct measures of genetic variability can be supplemented with information on naturalization outside species' native ranges and on the success of any past translocation efforts. Extrinsic factors likely to decrease dispersal success include the presence of geographical barriers such as mountain ranges, oceans and rivers. Anthropogenic transformation of migration routes or destination habitats increases species' susceptibility to negative impacts from climate change.

4.2   Crayfish translocations, biotic competition and the significance of crayfish invasions

Crayfish compete successfully with other freshwater invertebrates and will regulate the abundance of most of these, thus functioning as important keystone species (see Chapter 3). Interactions with other decapods, such as crabs, are rather rare because of their different distributions. However, interactions with invasive non-indigenous crayfish species (NICS) are among the main threats to indigenous crayfish species (ICS). This is accomplished through competition for food or shelter, through direct aggression or cross-mating, and – importantly – also through the transmission of disease. This aspect has received most study in Europe, where the spread of alien, disease-carrying crayfish has caused economic devastation for over a century (see Füreder *et al.*, 2006).

When crayfish are spread to habitats outside their natural range they can affect not only the distribution of indigenous species of crayfish, but also the dynamics and biodiversity of the invaded community. There are numerous examples of crayfish introductions, both intentional and accidental, throughout the world (Gherardi & Holdich, 1999; Holdich *et al.*, 2009b). Careless crayfish management, such as the stocking of NICS, is still causing the decline of indigenous crayfish populations in several European regions (Füreder *et al.*, 2006). In some areas, the ICS have suffered catastrophically from the introduction of NICS and are now endangered and declining, e.g. the white-clawed crayfish in France, Italy, Spain and Britain, and the noble crayfish and stone crayfish in Austria, Germany, Switzerland and the Czech Republic.

Superimposed on the natural distribution of organisms there is the product of a massive translocation of species between and within continents. Impacts of globalization, especially international trade and travel, have provided many pathways for the introduction of species to new areas. Some fragile indigenous species become critically threatened once non-indigenous species are introduced. Indeed, invasive non-indigenous species may constitute a higher level of threat than chemical pollutants, because chemical products are rapidly diluted and degraded and the ecosystem could rapidly recover once the pollution disappears, whereas invasive species are living organisms capable of reproduction, spread and even evolution, and so may persist indefinitely in the ecosystem if eradication is not possible.

Because of their size, longevity and relative resistance to desiccation, and their capacity to integrate into the food web at many levels (Nyström, 1999), crayfish are good candidates for invading aquatic systems (Moyle & Light, 1996). It has been estimated that between one-third and one-half of the world's crayfish species are threatened with population decline or extinction (Taylor, 2002). One of the greatest threats to crayfish biodiversity is from non-indigenous crayfish introduced either intentionally for harvesting for food, or unintentionally as unused bait or unwanted aquarium stock (Holdich, 1999; Taugbøl & Skurdal, 1999; Lodge *et al.*, 2000a; Gherardi, 2007c; Taylor *et al.* 2007). This is why the introduction of non-indigenous species is currently regarded as one of the most powerful drivers of change in inland waters (Gherardi, 2007a). In lakes, rivers and wetlands, non-indigenous species act with other anthropogenic sources of disturbance (impoundment of rivers, water quality deterioration, habitat degradation and fragmentation, overexploitation, etc.) to threaten the many endemisms and local adaptations that have characterized these ecosystems for millennia (Lodge, 2001).

In Europe, North America, Japan and elsewhere, indigenous crayfish have been displaced by non-indigenous crayfish through direct competition (Taylor, 2002). In Europe, the development of aquaculture has encouraged the introduction of non-indigenous species, the best example being the introduction to Europe of three American crayfish species, which has led to the loss of many indigenous populations because of direct competition but also through the resulting introduction of an induced pathology, the crayfish plague. This lethal disease first appeared in the middle of the nineteenth century and has proved even more difficult to control than the non-indigenous species themselves (see below). More recently, climate change has contributed to increasing stress on the indigenous crayfish while favouring those NICS with less strict ecological requirements. The situation is now grim in Europe, with only five widespread native species of crayfish. Among malacostracan species introduced into European inland waters (rivers, lakes, reservoirs, coastal lagoons and estuaries) are many Caridea and Brachyura (Holdich & Pöckl, 2007) (Table 4.1). The Astacida are the most often encountered, with nine non-indigenous species. More recently, the yabby *Cherax destructor* was also recorded in central Italy (Scalici *et al.*, 2009). The difficult situation in Europe, with few widespread ICS but often with several NICS per country, clearly illustrates the damage that the introduction of alien crayfish may inflict on indigenous communities (Souty-Grosset *et al.*, 2006).

Over the last few decades, a relatively small fraction of NICS globally – numbering just 24 species, according to Gherardi (2010) (Table 4.2) – have been subject to human-mediated translocations. Some of these translocations have been accidental, but most were deliberate: crayfish have been introduced for aquaculture and stocking into the wild, as live food, aquarium stock, live bait, and for snail and weed control (Lodge *et al.*, 2000a).

Upon their arrival in natural waters, crayfish almost inevitably establish self-sustaining populations. The invasion process may continue: crayfish become dominant in the colonized area and spread to adjacent areas, favoured in this by the ability of some invading species to travel long distances, sometimes overland, e.g. red swamp crayfish *Procambarus clarkii* (Gherardi *et al.*, 2000b, 2002c). Often, when established NICS populations become invasive, they induce modifications in the structure of freshwater food webs, decrease the biomass and species richness of macroinvertebrates, macrophytes and periphyton, transmit parasites and diseases to ICS, contribute to the decline of several animal taxa, including other crayfish, amphibians and fish, and even cause damage to human economy and health. The negative impacts on indigenous species are exacerbated by climate change, which increases stress on ICS while favouring NICS, with their less strict ecological requirements.

Crayfish species that cause concern in the areas of introduction include signal crayfish *Pacifastacus leniusculus* in California (USA), Europe and Japan, spiny-cheek crayfish *Orconectes limosus* in Europe, rusty crayfish *Orconectes rusticus* in North America, red swamp crayfish *Procambarus clarkii* in California, Africa, Europe and

Table 4.1. Non-indigenous Decapoda (Pleocyemata) in European inland waters (those marked with a + are considered to be highly invasive) (Holdich & Pöckl, 2007).

Scientific name, authority, (family)	Natural range	Introduced range and first records
Malacostraca, Caridea		
Atyaephyra desmaresti (Millet) (Atyidae)	Southern Europe	France (1843), Belgium (1888), The Netherlands (1916), Germany (1932), River Main (1983), Main–Danube Canal (1990), Bavarian Danube (1997), Austrian Danube (1999)
Palaemon macrodactylus Rathbun (Palaemonidae)	North-east Asia	England (2004)
Malacostraca, Brachyura		
Callinectes sapidus M.J. Rathbun (Portunidae)	USA	Widespread (France, 1901)
+ *Eriocheir sinensis* H. Milne Edwards (Varunidae)	Southeast Asia	Widespread (Germany, 1912)
Potamon sp. (Potomidae)	Unknown	France (1985)
Potamon fluviatile (Herbst) (Potamidae)	Italy, Balkans, Greece	France (early 19th century)
Potamon ibericum tauricum (Czerniavsky) (Potomidae)	Turkey	France (1960s)
Rhithropanopeus harrisii Maitland (Xanthidae)	USA	Widespread (Netherlands, 1874)
Malacostraca, Astacidae		
+ *Astacus leptodactylus* Eschscholtz (Astacidae)	Ponto-Caspian Basin	Widespread
Cherax destructor Clark (Parastacidae)	Australia	Spain (1983), possibly Switzerland
Orconectes immunis (Hagen) (Cambaridae)	USA	Germany (1997)
+ *Orconectes limosus* (Rafinesque) (Cambaridae)	USA	Widespread (Germany, 1890)
+ *Orconectes rusticus* (Girard) (Cambaridae)	USA	France (2005[a])
+ *Orconectes virilis* (Hagen) (Cambaridae)	North America	Netherlands (2005[a])
+ *Pacifastacus leniusculus* (Dana) (Astacidae)	North America	Widespread (Sweden, 1960s)
+ *Procambarus clarkii* (Girard) (Cambaridae)	USA	Widespread (Spain, 1970s)
+ *Procambarus fallax f. virginalis* (Cambaridae)	USA	Germany (2003), Netherlands

[a] Reported in that year but probably present earlier.

Table 4.2. Crayfish species moved between or within continents outside their native ranges (after Souty-Grosset *et al.*, 2006; Taylor *et al.*, 2007; Gherardi, 2010).

Family	Species	Common name	From	To
Parastacidae	*Cherax destructor* Clark	Yabby	Australia	Europe; Australia
	Cherax quadricarinatus (von Martens)	Redclaw	Australia	Africa; Asia; C, N & S America
	Cherax tenuimanus (Smith)	Marron	Australia	Australia
Astacidae	*Astacus astacus* (Linnaeus)	Noble crayfish	Europe	Africa; Europe
	Astacus leptodactylus Eschscholtz	Thin clawed crayfish	Asia; Europe	Asia; Europe
	Austropotamobius pallipes (Lereboullet)	White-clawed crayfish	Europe	Europe
	Pacifastacus gambelii (Girard)	Pilose crayfish	N America	N America
	Pacifastacus leniusculus leniusculus (Dana)	Signal crayfish	N America	Asia; Europe; N America
	Pacifastacus leniusculus trowbridgii (Stimpson)	Columbia River signal crayfish	N America	N America
Cambaridae	*Cambarus longirostris* Faxon	Atlantic slope crayfish	N America	N America
	Cambarus rusticiformis Rhoades	Depression crayfish	N America	N America
	Orconectes causeyi Jester	Western Plains crayfish	N America	N America
	Orconectes immunis (Hagen)	Calico crayfish	N America	Europe; N America
	Orconectes juvenilis (Hagen)	Kentucky River crayfish	N America	Europe
	Orconectes limosus (Rafinesque)	Spiny-cheek crayfish	N America	Africa; Europe; N America
	Orconectes neglectus neglectus (Faxon)	Ringed crayfish	N America	N America
	Orconectes palmeri creolanus (Creaser)	Creole painted crayfish	N America	N America
	Orconectes rusticus (Girard)	Rusty crayfish	N America	N America
	Orconectes sanbornii (Faxon)	Sanborn's crayfish	N America	N America
	Orconectes virilis Hagen	Virile crayfish	N America	Europe; N America
	Procambarus fallax f. virginalis	Marbled crayfish	N America	Africa; Europe
	Procambarus acutus (Girard)	White river crayfish	N America	N America
	Procambarus clarkii (Girard)	Red swamp crayfish	N America	Africa; Asia; Europe; C, N & S America
	Procambarus zonangulus Hobbs and Hobbs	Southern white river crayfish	N America	N America

Table 4.3. Vectors of crayfish introduction in Europe and North America (modified after Lodge *et al.*, 2000b).

Vector of crayfish introduction	Europe	North America
1. Canals	−	−
2. Legal stocking in natural waters	−	−
3. Illegal stocking in natural waters	+	−
4. Aquaculture	++	++
5. Live food trade	++	++
6. Aquarium and pond trade	+	++
7. Biological supply trade	0	++
8. Live bait	−	++

0 Not important; **−** Decreasing importance; **+** remains important; **++** increasing importance.

Japan, thin-clawed crayfish *Astacus leptodactylus* in some European countries, and yabby *Cherax destructor* in Australia (Holdich, 1999). However, this list is likely to be incomplete; species such as redclaw *Cherax quadricarinatus* in Ecuador (Romero, 1997) and marbled crayfish or marmorkrebs (*Procambarus fallax f. virginalis*) in Europe and Madagascar (Jones *et al.*, 2009; Scalici *et al.*, 2009) are expected to generate problems in the near future.

The threats posed by non-indigenous species are well illustrated at the European level. For instance, in Sweden the concomitant introduction of *Pacifastacus leniusculus* and its parasite *Aphanomyces astaci* (see below), together with water acidification and other environmental changes, has led, since its introduction in 1907, to a 95% decrease in populations of the economically important indigenous species, the noble crayfish *Astacus astacus* (Josefsson & Andersson, 2001). In 2007 alone there were 439 outbreaks of crayfish plague, and in 2008 there were at least 4000 populations of *P. leniusculus* compared with fewer than 1000 populations in 2009) (Edsman & Schröder, 2009).

4.2.1   Pathways of introductions

The human-mediated movement of crayfish around the world follows a multiplicity of pathways that result in either accidental (in ballast or via canals) or deliberate introductions of NICS for aquaculture, stocking, live food commerce, aquarium and pond trade, live bait, and biological supply, among others (Holdich & Pöckl, 2007). The relative importance of these pathways, however, may vary between the different socio-economic contexts of the recipient areas, as made clear by the comparison between Europe and North America (Lodge *et al.*, 2000a). Illegal stocking is still intense in Europe, but not in North America, whereas the introduction of crayfish species for aquarium and pond trade, biological supply and live bait is more frequent in North America than in Europe (Table 4.3) (Lodge *et al.*, 2000a).

A number of introductions have been driven by narrow objectives. *Procambarus clarkii*, for instance, was imported from Louisiana to Japan in 1927 as a food for the bullfrog, *Rana catesbeiana*, widely reared for human consumption; the introduction of only 20 crayfish led to the establishment in natural waters of extremely dense populations (reaching a density of 100 000 ha^{-1}). Sometimes introductions aimed to ameliorate human conditions; in Africa many releases into the wild of *P. clarkii* from the 1960s onwards were intended not only to broaden the range of commercial fisheries (Arrignon *et al.*, 1990; Mikkola, 1996) but also to control freshwater snails that carry human schistosomiasis (Hofkin *et al.*, 1991); unfortunately, they preyed on native fish and destroyed reed-beds.

However, the introduction of crayfish is most often motivated by our desire to eat them, which in turn generates economic interest and stimulates further human-assisted dispersal (Holdich, 1999). Some species are highly valued as gourmet food and in regions such as Scandinavia and Louisiana, feasting on them has become a cultural highlight (Lodge *et al.*, 2000a; Swahn, 2004). As a consequence, some NICS are commercially harvested from wild stocks or have become aquaculture commodities in countries such as Australia, the People's Republic of China, and the USA. For example, the yabby *Cherax destructor* was translocated within Australia (therefore becoming a NICS) to stock farm dams in semi-arid regions. The aquarium and pond trade is another powerful vector of NICS; it represents a great threat to regions such as southern Europe, where the climate is now amenable to species from subtropical regions – and will become more so in the near future with global warming. Associated with the aquarium trade is e-commerce, which is responsible for the easy and rapid translocation across the world of potentially dangerous invaders, such as the marbled crayfish (see below). Finally, the use of crayfish as live bait has also aided the spread of some NICS, notably in the case of *Orconectes rusticus* in North America.

4.2.2 Ecological impacts and loss of biodiversity

As predicted by Hobbs (1989), once added to an ecosystem, some NICS have the potential to exert considerable environmental stress and often induce 'irreparable shifts in species diversity'. In areas without any indigenous ecological equivalent, the modes of resource acquisition by crayfish, their capacity to develop new trophic relationships, and their action as bioturbators often cause several direct and indirect effects on the ecosystem, which in most cases are dramatic (Gherardi, 2007b). On the other hand, when NICS replace indigenous crayfish, their ecological effect may not be entirely novel to the colonized community but their overall impact can still be strong if the introduced crayfish species is able to build up high densities and/or to grow to a large size (Gherardi, 2007b). Indeed, several NICS reach significantly higher densities than the ICS. For instance, *Orconectes limosus* in Poland reaches a density of >70 m^{-2}, *O. rusticus* in North America >20 m^{-2}, and *Pacifastacus leniusculus* in the UK 30 m^{-2}; whereas the Shasta crayfish *P. fortis* in California has a density of about 1 m^{-2}, the northern koura *Paranephrops planifrons* in New Zealand and the white-clawed crayfish *Austropotamobius pallipes* in France up to 3 m^{-2}, and the Japanese crayfish *Cambaroides japonicus* in Japan up to 4 m^{-2} (Gherardi, 2007b).

A number of biological traits may contribute to the achievement by crayfish of high densities and/or large size. *Procambarus clarkii* is characterized by high fecundity, protracted spawning periods, rapid growth rates to 50 g in 3–5 months, and maturity reached at a small size of 10 g (Gherardi, 2007b). It is also extremely plastic in its life cycle and better at coping with pollution, habitat destruction and other anthropogenic sources of disturbance. When a species is introduced without a full complement of specific parasites, pathogens and enemies, a high survival rate is also expected. Large size, in its turn, makes crayfish both resistant to gape-size-limited predators (such as many fishes) and agonistically superior in resource fights. Invasive crayfish are also subject to the so-called 'aggression syndrome' that makes them both abundant and active at the same time despite the high intraspecific aggression they exhibit. Obviously, large size usually translates into a higher energy and nutrient demand, but many NICS are also more efficient energy converters when compared with similarly sized ICS.

NICS exert a negative impact at multiple levels of ecological organization (Gherardi, 2007b). At the individual level, they may outcompete or prey upon indigenous species, eventually leading to their extirpation. For instance, the intense predatory pressure by *P. clarkii* upon eggs of the newt *Taricha torosa* has led to the disappearance of this species from some streams in southern California (Gamradt & Kats, 1996).

Ecological impacts by NICS, coupled with predation, transmission of diseases/parasites, and induced genetic changes (Figure 4.1), enhance the effects of habitat loss, overexploitation and pollution in inducing the dramatic decline of indigenous crayfish diversity. Of the 67 threatened crayfish species in North America, for instance, over 5% are subject to interference competition by NICS. *Pacifastacus leniusculus* has contributed, along with urbanization and overexploitation, to the global extinction of the sooty crayfish *P. nigrescens*, once common in the creeks of the San Francisco Bay area (Bouchard, 1977), and it is now displacing the Shasta crayfish, *P. fortis*, in north-eastern California (Light *et al.*, 1995). Correspondingly, the European indigenous species *Astacus astacus*, *Austropotamobius pallipes* and *A. torrentium* are under the lethal threat of the oomycete *Aphanomyces astaci*, introduced to Europe via North American NICS.

Hybridization with the invaders is an additional threat for ICS. In Wisconsin (USA), the hybrids between indigenous northern clearwater crayfish *Orconectes propinquus* and the invader *O. rusticus* were found to back-cross with pure *O. rusticus*, leading to a massive genetic introgression of nuclear DNA from the indigenous to the invasive species and thus to the gradual elimination of *O. propinquus* genes from the population (Perry *et al.*, 2001a, 2001b). This hybridization results in fertile and vigorous offspring, but ultimately leads to the disappearance of *O. propinquus*. The competitive superiority of the hybrids helps exclude genetically pure *O. propinquus* faster than *O. rusticus* would without hybridization. Rusty crayfish were also found to hybridize with *O. limosus* (Smith, 1981). Recently Swecker *et al.* (2010) have suggested that *O. limosus* was eradicated by expanding *O. virilis* in eastern North America.

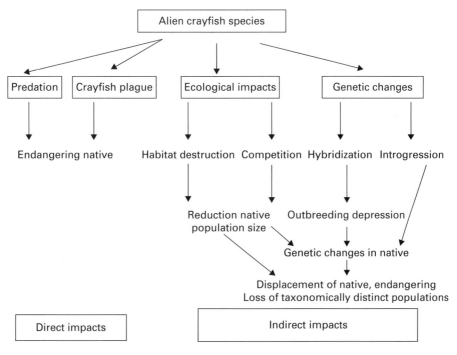

Figure 4.1. Ecological impacts by non-indigenous crayfish species (NICS) and consequences for habitat loss, overexploitation and pollution, inducing declines of native crayfish (drawn by Catherine Souty-Grosset).

At the community level, NICS exert both direct and indirect effects on the colonized ecosystems. Their dense populations graze intensely on aquatic macrophytes, coupled with non-consumptive plant clipping and uprooting, inducing a significant decline in plant abundance. Macrophyte destruction is generally followed by a switch from a clear to a turbid state dominated by surface microalgae, with the consequent reduction in light penetration and decrease in primary production of benthic plants. The biomass and species richness of macroinvertebrates are altered by NICS as the result of habitat disruption, direct consumption, increased drift through prey escape, incidental dislodgment by their foraging, and possible inhibition of invertebrate colonization. Mollusca are most affected; some gastropod species, particularly thin-shelled snails, have even been extirpated (Lodge, 1993). Crayfish predation may be light only on the species that move quickly enough to escape tactile-feeding crayfish (e.g. amphipods) or that are protected by cases (e.g. Trichoptera) or in the sediment (e.g. some Dipteran larvae). Through consumption of macrophytes and detritus, crayfish may also lead, in an indirect way, to the decline of macrophyte-associated taxa, particularly collector-gatherers, whereas their predation upon other zoobenthic predators such as Odonata larvae causes an increased abundance of their prey. Finally, NICS can be prey items for a large number of fishes, birds and mammals, such as eels, storks, herons, egrets and otters, thus representing a new resource for higher trophic levels in the areas of introduction.

At the ecosystem level, NICS may alter the pathways of energy flow through augmenting connectance by feeding at several trophic levels and through increasing the availability of autochthonous carbon as a food source for higher trophic levels. Their intense burrowing activity and locomotion often lead to bioturbation; as a result, water quality may be impoverished, light penetration and plant productivity may be reduced, and eventually benthic communities may be affected due to changes in the stream substrate.

4.2.3   Introduction of diseases and parasites

Since the first crayfish epizootics were observed, with their consequent impacts on harvest and profitability, there has been considerable interest in crayfish diseases. Crayfish may be attacked by a range of organisms, from viruses to metazoan parasites. Commenting on the pathogens, parasites and commensals found to infect or infest freshwater crayfish, Evans & Edgerton (2002) discussed the conditions caused by these organisms. Intranuclear bacilliform viruses, Birnavirus and Parvo-, Reo-, Toti- and Picorna-like viruses are among the viral pathogens; *Nocardia* sp. and Rickettsia- and Mollicute-like species are among the bacterial infective agents; oomycetes, microsporidians, *Psorospermum* sp. and *Tetrahymena pyriformis* are among the protists; and various platyhelminth species, nematodes, acanthocephalans and annelids are among the metazoan parasites and commensals that have been described. The worst is the oomycete pathogen causing crayfish plague.

The hard exoskeleton is the first line of defence. Once inside the cuticle, the intruder meets a typically arthropod and non-adaptive immune system. Haemocytes serve the function of vertebrate leucocytes, but close analogues of vertebrate lymphocytes and antibodies do not exist (Söderhäll & Söderhäll, 2002). Although crustaceans lack immunoglobulins, they are still capable of responding to microbial invaders by innate recognition of cell wall components. For example, a plasma protein in the haemolymph will recognize and bind to a fungal cell wall glucan and thereby activate the immune defence. Microbial polysaccharides involve pattern recognition proteins, initiating several defence mechanisms, some of which have been studied in *Pacifastacus leniusculus* (Söderhäll & Söderhäll, 2002). The intruding pathogen is typically coated by melanin deposition, a process primarily important in wound healing and cuticle sclerotization. A high level of prophenoloxidase activation results in efficient immobilization of the intruder.

The most severe epizootics result from oomycetes, distant relatives of fungi, including *Saprolegnia* spp. and *Aphanomyces astaci*, the causative organism of crayfish plague; and from the distantly related microsporidian *Thelohania contejeani*, which causes 'porcelain disease'. While *Saprolegnia* infections are not usually fatal, the others are invariably so. Porcelain disease is an intracellular infection caused by the microsporidian *T. contejeani* and related taxa, with a low prevalence generally between 0% and 30%, although it may be higher in certain restricted habitats (Emily Imhoff, personal communication, 2009). Dunn *et al.* (2009) have screened *T. contejeani* in *P. leniusculus* and *A. pallipes* for microsporidian infection. Three novel parasite sequences were also isolated from *P.*

leniusculus, with an overall prevalence of microsporidian infection of 38% within this species (Dunn *et al*., 2009). As the musculature of the host becomes replaced by spores it appears white, giving the disease its common name. Death results after several months or even years. There are two types of sporogony, resulting in different kinds of spores; their infectivity during transmission has been questioned (Diéguez-Uribeondo *et al*., 2006). The portal of infection is apparently the digestive tract, but transmission trials feeding infected crayfish have failed, and an intermediate host may be involved.

Crayfish plague outbreaks are characterized by rapid mass mortalities of indigenous crayfish species that result in 100% mortality within days or weeks but do not kill other fauna or flora. The history of crayfish plague in Europe is now well documented and understood (Diéguez-Uribeondo *et al*., 2006). The first outbreaks in Europe occurred in the mid-nineteenth century, presumably as a consequence of the introduction of North American crayfish species that are now known to be chronic carriers of this disease. Whole stocks and flourishing fisheries were wiped out. The first series of crayfish mortalities occurred in and around Lombardy in 1859. The second focus of plague started in France in 1874 and initiated a chain of outbreaks related to move-ments of commercial crayfish trappers and imports of infected crayfish. A third series commenced with the well-meaning introduction of the signal crayfish *Pacifastacus leniusculus* in 1969, spreading across Europe even to countries already affected by the disease. Several different genotypes of the plague organism have so far been identified in Europe (Söderhäll & Cerenius, 1999), apparently related to the various introductions into Europe.

Crayfish can become infected by a number of different pathways (Figure 4.2). Most commonly it is through swimming spores released from an infected carrier, but this does not have to be so. The zoospore may encyst and re-form a spore (repeated zoospore emergence), allowing more opportunities to find a new host. Matthews & Reynolds (1992) first identified plague in Ireland in the absence of any NICS, and suggested that spores may have come in with wet fishing gear.

While *P. leniusculus* is resistant to the pathogenic oomycete *Aphanomyces astaci*, as demonstrated by melanization in the cuticle, *Astacus astacus* is highly suscep-tible. During an infection, the level of prophenoloxidase increases in *A. astacus*, but it remains at a high level in *P. leniusculus* after the initial infection. As a result, the sig-nal crayfish is more vulnerable to stress and other parasites than the uninfected noble crayfish would be, and can even die of its own crayfish plague (Söderhäll & Cerenius, 1999; Javier Diéguez-Uribeondo, personal communication, 2009).

The additional effect of crayfish plague has meant that the devastation caused by NICS amongst indigenous crayfish species has been even greater. Crayfish diseases, and specifically, crayfish plague, are one of the main causes of crayfish decline in Europe (Edgerton *et al*., 2004). Knowledge of its causative agent, *Aphanomyces astaci*, is still one of the crucial aspects to be considered when action plans for restoring the European ICS are designed and implemented. *Astacus astacus*, *A. leptodactylus*, *Austropotamobius pallipes* and *A. torrentium* are examples of species shown to be highly susceptible to the disease. However, as revealed in laboratory-based studies, other crayfish species can be infected, including at least nine of the parastacid species from Australia and New

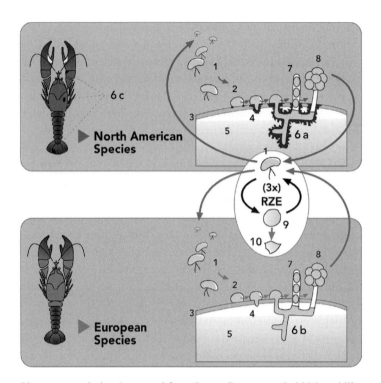

Figure 4.2.   Plague transmission (extracted from Souty-Grosset *et al.*, 2006, and illustrated by Javier Diéguez-Uribeondo): **1**, secondary zoospore (infective unit); **2**, encysting zoospore; **3**, crayfish epicuticle; **4**, germinating cyst; **5**, cuticle penetration; **6a**, melanized hyphae (chronic infection in North American crayfish); **6b**, unmelanized hyphae (acute infection in indigenous European species of crayfish or immune-stressed North American crayfish species); **6c**, black spots, i.e. usually a macroscopic sign of *A. astaci* infection; **7**, characteristic sporangium of *Aphanomyces*, the primary zoospores are formed and distributed in a single row within the sporangium; **8**, spore balls are clusters of primary cysts, these structures are characteristic of the genus *Aphanomyces*; **9**, secondary cyst – the zoospore responds to nonspecific stimuli, forming a secondary cyst that will not germinate and instead will form a new zoospore (i.e. repeated zoospore emergence: RZE); this process can be repeated up to three times depending on the conditions; **10**, unviable cyst. See also colour plate section.

Guinea, and even other decapods such as the Chinese mitten crab *Eriocheir sinensis* (Unestam, 1975). According to Diéguez-Uribeondo (2009), in each European country the number of detected and diagnosed mortalities due to crayfish plague varies from a couple of cases to a dozen cases per year. Thus, in Finland, Spain, Sweden and Estonia, around 10 cases of crayfish plague are diagnosed each year, in the Czech Republic from five to eight per year, in France around two per year, and in Italy just one, as recently reported. However, these numbers seem not to reflect the actual status but rather the intensity of surveillance carried out. In general, crayfish mass mortalities are detected by chance and the correct diagnosis is seldom supported by science.

    The first outbreaks of the plague in Europe seem to have occurred in 1859 in the Po River basin in Lombardy (Italy), which led to the extinction of several Italian populations of the indigenous *A. pallipes* (Alderman & Polglase, 1988). Since then, the parasite has continuously spread across Europe; many crayfish populations have been affected in Turkey (Baran & Soylu, 1989), Ireland (Matthews & Reynolds, 1992), England (Alderman, 1993), Norway (Håstein & Gladhaug, 1974; Taugbøl *et al.*, 1993), Sweden (Huang *et al.*, 1994), Austria (Alderman, 1996), Spain (Diéguez-Uribeondo *et al.*, 1997b), Finland (Vennerström *et al.*, 1998), France (Machino & Diéguez-Uribeondo, 1998), Germany (Oidtmann *et al.*, 1999) and the Czech Republic (Kozubíková *et al.*, 2009). Because of its virulence, *Aphanomyces astaci* has been classified among the world's hundred worst invasive non-indigenous species by the Invasive Species Specialist Group (ISSG) of the International Union for Conservation of Nature (IUCN) (www.issg.org/).

The origin of *A. astaci* was unknown until Unestam (1972) provided indirect evidence that North American crayfish are its natural hosts. More recently, molecular tools have directly proven the role of North American crayfish as vectors of *A. astaci* (Huang et al., 1994). So far, *Orconectes limosus*, *Pacifastacus leniusculus* and *Procambarus clarkii* have been shown to carry this parasite as a chronic infection (Unestam, 1969, 1972; Unestam & Weiss, 1970; Persson & Söderhäll, 1983; Vey *et al.*, 1983; Diéguez-Uribeondo & Söderhäll, 1993). In these species, *A. astaci* can be isolated from melanin deposits often seen as black spots on their cuticles (Söderhäll & Cerenius, 1992). In North American species, melanin is deposited on the wall of the penetrating hyphae and prevents or stops the growth of the parasite due to its fungitoxic and fungistatic properties (Söderhäll & Ajaxon, 1982), whereas the species sensitive to the plague lack this defence. When immersed in fresh water, *A. astaci* produces zoospores that can be carried considerable distances in flowing water or can encyst and remain 'dormant' for several days. Fishes and birds may act as vectors, transporting *A. astaci* to previously unexposed waters (Alderman & Polglase, 1988; Oidtmann *et al.*, 2002), but the oomycete can also be introduced to a new susceptible population from contaminated ropes, traps, fishing gear, boots, nets and other wet equipment. Should the spores encounter a susceptible crayfish, the hyphae may then penetrate the carapace and invade the body tissues, leading to death typically within 5–50 days from initial infection, depending on water temperature and the initial number of zoospores.

Investigations into the cause of mortality in European crayfish led to records of potential pathogens other than *A. astaci*, including virosis, porcelain disease caused by *Thelohania* spp., protozoans, bacteria, fungi and other fungus-like agents, and *Psorospermum haeckeli*. Although many of these organisms were originally described in crayfish over 100 years ago (Edgerton *et al.*, 2004; Figure 4.3), their pathogenic significance to European ICS still remains obscure. Other problems are related to high densities of ectoparasites or ectocommensals such as branchiobdellidan species (Diéguez-Uribeondo *et al.*, 2006). These diseases are only occasionally of particular importance and their economic impact is more relevant in crayfish farming than in natural populations.

Crayfish plague is the most studied invertebrate disease, and its causative agent *Aphanomyces astaci* is one of the best-known pathogens (see reviews by Söderhäll &

Figure 4.3.   Timeline of significant events in the field of crayfish pathology (not to scale). *Key*: # relates to Europe; * relates to USA; + relates to Australia (from Edgerton *et al*., 2004).

Cerenius, 1999; Diéguez-Uribeondo *et al*., 2006; Cerenius *et al*., 2009). The biology and phylogeny of *A. astaci* has been extensively researched and this knowledge has allowed us to achieve important goals in crayfish management. However, there are still some gaps in our knowledge that require further study, such as the existence of low-virulence strains. This aspect has been noted in Finland and Sweden (Viljamaa-Dirks & Heinikainen, 2006; Javier Diéguez-Uribeondo & Kenneth Söderhäll, personal communication, 2010). The presence of low-virulence strains could mean that some strains can survive in ICS for long periods, similar to chronic infection of *A. astaci* in North American crayfish, their natural carriers, and eventually manifest as acute plague. This is an important issue in management since it emphasizes the need for carrying out health controls in ICS for restocking. On the other hand, the presence of such strains could also mean that there could be ICS with an enhanced resistance. Further studies are needed in this exciting area of research.

4.2.4 Effects on human well-being

The introduction of non-indigenous crayfish species has certainly contributed in a positive way to human social systems; some of them have restored cultural traditions such as crayfishing (as in parts of Sweden), produced economic benefits in poorly developed areas (as in southern Spain), stimulated the development of extensive or semi-intensive cultivation systems (as in the People's Republic of China), and increased international trade (as in Spain) (Gherardi, 2007b).

However, the introduction of commercially valuable crayfish has also produced negative results in the marketplace. In Scandinavia, Germany and Spain, crayfish plague led to over 90% losses in the production of *Astacus astacus* and *A. leptodactylus*, with considerable economic damage. When the plague spread to Turkey in the 1980s, the annual catch of *A. leptodactylus* plunged from 7000 to 2000 tonnes, which almost eliminated exports from Turkey. In Africa, very few projects based on crayfish importations have been successful. This is clearly illustrated in the case of Lake Naivasha, Kenya, where *Procambarus clarkii* was introduced in 1970 to provide food for the introduced large-mouth bass; its commercial exploitation began in 1975 with catches of several hundred tonnes per annum that were exported alive, mainly to Europe (Sweden and Germany) (Gherardi *et al.*, 2010). However, since 1984 the species has been subject to dramatic fluctuations in its population size, and since 2000 the population has sharply collapsed (Foster & Harper, 2007) leading to reduced or, by 2009, zero catches in the lake.

NICS may damage other human activities. *P. clarkii* is a recognized pest in rice fields in various parts of the world, causing a decrease in profits amounting, for instance, to over 6% in Portugal. Burrowing by several NICS species can be a problem in agricultural and recreational areas, e.g. in irrigation systems, lawns and golf courses, and in river levees, dams, dykes and lakeshores, where they may destabilize the banks. Finally, the non-market economic damage of NICS due to their impact on ecosystem services is enormous. For instance, the restitution of *Pacifastacus fortis* in California cost US\$4.5 million and the (unsuccessful) eradication of *P. leniusculus* in Scotland has directly cost around £100 000 to date.

Little attention has been paid until now to the threat that NICS pose to human health. Invasive crayfish living in areas contaminated by sewage and toxic industrial residues may have elevated heavy-metal concentrations in their tissues. Their potential to transfer contaminants to their consumers, including humans, is thus high. *P. leniusculus* and

P. clarkii may also accumulate in their tissues the toxins produced by cyanobacteria (Tricarico *et al.*, 2008) and can transfer them to their predators, humans included (Cox *et al.*, 2005). Finally, *P. clarkii* is also suspected to be an intermediate host for numerous helminth parasites of vertebrates and to be a vector for transmission of the bacterium *Francisella tularensis*, the causative agent of human tularemia.

However, there may be some societal benefits deriving from NICS. *P. clarkii* is known to control the snails that host *Schistosoma* spp., the agents of human schistosomiasis (Foster & Harper, 2007). Due to the rapid spread of this crayfish in African waterbodies, the epidemiology of schistosomiasis is expected to be significantly altered over time, although the possibility remains that African snails will evolve measures to avoid crayfish predation, or that the parasite will change its host.

4.3   Case studies

4.3.1   Rusty crayfish *Orconectes rusticus*

The rusty crayfish, *O. rusticus*, is one of the most invasive NICS in North America. From its native range in the Ohio River basin, this species is currently undergoing an explosive expansion in the midwestern states and in Canada, particularly in Arctic watersheds and in the Great Lakes system. Its spread seems to be mediated by anglers who use it as live bait. It is also used as a biological supply in schools and universities, from which crayfish may be released into the wild.

Its natural dispersal has been estimated after long- and short-term studies. The rate of spread averages 0.5 km per year upstream and 3.7 km per year downstream in Thunder Bay (Canada), and 0.68 km per year in Trout Lake (Wisconsin, USA) (Wilson *et al.*, 2004). Using mark and recapture techniques in Trout Lake, Byron & Wilson (2001) showed that most crayfish remain in their original habitat, covering a distance of 0–58 m, whereas some move further, up to 221 m in 2 days.

There appear to be few constraints on the range expansion of the species. A first barrier might be acidic waters, a pH ranging from 5.4 to 6.1 being lethal to juveniles. A second barrier is water temperature. *O. rusticus* is most active from spring to autumn at temperatures above 6°–8°C and becomes torpid at temperatures below 4°C. The southern regions of the USA and Canada, where water temperatures are warmer for longer periods of the year, are most vulnerable to its invasion. Juveniles reach maximum growth rates between 26° and 28°C, although the greatest survival occurs between 20° and 22°C (Mundahl & Benton, 1990).

As with most other crayfish species, *O. rusticus* is omnivorous. It has, however, a higher metabolic rate than other crayfish of similar dimensions, reaching up to twice that of *O. virilis*, which means that its environmental impacts are significantly greater. It decimates beds of aquatic plants and macroinvertebrates, often leading to long-term and nearly irreversible changes in the biota of littoral zones (Lodge & Lorman, 1987). In Trout Lake, after 20 years of invasion by *O. rusticus*, the richness of submerged macrophytes declined by 80%, the abundance of Odonata, Amphipoda and Trichoptera significantly decreased, and the density of snails fell from >10 000 to <5 m^{-2} (Wilson *et al.*, 2004). Throughout the invaded range, *O. rusticus* has displaced some native species, such as *Orconectes bartonii*, *O. propinquus* and *O. virilis*, in Ontario lakes and waterways. Displacement may result from its superior competitive ability, for instance being able to force indigenous crayfish out of shelter and leave them susceptible to fish predation. A further threat posed by *O. rusticus* to native crayfish comes from hybridization and consequent introgression, as documented by Perry *et al.* (2001b, 2002) by the use of diagnostic nuclear and mitochondrial DNA markers. Over 6% of the crayfish sampled in the population of Trout Lake were F1 hybrids between *O. rusticus* and *O. propinquus*, hybridization being in the large majority of cases the result of *O. rusticus* females mating with *O. propinquus* males. F1 hybrids appeared to mate disproportionately with pure *O. rusticus*, leading to much greater genetic introgression of nuclear DNA from *O. propinquus* to *O. rusticus* than in the reverse direction. A consequence is the gradual elimination of *O. propinquus* genes from the population.

According to Olden *et al.* (2006), *O. rusticus* is one of America's best-known NICS, having been identified as extirpating indigenous crayfish and disrupting local aquatic ecosystems across a wide area. Over the past 40–50 years, rusty crayfish have spread from their historical range in the Ohio River drainage to waters throughout much of Illinois, Michigan, Wisconsin and Minnesota, and parts of 11 other states, Ontario (Canada) and the Laurentian Great Lakes. These authors found that rusty crayfish occurrences have increased from 7% of all crayfish records collected during the first 20 years of their invasion (1965–84) to 36% of all records during the last 20 years, and that rusty crayfish have now replaced the northern clearwater crayfish (*O. propinquus*) and virile crayfish (*O. virilis*) as the most dominant member of the contemporary crayfish fauna of eastern North America.

4.3.2   Red swamp crayfish *Procambarus clarkii*

The most notable example of an intercontinental invader crayfish is the red swamp crayfish, *P. clarkii*, native to north-eastern Mexico and south-central USA (Hobbs, 1972). In the southern USA it has been extensively cultivated since the 1950s, with production that, in 1999, reached a maximum of about 50 000 t, primarily in Louisiana (Huner, 2002).

Mostly due to its commercial value, it has been introduced into several states of the USA: its range now includes the east and west coasts and extends northwards into the states of Idaho and Ohio (Huner, 2002) (Figure 4.4). Outside the continental USA, *P. clarkii* has been successfully introduced into Hawaii, western Mexico, Costa Rica, Dominican Republic, Belize, Brazil, Ecuador, Venezuela, Japan, mainland China, Taiwan, the Philippines, Uganda, Kenya, Zambia, Republic of South Africa, and several areas in Europe (Huner, 2002). As a result of these extensive translocations, today *P clarkii* is the most cosmopolitan crayfish in the world, being found in various freshwater ecosystems in all continents except Australia and Antarctica (Huner, 1977).

The first introduction of *P. clarkii* into Europe was encouraged by the results from stocking with the North American *P. leniusculus* in Sweden and Finland. In June 1973, a batch of *P. clarkii* (100 kg) was imported from Louisiana into a farm in the Spanish

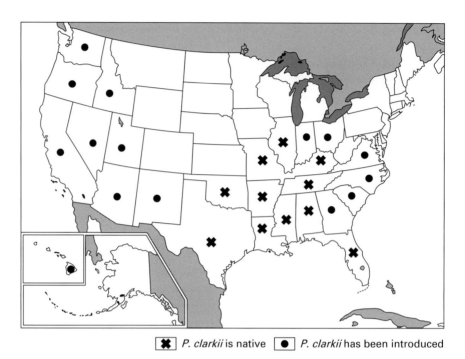

X P. clarkii is native   **●** P. clarkii has been introduced

Figure 4.4.   Distribution of *Procambarus clarkii* in the USA: crosses denote states where *P. clarkii* is native; circles denote states where *P. clarkii* has been introduced (drawn by Catherine Souty-Grosset).

province of Badajoz (Habsburgo-Lorena, 1986), and a year later a second larger batch (400 kg) was released into an eel pond in the Lower Guadalquivir, together with 100 kg of the white river crayfish *P. zonangulus* (Gutiérrez-Yurrita *et al.*, 1999). While this latter species did not prosper, *P. clarkii* soon became naturalized; the absence of filters in the sites of release allowed crayfish to escape and to colonize ditches and canals nearby. Because of the economic potential, crayfish expansion was accelerated by fishermen who distributed individuals throughout the entire Guadalquivir marsh zone and into the Doñana National Park. This was the first step of its subsequent expansion into the entire Iberian Peninsula and of its translocation to several other European countries as well.

P. clarkii has recently been included on the list of the hundred worst invasive species of Europe (Gherardi & Panov, 2006), being considered one of the top ten invasive species, with the highest number of different impact types on ecosystem services (Vilà *et al.*, 2009; Savini *et al.*, 2010). *P. clarkii* exhibits characteristics of an *r*-selected species, including early maturity at small body size (10 g), rapid growth rate (50 g in 3–5 months), large numbers of offspring at a given parental size (a female of an average size producing 400 pleopodal eggs, about four times the number of those produced by a similarly sized *Austropotamobius pallipes*), and relatively short life span (reviewed in Gherardi, 2006). It is also characterized by an enhanced plasticity of life cycle (Gutiérrez-Yurrita *et al.*, 1999; Gherardi *et al.*, 1996b, 2000b) that allows the species to invade a variety of environments. The invasive potential of the species is enhanced by its dispersal capability, as shown by radiotelemetry; its occupation of the habitat may be complete and movement or spread is fast, even exceeding 3 km per day (Gherardi & Barbaresi, 2000).

P. clarkii is highly tolerant and adaptable to extreme environmental conditions such as those encountered in temporary streams (Gherardi *et al.*, 2002a) and polluted habitats (Gherardi *et al.*, 2000b). Heavy metals accumulate in its hepatopancreas and exoskeleton at concentrations that exceed those found in indigenous decapods (*A. pallipes* and the river crab *Potamon fluviatile*; Gherardi *et al.*, 2002b). The ability of this crayfish to withstand environmental extremes is related to its burrowing activity (Huner & Barr, 1984), which in its turn increases water turbidity with the inhibition of primary production (Rodríguez *et al.*, 2003). In addition, the perforation of banks induces their rapid collapse, often causing damage to agricultural fields (Correia & Ferreira, 1995; Huner, 2002).

The species displays a generalist and opportunistic feeding habit, behaving as a keystone consumer in most invaded ecosystems (Gutiérrez-Yurrita *et al.*, 1998). Gut content analyses showed that *P. clarkii* feeds on the diverse items present in a given habitat in proportion to their availability and that its diet can change with the habitat (Gherardi & Barbaresi, 2008). As shown in field experiments, even low densities of *P. clarkii* can affect the abundance of snails and decrease the biomass of submersed macrophytes (Gherardi & Acquistapace, 2007). The reduction of the latter may be due both to its consumption and to non-consumptive cutting of the stems (Nyström & Strand, 1996). Such destructive activity on macrophytes may cause the loss of a large proportion of them, reaching about 80% in 20 years in Doñana National Park (Spain) (Gutiérrez-Yurrita *et al.*, 1998). The predatory ability of *P. clarkii* has led to the local extinction of several invertebrates, such as water beetles (Garth Foster, personal communication, 2008) and molluscs (Montes *et al.*, 1993). It also threatens species of conservation concern, such as amphibians (Gherardi *et al.*, 2001; Renai & Gherardi, 2004). In California, Gamradt & Kats (1996) found that the introduced *P. clarkii* were able to consume newt *Taricha torosa* larvae, despite them containing a tetrodotoxin poison that serves as an effective defence against indigenous crayfish predators. Crayfish activities may also affect the value of a pond as a breeding site for several amphibians that usually breed in habitats with abundant aquatic vegetation (Nyström, 1999). Finally, even the abundance and composition of surface microalgae (cyanobacteria and euglenoids) are affected by direct top-down effects of crayfish consuming the organically enriched film at the water surface (Gherardi & Lazzara, 2006).

Competitive exclusion adds to the dangers that *P. clarkii* poses to indigenous crayfish as a vector of *Aphanomyces astaci*. A laboratory-based study showed that *P. clarkii* outcompetes similarly sized *Austropotamobius pallipes* (Gherardi & Cioni, 2004), possibly reaching even higher levels of dominance over the indigenous species in nature. In fact, both the larger body size and the stronger chelae of *P. clarkii* can induce asymmetries in fighting ability (Gherardi *et al.*, 1999a, 2000a). Resources such as food and shelter influence fighting, and dominance translates into a differential ability to compete. In a competition-free context, shelters were more extensively occupied by

A. pallipes than by *P. clarkii*. The presence of a competitor, however, strengthened the latter's attraction to the shelter and its ability to evict other crayfish from it. This was also shown in the presence of the North American congeneric *P. acutus acutus*, which *P. clarkii* evicted, although it did not use the resource (Gherardi & Daniels, 2004).

4.3.3   Yabby *Cherax destructor*

The genus *Cherax* is the most widespread and diverse of the nine crayfish genera native to Australia, with centres of diversity in the south-west of Western Australia and in Queensland (Austin, 1996; Austin & Knott, 1996).

An eastern group includes the *C. destructor* lineage, in which four subspecies (*C. d. destructor*, *C. d. albidus*, *C. d. esculus* and *C. d. davisi*) have been recognized. The *C. destructor* complex is one of the principal cultured crayfish in Australia, contributing the majority of total crayfish production (Piper, 2000). It is widely stocked into artificial waterbodies by farmers and is commonly used as bait by recreational fishers (Nguyen, 2005). Thus, the species is highly susceptible to translocation, having the potential to become globally widespread, as indicated by Mills *et al.* (1994). Feral or cultured stocks have become established outside its natural range, in Tasmania (Elvey *et al.*, 1996) and in western Australia (Lynas *et al.*, 2007). Introductions have also involved Europe; the species was introduced into Spain in 1983 in Girona (Catalonia) and in 1984 in the Province of Zaragoza, and now four wild populations occur. Recently, an established population was found in a Natural Preserve in Italy (Latium), where *C. destructor* seems to have been introduced at the end of the 1980s to foster an experimental aquaculture (Scalici *et al.*, 2009). The species is farmed in several countries, including southern Italy, and is sold live at markets and restaurants in Switzerland, Germany and England. The potential for this species to be released and to become established in the wild is thus high.

Illustrative in this respect is the story of its translocation into the state of Western Australia. Although *C. destructor* was probably subject to extensive movement by aboriginal people and subsequently by the European colonizers, the modern introduction of *C. destructor* into Western Australia started in 1932, when 10 individuals were translocated from Merwyn Swamp, western Victoria, to the Narembeen district of the central wheatbelt of Western Australia (Morrissy & Cassells, 1992). From this founder stock, eight were transferred in 1935 to another dam in the district. By 1969, the species was established in most dams of the Narembeen and had been spread to other districts nearby in the central wheatbelt, Bruce Rock, Bonnie Rock and Bencubbin (Morrissy & Cassells, 1992).

This crayfish now co-occurs with two indigenous species, *Cherax quinquecarinatus* (gilgie) and *C. cainii* (smooth marron) in several river systems in the environs of Perth, which generates concerns about the survival of the two indigenous species. With respect to them, in fact, *C. destructor* has a higher tolerance to environmental fluctuations, faster growth, shorter life cycle, higher fecundity and capability to breed year-round. It is also aggressively dominant over gilgie and marron of similar size, as demonstrated by Lynas *et al.* (2004) in a laboratory-based experiment. Its intense burrowing behaviour may confer further competitive advantage to *C. destructor* over indigenous crayfish in an area where annual rainfall is decreasing. Fast growth and early maturity are two properties that make it able to displace the indigenous *Astacopsis franklinii* from the swampy habitats in the north of Tasmania, notwithstanding that the native crayfish may dominate one-to-one interactions with similarly sized *C. destructor* (Elvey *et al.*, 1996). Finally, *C. destructor* may outcompete and displace other aquatic species of conservation concern, such as the critically endangered western swamp turtle, *Pseudemydura umbrina* (Lynas *et al.*, 2004).

4.3.4 Marbled crayfish or marmorkrebs *Procambarus fallax f. virginalis*

The marbled crayfish or marmorkrebs was discovered in hobbyists' aquaria in Germany in the mid-1990s, and since then has been introduced into Germany and Austria through the aquarium trade. It is a parthogenetic crayfish of the genus *Procambarus* but its provenance and species identity were unknown. Scholtz *et al.* (2003) even raised the hypothesis that *Procambarus fallax f. virginalis* is a transgenic species created by laboratories, due to the apparent uniqueness of parthenogenesis among decapods. However, the recent finding by Yue *et al.* (2008) of four natural clones in *P. clarkii* from China indicates that parthenogenesis is more widespread in crayfish than previously thought. Through the analysis of six microsatellite loci, Martin *et al.* (2007) showed that the marbled crayfish produces genetically uniform clones. These results and the absence of meioses in the ovaries led to the conclusion that marmorkrebs propagate apomictically.

Naturalized populations seem to be restricted to two European sites, in Germany and the Netherlands (Souty-Grosset *et al.*, 2006). However, wild individuals have been sporadically found in other countries, as, for instance, in Italy (Marzano *et al.*, 2009). In Madagascar, introduced populations are spreading fast, being now sold in many markets (Jones *et al.*, 2009). Marbled crayfish are kept as pets in at least 13 states of the USA and one province of Canada (Jimenez & Faulkes, 2010). In both Europe and North America they can easily be purchased through the eBay website, which underlines concerns about e-commerce as a new but powerful pathway for the introduction of non-indigenous species.

The marbled crayfish has been defined as a new 'perfect invader' by Jones *et al.* (2009). According to Jones *et al.* (2007), there are a number of reasons to be seriously concerned about its spread, particularly in Madagascar. First, marbled crayfish may carry *Aphanomyces astaci* that might infect the indigenous *Astacoides* species of crayfish. Second, they may cause serious changes to aquatic communities, since they are voracious predators of tadpoles and aquatic invertebrates. Third, similarly to its congener *Procambarus clarkii*, the species may become important pests of rice fields, damaging banks and disrupting irrigation through burrowing and eating seedlings. As shown in laboratory-based experiments, the marbled crayfish is dominant over similarly sized *P. clarkii* (Jimenez & Faulkes, 2010), which suggests that competition would be unlikely to limit its spread or impact once released into the wild. In consequence, the potential threats to the indigenous communities posed by the marbled crayfish seem far from trivial.

4.4   Multiple ecological impacts of non-indigenous crayfish species (NICS)

In the face of climate change, the multiple ecological impacts of NICS and their effects on human well-being need to be assessed in a more integrated and dynamic context that includes the potential of new invasions and the ecological prevalence of the invaders (Figure 4.5).

Continued climatic warming will enable non-indigenous species to expand into regions where previously they were not able to survive and reproduce, and will make them more likely to persist, to occur more frequently, and to develop larger populations (Walther *et al.*, 2009). Superecological strategists, i.e. species able to thrive in very different habitats and even beyond the expected limits of physiological tolerance, such as *Procambarus clarkii*, will be favoured with respect to resident species with strict ecological requirements. The ability of some NICS to tolerate both desiccation by burrowing and a relatively wide range of salinity will enable them to survive the prolonged droughts and salinity changes that are expected in some regions. Global warming will also provide new opportunities for the deliberate introduction of NICS for commercial purposes into areas where, until recently, such species were not able to survive. Even now *P. clarkii* supports a flourishing industry in countries such as the People's Republic of China, and *P. leniusculus* in Scandinavia is being translocated further north than its expected climatic limits.

Induced pathology from invasive crayfish is also of the utmost importance because *Aphanomyces astaci* is a difficult organism to study and problems are associated with the submission of crayfish samples, the availability of expertise in laboratories, difficulties in isolating and maintaining strains of *A. astaci* and in interpreting the results of samples. The advent of molecular techniques has allowed the development of new methods for rapid and reliable identification of *A. astaci* (Oidtmann *et al.*, 2006; Ballesteros *et al.*, 2007; Hochwimmer *et al.*, 2009; Kozubíková *et al.*, 2009; Vrålstad *et al.*, 2009). More research is needed, however, on *Aphanomyces* biodiversity and molecular markers, since in recent years a number of new *Aphanomyces* species have been described, and it has been found that several such species are present in crayfish and may provide false positive results in tests (Ballesteros *et al.*, 2006, 2007; Oidtmann *et al.*, 2006; Diéguez-Uribeondo *et al.*, 2009). Improvement of the currently developed molecular techniques for diagnosing crayfish plague is also allowing us to improve the specificity of molecular tests. The combined knowledge of disease history, culture-based or histological studies, and molecular studies are key aspects for providing accurate diagnosis.

According to Holdich *et al.* (2009b), reviewing the ever increasing threat to ICS from NICS, recent evidence that Europe is home, as at February 2007, to 10 771 non-indigenous species (DAISIE, 2009) and that this number is rapidly increasing has spurred the European Commission to release its first ever Communication on invasive species (European Commission, 2008). The European Environment Commissioner, Stavros Dimas, noted at the launch of the Communication that 'the ecological, economic and social consequences of the spread of invasive species for EU countries are serious and need a harmonised response'. The Communication, which is currently

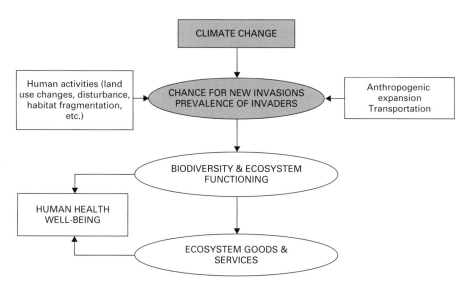

Figure 4.5.   Impacts of climate change and other aspects of global change (land-use change etc.) on species invasions, biodiversity, ecosystems and ultimately on human health and well-being and the associated processes (drawn by Francesca Gherardi).

open for consultation, proposes the development of a European Strategy on Invasive Species. It outlines three potential ways forward, each representing a different level of legislative cost and complexity.

It is clear from the above that the development of a transnational strategy on biological invasions in fresh water is needed. However, as Genovesi (2007) has pointed out, the main obstacles to this are: a lack of transboundary cooperation, limited ability to detect species early enough, ineffectual or delayed responses to the early stages of invasions, limited tools for eradicating or controlling invasive species in freshwater, deficiencies in and inconsistency of legal provisions, and the difficulty of trade regulation – all of which are very relevant to the NICS situation, and are discussed in detail in Chapter 8. The EU strategy on invasive species highlights the ever-growing problem of invasive non-indigenous species in Europe and emphasizes the importance of early detection of potentially invasive species and rapid action to eradicate them while it is still economically and environmentally viable (European Commission, 2008). This is very relevant to the 'new NICS' (recent arrivals) situation and also to the expansion of established 'old NICS' (Holdich *et al.*, 2009b).

In the changing world of the future, it will be increasingly difficult to evaluate the impact of some NICS and to prioritize interventions. New complex challenges will be posed to wildlife managers, scientists, decision-makers and other stakeholders in order to preserve biodiversity and at the same time ensure the sustainable management of wild and cultivated resources.

5   Crayfish exploitation systems: harvest fisheries, aquaculture and consequences for biodiversity

5.1   Introduction

For millennia, large crustaceans have been exploited as food in different parts of the world, tropical and temperate, in intertidal or inshore seas, and in fresh waters. The level of exploitation may lie anywhere along a continuum from casual fishing or poaching, through controlled and regulated exploitation (usually by trapping), to aquaculture, extensive or more or less divorced from the wild environment. Traps set for other species, such as eels and muskrat, may also catch crustaceans as by-catch. Harvesting would lead to holding pens and then basic aquaculture, and finally the emergence of crustacean superspecies that could be cultured across the globe. Genetic evidence suggests that humans in several continents moved around some freshwater species in prehistoric times (e.g. Lynas *et al.*, 2004; Reynolds, 2006). However, the live translocation of aquatic species for cash crop or culture purposes has thrown up its own problems for native faunal biodiversity, most either unforeseen or ignored because of economic opportunism.

Harvest systems were probably at first unregulated, until local recognition of scarcity led to agreements among fishermen to respect closed areas and seasons, particularly in fresh waters. In developing countries, parastacid harvests are lightly regulated, in practice often by traditions or taboos, but with current levels of human population growth and breakdown of traditions, this can lead to severe overfishing. However, regulation of crayfish fisheries was implemented in some developed countries, e.g. for noble crayfish in Europe or signal crayfish in western North America (examples discussed below). Crayfish were established early as a gourmet food among the aristocracy in Nordic countries (Swahn, 2004), and in some cases today, particularly in Europe and Australia, crayfish are exploited to provide for a luxury market rather than for subsistence food. This is often by recreational fishing, where the highly regulated fishing experience may be as enjoyable as the level of catch. In many areas, due to their simple life cycle and nutritional requirements, ease of reproduction in captivity and marketability, crayfish have become very attractive organisms for culture. Major extensive culture has developed to provide commercial-scale harvests. Examples of both harvesting and culture of crayfish are given below.

In the tropics freshwater crustaceans may provide valuable protein supplements. Freshwater crab harvests are little controlled, except to some extent locally and informally, and the produce is used variously, as human food or medicine, as a poultry feed and even as fertilizer. The larger freshwater crayfish are, however, recognized as a valuable foodstuff, e.g. in Madagascar, where regulations on indigenous fisheries for *Astacoides* spp. crayfish for food are almost unmonitored (Jones *et al.*, 2007), apart from local taboos on selling them, which may provide some protection to stocks. However, the impacts on these crabs and crayfish of both wide-scale changes in the landscape as forests are cleared for agriculture, and ecological changes from harvesting, are yet to be fully assessed.

Freshwater crayfish have large eggs and direct development, which makes their culture a relatively simple one-stage process, unlike that for marine decapods with their planktonic eggs and pelagic larval stages. Elements of crayfish aquaculture have been in place from the eighteenth century, while marine decapod culture showed its greatest development in the late twentieth century. Several crayfish species emerged early as candidates for global aquaculture status. Astacid crayfish have been traditionally cultured and moved around Europe for centuries. The noble crayfish *Astacus astacus* was the top value earner, and rearing stations developed in many parts of northern Europe. However, with the onslaught of crayfish plague, it was progressively replaced by a species long exploited in its native range in western North America, the signal crayfish *Pacifastacus leniusculus*, with many academic studies of its biology under controlled situations. Relevant aspects of the biology of other species were also investigated, for instance, the breeding biology of cambarid crayfish by Andrews (1907), based on the seminal studies of Huxley (1880) on the white-clawed astacid crayfish *Austropotamobius pallipes*.

From Louisiana in the south-eastern USA, red swamp crayfish *Procambarus clarkii* became the fast-growing species of choice, cultured in ponds and now widely introduced in Europe, Africa and eastern Asia. Market forces outweighed ecological considerations in the introduction of both signal and red swamp crayfish. Both species soon escaped into the wild, and as the negative impacts of these introductions became increasingly obvious, so too did the impossibility of undoing what had been done. Reduction of biodiversity and other ecological impacts are still being assessed, but damage by *P. clarkii* to river levees and to rice crops in Japan, Spain and elsewhere is among the quantifiable economic impacts. These introductions were discussed in Chapter 4 and their management and control feature in Chapter 8.

Although it was realized that introductions could have ecological impacts in their host ecosystems, action usually preceded reflection, and introductions for extensive aquaculture, or even into natural waters, were not thoroughly studied early in the process. In 1968, *Procambarus clarkii* was introduced to Lake Naivasha in Kenya, followed by highly deleterious impacts first on the vegetation and on the indigenous fishes, and then on the market economy of the region (Harper *et al.*, 2003). Then, in 1976, the signal crayfish *Pacifastacus leniusculus* was officially introduced to Britain, again without much study of its potential impact. Similar problems continue to arise today, as demonstrated by the finding of marbled crayfish (parthenogenetic *Procambarus fallax f. virginalis*) in Madagascar (Jones *et al.*, 2009). Such careless introductions must be considered unethical, as they may devastate unique ecosystems that took thousands or millions of years to develop.

The precise ecological status of individual crayfish species was not at first appreciated, and comforting concepts such as 'ecological homologues' were still being promoted in the 1960s and 1970s. However, many ecologists were pointing out the dangers of such thinking, including Unestam (1974), who wrote: 'We now have sufficient knowledge to realize that we are only part of a large ecological system where all organisms are interdependent ... but have we the humility to accept this?'

Added to direct ecological and economic harm was the wider damage to agriculture and fisheries. There were real risks of transferring disease, and in the last two decades it was finally accepted that the translocation of American crayfish would inevitably lead to the extinction of native species in other continents, as they all lacked resistance to the crayfish plague pathogen *Aphanomyces astaci* (Cerenius *et al.*, 2003; Javier Diéguez-Uribeondo, personal communication, 2008). Plague may be transferred between catchments by fishermen, boats, fishing gear, and even by fish, birds, mink and otter (e.g. Alderman *et al.*, 1987; Reynolds, 1988a; see also Evans & Edgerton, 2002). A common environmental result of plague, recognized early by Abrahamsson (1966), was overgrowth by aquatic vegetation, linked to more rapid lake senescence.

Pacifastacus leniusculus was sometimes screened for pathogens before implanting in European waters, and in the 1960s the Swedish rearing facility at Simonstorp bred from apparently healthy adults to produce early-stage juveniles for implantation. At that time, and probably even now, it was not in fact possible to provide a clean bill of health in regard to viruses, bacteria or fungi. Crayfish could also be vectors of damaging fish diseases, for instance, viral infectious pancreatic necrosis (IPN), transferred from North America to Europe with salmonids, but perhaps also with crayfish. The protection of salmon was the basis for the Irish ban on all introductions of live crayfish, which has resulted in Ireland being the only European country with no alien crayfish.

In the 1970s and 1980s the aquaculture potential of freshwater crayfish was a topic of great interest, and investigated from New Zealand and Australia (Morrissy, 1976; Jones, 1981) to Canada (Momot, 1984) and the USA (Nolfi, 1977; Nolfi & Miltner, 1978). Today, interest in native crayfish exploitation varies greatly – it is generally high in northern and eastern Europe, Australia, Madagascar and south-eastern USA, and relatively lower elsewhere. The existence or lack of such interest may affect the commercial success of an exploitation industry for local or export markets; and it may be difficult for crayfish farms to survive in isolation without a background of exploitation, even if there is some support in product management and diversification.

In all, about 15 species of crayfish are harvested on a commercial scale, less than 3% of the total number of species. The rest are mostly not widely harvested although, like freshwater crabs, their economic value is subject to change, particularly as human population pressure grows in developing countries such as Madagascar.

This chapter first describes capture and culture methods for crayfish. It next examines crayfish exploitation in Europe, where commercial harvesting of native species has gradually given way to farming and recreational fishing. It then turns to current harvest and culture situations in North America, Australasia and Madagascar.

5.2   Methods of exploitation

5.2.1   Capture

There are a number of crayfish capture methods in use, depending first on the habitat (whether a small stream, river or lake), and second on the behaviour of the target species. Monitoring of stocks may use the same methods as capture (Reynolds, 2009a); however, commercial capture methods may not give reliable information on the state of the stocks (monitoring of stocks is discussed in Chapter 7). Numerous capture techniques have been used: Somers & Stechey (1986) describe the use of dip-nets and seines for small areas, citing Brown & Bowler (1977); other examples include traps for larger areas (Goldman & Rundquist, 1977) and electro-fishing (Westman *et al.*, 1978).

In shallow water, the commonest capture method is by hand. By day, crayfish can be extracted by hand from refuges under stones or from their burrows (e.g. *Austropotamobius pallipes* in Spain) or, more damagingly, dug out from the banks (e.g. *Astacoides* in Madagascar; see Jones *et al.*, 2007). By night, crayfish are often captured by hand while illuminated by torchlight, as they move about foraging. The harvest area may be pre-baited to concentrate foraging activity. Baits are also pinned inshore by the bank in the 'baited stick' method (Policar & Kozák, 2005), and crayfish approaching the bait are taken by hand or with a small hand-net.

In deeper water, less direct methods are necessary; these include traps and various types of net. Many trap types and models are available on the market, with different mesh sizes and funnel types appropriate to different habitats and crayfish species (Figure 5.1). While most crayfish entering traps are mature, the size at maturity varies greatly between species, and a large mesh size will allow undersized crayfish to escape. The funnel may require modification to exclude predatory fish or otters. Traps are often baited with fish or offal, but will catch mature crayfish even if unbaited.

Where the substrate is fairly uniform, drop-nets or throw-nets can be used especially at night when crayfish may be moving around. In other situations, a lift-net or 'balance' (so called because it resembles the shallow pans of a weighing scales), sometimes baited in the centre, is often used; this must be lifted every few minutes to check and remove catches. Crayfish may sometimes be caught with rod and line, usually an unintentional catch while fishing with a baited hook. A baited, hookless line was the only legal method of catching *Astacopsis gouldi* in Australia. Finally, crayfish may form a significant by-catch in other fisheries, notably in seine-nets or fyke-nets fished for perch or eels.

5.2.2   Culture

There are many types of crayfish culture, relating chiefly to the economics and profitability of the cultured species. Methods are relatively simple, but in most cases, the value of the end-product will determine the degree of intensification, along with the cost of production in terms of land, labour and infrastructure. Thus, culture may range from extensive and semi-natural, where crayfish are stocked into a natural pond and

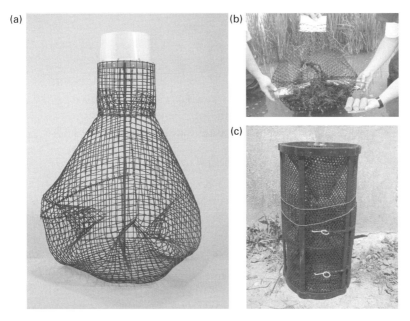

Figure 5.1. Crayfish traps: **a** and **b**: empty and filled traps with *P. clarkii* from Louisiana (photos courtesy of Jay Huner); **c**: trap used for *P. clarkii* in Brenne marshes, France (photo courtesy of Aurore Coignet).

harvested as and when they reach edible size, to more intensive situations where water and food are measured and provided, or where every stage of their life is controlled. Eggs may be stripped and incubated away from the female, and juveniles reared in cohorts. Temperature manipulation allows these processes to be speeded up or delayed, in theory making stocks available all year. Clearly, the length of time that a species takes to reach maturity, or marketable size (generally around 10 cm total length) will determine how much expenditure is necessary before obtaining a commercial product.

In the following sections, examples are given for capture and culture practices in Europe, North America, Australasia and Madagascar.

5.3 Europe

In Europe, as we have seen, there are only a handful of indigenous crayfish species (ICS), supplemented by more than ten non-indigenous crayfish species (NICS) which have been introduced over more than a century (Laurent, 1992; Holdich *et al.*, 2009b; Souty-Grossel *et al.*, 2006).

5.3.1 Indigenous and introduced crayfish stocks: history of exploitation

Crayfish were known to the ancient Greeks and Romans, with representations on coinage and a mention by Aristotle (Koutrakis *et al.*, 2007), but they were generally considered

Figure 5.2.   An early illustration of night capture of crayfish in Austria, from *Das Fischereibuch Kaiser Maximilians I* circa 1500. See also colour plate section (produced by the Lithographic Institute, K. Redlich, Innsbruck, 1901).

toxic or poisonous – an attitude which lingered on among country people in many regions, and was even repeated by Linnaeus (Swahn, 2004). However, different attitudes prevailed in different countries, and by the twelfth or thirteenth centuries freshwater crayfish were a food item in the larger monasteries, a habit that gradually filtered down to the laity (Swahn, 2004). In the ingenious minds of monks, crayfish were classed as fish (as too were many other aquatic animals – and even barnacle geese!) and so they could be eaten on Fridays and other fast-days, thus pleasantly diversifying the diet.

Lake and river fisheries developed early for noble crayfish *Astacus astacus* in northern Europe, particularly in Germany, Poland and Scandinavia (Füreder, 2009). A famous illustration from *c.* 1500 (*Das Fischereibuch Kaiser Maximilians I*) shows crayfish being taken from streams by torchlight (Figure 5.2).

Similar fisheries probably developed for *A. leptodactylus* further south and east in Europe. The wild harvest of crayfish in central Europe was regulated by Hapsburg Emperor Maximilian by the late fifteenth century, and by the 1700s crayfish ponds had been established in France to supply Paris.

Catches of indigenous European crayfish generally peaked around the end of the nineteenth century or early 1900s. Noble crayfish are still highly valued in certain regions, and are supported by breeding programmes and reintroduction policies (see

Chapter 10). In Austria, crayfish were a popular food up to the early 1900s, but today are less often eaten except in Salzburg. The earliest mention of noble crayfish in Hungary is in the sixteenth century, when cartloads of crayfish were exported to Vienna. Catches peaked around 1900 and stocks declined; reintroductions were at an important level between 1898 and 1914. Noble crayfish stocks continued to be exploited in Hungary until a few decades ago, with substantial numbers exported in 1956, but only about one tonne in 1980 (Puky *et al.*, 2005). However, a reintroduction and breeding programme has recently started in the Balaton Uplands National Park (Puky *et al.*, 2005).

By the nineteenth century, the valuable lake trap fisheries for *A. astacus* in northern Europe were in decline and becoming regulated, with fishermen restricted as to when and where they could use traps, and how many. Along with overfishing, plague was inevitably implicated, but the causative pathogen was not recognized until almost a century later. Strains of crayfish plague struck Italy before 1860, then France in 1874, Germany in 1878, Russia in 1880, and Finland in 1893, before hitting Sweden soon after 1900, at a time when catches of noble crayfish were around 200 t. Swedish production plummeted, and by 1972 unfilled demand led to imports of 1000 t of exotic crayfish, at an estimated cost of US$6 million. Regional losses of biodiversity represented by the dwindling native stocks would soon be joined by greater losses, as introduced crayfish species spread across Europe, wiping out indigenous members of the aquatic community (Westman, 1991; Kettunen & ten Brink, 2006).

The smaller white-clawed crayfish *Austropotamobius pallipes* species complex of southern Europe (including *A. italicus*) was also eaten in monasteries (Holdich *et al.*, 2009a), and widely fished in the streams of France, Spain and Italy for home consumption and to supply gourmets in Paris and other big cities. In the later nineteenth century *A. pallipes* was being increasingly harvested in the chalk streams of southern England for sale in London, encouraged by the availability of rapid bulk transport on the railways to Billingsgate Market in London. Occasional crayfish epizootics of unknown origin were recorded in England, as in mainland Europe (Pixell-Goodrich, 1956). Ecosystem changes resulting either from overfishing or from loss of crayfish through disease were, however, not yet being reported. In Ireland, *A. pallipes* was a food of the gentry; surprisingly, despite several devastating nineteenth-century famines, there are no reports of it being eaten by the common people in Ireland before the 1900s (Lucey, 1999; John Lucey, personal communication, 2009).

The American spiny-cheek crayfish *Orconectes limosus*, a carrier of plague, has been in Europe for over a century. Originally introduced from Mississippi to Poland around 1890, by the twentieth century *O. limosus* was becoming widespread in the region, and within decades had spread to many of the larger river systems of Europe and most of the north German lakes, and regrettably also to some large lakes such as Lake Annecy in Savoie and Lac Léman in Switzerland with their sparse populations of *A. pallipes* near inflowing streams. *O. limosus* is now moving down the Danube and threatening Lake Balaton (Hungary). The spiny-cheek crayfish was never popular with consumers, who complained about its small size, muddy flavour and difficulty of capture in the large, somewhat polluted rivers it inhabited. However, it has now become one of the most frequently caught crayfish in France, Poland and Hungary (Souty-Grosset *et al.*, 2006).

In the mid-twentieth century, the popularity and high prices of *Astacus*, particularly in Scandinavia, led to searches for new stocks to exploit, and for a few years in the early 1970s the shallow lakes of Turkey yielded thousands of tonnes of thin-clawed crayfish *A. leptodactylus* for the Scandinavian market (Erencin & Köksal, 1977). However, soon afterwards plague hit some of these stocks; this was perhaps not unconnected with their rapid exploitation and the use and transfer of fishing gear without sanitary controls. Around the same time, with the continued declines and unexplained losses of *A. astacus* from Scandinavian waters, the search was on for a replacement species, ecologically similar but, if possible, hardier. This was found in the shape of signal crayfish *Pacifastacus leniusculus* from western North America. *P. leniusculus* and perhaps two other species of *Pacifastacus* had been stocked into Lake Tahoe (California–Nevada) about 1895 (Abrahamsson & Goldman 1970), where a sustainable harvest developed. It was from Lake Tahoe in 1969 that, following some years of tests, 70 Swedish lakes were stocked with 70 000 signal crayfish, and the globalization of the species began.

Rearing stations were constructed at Simonstorp (Sweden) and elsewhere, where imported crayfish were held to check their environmental requirements and biological attributes such as growth and reproduction, and to monitor for diseases. Captive rearing was practised to produce 'disease-free' juveniles that could be implanted in natural systems. However, not enough was then understood about the transmission of the crayfish plague and the possibility that *P. leniusculus* could be an apparently healthy carrier of the *Aphanomyces* pathogen, and so the introduction of North American *P. leniusculus* in depleted waters was accompanied by further losses of *A. astacus*.

The success of *P. leniusculus*, and the high prices available for crayfish in Scandinavia, did not go unnoticed, and new export fisheries started to spring up in the USA (see below) at the same time as an interest in its rearing became widespread in Europe. By 1973, signals were being tested in France (Laurent, 1979) and were under consideration in Britain soon after (Richards & Fuke, 1977). A successful introduction for farming in England was allowed, on the false premise that native crayfish stocks had been decimated by plague. The scientific outcry that followed included pleas to consider exploiting native stocks first (Goddard, 1979) and a prediction, which proved correct, that the first plague outbreaks among native crayfish would be seen within 5 years.

Subsequent attempts to introduce *P. leniusculus* into Ireland included representations made direct to government ministers, but these were blocked by fisheries legislation to protect salmon in the Irish Republic, and by all-Ireland agreements for coordinated action with Northern Ireland. Ireland now remains the only part of Europe where no introduced American crayfish occur, and tellingly, the indigenous stocks of *Austropotamobius pallipes* are still widespread in lakes, rivers and streams, whereas elsewhere in their range they are now largely restricted to small fragmented stocks in isolated headwaters (Reynolds & Demers, 2006; see also Chapter 1).

Following the introduction of *P. leniusculus*, astacid fisheries in Scandinavia (of both noble and signal crayfish) have held fairly steady at around 1000–2000 t per year.

Finnish catches are still increasing (Japo Jussila, personal communication, 2008). The substantial *A. leptodactylus* pond fisheries of eastern Europe and the USSR slumped during recent changes in political systems, but attempts are under way in the last decade to redevelop this valuable cash crop.

There have been few commercial attempts to exploit *A. pallipes* in recent years, in part because of their smaller size, rapid decline across Europe and, most recently, their protected status under the EC Habitats Directive and national legislation (Souty-Grosset *et al.*, 2006). However, in 1987 an experimental crayfish fishery was established in a central Ireland lake with good stocks (Reynolds & Matthews, 1993), and market conditions were established for this species. Catches averaged two adult crayfish per trap night, slightly more females (54%) than males. Just 15% of 6659 crayfish trapped were 8 cm total length (TL) or greater, and only 2% exceeded 9 cm. Tested in a Dublin restaurant at a size of 8 cm and greater, white-clawed crayfish proved to be a less popular alternative to the popular marine Norway lobster *Nephrops norvegicus*. Crayfish prices rose only when sea-fishing conditions were unsuitable. Undersized crayfish in the catch were placed in an experimental farm for growing on (Reynolds, 1988b). A more intensive rearing facility was established in Northern Ireland in 2008 (Policar *et al.*, 2010), but it has yet to establish its markets.

The red swamp crayfish *Procambarus clarkii* was introduced to Spain in 1965 to the Guadalquivir near Seville (Albert P. Gaudé, personal communication, 2010), and in 1973 to the Guadiana at Badajos near the Portuguese border, perhaps through aquarium discards. It became an important commercial species within 10 years, even rejuvenating the economy around Seville (Thompson, 1990). Exports to France reached 2000 tonnes in 1982 (Albert P. Gaudé, personal communication, 2010). Recreational fishing of *P. clarkii* was at first regulated to limit their spread, but fishing regulations were relaxed in 1988 and 1990. As *Pacifastacus leniusculus* was considered a better substitute than *P. clarkii* for *A. pallipes* in the Spanish market, signal crayfish were introduced deliberately in the 1980s to north-central Spain as an 'ecological equivalent to European astacids' (Carral *et al.*, 1993) in an attempt to block the advance of *P. clarkii* up the major rivers of the Iberian Peninsula.

An epizootic of crayfish had been seen in Duero (Valladolid) in 1958, but plague was first documented in 1978 in Burgos (Carral *et al.*, 1993). Spores of the pathogen were disseminated by fishermen and gear. This aspect is well discussed by Diéguez-Uribeondo *et al.* (1997a) and Alonso *et al.* (2000). The first official regulations were promulgated in 1981, but *A. pallipes* populations were soon decimated, and those surviving the plague were heavily poached.

Other *P. clarkii* populations spread from introductions and discards into the extensive swamps, lagoons and marshes along the Mediterranean coast. After trying mechanical and chemical means of eradication in private ponds and rice fields, a profitable fishery developed, which today supplies thousands of tonnes every year. Production may reach 350 kg per ha, and some 3000 tonnes were trapped in 1980, valued at US$7.6 million. However, yield is variable; in drought years like 1983 it was only 700 t overall, but 5000 t in 1988 (Thompson, 1990), a level again reached in 2008 (Albert P. Gaudé, personal communication, 2010). International regulations prohibit its live transport, and the red swamp crayfish is now exported cooked and frozen, chiefly to Scandinavia. The damage caused to embankments and rice fields is well known (Escosa, 1990; Souty-Grosset *et al.*, 2006), and studies have recently commenced into its ecological impact on the original ecosystems and indigenous species. *P. clarkii* has had demonstrably adverse impacts on the native plants and animals (Gutiérrez-Yurrita *et al.*, 1998); for example, wiping out many water beetles, with only *Hydaticus leander* resisting its attentions (Garth Foster, personal communication, 2008). On the plus side, the introduced red swamp crayfish provides valuable feeding for otters and water birds in areas where native astacid crayfish never existed (Souty-Grosset *et al.*, 2006).

Although recent data are incomplete, Europe now produces between five and ten thousand tonnes of crayfish annually, mostly wild-harvested with traps, and more than 90% comprises NICS. Red swamp crayfish now form over half of total European crayfish production, chiefly from Spain. Thin-clawed crayfish (ICS in Eastern Europe but widely translocated into the west) make up less than 25% and signals more than 15%, while the indigenous noble crayfish now make up under 5%, chiefly in Nordic countries. Catches of spiny-cheek, stone and white-clawed crayfish contribute smaller amounts (Ackefors, 1998; Souty-Grosset *et al.*, 2006; unpublished data from the CRAYNET network). Yabby, redclaw and other species are also exploited in Europe, chiefly by culture in Italy.

A selection of regional case studies follows, describing the exploitation of noble crayfish in Finland and Norway, and of the white-clawed crayfish in southern and western Europe. Crayfish farming in Europe is then described, as well as a historical account of the farming of signals in Britain. This is followed by sections on the exploitation of crayfish in North America, Australasia and Madagascar.

5.3.2   Exploitation of noble crayfish in the Nordic countries

There have been commercial and recreational trap fisheries for noble crayfish in Scandinavia since the nineteenth century. Traditional fishing methods have evolved, and modern *Astacus* fisheries are now managed for sustainable exploitation (Skurdal & Taugbøl, 2002). Scandinavian crayfish fisheries continue to generate high prices and much related economic activity (Taugbøl, 2004a). The noble crayfish *Astacus astacus* still fetches significantly higher prices than the rather similar signal crayfish *Pacifastacus leniusculus*, indicating a discerning public (Lennart Edsman, personal communication, 2009).

Catch regulations for *A. astacus* vary across the Nordic countries, but as little is yet agreed about optimal management, most are empirical and modified as necessary. Westman *et al.* (1990) give the commercial importance of ICS in Nordic countries as around €30 million per year in Sweden, €7 million in Finland and €1 million in Norway. Finland provides a good example of exploitation of a valued resource, both of noble crayfish and increasingly also of introduced signal crayfish in southern lakes (Westman, 1991). Most is sport trapping, work-intensive, expensive to do, but producing a high-value product, further enhanced by marketing.

While elsewhere in Europe crayfish had been a luxury food item since the Middle Ages at least, they were not eaten in Finland until the sixteenth century, the habit spreading slowly from the Scandinavian royal families to the aristocracy and to the bourgeoisie, but meeting most resistance from the country folk. In the nineteenth century a fashion amongst city-dwellers for eating crayfish was spreading from Paris eastwards across Europe. As local stocks declined, the centre of exploitation shifted north, and by about 1840 Russian merchants were buying crayfish from Finnish peasants to supply the demand in St. Petersburg. The commercial capture of Finnish crayfish began in the 1850s for both the Russian and the Swedish markets, and export statistics were kept from 1856.

The practical minimum size was 10 cm TL for the commercial catch at that time. Currently, a 10 cm noble crayfish has a mean weight of 32 g, and 11 cm nobles average 49 g (Japo Jussila, personal communication, 2009). This would give estimates of between 32 and 51 tonnes per million crayfish, with a likely median value of 40 tonnes per million. Signal crayfish are slightly heavier per length, averaging 37 g at 10 cm and 51 g at 11 cm (Japo Jussila, personal communication, 2009).

Some 200 000 noble crayfish (perhaps 8 t) were exported annually in the 1860s, rising to 2 million (80 t) a year in the next decade, mostly by rail to Russia. By the 1880s Finland was also exporting large amounts to Germany, where the Berlin crayfish exchange paid the highest prices in winter. In 1891 the Finnish Fishery Association was established, and provided capture and marketing advice. The peak year for crayfish production was 1900, when 20 million crayfish were caught, of which 15.5 million (perhaps 600 t) were exported, still mainly to Russia. Finland was then the major European exporter of crayfish; in that year crayfish made up over 10% of all fish exports by value (Westman, 1991).

In 1893, crayfish plague was first noticed in Finland, but exports remained above 12 million (400 t) per year until 1907, when the best fishing waters became affected. Exports then dropped to 3 million (120 t), and by 1917 to just 240 000 (around 10 t). Exports to Russia ceased completely the following year. By 1925 exports started to recover, including 1 million (40 t) to Sweden. During the 1930s exports were around 2 million (80 t) per year. They declined during the war years, and then rose again. A sharp drop occurred in the 1960s, from a mixture of plague and river engineering works, recovering in the early 1970s to about 750 000 (30 t), then declining again. The total catch in 1988 was about 3.5 million crayfish, or about 140 t, mostly nobles. This made Finland the largest producer of noble crayfish, providing over 50% of total European catch of this species. In recent years, 3.5 million crayfish were caught (140 t), of which 98% were nobles. The value of the 1996 catch was 28 million Finnish marks (FIM) (US$5 million) (Westman, 1999). The market value of crayfish in 1990, at FIM 45 million, equalled the value of the Finnish salmon catch. Nonetheless, demand started to exceed supply in the 1960s, and crayfish have been imported since 1967, first nobles from the Soviet Union, then chiefly thin-claws from Turkey (1972–86) and latterly signals and red swamp crayfish, cooked and frozen, from the USA. Today imports run at 1.5–2 million crayfish (50–60 t) per year.

At the start of the twentieth century, the Finnish crayfishery supported thousands of professional fishermen. A century later, in Finland the number of professional fishermen has declined, most being part-time farmers, and most crayfish catchers are recreational fishermen from all walks of life, like recreational fishermen elsewhere. Today there are an estimated 100 000 recreational fishermen. Most use traps baited with fish; other capture methods range from hand-catching inshore and crayfish tongs for deeper water, to a baited rod and line (in use since 1690) and a balance net, used since the late 1800s. Most crayfish waters are privately owned, and the owners are obliged under the Fisheries Acts to safeguard and improve crayfish stocks by various means, including the reduction of predators and competing fish, and improving the habitat by liming.

There are usually size limits in force, crayfish not being marketable below 10 cm TL. As noble crayfish reach sexual maturity at 7–8 cm, their capture at 10 cm and above should not affect reproduction. Some lakes have dense, stunted stocks; production increases with the removal of the largest ones, and a reduction of the legal size limit from 10 to 9 cm has been recommended for such systems. Tulonen *et al.* (2008) investigated the impact of size regulations and exploitation with different trapping strategies and minimum catchable sizes of 9 or 10 cm TL on the population dynamics of *A. astacus*. Both size limits led to reduced numbers of large crayfish, but growth was not affected.

In conclusion, Finland has had a strong tradition for over a century of catching crayfish as a luxury foodstuff, much of it for export. However, demand exceeded supply 40 years ago, and today, instead of exports, increasing numbers of cooked, prepared crayfish are imported to make up the shortfall.

In Sweden, the home of crayfish summer festivals, crayfish have been esteemed and caught for many centuries (Swahn, 2004). Noble crayfish are believed to be indigenous, and genetic variability is demonstrable across the country (Edsman *et al.*, 2002), but some stocks were certainly imported from Germany in the sixteenth century by the Swedish Wasa kings, to plant in lakes of southern Sweden. Both noble and signal crayfish are caught, largely in recreational fisheries, with the former fetching considerably higher prices, for instance, in 2000 these were given as 300–400 Swedish kronor (SEK) for nobles and SEK 100–300 for signals (Kettunen & ten Brinck, 2006). Shallow, productive lakes can yield 20–40 kg ha^{-1}, but an average yield overall is closer to 3 kg ha^{-1} (Skurdal & Taugbøl, 2002). Many of the country's lakes have, however, been ravaged frequently by crayfish plague, now understood to be carried by the non-indigenous signal crayfish, and there is today a renewed emphasis on protecting the noble crayfish stocks. The distribution of both species in shown in Figure 5.3.

In Norway, Lake Steinsfjorden now produces several tonnes of noble crayfish each year, about 25% of all Norwegian crayfish (Skurdal *et al.*, 2002). Noble crayfish were introduced in the 1850s to this stony lake, about 14 km^2 in area and with a mean depth of 10 m, and the ensuing stocks have been exploited intensively since 1900.

Stocks showed a general decline over many years prior to 1991. Yield halved from 4.4 to 2.2 t, believed to be due both to the removal of undersized and possibly immature crayfish, and to the overgrowth of productive shallows by the Canadian waterweed

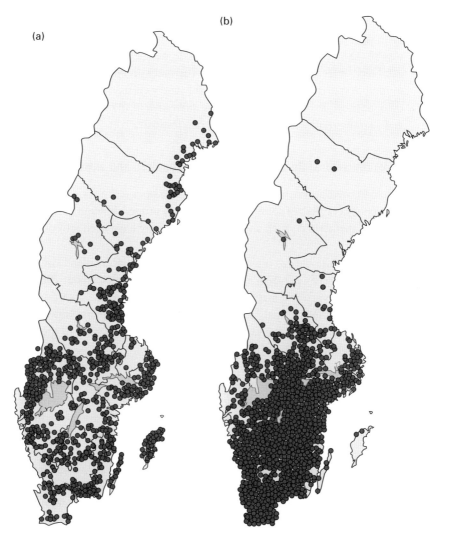

Figure 5.3.   Distribution of (**a**) *Astacus astacus* (1000 localities, a decrease of more than 500 in 8 years) and (**b**) *Pacifastacus leniusculus* (>4000 localities) in Sweden (2008). See also colour plate section. Reproduced with permission from Edsman & Schröder (2009) and Holdich *et al.* (2009b).

Elodea canadensis since 1977. Harvest regulations changed five times since the 1970s: trap mesh size was increased to allow undersized crayfish to escape, while the open season was reduced from 147 to 39 days in 1981, then to 14 days in 1989, and finally to just 10 days in 1995, taking in only the late summer period between the first and second moults. On opening night, up to 24 400 traps may be in use (18% of seasonal effort), dropping off thereafter (Skurdal *et al.*, 2002).

Monitoring of stocks is by pre- and post-season catch surveys. These at first differed greatly in the proportion of legal-sized crayfish, but latterly both seem to have stabilized at about 20% of the catch being of legal size, suggesting that the management regime was maintaining a stable population. The mean size of crayfish in catches was 83–88 mm, but the legal minimum size was held at 95 mm to ensure that females can breed at least once before capture. The main problem is policing the adherence to minimum size restrictions. This profitable and well-managed fishery is fostered by the outdoor lifestyle of many Norwegians: their love of fishing, familiarity with crayfish, and a strong tradition of summer crayfish festivals.

5.3.3   Exploitation of white-clawed crayfish in southern and western Europe

White-clawed crayfish (*Austropotamobius pallipes s.l.*, including *A. italicus*) are the indigenous crayfish of southern and western Europe, although recent genetic evidence suggests that British, Irish and Iberian stocks may have been introduced in the distant past.

Spanish white-clawed crayfish stocks sustained a large inland fishery up to the end of the 1970s, when crayfish plague struck Iberian waters. About 700 Spanish populations remain, very fragmented and isolated (Alonso *et al.*, 2000), while the species, never common in Portugal, is now believed to be extinct there. However, its traditional value remains high in Iberia and there is still some poaching of the species in Spain (Martinez *et al.*, 2003), as in France and Italy.

The first mention of crayfish capture in Spain is in the National Fishing Act of 1907. In the 1970s, exploitation regulations allowed the use of lift-nets only, and included the 'rule of eights' – a maximum of eight nets per fisherman, and a catch limit of eight dozen crayfish per day, with a postorbital TL of at least 8 cm. The season ran from April or May to September–October, depending on the region. Fishing for white-clawed crayfish has been forbidden since 1980, but today there is a generally low level of protection of the native species, with very complex fishing regulations for native and introduced species varying between regions, and low levels both of management and of public interest.

In France, ravaged by plague for over a century, white-clawed crayfish are still widespread but populations are small and sparse. There is no longer any professional fishing for white-clawed crayfish, but some poaching occurs in 34 of the 100 Départements (Changeux, 2003). Spiny-cheek crayfish (*Orconectes limosus*) are now the most sought-after species by fishermen in poorer-quality rivers (Changeux, 2003), while red swamp crayfish are fished in lagoons and marshes of the south. White-clawed crayfish may not be trapped in Belgium or Luxembourg, and there is no indication that white-clawed (*Austropotamobius pallipes*) or stone (*A. torrentium*) crayfish are harvested today in Austria. In Italy there are still illegal river fisheries for white-clawed crayfish in Latium and probably elsewhere.

Switzerland (not affected by the EC Habitats Directive) permits fishing for indigenous crayfish species, but the effective fishing pressure is low. The season lasts 12 weeks, and the minimum legal size is 12 cm for nobles and 9 cm for white-clawed and stone crayfish, though there is little economic interest in *Austropotamobius* species. White-clawed crayfish formerly occurred in low numbers in Lakes Annecy and Léman (Lake Geneva), mainly near influents. Since the 1970s, however, signals (*Pacifastacus leniusculus*), thin-claws (*A. leptodactylus*) and spiny-cheek (*O. limosus*) crayfish have all escaped into Lake Léman on the French side, today providing a sizeable commercial tonnage, while the white-claws are believed to have become extinct.

5.3.4   Farming crayfish in Europe

Noble crayfish have long been cultured in Scandinavian countries, as have signals since the 1960s. In Finland, where stocking and restocking is widespread, crayfish farming has been established since 1970, following on fisheries research into crayfish biology and the influence of environmental factors on rearing, including artificial incubation (Westman, 1973, 1991). Unlike Sweden and elsewhere, where crayfish are farmed for the table, private farms in Finland mainly concentrate on raising summerling nobles and signals for restocking, often through artificial incubation under raised temperatures. There are about 40 farms as well as state culture facilities, and a Producers Association was established in 1990 to promote and develop crayfish farming. By then, Finnish crayfish farming was the third largest in Europe after Sweden and the UK.

In 1990 around 60000 summerlings (0+ juveniles), 1000 year-old (1+) and 92000 wild-caught adult noble crayfish were stocked into suitable Finnish waters, while 18000 signal summerlings, 2000 1+ and 4000 wild-caught adults were restocked to plague-eradicated waters. Hatchlings (costing FIM 1–2) have a pre-reproduction mortality rate of 90–95% (Fürst, 1977), so summerlings are preferred, at 20–30 mm TL, each costing FIM 2–3, or 1+ (30–40 mm TL), chiefly signals, costing FIM 5–7 (at the time roughly equivalent to about €1 or US$1).

Noble crayfish are also farmed elsewhere in Europe within their general distribution range, e.g. in Latvia, where there has been a recent upsurge in interest since the 1990s, with a Crayfish Association, four crayfish centres and 18 farms, chiefly operating for the production of stocking materials (Arens & Taugbøl, 2005). Similar conditions operate in Lithuania and the Ukraine. In Germany, Max Keller's well-known farm in Augsburg, Bavaria produces summerlings for restocking and, in extensive stocked ponds, adult crayfish for the table. In the Czech Republic, crayfish ponds have operated since the early nineteenth century, yielding some 4 t per year.

In France, crayfish farming was important in the 1870s. The Marquis de Selve, among others, had an extensive hatchery for 10 million *Astacus astacus* to supply the Parisian market (André, 1960). The onset of plague late in the nineteenth century put an end to this industry, which is seeing a slow resurgence a century later with the rearing of noble crayfish, signals and thin-clawed crayfish. By the 1970s there were several state-sponsored farms. For example, Les Clouzioux (Loire) farmed *Pacifastacus leniusculus* following the Finnish system, using raised temperatures and Zug bottles for artificial incubation (Cabantous, 1974). La Canourgue (Lozère) was a CSP (Higher Fisheries Council) crayfish rearing station for native *A. pallipes*, with relatively low temperatures, principally for restocking karstic streams in the Massif Central. Guémené Penfao in Brittany reared both *Astacus leptodactylus* and *A. astacus*; under elevated temperatures their crayfish could reach a marketable size of 90 mm TL in their second summer, while Gournay (Oise) reared *A. leptodactylus* and *P. leniusculus.* Nowadays there is a pilot farm for noble crayfish and educational facility at Le Moulin des Écrevisses (Champagne-Ardenne). At Motiers in Neuchâtel canton, Switzerland, nobles and white-clawed crayfish are reared for restocking.

Further south, Italy's farms produced and exported more than 100 t of seven different species of crayfish in the 1990s, including an annual production of about 20 t of nobles and thin-clawed crayfish and some white-clawed and stone crayfish for restocking. Market prices were high for noble crayfish and lower for the other commercial species, at about US$20–26 per kilogram for nobles, US$10–13 for thin-clawed, US$14–17 for spiny-cheek, US$8–14 for yabby, and US$7–14 per kilogram for red swamp crayfish (D'Agaro *et al.*, 1999). Thus crayfish farming has supplemented or even replaced wild harvest in many parts of Europe where traditional interest persists and conditions and prices are favourable.

5.3.5   Exploiting NICS: signal crayfish in Great Britain

Interest in farming signal crayfish (*Pacifastacus leniusculus*) was generated in Britain from the early 1970s, and these crayfish were first introduced to England in 1976 from the Swedish rearing station at Simonstorp. The crayfish market was fostered entirely for commercial reasons, and controls were generally lax. Crayfish farming was promoted by Government as an opportunity for farm diversification in a time of recession, and as an extra crop for commercial fisheries, with the incentive of high prices for export (Richards & Fuke, 1977).

Signals were selected because of their resistance to plague, which was said to have 'devastated the native crayfish populations of Britain and Europe at the turn of the century' (Richards & Fuke, 1977) – an unsubstantiated statement disputed by Behrendt (1979) and Goddard (1979), among others. In Europe the market was mostly supplied by *Astacus astacus* and *A. leptodactylus*, reared or wild-caught, but the future was believed to lie with signal crayfish. Behrendt (1979) advised that strict controls were needed on imports.

The market for crayfish at Billingsgate, London, was then small and the market price was just £1.40 per lb (about £3 per kg) in 1979 (Behrendt, 1979). White-clawed crayfish were then for sale in Hampshire at £1.50 per lb, and Goddard (1979) recommended exploring the potential of native *A. pallipes* first.

Publicity continued to be generated; a retail price of around £5 per lb was predicted, and in 1989 there were optimistic reports of rising sales expected from UK crayfish farms. However, the market was actually in decline, and the following year the British Crayfish Marketing Association (BMCA) collapsed, despite its plans to establish a British Crayfish season from early July to the end of October. Just half of its 45 members produced crayfish for the market, totalling two tons in 1988, with a London price of £5.50 per lb (£12.10 per kg) for the top grade of crayfish (6–8 per kg) sold direct to restaurants. The BCMA had two holding stations to buffer supplies. However, restaurants could get Turkish or Russian *A. leptodactylus* or even Kenyan *P. clarkii* for about £3.50 per lb.

The UK scenario is worth a closer look (see, for example, Rogers & Holdich, 1995). Interest in crayfish farming peaked around 1980, but the table market never developed as anticipated. Production was expected to reach 100 tonnes; a crayfish marketing organization was set up in 1984, and, by 1989, 62 farmers were registered (Holdich *et al.*, 1995a). There was a profitable trade in fingerlings for stocking farms, but many crayfish escaped from these farms into the wild. Most farms failed to operate commercially.

The BCMA aimed to set a price at the start of the season in early summer, of around £5.50 per kg, and hold it firm throughout the season until the end of September. To do this, it needed a buffer stock, where surplus crayfish could be held and released to even out demand and supply; farmers paid 50p a pound into this scheme. However, the table market failed to develop as projected and was largely met by imports, chiefly of red swamp crayfish from Spain, where up to 5000 t are produced annually (Peay, 2000).

The BCMA ceased trading in 1990. Thompson (1989, 1990) reviewed the UK situation and market potential at that time. By 1993 the estimated number of crayfish producers was 95, but most farms had ceased trading by then and a few simply kept crayfish as a hobby, in farms and angling lakes. Total farm production was estimated at just 6 tonnes, but today there are no farms operating (Everard et al., 2009). Most signals were by then living in the wild in Britain, extending their range year by year, and eradication has proved impossible despite well-publicized and costly research attempts (e.g. Peay, 2006). A few tonnes each year were provided by wild fisheries of escaped signals out of a potential 100 t unharvested, while the native white-clawed stocks, once so widespread, are now in terminal decline through plague and competition (Sibley, 2003b).

5.4   North America

In general, crayfish in North America fetch rather low prices compared with crayfish in other continents or with marine decapods. Crayfish smaller than 10 cm TL are not commercially attractive, but among the several hundreds of indigenous forms of crayfish, several species of *Pacifastacus*, *Cambarus*, *Orconectes* and *Procambarus* reach or surpass this size.

5.4.1   Commercial exploitation of signal crayfish

In North America, as in Europe, crayfish were also being exploited by the nineteenth century, notably signal crayfish *Pacifastacus leniusculus* in north-western USA and red swamp crayfish *Procambarus clarkii* in Louisiana. *P. leniusculus* was stocked both into the Sacramento River system (McGriff, 1983) and into Lake Tahoe (California–Nevada) before 1900, and again in the next two decades (Abrahamsson & Goldman, 1970), and a sustainable harvest developed. As mentioned above, it was from Lake Tahoe in 1969 that Swedish lakes were stocked with *P. leniusculus*, and the globalization of the species began.

Signal crayfish (*P. leniusculus*), among the largest North American species and now perhaps the second most widespread outside North America, are today chiefly discussed in terms of their commerciality and negative ecological impacts in Europe. However, signals have been commercially trapped since the 1890s in their native range, centred on the Columbia River basin in Oregon and Washington (reviewed by Miller & Van Hyning, 1970). By 1900, more than 50 tons were being sold annually to homes, taverns and restaurants in Portland, with some demand from further afield in North America: Seattle, San Francisco, Salt Lake City and even St. Louis. There were two size grades – small (3.5–4 inches; 8.9–10.2 cm), generally used for tail and claw meat, and large (>4 inches; >10.2 cm), chiefly for restaurants, which classed those over 5 inches (>12.7 cm) as 'jumbo'. Before 1900, marketed crayfish averaged 3.3 oz (94 g) each. However, the proportion of jumbos declined and by 1968 small and large crayfish averaged just 1.8 and 2.3 oz (51 and 65 g, respectively). By 1957 the trade had declined to about 30 tons, but this now also included small crayfish for bait and specimens for biological supply houses.

The Oregon fishery was actively regulated from 1897. From 1911 there was a closed season between 1 November and 1 February. The seasonal restriction was removed in 1939, instead protecting all females and all crayfish less than 3.5 inches (8.9 cm) long. Later changes protected females or all crayfish in the spring months approaching egg hatching, and in 1957 a closed season was again implemented between 1 November and 31 March to protect egg-bearing females.

Despite such closely monitored regulatory controls, the fishery showed marked fluctuations, falling from 140 000 lb (about 70 t) in 1898 to under 10 000 lb (5 t) in 1906, then peaking again at over 177 000 lb (88 t) in 1930, when many were eaten at free-lunch taverns during the recession. Numbers fell back again to below 40 000 lb (20 t) in the mid-1950s. Among other things, this catch variability suggests that periods of intensive fishing (e.g. around the turn of the century) were not terminally damaging to the stocks. Between 20 and 50 fishermen took part, but only a handful of them made significant catches. Prices were low – from 1890 to 1900 the price rose from 5 to 10 cents per lb, but fell again to 3.5 cents in the next decade. From 1947 to 1956, annual landings were 70–145 t, in total value between US$4500 and almost US$9000. Landings diminished sharply after 1956, to 6 t –valued at US$6000 – in 1961 and to 2.5 t – worth just US$3000 – in 1969 (Miller & Van Hyning, 1970).

Several reasons have been put forward for the decline. Signal crayfish are cool-water species, and natural biological fluctuations in abundance may be caused by physical conditions affecting successful reproduction, or may be due to disease. However, economic reasons may be more important. In 1973, a report noted that production of the Oregon fishery was never established at a consistent high level, due to several possible causes, including low prices. Perhaps the availability of abundant marine crustaceans depressed the prices of freshwater ones. Fishermen were chronically underpaid, and many moved to higher-paid jobs in industry and, during certain periods, in the armed services (Weller, 1973). In low-production years, a market loss occurred due to changing consumer food habits, and domestic demand remained generally low. In Washington state, landings were a few thousand pounds in weight (1–2 t) at best. Renewed interest in crayfish in 1969 led to a rejuvenated fishery in both Washington and Oregon in order to supply signal crayfish to Sweden. The new fishery was, however, short-lived: it peaked in Washington in 1970 at 31 000 lb (8.5 t), and the fishery collapsed in 1972. The Oregon fishery showed a similar development and collapse.

There may, again, be a variety of causes for the more recent collapse in Washington. Some areas were closed to fishing after opposition from landowners, sports fishermen and recreationalists. A series of harsh winters and overfishing in Oregon led to poor reproductive success. The resultant low production was out of proportion to export demand, leading to an unstable market, and by 1972 European buyers had turned to alternative sources of supply.

In conclusion, the variably low volumes harvested, and low prices obtained for wild-caught signal crayfish in their native range meant that the public did not perceive these crayfish as desirable or luxury items, while most fishermen viewed them merely as supplementary income. Not enough was known about the stocks to ensure or predict levels for a dependable supply. Production stability depends on available stocks, a rational structure for the fishery, and supportive legislation. Opportunity is determined by market demand, but if local markets lack an economic incentive, only export markets are involved. Growth may occur only if local markets are developed, matched by the maintenance of stability in production and in marketing, as was attempted with *P. leniusculus* in the 1980s in Great Britain, as described above.

The commercial fishery is still extant in Oregon, but with a higher product value. Landings since 2000 have averaged nearly 70 000 lb (34 t), valued at over US$100 000 per year. In Washington, however, many lakes have been invaded by rusty and red swamp crayfish, and some 90 other lakes are closed to commercial crayfishing through management plans negotiated with treaty Indian tribes.

In neighbouring Canada, signal crayfish are found in lakes and streams in the southwestern corner of British Columbia from Vancouver Island east to Okanagan Lake and the Kootenays. Early interest in these crayfish (Mason, 1974) received a boost with the development of the north European import market, and *P. leniusculus* became a candidate species for farming in British Columbia (Thompson, 1990). There is small-scale exploitation of signals in a few spots in lower British Columbia, mainly sold live to hotels and restaurants. Most catches have come from Harrison Lake and Harrison River near Vancouver, with most licences issued to ethnic Scandinavians. However, *P. leniusculus* stocks in Pitt Lake, a tidal fjord lake near Vancouver from which signals (and the associated crayfish plague) were exported to Sweden in the 1980s (Huang *et al.*, 1994), were rather small and slow-growing, with 60% of the catch below the 90 mm size limit in 1988. Bondar *et al.* (2005) reviewed details of crayfish fisheries and regulation in British Columbia, but indicated that almost nothing was known about stock densities, reproductive rates, and other demographic information that would indicate the potential sustainable rate of harvest or conservation requirements.

By contrast, at the warmer end of its range in North America, *P. leniusculus* translocated into the Sacramento–San Joaquin Delta are fast-growing, juveniles reaching 60 mm TL in their first year and an average 98 mm at 2+, when at least half were mature (McGriff, 1983). The wild capture of *P. leniusculus* in Sacramento averaged

100–300 t per year in the 1990s, though declining more recently. In California, the capture, sale or transport of crayfish for commercial purposes such as for bait, for scientific or educational use, or for food, were all regulated. For example, no crayfish less than $3\frac{5}{8}$ inches (9.3 cm) could be taken for food, all undersized animals must be returned unharmed, and no cooked crayfish could be less than 3.5 inches long (8.9 cm). No minimum size limit, however, was established for either red swamp crayfish *Procambarus clarkii* or spiny-cheek crayfish *Orconectes limosus*, both established pests in ricefield levees in the Californian Central Valley, but it remains unlawful to import or release in California any cambarid crayfish. This dilemma – to market or to restrict harvesting of alien invasive species – remains unresolved in many countries to which they have been translocated.

5.4.2   Exploitation of *Orconectes* in eastern North America

In recent years there has been an upsurge in interest in exploiting cool-water *Orconectes* populations. Momot (1993) tested the impact of heavy harvesting pressure on two lake populations of virile crayfish (*Orconectes virilis*) for over a decade from 1976. Stocks were harvested in summer, removing 50% of large males (>30 mm CL) by day 5 of the harvest; smaller males and females could then enter the catch. Effort increased from 150 trap days in 1977 to 6000 in 1985 and the following years. Catch per unit of effort (CPUE) fell until 1981, then increased again. By 1982, 4000 trap days removed about 60% of exploitable age 1+ crayfish (70% of males and 50% of females). However, population size, weight and numbers harvested continued to increase (Momot, 1993). Exploitative removal of adult males allowed pre-recruitment survival rates to increase. By contrast, in the unexploited population, maturing males regulated growth and mortality rates, thus restricting the recruitment of hatchlings and juveniles. The studies show that increased trapping pressure on a short-lived cambarid population led to an expanding population.

Unexploited populations at low densities are dominated by males and are regulated by adjustments in hatchling growth and mortality rates, juvenile female mortality rates and shifts in sex ratios. Exploitation greatly diminishes hatchling growth–mortality interactions, resulting in better recruitment and an expanding population. Males will feed on immobile, moulting juveniles, but their main impact appears not to be cannibalism of hatchlings so much as inhibition of their activities.

Momot (1991, 1993) also suggested that restrictive harvest tactics as practised in Europe on northern crayfish populations should be re-evaluated. Despite their long historical use in Europe, there is little agreement on the best management of wild crayfish populations. Momot (1986) asks whether it is possible to overexploit crayfish stocks, and if the response of crayfish stocks to exploitation is similar to that of fin-fish. The evidence from *O. virilis* is that large size limits tend to protect breeding male stock, and could be counterproductive if they reduce juvenile recruitment and subsequent yield. However, *Orconectes* life histories are not comparable to those of the longer-lived European astacid populations. Also, studies of Australian marron, described below, show that protection of females can lead to stunting (see also Morgan & Momot, 1988).

As for overexploitation, short-lived cambarid crayfish, such as *Procambarus clarkii*, at lower latitudes can sustain very intense harvest rates; if not intensively fished, populations tend to stunt due to continuous recruitment and exhaustion of food supply (Momot & Romaire, 1982). Parastacids such as the yabby *Cherax destructor* can also withstand high exploitation rates (Morrissy, 1978). By contrast, astacids are better adapted to northern climes because of longer life spans, many more age classes, larger size, larger eggs and young, and different somatic growth and lipid storage relations, matched to periods of reduced winter activity. Yet they seem quite resilient to exploitation further south, e.g. in the Sacramento Delta abundant stocks of *Pacifastacus leniusculus* sustain up to 50% exploitation. Stocks adjust to fishing by varying the age of female maturity from 1+ to 4+ without increases in growth or fecundity (McGriff, 1983). Northern astacids are also quite resilient, for example the long-term yields from lake Steinsfjorden (Norway) are stable at up to 70% exploitation (Qvenild *et al.*, 1982) without variation in population parameters such as adult mean length, moult increment or fecundity.

Therefore, provided that habitat remains intact, adult crayfish can withstand high levels of exploitation, around the 50% level, without showing a growth or fecundity response. However, at high latitudes, unfavourable climatic years could affect the situation and, if overfishing continues, stock collapse is likely. Extensive long-term monitoring programmes could allow total exploitation to increase until overexploitation becomes evident, followed by management actions such as a reduction in exploitation, or a stocking programme. Suggested removal rates of around 50% for mature cambarids and astacids seem safe (Morgan, 1988).

Strong circumstantial evidence has linked commercial fishermen with the accelerated range extension of several crayfish species (e.g. Crocker & Barr, 1968; Berrill, 1978; Capelli, 1982; Butler & Stein, 1985) and this is considered the main reason for the dramatic extension of *Orconectes rusticus* (rusty crayfish) into northern Wisconsin (Capelli, 1975, 1982), displacing *O. virilis* (virile or fantail crayfish) and *O. propinquus* (blue crayfish). In some of these oligo-mesotrophic waters, *O. rusticus* has reduced or eliminated submersed macrophytes and associated invertebrates (Lodge & Lorman, 1987). *O. rusticus* is now the dominant *Orconectes* species in south Ontario, although restricted to areas where crayfish are a popular fishing bait; its further introduction or transfer into the nutrient-poor lakes of the Canadian shield could have significant effects. Rusty crayfish have higher metabolic rates, greater fecundity, larger size (Lorman, 1980) and higher population densities (Lodge & Lorman, 1987) than those species they displace. The 'Wisconsin syndrome', described by Lodge & Lorman (1987) and others, includes impacts on macrophytes and associated snails and insects, and on fishes (lake trout eggs eaten, recruitment failures in walleye and centrarchids).

With the collapse of *Astacus leptodactylus* fisheries in Turkey as a result of plague, an opening appeared for cool-water cambarid harvests in North America to fill an export gap. These had to be large enough to compete with astacid catches in northern Europe.

Of *O. virilis*, *O. rusticus* and *Cambarus bartonii*, the species *O. rusticus* appeared most suitable to supply large (>9 cm TL) individuals.

In Minnesota in 1979, crayfish exploitation was just developing, again stimulated by the burgeoning Swedish market. Crayfish were becoming available in the larger cities, and restaurants started to express an interest. The rusty crayfish (*O. rusticus*) had expanded into this area from its native range in Illinois, Ohio and Indiana, and its tendency to overpopulate some lakes was causing some concern, so a harvest was encouraged. Captures of rusty crayfish in lakes of the Detroit area by people of Swedish origin led to a small export market, no larger than about 5 tons, but in 1979 this was overwhelmed by orders from Sweden for about 100 t of crayfish, boiled and frozen. Harvest regulations and legislation about translocating them to other systems were drafted. However, a large-scale fishery for human consumption never developed.

Around the same time, Stechey & Somers (1983) evaluated four of the seven cambarid crayfish native to Ontario (*Orconectes immunis*, *O. propinquus*, *O. virilis*, *Cambarus bartonii*) for their potential for culture, studying growth rates, tail-meat yields and intraspecific aggression in captivity, using large Form I males. All showed low levels of aggression when adequate shelters were provided. When standardized at 30 mm CL, only *C. bartonii* (slowest growth rate) showed significantly heavier males than females – but perhaps larger individuals would have shown more allometry. Relative body weight was highest for *C. bartonii* and lowest for *O. virilis*. *O. immunis* had the heaviest tail-meat (17% of body weight), followed by *O. propinquus* and *O. virilis* (10%) and *C. bartonii* (<6%). *C. bartonii* was eliminated from further consideration for culture because of its high aggression, slow growth and low proportion of tail-meat. *O. propinquus* was too small (maximum 34 mm CL). *O. virilis* was also eliminated in this study, although it had been the subject of other culture ventures (Nolfi, 1977). Eventually, *O. immunis* was preferred as it had good tail-meat yield and low aggression in captivity; it is a pond species with tolerance to lowered levels of dissolved oxygen and fluctuating temperatures (Crocker & Barr, 1968; Bovbjerg, 1970). The reproductive cycle (Tack, 1941) permits delayed egg maturation with low temperatures, thus allowing hatching synchronization.

In Ontario, exploitation of *Orconectes virilis* seemed to lead to enhanced survival of young-of-year, and Morgan & Momot (1988) suggested that populations could sustain 50% harvest without size or sex restrictions. In Quebec, there is a commercial crayfishery for *Orconectes* species in the St. Laurence River, with annual catches of 15–20 t. The mean size of crayfish caught at Lac Saint Pierre is about 10 cm (Portelance, 1987).

5.4.3   Large-scale exploitation of *Procambarus* in Louisiana

In contrast to the cooler-water fisheries described above, some southern US states have developed warm-water crawfish fisheries in both natural wetlands and purpose-built ponds, until recently among the largest and most successful freshwater crayfish production systems in the world. Two species of crawfish, the red swamp crayfish

(*Procambarus clarkii*) and the white river crayfish (*P. zonangulus*) are cultivated in the southern USA, with over 90% of the crawfish farmland located in Louisiana (McClain *et al.*, 2007). This account follows Louisiana practice in referring to 'crawfish' in farming, exploitation and marketing; whereas we continue to use 'crayfish' for species biology.

As early as the 1700s, European immigrants to Louisiana caught and exploited local crawfish (Comeaux, 1972), and commercial sales records date back to the late 1800s. In 1908 a US Census report listed Louisiana's crawfish production at 88 000 lb (about 44 t), worth US$3600. Louisiana and many other southern states chiefly catch *P. clarkii*, yielding up to a maximum 50 or 60 thousand tons from 50–70 thousand hectares of water surface in Louisiana. This represented up to 80–90% of world crayfish production by the mid-1980s. More recent output levels are put at 30 000–40 000 tonnes (Huner, 2002). Lower production is attributed to drought conditions and to adverse trade with competition from imported materials.

In their natural range, red swamp crayfish are active from autumn to spring (during the cooler months), but are largely dormant during the summer, when low water forces them to retreat into burrows. At least 11 moults are required for *P. clarkii* to reach maturity, at anything from 45 to 125 mm TL. Males and females who are sexually active (Form I) develop large inflated chelae. Eggs are laid several weeks after mating. They develop in 2–3 weeks at 22°C, slower at lower temperatures, so at least two generations per year are possible (Huner, 2002). Once mating has ceased, surviving males moult back to the sexually inactive Form II, with smaller chelae. Females must wait until their young are released before moulting.

These short-lived crayfish are adapted to the region's dry summers and wet autumn-to-spring period and grow rapidly in 3–6 months to commercial size. Wild stocks are harvested in the Atchafalaya Basin floodway, yielding from 5000 to 20 000 tonnes depending on the wetness of the year. In culture, mature crawfish are stocked into shallow ponds in spring at around 30–40 kg ha^{-1}, where they mate and start to excavate burrows in the banks. The ponds are drained in summer, when rice may be planted – this or wild vegetation forming the basis for the crawfish diet of detritus (Huner, 2002). The ponds are reflooded in the autumn, and the crawfish with their offspring emerge from their burrows and are harvested throughout the wet season. Many crawfish burrow again, so restocking of ponds is unnecessary. Smallish (2–4 ha) ponds are often the most productive, yielding up to 2000 or even 3000 kg ha^{-1} (Huner, 1999). Crawfish harvesting is by baited traps, set and lifted from flat-bottomed boats (Figure 5.4). Because of the low value of the product, more intensive production methods are not economic, nor is the use of formulated foodstuffs.

The crawfish production process is a seasonal large-scale, low-cost culture/harvest system, susceptible to external fluctuations in cost and demand. However, the recent development of large-scale cultivation and wild harvesting of *P. clarkii* in China (70 000 t in 1999) has impinged on Louisiana crawfish production and, more recently, so too have exports from Spain. Production of large, more valuable crawfish is density-dependent (McClain *et al.*, 2007) and at high densities they may become 'stunted'. Such overpopulation is rarely a problem with crawfish–rice rotations. Farmers sometimes

Figure 5.4.   Capture of *Procambarus clarkii* in Louisiana. See also colour plate section (photo courtesy of Wray McClain).

move crawfish from stunted populations to underpopulated ponds with a dramatic increase in growth. A questionnaire survey of producers in the eastern USA from Florida to New England in 2004 indicated that crawfish production for food made up 64% of the total harvest, bait production 17%, and aquarium trade 19% (Eversole, 2008). Species not indigenous to certain states, including *P. clarkii*, were frequently involved, and the trade has resulted in a number of escapes and other threats to biodiversity (Eversole, 2008).

5.4.4   Red swamp crayfish and biodiversity

In the southern USA, where crawfish are grown in extensive culture in ponds, wetlands or rice fields, these 'working wetlands' are important habitats for both invertebrates and birds (Musumeche *et al.*, 2002; Huner *et al.*, 2009). In Louisiana the 160 000 ha mosaic of shallow water and moist soil habitats of working wetlands have replaced to some extent as habitat the 600 000 ha of adjacent coastal wetlands lost since 1950. Commercial production of rice in Louisiana's prairie grassland areas started in the early 1900s, and commercial production of crawfish in the 1950s. Within this landscape, grassland birds benefit from grassy fallow fields (Huner *et al.*, 2009). Clearing of wooded wetlands within the state's river basins dates from the 1960s. Here crawfish were the primary species, with rice added once tracked equipment became available for use in the soft substrates. In total, about 60 000 ha were in crawfish production in 2007, providing a substantial landscape of marsh and shallow-water habitats.

Flooding and draining of crawfish ponds creates a significant food resource for many waterbird species. Wading bird populations have increased dramatically in Louisiana, benefiting from this predictable resource. Impoundments used to culture crawfish, normally in a seasonal rotation with rice, provide both small vertebrate and macroinvertebrate food resources for predaceous waterbirds feeding on decomposing vegetation and seeds. Waterfowl also benefit from rice and weed seed and invertebrates prior to breeding (Huner *et al.*, 2009).

As the crawfish industry developed in the 1970s, farmers noticed very large concentrations of wading birds, especially egrets and ibises. They became concerned about the possible damage to their crops and subsequently began to complain to regulatory authorities about the perceived problems (Huner *et al.*, 2009). When large flocks of pelicans, cormorants, coots, gulls and terns began to use these habitats, this added to the farmers' concern about the welfare of their crawfish crops.

Conservation status of waterbirds regularly encountered in Louisiana's working wetlands is now a topic of concern by several authorities (see Brown *et al.*, 2000; Kushlan *et al.*, 2002; National Audubon Society, 2007). Surveys of the avifauna began in the mid-1990s, concentrating on waterbirds associated with perceived damage to crawfish crops (Huner, 2000; Huner *et al.*, 2002) in both the clayey bottomlands of the Mississippi and Atchafalaya Rivers and the lighter soils of prairie areas of south-central and south-western Louisiana. Over 100 species of waterbirds were recorded, and more than 180 other bird species utilized riparian areas and nearby wooded wetlands, together comprising over 60% of the state's total bird list (Huner *et al.*, 2002).

Surface water is a limiting factor in the life cycles of all waterbirds. Wetlands in Louisiana and adjacent states are generally dry from mid-summer into autumn. Surface waters accumulate from autumn rains and spring flooding of lowlands of major rivers including the Atchafalaya, Mississippi and Red Rivers. Dry years have a negative impact on nesting waders, through reduction in food. Likewise, migrants and wintering birds depend on shallow water and moist soil feeding grounds (Brown *et al.*, 2000; Frederick & Ogden, 2001; Kushlan *et al.*, 2002). When summer vegetation is flooded, a myriad of invertebrate organisms is produced, as well as small vertebrates such as minnows, fish fry and tadpoles, which serve as prey for crawfish, waterbirds and other predators, in addition to plant food resources including seeds, corms and tubers available to both crawfish and birds.

There is undoubtedly some competition between birds and crawfish. Herbivorous birds damage and consume emergent vegetation and seeds, especially lost rice grain that is important crawfish food. However, although the provision of crawfish and associated prey for wading birds has been documented by Fleury & Sherry (1995) and Fleury *et al.* (1999), there is only anecdotal data to show how carnivorous birds may adversely impact on crawfish production systems (Huner, 2000; Huner *et al.*, 2002; McClain *et al.*, 2007). Dabbling ducks and coots are generally assumed to be herbivorous but will, in fact, consume invertebrates, including crawfish, prior to the breeding season, so high densities of predaceous waterbirds can adversely impact crawfish production (Huner *et al.*, 2009).

5.5   Large-scale crayfish exploitation in Australasia

Crayfish in Australia tend to be more varied in size than elsewhere, reaching up to several kilograms in weight. There are local recreational fisheries for a number of crayfish species. In addition, at least three of the about 120 Australian species are widely exploited and have significant aquaculture potential. These are the marron (*Cherax tenuimanus/cainii*) in rivers of the south-western corner of Western Australia, the yabby (*C. destructor*) – widespread across the centre and east of Australia, and the tropical redclaw (*C. quadricarinatus*) in Queensland. The first two have been farmed for several decades, the third more recently, since the late 1980s. Farming is at best semi-intensive, and despite much experimentation there are as yet no commercially viable intensive operations.

The background to warm-water crayfish exploitation in Australia, with its barbecue culture and its large inland semi-arid farming areas where farm ponds are important for crayfish, differs strongly from that in the western USA. Generally good food price rewards means that rock-bottom prices were not hampering developments as in Oregon since the 1900s and in Louisiana today.

5.5.1   Recreational fishery for marron

Marron (*Cherax tenuimanus* and *C. cainii*) are large *K*-selected species with a limited natural range; they show relatively slow growth in the first year, reaching 30–50 g at 1 year old, and breed in the spring of years 2 or 3. Survival and growth of juveniles is related to cover and density. Growth is maximum at around 24°C but is very variable. Marron are usually harvested at 100–200 g, after 18–30 months (Morrissy, 2002).

The flavour of marron is locally considered superior to all other crustaceans, including lobsters. Recreational marron fishing has been very popular in Western Australia for more than half a century. In the 1960s the average size caught was greater than 200 g, with record specimens up to 2 kg and probably at least 14 years old. There was early concern for the conservation of these large crayfish, and so marron were protected in the south-western rivers of Western Australia from 1955 under state legislation; their commercial fishing and sale was banned, and a minimum carapace size limit imposed of 3 inches (76 mm CL), about 120 g in weight (Molony *et al.*, 2002, Wingfield, 2002).

The marron fishing experience is a positive one: family and friends go out in the afternoon, fish through dusk, and may have a 'cook-out' afterwards. Over 20 000 marron licences are issued each year. The open season runs from the first Saturday after 3 January to the last day in February, avoiding the mating and egg production periods. Only scoop-nets, drop-nets and snares are allowed, and the minimum size of 76 mm CL (about 150 mm or 6 inches TL) and daily bag limit of 10 crayfish are enforced.

Despite these controls, a downward trend has been seen in both total catch and catch per unit of effort (CPUE). This may partly be explained by a preference for fishing easy-access but suboptimal farm dams rather than rivers. Exploited populations of marron have a tendency towards stunting. Farm stock watering dams in the wheat belt of western Australia initially produce large crayfish, but with continued trapping, average size decreases until the majority are less than market size. This phenomenon was explained through experiments with exploited and unexploited populations. They showed that harvesting reduced the number of males, leading to a skewed sex ratio favouring the slower-growing females; while at the same time their increased reproductive potential gave rise to increased crowding (Lawrence *et al.*, 2006). These findings are somewhat at variance with some theories of exploitation (see above), where the growth of survivors appears enhanced following the exploitative removal of large, old individuals.

In unexploited wild stocks females spawn well below the legal size, but in many exploited stocks they are fast-growing and mature close to the legal limit; growth may reach 100 g in their first year and 300 g in the second. Thus, growth and production are both regulated by density. The favourable temperature range is 13°–30°C, with maximum growth at 24°C.

5.5.2 Recreational fishing for *Euastacus* and *Astacopsis* species

Euastacus species ('spiny crayfish') are recreationally fished in Victoria and New South Wales (but not in Queensland, where taking *Euastacus* spp. is illegal). The main targets are the larger species, e.g. *E. armatus* (Murray River crayfish) and *E. kershawi* (Gippsland crayfish); fishing for the Glenelg spiny crayfish (*E. bispinosus*) in south-western Victoria is now banned. Spiny crayfish may be taken with hookless baited lines or drop-nets, and the bag limit is five animals per person per day. The minimum takeable size is 90 mm orbital carapace length and, interestingly, there is also an upper size limit, in that only one animal in each daily bag may exceed 120 mm. The taking of berried females is banned. In Victoria there is a summer close season in waters inland of the Great Divide, and in New South Wales fishing for Murray River crayfish is also closed in summer.

The 'tayatea' or Tasmanian giant freshwater crayfish (*Astacopsis gouldi*) is found in northern Tasmania, almost entirely in rivers draining into Bass Strait. It prefers cool, clear, shaded waterways with undercut banks, logs and snags for shelter. It is listed as Vulnerable under the Environment Protection and Biodiversity Conservation Act 1999 and the Tasmanian Threatened Species Protection Act 1995.

Recreational fishing for, or any taking of, the Tasmanian giant freshwater crayfish *Astacopsis gouldi* or other *Astacopsis* species was banned in 1998 in response to declining numbers, especially of large animals, following its listing as Vulnerable under the Tasmanian Threatened Species Protection Act 1995. When fishing was legal it was restricted to the use of hookless baited lines and the original daily bag limit was 12 animals of carapace length greater than 130 mm. But in 1993 the taking of females was banned and the bag limit was reduced to three animals per day. In 1995 the Tasmanian Inland Fisheries Commission estimated that 10 000 animals were being caught each year, by about 2000 fishers.

Recreational fishing is a major problem for stocks of these large, long-lived freshwater crayfish, and its control and associated monitoring is anticipated to alleviate pressures. However, there are also problems in the often restricted habitats of the world's largest freshwater invertebrates. With this in mind, Tasmania launched a Recovery Plan for the Tasmanian giant freshwater crayfish (*Astacopsis gouldi*), scheduled for 2005–9 and incorporating both bans on fishing and protection of the habitat. *A. gouldi* is a flagship species with great potential for ecotourism if adequately protected. In contrast to some threatened species, there are clearly economic and social benefits that will follow from the success of the Recovery Plan for this species (see Chapter 11).

Following the biennial meeting of the IAA in the Gold Coast, Western Australia in August 2006, at which a resolution on *Astacopsis* was passed at the General Assembly, the IAA President wrote to Government to express the IAA's concerns for the future of the Tasmanian giant freshwater crayfish, to encourage measures for the conservation of Australia's globally significant freshwater crayfish fauna; in particular, to encourage the Minister to implement as soon as possible the Recovery Plan. The IAA supported the approach taken in the Recovery Plan, but was concerned at the length of time it had taken to prepare and implement, in view of the ongoing threats to the species and its habitats. IAA members had extensive experience in the management of crayfish populations in forested ecosystems in many countries, and felt that the measures recommended to safeguard essential habitat conditions might not be strong enough. In particular, they recommended firmer measures to protect habitat along the full length of streams. They further urged that if it was not feasible to protect the entire range of *A. gouldi*, strong measures be taken to protect a representative series of entire catchments supporting good populations of *A. gouldi* from siltation and temperature increases resulting from land clearance, whether for agriculture or forestry. This should be in addition to the protection of known localities through riparian buffer zones.

In response, the Tasmanian minister responsible for resource management and conservation said that he hoped to approve the plan soon, including the objective to eliminate or reduce fishing to such a low level that it no longer threatens population density or structure. However, catchments occupied by *A. gouldi* were also subject to forestry exploitation, and it did not appear to be possible to set aside whole streams for conservation. The Forestry Practices Authority, in consultation with stakeholders, was detailed to review and revise current management recommendations to protect *A. gouldi* and evaluate their effectiveness. Studies into habitat suitability for *A. gouldi* have continued since the release of the 2005 Draft Plan. It remains to be seen what benefits this plan has provided for this spectacular species.

In contrast to the increasingly controlled recreational and exploitative crayfisheries in Australia, there appears to be little protection for stocks in New Guinea. There are at least 13 crayfish species of the genus *Cherax*, all occurring south of the central mountain range and on Aru Islands and Misool on the Sahul Shelf, which would have connected Australia to New Guinea in the lowered sea levels of glacial times. There are some eight species in the Wissel Lakes at an altitude of 1700 m. The largest lake is 16 km long, and crayfish are fished by women with canoes, using large hand-nets 1.5–2 m in diameter in the shallows, and baited sink-nets (resembling a 'balance')

Figure 5.5. Catching *Cherax* spp. crayfish in New Guinea. See also colour plate section (photo courtesy of Chris Lukhaup).

woven from bullrushes, supported by a stick across the frame, which is fished for some hours before being lifted (Figure 5.5). The men catch crayfish by hand while diving (Holthuis, 1986).

5.5.3 Farming crayfish in Australia

Marron *Cherax cainii* are sensitive to low oxygen and high salinity, so eutrophication and salinization are threats in the wild and especially in culture. Extensive production is based on stocking small farm dams, but there is a trade-off between growth rates and biomass; the highest growth rates occur only at low densities (0.1 m^{-2}, and biomass below 1000 kg ha^{-1}). With increased density, growth declines but biomass increases. Farmed 1+ marron reach 50–100 g at densities of five per m^2, and 2000–4000 kg ha^{-1}.

Marron have been stocked into farm ponds in Western Australia since 1969, but more intensive aquaculture development was hindered by the sales and size restrictions protecting the recreational fishery until it was shown that capital-intensive farms needed to be able to sell all sizes for economic viability. Marron need adequate feeding and high levels of dissolved oxygen, the males must be removed after mating and the female parents after hatching, and there must be provision of dense artificial vegetation to shelter the young. In the wild, juveniles live away from the adults in masses of trailing weed.

Currently there are about 280 marron farmers licensed in Western Australia, with annual sales of *c.* 55 t, mainly to restaurants. Experimentally, intensive rearing of marron in Maine lobster-type battery units has so far proven uneconomic, and significant funding would be needed to develop and sustain intensive farming.

In many ponds, clay turbidity in the water maintains too high summer temperatures and oxygen stratification, while – on the positive side – protecting against bird predation. The more tolerant yabby *Cherax destructor* have subsequently been introduced to many such dams. Paddle-wheel aerators were introduced in 1979, and daily pellet feeding on demand is the norm. Feed levels need to be 35 g m^{-2} per week to sustain a biomass of 3000 kg ha^{-1}. Compared with marron, the smaller yabby are tolerant, *r*-selected, and can mature at 4 months and 20 g. They breed at over 15°C, maximum growth occurs at 28°C, and they have subsequently been introduced to many dams across Australia with low oxygen levels; however, they tend towards repeat breeding and stunting. Yabby are usually sold at 30–60 g, aged under 1 year old, but can reach 320 g. Yabby production rose rapidly to 290 t in 1993. Declared production of yabby in 1998–9 was about 88 t, distributed between New South Wales 40 t, Victoria 21 t, and Western Australia 27 t (Wingfield, 2002).

The third commercial species, redclaw crayfish *Cherax quadricarinatus*, live in tropical lakes and wetlands of northern Australia and Papua New Guinea but, unlike yabby, do not burrow. They mature in 6–9 months, breeding at temperatures above 22°C at 30–70 g and can eventually reach nearly 600 g. Redclaws grow in the temperature range 20°–34°C, with best growth at 28°C. They are usually harvested at 50–90 g, after 8–12 months. The average yield is 1200 kg ha^{-1}, at a minimum market size of 30 g, which is below the size at first maturity (Jones & Ruscoe, 2002).

Owing to their large size and suitability for aquaculture, redclaws have been widely translocated around the world, and their farming has recently been reviewed by Garza de Yta (2009). Their hardiness and conspicuous coloration has also made them popular in the aquarium trade worldwide. Unfortunately, they are often invasive, having established feral populations in South Africa, Mexico, Jamaica and Puerto Rico, and in Singapore (Ahyong & Yeo, 2007).

In the 1990s, total production of crayfish in Australia averaged 350 t per year, with yabby and redclaw producing about 90 t each, and marron about 50 t. Crayfish prices from culture or wild harvest vary with species and size. Prices per kilogram vary with size but also with species. In the early 2000s, yabby at a size of 30 g (about the minimum size of noble or signal crayfish when marketed) fetched A\$5 per kilogram, while larger ones fetched A\$9 per kg. Small redclaw fetched higher prices than yabby, with larger ones worth A\$16 per kg. Marron, the most valuable, fetched A\$15 per kg at a size of 80 g, while lobster-sized marron, at 250 g, fetched A\$24 per kg (Wingfield, 2002).

5.5.4   New Zealand *Paranephrops* exploitation

Paranephrops species, endemic to New Zealand, are called 'koura' by the Maori, a name equally applied to marine crayfish. Maori have long prized koura as a delicacy and many people have childhood memories of catching 'crawlies'.

Although genetic research is ongoing, there are two currently recognized species of koura found allopatrically in New Zealand. The larger and slower-growing species *Paranephrops zealandicus* has very hairy chelae and is found in the east and south of South Island and on Stewart Island. Northern koura *P. planifrons*, which are found on North Island and in Marlborough, Nelson and the west coast of South Island, are slightly smaller and less hairy.

The breeding cycle of these cool-water parastacid crayfish is not dissimilar to that of northern-hemisphere astacid crayfish. Female koura produce 20–200 eggs between April and December (mostly in May and June). The eggs hatch about 3–4 months later, clinging to the mother with their pincers until they are nearly 4 mm long. By about their fourth year they become adults at about 20 mm CL (Parkyn *et al.*, 2002; Kusabs & Quinn, 2009).

New Zealand freshwater animals such as the koura are in danger because their habitats are disappearing. Less than 9% of New Zealand's wetlands remain; most have been drained for farming. Many streams, rivers and lakes are now highly polluted, and the loss of riverbank vegetation can lead to erosion, making the water muddy and killing the food source for aquatic insects. Other threats include illegal harvesting; koura may legally be gathered for personal consumption up to a limit of 50 crayfish per day. However, the selling, trading, or possession of koura for the purposes of sale or trade is illegal.

There are now several koura farms, dependent on a good-quality water supply and designed to accelerate growth by temperature manipulation. One farm uses ensiled waste salmon from a farm as food in its raceways. By 1996, two farms were established to farm koura, one near Blenheim and one near Alexandra.

Broodstock either mate in the broodstock pond or are selectively mated in tanks. Berried females are removed from the broodstock pond 3–4 months after mating and transferred to the hatchery. Farmed female koura carry about 150–200 eggs on average; a large berried female about 120 g and 140 mm TL will have about 350 eggs. Females selectively mated are placed in the hatchery as soon as the fertilized eggs are cemented to the pleopods. When all hatchlings have left the female, she is returned to the broodstock pond. The hatchlings remain in the hatchery after four or five moults until about 10–15 mm TL, and then are transferred to a growing-on raceway.

Koura are harvested by trapping in 'opera house' traps, but can be caught less efficiently by dragging a scoop-net through the weed, or by draining the raceway and collecting the crayfish by hand. Sizes range up to 150–165 g for males, 80–95 g for females. Minimum marketable size of about 100 mm TL and 45–55 g weight is achieved in 20 months to 2 years, while up to 105–115 mm TL and 90–110 g is achieved in about 30 months. Larger-sized koura of around 130–150 mm TL and 120+ g have been produced in farms in about 3 years, and berried at 15 months of age.

5.6   Crayfish harvesting in Madagascar

Madagascar's freshwater crayfish belong to the endemic genus *Astacoides* (Parastacidae), currently containing seven species. Crayfish have been harvested in Madagascar at least since early colonial times (Sibree, 1915) and remain important in both subsistence use and trade. The species differ markedly in habitat requirements and also in growth rates, final size and aspects of their reproductive biology, though rather little detail is yet known about their ecology and how this affects their vulnerability to threats. Growth rates are apparently slow, with individuals of *A. granulimanus*, and perhaps other species, believed to live for more than 20 years.

Setting minimum size limits to ensure that females have spawned at least once before they are harvested is a common management tool for crayfish populations (Skurdal & Taugbøl, 1994). Official regulations in Madagascar impose a lower size limit of 100 mm TL (about 45 mm CL), but this is rarely respected. Even so, as *Astacoides* species become reproductive at different sizes (Jones, 2004), these regulations do not protect all species.

It would appear that current exploitation levels are unsustainable. All species currently suffer increasing exploitation by the expanding human population. Overharvesting has become a real and immediate threat to the large species *A. betsileoensis*, which first breeds at a large size, making this species vulnerable to exploitation. Only 30% of females were gravid at a carapace length of 60 mm (Jones *et al.*, 2007). In markets, 90% of *A. betsileoensis* examined were immature, compared with 65% of the more common *A. granulimanus*, indicating a pressing need for regulation. Crayfish price varies with season and with size, but not between the different species (Jones *et al.*, 2006).

Jones *et al.* (2005) assessed the sustainability of existing crayfish harvests in the humid forests of eastern Madagascar, focusing on *A. granulimanus* against the more general backdrop of promoting forest products as an incentive for communities to retain forest cover. Some villages had a traditional taboo (*fady*) against selling crayfish, resulting in uneven exploitation rates. However, in much of Madagascar, the rapid human population growth is driving the conversion of forest and wetlands to agriculture, particularly at low elevations. All native crayfish species require naturally vegetated banks, and habitat loss is an urgent threat to several species, especially to the forest-dwelling *A. caldwelli* and the slow-growing burrower *A. crosnieri* of swampy land that is being converted to rice fields.

A. granulimanus dominate the crayfish harvest, making up more than 95% of the crayfish harvested in one village, but almost 80% measured were smaller than the legal limit. The larger *A. betsileoensis* were taken in deep rivers by baited stick methods and seasonally in eel traps. *A. caldwelli* were rare in the area, while the endangered *A. crosnieri* were seldom targeted by harvesters because of their muddy taste, small size and the difficulty of harvesting this species in its swampy habitat.

In one harvesting village, more than half of all households were directly involved in the harvest, with mean annual earnings of US$83 (Jones *et al.*, 2007) – over half the mean annual income of the villagers. Subsistence use was widespread, particularly by children, to whom it may provide an important protein source, and crayfish with eggs were considered particularly flavourful. Communities reported that crayfish harvesting was more widespread in the past before the conversion of forest. Elders in these villages expressed regret at the loss of crayfish, saying they were valued both as a food source and for the recreational opportunities provided by crayfish harvesting.

In Madagascar, the current system of community-based conservation acknowledges their long-term interest in local natural resources and allows the implementation of management tools (such as avoiding reproductive females, size limits and no-take zones) at source, but this may not be sufficient to conserve rarer species, and there is

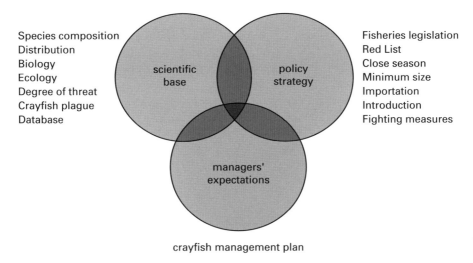

Species composition
Distribution
Biology
Ecology
Degree of threat
Crayfish plague
Database

scientific
base

policy
strategy

Fisheries legislation
Red List
Close season
Minimum size
Importation
Introduction
Fighting measures

managers'
expectations

crayfish management plan

Figure 5.6.   Crayfish management plan; the interaction of scientific knowledge and managers' expectations in formulating policy strategy (from Hefti & Stucki, in Souty-Grosset *et al.*, 2006).

now the added threat of introduced cambarid species which could drive some of the native species towards extinction (Jones *et al.*, 2009).

5.7   Outcomes from crayfish exploitation patterns

The interrelations of stock biology and exploitation are complex, and include threats particularly from crayfish plague, informal translocations, political strategies and managers' expectations. Figure 5.6 (from Hefti & Stucki, 2006) shows the interrelationships between science (biology, ecology, distribution, threats, impact of plague), political strategy, and managers' expectations, including fisheries, legislation (closed seasons, minimum size), and import and export regulations.

The exploitation of crayfish worldwide amounts to more than 100 000 tonnes per year, worth somewhere between US$100 million and US$1 billion, but prices vary enormously. Astacid harvests in northern Europe are sustained by the high value placed on the product, particularly of noble crayfish, as are harvests of Australian crayfish, particularly marron. Crayfish catches in North America are valued less, and price competition with the equivalent product of red swamp crayfish in Spain and China exacerbates natural fluctuations in annual yield. Low prices and inadequate producer rewards, as historically seen with signal crayfish in Oregon, may lead to irregular supplies, depending on alternative work opportunities; no capital for processing or market development; and a lack of price incentive for farming. Social priorities may reduce the potential for commercial developments. In developing countries such as Madagascar, crayfish exploitation tends to be lightly regulated, and stocks are under increasing threat. Such stocks may be unable to sustain the uneven but increasing pressures on them from unrestricted exploitation, with serious implications for native biodiversity.

The commercially exploited warm-water Australian crayfish are all much faster-growing than astacids. There is a differential in price among the *Cherax* species harvested. Marron are prized recreationally and protected by law from commercial fishing. Their capture ties in with the 'barbie and bush-tucker' traditions still prized by Australians, and the prices are enough to make extensive or semi-intensive culture a commercial proposition. The few farms supplying New Zealand koura charge restaurants around NZ$65 per kilogram.

Slow-growing northern astacids and southern parastacids such as koura are only profitable because of the high value placed upon them. Catch regulations for astacids are variable across Nordic countries; they tend to be empirical rather than based on known optimal management strategies. Finland has a strong tradition of over a century of catching crayfish as a luxury foodstuff, much of it for export. This tradition is maintained today, with numbers of recreational fishermen increasing – analogous to salmon fishing in Europe and North America.

Intensive aquaculture of crayfish is price-sensitive and is not at present profitable for cambarids, and just marginally so with parastacids in Australia and New Zealand. Aquaculture is still viable for astacids, despite their slow growth, but it depends on rearing juveniles for restocking at high prices, rather than on growing them on for the several years necessary to reach market size.

The lack of ongoing local traditions or well-developed local markets for crayfish in the UK has hampered the development of crayfish exploitation; crayfish farming was entered for short-term commercial profit, but the initiative largely failed and many stocks were allowed to escape, resulting in the destruction of native crayfish. Much of southern Europe is also coping with invasions of non-indigenous crayfish, which have caused the decimation of the formerly exploited native species; however, new traditions and larger fisheries are developing, particularly around signals and red swamp crayfish.

5.8   Conclusions: crayfish exploitation and biodiversity

We have seen that there are two fundamentally different aspects to crayfish exploitation – harvesting or rearing of ICS where their numbers allow (e.g. noble crayfish in Scandinavia, signals in western North America, yabby in Australia), and the exploitation of translocated NICS in many continents. Some of the more widespread indigenous crayfish have been exploited in the past, including translocations which have extended their ranges, and some of these continue to be exploited under increasingly careful management, providing an economic and social rationale for their conservation. These continental translocations may be relatively benign. However, where transcontinental translocations have taken place, the crayfish encounter a new situation where they are often competitively superior to members of the indigenous community. As NICS they may form stocks far denser than in their native range, disrupting the balance in their adopted ecosystems. In Europe, the urgent need to understand the impacts of alien species used in aquaculture led to EU funding for an international research project IMPASSE ('Environmental impacts of alien species in aquaculture'). Its overall goal is to develop procedures for assessing the potential impacts of invasive alien species in aquaculture and related activities. An important outcome is expected to be guidelines for environmentally sound practices for any necessary introductions and translocations in aquaculture, on quarantine procedures, and risk assessment protocols.

In the second part of this book ('Applying science to conservation management'), where we address the fundamental need to understand and manage biodiversity of fresh waters, we explain the need to conserve our indigenous crayfish as keystone species in their native communities. In Chapter 6 we examine the role of indigenous crayfish in maintaining biodiversity, and as bioindicators of community well-being. To do this, we must monitor their stocks (Chapter 7). This in turn links into the need to control and manage NICS stocks and reintroduce ICS where conditions are suitable (Chapters 8 and 9).

(a)

(b)

(c)

(d)

Crayfish from around the world: A *Astacoides betsileoensis* (Madagascar); B *Cherax holthuisi* (West New Guinea); C *Samastacus spinifrons* (South America); D *Pacifastacus leniusculus* (USA, invasive in Europe); E *Astacus astacus* (Europe); F *Austropotamobius pallipes* (Europe); G *Procambarus clarkii* (USA, invasive in Europe); H *Procambarus fallax* (marmorkrebs).

(a)

Figure 2.1.   (a) The large stream-dwelling crayfish *Astacopsis gouldi* (photography courtesy of Neil Doran).

(b)

Figure 2.1. (cont.) (b) A burrowing crayfish, *Engaeus orramakunna* (photography courtesy of Neil Doran).

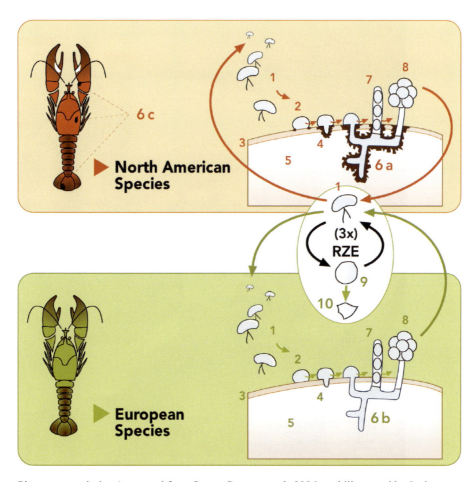

Figure 4.2. Plague transmission (extracted from Souty-Grosset *et al.*, 2006, and illustrated by Javier Diéguez-Uribeondo): **1**, secondary zoospore (infective unit); **2**, encysting zoospore; **3**, crayfish epicuticle; **4**, germinating cyst; **5**, cuticle penetration; **6a**, melanized hyphae (chronic infection in North American crayfish); **6b**, unmelanized hyphae (acute infection in indigenous European species of crayfish or immune-stressed North American crayfish species); **6c**, black spots, (usually a macroscopic sign of *A. astaci* infection); **7**, characteristic sporangium of *Aphanomyces*; the primary zoospores are formed and distributed in a single row within the sporangium; **8**, spore balls are clusters of primary cysts; these structures are characteristic of the genus *Aphanomyces*; **9**, secondary cyst – the zoospore responds to nonspecific stimuli, forming a secondary cyst that will not germinate and instead will form a new zoospore (i.e. repeated zoospore emergence: RZE); this process can be repeated up to three times depending on the conditions; **10**, unviable cyst.

Figure 5.2. An early illustration of night capture of crayfish in Austria, from *Das Fischereibuch Kaiser Maximilians I* circa 1500 (produced by the Lithographic Institute, K. Redlich, Innsbruck, 1901).

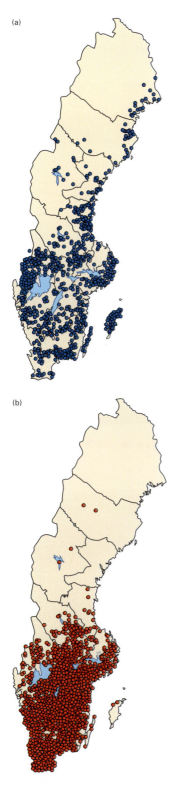

Figure 5.3. Distribution of (a) Astacus astacus (1000 localities, a decrease of more than 500 in 8 years) and (b) Pacifastacus leniusculus (>4000 localities) in Sweden (2008). Reproduced with permission from Edsman & Schröder (2009) and Holdich *et al.* (2009b).

Figure 5.4.   Capture of *Procambarus clarkii* in Louisiana (photo courtesy of Wray McClain).

Figure 5.5.   Catching *Cherax* spp. crayfish in New Guinea (photo courtesy of Chris Lukhaup).

Figure 6.1. Statue of *Astacopsis gouldi* (Tasmanian giant freshwater crayfish) in Burnie, Tasmania (photo courtesy of Alastair Richardson).

Figure 7.3. Surrogate signs of crayfish: (a) grebe catching *A. leptodactylus* (photo courtesy of Elinor Wiltshire), (b) otter feeding site (picture by Julian Reynolds).

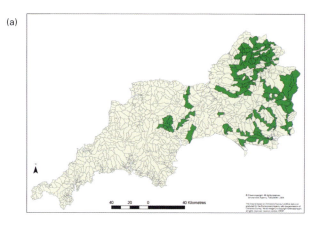

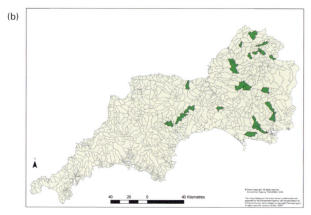

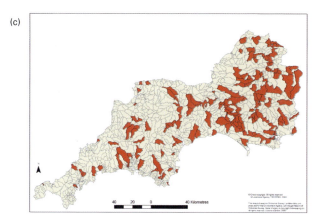

Figure 7.4. Crayfish distribution in river catchments in south-west England: (a) approximate distribution of *Austropotamobius pallipes* pre-1975, (b) distribution of *Austropotamobius pallipes* in 2009 (excluding recently translocated populations), (c) distribution of NICS, mainly *Pacifastacus leniusculus*, in 2009 (from Holdich *et al*., 2009b).

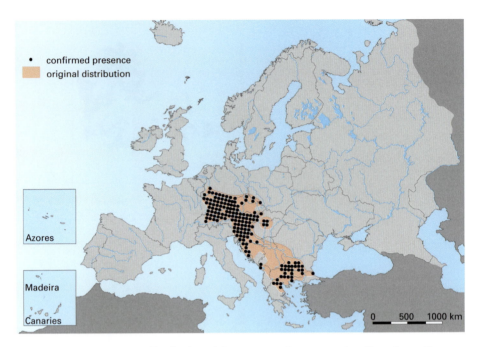

Figure 7.5. Map showing the European distribution of *Austropotamobius torrentium* (from Souty-Grosset *et al.*, 2006).

Part II

Applying science to conservation management

A   Protecting freshwater biodiversity through monitoring and conserving crayfish

6 Understanding and managing biodiversity using crayfish

6.1 Background to freshwater biodiversity and the role of crayfish

Some background to current ideas on biodiversity is provided in the Introduction to this book and developed with relation to aspects of crayfish ecology in Chapter 3. The pool of living diversity is dynamic, with continual changes in genetic variation, community structure and function. However, the biodiversity of an area is not just the sum of species present; for many organisms, particularly among the small and often unrecognized forms collectively known as 'cryptobiota' (Good, 2009), the relevant habitat or community is small or restricted. Also, introducing an extra species to a community does not necessarily increase biodiversity, and may often deplete it. Here we examine the value of biodiversity, the impact of changing freshwater systems on biodiversity, and the relationships of freshwater decapods, particularly crayfish, to community biodiversity.

As was mentioned in the introductory chapter, biodiversity in fresh waters is enormous in relation to the global extent of surface waters. Fresh water is also very fragmented and unevenly distributed across the globe, with a range of consequences for biodiversity (Saunders *et al.*, 1991). The extensive literature on biodiversity and habitat fragmentation can generate different conclusions depending on how species richness is measured, and whether the fragmentation reflects habitat loss or its subdivision (Fahrig, 2003). Much of the diversity of catchments may lie outside the main channels, in marshes, ditches and individual small ponds. Some organisms (including some freshwater decapods) are characteristic of such wetlands and marshes, while others are largely restricted to rivers, streams and/or small lakes.

A natural habitat may be valued for its high species diversity, or by an optimal structural environment for a particular species such as a freshwater crayfish. For communities occupying such a habitat, its quality is based on a range of complex parameters, often dominated by water flows; indeed, to many aquatic animals, a site's physical qualities (flow rate, temperature, substrate, etc.) are as important as the plant components of the habitat. However, although the value of a complex habitat has been well attested in marine and terrestrial situations and experimentally in lakes, there is rather little scientific evidence that habitat heterogeneity is important in determining stream biodiversity. For instance, an evaluation of 78 stream restoration projects that increased channel complexity or habitat heterogeneity showed that in most cases physical heterogeneity was enhanced; however, only two showed significant increases in macroinvertebrate biodiversity (Palmer *et al.*, 2010; Ormerod *et al.*, 2010). Despite this, however, many stream restoration projects focus primarily on physical channel characteristics, and we have seen that habitat heterogeneity is very important to stream-dwelling crayfish.

As fresh water is so limited, inland waters and their biodiversity constitute a valuable natural resource, both in economic terms and also in their cultural, aesthetic, scientific and educational value. But because of the patchy distribution of fresh waters in time and space, their relative scarcity and increasing use by humans, freshwater systems and biodiversity are under sustained and increasing pressures. An intriguing study by Harding *et al.* (1998) demonstrated that past catchment land-use activities in the 1950s were a good predictor of present-day diversity, whereas riparian and even catchment land use within the previous decade were comparatively poor indicators, for reasons that are not well understood. Preservation or restoration of natural riparian habitats may not be sufficient to maintain or restore natural diversity in streams.

The major threats to freshwater biodiversity are loss of habitat, pollution, the introduction of alien species, and overharvesting. The more sensitive species and communities in fresh water are under threat of extinction. Large forms such as astacid crayfish are at most risk because they are long-lived and slow to mature, and declines in their habitat quality are evident worldwide. In North America, the resulting extinction rates of freshwater animals, based on combined data sets for crayfish, unionid mussels, fish and amphibians, may be as much as 4% per decade – five times higher than species loss rates calculated from any terrestrial habitat (Ricciardi & Rasmussen, 1999).

It is generally assumed that biodiversity is closely related to ecosystem functioning, but this is far from proven. As described in Chapter 3, community functioning is often controlled by 'keystone' species – forms which by their activity maintain the status quo in a community. This is a role taken by many freshwater crayfish because of their large size, broad trophic niche, and burrowing or bioturbation activity. If such a functional species is lacking, food web disequilibrium is likely. Key functional species such as freshwater crayfish have often also been identified as useful indicators for conservation purposes. These points are further developed later in this chapter.

6.1.1   Anthropogenic threats to freshwater biodiversity and crayfish

Like the organisms within them, ecosystems are dynamic and evolving, and while species population growth, decline, migrations and extinctions are natural processes, humans have intervened in ecological systems for thousands of years. In some cases, human modifications appear to have contributed to high species richness for the whole system, though this cannot be equated to a higher conservation value (Gherardi *et al.*, 2003). Thus, when viewed at the whole-habitat level, a pre-existing marsh may have lower overall species richness than when modified to a patchwork of agricultural land, drains, pools and temporarily flooded areas, just as an exploited forest will have apparently higher biodiversity than the closed-canopy climax.

All 'natural' systems have been affected to some degree by multiple stressors largely inflicted by people, but also including climate change, so it is difficult to find any habitat in pristine condition. For example, streams are sensitive to a range of stresses including impacts from urbanization, mining, agriculture, deforestation, invasive species, flow regulation and water extraction. The impacts of such stressors, individually or in combination, typically lead to a decrease in biodiversity because of reduced water quality, biologically unsuitable flow regimes, dispersal barriers, increased inputs of organic matter and sunlight, and a degraded habitat.

The stressors associated with most human actions not only cause losses in biodiversity but also affect ecosystem functioning, thus reducing the ecosystem services provided. Fresh waters are experiencing declines in biodiversity far greater than those in the most affected terrestrial ecosystems. If rising trends in human demands for water remain unaltered and species losses continue at current rates, the opportunity to conserve much of the remaining biodiversity in fresh water will vanish before the 'Water for Life' decade ends in 2015 (Dudgeon *et al.*, 2006).

Because of conflicts in water use, fresh waters may be at particular risk of multiple stressor effects and, as these effects develop, non-linear 'ecological surprises' may sometimes emerge (Ormerod *et al.*, 2010). These can include losses of keystone species in the community, such as freshwater crayfish, and consequent changes in ecosystem functioning. For instance, multiple stressors in shallow, lentic systems can create multiple thresholds that may act in a hierarchical fashion. The characteristic seasonal wetlands, shallow lakes and temporary river pools of south-western Australia, some at least containing *Cherax* species crayfish, are subject to multiple anthropogenic impacts such as hydrological change, eutrophication, salinization and acidification (Davis *et al.*, 2010), affecting their indigenous denizens.

Streams are intimately connected to their landscapes and so are easily altered by multiple stressors that affect both adjacent land and the streams themselves. Statzner & Bêche (2010) have reviewed the use of biological traits as indicators of multiple stressor effects on running-water systems. In Hokkaido, Japan, about half the energy that sustains aquatic food webs falls directly into streams as terrestrial invertebrates, and a quarter of the energy needs for riparian birds is supplied by adult aquatic insects emerging from the stream (Fausch *et al.*, 2010). Single stressors in these Hokkaido streams – including deforestation, channelization, erosion-control dams, biological invasions and climate change – have drastic effects on stream food webs, the fishes they support and riparian predators (spiders, birds and bats). Each stressor reduced food web components, such as abundance of stream benthos or riparian spiders, to low levels, beyond which an additional or multiple stressor had little effect. Most single stressors caused 30–90% declines in foraging, growth, or abundance of aquatic or terrestrial predators. Indirect effects of stressors also cascaded throughout stream food webs and across the aquatic–terrestrial boundary.

The floodplains of larger rivers are highly complex dynamic ecosystems with pulses of flow, sediment and temperature which create distinct 'windows of ecological opportunity' (Tockner *et al.*, 2010). They are already among the world's most threatened ecosystems because of human interference through dams, levees and construction of settlements, as well as the rapid spread of non-native species. Human modifications that weaken or amplify these pulses will have cascading effects on river–floodplain interactions by shifting the thresholds of connectivity, resilience or resistance.

In line with these biodiversity trends, many freshwater decapod crustaceans have dramatically declined compared with their historical distribution, with serious implications for their value, either intrinsically or as indicator species. Human pressures on freshwater crayfish, from poaching to pollution, exemplify this process. Astacid crayfish, in particular, are thought of as bioindicators of a good environment, for even if many such crayfish are no longer recognized as strict water quality indicators (e.g. Füreder & Reynolds, 2003), they do not survive beyond certain levels of organic pollution (e.g. Demers & Reynolds, 2003), and different age groups together require a varied habitat for successful coexistence.

Freshwater crayfish are sensitive to a great variety of fertilizers and pesticides (Eversole *et al.*, 1995), and in countries with extensive agriculture, the decline and extinction of crayfish population may be a reflection of the use of harmful substances. Other forms of anthropogenic impacts on catchments, such as deforestation, reduction of riparian vegetation, and river regulation, may also have clear negative effects on crayfish habitat and food availability, as demonstrated by population decline; thus freshwater crayfish have value as indicators of ecosystem integrity. Studies in Italy and Austria showed that healthy crayfish populations were mostly found in less degraded systems, but a decline or extinction of crayfish was observed in areas with more extensive land use (Leo Füreder, personal communication, 2009). In France, the construction of small ponds along a stream, associated with changes in water chemistry, appeared to be linked to crayfish loss (Trouilhé *et al.*, 2008).

In much of Europe, most of the historical crayfish sites are no longer pristine, being located in intensively cultivated areas where arguments for biological conservation and nature protection often fail because of economic pressures on the land. Crayfish losses have been recorded from various European regions, e.g. Switzerland (Büttiker, 1987; Mickasch, 1999), Ireland (Matthews & Reynolds, 1995), Great Britain (Holdich & Rogers, 1997), France (Vigneux, 1997), Germany (Bohl, 1999), Italy (Gherardi *et al.*, 1999b), and Spain (Gil-Sánchez & Alba-Tercedor, 2002), demonstrating that this problem exists at a much larger spatial scale. In North America, a number of crayfish species are regionally extinct, and over 50% of all crayfish are considered endangered to some degree (Taylor *et al.*, 1996), while decreasing populations and even population extinctions have also been reported from Australia. Thus crayfish may be sentinels for water quality deterioration. If they are present, the habitat quality is satisfactory, but if a crayfish population is in decline, this can be an alarm signal that other sensitive freshwater organisms may follow.

6.1.2   Indicators of biodiversity

In conservation biology, some species may be used as surrogates (*sensu* Caro & O'Doherty, 1999) to portray broader conservation problems. As indicated in Chapter 3, they may be used in various ways, e.g. to indicate the extent of various types of anthropogenic impact (health indicator species), to track population changes of other

Figure 6.1. Statue of *Astacopsis gouldi* (Tasmanian giant freshwater crayfish) in Burnie, Tasmania. See also colour plate section (photo courtesy of Alastair Richardson).

species (population indicator species), to locate areas of high biodiversity (biodiversity indicator species), to act as 'umbrellas' for the requirements of sympatric species (umbrella species), or to attract the attention of the public (flagship species). Due to their special attributes and peculiarities, freshwater crayfish are often obvious surrogate species, fulfilling the majority of the prerequisites stated above.

When choosing species to use as indicators, some fundamental problems present themselves. One is to select those whose abundance and distribution reflect general trends in biodiversity, and which are sensitive at both regional and local scales. The choice of indicators may also have policy consequences. Indicators of habitat quality are different from those that measure biodiversity. If the indicators focus on habitat quality rather than biodiversity, then legislation will do likewise (see Chapter 10). Legislation tends to reward management practices that lead to good-quality habitats, sometimes including the presence of specific indicator species, but biodiversity may not increase.

The best universal indicator of biodiversity should be based on recognizable species richness and habitat complexity. Since our understanding of the biology of most invertebrates ('cryptobiota') and microorganisms is still poor, we need some focal or umbrella indicator species (Caro & O'Doherty, 1999) such as freshwater crayfish by which to categorize the system. Certain crayfish could be designated as suitable umbrella species for their habitats in regions of Australia (e.g. yabby or redclaw) or North America (e.g. calico or big water crayfish), as could any of the widely distributed indigenous crayfish species of Europe (noble, thin-clawed, white-clawed or stone crayfish).

It is often argued that indicators should be ecologically important components of a community, but rare or threatened species can also provide useful indicators for monitoring biodiversity, such as those in current IUCN Red Lists of threatened species. However, it is not clear whether rare or threatened indicator species, including crayfish such as the long-lived white-clawed crayfish *Austropotamobius pallipes* of western Europe, can be adequately monitored without risk to their status. Monitoring of crayfish populations is discussed in the following chapter.

6.1.3   Iconic species indicators for communities or habitats

Heritage or flagship species are ecologically significant organisms that also appeal to humans. This makes them very suitable for communicating conservation concerns, and they are often important in conservation monitoring and guiding management of fresh waters for the preservation of optimum biodiversity. Many are vertebrates, such as salmon, otters or platypus. Crayfish are prime players among invertebrates because of their relative size and longevity, and their reliance on benthic aquatic systems throughout life. Some have been identified as flagship species because of these qualities and also their interest to humans, who are either fascinated by seeing a 'lobster' in fresh waters, or because of their edible qualities, accessibility and tolerance of handling.

Being large and conspicuous, freshwater crayfish have been well known for centuries in some parts of the world, attracting the attention of the public, and they are widely used as flagship species to front conservation efforts not only in Europe but also in other parts of the world, e.g. iconic large Australian crayfish such as the Tasmanian giant freshwater crayfish *Astacopsis gouldi* in Tasmania, the esteemed marron *Cherax tenuimanus* in western Australia, or the Murray River crayfish *Euastacus armatus*.

In both New Zealand (Kusabs & Quinn, 2009) and Australia, freshwater crayfish have been a significant food source for aboriginal peoples, and some may be considered as heritage species. The widespread distribution and lack of genetic differentiation in the yabby *Cherax destructor* suggest that it was moved between waterbodies over very large distances by nomadic aboriginal people, perhaps to establish food sources at remote locations (Horwitz & Knott, 1996); it is thus justifiably a heritage species.

Astacopsis gouldi, the long-lived giant freshwater crayfish of Tasmania, was until quite recently merely the target of a casual recreational fishery (see Chapter 5) and was surprisingly little known outside northern Tasmania. With the decline in *A. gouldi* populations, and especially the larger specimens, and its listing as a threatened species in 1995, a moratorium was placed on fishing, with the intention of allowing an unfished generation of crayfish to grow unmolested. Its 'Vulnerable' status is due to habitat loss and overfishing, and the species is also threatened by stream siltation and the removal of woody snags, as decaying wood is a favourite food of this species. Recent captures of very large specimens suggest that this conservation strategy has been successful, although poaching remains a problem. The fishing ban and increasing levels of environmental awareness have raised the profile of this crayfish to iconic levels; there are now tourist excursions to view this animal in its natural habitat, and a large statue of it in the municipal park at Burnie (Figure 6.1), in the centre of the species' geographical range. Its conservation value as a heritage or flagship species is consequently enhanced.

Some large crayfish in North America, such as the big water crayfish *Cambarus robustus*, are locally considered iconic, while in Europe the designation refers particularly to the noble crayfish *Astacus astacus* in Scandinavia and elsewhere in northern Europe, and to the white-clawed crayfish species complex *Austropotamobius pallipes/A. italicus* in Italy, Spain, France, Britain and Ireland. These crayfish species have, or formerly had, a high value to ordinary citizens, particularly country-dwellers, and the culture associated with *A. astacus* is celebrated at festivals ('crayfish parties') across Scandinavia (Swahn, 2004). With the social-historical designation comes an economic value, which may have a multiplier in the form of associated festivals and leisure products, and so any loss of stocks of this species is felt keenly and their habitats are in general protected from gross pollution. This is particularly true for lake populations of *A. astacus* across the region. *A. pallipes* no longer has an economic value, but in many parts of its range its value is sentimental and nostalgic, evoking family outings with grandparents to catch crayfish.

6.1.4   Freshwater crayfish as surrogate species

Surrogate species may be assigned as representative indicators for a suite of less accessible species in the aquatic community, or as typifying environmental features (water quality, habitat quality). Appropriate surrogate species are needed to answer many relevant questions, and crayfish can evidently provide useful surrogates for the communities in a range of biotopes. This is already widely recognized for the noble crayfish *Astacus astacus* in northern Europe, and white-clawed crayfish are considered surrogate species in South Tyrol (Füreder *et al*., 2003).

   In several regions or countries, freshwater crayfish have large populations and a wide geographical range. Together with their sensitivity to human disturbance, this makes them effective surrogates and health indicators of anthropogenically induced environmental change. In this respect also, crayfish can act as umbrella species when used to define spatial and compositional attributes that must be present in a landscape. They may be used to specify the size and type of habitat to be protected rather than simply its location.

   Assessing relationships between human land-use activities and ecological resources is especially complex in a watershed in which multiple land uses, and interactions between those uses, are likely to be present (Diamond *et al*., 2002). In addition, when only relict populations are present in a region, it is difficult to provide the necessary correlations between population health and disturbance factors. However, given the various attributes of freshwater crayfish as surrogate species (including qualities of indicator species, umbrella species and flagship species), ongoing endangered-species protection programmes, combined with freshwater habitat improvements, will certainly help to advance the survival of crayfish.

Indicators of environmental health

Among other essential prerequisites for the use of freshwater crayfish as indicators of environmental health is a good existing knowledge of the species' natural history and ecological factors affecting their population growth rates (Holdich, 2002a). They may be monitored relatively easily and have accessible breeding sites, which reduces the costs of surveillance. In several regions or countries they have large populations and a wide geographical range. Together with their sensitivity to human disturbance this makes them effective health indicators of anthropogenically induced environmental change.

6.2   Managing freshwater biodiversity

6.2.1   Protection of the global freshwater resource

In response to the increasing threats to fresh waters, there has been an unprecedented number of actions and initiatives at an international level to safeguard and manage the resource and its associated ecosystems. These include the Water and Nature Initiative of IUCN's (International Union for Conservation of Nature) Water Programme (1985), the Rio de Janeiro Earth Summit's Convention on Biological Diversity (CBD) (1992), and the UN Environmental Programme's Ramsar Convention on Wetlands (2002), under which an total area of nearly 160 million hectares has been recognized. In 2003, the United Nations General Assembly adopted 'Water for Life' – the International Decade for Action from 2005 to 2015 – calling for a greater focus on water issues and development efforts and a renewal of the commitment to achieve the water-related goals of the 2000 Millennium Declaration and of Agenda 21. The Water for Life reso-lution comes at a time when biodiversity and the biological resources of inland waters are facing unprecedented and growing threats from human activities (Millennium Ecosystem Assessment, 2005). However, interim targets, such as halting biodiversity loss by 2010, have not been met.

Internationally there are other moves afoot to protect the aquatic environment and its biological diversity, which are discussed further in Chapter 10. The United Nations CBD proposal (UNEP/CBD/COP/7/4) aimed to establish a global network of protected areas by 2010, with the intention that all such areas should be integrated into a net-work by 2015, with particular attention being paid to the land–aquatic connections and buffer zones. Large areas have been set aside for conservation in Australia; unique pressures across that continent include fire, and fuel-reduction burning is widespread in order to reduce the widely perceived fire hazard both in the wooded south and in the northern savanna. Terrestrial savanna fauna and flora seem remarkably resilient to fire; however, stream and riparian biota suffer biodiversity and biomass losses with too frequent burning. The impact of this on crayfish has not been widely studied. In North America, the US Endangered Species Act of 1973 functions to protect plants and animals facing extinction, including some crayfish, and so provides programmes to conserve the ecosystems upon which they depend. In Europe, the 1979 Birds and 1992 EC Habitats Directives have led to the establishment of a network of Special Areas of Conservation (SACs) or Natura 2000 refuges, now totalling 26 000 reserves, many of them wetland, covering more than 18% of the total land area of the European Union.

Creating reserves is just the start of the process; in any protection programme the habitats and species present must be evaluated, current biodiversity levels measured, and the public made aware of the findings (see Chapter 10). However, suggested management solutions may lose public confidence if they do not reliably improve a complex situation. When applying scientific knowledge to decision making, the UN

Convention on Biological Diversity advises that precautionary measures should be taken if an activity raises a threat of harm to the environment or human health, even if some cause-and-effect relationships are not fully established scientifically. The precautionary principle has thus been recommended for almost two decades, although it has been widely ignored.

6.2.2 Protecting native habitats and species

Species losses have been identified in many parts of the world – the decimation of European native crayfish is one example widely discussed in this book – but it is rarer to see species recovery, although some crayfish have also shown some gains (see Chapter 7). Often the habitat needs to be improved before species can make any comeback; this is best done by addressing the drivers of biodiversity. Despite much active current research, we again emphasize that biodiversity of fresh waters is deteriorating faster than in other ecosystems. According to the CBD, the rate of loss of freshwater species diversity is the fastest of any of the world's major biomes. Taxonomic groups with the highest proportion of threatened species tend to be those that rely on freshwater habitats. For example, according to the Living Planet index, the rate of loss of freshwater biodiversity from 1970 to 2000 was almost twice that of marine and terrestrial biomes. This is probably because rivers are most often evaluated only in terms of fish productivity or water purification capacity. People value short-term economic profit and either underestimate or do not yet understand the value of the economic goods and services provided. As more water-related development projects are required, knowledge of their possible impacts on microbiological diversity, let alone faunal and floral, is urgently needed.

A first step in management is to provide an inventory and description of local knowledge of biodiversity and sustainable use of its contents. While networks of reserves such as the UNESCO Global Biosphere Reserves or the European Natura 2000 network, as systems to maintain biodiversity, may serve as a basis for assessment and comparison of actual biodiversity levels, there is also much natural variation related to latitude, size or isolation of land-masses. Because most ecological situations are complex, there is a high degree of uncertainty about the potential outcomes of management actions, which can hinder development of a consensus (Harwood & Stokes, 2003). The precautionary principle should then be applied. Most crayfish populations and habitats in some regions (such as South America, New Guinea or Madagascar) have not been monitored – even a basic global mapping of inland waters, classified by broad geomorphic categories, is largely lacking – and there are no global estimates of changes in the extent of lakes, rivers or wetlands (Balmford *et al.*, 2002).

We then need to understand the extent to which indigenous peoples either restrict access to local knowledge or treat it as a common good. Biodiversity provides a huge variety of goods and services, although often threatened by anthropocentric pressures (Gherardi *et al.*, 2003). More generally, climate change (whether caused or exacerbated by humans) will negatively impact on many biomes and reduce or alter biotic yields such as indigenous species fisheries.

6.2.3   Management of biodiversity in Europe

In Europe a water governance regime that specifically recognizes water as a life-support resource, the European Commission Water Framework Directive (2000) (EC WFD), puts the onus on states to restore their waters to a 'reference' (quasi-natural) condition, assessed using ecological methods such as long-term monitoring of fresh-water conditions and biodiversity. The assessment must establish the connections with human social systems, considering the impacts of pressures in freshwater ecosystems, such as fragmentation of habitats, constructed waterways, pollution, overexploitation of resources, and all associated human activities (irrigation, energy production, indus-trial development, tourism, domestic consumption), and must further consider the resilience and adaptive capacity of freshwater ecosystems to human pressures.

The WFD assumes that biodiversity is closely related to functioning, but it is not yet clear how, or even if, the WFD ecological status classes 'Natural, Good, Moderate, Poor and Bad' relate to aquatic biodiversity. Benthic invertebrates are one of four elem-ents of 'Good ecological status' used in monitoring biodiversity – the others being phytoplankton, phytobenthos and fish. However, native species such as crayfish are not specifically targeted, despite their keystone significance within Europe. The WFD also does not deal with specific invasive aliens, other than as a factor undermining natural-ness and as a cause of environmental pressures.

A Biodiversity Action Plan (BAP) is an internationally recognized programme addressing threatened species and habitats and is designed to protect and restore bio-logical systems. The UK has developed a BAP for the white-clawed crayfish and there are a number of regional Species Action Plans (SAPs). The original impetus for these plans derives from the 1992 Convention on Biological Diversity (CBD). However, as of 2009, only a fraction of the 191 countries ratifying the CBD have developed BAP documents. In Europe, habitat management for target species is moving away from a species-based approach (e.g. BAPs) to a habitat approach (HAP: Habitat Action Plan). In the UK, the Joint Nature Conservation Committee (JNCC) found that progress with Species or Habitat Action Plans was mostly limited by habitat loss or degradation (61% of cases) compared with pollution (16%) and intrinsic factors (7%) (Shore *et al.*, 2005). However, many UK Species Action Plans and Habitat Action Plans (SAPs and HAPs) were written for charismatic vertebrate or plant species, which were sometimes of little account in ecosystem functioning, and thus they may have missed important keystone species. BAPs need to assess whether Natura 2000 sites are really protecting a signifi-cant number of Europe's species. The findings need to be properly interpreted, includ-ing how to recognize and separate the impact of the Action Plan itself from the signals arising from some drivers such as climate change, ecological succession or land-use change, and even from species population dynamics.

In deciding whether we can conserve species better through habitat management or through more broadly based BAPs, we first need to establish the most appropriate techniques for habitat management to optimize species conservation. This requires a focus on metapopulation dynamics – effective habitat patch size for sustainable popu-lations, habitat resilience to perturbations, spatial bottlenecks to gene flow, networks and corridors. The protection of conservation priority areas (important habitats, bio-diversity hot-spots) – not just reserves or Natura 2000 sites – and the development of effective management and protection at the landscape level will increasingly become priorities.

6.2.4 Evaluating the current status and trends of crayfish biodiversity

We know that there are more than 600 species of freshwater crayfish around the globe, particularly in hot-spots in North America and Australia. Our knowledge of taxa is steadily improving; for example, the conservation status of crayfish in North America is documented in Taylor *et al.* (2007), and the European native species and their genetic variations are documented in Souty-Grosset *et al.* (2006), while increas-ingly comprehensive details of species worldwide are maintained by J. W. Fetzner, Jr on the Carnegie Museum of Natural History's *Global Crayfish Resources* pages (Fetzner, 2006). This level of baseline knowledge is needed to support management-led conser-vation (Reynolds *et al.*, 2006). The community in which crayfish operate is modified by these keystone species, with a potential addition of biodiversity through their food-web control.

An added complication is that because of their manageable size, hardiness and ease of transport, more and more types of crayfish have become translocated across the world, even to continents such as Africa which lack indigenous crayfish species. The impacts of such introductions are discussed in Chapter 8. The reasons are not hard to find: crayfish are prized as food, as a luxury item that is easily traded, and as an ornamental species for ponds or aquaria. About a dozen species, chiefly from North America, are now known to have been released into the wild in Europe, often with their associated pathogens (see Chapter 8), and this poses serious risks to the indigenous spe-cies there and hence to community biodiversity (Souty-Grosset *et al.*, 2006). There are comforting statements in the literature about 'ecological homologues' or 'ecological equivalents'. However, the degree to which non-native species can fully replicate the niche occupied and ecosystem functions performed by lost species that coevolved with local ecosystems is largely unknown. Introduced species therefore create risks both for ecosystem structure and function as well as for the services they provide, even where certain direct economic benefits from provisioning services such as harvesting for human food are quantifiable (Everard *et al.*, 2009). The precautionary principle advises against incautious assumptions about species substitution.

Research needs include better understanding of the impacts of specific non-indigenous crayfish species (NICS) on freshwater biodiversity and ecosystem func-tioning, in relation to their population biology and competitive capabilities.

Globally, Europe has been hardest hit by crayfish introductions. Its conventions on aspects of biodiversity, such as the Habitats and Species Directive, have Annexes list-ing important (often threatened) species and habitats central to the management of biodiversity, and each Member State has national regulations at least as strong as inter-national requirements. However, these are sometimes hindered by international agree-ments, particularly on the problems of free movement of animals and plants and the difficulty of controlling trade in known aquatic pests. As a result, many aquatic animals such as American crayfish have become widespread in Europe and are costly or impossible to control. The same is now happening elsewhere, e.g. in Central America, Africa and Madagascar, in each case involving North American crayfish. It has been claimed that mechanisms such as an Environmental Impact Assessment (EIA) can be used to curb the introduction of species known to be detrimental. However, most introductions are the result of accidental escapes or unauthorized releases of species, wanted or unwanted, and this cannot be controlled through EIAs.

The loss or diminution of indigenous crayfish populations because of both habitat deterioration and competition with alien or non-indigenous crayfish (most importantly, through their dissemination of crayfish plague) must clearly reduce freshwater biodiversity at the species level. Non-indigenous crayfish invaders have also diminished habitat complexity and species diversity in Kenya (Harper *et al.*, 2002; Harper & Mavuti, 2004) and many other countries.

6.2.5   Ecosystem services

Human dependency on biological processes

In contrast to their negative impacts on biodiversity, human beings have always been dependent on fundamental biological processes and systems for their sustenance, health, well-being and enjoyment of life. Thus, biodiversity conservation can have an economic basis if a species is a source of products useful to people. The benefits from conserving components of biological diversity can be ecosystem services (such as acceptable water quality), biological resources (e.g. crayfish as food) or social benefits (e.g. recreational or educational values) (Gherardi *et al.*, 2003).

The concept of ecosystem services provides a human-centric way of looking at biodiversity. The harmonization of ecosystem services into a unified classification under the UN's Millennium Ecosystem Assessment (MEA) then provides a framework supporting and integrating viewpoints on the implications for ecosystems and stakeholders dependent upon them, arising from management interventions and other modifications of the environment. The MEA classification of ecosystem services has also achieved consensus around the world as representing an imperfect, but adequate, basis for founding policy and legal action (Everard *et al.*, 2009).

Long-term studies integrating socio-economics with population and community ecology are required. These could determine how ecosystem services relate to changes in species composition, especially in terms of simplification of community biodiversity and reactions to climate change, and how societies manage the conflicts which arise when conserving biodiversity means restricting economic activities.

Many short-term actions destroy species and communities in the name of efficiency. In the longer term, this may represent a cost to society. The Earth's natural systems provide a range of ecosystem services such as water supply, soil formation, atmospheric gas balance, crop pollination and waste management. One study a decade ago estimated the global value of these services at US$33 trillion, which at the time was more than the GNP (gross national product) of all the world's economies. If some species are

Table 6.1. Examples of the types of ecosystem services lost due to or accompanied by the loss of biodiversity in 37 case studies in 18 EU Member States (from Kettunen & ten Brink, 2006).

Type of ecosystem service lost	Number of case studies
Provisioning services	
Food	19 (51%)
Fresh water	13 (35%)
Ornamental	1 (3%)
Regulating services	
Erosion control	13 (35%)
Water regulation	11 (38%)
Water purification and waste management	10 (26%)
Biological control (loss of natural predators)	8 (20%)
Climate regulation	8 (20%)
Loss of indicator species	2 (5%)
Cultural services	
Recreation and ecotourism	27 (69%)
Cultural diversity, educational, aesthetic	22 (56%)
Cultural heritage value	9 (23%)
Supporting services	
Nutrient cycling	7 (18%)

extinguished, not only will new sources of scientific information be lost, but potential biological wealth may be destroyed, including still undeveloped medicines, crops, pharmaceuticals, timber and fibres, soil-restoring vegetation, petroleum substitutes and other products and amenities. Ecosystem services also provide intangible benefits such as aesthetic and cultural values (see Table 6.1).

Generally speaking, the conservation of components of biological diversity, such as freshwater crayfish, can be justified because they produce benefits for humans through the protection of the aquatic environment and water resources, as well as the direct maintenance of both food sources and cultural heritage. The situation is less evident at first for smaller invertebrates such as hydroporine water beetles, water fleas or chironomids, which are unlikely to have iconic value, but the principles of ecosystem servicing are the same. In either case, a rare taxon is usually of less ecological significance than a more common member of a community, although the former may be useful in indicating the previous state or historical development of an ecosystem.

Wetland ecosystems may provide ecosystem services such as increasing landscape biodiversity and trapping nutrients moving from land to aquatic systems, as well as having considerable economic value. As a result, wetlands are often protected and restored and new ones even constructed. Hansson *et al.* (2005) analysed the physical, chemical and biological features of a large set of constructed wetlands and concluded that shallow wetlands with a large surface area and high shoreline complexity are likely to provide a higher biodiversity of birds, benthic invertebrates and macrophytes than a small, deep wetland. There are, therefore, opportunities to direct the ecosystem function of a specific wetland to boost the services provided.

At a larger catchment scale, ecosystem services are starting to be identified and evaluated. Wilson & Carpenter (1999) used various methods to assign economic values to non-market goods and services provided by freshwater systems, as described in 30 studies focusing on different aspects of social benefit associated with lakes, streams, rivers and wetlands. The authors conclude that creative interdisciplinary research is needed on the quantitative measurement of surface freshwater ecosystem goods and service values and the relation of these values to key limnological variables. These insights must be communicated to the public so as to facilitate and improve future management and research.

Use values of crayfish

Crayfish have a defined monetary and cultural value, now very obvious in both developing and developed countries. In Madagascar, wherever local taboos against their collection are not strong, *Astacoides* species of indigenous crayfish provide a valuable cash income and so are subject to increasing pressures from harvesting, although, in theory, these pressures could be regulated so as to sustain crayfish populations (Jones & Coulson, 2006). In Europe and Australia, some commercial and recreational harvests of *Astacus*, *Euastacus* or *Cherax* species provide support to the local economy comparable to that of globally traded marine lobster fisheries. Traditional Scandinavian crayfish-fishing festivals bring considerable tourist revenue, emphasizing the importance of managing these precious stocks.

In Scandinavia, sustainable exploitation of the noble crayfish *Astacus astacus* is a prerequisite for its conservation, and social benefits arise in terms of recreation, research and education. However, repeated outbreaks of crayfish plague have led to an estimated 95% loss of former Swedish crayfish stocks. In western and central Europe, the white-clawed crayfish *Austropotamobius pallipes* and the stone crayfish *A. torrentium* are increasingly recognized as being flagship species for environmental quality, and they both present high cultural and ecological values. In France *A. pallipes* still occurs in 72 of 95 departments, but many populations have been lost, with 68% of populations having been lost over 25 years, including 40% lost in the last 6 years. *A. pallipes* is now acknowledged as scarce and declining in France, where it is often considered both a bioindicator of high water quality and a heritage species (Grandjean *et al.*, 2002c). However, in Ireland, where its stocks are stable or in slight decline (Reynolds *et al.*, 2009), it occurs in many mildly polluted rivers (Reynolds & Demers, 2006). The difference appears not to be due to water quality, but to the presence of invasive, disease-spreading alien crayfish in France but not in Ireland. The expansion of non-native crayfish in Austria, together with habitat deterioration, has also led to losses of *A. torrentium* (Holdich *et al.*, 2009b).

The causes of biodiversity loss in these three species are well established (Persic, 2006) and the levels of perceived threat are high. Crayfish populations are under continuous pressure due to freshwater pollution and habitat loss, overexploitation, and the introduction of alien species and their associated diseases. To these direct drivers must be added indirect drivers, related to unsustainable management and development initiatives, that have led to the destruction and degradation of habitats. Lost ecosystem services include food provision through declines in fisheries and cascade effects on both predators and prey as well as on plant development, thus indirectly affecting ecosystem support in terms of water purification, nutrient cycling and primary productivity. There are also losses in cultural services, ecotourism, recreation and education, and restriction of research and study opportunities.

Economic costs affect stakeholders such as water managers, tourists and anglers, who are highly motivated to protect native species and who will inform the general public. Controlled exploitation may be important in such protection, particularly with *A. astacus* in Scandinavia. There are no identifiable benefits associated with the loss of native species. Short-term economic benefits may arise from land drainage, stream canalization and the introduction of non-native species; however, in the longer term, such practices have hidden costs for local biodiversity and ecosystem services. The costs of restoration of native crayfish populations and their habitats, by means such as improving water quality, liming water and restocking, are high.

An IEEP (Institute for European Environmental Policy) study by Kettunen & ten Brink (2006) of a range of European studies on ecosystem services demonstrated that quantifiable losses to biodiversity and associated services could have been avoided or minimized if the full implications to ecosystem services of decisions taken had been considered. The IEEP study analysed 37 cases from 18 European Member States, presenting 10 in detail as case studies. All examples were of biodiversity loss that led to the loss of ecosystem services. Estimates of lost value due to the loss of biodiversity-related ecosystem services, adapted from Kettunen & ten Brink (2006), are given in Table 6.2 for 10 aquatic case studies, including the crayfish waters study, the modification of Danube river ecosystems, the Swedish coastal archipelago and the Lake Karla wetlands in Greece. Restoration benefits include US$16 million a year from wetlands tourism and the same from river fisheries, as well as US$112 million for nitrogen and US$18 million for phosphorus recycling.

One case study on freshwater crayfish (Persic, 2006) analysed losses of ecosystem services related to the decline or disappearance of three European crayfish species from the Atlantic area, Scandinavia and the circum-alpine region (Table 6.1), associated – in part at least – with the spread of non-native invasive species. The benefits arising from conservation of freshwater crayfish include maintenance of food sources and cultural heritage, and the protection of the aquatic environment and water resources. While it is recognized that crayfish play a key role in the ecology and functioning of freshwater ecosystems, over the last century native crayfish species have been lost through a variety of anthropogenic pressures leading to degradation of water quality, and also directly, through poaching, overfishing and the introduction of non-native species (Table 6.3). This study on freshwater crayfish is based on the work of the European crayfish research network CRAYNET (Reynolds & Souty-Grosset, 2003a). It includes quantified losses such as the 40% decline in native crayfish populations in France

Table 6.2. Types of ecosystem services lost due to or accompanied by the loss of biodiversity in European aquatic case studies (modified from Kettunen & ten Brink, 2006).

	Type of ecosystem service lost	Study location
Provisioning services		
Food and fibre	Decline/loss of fish stocks	Danube
	Decline of crayfish stocks	Europe
	Decline of clam stocks	Venice lagoon
Fresh water	Decline in purification capacity	Danube
		Crayfish waters
		Lake Karla
Regulating services		
Erosion control	Increased erosion of basin	Danube
Water regulation	Loss of peak flow regulation	Danube
Water purification	Loss of purification capacity	Danube
		Crayfish waters
		Lake Karla
		Swedish coastal
Loss of indicator species		Crayfish waters
Cultural services		
Recreation and ecotourism	Loss of opportunity	Danube
		Swedish coastal
Cultural diversity, educational, aesthetic	Loss of amenity	Danube
		Crayfish waters
		Lake Karla
		Swedish coastal
Cultural heritage value	Loss of key species	Crayfish waters
		Lake Karla
Supporting services		
Primary production	Change in trophic web	Crayfish waters
Nutrient cycling	Loss of wetland capacity	Crayfish waters
		Danube
		Lake Karla
		Swedish coastal

in the preceding 6-year period and the 95% decline in native crayfish populations in Sweden since 1900. Many others are directly quantifiable, but there are important differences between the relevant stakeholders, as shown below.

The losses that have occurred are often indicated by declines in exploited resources or costs/benefits arising from restoration. This indicates that both losses and benefits accruing from improvements may be quantifiable. Ecosystem services necessarily

Table 6.3. Importance of threats to the indigenous crayfish populations of three regions of Europe. 0= none, 1=low, 2=medium, 3=high (after Souty-Grosset *et al.*, 2006, and Persic, 2006).

		Atlantic area *Austropotamobius pallipes*	Scandinavia *Astacus astacus*	Circum-Alpine area *Austropotamobius torrentium*
Threats	France	Ireland	Sweden	Austria
Crayfish plague	3	3	3	2/3
Other diseases	?	2	?	?
Non-indigenous spp	3	3	3	2/3
Predators	1	1	1	0
Exploitation	1	0	1	1
Habitat alterations	2/3	1	1	2
Water level reduction	2	2	1	1
Eutrophication	1	1	1/2	2
Acidification	1	0	1/2	1
Toxicants	3	2/3	1	2/3
Land-use	3	2/3	2	2/3
Fragmentation	3	1	2	3
Mean threat level	1.75	1.58	1.5	1.67

interact, so a benefit to enhance one service may be a cost to another. For example, improving the provision of agricultural goods may decrease the freshwater supply and recreation opportunities provided by aquatic ecosystems. Losses may also occur in a different ecosystem and/or socio-economic sector from the benefits. The distribution of costs and benefits is also biased between different stakeholders; benefits are often obtained privately, while the associated costs are often of a more social or public nature.

6.3   Managing crayfish and biodiversity in wetlands

Wetlands are among the most fragile of habitats. Conservation of their biodiversity is complicated by the landscape position of rivers and wetlands as 'receivers' of land-use effluents, and the complex problems posed by endemism and therefore non-substitutability. In addition, in many parts of the world there is severe competition for fresh water between many different human stakeholders, who are usually in denial of the need to protect the resource. Protection of freshwater biodiversity is perhaps the ultimate conservation challenge because it is influenced by the upstream drainage network, the riparian zone and surrounding land, and also by downstream areas (Dudgeon *et al.*, 2006).

Fresh waters are thus under severe threat because of expanding human demands for water. This is despite the fact that biodiversity underpins many freshwater processes (e.g. self-purification, protein production) that are of crucial importance for sustaining goods and services for human populations (Naiman *et al.*, 2006). Fresh water is essential for nearly every form of human activity, including industrial production, navigation, domestic water requirements, waste assimilation, health and food production. Identifying changes to water regimes and the inherent consequences of those changes to aquatic organisms and human societies has done little, however, to mitigate or alleviate them. The world's hydrological regimes are being fundamentally altered to meet the needs of rapidly expanding populations (Vörösmarty *et al.*, 2005), and across the globe, water shortages have been linked to wars and insurgencies (Ross, 2004).

With human population growth and a changing climate, the water regimes that helped shape the evolution of freshwater diversity and the life history adaptations of individual species are different today than in the past and will be very different in the future. These major changes to one of the Earth's most basic biophysical systems are taking place with an incomplete understanding of the organisms being affected, and less still of the larger-scale consequences of those changes (Dudgeon *et al.*, 2006, Balian *et al.*, 2008).

The Millennium Ecosystem Assessment (MEA) (2005) estimated that between 1970 and 2002, freshwater biodiversity declined by about 55%, while that of terrestrial systems and marine systems each declined by about 32%. The actual values for fresh waters may have been considerably higher, considering the incompleteness of the taxonomic database on freshwater biodiversity. Unfortunately, the systematics of freshwater organisms and their distributional patterns are only now beginning to become clear, even with the largest and best-known invertebrates, the freshwater crayfish (Souty-Grosset *et al.*, 2006), and many other groups lag behind. It is therefore critical that existing and emerging databases on species and distributions be underpinned by correct identifications and compiled in a manner that makes them interactive and integrated so that the broader research community and stakeholders can have access. Despite the concerns expressed by scientists, taxonomy has been in decline for decades, and there is a pressing need to train a new generation of taxonomists and ecologists with the most up-to-date techniques, in order to answer questions related to the distribution, monitoring and environmental requirements of freshwater organisms.

Although biodiversity has important social and cultural – as well as economic – value, most humans have difficulty in recognizing the cultural value of species other than themselves. Human exploitation, or indifference, has led to countless extinctions of populations and species and alterations to ecosystems; native crayfish are among those most threatened, as recognized by the IUCN. The real costs of investing in conservation management will necessarily lead to trade-offs and compromises between alternative lines of action; conservation is most difficult for politicians to support or sanction when the outcomes are complex and slow to be revealed. However, recent years have seen an evolving environmental ethic that places a high value on nature for its own sake. For example, the Earth Charter, developed as a grassroots measure in the

1980s under United Nations auspices and launched at Rio in 1992, urges that we recognize that all beings are interdependent and every form of life has value regardless of its worth to human beings.

We saw that both losses and benefits accruing from changes to freshwater systems may be quantifiable. Ecosystem services necessarily interact, so a benefit to enhance one service may be a cost to another. Losses may also occur in a different ecosystem and/or socio-economic sector from the benefits. There must be discussion of the various values and benefits of preserving biodiversity versus the idea of conserving only those elements of biodiversity that humans identify as procuring tangible biological resources (Gherardi *et al.*, 2003). Water managers need to understand the relative benefits and impacts of restocking and translocation of aquatic organisms, including the addition of parasites, pathogens and commensal species; a good example being the spread of crayfish plague across Europe with the widespread stocking of signal crayfish. The impacts of this invasive species on ecosystem services have been analysed most recently in Everard *et al.* (2009).

For most of the global land surface, trade-offs between conservation of freshwater biodiversity and human use of ecosystem goods and services are inevitable. Dudgeon *et al.* (2006) advocate continuing attempts to check species loss but, in many situations, urge the adoption of a compromise position of management for biodiversity conservation, ecosystem functioning and resilience, and human livelihoods in order to provide a viable long-term basis for freshwater conservation. Recognition of this need will require the adoption of a new approach to biodiversity protection and freshwater ecosystem management – one that has been appropriately termed 'reconciliation ecology' (*sensu* Rosensweig, 2003). This is the science of inventing, establishing and maintaining new habitats to conserve species diversity in places where people live, work or play.

In the following chapters we look further at conservation management in relation to crayfish; in particular how indigenous crayfish species are monitored for conservation (Chapter 7) and non-indigenous ones for their control (Chapter 8).

7 Monitoring in conservation and management of indigenous crayfish populations

7.1 Background to crayfish monitoring

Our knowledge of crayfish taxonomy and distribution is steadily improving; we now know that there are around 650 species of freshwater crayfish in many different habitats, although the ecological roles of most have not been studied or understood and only about 15 of these (less than 3%) are commercially exploited. The main commercial species are examined in Holdich (2002a) and all the European native species and their genetic variation are documented in Souty-Grosset *et al.* (2006). However, with such knowledge comes an awareness of possible differences in ecology, and indeed vulnerability, between related stocks.

Many crayfish species whose ecology has been studied are shown to play important roles in their ecosystems (Chapter 3). The community in which crayfish operate is modified and regulated by these keystone species, with a potential increase in biodiversity through food-web control. Management-led conservation needs the support of directed research. This should include evaluation of the current status and trends of freshwater biodiversity and of the drivers of change in fresh waters, including climate change and invasive species, and their impacts on freshwater biodiversity.

A number of countries have carried out national surveys of crayfish distribution and abundance. For example, the French Higher Fisheries Council (Conseil Supérieur de la Pêche) has surveyed crayfish in 1977, 1990, 1995 and 2001 (Changeux, 2003) and 2006 (Collas *et al.*, 2007), which allowed scientists to follow the development of the various crayfish species, both exotic and indigenous, present on national territory. In each successive survey, the large expansion of exotic species and decline of the natives was noted. In the preparation of the *Atlas of Crayfish in Europe* (Souty-Grosset *et al.*, 2006), 38 countries were involved. Some were persuaded to carry out such a survey for the first time.

Local surveys also provide valuable information, often leading to monitoring. The first requirement of conservation management of crayfish is information about where crayfish populations occur. This may be accomplished in two main ways: by compiling incidental records from landowners, anglers, ecologists and other stakeholders, and by carrying out specific surveys for crayfish. The areas surveyed may be selected to confirm incidental records, to investigate potentially suitable habitats for which there are no records of crayfish, or to assess the current status and abundance of crayfish in regions where there may be past records. The purpose of the survey may be to build a picture of the broad geographical extent of crayfish populations or to obtain localized information.

When resources are limited, one approach is to minimize the survey effort at individual locations in favour of a wide coverage of sites. However, as the effort per site declines, there is a decreasing probability of detecting crayfish populations at moderate to low abundance, and therefore survey effort may be wasted. Where survey effort is sufficient to give some confidence about the presence and relative abundance of the population, this provides a better basis for long-term monitoring. The variability of results from the survey method used and the confidence level required in the results determines the number of sample sites required.

Population monitoring is essential in the conservation and management of indigenous crayfish species (ICS), as well as keeping track of non-indigenous species (NICS) and of actions that might harm their habitat and other threats to their survival. Such monitoring involves not only locating and surveying populations, but continued surveillance of their presence and population dynamics over time and, where relevant, of habitat quality parameters. The more survey methods that are tried, the more chances there are of finding crayfish in a location. The objective is information on where the crayfish are located, the size of the populations, the existence of any threats to their survival, particularly from NICS and crayfish plague, and what changes are taking place over time. Managers need to monitor stocks regularly to provide such information. Monitoring crayfish stocks is not a standard exercise, but may be tailored to the particular situation. If a stock is economically important, then it is most usually monitored by the same methodology as is used for its harvest – thus changes in population parameters, such as sex ratios or proportions of the catch over the legal size limit, are quickly detected and can be evaluated and capture regulations altered to suit. However, such capture methods may not truly reflect population characteristics. Most crayfish stocks are not commercially harvestable, for reasons that may include population size, maximum size of individuals, behaviour, abundance and difficulty of capture. Some of these crayfish may be taken by hand or poached to some extent, while others are not considered of economic interest. However, like freshwater crabs, their economic value is subject to change as human population pressure grows, particularly in developing countries.

Crayfish species have increasingly been translocated across the world (Chapter 4). Most notably, about a dozen species, chiefly from North America, are now known to have been released into the wild in Europe, often with their associated pathogens, posing serious risks to the indigenous species there and hence to community biodiversity (Souty-Grosset *et al.*, 2006; Holdich *et al.*, 2009b). More research is needed to better understand the impacts of specific NICS on freshwater biodiversity and ecosystem functioning, in relation to their population biology and competitive capabilities. The threats from NICS cannot be properly assessed unless potential sites where they have not previously been recorded are first monitored. How monitoring is carried out often depends on resources – both financial and the availability of surveyors. Apart from national surveys, the most comprehensive picture of crayfish distribution is obtained where the maximum amount of data is provided from surveys by government agencies, researchers, consultants and amateur naturalists. However, in such cases, not all such records may be equally available for collation, and the invasion front or regional status of a NICS may therefore be unclear.

7.1.1   Why monitor?

When crayfish are detected, their populations should be monitored periodically with a clear stated objective. The question 'Why monitor?' should always be posed and answered before a monitoring programme is established, and appropriate survey methods then usually become evident (Holdich *et al.*, 2002). Monitoring could answer conservation questions such as: 'How are the crayfish populations changing within a region?' 'What are the changes over time?' 'Where are the most important areas for crayfish?' and 'How do crayfish populations respond to changes in management (e.g. catching season, minimum size, exploitation pressure)?' (Reynolds *et al.*, 2006).

It is important to clarify whether the main objective of monitoring is between-site comparisons (e.g. of densities or population structure) or changes over time at a spe-cific site. Accurate between-site comparisons require a common standard in site selec-tion and survey method(s), and often make it difficult to use existing data and data, for instance from naturalists or local fishermen. Monitoring changes over time for a specific site allows different methods and data sets to be used, including fishermen's own data – provided they are comparable between years – and the use of a simple and clear protocol for data collection. Whatever the method or methods used, monitoring programmes depend on repeatability, and therefore good records should be made of conditions at the time of the survey and of the suitability of the habitat for crayfish. The size distribution gives an indication of the selectivity of the method. Records obtained by different methods should not be aggregated, and the final results (population size, proportion of juveniles) should be compared with care (Reynolds *et al.*, 2006).

Irrespective of the survey method for monitoring populations, Peay (2004) recom-mends the use of a catchment-scale risk assessment for indigenous (native) crayfish (ICS). The nature of the threat will vary, but outside North America, and especially in Europe, the most widespread and serious threats are from disease carried by non-indigenous (alien) crayfish; competition from NICS; impacts of urban or agricultural pollution; and the reduction in habitat quality due to land use, such as the modification of watercourses for land drainage. Identification of risks helps to direct both conserva-tion management and monitoring requirements (Reynolds *et al.*, 2006).

7.2   Methods for monitoring crayfish stocks

There are no perfect methods for surveying crayfish. Many workers favour their own methodology for particular situations, and the topic continues to receive much study; reviews are provided by DiStefano *et al.* (2003), Peay (2004), Nowicki *et al.* (2008) Reynolds (2009a) and Price & Welch (2009). The methodology selected depends on crayfish ecology and habitat preferences (whether in streams, ponds or other wetlands) and also on the size and accessibility of stocks. The choice of method also depends on the purpose of the survey, the available resources, and the characteristics of the habitats to be surveyed (see Holdich & Rogers, 2000). Shallow waters can be entered and crayfish seen and handled; deep waters need to be accessed from a boat or from the shore. At least eight monitoring methods have been used for shallow-water stocks: night-viewing, manual survey, sweep-netting, baited stick lures, kick-sampling, various quadrat or timed area surveys for adults and/or juveniles, electro-fishing, and (passive) camera trapping. Five principal methods are commonly used for deep-water monitoring: traps, baited lift-nets, fyke-netting, throw-nets and diving.

There are many descriptions of monitoring methods in the literature – perhaps because each biotope appears to be unique and demands a different methodology (Somers & Stechey, 1986). Many involve the use of mark–recapture methods (Nowicki *et al.*, 2008). Published descriptions of techniques used and reasons for using them include: dip-nets and seines for small areas (Brown & Bowler, 1977); SCUBA diving (Emery, 1975) or traps for larger areas (Goldman & Rundquist, 1977); surveys along transects (Allison & Harvey, 1981); detailed investigations of quadrats (Capelli, 1975) or colonization samplers (Lorman, 1980); and electro-fishing (Westman *et al.*, 1979). Methods appropriate to different types of waterbody are summarized in Table 7.1.

Monitoring methods are largely derived from traditional capture methods. Indeed, when large crayfish are captured for food, the results are often used and interpreted in terms of stock stability and strength. In streams and shallow rivers, recreational capture of crayfish for food is labour-intensive; it is chiefly done by hand, sometimes at night, by turning over stones and reaching into burrows. In rather deeper water, various methods may be used to capture crayfish seen moving about, such as hand-netting crayfish attracted to a baited stick lure, or by the use of a throw-net. In deep water, capture is generally by the use of a lift-net, 'umbrella-trap' or 'balance', periodically retrieved by a pole or hook, or by using baited traps fished overnight. Catching by hand, baited stick or balance may yield lower results with greater physical effort than the use of traps. Finally, large crayfish (particularly NICS) may sometimes be an important by-catch of other fishing methods – as in seining, bottom-set gill nets, or summer fyke-nets set for eels. This is analogous to surrogate monitoring methods.

Monitoring for management of recreational or commercial crayfish fisheries has been addressed by Scandinavian and other workers, including Westman *et al.* (1993), Momot (1993) and Skurdal *et al.* (1993). Trapping methods, with their bias towards larger crayfish, are valuable for monitoring such commercial stocks. Recording trap catch per unit effort (CPUE) is an effective method of monitoring changes in commercial crayfish populations (e.g. Skurdal *et al.*, 1995). Survey methods used to monitor and update information on distribution, abundance and stability of population structure of the stocks may either be the same as capture methods, or may be treated as a separate exercise.

In contrast, many countries have adopted detailed protocols for monitoring protected crayfish species: e.g. the Irish lakes crayfish methodology (O'Connor *et al.*, 2009) or the Joint Nature Conservation Committee (JNCC) in the UK, using the methods of Peay (2003b). In shallow streams and rivers, stocks are usually monitored by turning

Table 7.1. Recommended survey methods for crayfish according to habitat type (in part after Paey).

Type of waterbody	Flow, substrate, habitats	Suitable survey method(s)
Headwater streams, larger stony rivers	Flow variable, substrate heterogeneous; boulders, cobbles, gravel and/or sand. Best habitats are under small boulders in glides and pools. Some crayfish found in banks and riffles.	Selective manual survey provides semi-quantitative abundance, or consider electro-fishing. Use night-viewing and hand-catching for adult crayfish per unit area.
Mid-gradient streams in gravel or clay	Flow variable, substrate mainly gravel or clay. Woody debris and urban detritus often the only refuges. Crayfish burrow in submerged banks, use tree roots, also stones at bridges and weirs. Calcareous streams have more stable flow.	Manual survey limited by availability of searchable refuges. Lift and sweep-net fine roots for juveniles. Check oval burrows in vertical banks. Sweep beds of submerged aquatic vegetation. Kick-sample in pebbles. These methods give presence only and have low reliability. Use baited traps or artificial refuges for semi-quantitative results. Night-viewing also effective if water is clear.
Lowland rivers, canals, lakes	Still or slow-flowing, often modified; substrate mainly silty clay or sand/gravel. Main crayfish habitats are steep clay banks, often with trees. May use submerged macrophytes or shallows with emergent reeds.	Usually too deep and turbid for manual survey. Sweep-netting of tree roots or macrophytes may be possible. Trapping usually best option, yielding semi-quantitative results.
Warm swamps, seasonally marshy ground	Standing water periodically present, well vegetated. Crayfish forage when wet, or burrow to the water table.	Sampled in wet phase by trapping, or by digging or counting chimneys.

stones identified as likely hiding places, by night surveys, by kick-sampling or sweep-netting in various habitats, or by juvenile surveys (Table 7.1).

Results may be expressed quantitatively by area, if using quadrats or surber samplers in waters with reasonably high densities of crayfish, or be semi-quantitative, e.g. kick or sweep-net sampling for a set time period or over a defined area. A recent study by DiStefano *et al.* (2003) recommended stratified quantitative sampling of the various microhabitats present in a stream.

Here we briefly outline the main methods used for monitoring crayfish. Many of these methods have been well described by Peay (2004) and other authors.

- **Night-viewing**: This method of spotting and catching active crayfish by hand has been widely used, e.g. by Abrahamsson (1983), Arrignon *et al.* (1999) and Peay (2004). The site must first be visited in daylight to determine the position of hazards. It requires a uniform substrate and water shallow enough for wading, unless

Figure 7.1.   Hand-search for lake crayfish while snorkelling (photo courtesy of William O'Connor).

SCUBA diving is used. Smaller crayfish can easily be missed, and good water clarity is essential. It has the benefit of providing counts of active crayfish per unit area, but is affected by the habitat, being less effective if the bottom is stony or covered by macrophytes. Camera traps can be substituted in good conditions.

- **Manual survey**: Like night-viewing, a manual survey is limited by the requirement for clear water. It may involve selective manual searches, where the likeliest refuges are examined (Peay, 2003b), or fixed area sampling using quadrats or surber samplers (e.g. Byrne *et al.*, 1999). Crayfish visibility may be enhanced by looking through a glass-floored viewing box or benthoscope, or by divers wearing a facemask while swimming. Hand-search while snorkelling disturbs the bottom less than by wading, but requires an assistant (Figure 7.1).

- **Sweep-netting**: This is widely used, often in conjunction with other methods such as transect or SCUBA surveys. It is not quantitative unless combined with areal quadrats, but can be rewarding in some circumstances, e.g. to determine whether crayfish are present or to locate juveniles. However, the method is less suitable on heterogeneous shores with cobbles, boulders and rocks.

- **Benthos samplers**: Trays containing bottom material or vegetation mats can be left in the water to be colonized by invertebrates, then later removed and examined. This method is particularly suitable for juveniles, which are often under-represented in survey results.

- **Electro-fishing** has been used successfully for many years to survey for crayfish, e.g. by Westman *et al.* (1979) and Eversole & Foltz (1993), provided that it is carried out in clear shallow water and in good weather. It requires a helper. The advantages over trapping are that smaller adults and juveniles are caught, and the catch is related

Figure 7.2. Trapping is frequently used for monitoring crayfish stocks: (**a**) for *Austropotamobius pallipes* in France (picture by Catherine Souty-Grosset), (**b**) for *Pacifastacus leniusculus* in Sweden (picture by Per Adolphson).

to a defined area (Peay, 2004), but crayfish may be under-recorded if they do not come out of their refuges, damage is sometimes caused to limbs, and the process can be destructive to the benthic community (Nowicki *et al.*, 2008).

• **Traps** are cages covered with mesh of a size that will retain all adult crayfish, with one or more entrance funnels (see Figure 7.2) and normally baited with fish or liver, placed in deeper water. They are usually set overnight, 3–5 m apart in strings of 10–50, and later retrieved from the bank or from a boat.

The size selectivity and seasonal variations in trappability are widely remarked on, e.g. by Brown & Brewis (1979), Reynolds & Matthews (1993) and Wright & Williams (2000). Trapping techniques should therefore be standardized as much as possible, including trap type, baiting and position (Peay, 2004). Trap retention varies considerably. Seasonal variation can be reduced by trapping in late summer to early autumn, when adult crayfish have finished releasing young and moulting, but before falling water temperature reduces activity and lowers catch efficiency. If traps are left out for more than one night, catches may increase, but not two-fold, and crayfish may be on average heavier (Reynolds & Matthews, 1993), but these increases mask various behavioural processes; e.g. some smaller trapped crayfish may find their way out, while there are interactions between large crayfish already in the trap and others seeking to enter. Thus, catch per unit effort (CPUE) from any trapping sessions longer than one night are not directly comparable with those from a single night unless some calculation is made of the rate of loss or gain of crayfish in longer periods.

Many authors have pointed to the different behavioural responses affecting crayfish trappability: Nowicki *et al.* (2008) suggest that capture sessions need to be separated by roughly 2-week intervals to avoid the strong but short-term negative effect of capturing crayfish on their likelihood of being recaptured.

Figure 7.3.   Surrogate signs of crayfish: (**a**) grebe catching *A. leptodactylus* (photo courtesy of Elinor Wiltshire), (**b**) otter feeding site (picture by Julian Reynolds). See also colour plate section.

- **Lures** include placing a dead fish or other animal in shallow water, often pinned by a stake to the bottom (the 'baited stick' method); this is observed and any approaching crayfish caught by hand or netted out with a hand-net. Another version, for deeper water and widely used, is the use of a baited 'balance' – a lift-net or shallow bag net suspended from a rigid rim and baited in the centre. This is lowered into the water and allowed to rest on the bottom; it is then raised at intervals to check for catches.
- **Surrogate or *ex situ* methods** may provide supplementary information of various kinds in both shallow- and deep-water situations. Surrogate evidence can be important in detecting crayfish populations in unsurveyed waterbodies, or can be used to amplify or enrich other records. Moulted shells or dead crayfish observed after pollution incidents may provide evidence of their presence, crayfish may be recorded from the faeces of aquatic mammals such as otter (*Lutra lutra*), or photography may record predation activity (Figure 7.3). Biological monitoring to establish water quality may also detect crayfish, although the methods used and fast-flowing, shallow stretches chosen are not best suited to the presence of crayfish. Routine fisheries surveys (electro-fishing of streams, or seine netting of fishing lakes) may also produce incidental catches of crayfish, while anglers may provide anecdotal evidence about crayfish taking angling bait or being found in the guts of fish. Finally, burrows attributable to crayfish may be seen in the banks, although actual crayfish presence should be verified.

7.2.1   Population estimation

All survey methods produce a biased sample of the true population. It is difficult to compare the degree of bias unless two or more methods can be used in the same area. Even then, the distribution of crayfish may be patchy in response to microhabitat, and habitat usage may vary in different portions of the population, as shown, for example, by Reyjol & Roqueplo (2002) and Demers *et al.* (2003). Methods yielding chiefly juvenile crayfish give different population information from those yielding adult females and males. The greater the size bias to larger crayfish, the lower is the proportion of the total population of crayfish sampled by the survey method.

Most methods need appropriate analysis techniques for population estimates. Rabeni *et al.* (1997) found that mark–recapture methods were more precise than depletion estimates of population size. Crayfish may be marked by temporary or semi-permanent methods, such as internal PIT tags (e.g. Bubb *et al.*, 2007), punching holes in the telson (e.g. Guan, 1997), or branding with a heated blunt needle to kill the pigment cells below the carapace (e.g. Brown & Brewis, 1979); this leaves an unpigmented pale spot which will survive a number of moults.

There are limitations to most methods; for example, catches from quadrats are highly biased towards smaller crayfish, electro-fishing is most effective in high-conductivity water, and night-viewing requires a uniform light-coloured substrate. Because of the size selectivity of trapping and the avoidance of traps by berried females, diving surveys are probably the most effective way of obtaining information on recruitment in deep waters (Peay, 2004). Rabeni *et al.* (1997) compared the efficacy of different methods for monitoring New Zealand parastacids, and recommended the use of electro-fishing to obtain the highest abundance estimates. While they found hand-netting to be effective, direct observations at night were not useful, nor were baited traps.

Peay (2004) compared the size frequencies of white-clawed crayfish obtained by different survey methods from a stream in Yorkshire, England, by trapping with coarse- and fine-mesh baited traps, by night-viewing, and by selective manual survey. Mesh size of Swedish Trappy® traps was approximately 20 mm, while that of the funnel traps (GB Nets) was 4 mm. The crayfish recorded in both types of trap were all mature or approaching maturity; they ranged from 27 to 53 mm carapace length (CL), but the modal value was lower in the fine-meshed traps. Crayfish from night-viewing and manual surveys ranged from 8 to 50 mm CL, with modal values similar to those for fine-meshed traps. Only 7% of the crayfish collected by night-viewing, and less than 1% of the catch using Swedish Trappy traps, were less than 30 mm CL, compared with over 70% of those from the manual survey and, even there, the juveniles were undoubtedly under-recorded compared with the true population. Thus, the choice of survey method has a major effect on the catch obtained, emphasizing that data sets obtained by different methods should be treated separately in population monitoring.

In deeper rivers, lakes and ponds, population density may be monitored by diving (SCUBA or snorkelling), or again by inshore sweep-netting or night surveys (O'Connor *et al.*, 2009). Quadrats may be used to define density (Lamontagne & Rasmussen (1993). Commercially important stocks in such habitats are usually monitored using traps similar to those used for capture; thus the adult population structure as seen in traps can be evaluated before and after the fishing season and related to catch and effort (e.g. Skurdal *et al.*, 2002). However, an early study of a reservoir feeder stream population of *Austropotamobius pallipes* showed that trapping significantly underestimated the population, compared with hand-catching (Brown & Brewis, 1979), and a study in a Czech reservoir found that hand-catches using baited sticks, which attracted a wide range of sizes, were more representative of the true population structure than were trap catches (Policar & Kozák, 2005).

For commercially exploited stocks, chiefly monitored by trapping, trap catches before and after the harvest season need careful interpretation. In addition, a number of bias factors may affect the use of information from catch methods (see also Price & Welch, 2009):

- **Traps used**: The mesh size and funnel width are designed to optimize catches of large crayfish, but a larger mesh will facilitate the escape of smaller individuals, thus falsifying population size structure.
- **Diel periodicity**: This will relate to maximum activity of crayfish, which is normally nocturnal, so traps are set overnight. If traps are not emptied soon after dawn, successive escapes will occur, especially on the following night. Additionally, a catch of large male crayfish may deter smaller crayfish from entering.
- **Time of year**: A monitoring campaign may operate full-time and year-round, but species activity patterns are determined by water temperature, flooding levels, moult periodicity and breeding periods. In temperate regions, temperature is the primary variable. Phases of the moon are also known to influence the catch (Reynolds & Matthews, 1993).
- **Water level and conditions**: Weather conditions obviously affect both the catcher and the catch. Crayfish catchability also varies with water conditions, with low activity or visibility when water is turbid or fast-flowing.
- **Bait use**: Traps may function as refuges and thus should not require baiting, but the use of lures or attractants is most usual. However, several studies have shown that different types of bait, and their freshness, vary in attractiveness and may affect catch size. In Algonquin Provincial Park, Ontario, *Cambarus bartonii* and *Orconectes virilis* were sampled with 60 minnow traps in four transects in October 1981, and a comparison of four different baits showed that meat baits caught larger crayfish (Somers & Stechey, 1986).
- **Species habitat preferences**: Even within a major habitat, such as a river or a swamp, not all crayfish show the same activity or habitat preferences. For example, in Europe, where noble crayfish *Astacus astacus* and white-clawed crayfish *Austropotamobius pallipes* are occasionally sympatric, they tend to occur in different parts of a catchment, while the introduced spiny-cheek crayfish *Orconectes limosus* prefers larger, deeper river stretches. Differences are also evident within the suites of *Orconectes* and *Cambarus* species in temperate North American rivers and these have been teased out by experimentation. Wetzel & Brown (1993) tested the growth of two very similar species, *O. virilis* and *O. immunis*; both showed best survival in the temperature range 15°–25°C, but *O. immunis* grew best at the lower end of this range.

In conclusion, the method of choice depends on the habitats encountered and on the purpose of the survey; whether for distribution (presence/absence), relative abundance (semi-quantitative) or population structure (quantitative, all size classes).

7.3 Regional case studies

This section describes a series of monitoring programmes from across the globe, arranged in three sections by general habitat (streams and ponds, rivers and lakes, and wetlands).

7.3.1 Monitoring stocks in streams and small waterbodies

Because of their small habitat size and ease of access, stream stocks of crayfish are most widely monitored, despite usually being of little economic importance. A number of methods are specifically employed in streams, as described above; they include surber samplers and other quadrat methods, stone turning while wading, or snorkelling (see Figure 7.1), sweep-netting, searching the bank for burrows and enticing the crayfish out, and night-search for foraging crayfish near the shore by torchlight. Direct observation is often possible in such shallow waters. The use of a hand-net may help to facilitate the capture of crayfish seen in quadrat or transect surveys, or to sweep around stands of vegetation or cobbles, particularly in juvenile surveys. A passive method analogous to the use of a balance in deeper water is the camera trap, primed to record at intervals. Rabeni *et al.* (1997) and Peay (2003b), among others, have evaluated the suitability of methods for crayfish in streams.

Europe

Because of a traditionally high level of European interest in crayfish as a harvestable delicacy, and their recognition as keystone species in aquatic systems, all European countries have taken note of the decline of indigenous crayfish species. This is most usually attributed to deteriorating habitat and water quality and to epizootic disease introduced by (North American) alien species. Populations of indigenous species are increasingly becoming restricted to fragmented habitats and occur at critical threshold levels for the loss of biodiversity. Monitoring of remaining stocks then becomes a priority, alongside monitoring of the environmental variables known to be relevant to crayfish survival.

The few indigenous crayfish species in Europe, all relatively large and subject to exploitation at some time, are generally well known, and their monitoring follows established methodology. In most of the continent, genetic and other evidence suggests that human actions have moved crayfish about for millennia (Chapter 1). Their population fluctuations and declines are well documented. See, for example, the proceedings of the European Inland Fisheries Advisory Commission (EIFAC) Workshop on Crayfish Management and Stocking, held in Kuopio, Finland in 1991 (EIFAC, 1992), and also symposia edited by Gherardi & Souty-Grosset (2006), Souty-Grosset *et al.* (2006), Füreder & Souty-Grosset (2005), Taugbøl & Souty-Grosset (2004), Reynolds & Souty-Grosset (2003b) and papers by Westman & Westman (1992) and Lodge *et al.* (2000a).

Each country has its monitoring scheme for crayfish in streams and rivers. For example, in France, national surveys have been made periodically since 1971 to determine changes in crayfish distribution (Changeux, 2003; Collas *et al.*, 2007). When analysed by habitat and region, they show that the native species *Austropotamobius pallipes*, *A. torrentium* and *Astacus astacus* are either rare or in decline, while the introduced species *Orconectes limosus*, *Pacifastacus leniusculus*, *Procambarus clarkii* and *Astacus leptodactylus* (native to eastern Europe but introduced widely in the west) are increasing.

In Britain, crayfish stocks have been monitored for several decades, in recent years using the standardized hand-search methods of Peay (2003b). The spread of NICS has become critical in recent years, with the transmission of crayfish plague and elimination of many native *A. pallipes* stocks. This has been well documented for south-western Britain in recent years, and the situation is summarized in Holdich *et al.* (2009b) (see Figure 7.4).

Spain once had large, economically valuable stocks of white-clawed crayfish. However, signal crayfish *Pacifastacus leniusculus* were introduced to Spain in 1974 (Habsburgo-Lorena, 1979) and plague outbreaks began in Spain in 1978 (Cuellar & Coll, 1983; Diéguez-Uribeondo *et al.*, 1997b). A survey by Lozano & Martín (1988) showed that most native populations had disappeared by 1985, and monitoring followed in several regions.

One of the most important crayfish fisheries in Spain was in Cuenca province in central Spain (Torre & Rodriguez, 1964). Crayfish populations in Cuenca have been monitored since the mid-1980s by different methodologies and intensities (Martinez *et al.*, 2003). In 2000, a new sampling programme was carried out in Cuenca to provide

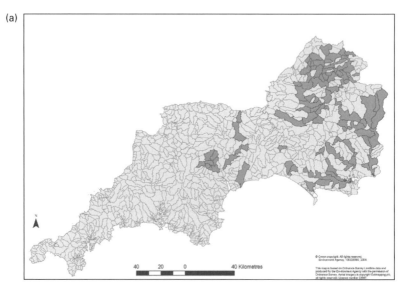

(a)

Figure 7.4.   Crayfish distribution in river catchments in south-west England: (**a**) approximate distribution of *Austropotamobius pallipes* pre-1975, (**b**) distribution of *Austropotamobius pallipes* in 2009 (excluding recently translocated populations), (**c**) distribution of NICS, mainly *Pacifastacus leniusculus*, in 2009 (from Holdich *et al.*, 2009b). See also colour plate section.

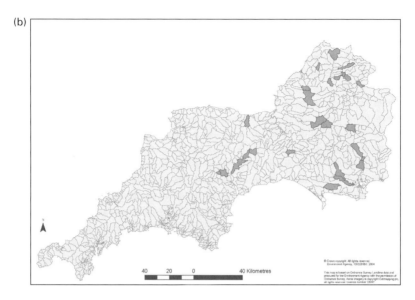

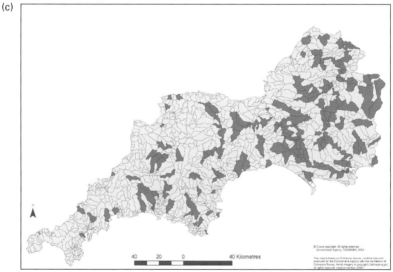

Figure 7.4. (*cont.*)

a baseline, using different sampling strategies and collecting information about cray-fish stocks, basin characteristics and habitat (Alonso, 2001). In total, 262 known cray-fish sites were surveyed, but just 39 crayfish stocks were found. Surviving populations of white-clawed crayfish were by then very small and restricted to isolated headwater creeks. Differences between sites with and without crayfish were noted, and several risk factors identified, including basin descriptors (river, creek, natural or artificial pond and their macrohabitats) and dimensions, mean slope and degree of channeliza-tion; whether refuges were in the bank or streambed; also riparian cover and whether the site was isolated from the main catchment by a cascade, dam, dry stretch or by heavy pollution. Lastly, percentage cover of macrophytes and evidence of aquatic vertebrates were assessed.

Crayfish survey methodology in Cuenca involved an active diurnal search for living or dead specimens, moults and signs of crayfish activity, a nocturnal search using flashlights, with or without previous baiting, and the overnight placement of baited traps, set 10 m apart. Diurnal searches were the favoured method, being both effective and time-saving. The size of the stock or length of water containing crayfish was estimated, and population size structure and data on moults, reproductive status and state of health, also any available stocking information, were recorded. Relevant conservation problems were noted, such as the proximity of American crayfish species, their date of introduction if known, the intensity of fishing activity or of poaching, and also more general constraints to conservation, such as water use, agriculture, forestry or industrial activity.

Results of surveys showed that the few remaining stocks were located at an elevation of 870–1560 m, almost all in natural headwater streams, with annual temperature means of 8.8°–11.4°C and a range of 0.5°–24°C (Alonso, 2001). Permanent dry stretches were the most usual barriers isolating populations. The nearest settlement was on average 2 km distant. Few populations were within reserves, and there was strong evidence of poaching in nearly 30% of stocks. The surveys showed that 77% of populations were within 15 km of American crayfish populations, and 36% were in sites previously stocked from state-owned hatcheries.

In Croatia, where crayfish are restricted to limestone rivers flowing to the Adriatic Sea, stocks are also in decline. The current distribution of crayfish was surveyed by Maguire *et al.* (2003). Crayfish were caught by hand or with baited traps. Many stocks had been eliminated from lower reaches of rivers, where dams, agriculture or pollution were prevalent. Two cave populations of *Austropotamobius pallipes* (in an artificial tunnel and in a sinkhole) were found, both apparently of epigean origin (Maguire *et al.*, 2003), and populations of *Astacus astacus*, probably introduced in the first half of the twentieth century, were recorded in Istria.

In preparation for the CRAYNET *Atlas of Crayfish in Europe* (Souty-Grosset *et al.*, 2006), the long-recognized but little-studied stone crayfish *Austropotamobius torrentium* was surveyed across its possible European range (Figure 7.5). Laurent (1988) suggested that this is a Danubian species that probably originated in the south-western part of the Pannonian Basin, towards Serbia and Croatia, thereafter spreading both upstream and downstream. Detailed sampling in Austria and across eastern Europe by Machino & Füreder (2005) documented its current extent and showed that it is always accompanied by other Danubian faunal elements.

Survey methods followed three phases. First, the biogeographical literature on Danubian fauna, particularly fish and crayfish, was analysed to suggest potential occurrences of stone crayfish, then detailed topographical maps were studied to indicate the most likely regions. Here, key sites were targeted using topographical and ecological information. Finally, a daytime site visit looked for the likeliest spots, which were then surveyed by hand-searches, night-searches and traps set overnight.

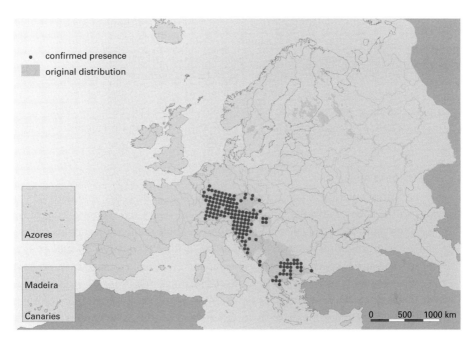

Figure 7.5.   Map showing the European distribution of *Austropotamobius torrentium* (from Souty-Grosset *et al.*, 2006). See also colour plate section.

The findings showed stone crayfish to be predominantly denizens of gravelly or stony streams in the Danube Basin. These streams were less than 15 m wide, not too cool, and with a stable slow flow, although stone crayfish also occurred in some lakes. Unlike *A. pallipes*, this species appears intolerant of mud and also of water pollution from houses or agriculture.

Stone crayfish were also found outside the Danube system. For instance, in the Czech Republic the species was found only in the Elbe catchment, where it is possibly an introduction (Kozák *et al.*, 2002), while in Germany it was found in a tributary of the Elbe, as well as in the Middle and Upper Rhine. Stone crayfish were recently discovered in the eastern Struma and Mesta rivers of Greece, while in Turkey they were found in the Velika drainage (Souty-Grosset *et al.*, 2006; Holdich *et al.*, 2009b).

In Hungary a survey of decapod (crab and crayfish) distribution was carried out initially through literature searches from 1909 to 2004 and interviews with field workers (Puky *et al.*, 2005). Field data were obtained by hand-searching by day and/or night, by trapping, and from results from electro-fishing during fish surveys. Data from drained fish ponds and other signs (dead crayfish along banks) were also used. The most widespread native species was *Astacus astacus*, followed by *A. leptodactylus* and *Austropotamobius torrentium*, the last in two separate Danube locations. Alien species were fairly restricted, including *Orconectes limosus* in the mainstem Danube and *Pacifastacus leniusculus* in the Raba.

A detailed survey of the crayfish of the low-lying Po catchment in north-eastern Italy was carried out by Nardi *et al.* (2005). All tributary streams and canals were investigated by hand, dip-net or trap. This area is primarily agricultural, with a mixed land use comprising grasslands, woodlands, orchards, vineyards and arable land. Of 409 sites investigated, just 13% had crayfish, all indigenous *A. pallipes*, and no NICS were found. However, only one of 18 former sightings was confirmed, indicating a substantial contraction. Where they occurred, summer temperatures were up to 21°–25°C, hardness was very high (127–545 mg/L $CaCO_3$) and there was often an oxygen deficit. The main requirement was for permanent water, and preferably no human habitation nearby.

North America

North America is the largest centre of crayfish diversity, and here cambarid crayfish have been exploited commercially in lakes, rivers and swamps, as have river stocks of astacids. Not all species are equally susceptible to the main capture methods. Different monitoring programmes have developed for *Pacifastacus* species in the north-west, *Orconectes* species in the north-east, and *Procambarus* species in the south-east.

Populations of signal crayfish (*Pacifastacus leniusculus*) in a woodland headwater stream in Oregon were investigated over two years in a landmark study by Mason (1975), using minnow traps for adults and benthos samplers or fine-mesh seines for juveniles in three age classes, sampled in shallow riffles, glides and small pools. Interestingly, females of at least five age classes dominated summer trap catches, giving way to male dominance at and after breeding. The study provided insights into the production of the stream population, and its important community function in conditioning the allochthonous detrital component, the chief basis of crayfish diet. At the southern end of their distribution, signals have been translocated into the warm waters of the Sacramento–San Joaquin delta, where population surveys using traps followed seasonal growth, maturity and fecundity (McGriff, 1983), important in demonstrating how environmental differences explain enhanced growth and productivity.

Signal stocks have been commercially fished in backwaters of the Columbia River basin in Oregon and Washington since the late 1800s (Miller & Van Hyning, 1970), using baited traps deployed from small boats. However, the basis for regulating the early fishery appears not to have been by monitoring commercial catches, but rather the application of empirical ideas from hunting, with closed seasons and restricted areas, imposed as far back as 1897 and modified over the years. Despite such closely policed regulatory controls, the fishery showed marked fluctuations, falling to less than 5 t in 1906, then peaking again in 1930 at around 88 t before falling back again in the mid-1950s. Fishermen were poorly rewarded, so that most viewed the *Pacifastacus* fishery as supplementary income until renewed interest in 1969 led to a rejuvenated, but short-lived, fishery to supply signal crayfish to Sweden. However, this collapsed in 1972. Although the fishery was regulated, it seems that, without scientific monitoring, not enough was known about the stocks to ensure or predict levels for a dependable supply, and with a low domestic demand, the fishery was likely to remain small.

There are numerous studies describing the results of surveys of stream-dwelling cambarids in North America. For other crayfish, a recent survey of *Procambarus* and *Fallicambarus* species in streams evaluated the relative success of four semi-quantitative crayfish monitoring techniques in South Carolina waters, and found electro-fishing to yield the most crayfish, followed by seines, baited minnow traps and dip-nets, although sex, size range and species obtained varied with method (Price & Welch, 2009). *Orconectes* and *Cambarus* species in ponds and streams of eastern North America have been monitored in several studies relating to their population structure and productivity, sometimes with a view to exploitation. These are well exemplified by a series of recent papers covering crayfish distribution and life histories in a special issue of the *Southeastern Naturalist* in 2010 (Volume 9). Many studies have looked at habitat selection by sympatric species, since habitats determine the availability of food and shelter. However, surveys by Stewart *et al.* (2010) failed to find any micro-habitat partitioning among crayfish assemblages in streams of south-eastern Alabama. The stream runs were dominated by *Procambarus suttkusi*, *P. versutus* and *Cambarus graysoni*, all occurring on sand and among woody debris. However, no species showed a microhabitat preference, perhaps due to the limited habitat available in these streams and their lack of variety in cover and substrates.

Australasia and Japan

Across the region, crayfish are monitored to various intensities, to support their conservation or underpin their exploitation. In Japan, the declining indigenous Nippon zarigani *Cambaroides japonicus* has been the subject of some study, but there is more interest in the introduced signal crayfish, and monitoring of the native species lags behind other scientific study (Hiruta, 1999). In Australia, the largest parastacid species, such as *Astacopsis gouldi* of forested streams, are now monitored in order to provide a baseline for conservation. The profitable recreational river fisheries for marron, *Cherax cainii*, in western Australia are also regularly surveyed, while in New Zealand the slower-growing koura (*Paranephrops* spp.) are also monitored: partly for conservation, partly to underpin farming of these cool-water, slow-growing species.

Astacopsis gouldi, the endemic Tasmanian giant freshwater crayfish, is a slow-growing and long-lived freshwater crustacean. Its fishery is now controlled and stocks are monitored as part of a recovery plan; PIT tags allow long-term identification of individuals. The biology of *A. gouldi* has been documented by Hamr (1997), chiefly from monitoring studies carried out in the Inglis River, using a variety of methods including drop-nets, baited tangle-nets and baited lines, as well as hand-search while snorkelling. Two major threats to the species are cumulative effects of past and current (illegal) fishing pressure, and large-scale habitat disturbance for agricultural, urban and forestry land use. These threats have reduced the species' abundance and the viability of some populations. Continued monitoring of this long-lived iconic species is essential if its stocks are to survive.

Marron (*Cherax cainii/C. tenuimanus*) are large *K*-selected species with a limited natural range in perennial rivers of Western Australia, particularly the hairy marron *C. tenuimanus*, which is restricted to the Margaret River. Marron breed in the spring of years 2 or 3 (Morrissy, 2002) and studies show that juvenile survival and growth is related to weed cover and density. Recreational marron fishing has been very popular in the rivers of Western Australia and so these large crayfish have been protected in the south-western rivers since 1955 under state legislation; with a lower size limit, a short open season, gear controls and a daily bag limit. However, these regulations are primarily based on catch controls and inspection feedback, rather than population monitoring. The Western Australia Department of Conservation and Land Management and Department of Fisheries are now working together with the public to develop and implement a Recovery Plan for the hairy marron.

Madagascar

Most of the seven species of freshwater crayfish currently recognized in Madagascar, belonging to the endemic parastacid genus *Astacoides*, are practically unstudied (Jones *et al.*, 2005) and monitoring is not yet widespread (Jones *et al.*, 2006). In 2004, *Astacoides crosnieri* and *A. petiti* were categorized by IUCN as 'Endangered' and *A. betsileoensis*, *A. caldwelli*, *A. granulimanus* and *A. madagascariensis* as 'Data Deficient' (IUCN, 2004). Crandall (2003) recommended that all described species should be listed as 'Threatened' under the IUCN Red List criteria; however, the 2010 status recommended for all is 'Data Deficient'.

Malagasy crayfish are important to local people for both subsistence and small-scale trade. Many rural people rely, at least partly, on harvesting forest products including freshwater crayfish (Shyamsundar & Kramer, 1997; Kremen *et al.*, 1998; Ferraro, 2002). State regulations say that only crayfish larger than 100 mm total length should be harvested, but this regulation is widely ignored, and in any case it takes no notice of the different sizes attained by each species. Regulations are not widely enforced and monitoring is rare; there is concern that some populations, and even species, are threatened by overexploitation. Jones *et al.* (2005) suggested that commercial exploitation of the most common species, *A. granulimanus* could be sustainable. To investigate this, Jones *et al.* (2006) monitored the crayfish harvest of four species in and around a national park in eastern Madagascar, and discussed the potential of community-based conservation, through forest management by local people, in promoting improved management practices.

The natural vegetation of the national park was humid evergreen forest at between 500 and 1500 m altitude, intersected by numerous streams and rivers. The crayfish harvest from streams was dominated by hand-caught *Astacoides granulimanus*, with smaller numbers of *A. betsileoensis* and *A. caldwelli* from larger rivers (Jones *et al.*, 2005, 2006). Almost 80% of stream-caught *A. granulimanus* offered for sale were under the legal size limit. *A. betsileoensis* live in deep rivers and are sometimes caught in eel traps or fished from the bank with baited sticks; this method appears to be more selective for large size than entering the river to turn rocks but, even so, 32% were below the legal size. However, no species is comprehensively monitored, and no single monitoring method would suffice for all species. Among problems affecting conservation, the crayfish reproductive period (July–December) overlaps with a season of food scarcity, so all crayfish harvesters will collect crayfish that are bearing eggs (Jones *et al.*, 2006).

The findings indicate that existing regulations are not adequate for a mixed-species harvest, and development of a range of monitoring methods is urgently required

(Hockley *et al.*, 2005). Jones *et al.* (2006) suggest that a number of management tools to protect crayfish stocks from overexploitation could be introduced and enforced at the local level. The simplest way to protect broodstock is for communities to ban the harvest of all female crayfish with eggs or young, or of all females during the breeding period. Setting minimum size limits would ensure that females have spawned at least once before they are harvested. However, *Astacoides* species become reproductive at different sizes (Jones, 2004), so appropriate size limits need to be determined for each species. In addition, the species inhabit different biotopes (rivers, streams and swamps), requiring different capture methodologies. Fishing methods may also need regulation, and destructive methods, such as digging out crayfish, should be banned. Only a few species may supply the resource needs of communities, and thus people may have little incentive to conserve the full range of biodiversity (Adams & Hulme, 2001). Rarer crayfish species may require additional protection or monitoring.

Scientific monitoring of these endemic Malagasy crayfish is particularly needed at present, in order to establish whether changes in tenure are resulting in positive or negative outcomes in terms of the resource. Monitoring with sufficient power to detect declines is costly in terms of effort (Sheil, 2001), but simple monitoring of the number, species, size and breeding status of individuals caught per day at a given site could give useful information.

7.3.2   Monitoring crayfish stocks in large rivers, lakes and ponds

Most commercially harvested crayfish stocks occur in large waterbodies, and the main catch methods used for such stocks, appropriate to the size and depth of such habitats, are traps and lures (Reynolds *et al.*, 2009; see also Chapter 5). These are also the monitoring methods of choice, although it is sometimes done by hand-collecting by divers. Traps are the standard method of much crayfish monitoring in Scandinavia (e.g. Skurdal & Taugbøl, 1994). Disadvantages are that smaller crayfish can escape from traps, especially if they have not been modified to prevent this; also trapping is time- and effort-consuming and the operators must return a second time to the lake to retrieve the traps, which could be interfered with in remote areas. Other traps used are the unbaited fyke-nets designed and used to catch eels, which may also yield many crayfish, usually as a by-catch.

Results differ with the method and with conditions, as described above. A good method will provide a reasonable catch per unit effort (CPUE) and will also show an explainable variability in CPUE between waterbodies. Summary statistics for catches (e.g. of lengths or weights) will also vary between methods. In a survey of white-clawed crayfish (O'Connor *et al.*, 2009), hand-searching caught a wide range of sizes except for the smallest juveniles, traps caught only mature and maturing adults and more large males than other categories; while sweep-nets yielded predominantly juveniles.

Europe

Noble crayfish *Astacus astacus* are a well-monitored harvestable resource in Scandinavian countries. A commercial/recreational fishery for noble crayfish has existed in Scandinavia since the nineteenth century. Most are fished by sport trapping, and stocks of this high-value product are well monitored and managed.

Finland provides a good example of exploitation of a valued crayfish resource, currently utilizing both signal and noble crayfish. By 1900, the peak year for crayfish production, yielding over 20 million crayfish (Westman, 1992), the crayfish industry supported thousands of professional fishermen catching chiefly for export. Today these have been largely supplanted by 100 000 recreational fishermen, most of whom use traps. Most crayfish waters are privately owned, and under the Fisheries Acts the owners are obliged to safeguard and improve crayfish stocks by various means, usually monitoring-based using traps.

Noble crayfish were introduced in the 1850s to Lake Steinsfjorden, a stony Norwegian lake of 14 km² and about 10 m mean depth, and the ensuing stocks have been exploited intensively by trapping since 1900. The lake now produces several tonnes of crayfish each year; some 25% of all Norway crayfish catches (Skurdal *et al.*, 2002). Stocks, and the lake habitat, varied over the years, and harvest regulations were adjusted to accommodate these changes. Monitoring involves catch surveys using commercial traps pre- and post-season. At first these differed greatly in the proportions of legal-sized to undersized crayfish, but latterly this has stabilized, with about 20% of the catch of legal size, suggesting that the management regime was maintaining a stable population. The legal minimum size was held at 95 mm total length, to ensure that females can breed at least once before capture. However, the main problem is policing the minimum size restrictions.

Although white-clawed crayfish *Austropotamobius pallipes* are usually associated with streams (see above), there are substantial lake populations in some countries, particularly Ireland, where a monitoring protocol has recently been developed for lake stocks. This uses selective manual survey methods (adapted for monitoring streams) in stony shallows (see hand-search), with traps resorted to where conditions are unsuited to manual survey (O'Connor *et al.*, 2009).

Table 7.2 shows recent comparative data for monitoring methods for white-clawed crayfish stocks in Irish lakes.

North America

Momot and co-workers have monitored cool-water *Orconectes* spp. stocks in Canadian and northern US lakes and rivers independently of the development of a small-scale exploitative fishery. In a study of the range extension of *O. rusticus* into rivers and lakes around Lake Superior, Momot (1997) deployed baited minnow traps at ten locations, documenting its spread (slowed by beaver dams and halted by impoundments) and found that this invasive species has eliminated *O. virilis* populations at a number of sites. Catch rate ranged from <1 to 18 rusty crayfish per trap-day, which is higher than that of native orconectids.

Many authors have shown that the life history of signal crayfish varies with habitat (e.g. Westman *et al.*, 1993), so management needs to be population-specific, linked to each area exploited. The inundation of part of the Deschutes River in Oregon to form Lake Billy Chinook provided an opportunity to examine the developing lacustrine signal crayfish populations. Lewis & Horton (1997) used baited minnow traps to survey these,

Table 7.2. Catch per unit effort (CPUE) for white-clawed crayfish surveyed by different quantitative methods in Irish lakes in 2007 (after O'Connor *et al.*, 2009).

Lake	Month	Hand-searching	Sweep-netting	Trapping	Night-search
Labe	August	0.21			
Labe	September	0.39	0.05	0.8	
Gowna	August	0.03	0		
Gowna	October	0.25	0	0.05	
Kilrooskey	August	0.04	0		
Kilrooskey	October	0.07	1.75	1.95	1.2
Nageage	October	0.05	0	0.05	
Talt	August	0.47	2.15		
Owel	June	0.50	0.15		

Calculation of CPUE: hand-searching – number of crayfish/refuge; sweep-netting – number of crayfish per standard sweep; trapping – number of crayfish/trap; night-searching – number of crayfish per 3 metres of shoreline.

in order to establish management practices. Crayfish started to mature and be trappable at around 26 mm CL, with high catches of up to 50 crayfish per trap. Continued careful monitoring should allow management of this stock to produce a sustainable fishery.

For many years, Huner and extension service co-workers at Louisiana State University have been monitoring the stocks and extensive harvests of red swamp crayfish *Procambarus clarkii* in swampy bottomlands of the Louisiana rivers, now increasingly converted to rice fields, and in other ponds developed in the area for the same purpose (e.g. Huner, 1997). The life history of this species is now very well understood, and major fluctuations in harvests are often cost-led and predictable.

The same species is now among the most widespread of NICS in Europe, causing nuisance problems in rivers and rice fields and showing a remarkable ability to adapt to conditions outside those in its native range (Holdich *et al.*, 2009b). In southern Europe, where populations of red swamp crayfish have become established, there are now important commercial harvests, but monitoring is not always carried out at the same level at all sites, or with similar aims. Ilhéu & Bernardo (1997) studied population structure and recruitment in a small semi-permanent reservoir in southern Portugal using a variety of methods: electro-fishing for adults, hand-netting for juveniles, and digging out burrows in dry periods. As in Louisiana, hydrological events such as the timing and degree of winter flooding determined the success of the subsequent year-class.

Australasia

An indigenous capture method has been adapted for monitoring parastacid crayfish in New Zealand lakes. Kusabs & Quinn (2009) describe the use of a traditional Maori sampling method for the northern koura *Paranephrops planifrons* to assess population abundance and structure in Lake Rotoiti (mean depth 32 m), North Island, New Zealand. The *tau koura* is a traditional Maori method used to catch koura in central North Island lakes by placing *whakaweku* (bundles of the bracken fern *Pteridium esculentum*) on the lake bed, which the crayfish then colonize. These authors demonstrated its use to monitor koura populations and to discern seasonal breeding patterns. It has some advantages as a monitoring tool over conventional methods, such as baited traps and diving surveys, as it samples all koura size classes, can be used in turbid waters and at a wide range of depths, and does not require expensive equipment or specialized expertise (e.g. the use of SCUBA diving).

7.3.3 Monitoring quasi-terrestrial crayfish stocks in wetlands, swamps, seasonally saturated ground and in caves

Stocks in these heterogeneous and traditionally understudied habitats are chiefly monitored as a background to their exploitation; for example, *Procambarus* in Louisiana wetlands and in French and Spanish delta marshes, where the harvesting method, almost always trapping, is used for monitoring, or because their abundance may reach pest levels from the viewpoint of other users of such wetlands. Huner (1997) used commercial pyramid traps to document the effect of early flooding date on increased production of red swamp crayfish in experimental temporary ponds in Louisiana, and found higher yields when ponds were planted in the dry phase with rice or soybean.

In their native ranges, *Procambarus clarkii* and *P. zonangulus* often occur together in temporary ponds and ditches, where seasonal dewatering promotes vegetation growth, reduces aquatic predators, and limits anoxia in sediments. Standard mark–recapture methods are impractical for use in commercial ponds. Juveniles may be monitored using hand-held nets and small-mesh traps (Huner & Barr, 1991) and/or seines with weighted bottom ropes for use in dense vegetation (Momot & Romaire, 1982). However, juvenile monitoring provides information on relative abundance only, and predictions of potential crop yields are not very accurate, although Romaire (1990) has developed computer simulation models for *Procambarus clarkii* culture ponds in Louisiana. Cannibalism among cohorts of the two species may have a major but unpredictable outcome, and there are also a myriad of aquatic and semi-aquatic predators; finally, physical and chemical conditions in the drying pond can be inimical.

Crayfish in Louisiana are almost exclusively harvested with baited traps (Huner & Barr, 1991; Romaire, 1995); these can also be used to catch smaller crayfish for relaying (to improve densities) and other forms of stock manipulation. The traditional cylindrical pillow traps or pyramid traps with three openings (see Figures 5.1 and 5.4) are placed vertically at trap densities generally of 25–35 ha^{-1}, fixed with rods into the substrate and protruding above the surface. The top of the trap is open to remove crayfish or add bait. Other methods that have been used are seines and trawls, but seines are generally ineffective in dense vegetation in these shallow ponds. Several types of bow-mounted trawl have been used, with varying success, such as in combination with a direct current (DC) electro-fishing device, chiefly used to harvest high-value, soft-shell crayfish (Huner, 2002).

Procambarus clarkii has been widely introduced outside its native range, and its ecological plasticity has been demonstrated in response to hydrological and climatic factors. For instance, Sommer (1984) has studied its biological response to transplantation into Californian rice fields, where such factors have led to strong variation in reproductive cycles. In French and Spanish delta marshes, invasive *Procambarus clarkii* are increasingly trapped and harvested as a cash crop, and are monitored to varying degrees (e.g. Bravo *et al.*, 1994, studying the Doñana marshes). In Spain, unbaited cylindrical eel traps have been set in irrigation channels and canals as ponds are drained (Habsburgo-Lorena, 1983). A similar 'flow box' harvest system is used for redclaw in northern Australia (Lawrence & Jones, 2002).

Burrowing, semi-terrestrial crayfish in Australia and the Americas require different sampling methods, including tangle-traps or mist-nets as used by Welch & Eversole (2006) and Ridge *et al.* (2008), and specialized traps that fit over burrow openings (Norrocky, 1984). Determining absolute numbers is difficult, environmentally damaging, and labour-intensive, as most studies of 'land crayfish' involve digging up burrows to obtain information on numbers, sizes and reproductive status (e.g. Hamr & Richardson, 1994). However, to monitor changes in activity or relative abundance over time, a good approach is setting up permanent plots and counting the number of burrow entrances, as is done in Tasmanian sedgelands. This is less reliable where the substrate is unstable and the animals are constantly re-excavating; for example in mobile sediment beside streams (Alastair Richardson, personal communication, 2010).

A recent ecological study of upland burrowing crayfish *Cambarus dubius* was conducted in a wooded swampland at 781 m elevation (Loughman, 2010), to provide monitoring data relevant for population management and conservation. Size at maturity did not differ significantly for males and females, and form change occurred synchronously within the population – a phenomenon not previously documented in primary burrowing Cambaridae. The central importance of this burrowing species in the swamp community was shown in that many commensal species, both invertebrate and vertebrate, used *C. dubius* burrows.

Cave populations of crayfish are best known and studied in North America. Obligate troglobites occur only among the Cambaridae of North America (Hobbs, 1988) and may be diverse (e.g. 13 cave-dwelling crayfish of 62 known species in Florida, and 6 species in Indiana). Both pigmented (e.g. *Cambarus laevis*) and unpigmented forms (e.g. *Orconectes inermis*) are known. However, cave populations are usually small, cave habitats are variable, and survey methods have not been standardized.

Astacid crayfish have seldom been recorded from hypogean habitats, apart from a few populations in some Mediterranean karstic systems. Bott (1972) found troglophilic specimens of *Austropotamobius torrentium* in the Tkalca Jama cave in Slovenia, and both *A. torrentium* and *A. pallipes* have been recorded from other caves there (e.g. Stammer, 1932), while in Romania, a number of *Astacus astacus* were caught in the Paros cave, down to a depth of 300 m (Chappuis, 1927). Crayfish were surveyed in a karstic tunnel in northern Greece by Koutrakis *et al.* (2005). The Aggitis cave is at least 9 km long, divided into sections by narrow siphons. Between the siphons are wide-bore tunnels partly filled with sediments. Epigean crayfish have been found at the cave entrance and in the outflowing river. In the first two kilometres of tunnel, crayfish were surveyed using two traps baited with fish, placed 1150 and 2100 m from the entry, also by electro-fishing and a bag seine. In a second survey, divers penetrated down to 7800 m from the entrance, where some 20 crayfish were seen and caught using a small dip-net. All were pigmented, but distinguishable from surface forms by their bluish pereiopods. It is unlikely that they entered the cave recently from upstream because of a sediment block, but 50 years earlier the cave was not blocked by sediments and crayfish could enter.

7.4   Monitoring habitats and biological water quality

In addition to surveying and monitoring crayfish stocks, parallel monitoring of their habitat is usually carried out. Adults and juveniles usually depend on different habitats. High water speeds may limit the diversity of lotic crayfish, while levels of dissolved oxygen and pH may be critical for crayfish survival, particularly in warmer waters. In warm-water wetlands, conditions can deteriorate fast, and periodic water quality monitoring, particularly temperature, dissolved oxygen, hydrogen sulphide and dissolved iron, as well as pesticide levels, is essential where crayfish are at risk or are economically important.

Habitat management and restoration are important aspects of any crayfish conservation programme. Crayfish species are often considered as bioindicators of a particular water quality or habitat type (e.g. rocky stream, vegetated lake or warm wetland), but they will on occasion be found elsewhere (for example, the normally epigean crayfish found in karstic cave systems, described above). As part of the conservation efforts to maintain *Astacopsis gouldi* in Tasmania, a predictive geographical information system (GIS) habitat model is used in planning and regulating forestry activities (Davies *et al.*, 2005, 2007). Where high-quality habitat is predicted, a 30-m buffer strip is protected alongside streams, whether or not the species has been detected.

Peay (2003a) described the potential impacts of various physical works such as bank reconstruction, and listed mitigation measures designed to create or improve provision of refuges. Habitat alteration may include impoundment, bank grading, canalization, drainage or infrastructural projects (see Chapter 2). The bank is known to be particularly important; Naura & Robinson (1998) showed that riparian tree roots act as essential refuges for juvenile crayfish, while the trees themselves provide shade and also nutrients through insects and leaf-fall.

Biological water quality is usually monitored through the periodic collection of organisms from representative habitats and assigning a quality score based on the proportions of organism types present, often including crayfish. Indigenous European freshwater crayfish and many cool-water cambarids have often been considered as bioindicators of good water quality. Deteriorating water quality may have little impact at first, as crayfish adopt behavioural reactions to decreases in dissolved oxygen associated with eutrophication. When other conditions are not limiting, recent studies have shown that some crayfish species may form long-persisting, dense populations in water of only moderate quality (Demers *et al.*, 2003; Füreder & Reynolds, 2003), but rarely below this level (see Chapter 3). On the other hand, they also need a heterogeneous habitat where the different requirements for shelter and food of the different life stages can be accommodated, so abundance may be proportional to the number and types of available refuges (Lodge & Hill, 1994). Muddy stretches of waterways may hold surprising numbers of crayfish (Holdich *et al.*, 2006; Peay *et al.*, 2006b), with the juveniles presumably living among tree roots along the bank.

Known crayfish population declines and extinctions have been variously linked to disease, instream pollution, bank or bed alteration, or overfishing. Studies show that major physical or chemical changes in watercourses may be associated with a decline or loss of crayfish. For example, Lyons & Kelly-Quinn (2003) documented declines in stream crayfish populations in parallel with decreasing chemical quality. Indeed, Scalici & Gibertini (2005) addressed the possibility of using one subspecies of white-clawed crayfish, *Austropotamobius italicus meridionalis*, as a monitoring instrument and possible bioindicator in central Italy. The most natural watercourses (Class I) had most crayfish, and the best age- and sex-structured populations. Class II had few specimens, while none were found in most altered streams.

7.5   Importance of monitoring for management

As crayfish come under increasing pressure, scientific monitoring of populations becomes essential. The choice of crayfish survey and capture methods depends on many factors: these include the size and accessibility of stocks and ease of capture, whether stocks are in streams, rivers or lakes, and details of the habitat (e.g. permanent or temporary; muddy, weedy or stony; water clear or turbid); also whether the methodology is to be used to sample or to deplete the population, or to catch and mark for release and subsequent recapture. With all methods, the habitat preferences of juveniles and adults affect the catch success (e.g. Richards *et al.*, 1996; Price & Welch, 2009). Surrogate records have most value if they are added to a crayfish database locally and nationally, and are used to inform decisions about future surveys for crayfish

Different methods have different levels of impact on their target stocks and habitats. Traps and lift-nets used for deep-water capture are essentially passive methods and, as such, are less damaging to the environment than actively netting or disturbing the substrate. Studies by divers using SCUBA or snorkelling have a generally lower impact than those involving wading. Camera traps and surrogate monitoring cause least disturbance.

Traps continue to be very widely used, but results may not be predictable. Dorn *et al.* (2005) evaluated the sampling efficacy of an active throw-trap against that of baited passive traps across an experimental density gradient of crayfish (*Procambarus fallax*). The throw-trap catch estimates correlated well with crayfish density and size distribution, whereas minnow traps caught relatively fewer as density increased, and chiefly larger males. Among passive fishing methods, Policar & Kozák (2005) found baited sticks to attract a wider range of crayfish sizes and reproductive stages, both male and female, than were retained in traps. Thus, traps might serve a capture fishery well, while not necessarily providing good population information.

We have seen that surveys can be biased by a number of other factors. Trap mesh size and funnel dimensions both select for crayfish size, which relates principally to size at maturity and would affect the number of each species caught. Periodicity of trapping and of lift-net examination also affects the number caught. Lift-nets are best examined every 20–30 minutes if crayfish are active. Trap catches are highest if set over one night and lifted the following morning. Bait type for traps and lift-nets may provide different levels of attractiveness, and may even repel if stale; in some circumstances traps provide a refuge whether or not they are baited. Weather, water levels and water conditions may all affect catches. Crayfish may not venture far from their refuges in poor weather conditions. Lake catches of many crayfish are highest if there is a full moon and clear skies (Reynolds & Matthews, 1993). Crayfish are most active and trappable in the warmer months, after their moult period.

Population parameters, such as age, sex ratios and maturity status, may be different in traps than in the general population. Because females are less predictably active than males and the sex ratio is usually equal, Nowicki *et al.* (2008) recommend monitoring only male numbers to estimate population sizes.

In conclusion, monitoring of crayfish stocks is a necessity because of the socio-economic implications of native crayfish decline or spread. Monitoring makes sense for economic stocks, where it provides information on the performance of catch regulations. Periodic monitoring is also needed for keystone species or for rarer species in need of conservation. It is also imperative to monitor and check crayfish habitats and water quality, and to restore them if necessary. Finally, the ecological and economic damage done by non-indigenous crayfish species requires regular monitoring of their status and, in particular, their degree of carrying and disseminating crayfish plague to indigenous crayfish stocks. This scenario is developed further in the next chapter.

Part II

Applying science to conservation management

B   Management for conservation

8 Control and management of non-indigenous crayfish

(with Francesca Gherardi)

8.1 Background

Species that have been introduced outside their native range (alien or non-indigenous species) have the potential to cause irreparable ecological and economic damage. Although the proportion of introduced species that become invasive is usually relatively small (just 1% of those released and about 10% of survivors of translocation; according to the 'ten percent rule' for non-native species released into new ecosystems (Williamson & Fitter, 1996)), the significant risks that these few organisms pose require the adoption of precautionary approaches to prevent the deliberate or accidental introduction of potential invaders and to design contingency plans detailing the actions needed to rapidly mitigate and remediate their impacts (Manchester & Bullock, 2000). We will see that crayfish do not follow the 10% rule for invasive species, as a much larger percentage of crayfish introductions seem to thrive.

Hundreds of freshwater species have been moved outside their native ranges by vectors such as ballast water, canals, deliberate introductions, and releases from aquaria, garden ponds and bait buckets. Some invaders have had profound effects on the ecosystems that they invade. Classes of ecologically important invaders in fresh waters include molluscs that are primary consumers and disrupt the food web from its base, fishes that disrupt the food web from its apex or centre, decapods that act as powerful omnivores, aquatic plants that have strong engineering effects and affect the quality and quantity of primary production, and diseases, which have probably been underestimated as an ecological force (Strayer, 2010). Interactions between alien species and other contemporary stressors of freshwater ecosystems are important and varied. Because disturbance is generally thought to favour invasive species, stressed ecosystems may be especially susceptible to invasions, as are highly artificial ecosystems. In turn, alien species can strongly alter the hydrology, biogeochemical cycling and biotic composition of the invaded ecosystems, and thus modulate the effects of other stressors.

The implementation of mitigation and remediation measures to deal with invasive alien species was viewed as a priority by the United Nations Convention on Biological Diversity (CBD) at the 1992 Earth Summit in Rio de Janeiro. Signatories to the CBD called on governments 'as far as possible and as appropriate, (to) prevent the introduction of, control or eradicate those alien species which threaten ecosystems, habitats or species' (Article 8(h)). In 2002, the CBD Conference of the Parties adopted the Decision

VI/23 on *Alien species that threaten ecosystems, habitats and species* (COP-VI, The Hague, April 2002), which emphasized the urgency of prioritizing the development of strategies and contingency plans against invasive species at national and regional levels. At the same time, the CBD Conference formulated Guiding Principles for the *Prevention, introduction and mitigation of impacts of alien species that threaten ecosystems, habitats or species* to be promoted and implemented by governments and organizations.

This latter document set out a hierarchy of actions composed of

(1) the prevention of introductions of invasive alien species between and within states;
(2) early detection and rapid response if an invasive alien species has been introduced;
(3) containment and long-term control measures, where eradication is not feasible or resources are not available.

The recent *European Strategy on Alien Species* (Genovesi & Shine, 2003) has developed the above-listed actions and has also included

(4) raising awareness and disseminating information on invasive species and on ways to tackle them;
(5) strengthening national and regional capacity and cooperation to deal with invasive alien species issues;
(6) recovering species and restoring natural habitats and ecosystems that have been adversely affected by biological invasions.

We have seen that a high proportion of introduced non-indigenous crayfish species (NICS) may become established. Given that the impacts resulting from the introduction of NICS are generally severe, can occur across many levels of ecological organization, and result in the loss of native crayfish populations (see Chapter 4), the CBD approach, as complemented by the European Strategy, is usually promoted as a priority to prevent the introductions of NICS and to alleviate or eliminate the damages they inflict (Holdich *et al.*, 1999). However, attempts to manage invading populations often fall short of achieving their objective; none of the attempts made to contain the spread of NICS in the last decade have provided a definitive methodology or have achieved eradication (e.g. Blake & Hart, 1995; Frutiger *et al.*, 1999; Stebbing *et al.*, 2003; Peay *et al.*, 2006a).

This chapter presents a summary of the different methods used to control or eradicate invasive alien crayfish, along with a discussion of their pitfalls and potentialities, together with a brief glance at ongoing research in this field. Finally, we examine crayfish plague in some detail. The plague pathogen, the oomycete *Aphanomyces astaci*, is carried by resistant crayfish (apparently all North American in origin) and has had heavy impacts on susceptible crayfish in all other parts of the world. Its potential for controlling invasive alien crayfish is therefore somewhat limited, as most NICS are North American in origin. However, even if the invasive crayfish are controlled by other means, the plague pathogen may still induce pathology in indigenous crayfish populations and eradicate them.

8.1.1   An overview of invasive crayfish worldwide

As with other invasive species, it is far more cost-effective to prevent the introduction of NICS, and environmentally more desirable, than to take reactive measures after their introduction and establishment. NICS can be hard to detect and may disperse rapidly, making their eradication or control extremely difficult and expensive. Much effort should, therefore, be directed to minimize the risk of intentional introductions, and this is now being tackled by legislation in force in several countries (see also Chapter 10). For instance, in the UK, *Astacus astacus*, *A. leptodactylus* and *Pacifastacus leniusculus* have been designated as pests under the Wildlife and Countryside Act. In addition, much of Britain has been declared a no-go area for the keeping of *P. leniusculus* and the whole of Britain for the keeping of all other NICS (except the tropical *Cherax quadricarinatus*). Similarly, in Japan, all species of *Astacus* and *Cherax*, *Orconectes rusticus* and *P. leniusculus* have been designated as invasive alien species under the Invasive Alien Species Act and their import and keeping alive are banned except for scientific purposes. In the EU, the Council Regulation No 708/07 'concerning use of alien and locally absent species in aquaculture' has been in force since 2007. Its novelty is to take a 'white list' approach, in that only the importation of species that have been appropriately screened after a thorough risk assessment analysis can be approved, which contrasts with the homologous regulation in the USA, which permits the importation of species unless these are on a 'black list' (Injurious Wildlife Species, US Fish & Wildlife Service) (Lodge *et al.*, 2000b). Recently, the Freshwater Invertebrate Invasiveness Scoring Kit (FI-ISK) has been proposed by Tricarico *et al.* (2010) as a screening tool for identifying potentially invasive freshwater invertebrates. Using receiver operating characteristic (ROC) curves, FI-ISK was shown to distinguish accurately and with statistical confidence between potentially invasive and non-invasive species of alien crayfish (Astacidae, Cambaridae, Parastacidae) (Figure 8.1). However, regulations seem not to be well harmonized with those concerning the aquarium trade. For instance, it is extremely easy to buy NICS for ornamental use, using e-commerce, as shown in the case of the marbled crayfish. To make prevention more difficult, there are many records of illegal release of NICS into the wild and of their accidental introduction as undetected contaminants in batches of regulated fish species (Gherardi, 2010). As a consequence, it is imperative that post-introduction mitigation and remediation protocols and processes, such as contingency plans, are always in place. These should enable rapid detection and response in order to minimize and, ideally, eliminate the threats posed by NICS.

Eradication consists of eliminating the entire invading population. It is considered the best and least expensive remediation tool, certainly in the long term. Yet eradication programmes are viewed with scepticism by many conservation biologists, particularly in Europe. In general, eradication is seen as an impossible goal (e.g. Bertolino & Genovesi, 2003) that might have the potential to incur 'horrendous non-target impacts' (Simberloff, 2002). In a review published in 2005, Genovesi reported only 37 successful eradication programmes against vertebrates in Europe, mostly on islands (33); while no eradication of invertebrates has ever been achieved, even if attempted. As

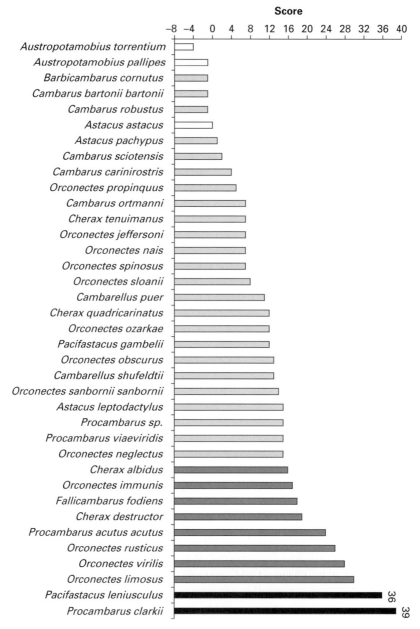

Figure 8.1.   FI-ISK (Freshwater Invertebrate Invasiveness Scoring Kit) model proposed by Tricarico *et al.* (2010) for identifying potentially invasive freshwater crayfish. The use of receiver operating characteristic (ROC) curves allows FI-ISK to distinguish accurately and with statistical confidence between potentially invasive and non-invasive species of alien crayfish (Astacidae, Cambaridae, Parastacidae). '*Procambarus* sp.' is now known to be *P. fallax f. virginalis*

recently stressed by Simberloff (2009), part of the pessimism about controlling invasions arises from widely publicized eradication failures, while successful eradications are rarely mentioned in the popular press or scientific literature. However, the number of invasions for which eradication is seriously attempted is negligible, and many of these have failed.

Such failures might be ascribed to the several requirements to be fulfilled in order to make eradication an effective remediation tool against invasive species, including invasive NICS.

1. Any method designed to eradicate invasive crayfish must be capable of removing enough individuals to ensure population extinction, and this must be demonstrable. A density threshold – the Allee threshold (Keitt *et al.*, 2001) – exists for all animal populations, below which the population will cease to be self-sustaining. Thus, any method considered as having potential for achieving eradication must reduce the population density to below such a threshold. If the number of individuals that survive the eradication attempt exceeds this, the population will maintain itself in the long term.

2. The best opportunities for eradicating an invasive species are in the early stages of invasion, in the lag phase before population increase and spread. Some NICS can remain relatively uncommon and seem harmless for long periods of time before suddenly becoming invasive, perhaps following a genetic change, local environmental change, or the arrival of another alien species which might favour its population expansion and spread. The early detection of new biological invasions is therefore crucial, and rapid response is required to eradicate or contain the new invader once it is detected. To achieve this, local knowledge should be used and immediate reporting to local biosafety authorities encouraged, so that managers detect invasions as early as possible. Rapid response teams of local experts could be formed in order to detect and evaluate new invaders at the earliest stage and to make recommendations for action. In these instances, delay and procrastination is likely to be disastrous.

3. Programmes against well-established invasive populations are only successful where the area of invasion is relatively small. Where large-scale eradication has been attempted against established invasive alien species, an extremely high failure-to-success ratio was recorded.

4. Another requirement is that the ecosystem concerned should be sufficiently isolated from potential sources of recolonization by the invader.

5. Before starting any eradication programme, managers should ensure that adequate funds and commitment exist to complete the eradication, that monitoring of the target species is feasible in order to ascertain a decrease in the population size, and that eradication will be followed by the restoration or management of the community or ecosystem after the removal of the target species.

There are a few cases in which the above-listed requirements can easily be met with invasive populations of NICS. One is the recently recorded population of *Cherax destructor* in Italy (Scalici *et al.*, 2009). Its confined distribution in abandoned aquaculture ponds, the low temperatures of the surrounding waters that act as a barrier against its natural spreading, and the absence of neighbouring populations all make eradication feasible and economic when compared with the enormous costs that this species might inflict if allowed to spread. For most of the already established populations of invasive NICS, on the other hand, the only option is to adopt some mitigation tools that might maintain their density at a low level and thus reduce their negative impact.

In every case, both eradication and maintenance management of NICS should be socially and ethically acceptable, efficient, non-polluting, and should not damage native flora or fauna, humans, domestic animals or crops. Although all of these criteria are difficult to address, genuine attempts should be made to do so.

The type of intervention should be chosen on a case-by-case basis. It is important to evaluate the situations for which a given intervention is biologically feasible, as well as acceptable with respect to ecological, economic, political and ethical viewpoints. Attempts to prevent the introduction of NICS and to mitigate their damage should be based on a thorough understanding of their threats by the general public, decision-makers and other stakeholders. However, as recently shown in southern Spain (García-Llorente *et al.*, 2008), most stakeholders have a limited knowledge of what invasive species are and demonstrate different perceptions of their impacts and different attitudes toward their management. Thus, education and public awareness campaigns seem to be an essential step in order to develop the shared responsibility needed to address any intervention against biological invaders, crayfish included – an area further developed in Chapter 10.

8.2   Methods for controlling non-indigenous invasive crayfish species

Several different methods have been used to eradicate, or at least mitigate, the negative impacts of invasive NICS. These can be classified into five broad categories: mechanical removal of a target invasive population from an area, physical methods, and reduction of the size of the target population by the use of biological control methods, biocides or autocidal methods.

8.2.1   Mechanical removal

Mechanical removal by the use of traps of various designs (e.g. Louisiana pyramid traps, Swedish Trappy traps, collapsible minnow traps, fyke-nets), by seine-nets (e.g. Westman *et al.*, 1979; Fjälling, 1995) or by electro-fishing (Westman *et al.*, 1978, Laurent, 1988) may have some effect on the size of invasive populations of NICS (see also Chapters 5 and 7). For example, catches of an invasive population of *Orconectes rusticus* in the USA declined from 6500 to 206 after 6 weeks of continuous trapping (Bills & Marking, 1988). However, while a decrease in the population size may be achieved in the short term, it does not necessarily lead to eradication. For reliable results, trapping should be conducted for an extended period of time. For instance, 900 trap nights were needed to reduce *Pacifastacus leniusculus* populations from 4000 to 1500 in carp ponds in England (Rogers & Holdich, 1997), yet – in the absence of continuous trapping after that period – populations returned to their former levels within a couple of breeding seasons (Holdich *et al.*, 1999).

Mechanical removal is often affected by crayfish size and sex, as shown by several studies. Traps are known to select for adult males, as in catches of *O. rusticus* in the USA (Bills & Marking, 1988) and *P. leniusculus* in the UK (Holdich *et al.*, 1995b) and in the Czech Republic (Kozák & Policar, 2003). While to some extent affected by mesh size, the size of captured crayfish seems to relate more to the avoidance behaviour by juveniles towards adults (Guan & Wiles, 1996). One consequence of the greater trappability of large males is the reduction of competitive interference by these over juveniles, allowing the latter to grow and to produce dense populations (Skurdal & Qvenild, 1986). Intensive trapping of *P. leniusculus* in one section of the River Thames in England depleted larger crayfish in the population and thus enhanced population expansion in adjacent areas by the younger size classes (Holdich *et al.*, 1999). Female crayfish, in particular ovigerous females, are less frequently trapped. However, removing some ovigerous females might lead to feedback mechanisms so that crayfish, as with most animals, would probably respond to low numbers in the population by producing more eggs and reaching maturity earlier (Holdich *et al.*, 1999).

8.2.2 Physical methods

Drainage of ponds, diversion of rivers and construction of barriers may be used in the case of confined populations of NICS, but very little is known about their efficacy. Drainage, for instance, is not effective with burrowing marshland species such as *Procambarus clarkii*, which can survive out of water for long periods. Even species such as *P. leniusculus*, which in their native range rarely burrow, can do so extensively in suitable substrates (Holdich *et al.*, 1999) and therefore survive drying. Rivers may be diverted via a channel or pipeline and the remaining water pumped out to isolate populations of NICS. The isolated stretch can then be thoroughly searched for crayfish, and burrows can be chemically treated or crayfish removed from their burrows by hand. In 2006, a barrier was erected in the River Buåa on the border between Sweden and Norway to prevent migration of *P. leniusculus* to the Norwegian part of the river. However, the barrier did not work as expected; during July 2008, signal crayfish were detected in the lower parts of the Halden transborder watercourse in the far south-east (Trond Taugbøl, personal communication, 2008).

Other physical methods may include electric fences, used to discourage migration of crayfish (Håstein & Gladhaug, 1973, 1974) and vibrations. Anecdotal evidence showed higher mortalities of crayfish possibly resulting from vibrations from aerators and pumps (Holdich *et al.*, 1999).

8.2.3 Biological control methods

Biological control, or biocontrol, is a term that includes a variety of interventions based on the use of natural enemies of the invader. It is, in theory, preferable to biocides or other chemical methods because it is permanent and non-polluting. Risks lie in that these enemies are not always specific to the target organism and may instead attack indigenous organisms. Control agents must therefore be thoroughly checked for specificity and for non-target effects before their release into the wild.

Traditional enemies of crayfish are predators such as birds and fish, disease-causing organisms, and microbes that produce toxins, e.g. the bacterium *Bacillus thuringiensis*. However, only predaceous fish are worth considering as control agents, as will be shown below, and only the oomycete *Aphanomyces astaci*, the etiological agent of the crayfish plague, is of any significance among disease-causing organisms (Holdich *et al.*, 1999). *A. astaci* has been used in Spain for biological control of the invasive species *Cherax destructor*, according to Diéguez-Uribeondo & Muzquiz (2005). In theory, *A. astaci* could be used to eliminate other invasive populations of NICS susceptible to it, such as *Astacus leptodactylus*, and genetically modified strains might overcome the defence system of North American crayfish. However, in both cases, there is the likely risk that the disease might spread to indigenous crayfish. Finally, the potential use of *B. thuringiensis* and its varieties such as subsp. *israeliensis*, which is already used to produce natural insecticides, is worthy of investigation.

Several studies have revealed that fish predation has an impact on crayfish populations. In Europe, eels, burbot, perch and pike are well-known predators of crayfish (Westman, 1991). Eels introduced into the Rumensee in Switzerland reduced an expanding *Procambarus clarkii* population to less than 10% within 3 years, whereas pike, introduced at the same time, had no obvious effect (Müller & Frutiger, 2001; Frutiger & Müller, 2002). In the Lower Guadalquivir Basin in Spain, before the introduction of *P. clarkii*, eels mostly preyed upon fish species such as mosquitofish and carp; whereas after crayfish introduction the dominant prey item was *P. clarkii*, occurring in up to 67% of eel stomachs (Montes *et al.*, 1993). However, a number of North American studies showed little correlation between the presence of fish such as largemouth bass and yellow perch, and crayfish abundance (e.g. Lodge & Hill, 1994), and others even suggested a positive effect on NICS densities when stocking with fish predators such as the brook trout in Canada (Gowing & Momot, 1979) or brown and rainbow trout, perch and carp in England (Holdich & Domaniewski, 1995). Predatory fish may also have subtle sublethal effects that, in the long term, may reduce crayfish growth, reproduction and survival (Holdich *et al.*, 1999).

Few experimental studies have been aimed at understanding, at least in the short term, the impact of fish predation on crayfish densities. Interactions between three carnivorous fish species – pike, perch and sander – and invasive populations of two NICS (*Pacifastacus leniusculus* and *Procambarus clarkii*) have been analysed in mesocosms, enclosures and small ponds in France (Neveu, 2001a). Pike appeared to be the most efficient predator of both crayfish species, independent of size, whereas perch and sander were found to prey on significantly smaller crayfish. In a mesocosm, pike more than 16 cm long ate crayfish all year round. The maximum size of the ingested crayfish was positively correlated with pike size; thus pike of 40–50 cm length swallowed adult crayfish over 8 cm in length. In enclosures and natural ponds, shelter seemed to be ineffective against pike, the few surviving crayfish showing reduced

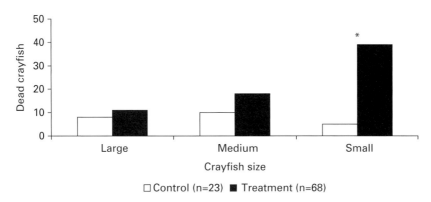

Figure 8.2. Eel predation and crayfish size: eel inclusion (treatment, black columns, *n* = 68)/exclusion (control, white columns, *n*=23) laboratory experiments used by Aquiloni *et al.* (2010) to investigate the impact of European eel on an invasive population of *Procambarus clarkii* in Italy: eels usually avoid larger crayfish, except when they are soft-shelled, and always attack the smaller ones from behind. Asterisk denotes significance at *P*>0.00l.

growth and delayed sexual maturity. Interestingly, when crayfish were isolated by nets, their growth was reduced by the mere sight of a perch.

In a similar experiment, interactions between 11 omnivorous resident fish species and two NICS (*Pacifastacus leniusculus* and *Astacus leptodactylus*) were studied within enclosures and in 100 m² ponds (Neveu, 2001b). Young carp and tench preyed on young-of-year crayfish, also inducing decreased growth in the survivors. However, roach, rudd, grass carp, crucian carp and mosquitofish had little or no effect on young-of-year crayfish in enclosures. Finally, white aspe seemed to disturb crayfish by their intense activity.

Inclusion/exclusion experiments were used by Aquiloni *et al.* (2010) to investigate the impact of European eel on an invasive population of *Procambarus clarkii* in an Italian wetland. *Anguilla anguilla* is a good candidate for mitigating the damage caused by *P. clarkii* in Italy; it has a benthonic feeding habit and is able to tolerate partially deoxygenated waters – properties that match these crayfish and the typical habitats they occupy. In addition, eels may be more efficient as predators than other fish species because they are able to detect crayfish by odour (Blake & Hart, 1995) and can enter crayfish burrows. The study confirmed that *A. anguilla* preys on *P. clarkii* but, like other fish such as smallmouth bass and rock bass (Hein *et al.*, 2006), it is gape-size limited, mostly catching small crayfish (Figure 8.2). Indeed, as confirmed by a laboratory experiment (Aquiloni *et al.*, 2010), eels usually avoid larger crayfish, except when they are soft-shelled, and always attack the smaller ones from behind. However, their effectiveness for control is limited by their low consumption of crayfish. Eels were less voracious than the other fish tested, e.g. smallmouth bass (Rach & Bills, 1989) or pike (Elvira *et al.*, 1996), consuming about one crayfish every four days (*c*. 1.3% of average eel weight) possibly due to its temperature-related lower metabolic rate than other fish species (Owen, 2001).

Fish predators may also modify the behaviour of crayfish, inducing either a reduction of activity or a shift in its peak and a corresponding increase in the time spent in shelters (Stein & Magnuson, 1976; Stein, 1977; Hamrin, 1987; Blake & Hart, 1993, 1995; Aquiloni et al., 2010). It was also found that the greater the number of hides provided, the better the survival of the crayfish (Saiki & Tash, 1979; Blake & Hart, 1993). The reduced activity of crayfish in the presence of a fish predator may translate, on the one hand, into decreased trophic activity followed by an increased mortality of crayfish due to starvation and, on the other, a decreased impact on the most affected components of the community such as macrophytes and snails.

8.2.4   Biocides

Biocides or pesticides are general terms that cover all the chemicals used to control invasive and noxious organisms, including insecticides when used for the control of insects, and herbicides when used for the control of plants. Many effective maintenance management projects and successful eradications employ chemicals, either alone or in concert with mechanical or physical methods. However, the expense of chemicals, especially when used for environmental purposes over large areas, is high. Additionally, the evolution of resistance is frequent; there are no species-specific biocides and concerns arise from the possibility of bioaccumulation and biomagnification in the food chain. As indicated by Williams (1997), the use of chemicals may also generate ideological opposition and thus may foster opposition by local people against the intervention. However, there are some biocides registered today that, if used properly, have far more limited non-target impacts, and in some instances they may be the only means currently available to stop irreversible damage from an invasion, at least until some other method is developed (Simberloff, 2009).

Biocides that have been used to control invasive NICS include organophosphate, organochlorine and pyrethroid insecticides, rotenone and surfactants. Since no biocides are selective for crayfish, most attention has been given to chemicals that are not persistent in the environment, are readily available, and are relatively inexpensive. This has led to the discovery of two methods capable of eradicating a crayfish population from small bodies of water.

The first, some derivatives of natural pyrethrum, such as 'Pyblast' (3.0% w/w pyrethrins plus piperonyl butoxide and alcohol ethoxylate), applied in the water and as a spray for treatment of the shoreline, were found to be the most cost-effective and easy to use. Natural pyrethrum is the oldest known insecticide; it is produced primarily from the flowers of Chrysanthemum cinerariaefolium and C. cineum, as extracts composed of several natural pyrethrins. It is widely used as an organic insecticide on crops, where it can be applied up to harvest. It is used in food-handling premises, for the control of insects, for public hygiene or avoidance of nuisance, and also as a treatment for head lice. It was first used against crustaceans in 1947 to clear infestations of the water hoglouse Asellus aquaticus from public water mains (Hart, 1958) and is still used in this way (Peay et al., 2006a). The advantages of natural pyrethrum are its low toxicity to mammals and birds, its rapid breakdown in sunlight, the absence of toxic residues, and its harmlessness to plants; it is, however, toxic to other crustaceans, insects and fish (Peay *et al.*, 2006a). Pyblast was chosen as the biocide for the attempted eradication of the signal crayfish *Pacifastacus leniusculus* in the North Esk catchment in Aberdeenshire, Scotland, because it was considered to have lower environmental impact than more stable and persistent insecticides. It was also decided that it was better to have a short-term, fully recoverable impact on a waterbody in a controlled, localized area than to allow signal crayfish to spread throughout the drainage, with the associated long-term impacts. The intervention consisted of different phases: the inflow/outflow of water was prevented, fish were removed, and margins were sprayed with Pyblast to prevent any escape over land, the whole waterbody was treated with Pyblast, and the treated water was contained throughout the recovery period to prevent any adverse effects in non-target areas. Biomonitoring was carried out using amphipods (*Gammarus* sp). No crayfish were found in a summer survey after the treatment (Peay *et al.*, 2006a), but monitoring may be required for up to 5 years before claiming the complete success of the treatment.

The synthetic pyrethroid BETAMAX VET, followed by draining of the ponds, was used to eradicate *Pacifastacus leniusculus* and the associated pathogen *Aphanomyces astaci* in the Dammane area, Telemark county, Norway (Sandodden & Johnsen, 2010) after the first discovery of the invader. This biocide is a cypermethrin-based pharmaceutical developed for the treatment of salmon lice (*Lepeophtheirus salmonis*) infestations of farmed Atlantic salmon, and is highly toxic to aquatic crustaceans (Haya, 1989). A double administration of BETAMAX VET was carried out with powerful pumps placed in a boat or on the shore. The chemical was dispersed both on the surface and along the bottom of the ponds, and the ponds were subsequently drained. During and after the second treatment and draining of the ponds, no signal crayfish were discovered. A post-treatment surveillance programme is ongoing to document the success of the intervention.

Alternative approaches include the use of ammonium in the presence of high pH with prior deoxygenation, and organophosphate (e.g. fenthion and methyl parathion) and organochlorine insecticides (e.g. mirex). Examples of their application to control invasive populations of NICS have been discussed by Holdich *et al.* (1999). Among others, Laurent's (1995) study is worth mentioning. The author tested various organophosphate insecticides on *Orconectes limosus* from Lake Geneva in France and found that Baytex PM 40 (active ingredient fenthion) was effective at low doses. Laboratory studies showed a 24-h LC_{50} of 46 $\mu g\ L^{-1}$ and 48-h LC_{50} of 12 $\mu g\ L^{-1}$. Total mortality was achieved after 24 hours with concentrations of 90–100 $\mu g\ L^{-1}$ and after 48 hours with 50 $\mu g\ L^{-1}$. These levels are much lower than those required to kill fin-fish. The author also found that the toxicity of the biocide lasted several weeks. Field trials were effective at levels as low as 60 $\mu g\ L^{-1}$, with total mortality after 87 hours. Fish, frogs, mammals, many species of Rotifera and molluscs were not affected, but insects and other Crustacea were killed, with the exception of Copepoda. The relatively long time needed for total mortality of crayfish is a limitation of the method. Additionally, studies on the fenthion residue in the food web are lacking and comparison with the results of other studies is difficult due to the large number of commercial formulations of Baytex available.

Surfactants have been used to control crayfish activity by inhibiting oxygen consumption through morphological and physiological changes on the surface of the gills (Cabral *et al.*, 1997; Fonseca *et al.*, 1997), but their application showed limited success in eradicating crayfish populations. The efficacy of another biocide, Ivermectin (a synthetic derivative of abamectin, a natural fermentation product of the actinomycete *Streptomyces avermitilis*) has never been investigated against invasive populations of NICS; it seems, however, unlikely that permission for its general use would be given before much more is known about its environmental impact (Holdich *et al.*, 1999). Rotenone is a toxin associated with certain leguminous plants such as *Derris*, which acts as a vasoconstrictor, narrowing the blood vessels in fish gills, thus preventing oxygen uptake. Rotenone might be acceptable for crayfish eradication. It is toxic to fish and amphibians at levels lower than those needed to kill crustaceans, so removal of these would have to be considered before its use was contemplated. Rotenone is widely used as a piscicide in fisheries management, but it has rarely been tested on crayfish (Bills & Marking, 1988). Holdich *et al.* (1999) reported the results of experiments conducted on *Astacus leptodactylus* and *Pacifastacus leniusculus* showing the relative tolerance of these species to rotenone, with the former species surviving levels of 100 mg L^{-1} for 24 hours. Because of the higher tolerance of crayfish than fish, considerable cost would be involved in applying sufficient levels of rotenone to eradicate them.

8.2.5   Autocidal methods

Autocidal methods include the sterile male release technique (SMRT) and the use of sex pheromones to interfere with reproduction. SMRT is based on rearing, sterilizing and releasing large numbers of males to mate with wild females, who will then produce non-viable eggs. It has been successful in the control of some insect pests (e.g. Knipling, 1955; Curtis, 1985) and aquatic vertebrates such as sea lamprey *Petromyzon marinus* (Twohey *et al.*, 2003). The potential use of SMRT for the management of invasive crayfish has recently been tested in the laboratory (Aquiloni *et al.*, 2009). This technique, although initially expensive, causes no environmental contamination or non-target impacts. It is species-specific and offers the additional advantage that, at low density, sterile specimens may seek and mate with the remaining fertile individuals. The high mitotic rate in male gonads makes them particularly radiosensitive, so irradiation can kill cells or inhibit their growth, eventually leading to the partial or total sterility of the treated subjects (Aquiloni *et al.*, 2009). Risks of the treatment include a reduced competitiveness of males and thus their lessened ability to mate in the presence of wild males, a decreased life span, and an effect on female choice (Lance *et al.*, 2000; Lux *et al.*, 2002). Information on the use of ionizing irradiation in decapods comes from studies aimed at preventing unlicensed breeding of the prawns *Palaemonetes pugio* (Rees, 1962), *Macrobrachium rosenbergii* (Lee, 2000) and *Penaeus japonicus*, both males and females (Sellars & Preston, 2005). With crayfish, an irradiation dose of 20 Gy did not appear to alter either the survival or mating ability of *Procambarus clarkii* males but significantly affected their reproductive success by reducing by 43% the number of hatchlings. The damage recorded in the testes (i.e. decreased gonado-

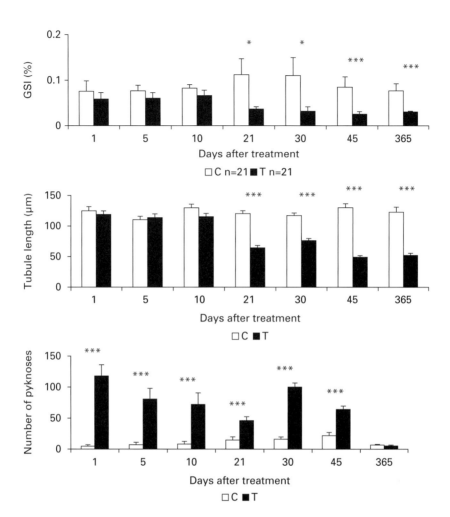

Figure 8.3. Sterilization of crayfish: an irradiation dose of 20 Gy significantly affected the reproductive success of *P. clarkii* by reducing by 43% the number of hatchlings. The damage recorded in the testes (i.e. decreased gonado-somatic index (GSI) and shortened tubule length) and in their tissues (i.e. increased number of pyknoses) increased with the duration of treatment (from Aquiloni *et al.*, 2009). One and two asterisks denote significant differences at $P<0.05$, and $P<0.001$, respectively, after the application of one-tailed Student's *t* tests for independent data.

somatic index (GSI) and shortened seminiferous tubules) and in their tissues (i.e. increased number of pyknoses) increased with the duration of treatment. Except for the number of pyknoses, the damage lasted for at least one year, thus probably affecting the subsequent reproductive season (Figure 8.3). Taken together, these data suggest that the release of sufficient numbers of irradiated males can, in theory, decrease the size of the invasive population, and that their reduced fertility might persist for more than one reproductive season (Aquiloni *et al.*, 2009). It should be noted, however, that 43% sterility is relatively low when compared with the results achieved with some insect species (Bakri *et al.*, 2005). Thus, it is unlikely that this rate of sterility will reduce the density of *P. clarkii* below the 'Allee threshold' (see above), where dispensatory density-dependent processes may accelerate further population decline and cause the eventual extirpation of the invader (Aquiloni *et al.*, 2009).

Sex pheromones are widely used to control insect pests. The release of large quantities of sex pheromones in an area can confuse the males and prevent them from finding females, or they may function as attractants, usually of males, during the mating season. Once most males have been removed from the population, few matings might take place and a quick reduction in the size of the population may be achieved. This procedure is environmentally sound because the sex attractants are in most cases species-specific. An apparent limitation is that it can be applied only during the breeding season. Crustacean decapods use similar sex pheromones to insects, as shown for several species in the laboratory: *Callinectes sapidus* (Gleeson, 1980), *Carcinus maenas* (Hardege *et al.*, 2002), *Erimacrus isenbeckii* (Asai *et al.*, 2000), *Homarus americanus* (McLeese, 1970, Dunham, 1979; Cowan 1991) and the crayfish *Orconectes virilis* (Hazlett, 1985), *Pacifastacus leniusculus* (Stebbing *et al.*, 2004) and *Procambarus clarkii* (Ameyaw-Akumfi & Hazlett, 1975; Bechler *et al.*, 1988; Dunham & Oh, 1996). This suggests that sex pheromones could be used for the control of decapod pests. A limitation is that up until now, attempts to identify the molecular structure of pheromones in decapods have had little success, so the ongoing studies must rely on natural sources of the putative sex pheromones (Stebbing *et al.*, 2004; Aquiloni & Gherardi, 2010).

In the UK, Stebbing *et al.* (2004) used standard traps baited with gel infused with water that had been preliminarily conditioned by mature *P. leniusculus* females. The results of this study, however, were not able to prove the efficacy of the method, since control traps baited with food attracted a similar number of crayfish as did traps baited with sex pheromones. Another field study was conducted in a wetland in Italy invaded by *Procambarus clarkii* (Aquiloni & Gherardi, 2010). Here, standard traps were baited with live sexually receptive individuals, either males or females, and the number, sex and size of the catches were compared with empty traps and with traps baited with food. The results of this study were also contradictory. The traps containing receptive females attracted more males than females, confirming that crayfish females release sex pheromones and suggesting that these putative sex pheromones might orient the males to the female location. Laboratory studies have shown that males rely on chemicals to recognize the other sex, whereas sex recognition by females requires both chemical and visual stimuli emitted together by a potential mate (Aquiloni *et al.*, 2009). A second interesting result was that the crayfish attracted by receptive individuals were smaller than those captured using food as bait. Since in this species body size is related to age (Huner, 2002), the ability of sex pheromones to attract young individuals with more reproductive seasons ahead might be an advantage when invasive populations need to be managed.

It appears that the efficacy of the method is low due mainly to three limitations. First, as with the results of Stebbing *et al.* (2004), sex pheromones attract relatively fewer crayfish than does food. Indeed, confinement in traps might cause stress, with the consequent reduced emission of sex pheromones (Hazlett, 1999). Purification and concentration of the molecules involved in sexual communication might improve the efficacy of the method, but the chemical nature of sex pheromones is still unknown and research in the field is time-consuming and expensive (Holdich *et al.*, 1999). Second, the females do not respond to putative sex pheromones released by males, so only a part of the population can be affected by catches. Third, the removal of mature crayfish may not necessarily induce an effective decrease in the invasive populations. As explained above, removing large males might reduce the pressure on the smaller individuals, allowing them to grow, and might lead to a large population of individuals whose growth is stunted due to competition for resources. In addition, due to feedback mechanisms, crayfish might respond to reduced numbers in the population by producing more eggs and reaching maturity earlier (Holdich *et al.*, 1999).

The evidence presented here has shown that mitigation and remediation options for invasive NICS have not been widely explored, and have so far met with limited success. Few studies have reported the results of long-term control of invasive populations and none has achieved eradication. This is clearly illustrated by the case study of *Orconectes rusticus* in Sparkling Lake in Wisconsin, USA. In this lake, intensive trapping of adult crayfish and restrictions on harvesting fish predators (smallmouth bass *Micropterus dolomieu* and rock bass *Ambloplites rupestris*) were used from 2001 to 2005 (Hein *et al.* 2006, 2007), leading to the removal of a substantial proportion of the invasive population of *O. rusticus*. Trapping removed crayfish of highest reproductive value, while fish predation caused a large decline in the population growth rate, so that catches decreased by 95%, from 11 crayfish per trap per day in 2002 to 0.5 crayfish in 2005 (Hein *et al.*, 2006). Overall, five summers of intensive trapping and fisheries management practices led to the removal of 88 602 crayfish, corresponding to a biomass of 1193 kg (Hein *et al.*, 2007), but this large effort was not sufficient to extirpate the *O. rusticus* population. Recent studies by Freeman *et al.* (2010) showed that removal of *Pacifastacus leniusculus* using traps, and pond trials with biocides met with moderate success in reducing crayfish numbers and containing their populations. Signal crayfish have populated many habitat types in the UK, each of which may require a different control strategy; hence no single strategy or universal solution is likely to be attainable. Signal crayfish are susceptible to various biocides and microbial pathogens, but more scientific research will be required to develop safe biological control methods and integrated pest management strategies to control these invasive organisms.

8.3   Control of crayfish plague induced by non-indigenous crayfish

One of the worst effects of invasive crayfish of North American origin is that they are usually accompanied by the oomycete pathogen *Aphanomyces astaci*, which causes lethal crayfish plague in susceptible species. Thus, their spread into a new area may not only disrupt the receiving community, it may also speed the extinction of indigenous crayfish stocks. Even if North American crayfish are not present in a region, a plague outbreak may occur, as happened in Ireland in the 1980s (Matthews & Reynolds, 1992). It is therefore necessary to consider plague control as well as NICS control.

It is first important to examine the state of knowledge about the crayfish plague in American species in their native area, compared with their capability to develop and disseminate the crayfish plague in Europe. For example, *Pacifastacus leniusculus* is more susceptible to *Aphanomyces astaci* than is *Procambarus clarkii*. *P. leniusculus* might need up to 10 000 zoospores mL^{-1} to kill it (Persson & Söderhäll, 1983; Persson *et al.*, 1987) while *P. clarkii* requires about 50 000 zoospores mL^{-1} (Diéguez-Uribeondo & Söderhäll, 1993). *P. leniusculus* is also more susceptible to *Saprolegnia parasitica* than is *P. clarkii* (Diéguez-Uribeondo *et al.*, 1994). Cerenius & Söderhäll (1992) also found that the chronic infection carried by *P. leniusculus* renders them susceptible to all kinds of environmental change and to new pathogens, which has serious implications for the use of this species for stocking or aquaculture purposes. To date, however, no investigation of the natural and original distribution of *Aphanomyces astaci* has been carried out in the USA.

North American species of crayfish (e.g. *P. leniusculus* and *P. clarkii*) are quite resistant to crayfish plague, but become susceptible under conditions of stress: e.g. low haemocyte number in haemolymph (Persson *et al.*, 1987), pathogens (e.g. *Psorospermum* – Thörnqvist & Söderhäll, 1993; *Saprolegnia* – Diéguez-Uribeondo *et al.*, 1994), immuno-depressors such as zymosan (Persson *et al.*, 1987; Diéguez-Uribeondo & Söderhäll, 1993) or pesticides (Javier Diéguez-Uribeondo, personal communication, 2009).

No comparative studies among crayfish species on their susceptibility under stress conditions have been done except for the study of *Saprolegnia* virulence by Diéguez-Uribeondo *et al.* (1994). A recent literature search for crayfish plague events referenced at the level of native distribution found no reports on crayfish plague published in the USA, Mexico, Central or South America. This is because *Aphanomyces astaci* may live almost as a symbiont in the geographical region and in a host where it has coevolved, while causing a dramatic disease, crayfish plague, in susceptible hosts in other geographical regions where this organism has not coevolved (see Cerenius *et al.*, 2003). Further, the degree of threat by crayfish plague in its native area and in aquaculture is evidently low, since it has never been reported or come to the attention of scientists, again probably because *A. astaci* lives as a symbiont. Other possibilities for not having detected crayfish plague mortalities (or evidence of the so-called 'acute plague') in North America are that *Procambarus clarkii* is the only species farmed. This is a highly resistant species and is also farmed extensively, which is not as stressful as in intensive culture, and the risk is therefore low. In *Pacifastacus leniusculus* the risk would theoretically be higher (especially in intensive aquaculture) because of the potential stressing factors of pathogens and pollution, and because this species always harbours *Aphanomyces astaci*. However, this species is not farmed in the USA.

In South America, on the other hand, the risk of crayfish plague could be extremely high, as it is outside the original area of distribution of this pathogen. South America has only parastacid species, which are susceptible to *A. astaci* (Unestam, 1972). We do not know how far down the American continent plague may exist; Unestam (1972) is the only worker to have checked the presence of *A. astaci* in America. Javier Diéguez-Uribeondo has recently studied samples from Ecuador, but has not found *A. astaci* (personal communication, 2009). Experimentally, it has not been tested as to whether a crayfish species could be killed by a different strain of plague coming from another species (e.g. *P. leniusculus* versus *P. clarkii*). All that is known is that temperature differences make some strains more virulent than others. For example, the *P. clarkii* strain is more virulent than strains from *P. leniusculus* at temperatures higher than 20°C, but below 17°C they seem to be about the same (Diéguez-Uribeondo *et al.*, 1995).

8.4   Protection of European natives in a plague situation

According to Holdich (2003), the restocking of rivers previously infected by plague is possible if the source of infection, i.e. North American crayfish, is no longer present. In Europe, where plague is an ever-present risk, the importance of sanitary control during reintroduction procedures of indigenous crayfish is paramount (see Chapter 9). In Spain such controls are currently applied in reintroduction studies with *Austropotamobius pallipes*. The restoration plan for native crayfish in Navarra has been successful, since they have increased the number and size of populations in many places in spite of having inadequate policies regarding fisheries of alien species. The sanitary control protocol is described in Diéguez-Uribeondo *et al.* (1997a) and is still valid. Wherever it is shown that there are no American crayfish and native crayfish can survive in cages, the natives can be successfully reintroduced. As an example, in 2008, over 25 000 natives were fished from one such reintroduction site (Javier Diéguez-Uribeondo, personal communication, 2009).

The problem of crayfish plague is more difficult to solve, because the plague can be transmitted without the presence of aliens but transported by water (e.g. with trout introduced from fish farms that also rear American crayfish), by fishermen (water and wet fishing gear, as suspected in the case of Ireland in the 1980s; Matthews & Reynolds, 1992), or by crayfish used as bait in the past. This is why the crayfish plague, caused by this fungus-like organism *Aphanomyces astaci*, is listed among the top 100 of the world's worst invaders by the IUCN (Lowe *et al.*, 2000) and is considered to be a worse invader than the host itself. Once a watershed is infected, control of the spread of infection is almost impossible; therefore only preventative measures are effective. As the pathogen is obligate and lethal, it cannot persist in ICS alternative hosts, nor in the environment, so the transmission could only occur during the brief period of a few days while zoospores are viable. Oidtmann *et al.* (2002) stated that *A. astaci* remains viable for 5 days, and possibly longer in crayfish kept in water at 21°C after dying of crayfish plague. It was also found that *A. astaci* is unlikely to survive passage through the gastrointestinal tract of either mammals or birds, although there is a risk of transmission of crayfish plague via fish faeces.

A. astaci can be physically controlled by disinfection of water and equipment, or drying of equipment (>24 hours), as the oomycete spores are not resistant to desiccation. *A. astaci* does not survive at −5°C or below for more than 24 hours. Chemical control was tested by Rantamäki *et al.* (1992) by *in vitro* prevention of spore production by *A. astaci* through the addition of $MgCl_2$ at a concentration of 20 mM. When zoospores were used for infection, at least 100 mM of $MgCl_2$ was needed. Cerenius *et al.* (1992) also found that the fungicide Ampropylfos was capable of reducing zoospore numbers of *A. astaci*.

Biological control of *A. astaci* was tested by Diéguez-Uribeondo & Cerenius (1998), by purifying three different proteinase inhibitors from crayfish blood, then testing for their inhibitory activity against extracellular proteinases from *A. astaci*. The authors found that these proteinase inhibitors may reduce proteolytic breakdown exerted by *A. astaci* proteinases during an infection.

8.5   Future developments

The global expansion of non-indigenous crayfish and the damage caused by them to indigenous species and habitats is a cause for increasing concern. This is particularly true in Europe, where it has stimulated much research-led management (see, for example, the evaluation by Scalera, 2008). Yet there is a great deal of variation in the measures put in place to control introductions of crayfish in different European countries, and indeed within individual countries. Table 8.1 summarizes potential control methods for NICS and, by highlighting the negative and positive aspects associated with each, underlines the continuing difficulty of eradicating them.

Freeman *et al.* (2010) note that legislation is beyond the scope of their review of control methods. However, recommendations from a conference on the future of native crayfish in Europe were summarized by Peay (2009a), who outlined the need for much tighter regulation on the sale of non-indigenous crayfish within Europe, including a pressing need to prevent the introduction of more exotic species via the aquarium trade. There is a clear requirement to identify the threats to remaining populations of indigenous crayfish regionally and nationally, and to provide well-enforced biosecurity measures to help protect these populations. As we show in Chapter 10, it is recognized that this can only be done through a concerted effort on education and by information-sharing, because without public cooperation, the ongoing trend of decline in indigenous crayfish will continue.

Aphanomyces astaci is a difficult organism to study, and problems include the timely submission of crayfish for testing, availability of expertise in laboratories, difficulty in isolating and maintaining strains of *A. astaci*, and interpreting the results of samples. The advent of molecular techniques, however, has allowed the development of new methods for rapid and reliable identification of *A. astaci* (Oidtmann *et al.*, 2006; Ballesteros *et al.*, 2007; Hochwimmer *et al.*, 2009; Kozubíková *et al.*, 2009; Vrålstad *et al.*, 2009). Nonetheless, more research is needed on *Aphanomyces* diversity and molecular markers, since in recent years a number of new *Aphanomyces* species have been described, and it has been found that some of these are present in crayfish and provide false positive results (Ballesteros *et al.*, 2006, 2007; Oidtmann *et al.*, 2006; Diéguez-Uribeondo *et al.*, 2009). Improvement of the currently developed molecular techniques for diagnosing crayfish plague is also allowing us to improve the specificity of molecular tests. The combined knowledge of disease history, culture-based

Table 8.1. Summary of potential crayfish control methods, highlighting the negative and positive aspects for each method (Freeman *et al.* 2010).

Control method	Negative aspects	Positive aspects	Conclusions
Mechanical			
Netting	Very labour-intensive and site-sensitive.	Removes crayfish and also effective against juveniles.	Unlikely to eradicate a population. Not sustainable.
Trapping	Very labour-intensive and site-sensitive. Not effective against juveniles. May risk encouraging a market for non-native crayfish, and hence increase illegal introductions.	Removes crayfish effectively and reduces population density in the short term.	Unlikely to eradicate a population. Not sustainable. In the long term tends to promote earlier sexual maturity in the population and lead to a state of 'sustainable harvest'.
Electro-fishing	Very labour-intensive and site-sensitive. Potential to harm non-target organisms and potential vector.	Effective against all age classes.	Only removes a portion of a population. Too site-sensitive to be practical.
Chemical			
Biocides	Not appropriate in large areas such as river systems, hence very site-sensitive.	Can cause high crayfish mortality. Not as labour-intensive as mechanical methods.	Most biocides seriously impact non-target organisms. Scope for future development of novel crayfish biocides.
Semiochemicals	Expensive to develop and purify, and dependent upon trapping.	Species-specific, increases the efficiency of trapping.	Not sustainable and not effective against juveniles and sub-adult crayfish.
Physical			
Habitat alterations	Extremely site-sensitive. Causes excessive damage to the environment.	An option for small ponds or closed systems.	With unlimited resources may work for certain sites. Not practical.
Biological			
Microbial	Possible impact to native and aquaculture species. Current lack of scientific knowledge and techniques.	Potentially very host-specific, and self-maintaining in the environment. Both acutely and chronically acting pathogens have potential.	Burdened with legislative issues, but could, given the research effort, provide a long-term strategy for the control of invasive crayfish.
Predators	Site/habitat-sensitive. Native species not always good candidates.	Native predators pose a low risk to the environment.	Difficult to evaluate, may have a role in an IPM strategy for some sites.

With permission from Mark Freeman.

or histological studies, and molecular research are key aspects for providing accurate diagnosis (Diéguez-Uribeondo, 2009).

In spite of the general failure of any attempts to eradicate NICS, an intensification of scientific research into bioinvasions and a greater public understanding of their negative impact are expected to catalyse the development of novel approaches for the mitigation and remediation of invasive populations of crayfish (Gherardi, 2007b, 2010). Success in these efforts will be crucial for the long-term conservation of the highly threatened freshwater communities in Europe as well as for parastacid crayfish elsewhere in the world, though currently less threatened.

In Chapter 7 we emphasized the importance of monitoring the current distribution of crayfish species. In Europe, interest in crayfish distribution was stimulated by the CRAYNET programme, culminating in the production of the *Atlas of Crayfish in Europe* (Souty-Grosset *et al.*, 2006) and other educational aids. Nonetheless, the ongoing invasion by various NICS and the additional human-assisted introductions occurring in most countries means that the distribution of crayfish species is changing every year. The picture has already been updated in a detailed review of the current status of ICS and NICS in all the countries and regions in Europe (Holdich *et al.*, 2009b). It is apparent that there is a need for a coordinated approach to surveillance and monitoring at a range of scales, not only in Europe but across the world. The production of distribution maps of crayfish species will always lag behind the actual distribution of the species. In some areas, web-based recording systems have been set up to encourage members of the public to inform authorities about new locations of invasive non-native species. For example, there is an 'alien watch' scheme in Ireland (www. invasivespeciesireland.com), where sightings anywhere in Ireland can be reported, both from the Republic of Ireland and Northern Ireland (part of the UK). This is a good example of transboundary cooperation on the issue of non-native species, but more work is needed, especially given the observed transboundary spread of NICS in mainland Europe. DAISIE (Delivering Alien Invasive Species Inventories for Europe) was a response at a European scale to the need for distribution data on non-indigenous species (DAISIE, 2009) and the journal *Aquatic Invasions* was set up to encourage the rapid publication of information on newly arrived aquatic species, as an early warning of new potentially invasive species (Panov & Gollasch, 2006).

Peay (2009b) also noted the importance of assessing the risks caused by invasive crayfish before they become widely established, as recommended by the IUCN (2000), and of using legal instruments to prevent further introductions. Some European countries have started carrying out risk assessments, for example for the several NICS already present in Great Britain, predicting their impacts and potential for expansion of range (Non-Native Species Secretariat, 2008; Stephanie Peay, personal communication, 2008).

The aquarium trade is now the most probable source of new crayfish species entering Europe. While some of these are tropical species, it is very likely that some could survive in the wild in Europe and become invasive. Consequently there should be a Europe-wide ban on the supply or keeping of crayfish in aquaria, with the exception of keeping them for scientific purposes, under strict regulation. In Ireland and Scotland, there is a total ban on aquarium trade in crayfish and it is illegal to keep any species. In England and Wales, only one species is permitted, the redclaw crayfish *Cherax quadricarinatus*. By contrast, many crayfish species are available for sale in the Czech Republic and at least 20 cambarid species are sold in Germany, some of which are advertised as pond species. Marbled crayfish *Procambarus fallax f. virginalis* have been found in the wild in Europe and in Madagascar, and could also be a potential carrier of crayfish plague. At present, an aquarium wholesaler in a European country where the sale of NICS is legal can sell a new species of NICS to anyone in Sweden, Ireland or other countries where the species is banned. As a minimum, there needs to be regulation of exports included in the rules of receiving countries.

The European Union is now working 'Towards an EU strategy on invasive species' and options for a legislative framework in Europe have been outlined (Genovesi & Shine, 2003), with four options ranging from no change through to a complete new European Directive, but the progress of consultation has been slow (Commission of the European Communities, 2008; European Economic and Social Committee, 2009). The Committee of the Regions was critical of the delay in action on a strategy. It called for specific EU legislation to deal with the problems of invasive species as a matter of urgency and a European Agency to monitor implementation. Failure to deal with invasive species was seen as an issue that could prevent the EU from achieving its agreed target of 'Halting the loss of biodiversity by 2010 and beyond'. The committee reported that rapidly growing trade and transport activities are expanding the opportunities for IS (invasive species) introduction, resulting in environmental pressures. The existence of the single market means that once a species is introduced in the territory of one Member State, it can be dispersed rapidly throughout the whole European Union. Therefore, addressing trade-related issues can only be done effectively at the EU's external frontier. Given the way that these species become established and spread, measures taken by one Member State can be totally negated, if neighbouring countries fail to take action or respond in an uncoordinated manner (European Economic and Social Committee, 2009).

These aspects, of regulation and the associated need for public and official education, will be taken up again in Chapter 10.

9 Biodiversity management through the reintroduction of heritage crayfish species

9.1 Introduction

Freshwater ecosystems, communities and populations can be managed in various ways, including controlled harvesting, restocking and habitat restoration. The restoration of habitats and communities may involve the reintroduction of keystone or heritage species which were formerly present. The principal aim of any reintroduction should be to establish a viable, free-ranging population of a species, subspecies or race which had become globally or locally extinct in the wild. It should be reintroduced within the species' former natural habitat and range, and should require minimal long-term management. The objectives of reintroductions may include the enhancement of the long-term survival of a species, re-establishment of a keystone species (in the ecological or cultural sense) in an ecosystem, maintenance or restoration of natural biodiversity, provision of long-term economic benefits to the local and/or national economy, promotion of conservation awareness, or a combination of these objectives.

While in other regions of the world where crayfish are important, the situation is developing more slowly, in Europe there has been a drastic reduction in the distribution and abundance of the indigenous crayfish species (ICS), despite programmes of habitat restoration (Chapters 3 and 6). For example in Poitou-Charentes (France) successive surveys carried out from 1978 to 2003 revealed a high rate of disappearance of *Austropotamobius pallipes* populations from the region and the alarming spread of non-indigenous species such as *Procambarus clarkii* and *Pacifastacus leniusculus*. Represented by 137 populations in 1978, *A. pallipes* is now almost completely restricted to only one department, with just 45 populations recorded, representing a decrease of 68% of population numbers in 25 years and a loss of 40% of populations in the last 6 years (Bramard *et al.*, 2006). This reflects the situation in the rest of Europe, as the IUCN is considering an overall rate of decline for European crayfish somewhere between 50% and 80% over the last 10 years (IUCN, 2009). This appears to be due to the direct and indirect results of human activities (e.g. destruction and fragmentation of habitats, pollution, poaching, and the introduction of invasive non-indigenous crayfish species (NICS), resulting in both competitive exclusion and dissemination of crayfish plague caused by *Aphanomyces astaci*). This disastrous situation led to the inception of the EC thematic network CRAYNET, which brought together scientists and water managers from 11 European countries. Reintroductions or restocking are often emphasized as a management strategy for the conservation of indigenous freshwater crayfish. Norway had especially good conditions for reintroduction of *Astacus astacus* after crayfish plague, because at the time there was no alien plague-carrying crayfish species in this country (Taugbøl, 2004a).

Among the three crayfish species native to western Europe, *Astacus astacus* and *Austropotamobius torrentium* are listed in Annex V of the EU Habitats Directive (Annex E of DPR 357/97), while *Austropotamobius pallipes* is listed in Annexes II and V (Annexes B and E of DPR 357/97). Because *A. italicus* has only recently been proposed as a separate species distinct from *A. pallipes* (Fratini *et al.*, 2005; Bertocchi *et al.*, 2008), it is yet to be included in legislative protection. For all species protected under the Habitats Directive in Europe, each Member State must submit regular 'favourable status reports', based on an assessment of the species' current status (i.e. in decline, stable or increasing), with an assessment of the pressures and threats acting on it. Conservation measures may be required in the case of declines; these include protection of the habitat and reintroductions to favourable areas within the broad range of the species. Indeed, measures to reintroduce native crayfish into surface waters have been suggested as a crucial part of management and conservation strategies in Europe (Schulz *et al.*, 2002). However, there is still considerable uncertainty as to how best to perform such actions and what questions need to be answered relating to reintroduction or restocking exercises (in the crayfish literature, Schulz *et al.* (2002) comment that the term 'restocking' is sometimes used for actions that should properly be called 'reintroductions').

The CRAYNET programme has helped to stimulate interest in assessing the current distribution of crayfish species, culminating in the production of the *Atlas of Crayfish in Europe* (Souty-Grosset *et al.*, 2006). This has been updated in a detailed review of the current status of crayfish in all the countries and regions in Europe, and the overall status of the various ICS and NICS (Holdich *et al.*, 2009b). Requirements of the EU Species and Habitats Directive cover monitoring of ICS, whether or not in Natura 2000 sites, and another major driver in future will be the EU Water Framework Directive (adopted by the European Parliament in 2000), which requires Member States 'to protect, enhance and restore all bodies of surface water' with the aim of achieving good surface water status in 15 years at the latest. Measures to reintroduce native crayfish into surface waters have been suggested as a crucial part of management and conservation strategies across Europe (Reynolds, 1997; Dehus *et al.*, 1999; Souty-Grosset, 2005).

Once the habitat has been restored, the next step is to reintroduce heritage crayfish species, but there are current problems with regard to the loss or very low density of remaining populations and the difficulty of halting the expanding distribution of aliens, leading to a loss of freshwater biodiversity (see Chapter 8). However, studies have shown that the present distribution of European crayfish is the result both of natural events that occurred from the Pleistocene until recent historical times, and of translocations caused by human activities. With respect to the complex taxonomy of the white-clawed crayfish, knowledge of the present distribution and composition of populations is a prerequisite before undertaking reintroductions of this crayfish (Souty-Grosset *et al.*, 2006).

There is still considerable uncertainty as to how such reintroduction or restocking exercises should actually be performed. There are, however, a number of studies referring to the general water quality parameters and habitat requirements of native crayfish in each continent (e.g. Bohl, 1999; Garcia-Arberas & Rallo, 2000; Trouilhé *et al.*,

2008). Among the basic aspects such as the range of water temperatures, the substrate, and the presence of morphological structures for hiding places, geographical isolation of the habitat seems to be of importance in Europe. Currently, many stocks occur in small, isolated lakes (Schulz, 2000) or isolated stretches of small rivers (Alonso *et al.*, 2000). One general aspect, often associated with geographical isolation of a freshwater body, is the absence or low amount of human impact such as fishing pressure by anglers or commercial fishermen, swimming or other recreational activity or, indeed, the likelihood of aquarium owners releasing alien stocks of fish, plants or crayfish (Skurdal, 1995; Dehus *et al.*, 1999).

It is of prime importance to check whether a habitat intended for reintroduction is free of crayfish plague arising from the oomycete *Aphanomyces astaci* (Schulz *et al.*, 2002). The most effective test is *in situ* exposure of native crayfish in the target habitat. Thus, Spink & Frayling (2000) exposed ten white-clawed crayfish *Austropotamobius pallipes* in 46 × 46 × 31 cm cages for a period between 6 months and 1 year in two UK streams to test for crayfish plague prior to reintroduction.

Another aspect that needs to be considered is the plant and animal assemblage of the target habitat before the reintroduction takes place. As it is well known that crayfish influence aquatic community structure (Hart, 1992; Nyström *et al.*, 1999), it is important to make sure that the introduction of crayfish does not cause any negative effects on any other protected species already in the target habitat. It is therefore recommended to undertake a full risk assessment of the effects of crayfish introduction if a habitat has not contained crayfish for a period of 5 years or longer.

An important aspect of reintroductions is to monitor their success rate, in order to evaluate the procedure itself and to follow up the state of the stock and of the aquatic habitat. Follow-up surveys of the success of numerous reintroduction measures have been carried out in Finland (Lennart Edsman, personal communication, 2006). Monitoring may not be required directly following the first reintroduction because dispersal of the colonists may make them hard to detect. It is therefore often recommended to start monitoring 3–5 years after the first reintroduction, depending on the size of the waterbody and the number of individuals used for restocking. According to Abrahamsson (1966), densities of about 8000 *A. astacus* per hectare of lake area or about 2.5 adult individuals per metre of shoreline represent natural stock densities in suitable habitats, while Matthews & Reynolds (1995) documented about five trappable (adult) *A. pallipes* per square metre of suitable shoreline in Blessington Lake, Ireland.

Most work on restocking has been done in Europe, because of the historic importance of crayfish there and the large-scale losses of native crayfish. Reintroductions of extirpated native crayfish populations are less common elsewhere in the world (see selected case studies for Australia and North America, below), and we know of none in South America or Madagascar.

A (re)introduction may be appropriate to re-establish a population recently lost, extend the distribution of an indigenous crayfish species into its historic range, or create new or isolated populations to conserve genetic diversity or the species. Genetic distinctiveness and possible spread of diseases must be considered. Restocking methods may include population monitoring, water quality surveillance, and population

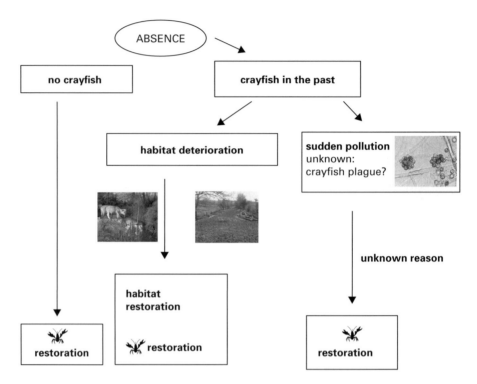

Figure 9.1.   Monitoring sites for the feasibility of European crayfish restocking in streams (drawn by
Catherine Souty-Grosset). Photographs show stream bed trampled by cattle and riparian
tree loss.

genetic monitoring. Reintroduction of indigenous crayfish and habitat restoration are
included so as to provide practical recommendations of value to environmental authorities, decision makers and local managers. General recommendations are to use adults
and juveniles as available, to stock as many crayfish as can be afforded and in several
batches and, if short of stock, to boost the numbers with hatchery rearing. Major constraints in a restocking project are funding limitations and the availability of stocking
material (see Figures 9.1 and 9.2).

9.2   Case studies

9.2.1   North America

In several areas of North America, combinations of environmental degradation and
range expansions or introductions of non-native crayfish have led to declines in indigenous species (Lodge *et al.*, 2000a). Despite the importance of their ecological roles,
there has sometimes been a deficit of knowledge about crayfish distributions, life histories and taxonomy, although this situation is changing (e.g. Welsh *et al.*, 2010). In the
USA and Mexico, many species still await description and, as in Europe, several crayfish 'species' are actually species complexes consisting of more than a single taxon, for

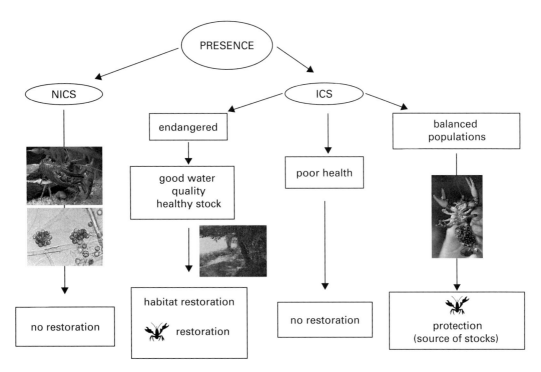

Figure 9.2. Monitoring European crayfish populations in streams (drawn by Catherine Souty-Grosset). Photographs show (from left) *P. clarkii* and the oomycete *A. astaci*; an undisturbed *A. pallipes* site; female with eggs.

example, the species complex including *Orconectes virilis* in North America (Mathews *et al.*, 2008). Many species have naturally small native ranges and are therefore vulnerable to environmental change.

The topics of 'recolonization' of native crayfish species into their former range or 'assisted colonization' (conservation translocations into a new range if the former range is becoming unsuitable) are arousing some interest, but have rarely been proposed for native crayfish in North America; with the cautionary example of *Orconectes rusticus*, which has caused substantial problems after having been moved a small distance within its native continent (Eric Larson, personal communication, 2010). There have, however, been experiments in which endangered crayfish species that had been displaced from their former range were returned there in stream enclosures to determine whether they could survive in their original setting. These experiments were conducted to see if their extirpation might have been due to abiotic or habitat factors, or to biotic factors such as an invasive crayfish species (Robert DiStefano, personal communication, 2010).

Only a few recent studies of reintroduction programmes have been undertaken, among them Phillips *et al.* (2009), who demonstrated that the reintroduction of functionally important species is considered a key strategy for restoring damaged ecosystems. However, noting that the sudden reappearance of an extirpated species may have adverse ecological impacts, even degrading ecosystem services, these authors experimentally reintroduced the crayfish *Orconectes virilis* into a biologically recovering, formerly acidified Boreal Shield lake in Canada, to determine its effect on the littoral food web following a 17-year absence. Their findings highlight that reintroductions of *O. virilis* must be balanced by adequate fish predation to prevent this species from becoming an invader and negatively affecting the productive capacity of boreal lakes. Interest in reintroductions is growing, and candidate species could include endangered *Pacifastacus* species in the north-west of the USA.

9.2.2   Australia

With its large and uniquely varied crayfish fauna, Australia has fortunately resisted the importation of exotic crayfish from other countries. However, live freshwater crayfish from Australia, particularly the three commercially important species, *Cherax cainii* / *tenuimanus*, *C. destructor* and *C. quadricarinatus*, have been translocated extensively internationally and within Australia. While controls exist to prevent the importation of live freshwater crayfish, and to regulate their export, there is a lack of consistency in attitudes and regulations across Australia for the control of their translocation between and within states. Potential problems relating to the translocation of freshwater crayfish include the introduction of diseases, competitive interactions between introduced and indigenous species, habitat alteration, the loss of unique combinations of characteristics by hybridization, and the loss of unique combinations of epibiotic species (Horwitz, 1990b).

In the south-west of Western Australia a suite of large crayfish have restricted distributions, complicated by translocations of one more widespread species, the marron *Cherax cainii*, and a species from central and eastern Australia, the yabby *C. destructor* (Austin, 1996). The crayfish of the Canning River system near Perth constitute a fauna of composite origins and include the gilgies *C. quinquecarinatus*, marron and yabby (Lynas *et al.*, 2004). Only gilgies, are indigenous; marron are native to more southern rivers and freshwater lakes in south-western Australia (Austin & Ryan, 2002) and their occurrence is exotic in more northern rivers, including the Canning River system. The endangered hairy marron *C. tenuimanus* has a natural range limited to the Margaret River, where it is threatened by translocated *C. cainii*, particularly by hybridization, and by translocated yabby. There is now a restocking programme for hairy marron through captive breeding, with up to 10 000 tagged juveniles being released each year, but the problem of sympatric exotic species remains.

Restocking is popular among angling bodies across Australia. In 2006, the Government of Western Australia recommended that restocking of marron only be considered as a strategy to assist in the recovery of a stock which had been endangered through depletion, and must be evaluated against disease risks, biodiversity and genetic diversity criteria. Fifteen years earlier, Horwitz (1990b) urged that new regulations for intra- and interstate translocations should be consistent across Australia, and the current ban on imported crayfish must be maintained. Education programmes and an increased level of funding for disease research are seen as essential. He noted that such recommendations might be of value to other countries if acted upon before problems are identified (Horwitz, 1990b).

9.2.3 Europe

Because Europe has been worst hit by crayfish plague and expansions of invading NICS, we present the most detail in this section, looking at restocking projects for *Astacus astacus* and *Austropotamobius pallipes*, followed by an analysis of restocking methods and success with the latter widespread European species.

Astacus astacus restocking

As the noble crayfish *A. astacus* is of high social and cultural value in Scandinavia, inspiring the famous crayfish parties in August, a number of experimental reintroductions have been carried out, especially following stock losses brought about by crayfish plague events initiated by the introduced signal crayfish *Pacifastacus leniusculus*. For example, Jussila *et al.* (2008) reintroduced the noble crayfish into western Finland; the crayfish plague (*Aphanomyces astaci*) and watercourse construction having devastated *A. astacus* stocks in the large river systems there during the first half of the 1900s. Since then, there have been several other attempts to reintroduce noble crayfish to rivers and, in addition, resources have been made available to improve the aquatic habitat for the general requirements of crayfish. Crayfish stocks in the River Pyhäjoki were wiped out by crayfish plague at least twice, in 1960 and 1979, while on another occasion (1988) the reason for mortality was unknown. The most recent reintroduction programme was initiated at the turn of the millennium (in the year 2000), involving a carefully planned project funded by the EU and fisheries administration, with other finance from national and private sources. After two years of introductions, unfortunately crayfish plague was again introduced to the river system. The spread of the plague has been sporadic in the river system and, amazingly, it did not affect all the stocks, even in the main channel of the river. The plague also wiped out one of the source stocks 50 km from the River Pyhäjoki. Later it was shown that the plague fungus could have originated from signal crayfish, either directly or indirectly, but there are no known occurrences of signal crayfish in this area. Furthermore, the stockings were more successful in the small rivers upstream than in the main channel of the River Pyhäjoki itself. However, due to a severe lack of rainfall and resulting drought, some of the small river populations were also lost. This example shows the difficulty of achieving success in the face of unexpected events, and especially the problem of crayfish plague introduction even in the absence of the host.

In Norway, reintroduction was attempted in the Glomma and Halden watercourses, which were contaminated by crayfish plague in 1987 and 1989 (Taugbøl, 2004a). Reintroduction of the noble crayfish started in 1989 in the Glomma and in 1995 in the Halden watercourse. Norway has especially good conditions for reintroduction of the native crayfish after crayfish plague, with no alien plague-carrying crayfish species established in the country. In the Glomma watercourse, 15 000 adult crayfish and 10 000 juveniles were stocked, while 19 000 adults and 26 500 juveniles were stocked into the Halden watercourse. All stocking sites were previously regarded as very good crayfish localities. Four years after stocking, natural recruitment was recorded at all adult crayfish stocking sites in the Glomma watercourse and at most sites in the Halden watercourse.

Current crayfish density is, however, much lower than pre-plague densities, even at the sites where the population has been increasing for more than 10 years. Extensive post-stocking movements were recorded among adult crayfish. Some sites seemed more suitable for settling, resulting in a great variation in catch between the different test-fishing sites. Taugbøl (2004a) advised that juveniles would seem more appropriate as stocking material than adults if the goal is to re-establish a population in a particular area, due to their more stationary behaviour, which seems to persist as they grow larger.

Introductions and reintroduction experiments have also been carried out with the noble crayfish in northern Sweden, an area still free from the disease, but many areas showed a decline and extinction of the crayfish (Jenny Zimmermann, personal communication, 2009). The crayfish population in the river Ljungan crashed and went extinct in 1999, apparently due to overfishing. Analysing the data with a linear model, total extinction was predicted after 2003. In 2004 a large-scale reintroduction of noble crayfish was made from populations remaining in the surrounding areas, with up to 60 000 crayfish being reintroduced. The controlled reintroduction of noble crayfish in the river Ljungan provided a unique opportunity to develop a sustainable harvest system, maintain viable populations, and provide for the conservation of the species in northern Sweden.

Austropotamobius pallipes restocking

There have been a number of recent projects to restock native crayfish into devastated areas of France, Spain and Italy. In France, genetic studies now show that the northern and southern stocks of white-clawed crayfish *A. pallipes* have separate evolutionary origins, and there are also some stocks attributable to *A. italicus* (Gouin *et al.*, 2006). Decisions on restocking are therefore complex. An *A. pallipes* hatchery and rearing station at La Canourgue, which had provided stocking materials since the 1980s, is now closed.

In Navarra (Spain), red swamp crayfish have invaded chiefly from the south and signals further north, and native crayfish are now sparse and scattered. The northern part of Navarra has now been designated for native white-clawed crayfish. The conservation plan involves preserving and re-establishing populations within its suitable habitat range – a programme of detecting suitable watercourses, restocking them, and preventing the spread of alien crayfish by banning their live transport or commerce. Today, red swamp crayfish may only be caught in the southern 'aliens' zone, except under special conditions. All NICS must be killed when caught, by removing their telsons. The conservation plan involved a yearly monitoring programme and an education and awareness campaign (Diéguez-Uribeondo *et al.*, 1997a).

In Italy, there is an annual production for restocking of about 5 t of white-clawed and stone crayfish, in 25 farms, centred on 10 small astacifactories. In addition to these native species, however, noble and thin-clawed crayfish can also be purchased from farms for restocking, costing 50–70 cents each (D'Agaro *et al.*, 1999).

In Ireland, there are good opportunities for restocking the white-clawed crayfish because the species is still widespread and often numerous in large rivers and lakes of the low-lying limestone midlands (Reynolds, 1997, Reynolds *et al.*, 2002a; Demers *et al.*, 2005) and, uniquely in Europe, there are no non-indigenous crayfish species

(Reynolds, 2009b). Irish crayfish are genetically fairly close to those in Great Britain and northern France and show high genetic uniformity between catchments, suggesting that they may be derived from a single stock translocated from western France (Gouin *et al.*, 2003). There could therefore be the potential to supply white-clawed crayfish for restocking from Ireland, where there is a currently operating crayfish hatchery (Policar *et al.*, 2010. Where genetic composition is not known, the precautionary principle suggests using stocks from a contiguous catchment for rearing and restocking. Thus, transfer of crayfish stocks between Northern Ireland and the Irish Republic should not be a problem, as many catchments are shared. White-clawed crayfish in Britain are genetically quite close to Irish ones, but despite precipitous declines in abundance (Holdich *et al.*, 2009b) it appears that, as long as local stocks persist, British authorities are unlikely to restock with material from outside the mainland.

While white-clawed crayfish have been lost in recent years from many areas of continental Europe, potential opportunities for their restocking using Irish crayfish are becoming increasingly limited, as the genetic specificity of stocks to specific catchments is now better understood and written into Species Action Plans (SAPs). On the European continent, restocking of *A. pallipes* is generally done using hatchery-reared stock, particularly where plague is rife and native populations have been seriously depleted, e.g. in France and Spain.

In France, some northern and western stocks are genetically very close to Irish ones (Gouin *et al.*, 2006) and the use of Irish stocks would not be ruled out. There are two possible scenarios: Irish stocks could be used in western areas of France where the same haplotype is frequent; however, this would require a pilot project to establish procedures and protocols (see, for example, Table 1 in Schulz *et al.*, 2002). Alternatively, Irish stocks could be used to restock other catchments from which crayfish within the same evolutionary family have disappeared, and where there are no suitable donor stocks remaining. In such cases, arguably, the precise genetic make-up of introduced stocks may not be as important as the restoration of the species. However, for such areas, development of alien no-go areas seems a first prerequisite, and also a programme of habitat restoration or improvement in the recipient sites (Rogers *et al.*, 2002).

9.3   Analysis of methodology in European *Austropotamobius pallipes* restockings

While measures to reintroduce native crayfish into surface waters have been suggested as a crucial part of management and conservation strategies in Europe (Schulz *et al.*, 2002), there is still considerable uncertainty as to how best to perform such actions and what questions related to reintroduction or restocking exercises should be answered.

9.3.1   Reintroduction procedures

The European thematic network CRAYNET recommended that the crayfish reintroduction process be considered as three separate phases:

I Pre-introduction feasibility

II Implementation

III Post-introduction monitoring.

These phases formed the basis for an analysis of 59 case studies of reintroductions across Europe (Souty-Grosset & Reynolds, 2010). Under each main heading or phase is listed a series of stages identified in the reintroduction process, and a number of possible situations within each stage (see Box 9.1).

Box 9.1.   Sequence of phases, stages and steps in the analysis of reintroduction success of white-clawed crayfish populations in Europe

Phase I   Pre-introduction feasibility check

For the success of the procedure, four preliminary steps are required:

1. Government and stakeholders consulted,
2. Necessary permits obtained,
3. Pilot survey to ascertain if crayfish absent and no sign of plague,
4. Enhancement of habitat if necessary.

Stage Ia   Suitability of target habitats

1. Site is within natural range of species, but contains no current populations and recolonization is unlikely; streams with native crayfish in the past will be prioritized.
2. There are no NICS within 50 km in adjoining waters (at least 20 km, according to Peay, 2003a).
3. Site meets ecological requirements for habitat and water quality (EU Water Framework Directive 2000/60/EC), including a low risk of pollution.
4. Suitable surplus habitat for population expansion (bedrock crevices, boulders, cobbles, gravel for adults, small roots, bryophytes, leaf litter, sand for juveniles).

Stage Ib   Crayfish donor population for restocking

(Stocking material will originate either from existing wild stocks or from crayfish farms).

1. Donor population sourced from same or adjacent catchment following precautionary principle (see also transport).
2. Donor stocks should be in high abundance (no more than 10% of the donor population must be removed).
3. Donor stocks free from plague, *Thelohania* <10%, and health screening carried out.
4. Legislative regulations should be considered, because the direct transfer of crayfish from one waterbody to another usually requires specific permits.

Phase II   Implementation

Stage IIa   Suitable stock

1. Use adults, or ideally a balanced donor population with all size classes, in several introductions over at least 3 years and during the period from August to October (Peay, 2003a).
2. Use a suitable M:F ratio (1:1 to 1:3) among adults.
3. Use a range of size classes.
4. Use 50–100 individuals minimum.
5. Know the genetic origin of donors (preferable to precautionary principle).

Stage IIb   Transport

1. Provide interim storage if transport time exceeds 18 hours; another reason to work within a catchment, to minimize the time needed for translocation.
2. Minimize disturbance or aggression by providing ample hides, cool conditions, and water from the stream of origin.
3. Before release, the crayfish can be acclimatized for 1–4 days in the new habitat, in net cages supplied with adequate refuges.

Stage IIc   Release

1. Introduce to suitable refuges (natural or created).
2. Take appropriate measures to avoid the spread of crayfish plague (e.g. disinfect boots and equipment).
3. Keep accurate records of reintroduction process.

Phase III   Post-introduction stages

1. Annual or biennial monitoring for population presence and density estimates for at least 5 years.
2. If sites deteriorate, carry out management works.
3. Report all works and findings to statutory agency.

From Souty-Grosset & Reynolds (2010).

Phase I   Pre-introduction feasibility

For the success of the procedure, four preliminary steps are required. Government and stakeholders must be consulted and necessary permits obtained. There must be a pilot survey to ascertain whether crayfish are indeed absent, and that there are no signs of plague, and finally, the habitat should be enhanced if it is considered necessary.

Stage Ia   Suitability of target habitats

Several studies refer to the general water quality parameters and habitat requirements of native crayfish. For example, despite a growing acceptance that *A. pallipes* is not a strict bioindicator of high water quality (Füreder & Reynolds, 2003), the heterogeneous nature of the habitat for crayfish must be maintained and enhanced, and water quality monitored in both rivers and lakes (Demers & Reynolds, 2002; Renai *et al.*, 2006). The bottom substrate, the presence of morphological structures acting as potential hiding places, and the geographical isolation of the habitat all seem to be of importance. Among some basic water quality aspects it was found that white-clawed crayfish were able to tolerate unexpectedly wide ranges of values of some of the measured parameters, such as water temperature and hypoxia (Demers *et al.*, 2006). Principal component analysis (PCA) suggested, however, that an increase in organic matter was a reliable indicator for the loss of *A. pallipes*. (Trouilhé *et al.*, 2008).

Four situations were selected as important for ultimate success. The site must be within the natural range of the species but should contain no current populations, and recolonization by natural means would be unlikely. Streams which held native crayfish in the past would be prioritized. There should be no NICS nearby (within 50 km in adjoining waters, as suggested by CRAYNET, or at least 20 km according to Peay, 2003a). The site should meet ecological requirements for habitat and water quality (EU Water Framework Directive 2000/60/EC), including a low risk of pollution. Finally, there should be suitable surplus habitat for population expansion (e.g. bedrock crevices, boulders, cobbles or gravel for adults, small roots, bryophytes, leaf litter and sand for juveniles).

Stage Ib   Crayfish donor population for restocking

Stocking material will originate either from existing 'donor' stocks in other streams or ponds, or from crayfish farms. The best situations are that donor populations are sourced from the same or an adjacent catchment following the precautionary principle, that donor stocks should be in high abundance (no more than 10% of the donor population must be removed) and free from plague, with low levels of *Thelohania* (<10%) and health screening carried out. Legislative regulations should also be considered, because the direct transfer of crayfish from one waterbody to another usually requires specific permits.

Phase II   Implementation

Stage IIa   Availability of suitable stock

While adults have the advantages of good dispersal activity for rapid colonization and lower mortality than juveniles, they have the disadvantages of male aggression and a lower life expectancy for the oldest crayfish. If juveniles are introduced, they are easily predated by fish but one could expect better adaptation to a new environment and lower mobility, and a larger number could be introduced.

Recommended procedures are to restock ideally with a balanced donor population with all size classes, in several introductions over at least 3 years and during the period from August to October (Peay, 2003a). Otherwise, restock with adults with a suitable M:F ratio (1:1 to 1:3), a range of size classes, and a minimum of 50–100 individuals each year.

Ideally, the genetic origin of donors and original inhabitants should be known, since *Austropotamobius pallipes* is now recognized as a species complex. As a declining species, *A. pallipes* is subject to a loss of genetic diversity. Consequently, a certain degree of genetic variability needs to be maintained within the species because it governs its adaptation potential; the populations must be capable of responding to new environmental conditions. The first step is to define management units within the species. At present, the identity of the complex taxon *A. pallipes* is clear across its northern and western range (particularly in France, Britain and Ireland). The situation is more complex with *A. italicus*, which is shared between three subspecies in Spain, Italy, Austria and the Balkans. Where there are subspecies, and perhaps sibling species, conservation programmes cannot be undertaken without a thorough knowledge of taxonomic entities, particularly in zones where these overlap (reviewed in Souty-Grosset *et al.*, 2006; Souty-Grosset, 2009). For the other native European species such as *Astacus astacus* and *Austropotamobius torrentium*, the genetic relationships should also be carefully considered. It is still difficult to draw any final conclusions from the studies to date on the genetic structure of these crayfish stocks in relation to reintroduction measures. However, the precautionary principle would recommend the use of local populations whenever possible.

Stage IIb   Transport

If the transport time for stocks exceeds 18 hours, interim storage must be provided (another reason to work within a catchment, so as to minimize the time needed for translocation). The provision of ample hides, cool conditions, and water from the stream of origin while the crayfish are in storage will all minimize disturbance or aggression. Before release, the crayfish can be acclimatized for 1–4 days in the new habitat, in net cages supplied with adequate refuges.

Stage IIc   Release

Crayfish should be introduced to areas with suitable refuges (natural or specially created), and accurate records kept of the reintroduction process. Following release, appropriate measures should be taken to avoid the spread of crayfish plague (e.g. disinfecting boots and equipment).

Phase III   Post-introduction monitoring stages

Annual or biennial monitoring should be carried out for population presence and density estimates for at least 5 years, during which period at least two breedings should have taken place. If the restocking sites deteriorate, management work should be carried out, and all works and findings reported to the statutory agency. Surprisingly, these stages are not always observed, which is perhaps indicative of a lack of professionalism in the restocking process.

9.3.2   Analysis of reintroduction studies

The final step is to analyse the reasons for success or failure, because there is still a lack of consensus on how the reintroduction measure itself should be done. An analysis of

59 case studies of reintroductions of the white-clawed crayfish species complex across Europe (France, Ireland, UK, Spain, Italy and Austria) was attempted (Souty-Grosset & Reynolds, 2010), but while the results listed a wide range of methodology, no clear-cut optimal strategy emerged for *A. pallipes* over this geographical region, indicating that more consideration of methodology and more careful recording of results for each step might be needed.

The process of reintroduction was analysed under the three main phase headings: Pre-introduction feasibility, Implementation and Post-introduction monitoring. Eight stages were identified, involving 26 possible steps or decisions, as described in Box 9.1 and discussed above. Each situation was codified as positive, negative or unknown. In the 59 studies, 26 reintroductions were successful and 33 unsuccessful. However, both regional and taxonomic differences are apparent. With *A. pallipes* in the UK, Ireland and France, successful attempts had more positive scores during the reintroduction process (i.e. the desired conditions complied with) than did unsuccessful ones. However, in studies in Spain and Italy with *A. italicus*, no such clear-cut differences were seen either in positive or negative scores. Thus, in Spain, where 13 reintroductions were successful and 12 unsuccessful, in both cases there were the same number of positive and negative scores; and in Italy, with five successful and four unsuccessful reintroductions, each averaged the same high number of positive scores, indicating no greater success rate despite apparently paying close attention to detail. It therefore seems that the number of stages or steps scored in each study was not an indication of success or failure in most studies. However, the number of positive scores was correlated with successful reintroductions of *A. pallipes* in several northern countries in which the taxonomy was clear.

From the 59 study findings, the conclusions were as follows.

- **Within the pre-introduction feasibility phase**, only one stage, that of target habitat choice, seemed important: steps 1 (site is within natural range of species, with no current populations, and recolonization unlikely) and 4 (suitable surplus habitat for expansion) appeared to influence success or failure. Neither donor populations nor site preparation showed clear patterns in most regions. More information would appear to be needed on target sites, e.g. whether they are in the same or different catchments as donor sites.
- **In the implementation phase**, no clear pattern was seen in most regions as regards suitable stock, transport and release. These findings are counterintuitive, but may suggest that if plague or other disease is perceived as a problem locally, the outcome may be poor, despite taking precautions.
- **The post-reintroduction monitoring phase** again showed no consistent pattern in most regions.

Among the conclusions, it appears that the more meticulously planned and recorded is the process of reintroduction, the more chance there is of a positive outcome. However, donor populations and site preparation do not appear to influence results overall. It seems that *A pallipes* and *A. italicus* may be fundamentally different in their reintroduction success; either because of different climatic conditions and environment, or because the methodology of reintroduction may not correspond between different studies, although they have been coded in the same way. Comparable analyses of reintroductions of other crayfish species are awaited.

9.4   Discussions on a general model

This analysis of reintroduction projects for *A. pallipes* was further discussed at a regional crayfish conference in the Czech Republic in 2009 on native crayfish reintroductions, between scientists from ten countries encompassing the range of the species (Souty-Grosset & Reynolds, 2010).

On the need for general Europe-wide protocols for restocking, it was concluded that, while the methodology could follow general principles, the details must depend on individual species, geography and available habitats. Detailed baseline methodology would require an analysis of successes and failures for each species and region, as carried out for the *A. pallipes* species complex described above; however, few generalizations emerged from that analysis. Moreover, strategies applicable to streams will be different to those for ponds or lakes. In the latter, it is recommended to restock from cages, where health checks can be implemented, but in streams this is seldom feasible.

CRAYNET scientists recommended that reintroduction sites be at least 50 km from a NICS site. However, it was noted in discussion that it would be difficult to find anywhere in much of Europe so far from a NICS site, and even sanctuary (Ark) sites in the UK are much less than 50 km from NICS stocks. Therefore, identifying the barriers to migration becomes essential. A stream is always a possible corridor for NICS, but an impassable waterfall or culvert can improve isolation. Crayfish may fall down an outflow, and NICS such as *Procambarus clarkii* or *Pacifastacus leniusculus* show particular ingenuity in circumventing barriers. Crayfish can also bypass barriers by land, or with human assistance, so target sites must be isolated from tourists and anglers. In the Czech Republic, new ponds in forest areas may appear to be safe reintroduction sites, but most are stocked for fishing; only drinking water reservoirs would be safe.

Importance of genetic variation at the proposed reintroduction site

It makes sense to consider between-watershed genetic differences developed over hundreds of generations. Variation can, however, arise quite fast, as shown in the Liffey catchment (Ireland), where *A. pallipes* stocks in the Blessington Reservoir created 80 years ago now show genetic variation different from that in the tributary Brittas Stream, presumably through adaptation to a lake habitat (Reynolds *et al.*, 2002b). However, Irish crayfish stocks are relatively very uniform (Gouin *et al.*, 2003), and differences between Blessington and Brittas crayfish are well within this range. Genetic screening is essential, including determining what alleles are present. The importance of genetic information was demonstrated by Bertocchi *et al.* (2008) for *A. italicus*. Using a fragment of the mitochondrial DNA 16S rRNA gene, they identified eight haplotypes, six corresponding to *A. i. italicus* and two to *A. i. meridionalis*, the two clades being found in syntopy in one stream. Eight populations of *A. i. italicus*, analysed for their microsatellite loci, showed a low intrapopulation genetic variability and a high interpopulation genetic divergence. Populations sampled in one basin showed no heterozygotes and a high level of inbreeding. Thus, knowledge of the genetic structure of studied populations, combined with information on their ethology, ecology and demography, is an essential prerequisite for any action aimed at reintroducing or restocking this threatened species.

For a fragmented population, the best approach is to restore the environment. Existing small, fragmented populations and their range should first be maintained, preventing further fragmentation and loss. Perhaps a bigger impact can be made through restoration of parts of a stream, leading to an expanded population, rather than restocking.

Some population mixing is inevitable with restocking, but perhaps genetic variability or mingling of donor stocks is not a serious problem. For example, a successful project to reintroduce Atlantic salmon to the Rhine used hatchery stocks from western Ireland as source material (Kenneth Whelan, personal communication, 2007), while another, to increase alpine populations of brown trout, involved adding both Atlantic and Danube stocks to increase variation. However, information from molecular monitoring indicated that after catastrophic events such as floods, only the well-adapted local stocks survived (Medgyesi *et al.*, 2009).

There has been much debate on whether it is better to restock with captive-bred donor stock or to harvest a possibly threatened donor stock, with responses covering *Astacus astacus*, *Austropotamobius pallipes* and *A. torrentium*. It is certainly important to know the source of donor stocks, and preferable to use a good donor stock and harvest it heavily, than to take a few crayfish from a feeble population. Captive breeding is best, but it is necessary first to ensure that such crayfish culture has a local (genetic) basis. Different stocks can be maintained in separate lines in a modern hatchery. The use of small donor populations is questionable. In Spain most white-clawed crayfish populations are now too small to risk harvesting for stocking, with too few donors available. Finland and Sweden will soon stop stocking from wild harvests, only allowing stocks from aquaculture (with known genetics, large numbers available, and complete control of disease status possible). It is now known that wild *A. astacus* stocks can 'hide' plague for several years, but this tends not to happen in culture, where stress will bring it out. The optimum strategy seems that if the local genetic strains are known, they should be used. However, this has not happened with *A. astacus* across much of Europe, since many introductions or reintroductions have been of the Augsburg selected strain.

The preferred restocking situation likely to lead to the best survival of donor populations is to reintroduce at least 50 crayfish each year for good genetic variation, in three annual sessions to ensure a range of ages in the new population. Survival is best if juveniles are stocked in autumn, when crayfish feeding slows or stops. Suitable sanctuary sites are best looked for in isolated pristine headwaters, remote from human activities. If using water-filled quarries (recommended as Ark sites in the UK) it would be necessary to control access by recreational SCUBA divers to protect implanted crayfish.

The legal situation with restocking is quite variable across Europe (see Chapter 10), and there are often local and bio-political problems involved. Some EU countries permit the sale of live crayfish. However, in the Czech Republic an individual who constructs a pond is not legally permitted to buy crayfish for stocking, even near native crayfish sites. In Spain, state-run native crayfish farms produce crayfish for restocking, but these crayfish cannot be bought. In both these cases, there is a risk that pond owners will stock with non-native crayfish obtained illegally or from pet stores. Therefore, uniform Europe-wide legislation is needed to protect native stocks, and it may be best to provide restocking materials legally from an approved aquaculture supply.

When establishing new populations or sanctuary areas, as in the UK Ark programme, opinions differ over whether or not these should be indicated to the public. Public access to land is a key to any education policy; however, ownership of land and of water varies across the EU. It is certainly necessary to involve local people and other stakeholders. Fishermen are often justifiably proud of their ponds, and it is therefore better to make positive suggestions than to provide further restrictions. Education must explain the role of crayfish in the freshwater ecosystem, and the wider focus – their value as sentinels for water quality, and their disappearance as alarm signals that other fauna, e.g. trout, are also in danger of extinction.

Climate change is a longer-term consideration, but one which must influence the choice of restocking site. In France and Italy in recent years high temperatures ('heat waves') have been the main cause of extinction of white-clawed crayfish populations, with these generally surviving only in regions of hyporheic flow or percolating cool groundwaters (Renai et al., 2008). Stocks are in particular danger when fragmented and restricted to headwaters with small flows. Climate change outcomes predict not just temperature extremes, but also local flooding and droughts. A 10% increase in such events in future is expected, and sudden flooding could result in a wash-out of introduced stocks.

9.5 Current feasibility of crayfish reintroduction

According to Taugbøl & Peay (2004), a reintroduction is particularly appropriate for a population recently lost, for extending the distribution of an indigenous crayfish species into its historic range, or for creating new or isolated populations to conserve genetic diversity of the species. However, the outcomes of experiences in European countries suggest that crayfish reintroductions are successful only when they are preceded by a feasibility study in order to verify the taxonomic status of the species and identify genetically the crayfish management unit that was originally present in the area of reintroduction, and also to select the target area for reintroduction.

The suitability of the area to be repopulated is assessed according to general characteristics of the catchment, its physico-chemical and ecological particulars, including the absence of and prevention of access by non-indigenous crayfish species and the absence of Aphanomyces astaci and other potential pathogens. General recommendations are to use both adults and juveniles as available, to stock as many crayfish as can be afforded and over several seasons and, if short of stock, to boost through hatchery rearing. Projects that were successful in establishing stable and self-sustaining white-clawed crayfish populations had reintroduction numbers of at least 100–200 sexually mature individuals of various size classes, with a ratio of one male to three female crayfish. Harvesting from a donor population should be carried out in summer, after females have released young and before mating. Before their release the crayfish can be acclimatized for 1–4 days in net cages supplied with adequate refuges. Their release must occur in favourable physico-chemical conditions and with the availability of ample natural and/or artificial shelters. After the reintroduction (to be repeated annually in the same watercourses for 3 years at least), regular monitoring of the reintroduced population and checking the physico-chemical and biotic parameters of the habitat of reintroduction are essential.

In general, the major constraints in a restocking project are money and availability of stocking material. The current UK focus on Ark sites – new, isolated sites, such as abandoned quarries, where populations can be established in relative safety from the widespread signal crayfish – is now backed by a stage-by-stage methodology for Ark site selection (Buglife, 2010).

9.6   Key needs for successful restoration

The chapters in Part II have shown that management of biodiversity is a complex and often changing task. The situation with NICS is especially complex. While their exploitation may appear to help to reduce stocks, it has been shown also to spread awareness of these species and to lead to further introductions. Fisheries officials may transfer plague spores while restocking young trout, fishermen may transfer plague directly or indirectly, and uninformed people are equally dangerous if they give a child a crayfish as a pet and later dispose of its offspring into a pond or waterway. Finally there is strong and increasing concern about the aquarium trade for NICS, particularly through internet access, and scientists and managers recommended that a resolution on control of trade in live crayfish be considered for submission to the International Association of Astacology (IAA). Positive approaches are thus needed both in educating the public and in developing uniform legislation to protect European native stocks (see Chapter 10). Europe is now more amenable to broad-scale protection of native stocks, and it is hoped that there will be a decision for common harmonization of rules.

A key factor in the protection of indigenous and reintroduced crayfish populations is the knowledge and attitude of people locally. The objectives and actions of all projects should be agreed with local stakeholders to improve their chances of success. As seen with *Astacus astacus* in Scandinavian countries, there need be no contradiction between exploitation and conservation provided that a balance between utilization and overexploitation can be found. In some European countries where there are strong traditions connected to crayfish fishery, crayfish exploitation, in the form of a controlled fishery, may be an essential tool in conservation by involving more people in the task of protecting the species and by increasing general awareness. In these cases, local guidelines for sustainable exploitation should be produced. Other ways of utilizing indigenous crayfish e.g. farming indigenous crayfish for restocking purposes, are possible. The ultimate aim should be to restore community functioning in fresh waters to as near a natural state as possible.

Part III

Knowledge transfer for successful crayfish management

10 Effective legislation and public education for adequate conservation of crayfish and biodiversity

10.1 Legislative controls on crayfish: the international situation

As earlier chapters have shown, much of global biological diversity resides in fresh waters, but proportionately more freshwater species are endangered than in other biomes, largely because of increasing human demands on a restricted resource. Decapods (crabs and crayfish) are considered among the most threatened of fresh-water invertebrates, with 168 decapod species on the *IUCN Red List of Threatened and Vulnerable Species* (2003). On average, 40% of crayfish are considered threatened. Many crayfish species also appear on international and national Red Lists and are afforded some protection. However, not enough is being done to publicize this situation and to explain to the public why this is so important. Furthermore, working against national or international protection are some international conventions, such as the World Trade Organization treaties to which many countries are signatories. In some specific cases, this has forced the importation of alien species despite their known damaging impacts. Some case examples are given later in the chapter.

For the first time in international law, the 1992 Convention on Biological Diversity (CBD) recognized that the conservation of biodiversity is a common human concern and integral to the development process. The agreement covers all ecosystems, species and genetic resources, and links traditional conservation efforts to the economic goal of sustainable use of biological resources. While past conservation efforts were aimed at protecting particular species and habitats, the Convention recognizes that ecosystems, species and genes must be used sustainably for the benefit of humans in such a way that it does not lead to the long-term decline of biological diversity.

The Biodiversity Convention also obliges decision makers to base their actions on the precautionary principle that, where there is a threat of significant reduction or loss of biological diversity, the lack of full scientific certainty should not be used as a reason for postponing measures to avoid or minimize such a threat. The Convention acknowledges that substantial investments are needed in order to conserve biological diversity. It argues, however, that conservation will bring us significant environmental, economic and social benefits in return. A legislative response is needed, and most of the Parties have now established National Biodiversity Strategies and Action Plans (NBSAPs) to implement the Convention. For example, the UK and New Zealand have both carried out elaborate responses including recovery plans to conserve individual species and specific habitats, while the USA, although it has not yet ratified the treaty, has long had species recovery programmes and other mechanisms in place for species conservation.

Legislative controls are designed both to confer protection on indigenous crayfish species (ICS), and to provide regulatory controls for non-indigenous, exotic or alien crayfish species (NICS) or to prevent their introduction. The most pressing case is that of controlling invasive North American crayfish species, carriers of various strains of the crayfish plague organism *Aphanomyces astaci*, which is lethal to crayfish on other continents. American crayfish have been widely introduced to Europe and Africa, and legislative controls have struggled unsuccessfully to keep up with the damage caused. Several pieces of legislation protect indigenous crayfish both through prohibitions on imports and through regulation of implantation (Vigneux *et al.*, 2002). However, in many countries such legislation was weak or non-existent until it was too late and NICS were already well established. It tended to be seen as counter to free trade and movement of goods agreements.

10.1.1   International resolutions on crayfish

In 2000 an open forum of the International Association of Astacology (IAA), an international scientific body for the study of crayfish, meeting in Perth, Western Australia, led to consensus amongst astacologists from many disciplines, including science, aquaculture, trade and conservation, on a range of issues related to biodiversity and methods of combating the potential extinction of crayfish species.

The following points arose (many of them covered in earlier chapters):

- The concepts of 'maintenance of biodiversity' and 'sustainability' are central to the conservation of crayfish species.
- Maintenance of biodiversity in the case of endangered native crayfish species (e.g. the Tasmanian giant freshwater crayfish *Astacopsis gouldi*) can be equated with prevention of extinction; whereas in the case of invasive crayfish species (e.g. red swamp crayfish *Procambarus clarkii*) prevention of indiscriminate dispersal is most important.
- Crayfish producers seek the greatest return on their investments, which are often obtained by exporting live crayfish to national and international markets. There has been strong opposition from producers, as well as from researchers studying introduced species as potential aquaculture or experimental animals, to a ban on translocations. However, although many want to continue their crayfish translocation activities, there was an appreciation amongst astacologists that biodiversity should be maintained and not threatened by non-native crayfish trade or projects.
- Indiscriminate intercontinental translocation of crayfish is known to have had adverse effects on biodiversity (Gherardi & Holdich, 1999), but local translocations can also be devastating. In western Australia, local translocation has resulted in demonstrable and significant reduction in the gene pool of *Cherax tenuimanus* (Nguyen *et al.*, 2002).
- World Trade Organization (WTO) member countries must base the measures taken to reduce adverse risks associated with trade in animals and their products on international standards developed by the World Organization for Animal Health (OIE).

In response, the IAA Perth Meeting in 2000 passed two resolutions relating to these findings: that IAA will promote crayfish as flagship or keystone species, and that IAA supports causes that are congruent with the maintenance of biodiversity. The following year (2001), a roundtable workshop at the IAA European meeting in Poitiers (France) emphasized the importance of crayfish in European national traditions, and welcomed non-governmental organization (NGO) educational initiatives by France, Spain and Ireland to promote the heritage value of white-clawed crayfish (Puky *et al.*, 2002). Another Poitiers roundtable examined the difficult situation of indigenous European crayfish and the legislative basis for protection of ICS and controls of NICS in Europe (Vigneux *et al.*, 2002). In addition to pressures from human activities resulting in water pollution and the physical destruction of habitats, they are subjected to competition and transmission of disease from exotic NICS introduced or translocated across Europe.

By 2008, the widespread negative consequences of movements and translocations of crayfish within and between countries, as well as between continents, had become of great concern to IAA members gathered in Kuopio, Finland. Trade and introductions of non-native crayfish species for economic reasons have had a severe impact on native species and habitats by spreading disease and parasites and through altering the original ecosystem. IAA members also expressed their concern that climate change would further jeopardize the survival of species in their native habitats. Higher temperatures might change disease risk profiles for crayfish and alter the resilience of the natural ecosystem to invasions by non-native species. Drought and rainfall decline would increase pressure on water resources and threaten locally restricted crayfish. Very few countries in the world would be unaffected by this sort of change.

The IAA in 2008 also called upon governments to adopt the following two recommendations:

• that no translocations of crayfish should be authorized or encouraged until the consequences are carefully evaluated and fully understood;
• that the implications of changing climates and increasing pressures on water resources form a component of all species management plans for freshwater crayfish.

Even though the IAA is an international body composed of crayfish producers, marketers and scientists, and it is a measure of their responsibility that meetings consistently reflect conservationist concerns, such resolutions and recommendations still need to be translated into regulatory action, and then publicized through appropriate education programmes. The legislative controls across the world, on the conservation of indigenous crayfish stocks and on trade and movement of crayfish, are summarized below, followed by a discussion on how conservation is assisted by education.

10.2   Legislation protecting ICS or controlling NICS

10.2.1   Legislation protecting ICS in Europe

In much of Europe, monitoring has revealed declines in ICS and advances by NICS (Holdich *et al.*, 2009b); however, there are no uniform protective policies within the

EU. In Sweden and France, a ban on live transport of all introduced species originating from outside Europe did not stop this process, and other measures such as fishing regulations and reintroduction plans have not reversed the declines; so a different conservation policy is needed, based on habitat preservation and on the enforcement of prophylactic rules. A start could be made in implementing such actions for the 55 French habitat decrees and 154 Natura 2000 zones with their management plans.

Among influential EU Directives, the 1992 EC Habitats Directive (*Directive for the Conservation of Natural Habitats and Wild Flora and Fauna*: 92/43/EEC and 97/62/EU) defines species and their habitats for protection, and the 2000 Water Framework Directive (2000/60/EC) sets out how water quality is to be maintained and improved across Europe. Both have maintenance or enhancement of biodiversity as a goal. The European Directive 91/67/EEC regulating fish diseases, under which areas can be designated and protected if disease-free, could also be used to protect ICS (e.g. from crayfish plague) – but this has not yet been done.

It would be excellent to harmonize national and regional regulations for ICS in Europe, considering that the legislative basis protection varies considerably (see below and Appendix 10.1). For example, laws in the UK, Austria, France, Italy and Latvia consider crayfish as fish, while other countries treat them as species in their own right. Legal capture size limits may also vary; for example, the minimum legal size for stone crayfish *Austropotamobius torrentium* is 9 cm in Switzerland, 10 cm in Styria and 12 cm in Lower and Upper Austria: the last three being provinces of Federal Austria. There are also transborder considerations requiring eventual harmonization, e.g. the different treatments of stone crayfish along the Danube corridor. Finally, there are legal implications with taxonomy, e.g. the species complex *A. pallipes s.l.* is protected in southern Europe, but not *A. italicus* or subspecies recently recognized through new genetics-based taxonomy. The legal situation plainly lags behind scientific discoveries, and issues of infraspecies, genetic species and redefined species urgently need integration in law. State veterinarians and customs officers have a crucial role to play, as do wildlife inspectors and water managers, but if they cannot recognize the species named in the legislation in order to take appropriate action, the law is useless.

Definition of the terms 'indigenous' or 'native' has caused problems in interpreting the law in France, Germany and some other countries. In Germany, for example, under conservation legislation, all species – native or alien – that can breed in the wild are protected equally. The IUCN now defines 'native' or 'indigenous' as demonstrably present in a country before 1500, the date relating to the voyages of discovery to North America and subsequent introduction of many exotic plants ('neophytes') and animals. This ruling may affect some heritage species generally considered native but for which evidence is lacking. Noble crayfish were certainly introduced to Norway in recent centuries, while people may actually have brought the 'native' white-clawed crayfish to Britain and Ireland from France some time in the last millennium, and probably also to the Iberian Peninsula from southern Europe; but documentation is scant or lacking (Holdich *et al.*, 2009a).

Three indigenous crayfish species (ICS), the white-clawed crayfish *Austropotamobius pallipes*, the stone crayfish *A. torrentium* and the noble crayfish *Astacus*

astacus, are protected across Europe under Appendix 3 of the Bern Convention (1979), which limits their exploitation. The Habitats Directive confers legal protection on the Bern species and on their habitats, and lists the three indigenous crayfish species in its Annex II, requiring Special Areas of Conservation (SACs) to be set up for them in each country under the Natura 2000 umbrella. White-clawed, stone and noble crayfish are also listed in Annex V of the Habitats Directive, which allows exploitation provided that conservation status is favourable. However, commercialization of ICS is only important for noble crayfish in the Nordic countries, where it had an estimated value of some €40 million per annum in 2004, including Sweden €30 million, Finland €7 million, and Norway €1 million per annum (Holdich & Pöckl, 2005). Exploitation of noble crayfish continues, although recent assessments under the Habitats Directive in 2008 have shown their conservation status to be unfavourable in most, if not all, European countries. The commercial value of ICS is nowadays less important than formerly in France, Italy, Poland, Germany, Austria and Spain, and is negligible in the UK and Ireland (Chapter 5).

In addition to European legislation, EU Member States have national legislation, usually inserting EC Directives into national law, though they may go further (Vigneux *et al.*, 2002; Holdich & Pöckl, 2005). States may also have other regulations and by-laws adapted to the particular national or regional situation, such as the Freshwater Biodiversity Conservation Initiative of the UK Nature Conservancy, which produces scientific syntheses of major issues (e.g. Dudgeon *et al.*, 2006). National protection regimes, including legislation, education measures and restocking protocols, are summarized in Reynolds *et al.* (2006). Within federal states, such as Germany and Austria, and countries with strong autonomous regions, such as Italy and Spain, regional regulations may differ.

Species Action Plans (SAPs) for native crayfish now exist in many European countries, e.g. France (Laurent *et al.*, 1993), Britain (Environment Agency, 1995; Holdich and Rogers, 1995), Norway (Taugbøl *et al.*, 1993; Taugbøl & Skurdal, 1998), Sweden (Söderbäck & Edsman, 1998), Finland (Mannonen & Halonen, 2000), Estonia (Tuusti *et al.*, 1998) and Lithuania (Taugbøl *et al.*, 1998). While the federal states of Germany (Lukowicz, 1999) and Austria (Pöckl, 1999) do not have nationwide Species Action Plans, they do have action plans for certain areas.

Assessment of threat

In 1996, noble crayfish *Astacus astacus*, white-clawed *Austropotamobius pallipes* and stone crayfish *A. torrentium* were assessed as Vulnerable using criterion B2bce + 3bcd by the IUCN (Baillie & Groombridge, 1996). These assessments still stood in 2009 (IUCN, 2009), although updating is in progress (Nadia Richman, personal communication, 2011) and current population estimates indicate that some of these species are likely to change category. However, any change in category cannot be interpreted as a decline or increase in abundance since the 1996 assessments. Those previous assessments of Vulnerable were made on the basis that these species had an Extent of Occurrence (EOO) of less than 20 000 km^2, but recent calculations of the EOO for each species indicate that they far exceed 20 000 km^2 and so no longer qualify for listing under criterion B. Both *A. astacus* and *A. pallipes* now qualify for a listing under criterion A, which utilizes population data to infer rates of decline over a 10-year period or three generation lengths, whichever is greater. Trends in abundance have been calculated using both presence/absence data, and harvest data. It is, however, acknowledged that calculations of these trends are based on the assumption that rates of decline for parts of a country can be translated into what is happening in the whole country, that the population is equally distributed across the country or has been in the last 10 years, and that the rates of decline that have been obtained from presence/absence data are reasonably indicative – or at least conservative – estimates, of changes in population numbers. Preliminary results suggest that *A. pallipes* has declined over the last 10 years by around 60% in the UK, *c.* 50% in France, and *c.* 75% in Italy. Population estimates for *A. astacus* indicate declines of around 87% for Sweden and 15% for Finland over the last 10 years. Data on population trends for *A torrentium* are seriously lacking, and so it is unlikely to qualify for a listing under criterion A. As declines are known to be occurring, this species may be listed by IUCN as Data Deficient (DD), with a caveat acknowledging that it is likely to be threatened, but that data to assess it under the criteria are not available. Based on the available data, Holdich *et al.* (2009a) suggested a revised listing of Endangered for *A. pallipes* and to maintain a listing of Vulnerable for *A. astacus*.

10.2.2   Legislation controlling NICS in Europe

Several pieces of legislation in Europe confer additional protection on indigenous crayfish through prohibitions on imports of NICS and/or regulation of their implantation (Holdich & Pöckl, 2005). However, this tended to be seen as counter to agreements on free movement of goods and, in some countries such as the UK, such legislation was weak or non-existent until it was too late and NICS were already well established. The commercial value of NICS varies across Europe, and harvesting may be encouraged or prohibited depending on its perceived impact. The NICS red swamp, spiny-cheek and signal crayfish are harvested in France, Italy, Poland, Germany, Austria, Spain and the UK. In Italy, parastacids such as the marron and yabby are also farmed (Chapter 5) and are likely to escape. A new EU Directive is in preparation on alien species, which will be likely to have particular impacts on those countries where NICS harvests are significant. Currently, the European Network on Invasive Alien Species, NOBANIS (www.nobanis.org/Regulations_International.asp) provides a gateway to regional directives.

In addition, Council Regulation (EC) No 708/2007 of 11 June 2007 deals with the introduction or translocation of alien and locally absent species in aquaculture. It covers both animals and plants, and applies to all types of aquaculture in the EU or within Member States if there is a risk to the environment. This Regulation aims to ensure adequate protection of the aquatic environment from the risks associated with the aquaculture of non-native species. It provides measures to limit the environmental risks from movements of non-native aquatic species by requiring translocation permits, preventive measures such as quarantine, and monitoring measures. However, it does not apply to pet shops, garden centres or aquaria where there is no contact with

EU waters. Despite the last exclusions, the Regulation notes that Member States must take all appropriate measures to avoid adverse effects on biodiversity resulting from the movement of aquatic organisms for aquaculture purposes and from the spread of those organisms.

As NICS become more abundant, ecosystem changes are to be expected, resulting in community simplification and loss of biodiversity. Realizing the devastation that NICS can cause to native crayfish, most EU countries now ban importation of live crayfish, including Finland, France, Ireland, Norway, Poland, Spain and Sweden, but not Austria, Germany or Italy. However, a German ban was overturned by the European Courts of Justice in 1994, citing free trade principles; as a result an Austrian ban was not instigated, perhaps for fear that it would meet the same fate (Manfred Pöckl, personal communication, 2008). Sweden's ban on live imports was also challenged in 1997 and the law rescinded, but the ban was finally upheld and reintroduced in 2003, because by this time EC environmental legislation was deemed more important than free trade in such cases.

The European situation provides a good example of how crayfish conservation may operate in a loose federation of cooperating states. In Europe, state laws and regulations may relate to controls on imports and exports, or to protection of indigenous stocks and habitats; while fishing regulations may relate to ICS, NICS or both. The relevant legislation relating to freshwater crayfish varies across Europe (Vigneux *et al.*, 2002; Edsman & Śmietana, 2004; Reynolds *et al.*, 2006) and within states (Puky *et al.*, 2005), and its efficacy has been questioned (Holdich & Pöckl, 2005).

Variable controls in transnational catchments, notably the Danube system, are particularly problematic in regard to the spread of species (Puky *et al.*, 2005; Pârvulescu *et al.*, 2009), and European legislation is not strong enough in this regard. Table 10.1 shows how indigenous crayfish species in one state (Hungary) can be affected by regulations in neighbouring regions. There are also problems of enforcement, particularly in internet-based trade of NICS (Holdich *et al.*, 2009b).

Recent legislation and conservation measures relating to ICS and NICS in Europe (see also Appendix 10.1)

In the past decade, the situation has changed markedly in northern Europe, where the ICS *Astacus astacus* is in decline while NICS (chiefly *Pacifastacus leniusculus*) expand their range. The legal response has been variable. Swedish legislation restricting live crayfish imports was lifted in 1997, but reinstated in 2003, indicating the new importance at the European level of environmental and conservation legislation over the previously dominant free trade agreements (Edsman, 2004). A revised national action plan for the conservation of *A. astacus* in Sweden was launched in 2009, and county administrations can now assign special protected areas for *A. astacus*, with restrictions on moving live crayfish, fish and gear in and out of the area to avoid spreading diseases such as crayfish plague. In addition, funds have been allocated for actions such as information, extermination of illegally introduced *P. leniusculus* populations, reintroduction of *A. astacus* after crayfish plague, and habitat improvements. The action plan also notes that with NICS readily available, the largest threat is not

Table 10.1. Examples of national or regional protection status (+) of decapod species native to Hungary in neighbouring countries and by international organizations (after Puky *et al.*, 2005).

Country, region or organization	*Austropotamobius torrentium*	*Astacus astacus*	*Astacus leptodactylus*
Croatia	+	+	
Czech Republic	+	+	+
European Union	+	+	
Hungary	+		
IUCN	+	+	
Provinces of Vienna & Tyrol, Austria	+	+	+
Romania	+		
Serbia & Montenegro	+	+	
Slovenia	+	+	
Slovakia	+		+
Ukraine		+	
Thüringia	+	+	

overfishing but people illegally introducing plague-carrying *P. leniusculus*. The best protection against illegal stocking of non-indigenous crayfish is that local people are allowed to catch and benefit from *A. astacus*. Exploitation, in the form of a sustainable fishery, is thus the key to successful conservation of *A. astacus* in Sweden (Edsman & Schröder, 2009, Holdich *et al.*, 2009b).

In Norway, there is a law that forbids stocking of any freshwater organism without permission from environmental authorities. There is central regulation of noble crayfish harvesting, involving legal periods, minimum size and legal mesh size on traps. Another law forbids live imports of NICS. In watersheds with crayfish plague, local regulations prohibit fishing for crayfish and restrict other uses or activities in the watershed. The Finnish fisheries legislation has included crayfish since the 1920s, and the national crayfisheries strategy, published in 2000, involves both *A. astacus* and *P. leniusculus*. To be allowed to catch crayfish, one must have a governmental fishing licence and a permit from the water owner; the crayfish season runs from noon on 21 June until the end of October.

German federal law remains a major hole in the defences against NICS (see Appendix 10.1) as all species naturally reproducing over several generations are defined as native or indigenous; thus NICS already established in natural habitats, such as *Orconectes limosus* and *P. leniusculus*, are not specially controlled. The introduction of NICS is not allowed, but live imports are permitted. The ICS *A. astacus* and *Austropotamobius pallipes* are protected under the Federal Nature Conservation & Protection Act (NCPA) and the Federal Species Protection Ordinance. The state fisheries laws of some federal states include additional restrictions on the stocking of crayfish; for example, in Bavaria, only *A. astacus* may be stocked in all kinds of waters (Holdich *et al.*, 2009b).

UK and Irish legislation differs (Holdich *et al.*, 1999; see Appendix 10.1), although in both jurisdictions the EU Habitats Directive provides some protection for the widespread and indigenous white-clawed crayfish, *Austropotamobius pallipes*. British legislation sets out 'no-go areas' where NICS may not be introduced, but still allows some importation and movement of non-indigenous stocks. The whole of Northern Ireland (part of the UK) is one such no-go area. Irish fisheries legislation has discouraged the importation of NICS, among other hygiene measures to protect the valuable salmonid stocks (Gibson, 1979; Reynolds *et al.*, 2002b). Northern Ireland cooperates with the Irish Republic on this. However, there is a danger that UK citizens may assume that all British legislation applies in Northern Ireland, and some British media programmes have given a false impression that NICS are already present in the province, further endangering the Irish white-clawed crayfish stocks.

Recent evidence that Europe may be home to 11 000 alien species has spurred the European Commission to release its first ever Communication concerning invasive species (European Commission, 2008). This proposes the development of a European Strategy on Invasive Species, and outlines three potential ways forward, from using or adapting existing legislation to developing a dedicated legal instrument to address invasive species. A recent paper by Hulme *et al.* (2009) suggests that legislation is only part of the answer and that Europe lacks appropriate governance and institutional coordination across Member States to tackle the problem of invasions effectively. Currently, the responsibility for invasive species management lies within too many different European institutions, where invasions are only one topic among many areas of activity. They further note that some organizations have not seen eye to eye when it comes to assessing the risks to Europe of different alien species, while funding for research and management is often prioritized differently by the various Directorates-General in Brussels. This makes a single coordinating body essential, and Hulme *et al.* (2009) recommend the establishment of a European Centre for Invasive Species Management (ECISM), to bring together currently dispersed European resources and activities related to invasive species. ECISM would coordinate surveillance activities across Member States to monitor emerging threats, support rapid response, and raise public awareness around the issues of invasive species. However, such a Centre would face considerable challenges. For example, the single EU market for goods and people favours the spread of invasive species; the number of alien species introductions continues to increase year on year, and public awareness of the impact of those species is little more than 2% (Holdich *et al.*, 2009b). These factors are likely to mitigate against the formation of such a body.

While it is clear that a transnational strategy on biological invasions in European fresh waters is needed, the main obstacles are a lack of transboundary cooperation, limited ability to detect species early enough, ineffectual or delayed responses to the early stages of invasions, limited tools for eradicating or controlling invasive species in fresh water, the deficiencies and inconsistency of legal provisions, and the difficulty of trade regulation (Genovesi, 2007) – all of which are very relevant to the NICS situation. The EU Communication on invasive species emphasizes the importance of early detection of potentially invasive species and rapid action to eradicate them while it is still economically and environmentally effective (European Commission, 2008; Holdich *et al.*, 2009b).

Perhaps most worrying for the survival of ICS in Europe is the rapid spread of *Orconectes limosus* and *Pacifastacus leniusculus* through the rivers of eastern Europe. *O. limosus* has reached Romania through the River Danube (Pârvulescu *et al.*, 2009) and *P. leniusculus* has reached the Mura River in Croatia (Hudina & Lucić, 2009). This does not bode well for stocks of *Astacus astacus* and *A. leptodactylus* in these regions and further east, although *Austropotamobius torrentium*, because of its habitat preferences, may be protected to some extent. Another worrying issue is the popularity of marmorkrebs *Procambarus fallax f. virginalis* amongst hobbyists, particularly in central and eastern European states (Holdich *et al.*, 2009b).

In their discussion on the future of ICS in Europe, Taugbøl & Skurdal (1999) predicted that if effective conservation plans were not put in place, then in 100 years' time all catchments suitable for crayfish in Europe could be occupied by NICS, with all ICS critically endangered and surviving only in a few protected localities. To avoid this scenario, they suggested a number of actions, including protection of ICS as a national aim and implementing effective legislation. Taugbøl & Skurdal (1999) and Taugbøl (2004b) maintain that exploitation and protection are closely linked in Scandinavian countries, as those who exploit are usually concerned about the resources and will protect them. Taugbøl & Skurdal (1999) further suggested that the setting up of 'native crayfish areas' (NCAs) was of prime importance for ensuring the future of ICS. These could range in size from a country, a region, a catchment basin, or even a single watercourse or waterbody. They highlighted Ireland and Norway as suitable NCAs for *Austropotamobius pallipes* and *Astacus astacus*, respectively, as both countries were at the time free of NICS. Sweden is in the process of setting up protected areas for *A. astacus*, including the whole of the island of Gotland (Lennart Edsman, personal communication, 2009). In Britain, in addition to designated no-go areas, smaller secure locations or 'Ark sites' are being developed into which threatened populations of ICS are being moved (Peay, 2009a), but so far these have no legal basis.

The conceptual model presented in Figure 10.1 (Holdich *et al.*, 2009b) shows the different actions necessary for the protection of ICS in Europe, under two main groupings: general management, including implementing legislation, developing public education strategies and coordination; and specific actions – distribution surveys, site protection and habitat restoration, fisheries controls for ICS and NICS, and actions to restrict NICS and the spread of plague. In the decade since Taugbøl & Skurdal (1999) published their guidelines, there has been activity at a European level (e.g. EU Habitats Directive, CRAYNET) and in EU Member States. Legislation has been tightened, and the attitudes of the EU and Member States to international treaties dealing with the environment and with free trade have changed somewhat (Reynolds *et al.*, 2006). A number of countries have set up national plans for their ICS and NICS, e.g. Austria (Pöckl, 2002), Switzerland (Stucki *et al.*, 2005; Hefti & Stucki, 2006) and Sweden (Edsman & Schröder, 2009).

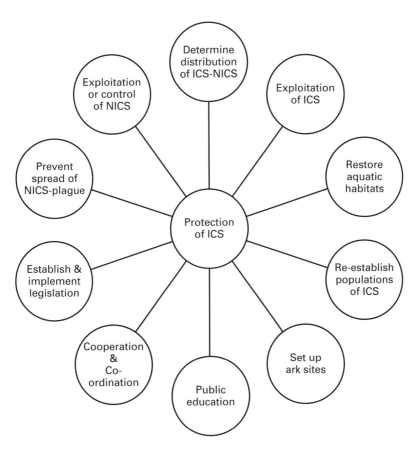

Figure 10.1. Conceptual model showing paths that could be taken to try and protect ICS. Modified from Taugbøl & Skurdal (1999) in Holdich *et al.* (2009b).

10.2.3 Legislation protecting ICS or controlling NICS in North America

In the USA, a wide array of international, national, state and local government agencies and non-governmental organizations have responsibility for protecting biodiversity and managing introduced species. Species Action Plans are developing rapidly in some individual states, but a national policy has not been developed. Unlike Canada, the USA has not ratified the Rio Convention on Biological Diversity, leading to widespread frustration among conservationists in the USA (Lodge *et al.*, 2000a, 2000b).

The US Endangered Species Act of 1973 was a milestone in conservation legislation. Its purpose is not only to protect plants and animals facing extinction, but also to provide a means for protecting and conserving the ecosystems upon which those species depend and provide programmes for their conservation. The Act has undergone many changes throughout its 30-year history and has been tested repeatedly, but it still stands as one of the most important pieces of legislation for the protection and conservation of threatened plant and animal species, including some crayfish, in the USA.

Another purpose of the Endangered Species Act is to protect individual endangered and threatened plants and animals from 'take' (here defined as to harm, harass, injure or kill a species or destroy essential habitat), without finding ways to minimize the threats and provide for the long-term survival and recovery of the species. 'Take' of listed species is prohibited and carries severe penalties, but the Endangered Species Act also provides for take that is incidental to otherwise lawful activities. Thus, federal agencies are protected from violation of the Act's take provisions through consultation with the US Fish and Wildlife Service, but non-federal agencies and private landowners would face possible prosecution for take of listed species. In 1988, however, amendments to the Act authorized the issuance of permits to private landowners and non-federal agencies conducting lawful activities to take species, but required them to minimize and mitigate the take to the greatest extent practicable. Some protected cave crayfish species have total known population sizes of under a hundred.

Taylor *et al.* (2007) have reassessed the conservation status of crayfish in North America, nearly a decade since their first assessment (Taylor *et al.*, 1996; Taylor, 2002). There have been no changes to the conservation status of crayfish at the federal level since then, and no crayfish have been proposed for or received protection under the Federal Endangered Species Act since 2007 (Chris Taylor, personal communication, 2009).

Historically, responsibility for the introduction of non-native crayfish species has been assigned to fishermen dumping bait crayfish into waters where they do not naturally occur. Most states now have laws prohibiting bait bucket introductions of non-native crayfish, and many states also have laws that regulate crayfish in the aquarium trade. However, a quick search of internet auction sites will find numerous species of native and exotic crayfish advertised for sale with shipment almost anywhere.

In the USA, the responsible federal agencies include the US Department of Agriculture's Animal and Plant Health Inspection Service, Forest Service and Natural Resource Conservation Service, the US Department of the Interior's Fish & Wildlife Service and the National Park Service. The US Environmental Protection Agency is particularly concerned with invasive species in waters of the USA. These agencies also have an educational role: the Biological Resources Division of the US Geological Survey has extensive web resources on topics including invasive and non-indigenous species, and maintains the National Biological Information Infrastructure (www.nbii.gov/) and a guide to resources in each state.

At the next level, US states regulating the import or sale of crayfish include Arizona, California, Minnesota, Utah and Wisconsin, and among Canadian provinces, Manitoba and Saskatchewan. A number of states including Alabama, Arkansas, Florida and New Hampshire, and Canadian provinces Newfoundland–Labrador and Ontario, prohibit the release of crayfish into local waters. Details of regulations at a state or provincial level in North America are summarized on the web-page 'North American laws concerning crayfish' on the website Marmorkrebs.org, created and maintained by Zen Faulkes.

As an example of such state regulations, the state government of Massachusetts has taken several initiatives to go beyond fighting battles against individual invaders to look at the larger picture of how best to conserve biodiversity. The Natural Heritage and Endangered Species Program, part of the Massachusetts Division of Fisheries & Wildlife, researches and inventories biological resources, and has responsibilities for protecting non-game, especially endangered species, habitat. There are also associated educational activities. Many other states have comparable regulations. For instance, in Missouri a recent survey of crayfish controls for NICS is in review (DiStefano *et al.*, 2009; Robert DiStefano, personal communication, 2009).

In Mexico, taxonomy and distribution of native and alien crayfish stocks is still imperfectly known. The NICS redclaw *Cherax quadricarinatus* has been introduced into dams where ICS are not known, and used for aquaculture. There are some efforts to control the introduction and spread of NICS, chiefly through Best Management Practices (BMP) (Antonio Garza de Yta, personal communication, 2009).

10.2.4   Legislation in Australia and New Zealand

Conservation of Australian crayfish is tackled at both state and federal (Commonwealth) levels. The main Commonwealth law is the Environmental Protection and Biodiversity Conservation Act (EPBC) of 1999. Several freshwater crayfish appear on threatened species lists generated under state and Commonwealth legislation in Australia. Tasmania lists six species (two endangered, four vulnerable), Victoria 12 species (status unclassified), Western Australia four (rare or likely to become extinct) and Australian Capital Territory one species (vulnerable). These threatened species include some that are widely distributed, such as the Murray River crayfish *Euastacus armatus*, which is under threat as a result of declining habitat quality, and also burrowing species with highly restricted distributions that are threatened by local habitat loss, such as the Furneaux burrowing crayfish *Engaeus martigener* from Flinders Island, threatened by feral pigs and habitat loss due to climate change. Among the most endangered Australian crayfish are burrowing species, which live in seasonally inundated swamps and are threatened by rapid changes of land use and pressures from agriculture, affecting groundwater and surface water levels. The Australian EPBC Act lists one critically endangered species (the hairy marron, *Cherax tenuimanus* from Western Australia), three endangered species (all burrowing *Engaeus* species from Tasmania), and three vulnerable species (*Astacopsis gouldi* and two more Tasmanian *Engaeus* species). In northern Tasmania some further species of burrowing crayfish in the genus *Engaeus* have only been described relatively recently (Horwitz, 1990b). *E. granulatus*, the central north burrowing crayfish, is one of those listed as endangered under the EPBC Act.

Burrowing crayfish of the genus *Engaewa* are small, up to 5 cm total length, and are only found in seasonally inundated freshwater swamps and seepages in high-rainfall areas of south-western Australia. In Western Australia, three threatened species of burrowing crayfish are located in the state's south-west: the Walpole burrowing crayfish *Engaewa walpolea*, Dunsborough burrowing crayfish *E. reducta*, and Margaret River burrowing crayfish *E. pseudoreducta*. All are listed as threatened under state legislation, and the Western Australia Department of Environment and Conservation (DEC) has prepared a Recovery Plan to ensure their survival. The DEC has also recently nominated all three species of *Engaewa* crayfish for listing under the EPBC Act.

The Threatened Species Scientific Committee (Department of the Environment, Water, Heritage and the Arts) issued Commonwealth Conservation Advice on *Engaeus granulatus* in 2008. It is likely that this species was quite common throughout its range prior to its habitat becoming highly modified. *E. granulatus* is now restricted and fragmented, with limited connectivity between populations, and has not to date been recorded from any secure conservation reserves (Nelson, 2003).

The central north burrowing crayfish *Engaeus granulatus* is associated with several other burrowing crayfish listed under Tasmanian state environmental legislation. The Mount Arthur, Scottsdale and Burnie burrowing crayfish (*E. orramakunna*, *E. spinicaudatus* and *E. yabbimunna*, respectively) are currently all listed as vulnerable under the Tasmanian Threatened Species Protection Act 1995, and the Burrowing Crayfish (*Engaeus*) Group Recovery Plan 2001–2005 is among the EPBC Action Plans. The species' ranges are highly modified by agriculture, forestry and urban development. *Engaeus* species is most at risk at periods when it is moulting, visiting the surface, mating or nurturing young (Horwitz, 1990b).

The freshwater yabby *Cherax destructor* has recently been recorded from a dam in Tasmania near where central north burrowing crayfish were present and may pose a threat to the burrowing crayfish through competition for food and habitat. The yabby is fairly widespread in Tasmania and is regarded as an introduced pest (Nelson, 2003; DPIW, 2007; DEWHA, 2008).

Marron, which support a popular recreational fishery, have been protected under state legislation in the south-western rivers of Western Australia since 1955; their commercial fishing and sale was banned, and a minimum carapace size limit imposed of 3 inches (76 mm CL), equivalent to about 120 g in weight (Molony *et al.*, 2002; Wingfield, 2002). The restricted hairy marron *Cherax tenuimanus* has recently come under even more stringent protection.

In New Zealand no alien potentially invasive crayfish are permitted entry. Two species of koura *Parastacus* spp. occupy rivers and lakes of both main islands, and both are considered threatened. There are now several koura aquaculture projects aiming to help protect wild stocks from overexploitation.

10.2.5   Legislation protecting ICS or controlling NICS elsewhere

In other parts of the world where native crayfish occur, legislation is variable but generally not strong. Native parastacids occur in the southern hemisphere (South America, Madagascar) and cambarids in Japan, Korea and China.

South America

Indigenous species of the parastacid crayfish genera *Parastacus*, *Samastacus* and *Virilastacus* occur on both sides of the Andes, from Ecuador to southern Brazil, Argentina and southern Chile. Many are burrowers. There are also a number of aeglid freshwater crabs known, several endangered and at least two of them extinct. In addition, two Australian parastacid NICS, the marron *Cherax cainii* and the redclaw *C. quadricarinatus* were introduced in 1998 and 2004 for aquaculture trials in Chile, the latter species also to Peru, Argentina, Paraguay, Uruguay and Ecuador. Finally, in the 1980s *Astacus astacus* was introduced from Austria to the south of Chile, for culture experiments. These culture experiments were not successful and the last destination of all these specimens is not known (Erich Rudolph, personal communication, 2010). Escapes are probable but have not been reported. No relevant laws protecting ICS or controlling NICS are known.

There are, however, federal laws in Brazil both to protect native species and to control certain invasive species, but they are rather general. The native species *Parastacus brasiliensis* is considered not threatened across Brazil, including in the Departmento do Rio Grande do Sul (RS). Other natives (*P. varicosus*, *P. defossus*, *P. pilimanus* and *P. saffordi*) are also not considered threatened in RS but their situation in the whole country is unknown. The invasive *Procambarus clarkii* has been noted and, as it is both aggressive and a plague-carrier, there are strong fears that it will affect native stocks. It is sold as a pet without restriction around São Paulo, and later often discarded into lakes (Mauricio Almerão, personal communication, 2009).

Madagascar

Regulations controlling minimum crayfish size for capture are not widely observed. Existing regulations providing protection for ICS seem ineffective to prevent exploitation of undersized and immature forms. Moreover, the parthenogenetic marmorkrebs *Procambarus fallax f. virginalis* is spreading rapidly and is now found in markets (Jones *et al.*, 2009).

Mainland Africa

No crayfish are native to the African continent, but in some regions *Procambarus clarkii* has been introduced and is spreading, causing massive damage to ecosystems such as Lake Naivasha in Kenya (Harper *et al.*, 2007); however, no scientific controls are implemented.

East Asia

There is a native species of *Cambaroides* in China and another in Korea. Chinese environmental legislation includes the Environmental Protection Law of the People's Republic of China, but this does not cover invasive species and their control. Aquaculture of exotic species is very important. Farming of *Procambarus clarkii* is practiced on a large scale in China, principally in Anhui, Hubei, Hangsu and Jiangxi provinces, where production reached 130 000 tonnes in 2006 (FBMA, 2007, Wu & Gao, 2008). However, negative impacts on *Cambaroides* have not been reported. Agricultural legislation regulates the introduction of exotic species and the processes of examination, approval and registration, along with the relevant safety measures to be taken.

In Japan, there are currently three crayfish species: the native *Cambaroides japonicus* and two NICS, *Pacifastacus leniusculus* and *Procambarus clarkii*. *C. japonicus* is now considered endangered and is on the Japanese Red List; it is vulnerable to crayfish plague. Many alien species (including over 1500 plants and hundreds of animals) have been introduced into Japan, some becoming invasive, but legal controls were at first fragmentary. However, after adopting the Convention on Biological Diversity, the Japanese Parliament formulated and passed the Invasive Alien Species Act in 2005 (Mito & Uesugi, 2004).

Under the Act, invasive alien species (IAS) are designated as having adverse effects on ecosystems, human safety, or agriculture, forestry and fisheries. Various actions dealing with IAS – such as importing, rearing, planting and transporting – are prohibited in Japan except under permit. Government, local councils and non-profit organizations are required to take appropriate measures to mitigate the impact of IAS already present in Japan. Finally, all uncategorized alien species (UAS) must be investigated by government before being allowed to be imported into Japan (Mito & Uesugi, 2004). Tens of IAS and thousands of UAS were expected to be designated in the first step. Among IAS are the competing crayfish *Pacifastacus leniusculus* and *Orconectes rusticus* and all *Cherax* species, while all crayfish except the widespread *Procambarus clarkii* are UAS. Thus, there are ongoing problems with legislation for endangered crayfish (Usio, 2007). The Invasive Alien Species Act remains the main means of control: all species of *Astacus* and *Cherax*, *O. rusticus* and *P. leniusculus* have now been designated as IAS under the Act and their import and keeping alive are banned except for scientific purposes (Usio *et al.*, 2007, 2009; Nisikawa Usio, personal communication, 2009).

10.3   Lessons from legislation

While legislation has been considered from the twin approaches of protecting ICS and regulating NICS, the aim of both is biodiversity conservation. The three-stage hierarchical approach (prevention, early detection/rapid response, and containment or control) set out by the Convention on Biological Diversity applies well to the management of invasive crayfish. The first stage, prevention, is particularly critical; NICS can initially be hard to detect and can disperse rapidly, making eradication or control both extremely difficult and expensive. Much effort should therefore be directed to minimizing the risks of intentional and unintentional introductions, currently covered in part by laws in force in several countries. For instance, in Japan *Orconectes rusticus*, *Pacifastacus leniusculus* and all species of *Astacus* and *Cherax* have been designated as invasive alien species and it is illegal to import and keep them except for scientific purposes. In the UK, *Astacus astacus*, *A. leptodactylus* and *P. leniusculus* have been designated as pests under the Wildlife and Countryside Act; much of Britain has been declared a no-go area for the keeping of *P. leniusculus*, and the whole of Britain for the keeping of all other NICS (except the tropical *Cherax quadricarinatus*). The complexity of UK law as it applies to crayfish management has been summarized by a number of authors, including Bean *et al.* (2006) for Scotland, and Holdich (2003), Sibley (2003a) and Everard *et al.* (2009) for the whole of the UK.

EU Council Regulation No 708/07 'Concerning use of alien and locally absent species in aquaculture' has been in force since 2007. Its novelty is to take a 'white list' approach, in that only the importation of species that have been appropriately screened after a thorough risk assessment analysis can be approved. This contrasts with the equivalent regulation in the USA, which permits the importation of species unless they are on a 'black list' (Injurious Wildlife Species; US Fish & Wildlife Service). Again, all these regulations seem poorly harmonized with legislation controlling the aquarium trade, as it is easy to buy NICS such as the marbled crayfish as pets, particularly through web commerce. Finally, illegal translocations of NICS by fishermen are very difficult to police, while accidental introductions, for example with stocked fish, are common (see Chapter 8).

We have seen that legislation protecting ICS and restricting NICS is quite variable across the world, and where it has been developed, as in Europe, it has been weakened by international regulations concerning trade. The British situation shows the dangers of allowing introductions for agricultural purposes without a full review of the possible consequences. Seven of the top ten 'high-impact' non-native species affecting water-bodies in the UK, according to a recent risk assessment for the EC Water Framework Directive (WFD), are in fresh water. The plants mostly come from aquarium discards, and the listed animals – all invertebrates (decapod crustaceans and molluscs) – from more varied sources (Table 10.2).

Everard *et al.* (2009) used the framework of 'ecosystem services' (discussed in Chapter 6) to assess the ecological impacts associated with the invasive signal crayfish *Pacifastacus leniusculus* in British freshwater ecosystems. The ecosystem services assessment found an overwhelming predominance of negative impacts associated with signal crayfish invasion, which supported calls for action to speed up the strengthening of legal and procedural safeguards (Everard *et al.*, 2009). The implications were sufficiently strong to suggest that further quantitative analysis may only introduce unnecessary delays and expense to framing policy responses. Any calls to compensate private crayfish farmers could be set against the potential damage to a wide range of public 'goods' arising from the spread of non-native crayfish and the diseases that they carry, as running counter to the 'polluter pays' principle. There is thus a tenable case for a complete ban on any further farming of all crayfish, and potentially also a ban on trapping where this increases the risk of spread or creates an incentive for illegal seeding, in order to safeguard the wide range of public benefits highlighted by the ecosystem services analysis (Everard *et al.*, 2009).

European legislation for aquaculture, in particular Council Regulation 708/2007 on alien species in aquaculture, appears adequate to control the spread and import of invasive species such as non-native crayfish. However, the current legislation regulating trade in aquatic species and in human food is inadequate to stop the import and spread of organisms and their diseases. Changes are urgently needed to tighten current regulations in order to reduce the impacts of non-native crayfish and other non-native species before further new introductions occur, and to minimize further damage to the public good, as revealed by ecosystem services appraisal (Table 10.3; Everard *et al.*, 2009). This is also consistent with the requirements of the Habitats Directive and the WFD.

As illegal and unintended activities are also contributing to the spread of signal crayfish and their associated diseases, strong enforcement of the law and codes of

Table 10.2. Seven of the top ten 'high-impact' non-native species listed in the UK Environment Agency Water Framework Directive risk assessment are freshwater species (modified after Everard *et al.*, 2009).

Plants	Origin
Swamp stonecrop (*Crassula helmsii*)	Australia and New Zealand
Floating pennywort (*Hydrocotyle ranunculoides*)	North America
Water fern (*Azolla filiculoides*)	North America
Parrot's feather (*Myriophyllum aquaticum*)	South America
Animals	
Signal crayfish (*Pacifastacus leniusculus*)	Western North America
Zebra mussel (*Dreissena polymorpha*)	Ponto-Caspian region
Chinese mitten crab (*Eriocheir sinensis*)	East Asia

conduct may also be required to close these avenues of ecosystem damage, and some mechanism may need to be introduced which would place a liability upon consumers to purchase crayfish only from legal sources and so eliminate the markets for illegally supplied stock (Everard *et al.*, 2009).

10.4   The role of education in conservation

Native animals are crucially important in biodiversity and conservation issues, and freshwater organisms especially so because the aquatic habitat, with its often rich biodiversity, is threatened worldwide. For various reasons, crustacean vulnerability is greater than that of most other groups using the same limited habitats, so they have high presence in regional and international Red Lists (e.g. IUCN).

Estimates place up to one-half of the world's crayfish species at risk of serious population decline or extinction (Taylor, 2002). We have also seen that crayfish conservation produces benefits relating to the protection of the aquatic environment as well as to the maintenance both of food sources and of cultural heritage values. Legislation may have an input. In some cases, as for European species listed in Annex 5 of the EU Habitats Directive, their controlled exploitation may be a benefit both to mankind and to the species themselves; this has been demonstrated in earlier chapters for noble crayfish *Astacus astacus*. It has become clear that education is the key to the effective operation of all such controls and regulations, whether exploitative or conservation-based. Little can be implemented without some ability to recognize the species of concern, and how to distinguish native from non-native species which may pose a risk to conservation.

To change prevailing attitudes and generate awareness and concern, information must be widely available, accurate and regularly updated, and promoted by an interest-specific approach to education, addressing those not interested as well as those already somewhat interested. Suggested target groups include politicians, environmental and fishery managers, watercourse owners or dwellers, school-goers, third-level students,

Table 10.3. The negative impacts of invasive crayfish and crabs on ecosystem services, chiefly through habitat simplification (modified after Everard *et al.*, 2009).

MEA categories and ecosystem services	Assessment of NICS impact
PROVISIONING SERVICES	
Fresh water	Burrowing releases silt and contaminants
Food	Displacement of salmonids etc.
Fibre and fuel	Reeds and riparian trees reduced
Genetic resources	Loss of biodiversity
REGULATORY SERVICES	
Climate regulation	Reduced carbon sequestration
Water regulation	Hydrology modified
Natural hazard regulation	Burrowing reduces resilience
Disease regulation	Devastating spread of crayfish plague
Erosion regulation	Bank damage and vegetation grazed
Water purification & treatment	Reduced biofilm surfaces
CULTURAL SERVICES	
Cultural heritage	Lost heritage species, simplified landscape
Recreation and tourism	Degraded or simplified systems, birds, fish
Aesthetic value	Lost heritage species, simplified landscape
Social relations, e.g. fishing groups	Reduced angling potential
SUPPORTING SERVICES	
Soil formation	Bank damage slows natural soil formation
Primary production, photosynthesis	Loss of aquatic plants and biofilm surfaces
Nutrient cycling	Sediment and contaminant mobilization
Water recycling	Degraded habitat reduces storage, cycling
Provision of habitat	Degradation of riverine habitat

MEA: Millennium Ecosystem Assessment.

non-governmental organizations (NGOs) and green activists. Suggested methods include regular and accurate news media briefings, exhibitions, excursions, posters, television and the most powerful tool, the internet. These days, people can find a wide array of images of crayfish from all over the world. However, there is no guarantee of accuracy on the internet, and some postings and photos may be incorrectly labelled or misleading in terms of the associated information.

Conservation education has three main target groups: the policy-makers and state officials who must make and implement legislation, the stakeholders in any affected catchment (such as managers, fishermen and riparian owners), and the general public, both interested and neutral (Reynolds & Puky, 2005). While a great deal of 'educational' material already exists relating to crayfish, there is a perceived need for such material to be tailored to specific groups such as government officials, water managers and educators.

Conflict resolution between conservationists and stakeholders may also be educational. In some countries, such as Sweden and France, conservation biologists engage in dialogue with farmers, other managers and NGOs, thus strengthening the scientific approach as well as the practical one. But significantly more input from scientists is needed if the loss of freshwater biodiversity is to be slowed, let alone halted, as was the aim of the CBD by 2010.

Educational activities involving crayfish are highly organized in Sweden and Norway, where crayfish have a recognized broad economic and cultural value, and where a price differential exists between indigenous and non-indigenous species. Even in those countries where crayfish historically have less cultural value in terms of culinary or commercial exploitation, their importance as flagship and keystone species is assured (see Chapter 3), and education in applied conservation strategies can play a vital role to promote this.

As crayfish have great potential to act as iconic symbols of a good-quality habitat in national and international campaigns to protect fauna and landscape (Puky *et al.*, 2002), related educational activities can also be beneficial to other species and to aquatic habitats in general. A key issue here is the relatively limited ability of homotopic crayfish, tied to their habitats, to recolonize freshwater sites after pollution events, in contrast to aquatic insects capable of colonization by flight.

10.4.1   Education of specific interest groups: spreading the word

Education of scientists

The scientist's role is to investigate and clarify issues so as to provide education and information for all citizens, and arguably especially for managers, decision makers and legislators. But scientists must also make their subject interdisciplinary by informing each other. For many organisms, and specifically for freshwater crayfish, taxonomy is in a state of flux. Recent changes already described which affect the conservation situation of crayfish species include the recognition of two species of marron in western Australia, *C. tenuimanus* and *Cherax cainii*, one apparently endangered by the spread of the other (Lynas *et al.*, 2007), and the realization that white-clawed crayfish *Austropotamobius pallipes* in Europe is a species group that becomes more complex (and therefore more difficult to conserve) in the south of its range, notably in Italy, Spain and Austria (Grandjean *et al.*, 2000).

Therefore, the scientist needs to transfer knowledge in understandable language to other interest groups. In particular, science must keep the public informed. Everyone has a right to be informed, but possibly country-dwellers and those associated with water (riverine stakeholders) are more likely to be involved, and hence potentially more 'dangerous', and so they need education more than city-dwellers. Anglers are a particular case. Fishermen tend to be good reporters of the distribution limits of a crayfish species, of mortalities, and of changes in its abundance. With the angling licence now being almost a universal requirement, there is a unique opportunity to educate; in some countries it comes with a periodic newsletter informing the holder of new regulations or close seasons and a variety of articles about the freshwater environment and its denizens. This, directed at an already interested stakeholder group, can be a powerful educational tool.

Finally, as well as the promotion of conservation and an increase in knowledge about crayfish, educational activities by scientists can also help in collecting information from uninvestigated areas, which for crayfish was around 30% of Europe in 2006 (Souty-Grosset *et al.*, 2006; Patrick Haffner, personal communication, 2006) and likely to be even greater for most of the globe.

Education of managers and officials

Legislation, as outlined above, can only help protect native endemic crayfish if it is correctly implemented. Education is the key to the effective operation of controls, whether exploitative or conservation-based. State veterinarians, customs officers, wildlife inspectors and water managers all have a crucial role to play in protecting habitats and species at risk, but the law is useless if these officials cannot recognize the species named in the legislation in order to take appropriate action. Specific information must therefore target these groups, with a high standard of accuracy and clarity of identification, wherever a number of species may be encountered. In addition, as crayfish require a range of habitats over their life cycle (Chapter 3), good background knowledge of crayfish ecology, population biology and life cycles is essential wherever wetland or stream modifications are planned in the course of development works.

Among the items required are taxonomic keys for the determination of species, and methodological instructions for the recognition of crayfish plague and other serious diseases, preferably through the World Organization for Animal Health (OIE). Managers can be referred to a pre selected range of educational material produced through the IUCN, online research sites such as DAISIE, the global invasive species database of the Invasive Species Specialist Group (ISSG), the Encyclopedia of Life Support Systems (EOLSS), the European research network CRAYNET, and many more.

By contrast, politicians may not have time to assimilate long explanations and background detail, so they need a concise, easily understood message with suggested action points. This is also useful if an elected politician persists in giving incorrect information to back up his/her views.

Education of the public

One promising approach is to educate the public and, through them, the politicians and decision makers. Public natural history education has developed greatly in the last 30 years, and most current approaches to conservation focus on wide dissemination of information (Reynolds & Puky, 2005). However, if such information has to be bought or requested by the interested public (as in the UK and some other countries), it presupposes a prior level of awareness and enthusiasm. 'Bad news' stories are also important for the underlying messages; e.g. a story about the spread of crayfish plague underlines the need to be able to recognize and identify plague carriers and to distinguish such causes of mortality from others due to pollution.

Because of their traditional importance in recreational fishing, crayfish may be natural flagship species that appeal to the public and are intrinsically suitable for communicating conservation concerns. The European research network CRAYNET in 2006 produced and disseminated educational illustrated strip cartoons, posters, leaflets and brochures, and there is now comparable literature available in many other countries, such as the UK Buglife website (www.buglife.org.uk/). In the USA and Canada, there are excellent examples of educational folders and posters. For example, in Canada, Toronto Zoo and Ontario Nature sponsored a 2008 folder by Aleta Karstad and Premek Hamr, illustrating the six native species and their distribution, with a key to their accurate identification and an invitation to contribute to knowledge about Ontario crayfish.

Practical education: monitoring of crustaceans by the public

Many crayfish require a clean habitat, and so tie in well with people's concerns about their environment. Crayfish also have a limited ability to recolonize stream sections that have been polluted; therefore they are often used by non-governmental organizations (NGOs) in campaigns for faunal protection and habitat conservation. NGOs monitoring the status of protected crayfish may need to set up special links with governmental conservation agencies, including being licensed to handle such crayfish. Activities may involve catch, mark and release, photography and video.

Protected areas, with a degree of wardening by the state, might also be the best sites in which to involve the public initially. The discredited idea that most people are best kept in ignorance of the existence of a rare species or excluded from an important site has given way to today's approach of encouraging public education through the wide dissemination of information, in the belief that the species or habitat stands an improved chance of survival if many people are aware and concerned. Discussions now focus, for example, on which section of the public to target, and which approach is most likely to bear fruit (see Puky *et al.*, 2002).

Delivering the education message

There are many different ways in which the education message can reach target groups, and specific messages should be promoted using the most effective media for each group. Television programmes, videos, postcards, stamps, stickers, leaflets, wallcharts – all can contribute to such campaigns.

The best targets for these campaigns are probably children and young adults, including third-level students. Children are naturally interested; they lack *a priori* attitudes to invertebrates as dangerous, alien or unpleasant, are receptive to interesting and novel messages, and will spread the information through homes and friends in a way not duplicated by their parents. Schools are receptive to new educational material, such as posters and information packs. It is essential to maintain a fresh approach and to introduce new material at regular intervals. In this way, the depicted biota, such as crayfish, may become a part of everyday life for the younger generation. Children will communicate a positive message about conservation to their parents. Natural history societies, by organizing walks and talks, can also play an important role in stimulating interest in both adults and children. This is most effective in conjunction with special nature conservation days. Many decapods, being large and robust, can be handled and tracked, so that students are encouraged to gather information and form their own ideas on habitat and species conservation.

Images in art and on postage stamps

Crustaceans can be eye-catching, and a surprising number of paintings and carvings in public collections feature crayfish and other decapods. National postage stamps are often used to promote a conservation message, for birds, flowers, butterflies and so on. Spain has featured the protected white-clawed crayfish *Austropotamobius pallipes* on their postage stamps, and at a recent count, other crayfish have been shown on European stamps from Romania (1966), Spain (1979), Finland (1991), Poland (2004) and Croatia (2007), and outside Europe, from USA, Australia, New Zealand and South Korea.

10.5   Case studies

10.5.1   Europe

We have emphasized the important heritage image of native crayfish in Europe, as large, long-lived and edible inhabitants of good-quality streams and ponds. They represent an integral part of the folk traditions of many countries, most notably with *Astacus astacus* in Scandinavian countries (Swahn, 2004), but also throughout their range. National traditional celebrations in Sweden, Norway and Finland have led to catch restrictions and other conservation measures to ensure continuity of stocks for the August festival. The catch has high economic added value compared with the equivalent marine decapod stock, making the loss of a crayfish lake to pollution or crayfish plague very serious.

Austropotamobius pallipes also has a heritage value in western continental Europe – France, Italy and Spain – where it was formerly widely fished (Chapter 5) and is still sometimes poached. However, traditions relating to this species are less obvious in the UK and almost absent in Ireland. Reasons for this lack in Ireland are perhaps because the nineteenth-century Irish famines mostly affected people farming the acid uplands, while the lakes, rivers and lime-rich wetlands containing crayfish were mainly under the control of landlords.

Puky *et al.* (2002) examined the European knowledge base on crayfish, and how this might be directed towards national or international goals of management and conservation. A questionnaire on public awareness of crayfish across Europe, distributed among European crayfish scientists, yielded responses from 15 countries. Although too small for statistical rigour, the survey gave a useful snapshot of different countries (Puky et *al.*, 2002) and showed major regional differences. Not surprisingly, the greatest public awareness was indicated for Scandinavian countries, mainly because of the living tradition of wide-scale exploitation of the heritage noble crayfish, and this awareness was reinforced by easily available documentation. Elsewhere, the availability of information to the general public was either patchy or non-existent. Respondents considered British people to be generally quite aware, more so than the public in France, Germany and Poland, who could not discriminate between species. For different reasons, the Irish and Croatian public are unlikely to know what a crayfish is (in Ireland, perhaps through a lack of utilization or because of restrictions on fishing in fresh water; in Croatia perhaps related to recent civil strife rendering the countryside unsafe). Public awareness of the threatened status of endemic crayfish was judged good in Sweden, Norway, Czech Republic and the UK. There is recognition in the UK and Sweden of negative impacts of the expansion of signals, but apparently less so in Finland, where this expansion is officially fostered.

The availability of information about crayfish for the general public, in 2002, was judged best in Finland, Sweden and Austria; moderate in Germany, the UK and Italy; and minimal or lacking in Hungary, Ireland, France and Spain. Regional differences were noted within France, Spain, Federal Germany and Poland, where, for example, Szczecin had its own crayfish initiative.

Crayfish thus have considerable potential to act as symbols of a good-quality habitat in national and European campaigns to protect fauna and landscape. Crayfish have been used successfully as the focus of a conservation campaign in Hungary (Puky *et al.*, 1999). From a small NGO base, volunteer teachers went out to talk to voluntary groups, teachers and schoolchildren, and provided them with illustrative materials. Television programmes, videos, postcards, wall-charts and stickers all contributed to the campaign; each could be seen as a separate fund-raising opportunity rather than as an added cost to the campaign. There are many comparable examples involving flowers, amphibians and birds across Europe and North America.

It was clear that in many other parts of Europe, however, available information on decapod species was often limited for various reasons (for a detailed analysis see Reynolds & Puky, 2005) and there is a need to develop this field. International projects are needed to effectively protect threatened European crayfish species, as their distribution areas cover many countries; international projects would also often result in better-quality educational materials and greater media attention.

There are different amounts of crayfish-specific media material available in different countries. In the mid-1990s, Hungary launched a conservation-oriented survey, with publication of a crayfish survey manual containing detailed general, observational and methodological information, including some on *Austropotamobius torrentium* (Harsányi & Rogovsky 1996). In Austria, recreational fishermen must pass a test on biology, ecology, legislation and fishing methods. Licensed fishermen receive a quarterly newsletter which may contain information on threatened species or responsible actions to halt the spread of aliens. Swedish newspapers contain colour supplements on a variety of related topics at the start of the crayfishing season. Such supplements can educate and influence a very wide section of the public, but the associated commerce must be there also.

There are also many campaigns for most of the European crayfish species, not just the annual orgy of information and advertisement that surrounds the short fishing season for *Astacus astacus* in Scandinavian countries. Educational campaigns around the non-commercial and protected *Austropotamobius pallipes* have a different approach, targeting its reclusive and threatened nature. However, specific educational programmes were fewer for the similarly sized stone crayfish *A. torrentium*, which occurs widely in central and eastern Europe, often outside Natura 2000 sites. Puky *et al.* (2002) concentrated on how to stimulate discussion about and interest in this little-known native European crayfish, and how best to educate the public about its situation and status. It occurs in 20 countries, from France and Germany to Italy and Romania (Holdich *et al.*, 2009b). There is much recent information on its distribution and preferred habitats in circum-alpine regions, where populations are more patchy and biotopes more threatened. However, the species is also distributed widely in central and eastern Europe. Educational programmes are generally lacking for *A. torrentium* and no European legislation covers this species (see Holdich & Pöckl, 2005; Souty-Grosset *et al.*, 2005, 2006; Holdich *et al.*, 2009a). *A. torrentium* lives not only in pristine lakes and streams, many in already protected habitats, but also in less good habitats, comparable to those of *A. pallipes*. Although *A. torrentium* grows to the same size as *A. pallipes*, no commercial fishing exists, although there is some recreational fishing. It was the general consensus of crayfish scientists at Innsbruck in 2004 that a series of leaflets on the stone crayfish should be prepared and agreed for the widest possible distribution in various languages – on its distribution, habitats, life cycle, significance as a heritage species, and why we should conserve it. At the same time, a need to clarify and strengthen its legal status was addressed by promoting its addition to the EU Habitats Directive.

In many countries, Fisheries Boards and Environmental Agencies may produce relevant posters and leaflets; good examples for Europe being the UK Environmental Agency's *The Crayfish Code: Protecting Native Crayfish in the Midlands*, and the Fiskeriverket Sweden poster about crayfish, printed in Swedish, English and Spanish. Larger documents and manuals are sometimes available from governmental services (e.g. Reynolds, 1998). There may be scope for further educational material/programmes aimed at *A. torrentium* and, more generally, at all European crayfish. Details and approaches are likely to be country-specific.

At present in the UK, where American crayfish are now widespread and increasing, there are many campaigns aimed at conserving native crayfish through education. For instance, the Lowland Derbyshire Local Biodiversity Action Plan includes a white-clawed crayfish Species Action Plan, which includes awareness-raising. There are several aspects to this: distribution of appropriate land management information to landowners and angling clubs, liaising with angling clubs to inform them about the Environment Agency's crayfish code and encourage its adoption, and provision of information on crayfish issues to the general public via formal education, guided walks, events, newsletters and media interviews.

In south-west Britain, where losses of white-clawed crayfish have become acute, there is a new conservation campaign for white-clawed crayfish, based in Bristol Zoo Gardens and involving the Environment Agency and Avon Wildlife. The campaign has among its strategic aims to work in partnership to identify remaining wild populations of white-clawed crayfish in the region and to identify potential Ark sites where populations can be maintained safely. It also aims to implement a programme of intervention with those populations most at risk of extinction, by carrying out translocations to Ark sites across the region; to establish viable populations by establishing and maintaining viable breeding populations *ex situ* to provide plague-free broodstock; and by running a targeted education programme alongside the project, highlighting key threats to white-clawed crayfish and publicly promoting measures for their conservation. This involves the development of a regional awareness campaign including outreach programmes to fisheries workers and landowners, a media campaign, and production of publicity materials. The performance measure is a target of 500 000 zoo visitors and schoolchildren, and 30 angling clubs or landowners targeted and evaluated to discover whether they respect the 'crayfish code'.

In France, on World Wetlands Day on 2 February 2009 (the anniversary of the 1971 signing of the Ramsar Convention on Wetlands), a motion was launched on an action plan to control *Procambarus clarkii* and other NICS. This motion was signed by scientists, managers and stakeholders. It called for national action for effective legislation and the establishment of networks of scientists and managers to detect the arrival of new NICS, to evaluate the resulting damage to ecosystems, and to control the populations. It also demanded greater information for the public. Sixteen months later, a national surveillance network of experts was set up to track and monitor new invasive species in the country.

Public education into the dangers of spreading NICS is increasing at a national and local level in Europe. Surveys have established the recent distribution of ICS and NICS in Europe (Souty-Grosset *et al.*, 2006; Holdich *et al.*, 2009b), and research in the UK has shown the difficulty of eradicating NICS stocks (Peay *et al.*, 2006a). A costly attempt to eliminate them from the River Clyde in Scotland was unsuccessful (Collins, 2006). Prophylactic measures to prevent the spread of plague, already promoted in Scandinavia (e.g. Taugbøl *et al.*, 1993), are now more widely established as transmission of the plague organism has become better understood (Diéguez-Uribeondo, 2006). The real problem is in the persistent power of myths about the superiority of the signal crayfish, *Pacifastacus leniusculus*, and the main culprit remains the illegal transfer of NICS into waters containing indigenous crayfish stocks, particularly in Scandinavia and Britain (Lennart Edsman, personal communication, 2008). Whether or not European ICS survive the next 100 years is up to each country and the action it takes, but it should be borne in mind that a lack of action may well impinge on the survival of ICS in neighbouring countries (Holdich *et al.*, 2009b).

On a broader international scale, as governments prioritize food production over natural resource conservation, it is important to emphasize the value of animals such as heritage indigenous crayfish species through public education. Crayfish are important in overall biodiversity for a number of reasons, including food resource and keystone species impacts on communities, which may result in altered Water Framework Directive categorization for a given site (Julie Bywater, personal communication, 2006), as well as their intrinsic or amenity value (Taylor, 2002; Gherardi *et al.*, 2003). Through such education, the groundwork is laid for good conservation legislation.

10.5.2   North America

The North American situation is of particular interest because of the high diversity of crayfish on this continent. Many US states have publicly funded Departments of Biodiversity and Conservation – for example, Kentucky and Texas – with the equivalent in some Canadian provinces (e.g. Ontario's Ministry of Natural Resources). In each case there are websites providing valuable educational material.

In the state of Massachusetts, associated with conservation regulations, there are educational activities such as Biodiversity Days and the Visible Species of Massachusetts database, designed to challenge citizens to familiarize themselves with the wealth of animal and plant species present in Massachusetts communities. There is also an Exploring Biodiversity workbook in PDF format. The BioMap Project, a spatial representation of the areas deemed most critical to the long-term conservation of the known biodiversity, is an initiative designed to identify land areas crucial to the survival of Massachusetts' native species and exemplary natural communities, and to help conservationists prioritize land protection efforts.

Texas Crawfish Biodiversity and Conservation sponsors a website with pictures of species and indications of their habitat and restricted distributions. The website warns that habitat loss is a major threat to Texas crawfish biodiversity. Particularly vulnerable are species occupying a very limited range or a specialized habitat niche, such as the Texas prairie burrower species *Procambarus steigmani* and *P. regalis*. Visitors are advised about habitat modifications that threaten native crayfish populations, including dams which disturb flow regimes and floodplains, urban development and drainage modifications, water pollution, destruction of wetland habitat types, or the lowering of the local water table to below the reach of burrowing species due to groundwater pumping or diversion of natural instream flows and recharge.

The Texas website, like many state websites, also warns about the dangers of spreading invasive species by discarding either bait or aquarium specimens, because of the risk of displacing or outcompeting other native species in whatever local habitat remains undisturbed. A particular example is the rusty crayfish *Orconectes rusticus*, a relatively aggressive crayfish with high fecundity, native to the Ohio River basin. This crayfish has become a problem invasive species in many places outside its native range and, where introduced, is a major threat to native crayfish species. *O. rusticus* introductions have been reported from the Canadian River drainage in New Mexico, and it is probably only a matter of time before it is also reported from the Canadian River drainage within Texas. Education is of vital importance here.

10.5.3   Australia, New Zealand

Australia has considerable interest and activity in conservation education, with educational projects associated with the major species' recovery plans, particularly for burrowing crayfish and for the threatened large crayfish of the genera *Euastacus* and *Astacopsis*. The identity of burrowing species has been reinforced by giving them local or geographical names. Increased public awareness and involvement in threatened species protection through community education and involvement was seen to greatly assist the recovery process for these crayfish species. Through the work of the Burrowing Crayfish Recovery Team, public awareness of several other Tasmanian burrowing crayfish has been raised by school and community talks and by a series of magazine, press and newspaper articles (Doran, 1999). Other suggested conservation measures include targeting of private landowners for conservation covenants, creating new reserves, establishing water watch monitoring programmes in catchments (G. Marsden, personal communication, 2005), and protecting existing colonies (Alastair Richardson, personal communication, 2004).

In New Zealand, the two native species of crayfish or koura *Paranephrops planifrons* and *P. zealandicus*, are well displayed on the website www.crayfishworld.com/nz.htm ('New Zealand crayfish and shrimps'), with photos, brief biological information, and a sentence on conservation status. The attractive display is undoubtedly educational and would engage anyone with an interest in freshwater life, but concerns have been raised that such websites may encourage the aquarium fancier to look for supplies, and this has already been shown to be the source of many non-native crayfish species in Europe and the USA.

10.6   Twin prerequisites for protecting crayfish biodiversity

Legislation and education are two approaches with the same aim: that of protecting biodiversity. Freshwater crustaceans have the potential to be very useful in education and in promoting conservation, in part through an interest in their preservation. Their habitats may also receive protection, resulting in improved water quality.

Other smaller crustaceans may have a lesser impact on the popular psyche but might be almost equally important in terms of ecosystem modelling, biomonitors or bioindicators. However, the larger decapods provide very suitable visual examples to demonstrate a range of biological phenomena – behavioural interactions, burrowing, breeding cycles, longevity, articulated limbs – to a lay audience. Overall, crayfish have a positive image and educational potential possessed by few other invertebrates. They are also fascinating and easy to handle (large enough, widespread, and not dangerous).

For legislation to be effective, there must be proficiency in identifying the biota subject to those laws, at least among wildlife and customs officers. This proficiency has usually proved lacking. A wider ability to distinguish NICS from ICS is important, and especially an understanding of why this is important – in terms of ecology, competition, disease transmission, ecosystem impacts, environmental damage, etc. For all of these, the active involvement of an informed public is essential, and education programmes should target different interest groups, and also those who are not interested.

Crayfish that are restricted or threatened require their own education campaigns, before it is too late to save them. To generate awareness and help counter the loss of native stocks, basic information should be accurate and widely available, both for decision makers and the general public. There already exist many good examples of public awareness campaigns focused on crayfish across developed countries. The next priority must be to assess their effectiveness, and to find out whether the diversified approach suited to each specific region can be merged into a country- or continent-wide coordinated strategy.

Appendix 10.1 Legislation affecting crayfish in individual European countries in 2009

AUSTRIA (Federal): Exploitation is allowed as a means to conservation. The minimum legal capture size is 12 cm in most states, 14 cm in Burgenland; closed seasons vary. Stone crayfish males >12 cm can be harvested in Lower and Upper Austria, >10 cm in Styria (Holdich & Pöckl, 2005).

BELGIUM, LUXEMBOURG: NICS may be trapped, but not white-clawed crayfish.

CZECH REPUBLIC: Act No 114/92 SB forbids commercial exploitation of ICS. However, this strong protective legislation means that people have rarely seen crayfish in nature (Policar & Kozák, 2005).

FINLAND: All anglers over 18 years old must have a state licence in addition to permission from the lake owner. Under the Fishing Act 1982/286, the importation of crayfish is not allowed to endanger crayfish species found in the wild in Finland. Therefore, crayfish imported for cooking cannot be marketed live to the consumer, they may not be kept even temporarily in natural waters, and they must be prevented from getting into the natural waterways. Importers of live crayfish to Finland from the EU and Norway for use as food must be registered as first-destination operators with the municipal food control authority, under decree 118/2006 of the Ministry of Agriculture and Forestry on first-destination operations. Live crayfish brought to Finland must originate from an approved establishment, and either be cooked at the first destination or be delivered to approved food premises for cooking (for example, a fish processing establishment or a restaurant). Importing foreign crayfish for stocking or farming requires either a registration (crayfish imported for farming) or an import permit (crayfish imported for restocking purposes) (decrees 977/2006 and 312/2007 of the Ministry of Agriculture and Forestry; restocking requires a permit issued by the local Employment and Economic Development Centre (TE-Centre)). In addition, the import of new species and populations of crayfish requires an import permit issued by the Department of Fisheries and Game of the Ministry of Agriculture and Forestry. Current crayfisheries policy is based on the national crayfish strategy (2000) drawn up by working groups led by Ari Mannonen. The EU Alien Species policy in preparation will probably cause changes to the position of NICS and ICS in Finland (Japo Jussila, personal communication, 2009).

FRANCE: Measures to protect ICS include no-kill zones, increases in legal size and limits on fishing effort, some imposed by fishermen themselves to protect native species (Changeux, 2003). NICS (signals and spiny-cheek crayfish) cannot be transported or introduced to specific types of waterbody.

GERMANY: ICS (noble and white-clawed crayfish) are protected under the Federal Nature Conservation & Protection Act (NCPA) and Federal Species Protection

Ordinance. The introduction of NICS is not allowed, but all species naturally reproducing (e.g. spiny-cheek and signals) are defined as native. EC courts refused a ban on live imports in 1994, citing free trade legislation; now Germany is the source of many damaging exotics such as the continuously breeding marmorkrebs. Federal law has not been improved since 2005. State fishing laws in some federal states now include additional restrictions for the stocking of crayfish; e.g. in Bavaria, only *A. astacus* is allowed to be stocked in all kinds of waters (Holger Schulz, personal communication, 2009).

HUNGARY: ICS are protected by law, with a legal conservation value (i.e. a fine for damaging it) for the noble crayfish of €40 per head (Puky *et al.*, 2005). In June 2008, under an additional decree, all three ICS were protected with the same legal conservation value, thin-clawed and stone as well as noble crayfish. Active conservation measures are still required to safeguard their future (Miklos Puky, personal communication, 2009).

IRELAND: Ireland is probably the only EU country without American alien crayfish. Its internal border with the UK cuts across catchments and its legislation in both territories has aroused interest. The UK Wildlife & Countryside Act is enacted into Northern Ireland law by Wildlife Protection Orders, and the white-clawed crayfish Species Action Plan has been valid in Northern Ireland since 1994. The Wildlife (NI) Order 1985 prohibits release into the wild of alien species. Section 14 of the Wildlife and Countryside Act covers introduced pest species listed on Schedule 9: noble, thin-clawed and signal crayfish. Red swamp and spiny-cheek crayfish were not then added. The Prohibition of Keeping of Live Fish (Crayfish) Order 1996 states that signal crayfish cannot be kept without a licence in the no-go area making up the whole of Northern Ireland. In the Republic of Ireland, where *Austropotamobius pallipes* is still widespread (Demers *et al.*, 2005) white-clawed crayfish are listed in the Wildlife Act 1976 – neither the species nor its habitat can be interfered with without a licence. Fourteen SACs were set up for crayfish, covering both lakes and rivers. Fisheries Acts prohibit the importation of exotic crayfish as potential vectors of salmonid virus.

ITALY: The Habitats Directive was received into Italian law as DPR 357/97, DRR 120/2003. Some regional administrations are more stringent – e.g. Piedmont forbids capture, transport, keeping and trade in captivity, requiring waterbodies to be regularly repopulated from breeding stock (art.29, LR n.32 of 2/11/1982. (Nardi *et al.*, 2005).

LATVIA: Only noble and thin-clawed crayfish are mentioned in law. Live crayfish imports are permitted with a veterinary certificate, but live crayfish are not allowed as bait (Arens & Taugbøl, 2005).

NETHERLANDS: New legislation is in preparation by the Fisheries Department (Bram Koese, personal communication, 2009).

NORWAY: One species (noble) is present and considered native. One law forbids live imports of NICS. A new law forbids stocking of any freshwater organism (including NICS) without a permit. There is central regulation of crayfish harvesting, including legal harvest periods, legal mesh size for traps, and minimum size. In watersheds with plague, local regulations prohibit all crayfish fishing and restrict other activities in the watershed. However, since 2005, signal crayfish have been recorded in three locations (Trond Taugbøl, personal communication, 2009).

SWEDEN: Legislation banning live imports was changed in 1997 following an EC challenge, but the ban on live imports, both from other EU countries and abroad, was eventually reinstated in 2003. The Swedish example indicates the new importance at European level of environmental and conservation legislation over the previously dominant free-agreements (Edsman, 2004). A revised action plan for the conservation of noble crayfish was launched in 2009, and county administrations can now assign special protected areas for the noble crayfish with restrictions on moving live crayfish, fish and gear in and out of the area, in order to avoid spreading crayfish plague (Lennart Edsman, personal communication, 2009).

SWITZERLAND: Crayfish are regulated under the National Fisheries law of 1994. ICS include noble crayfish, originally introduced in the Middle Ages and still exploited, and white-clawed and stone crayfish, native since the last glaciation, which have low economic value. Catching of ICS is allowed, but the effective fishing pressure is low. There is a 40-week closed season, and minimum legal sizes of 12 cm for nobles and 9 cm for white-clawed and stone crayfish. Thin-clawed crayfish (NICS) were introduced in the 1870s to compensate for a decline in noble crayfish. Spiny-cheek crayfish were also introduced in the 1870s, signal crayfish in the 1980s, and red swamp crayfish in the 1990s. Legally, importation, transport, and introduction of NICS are forbidden except for Australian *Cherax* species. Elimination measures are targeted at signals and red swamp crayfish, and include supervised angling; all crayfish caught must be killed immediately.

UNITED KINGDOM: The white-clawed crayfish is considered indigenous and has been documented from before 1500 (Holdich & Rogers, 1997). The EU Habitats Directive is implemented in the UK by the Wildlife & Countryside Act 1981, which places white-clawed crayfish on Schedule 5, preventing its capture or sale without a licence. The Conservation (Natural Habitats) Regulations of 1994 of the Salmon and Freshwater Fisheries Act 1975 regulate crayfishing and allow the creation of by-laws (Sibley, 2003a). The UK Species Action Plan covers white-clawed crayfish (Palmer, 1994, JNCC Report No. 193), and further regulations oblige conservation and environmental bodies to implement the Plan. An Environment Agency by-law prohibits the use of crayfish as bait. No-go areas excluding alien crayfish were set up under the Keeping of Live fish (Crayfish) Order 1996 to provide refuges for native crayfish. Signal crayfish were introduced in 1976, but with few controls until 1992, when they were added to Schedule 9 of the Wildlife & Countryside Act, making it an offence to release them into the wild. Noble and thin-clawed crayfish were also added to the Act at the same time. The law has many loopholes. No other alien crayfish are permitted in Britain, except where already established. The 1996 legislation introduced a ban on keeping such crayfish in designated areas affecting all areas north of a line from the Severn to the Wash and also some catchments south of that line, except with the approval of MAFF (Ministry of Agriculture, Fisheries and Food). However, 'go' and 'no-go' areas were defined by postcode, not by catchment! Any signals kept in a no-go area must be kept securely indoors, but where signal populations were already established prior to 1996 the landowner cannot be compelled to stop keeping signal crayfish. However, signal crayfish continued to be advertised for sale, flouting the law, and to be released casually into ponds and streams (Peay, 2000), but up until 2000 no prosecutions had been brought under the Act. Difficulties in prosecution include a definition of release into 'the wild', and in proving either the sources of introduction or the intent to release (Peay, 2000). The government eventually defined 'release or escape to wild' in 2000, ending the establishment of farms in most areas. Crayfish were belatedly classed as fish in 2003, under the Salmon and Freshwater Fisheries Act 1975.

11 Management strategies to protect crayfish and biodiversity

11.1 Background to the effective management of biodiversity

11.1.1 Biodiversity in fresh waters

In most countries today there are marked gradients in species distribution and richness, often arousing some concern. Such gradients may be produced by natural drivers, including evolutionary pressures through habitat restriction, isolation, change over time associated with mountain building or infilling of lakes, and climatic change. However, observed gradients in biodiversity in fresh waters are frequently due, directly or indirectly, to human intervention – diffuse or point source pollution, climate change and introduced alien species – resulting in local biodiversity loss. Conservation of wetland biodiversity is complicated by the landscape position of rivers and wetlands as 'receivers' of land-use effluents, and by competition for fresh water between many different human stakeholders, usually in denial of the need to protect the resource. Even if the headwaters of a catchment maintain biological diversity that underpins ecosystem services, this biodiversity is easily threatened because of the small size and fragmentation of these habitats.

Decapods are important in many freshwater bodies, and we have concentrated on indigenous crayfish as indicators for biodiversity, on their threats and losses, and on management to restore them. There are hundreds of freshwater crayfish species, chiefly in temperate and subtropical zones, and twice as many species of freshwater crab, reflecting their more restricted ranges in the tropics. Indigenous crayfish species are often important components of freshwater communities, acting as keystone species in shaping community function and biodiversity. There are major crayfish threat hotspots in the south-east of North America and southern Australia. Over half of North American crayfish are considered at risk (Jay Cordeiro, personal communication, 2010), while almost half of all Australian crayfish are considered to be threatened because of habitat loss and degradation, and the effects of climate change, further exacerbated by their small ranges (Nadia Richman, personal communication, 2011).

Invasive species are another threat to freshwater biodiversity and to decapods, as seen particularly in Europe. Translocated species may take on new and unexpected roles in the alien environment and lead to loss of native biodiversity. Thus, in brief, while indigenous crayfish species (ICS) enhance freshwater biodiversity, non-indigenous ones (NICS) tend to reduce it.

11.1.2   Indigenous crayfish ecology and management

Some crayfish are exclusively aquatic; others are amphibious or will forage on land, often from burrows. Many crayfish are long-lived and may attain a large size, in contrast to most other benthic freshwater or terrestrial invertebrates. The ecology of crayfish species also appears more individualistic than that of most other invertebrates and may be closer to that of cold-blooded vertebrates. As the dominant shredders in many systems, they are significant ecosystems engineers. Their broadly omnivorous diet allows certain species to be more abundant in a habitat than would be the case with more specialized feeders. Generally, where resources are abundant, crayfish are r-selected and breed early, e.g. red swamp crayfish *Procambarus clarkii* from Louisiana. In a less benign environment, crayfish may benefit by delaying reproduction until later in life (K-selected), e.g. the European white-clawed crayfish *Austropotamobius pallipes*.

Around half of all crayfish species require relatively cool-water, good-quality streams and lakes, where they shelter under stones or create shallow burrows, emerging to forage by night. These crayfish are typically long-lived and K-selected, achieving relatively large maximum sizes. As keystone species they may control the abundance of macrophytes and their associated invertebrates, increasing habitat biodiversity by controlling the commoner species. Crayfish of lower-quality, warm-water wetland habitats, some 20% of the total, are shorter-lived, living among weeds and roots in warm-water ponds and ditches.

Practically all crayfish have some propensity to burrow, but this habit becomes obligate in another 20% living in swampy or seasonally wet ground. Primary burrowers are restricted to their burrows for most of their lives; secondary burrowers leave their burrows to wander during the rainy season when the ground is flooded. A few burrowing crayfish are considered significant pests, either as a result of their foraging or their burrowing. Burrowing crayfish function as biodiversity drivers and ecosystem engineers. They can produce prodigious tunnel systems that have a significant impact on the surrounding ecosystem. Finally, a small number of cave-dwelling crayfish are highly K-selected and apparently very long-lived.

Many freshwater crayfish are keystone species because of their large size, trophic niche, and burrowing or bioturbation activity; they enhance community biodiversity by controlling the abundance of plants and plant-living invertebrates, also shredding and comminuting plant debris to the benefit of detritivores. However, multiple stressors may lead to the loss of key freshwater species such as crayfish, and substantial changes in ecosystem functioning. The loss of indigenous crayfish populations (ICS) must clearly reduce freshwater biodiversity at the species level.

Reintroductions of ICS may be appropriate to restore a recently lost population, extend the distribution of an indigenous crayfish species into its historic range, or create new or isolated populations to conserve genetic diversity or the species. Reintroductions are more widely important to re-establish a keystone species in an ecosystem, maintain and/or restore natural biodiversity, and to promote conservation awareness.

Many short-term human actions destroy species and communities in the name of efficiency but, in the longer term, this may represent a cost to society. Ecosystem services include provisioning services (e.g. fisheries, food for predators), regulating and supporting services (e.g. trophic cascade impacts including overgrowth of macrophytes), and cultural services, both quantifiable (e.g. ecotourism) and intangible benefits (aesthetic and cultural values). Persic (2006) has analysed losses of ecosystem services related to the decline or disappearance of three European crayfish species, one of which is currently exploited. The costs of ecosystem services lost are mostly unquantified at present, while restoration costs of native crayfish populations and their habitats, by such actions as improving water quality, liming water and restocking, are high.

Crayfish that are heritage or flagship species – iconic, edible, ecologically significant species used in conservation to attract the attention of the public – may have an economic value with a multiplier in the form of associated festivals and leisure products, so any loss of stocks is felt keenly and their habitats are in general protected from gross pollution. Across the globe, about 15 species of crayfish are harvested on a commercial scale and some, depending on costs and prices, are farmed to marketable size (at least 10 cm total length). Culture may be extensive and semi-natural or more intensive, where water and food are measured and provided or where every stage of their life is controlled, and may involve indigenous or non-indigenous species.

11.1.3   Management problems with alien crayfish

Large crayfish can survive prolonged transport for stocking or aquaculture, and can integrate into the food web at many levels (Nyström, 2002). Escaped crayfish are therefore good invaders, with a high likelihood of success (Moyle & Light, 1996). When crayfish become invasive, they may reach high densities, with the ability to greatly affect their environment, inducing modifications in the structure of freshwater food webs, decreasing biomass and biodiversity, contributing to the decline of other crayfish, and inflicting damage to human economy and health. Competition by invasive NICS is among the main threats to indigenous crayfish, accomplished through competition for food or shelter, through direct aggression or cross-mating, but also through disease transmission. Climate change has also increased stress on some indigenous crayfish species (ICS) while favouring NICS.

The European continent has been hardest hit by crayfish introductions and plague, but the same thing is now happening elsewhere, e.g. in Central America, Africa, Madagascar and Japan, in each case driven by North American crayfish. A high proportion of non-indigenous crayfish species introductions may become established, yet we have seen that attempts to manage invading populations often fail. Actions include early detection and rapid response, and long-term control measures where eradication is not feasible. Preventing the introduction of NICS is far more cost-effective and environmentally desirable than measures taken after their introduction and establishment. Attempts to control NICS may involve physical barriers, biological control agents (but traditional predators and disease-causing organisms are not always specific to the target organism), pyrethrum-based biocides, and surfactants which inhibit oxygen consumption through the gills. Autocidal methods such as the sterile male release technique (SMRT) and the use of sex pheromones to interfere with breeding have been rather ineffective.

Plague adds to the dangers of NICS. *Aphanomyces astaci* may live almost as a symbiont in its native geographical region, although North American species of crayfish may become susceptible to plague under conditions of stress. *A. astaci* has even been used in Spain for biological control of the invasive species *Cherax destructor* (Diéguez-Uribeondo & Muzquiz, 2005).

Newly arrived alien crayfish present different problems from those of established NICS. Populations are smaller and ranges still limited, and they may not yet have become invasive. The options for spot eradication using extreme methods are greater, and should be seized, along with the opportunity to target the area with educational materials.

11.2   The international legal and regulatory background

Legislative controls may be designed to protect indigenous crayfish species (ICS), or to regulate non-indigenous, exotic or alien crayfish (NICS) or prevent their introduction. The aim of both approaches is biodiversity conservation. To conserve a native species is to maintain community equilibrium and the existing functional food webs, which are often disrupted by the presence of alien species.

American crayfish have been widely introduced to Europe and Africa, and legislative controls have struggled unsuccessfully to keep up with the damage caused, including defining the species in law. There are also problems of enforcement, particularly with internet-based trading of NICS (Holdich *et al.*, 2009b). The aquarium trade is now the most likely source of new crayfish species entering Europe, indicating the need for Europe-wide control. Realizing the devastation that NICS can cause to native crayfish, most EU countries now ban the importation of live crayfish, as do Australia and New Zealand.

Education is the key to effective operation of all such controls and regulations, whether exploitative or conservation-based. Education should target different sectors. The angling licence provides a unique opportunity to reach the important stakeholder group of water users. There is also a specific need for educational material dealing with biodiversity to be tailored to government officials and water managers. The law is useless if officials cannot recognize the species named in the legislation in order to take appropriate action.

International declarations

There is now substantial agreement that invasive alien species (IAS) are deleterious to biodiversity through their impacts on indigenous species (McGeogh *et al.*, 2010). Biodiversity of fresh waters is a topic tackled by a number of declarations, conventions and international organizations both inside and outside the UN system (*inter alia* the Bonn Convention, FAO, Global Water Partnership, IUCN, Wetlands International, World Water Council and the World Bank). Happily, there is increasing cooperation between the many international conventions on water because of rising awareness of the vulnerability of functions and services of freshwater ecosystems to threats to their bio-diversity. In particular, with the Convention on Biological Diversity (CBD), the Ramsar Convention, the UN Framework Convention on Climate Change (UNFCCC) and the Convention on International Watercourses, there is an emerging global framework for action aiming to preserve the integrity of freshwater ecosystems and to foster fresh-water biodiversity. Furthermore, the CBD and Ramsar have initiated cooperation with many other actors influential in international water policy. This emerging network has intensified scientific and political discussion and can potentially lead to more coher-ent actions at the global level. Such cooperation in the field of biodiversity-oriented water policy proves that institutional obstacles can to some extent be overcome.

In general, therefore, the weakness of international policy relating to freshwater bio-diversity is less the result of insufficient global cooperation but can instead be traced back to weak political support at the regional and national levels. McGeogh *et al.* (2010) note that since 1951 the number of international agreements relevant to the control of IAS and the number of countries party to these agreements has increased expo-nentially, but that under half of all signatories to the CBD have not enacted any IAS-relevant national legislation. To stimulate national activity, we now urgently need to integrate the global initiatives with our enhanced understanding of how freshwater systems function. Because of their keystone and flagship qualities in fresh waters, we advocate bringing freshwater crayfish to the forefront of our planning.

11.3   Management-led conservation of crayfish populations

A summary of the management options for protecting freshwater crayfish and their habitats is presented in Figure 10.1 (from Holdich *et al.*, 2009b). This conceptual model shows the different actions necessary for the protection of ICS in Europe, grouped under two main headings:

1. **General management** involves coordination at a regional scale, the implementa-tion of strong and appropriate legislation and, most important, public education.
2. **Specific management** actions include distribution surveys, site protection and habitat restoration, fisheries controls for ICS and NICS, and actions to restrict NICS and the spread of plague. Where invasive NICS have become dominant, this may require setting up Ark sites or sanctuaries.

Suitably modified, the model in Figure 10.1 could form the basis of management plans for crayfish on all continents, so it would be instructive to test the model elsewhere, e.g. the USA, Canada or Australia, if not yet suitable for Brazil, Chile or other South American countries, or for Madagascar.

In the decade since Taugbøl & Skurdal (1999) published their guidelines, there has been increased crayfish conservation activity in Europe, involving the EU Habitats Directive (1992) and CRAYNET, and in individual European states, particularly the UK – with initiatives such as no-go areas for NICS and Ark sites for ICS. Legislation has been tightened and the attitudes of the EU and its Member States to international treaties dealing with the environment and with free trade have started to change. In Scandinavia, the value of exploitation as a conservation tool is emphasized by Taugbøl (2004b), while the Swedish story, involving relaxation of legislation in 1997 to permit live crayfish imports under free trade regulations, and their eventual re-imposition 5 years later, has been described by Edsman (2004). This model was originally devised by Taugbøl & Skurdal (1999) for Europe, specifically for the situation in Scandinavia, and it has since been suggested as a basis of conserving indigenous crayfish species in Austria (Pöckl & Pekny, 2002), south-west England (Holdich *et al.*, 2009b) and elsewhere, except that in the UK, indigenous crayfish are fully protected and no exploitation is permitted.

In light of what was happening in Europe in the 1990s, Taugbøl & Skurdal (1999) suggested that the setting up of 'native crayfish areas' (NCAs) was of prime importance for ensuring the future of ICS. These could be as large as a country, or could comprise a region, a watershed, or just a single watercourse or waterbody. Such areas are comparable to the no-go areas in operation in the UK since 1996. Taugbøl & Skurdal (1999) highlighted Ireland and Norway as being suitable NCAs for *Austropotamobius pallipes* and *Astacus astacus*, respectively, as both countries were at the time free of NICS. Unfortunately, Norway has since had a number of incursions of *Pacifastacus leniusculus* into its waters, although in one case they might have been eradicated (Johnsen *et al.*, 2007; Johnsen & Vrålstad 2009). Ireland retains its status as the only country solely occupied by *A. pallipes* and with no NICS (Gallagher *et al.*, 2005; Reynolds, 2009b; Reynolds *et al.*, 2010), although still under continuing threat of illegal importations. Northern Ireland (part of the UK) has also been declared a no-go area for NICS. In 2000, the suggestion of 'native crayfish areas' was further developed on a smaller scale. In south-west England (Sibley *et al.*, 2007) and at a number of other sites in Britain (Peay, 2009a), secure locations or 'Ark sites' are being developed, into which threatened populations of ICS are being moved. The concept of Ark sites is also being taken forward in Northern Ireland (Horton, 2009; Reynolds, 2009b). Sweden is in the process of setting up protected areas for *A. astacus*, including the whole of the island of Gotland (Lennart Edsman, personal communication, 2009).

The most important management option is prevention of the spread of NICS and their associated crayfish plague, so their control or management by whatever means is essential. Prophylactic measures to prevent the spread of plague, already promoted in Scandinavia (Taugbøl *et al.*, 1993), are now more widely implemented as transmission of the plague organism has become better understood (Diéguez-Uribeondo, 2006). The main problem lies in the persistent power of myths about the superiority of the signal crayfish *Pacifastacus leniusculus* (Lennart Edsman, personal communication, 2009); and the real culprits remain those who illegally transfer NICS into waters containing indigenous crayfish stocks, particularly in Scandinavia and Britain.

Education of the public is thus an essential part of any management strategy, whether for the need to control invasive alien crayfish or to protect restricted or threatened species. To generate awareness and help counter the loss of native stocks, basic information should be accurate and widely available, both for decision makers and the general public. There already exist many good examples of public awareness campaigns focused on crayfish across developed countries; thus a priority must be to assess their effectiveness, and to find out whether the diversified approaches suited to each specific region can usefully be merged into a country- or continent-wide coordinated strategy, involving regular monitoring and inventories, an 'alarm system' to signal new arrivals, and an agreed methodology to prevent their dissemination.

It seems clear that if we are to reduce losses of crayfish species and hence maintain their functional roles in aquatic and semi-aquatic environments, and also to optimize the use of exploitable species, we need to adopt an effective code of management based on the model. In simplest terms, the management recommendations might read:

- Exploit worldwide species
- Conserve restricted species
- Control invasive species.

11.3.1   Exploitation of worldwide species

Some aquatic animals and plants valued for food by humans (many of them, like the rainbow trout, originally from North America) are now globally distributed, and their exploitation is both economically important and highly developed, sometimes involving intensive rearing. Best management practice relates to habitat and community conservation in semi-natural situations.

While some of the best crayfish species for culture, in terms of both growth characteristics and flavour, are of Australian origin, most global crayfish come from North America, their relative immunity to crayfish plague helping their survival and competitive exclusion of other forms. For similar reasons, the esteemed European noble crayfish *Astacus astacus* is also less widely utilized than might be expected, even in its native range.

Examples of exploiting worldwide species: The red swamp crayfish *Procambarus clarkii* from Louisiana is now widespread in southern Europe, in Africa, and in east Asia, where it spans a wider range of climatic and environmental conditions than found in its native range. This species is essentially detritivorous, with an annual life cycle; it is an ecological engineer and modifies both wetland environments and native communities wherever it colonizes. The signal crayfish, *Pacifastacus leniusculus* from northwestern North America is now widespread in cooler parts of the world. Like other astacids it is omnivorous, long-lived, and prefers good-quality water. It modifies native communities through competition and the transmission of crayfish plague pathogen, to which it is not itself entirely immune. The tropical redclaw *Cherax quadricarinatus* is becoming naturalized in various parts of the world, including the Kafue River in Zambia, where dense stocks have developed and are now falling prey to some of the more voracious fishes of the Zambezi system (John Foster, personal communication, 2010). None of these global species has shown susceptibility to heavy exploitation, and should be exploited. However, there are still conflicts between exploiting to control these NICS, and fears of encouraging their spread for the sake of further exploitation.

11.3.2   Conservation of restricted species through sensitive management

It is recognized that species may be deemed restricted under different IUCN threat categories. They may be restricted in the physical sense, limited to a small area, and also in the sense of being in strong decline, with populations becoming increasingly small, fragmented and isolated.

There are numerous examples of physically restricted aquatic animals, including cool-temperate relict salmonids and coregonids from Europe, Asia and North America. Such species may have colonized pristine favourable areas shortly after the last glaciation and are now facing threats, both from increasingly adverse conditions of climate and from dense human populations, causing worsening water quality. Most crayfish stocks are cool- or warm-temperate in origin, and many stocks are also declining, for a variety of reasons.

Examples of conservation of restricted species: Some Cambaridae and Astacidae are among restricted species needing protection. In Japan, the native *Cambaroides japonicus* is diminishing sharply as its natural habitat deteriorates and North American crayfish spread. European astacid crayfish are also in sharp decline. *Austropotamobius pallipes* is considered to be well understood, including the geography of its rapid post-glacial expansion to colonize all available areas, but we still do not know enough about its requirements to guarantee successful conservation through restocking. Reintroduction successes and failures in several European countries have been evaluated by Souty-Grosset & Reynolds (2010). The suitability of the target habitat, the stocking material, and the stocking procedure itself are paramount during any reintroduction measure. It is, above all, essential that the target habitat is free of crayfish plague. Apart from generally good water quality and a heterogeneous environment, a suitable site for reintroduction is ideally geographically isolated from other surface waters and from human activities such as intensive fishing pressure and agricultural practices. Genetic aspects should also be considered in the choice of stocking material because there is unresolved infraspecies-level variation in *Austropotamobius* (Souty-Grosset *et al.*, 2006).

There are many restricted and threatened species in the southern hemisphere, notably in Madagascar, where overexploitation, habitat deterioration and introduced *Procambarus fallax f. virginalis* (marmorkrebs), are all having an effect; but no conservation programmes are yet developed. Habitat deterioration is the main problem for Australian crayfish such as the Tasmanian giant freshwater crayfish *Astacopsis gouldi* and the Murray crayfish (*Euastacus armatus*) in south-eastern Australia. These large crayfish are used as 'surrogate species' for ecosystem conservation goals. Surrogate species are designated to provide a protective umbrella for either a habitat or a community, in particular for other sympatric members of the same guild or for lesser-known community members.

The 5-year Recovery Plan for the *A. gouldi* of northern Tasmania includes habitat protection and rehabilitation, and encourages communities to undertake compatible activities, including enhancing awareness. Benefits to other species and ecological communities are noted through managing Tasmanian freshwater ecosystems for *A. gouldi*, with an improved status for many other threatened native aquatic fauna.

These include over 40 species of threatened aquatic invertebrates, especially four species of threatened burrowing crayfish and two closely related *Astacopsis* species where an overlap in range occurs. Other native species that will also benefit from the implementation of these recovery actions are platypus, native frogs and many freshwater fish, notably endemic galaxiids.

Other restricted species are well exemplified by two ecological groupings of crayfish; burrowing crayfish (*Engaeus* and *Engaewa* species) in Australia and cave-dwelling crayfish in North America such as *Cambarus aculabrum* and troglophilic *Orconectes* species (examples were considered in Chapter 10). Many crayfish species under state protection in both jurisdictions have very restricted distributions and some are the subject of recovery plans. A high proportion of crayfish in the USA is listed as threatened or vulnerable (Taylor *et al.*, 2007), with some of these coming under Endangered Species Programs, through conservation candidature, listing, conservation of habitat and recovery programmes under the aegis of the US Fish & Wildlife Service working in consultation with other federal agencies, and in partnership with state and non-governmental organizations. The main conflicts are associated with deterioration in water quality, of particular concern for cave crayfish but more generally for many crayfish species worldwide.

11.3.3   Control of invasive species

In Europe especially, but also in parts of the USA, Australia, Japan and Madagascar, invasive crayfish have changed the original patterns of biodiversity, and their control is the most difficult part of any action or management plan for conservation. To have any chance of success, NICS must be controlled as soon as they are detected and ideally before they have become established or invasive. Holdich *et al.* (2009b) separated non-indigenous crayfish in Europe into 'old NICS' which have been established for at least 45 years and are now widespread, and 'new NICS' which have more recently invaded. The latter may be restricted to one or a few ponds into which they were released, which provides more chance of eradication than for a species which has colonized and is expanding in major river catchments.

Public education about the dangers of introducing NICS and fostering their spread is vital. Research in the UK has shown the difficulty of eradicating NICS (Collins, 2006, Peay *et al.*, 2006a; Peay, 2009b). In areas where NICS are already widespread and expanding their range, the remaining populations of indigenous crayfish are under threat from NICS or from crayfish plague, especially in river systems, and there may be no measures possible to safeguard them *in situ*. In this regard, the white-clawed crayfish populations in Ireland are crucial to conservation of the species in that they are the only stocks in Europe not sympatric with American non-indigenous species (Reynolds *et al.*, 2002a; Reynolds, 2009b), but are under strong and increasing threat from the misplaced interest in alien crayfish in Europe. In most other cases, the only option for retaining native populations within their original region may be to find or create sanctuaries in isolated locations (Holdich *et al.*, 2004).

Examples of control of invasive species: Examples of invasive crayfish and the difficulties of controlling them have formed the bulk of this book and so will not be further developed here. Control efforts for 'old NICS' such as signal crayfish *Pacifastacus*

leniusculus in Britain have not been successful (Peay, 2009b). Continental translocations of *Orconectes rusticus* in the USA and in Canada or of *Cherax destructor* have
led to invasions and disequilibrium, as documented in Chapter 8. One complication is
hybridization between related species of crayfish brought into sympatry. Finally, there
are current and future problems caused by aquarists and hobbyists, which have resulted
in the release of exotic species such as the marmorkrebs, whose control will undoubtedly involve legislation.

11.4   Costs of the different management strategies

The value of flagship species in defining desirable outcomes for fresh waters and direct-
ing their management has been demonstrated. The various management strategies have
widely different costs and benefits; the benefits often locally enriching while the costs
are more widely spread. Some are local and direct, and might be funded through licens-
ing or harvest sales, while others would be restrictive or prohibitive without special
funding, perhaps buried in regional or state administration. In the Nordic countries,
for instance, the right to catch crayfish generally belongs to the riparian landowners,
but in some other countries the fishing rights in general belong to the state but can be
rented out to private persons or associations. Activities related to crayfish culture or
capture have been considered to play an economic role in rural development, at least in
the Nordic and Baltic countries. Similar activities could be expanded to other crayfish
regions of the world (Reynolds *et al.*, 2006).

   Many conservationists and environmental protection officers not familiar with the
socio-cultural aspects of crayfish utilization believe that red-listed species like the
European indigenous crayfish should be protected from exploitation. However, market
value and the possibility for exploitation may be important components of a conservation strategy. This is especially true for the noble crayfish in areas with existing
catching traditions, but has also been suggested for white-clawed crayfish (Reynolds
& Matthews, 1996). The greatest threat against indigenous crayfish is the human-
facilitated spread of non-indigenous crayfish species (NICS) and, with them, crayfish
plague. The possibility of utilizing indigenous crayfish for recreational and economic
purposes is of major importance in the struggle to protect them and to avoid illegal
stocking with NICS. Information directed to fishermen and landowners should stress
the economic and recreational value of the indigenous crayfish and provide good arguments against the introduction of NICS; for example that NICS can be detrimental to
recreational fisheries (Peay & Hiley, 2004). It is impossible to prevent the spread of
such species if local people have a different agenda.

11.5   The outlook ahead

Since the beginning of the 'Anthropocene' in the latter part of the eighteenth century, the loss of biodiversity has been devastating, particularly in fresh waters, with

accompanying repercussions for human and environmental well-being (Naiman & Dudgeon, 2010). Most human societies are not yet at the point of realizing that the deterioration of fresh waters puts us all at risk. It is particularly important to understand how virtual global water trading – the use of water resources in one region for the production of crops and goods, and their subsequent export to other parts of the world – exposes natural systems to short-term economic profit, but may result in fragmentation and loss of ecosystem services.

Naiman & Dudgeon (2010) echo Bernhardt *et al.* (2006) in making a plea for balancing water-resource development and environmental well-being, by recognizing that natural systems are inherently dynamic and unpredictable, and accepting that rivers and estuaries need environmental flows – the right quality of water at the right times in the right amounts to sustain ecosystem services and biodiversity. On top of this, it is important to understand the aggregative effects of multiple stressors from human activities within a catchment and the consequences of biodiversity loss for ecosystem services. As freshwater systems and their communities become increasingly fragmented, their connectivity must be maintained and managed.

The complexity of the impacts of biological invasions in fresh waters and the progressive mixing of biota from across the globe is intimately tied up with human pressures such as trade, travel and transport (Pyšek *et al.*, 2010). These authors reviewed recent European data in order to partition between macroecological, economic and demographic variables the variation in alien species richness of many groups, including bryophytes, aquatic invertebrates, fish, amphibians and mammals. Only national wealth and human population density were found to be statistically significant predictors in the majority of models, when analysed jointly with climate, geography and land cover. The strong influence of economic and demographic variables on invasion by alien species demonstrates that future solutions to the problem of biological invasions must lie in mitigating the negative environmental consequences of human activities that generate wealth, and by promoting more sustainable population growth.

The evidence shows that one way to protect the aquatic environment and water resources is by conserving freshwater crayfish, as in the maintenance of freshwater food sources and the cultural heritage. As a result, crayfish have a positive image and educational potential possessed by few other invertebrates. Other large (decapod) crustaceans in fresh waters have a lesser impact on the popular psyche and traditions, but may also be important as keystone species, biomonitors or bioindicators. Such freshwater crustaceans are also large enough to be easily handled, and are widespread and fascinating. They may thus be very useful in education and in promoting conservation, and – through an interest in their preservation – their habitats may also receive protection, so that improved water quality would often result.

One inescapable conclusion is that if anyone, whether stakeholder, scientist, manager or legislator, wishes to act for the restoration of good freshwater environmental quality, and particularly for the management of heritage species such as indigenous crayfish, he or she must first be able to identify them. A species inventory is useful both to scientists and also to conservation organizations in the development of action plans. Above all, such an inventory informs the public, and indeed all stakeholders, showing accurately how many indigenous species are present, where they occur and how many non-indigenous species have been introduced, and thus help people to understand why these are such a serious threat.

In Europe and the Americas, 'native' status tends to be defined individually at state level (Holdich, 2002c; see also Holdich, 2002a) rather than following a catchment-based approach or one based on large geographical regions. Some 'native' crayfish species are already afforded statutory protection at regional, state and transnational levels, but the identification of members of species complexes is still not agreed, leading to legal complications. The first imperative is therefore to agree on taxonomic ranks and then to recognize appropriate statutory protection for all indigenous crayfish, with clear definitions of what responsibilities are placed on authorities and the public (Reynolds *et al.*, 2006).

With global increases in human demand for food, aquaculture is undergoing a rapid worldwide expansion. Of significant concern is the increasing use of non-native species (Cook *et al.*, 2008), with subsequent escapes of these species and their associated pathogens and parasites posing a serious threat to native biodiversity, economic value and ecosystem function, particularly in regions rich in endemic species. The contribution of non-native species to the growth of the global aquaculture industry and the economic benefits that this has brought to many developing countries cannot be underestimated. However, limiting or minimizing the escapes of non-native aquaculture species must be a high priority for resource managers, conservationists and the aquaculture industry. Cook *et al.* (2008) reviewed the environmental consequences that escapes can have on the aquatic environment and presented a potential system of risk evaluation, management and funding mechanisms to assist in the long-term sustainable development of the aquaculture industry.

11.5.1   Lessons from Europe

Invasive crayfish are most widespread in Europe, so what happens to European fresh waters will provide lessons for the rest of the world. Taugbøl & Skurdal (1999) predicted that if effective conservation plans were not put in place, then eventually all the watersheds suitable for crayfish in Europe might be occupied by NICS, with all ICS critically endangered and surviving only in a few protected localities. To avoid this scenario, they suggested remedial actions including restoration of aquatic habitats, protection of ICS as a national aim, obtaining a good knowledge of the status and distribution of crayfish, identifying and establishing 'native crayfish areas' (since established as no-go areas, sanctuaries or Ark sites), preventing the further spread of NICS, implementing effective legislation, re-establishing ICS where they have been eradicated, informing the public, and exploiting ICS (see Figure 10.1). While most of these actions are commendable, the last one is contentious. Taugbøl & Skurdal (1999) and Taugbøl (2004b) maintain that exploitation and protection are closely linked, as those who exploit are usually concerned about the resources and will protect them. This may be the case for countries where there is a strong tradition of harvesting and consuming crayfish, but not where the ICS are protected from harvesting by law, as in Britain and Ireland.

Directed surveys have established the distribution of ICS and NICS in Europe up to 2006 (Souty-Grosset *et al.*, 2006), and a number of countries have set up national plans for their ICS and NICS, e.g. Austria (Pöckl, 2002) and Switzerland (Stucki *et al.*, 2005; Hefti & Stucki, 2006). Public education into the dangers of spreading NICS is increasing at a national and local level, for example in France, and public interest is expanding. Research in the UK has shown the difficulty of eradicating NICS stocks (Peay *et al.*, 2006a). An attempt to eradicate them from the River Clyde in Scotland cost over £100 000 but was unsuccessful (Collins, 2006). However, prophylactic measures to prevent the spread of plague, already promoted in Scandinavia (e.g. Taugbøl *et al.*, 1993) are now better and more widely established as transmission of the plague organism has become better understood (Diéguez-Uribeondo, 2006).

The European Community, as a signatory to the 1992 Convention on Biological Diversity, has a Biodiversity Strategy published in 1999. This states:

Biodiversity is essential to maintain life on Earth and has important social, economic, scientific, educational, cultural, recreational and aesthetic values.

Without active conservation, more species will disappear and habitats will decline further. Generally, the conservation of key components of biological diversity, such as freshwater crayfish, produces benefits arising from the protection of the aquatic environment and water resources, as well as from the maintenance of both food sources and cultural heritage.

In most European countries, crayfish are still of commercial and conservation importance. The final conclusions of CRAYNET: *Conservation of European Crayfish* noted that the five indigenous crayfish species (ICS) are still widespread, despite the ravages of a disease – crayfish plague – introduced in the nineteenth century by invasive alien species introduced deliberately or unintentionally outside their natural occurrence areas. ICS are considered to be under constant threat from the introduction of non-indigenous species of crayfish (NICS) as superior competitors, as well as from the effects of human activity (agricultural practices, industry, destruction of the river bed and riparian vegetation). The threat to biodiversity due to invasive alien species is considered as important as habitat loss.

Whether or not European ICS survive the next 100 years is up to each country and the action it takes, but it should be borne in mind that taking no action may well impinge on the survival of ICS in neighbouring countries. Territories without invading populations of NICS, or in early stages of the problem, could do well to look at the mixed experiences of Britain in trying to protect its single ICS, *Austropotamobius pallipes*, in the face of an ever-growing number of NICS (Peay *et al.*, 2010; Sibley *et al.*, 2009; Holdich & Sibley, 2009).

12 Maintaining biological diversity and human well-being

From analysis made through IUCN 2010 Red List assessments, south-east Australia was highlighted as one of the most threatened regions for crayfish species, with almost half of all species threatened with extinction. The most significant threats to these species were climate change and severe weather events, and habitat degradation and loss; while in North America habitat degradation and loss were considered a major threat, along with pollution, particularly sedimentation from land-use change. Multiple threats were found to European species with equal impacts from invasive species, pollution, and habitat degradation and loss. Madagascar was the only region in which harvesting was considered a principal threat; its impacts, though, were found to be compounded by the increasing affect of habitat fragmentation, and the long-lived nature of some of these species.

Strayer & Dudgeon (2010) have reviewed recent progress in the conservation of freshwater biodiversity. Important challenges for freshwater conservation include climate change and further freshwater extinctions, and these authors join with other voices in urging that scholarly societies, scientists, conservationists and other stakeholders must concentrate on disseminating information on conservation ecology if the world's fresh waters are not to be dramatically impoverished.

Among ecologically important aquatic invaders are molluscs that are primary consumers and disrupt the food web from its base, fish that disrupt the food web from its apex or centre, decapods that act as powerful omnivores, aquatic plants that have strong engineering effects, and diseases which probably have been underestimated as an ecological force (Strayer, 2010). Decapods and other successful invaders in fresh waters are highly non-random with respect to their biological traits and, indeed, taxonomic identity, the ecological characteristics of the invaded ecosystems, and the geographical location of the ecosystems that supply and receive the invaders (Strayer, 2010). Some invaders have had dramatic effects on the ecosystems that they invade; most stressed ecosystems are susceptible to invasion, and the result must be new and unpredictable freshwater systems with unknown ecological services, costs and benefits.

The spread of invasive alien species is one of only two indicators of threat to biodiversity forming part of the Convention on Biological Diversity's framework for monitoring progress toward its 2010 target (i.e. the commitment to achieve, by that date, a significant reduction in the current rate of biodiversity loss – a target that was not met). However, there is as yet no indicator for invasive alien species (IAS) that combines trends across species groups, ecosystems and regions. In one approach, McGeogh *et al.*

(2006) suggested single and composite indicators of trends in IAS that include problem-status and management-status measures. The single indicators, at national and global scales, are the number of IAS and number of operational management plans for IAS. Global trends in IAS are measured as the progress of nations toward the targets of stabilizing IAS numbers and the implementation of IAS management plans that aim to maximize national participation. This global indicator then required testing to assess its accuracy, sensitivity and tractability.

McGeogh *et al.* (2010) examined over 500 invasive alien species (IAS) with demonstrated negative impacts on biodiversity, across 57 countries; numbers ranged from 9 in New Guinea to 222 in New Zealand. While no freshwater invertebrates were included, 44 freshwater fish species and 15 amphibians were assessed. The authors assessed species numbers and biodiversity impact in global indicators of biological invasion. Overall, the IUCN threat level was increased for 245 species, while the eradication of IAS led to a reduction of IUCN threat status for 17 species. IAS constituted the most important driver for amphibians, although their relative importance in terrestrial groups was less than that of agriculture for birds and mammals, and less than that of logging and hunting for mammals. This underlines the critical nature of invasions by alien species into fresh waters. McGeogh *et al.* (2010) comment that although it may not have been possible to achieve the objective for a global indicator of biological invasion by 2010 as comprehensively as desired, it should be possible to obtain trend estimates for components of the taxa, ecosystems and regions involved. Importantly, current indicator development initiatives will also contribute to developing the mechanisms necessary for monitoring global trends in IAS beyond 2010.

Having analysed and discussed the biodiversity indicators for 2010 (Mace & Baillie, 2007), and noting that there is now abundant evidence that biodiversity, both its variability and its composition, significantly influences the ability of an ecosystem to deliver ecosystem services, Mace *et al.* (2010) noted that management tends to be local, but its consequences are felt globally. They therefore advocated a return to a simpler series of targets after 2010. 'Red' targets are those biodiversity outcomes, such as collapses of fish stocks or the dissemination of global zoonoses, to be avoided in order to avert situations deleterious to people; 'green' targets are those highly valued biodiversity conservation priorities such as protection of the biota of Madagascar or the Great Barrier Reef; and 'blue' targets are the improved scientific understanding necessary for adaptive management into the future.

This would be a very appropriate model for the conservation of crayfish, which we have shown are effective for the maintenance of freshwater biodiversity and well-being. Red targets would comprise the avoidance of the spread of crayfish plague, and green targets would include the continued protection of crayfish biodiversity in diverse habitats such as lakes and caves. Blue targets would include the demonstration of the need for education among management priorities and the use of the precautionary principle when dealing with potentially damaging situations where the outcome is not certain.

Thus, conservation of crayfish in the future will require the integration of current knowledge of conservation biology and resource management, and also effective information dissemination and legislation development and enforcement. Although there is some transnational legislation in the USA, Canada, Europe and Australia protecting indigenous crayfish and providing a basis for management policies, a national and regional approach is also required in order to address specific situations. Island countries such as Ireland, Tasmania and New Zealand, where stocks of indigenous crayfish are important and widely distributed and where no non-indigenous crayfish yet occurs in the wild, can elaborate a nationwide or regional conservation strategy based on habitat preservation and the prevention of the invasion of alien species or diseases. Key factors include rigorous import controls, a ban on the use of crayfish as bait, and raising public awareness of the issue, both among residents and visiting anglers (Reynolds & Demers, 2006). On the other hand, in continental countries such as France and Italy, where indigenous crayfish distribution is now increasingly restricted and fragmented, catchment-based or even site-based strategies will be much more effective in protecting the remaining populations (Reynolds *et al.*, 2006).

The moral of this book is surely that

> ***Conservation of crayfish is a challenge involving everybody,***
> ***from the citizen to stakeholders, scientists and decision-makers.***

References

Abele, L. G. & Felgenhauer, B. E. (1986). Phylogenetic and phenetic relationships among the lower Decapoda. *Journal of Crustacean Biology*, **6**, 385–400.

Abell, R., Thieme, M., Dinnerstein, E. & Olson, D. (2002). *A Sourcebook for Conducting Biological Assessments and Developing Biodiversity Visions for Ecoregion Conservation. Volume II. Freshwater Ecoregions.* World Wildlife Fund. Island Press, Washington, DC: 201 pp.

Abrahamsson, S. (1966). Dynamics of an isolated population of the crayfish *Astacus astacus* Linne. *Oikos*, **17**, 96–107.

Abrahamsson, S. (1973). The crayfish, *Astacus astacus*, in Sweden and the introduction of the American crayfish *Pacifastacus leniusculus. Freshwater Crayfish*, **1**, 27–40.

Abrahamsson, S. A. A. (1983). Trappability, locomotion, and diel pattern of activity of the crayfish *Astacus astacus* and *Pacifastacus leniusculus* Dana. *Freshwater Crayfish*, **5**, 239–53.

Abrahamsson, S. & Goldman, C. R. (1970). Distribution, density and production of the crayfish *Pacifastacus leniusculus* Dana in Lake Tahoe, California-Nevada. *Oikos*, **21**, 83–91.

Ackefors, H. (1998). The culture and capture crayfish fisheries in Europe. *World Aquaculture*, **29**, 12–24, 64–7.

Adams, W. M. & Hulme, D. (2001). If community conservation is the answer in Africa, what is the question? *Oryx*, **35**, 193–200.

Ahyong, S. T. & O'Meally, D. (2004). Phylogeny of the Decapoda Reptantia: resolution using three molecular loci and morphology. *Raffles Bulletin of Zoology*, **52**, 673–93.

Ahyong, S. T. & Yeo, D. C. J. (2007). Feral populations of the Australian red claw crayfish (*Cherax quadricarinatus*, von Martens) in water supply catchments of Singapore. *Biological Invasions*, **9**(8), 943–46.

Ahyong, S. T., Lai, J. C., Sharkey, D., Colgan, D. J. & Ng, P. K. (2007). Phylogenetics of the brachyuran crabs (Crustacea: Decapoda): the status of Podotremata based on small subunit nuclear ribosomal RNA. *Molecular Phylogenetics and Evolution*, **45**, 576–86.

Alderman, D. J. (1993). Crayfish plague in Britain, the first twelve years. *Freshwater Crayfish* **9**, 266–72.

Alderman, D. J. (1996). Geographical spread of bacterial and fungal diseases of crustaceans. *Revue Scientifique et Technique Office International des Epizooties,* **15**(2), 603–32.

Alderman, D. J. & Polglase, J. L. (1988). Pathogens, parasites and commensals. In: D. M. Holdich & R. S. Lowery (eds) *Freshwater Crayfish: Biology, Management and Exploitation.* Croom Helm, London: 167–212.

Alderman, D. J., Polglase, J. L. & Frayling, M. (1987). *Aphanomyces astaci* pathogenicity under laboratory and field conditions. *Journal of Fish Diseases*, **10**, 385–93.

Alikhan, M. A., Bagatto, G. & Zia, S. (1990). The crayfish as a 'biological indicator' of aquatic contamination by heavy metals. *Water Research*, **24**, 1069–76.

Allan, J. D. & Flecker, A. S. (1993). Biodiversity conservation in running waters: identifying the major factors that threaten destruction of riverine species and ecosystems. *BioScience*, **43**, 32–43.

Allison, W. R. & Harvey, H. H. (1981). Methods for assessing the benthos of acidifying lakes. In: R. Singer (ed.) *Effects of Acidic Precipitation on Benthos*. North American Benthological Society, Lawrence, KS: 1–13.

Almeida, A. O. & Buckup, L. (1999). Caracteres sexuals primários e secundários do lagostim *Parastacus defossus* Faxon, 1898 (Crustacea, Parastacidae). *Nauplius*, **7**, 113–26.

Almeida, A. O. & Buckup, L. (2000). Occurrence of protandric hermaphroditism in a population of the neotropical freshwater crayfish *Parastacus brasiliensis* (Parastacidae). *Journal of Crustacean Biology*, **20**, 224–30.

Alonso, F. (2001). Efficiency of electrofishing as a sampling method for freshwater crayfish populations in small creeks. *Limnetica*, **20**, 59–72.

Alonso, F., Temino, C. & Diéguez-Uribeondo, J. (2000). Status of the white-clawed crayfish, *Austropotamobius pallipes* (Lereboullet, 1858) in Spain: distribution and legislation. *Bulletin Français de la Pêche et de la Pisciculture*, **356**, 31–54.

Ameyaw-Akumfi, C. (1976). Some aspects of the breeding biology of the crayfish. DPhil thesis, University of Michigan, Ann Arbor, MI.

Ameyaw-Akumfi, C. & Hazlett, B. A. (1975). Sex recognition in the crayfish *Procambarus clarkii*. *Science*, **190**, 1225–6.

Andersen, A.N. (1999). My bioindicator or yours? Making the selection. *Journal of Insect Conservation*, **3**, 1–4.

André, M. (1960). *Les Écrevisses Françaises*. Editions Paul Lechevalier, Paris: 293 pp.

Andrews, J. A. (1907). The young of the crayfishes *Astacus* and *Cambarus*. *Smithsonian Contributions to Knowledge*, **35** (1718), 11–77.

Aquiloni, L. & Gherardi, F. (2010). The use of sex pheromones for the control of invasive populations of the crayfish *Procambarus clarkii*: a field study. *Hydrobiologia*, **649**(7), 249–254.

Aquiloni, L., Becciolini, A., Berti, R., et al. (2009). Managing invasive crayfish: use of x-ray sterilisation of males. *Freshwater Biology*, **54**, 1510–19.

Aquiloni, L., Brusconi, S., Cecchinelli, E., et al. (2010). Biological control of invasive populations of crayfish: the European eel (*Anguilla anguilla*) as a predator of *Procambarus clarkii*. *Biological Invasions*, **12**(11), 3817–24.

Arens, A. & Taugbøl, T. (2005). Status of crayfish in Latvia. *Bulletin Français de la Pêche et de la Pisciculture*, **376–7**, 519–28.

Arrignon, J. C. V., Huner, J. V. & Laurent, P. J. (1990). *L'Écrevisse Rouge des Marais*. Maisonneuve et Larose Editions, Paris: 87 pp.

Arrignon, J. C. V., Martini, M. & Mattei, J. (1999). *Austropotamobius pallipes pallipes* (Lereb.) in Corsica. *Freshwater Crayfish*, **12**, 811–16.

Asai, N., Fusetani, N., Matsugana, S. & Sasaki, J. (2000). Sex pheromones of the hair crab *Erimacrus isenbeckii*. Part 1. Isolation and structures of novel ceramides. *Tetrahedron*, **56**, 9895–9.

Austin, C. M. (1996). An electrophoretic and morphological taxonomic study of the freshwater crayfish genus *Cherax* (Decapoda: Parastacidae) in Northern and Eastern Australia. *Australian Journal of Zoology*, **44**, 259–96.

Austin, C. M. & Knott, B. (1996). Systematics of the freshwater crayfish genus *Cherax* (Decapoda: Parastacidae) in south-western Australia: electrophoretic, morphological and habitat variation. *Australian Journal of Zoology*, **44**, 223–58.

Austin, C. M. & Ryan, S. G. (2002). Allozyme evidence for a new species of freshwater crayfish of the genus *Cherax* Ericson (Decapoda; Parastacidae) from south-western Australia. *Invertebrate Systematics*, **16**, 357–67.

Baillie, J. & Groombridge, B. (eds) (1996). *1996 IUCN Red List of Threatened Animals*. IUCN, Gland, Switzerland.

Bakri, A., Metha, K. & Lance, D. R. (2005). Sterilizing insects with ionizing radiation. In: V. A. Dyck, J. Hendrichs & A. S. Robinson (eds) *Sterile Insect Technique: Principles and Practice in Area-wide Integrated Pest Management*. Springer, Dordrecht, The Netherlands: 233–68.

Balian, E. V., Segers, H., Lévèque, C. & Martens, K. (2008). The freshwater animal diversity assessment: an overview of the results. *Hydrobiologia*, **395**, 627–37.

Ballesteros, I., Martín, M. P. & Diéguez-Uribeondo, J. (2006). First isolation of *Aphanomyces frigidophilus* (Saprolegniales) in Europe. *Mycotaxon*, **95**, 335–40.

Ballesteros, I., Martín, M. P., Cerenius, L., et al. (2007). Lack of specificity of the molecular diagnostic method for identification of *Aphanomyces*. *Bulletin Français de la Pêche et de la Pisciculture*, **385**, 17–24.

Balmford, A., Bruner, A., Cooper, P., et al. (2002). Economic reasons for conserving wild nature. *Science*, **297** (5583), 950–3.

Baran, I. & Soylu, E. (1989). Crayfish plague in Turkey. *Journal of Fish Diseases*, **12**, 193–7.

Barbaresi, S. & Gherardi, F. (1997). Italian freshwater decapods: exclusion between the crayfish *Austropotamobius pallipes* (Faxon) and the river crab *Potamon fluviatile* (Herbst.). *Bulletin Français de la Pêche et de la Pisciculture*, **347**, 731–47.

Baron, J. S., Poff, N. L., Angermeier, P. L., et al. (2003). Sustaining healthy freshwater ecosystems. *Issues in Ecology*, **10**, 1–16.

Bean, C. W., Maitland, P. S. & Collen, P. (2006). Crayfish in Scotland: a review of current status and legislative control. *Freshwater Crayfish*, **15**, 220–8.

Bechler, D. L. (1981). Copulatory and maternal-offspring behavior in the hypogean crayfish, *Orconectes inermis inermis* Cope and *Orconectes pellucidus* (Tellkampf) (Decapoda, Astacidea). *Crustaceana*, **40**, 136–43.

Bechler, D. L., Deng, X. & McDonald, B. (1988). Interspecific pheromonal communication between sympatric crayfish of the genus *Procambarus* (Decapoda, Astacidae). *Crustaceana*, **54**, 153–62.

Behrendt, A. (1979). Export push needed to open market for crayfish. *Fish Farmer*, **2**, 44–6.

Belchier, M., Edsman, L., Sheehy, M. R. J. & Shelton, P. M. J. (1998). Estimating age and growth in long-lived temperate crayfish using lipofuscin. *Freshwater Biology*, **39**, 439–46.

Bernhardt, E., Bunn, S. E., Hart, D. D., et al. (2006). The challenge of ecologically sustainable water management. *Water Policy*, **8**, 475–9.

Berrill, M. (1978). Distribution and ecology of crayfish in the Kawartha Lakes region of southern Ontario. *Canadian Journal of Zoology*, **56**, 166–77.

Berrill, M. & Chenoweth, B. (1982). The burrowing ability of non-burrowing crayfish. *American Midland Naturalist*, **108**, 199–201.

Bertocchi, S., Brusconi, S., Gherardi, F., Grandjean, F. & Souty-Grosset, C. (2008). Genetic variability in the threatened crayfish *Austropotamobius italicus* in Tuscany: implications for its management. *Fundamental and Applied Limnology (Archiv für Hydrobiologie)*, **173**(2), 153–64.

Bertolino, S. & Genovesi, P. (2003). Spread and attempted eradication of the grey squirrel (*Sciurus carolinensis*) in Italy, and consequences for the red squirrel (*Sciurus vulgaris*) in Eurasia. *Biological Conservation*, **109**, 351–8.

Bills, T. D. & Marking, L. L. (1988). Control of nuisance populations of crayfish with traps and toxicants. *Progressive Fish-Culturist*, **50**(2), 103–6.

Blake, M. A. & Hart, P. J. B. (1993). Habitat preferences and survival of juvenile signal crayfish, *Pacifastacus leniusculus*: the influence of water depth, substratum, predatory fish and gravid female crayfish. *Freshwater Crayfish*, **9**, 318–32.

Blake, M. A. & Hart, P. J. B. (1995). The vulnerability of juvenile signal crayfish to perch and eel predation. *Freshwater Biology*, **33**, 233–44.

Boas, J. E. V. (1880). *Studier over Decapodernes Slaegtskabsforhold*. Kongel, Danske Videnske Selsk. Skr. 6: 25–210.

Bocic, V., Rudolph, E. & Lopez, D. (1988). Biologia reproductiva y dinamica poblacional del camaron de rio, *Samastacus spinifrons* (Philippi, 1882) (Decapoda, Parastacidae). *Boletín de la Sociedad de Biologia de Concepción, Chile*, **59**, 9–21.

Bohl, E. (1999). Crayfish stock situation in Bavaria (Germany): attributes, threats and chances. *Freshwater Crayfish*, **12**, 765–77.

Bondar, C. A., Zhang, Y., Richardson, J. S. & Jesson, D. (2005). *The Conservation Status of the Freshwater Crayfish*, Pacifastacus leniusculus, *in British Columbia*. Fisheries Management Report No. 117. BC Ministry of Water, Land and Air Protection.

Bott, R. (1972). Beseidlungsgeschischte und Systematik der Astaciden W-Europas unter besonderer Berücksichtigung der Schweiz. *Revue Suisse de Zoologie*, **79**, 387–408.

Bouchard, R. W. (1977). Distribution, systematic status and ecological notes on five poorly known species of crayfish in western North America (Decapoda: Astacidae and Cambaridae). *Freshwater Crayfish*, **3**, 409–23.

Bovbjerg, R. V. (1961). Mechanisms affecting isolation for species of crayfish. *American Zoologist*, **1**, 345.

Bovbjerg, R. V. (1970). Ecological isolation and competitive exclusion in two crayfish (*O. virilis* and *O. immunis*). *Ecology*, **51**, 226–36.

Braband, A., Kawai, T. & Scholtz, G. (2006). The phylogenetic position of the East Asian freshwater crayfish *Cambaroides* within the Northern Hemisphere Astacoidea (Crustacea, Decapoda, Astacida) based on molecular data. *Journal of Zoological Systematics and Evolutionary Research*, **44**, 17–24.

Bracken, H. D., Toon, A., Felder, D. L., et al. (2009). The decapod tree of life: compiling the data and moving toward a consensus of decapod evolution. *Arthropod Systematics & Phylogeny*, **67**(1), 99–116.

Bramard, M., Demers, A., Trouilhé, M. C., et al. (2006). Distribution of indigenous and non-indigenous crayfish populations in the Poitou-Charentes Region (France): evolution over the past 25 years. *Bulletin Français de la Pêche et de la Pisciculture*, **380**–1, 857–65.

Bravo, M. A., Duarte, C. M. & Montes, C. (1994). Environmental factors controlling the life history of *Procambarus clarkii* (Decapoda, Cambaridae) in temporary marsh of the Doñana National Park (SW Spain). *Verhandlungen der Internationale Vereinigung für Limnologie*, **25**, 2450–3.

Breinholt, J., Perez-Losada, M. & Crandall, K. A. (2009). The timing of the diversification of the freshwater crayfishes. In: J. W. Martin, K. A. Crandall & D. L. Felder (eds) *Decapod Crustacean Phylogenetics*. CRC Press, Taylor and Francis Group: 335–43.

Brook, B., Grant, A. & Bell, D. (2009). Can land crabs be used as a rapid ecosystem evaluation tool? *Acta Oecologia*, **35**(5), 711–19.

Brown, D. J. & Bowler, K. (1977). A population study of British freshwater crayfish *Austropotamobius pallipes* (Lereboullet). *Freshwater Crayfish*, **3**, 33–49.

Brown, D. J. & Brewis, J. M. (1979). A critical look at trapping as a method of sampling a population of *Austropotamobius pallipes* (Lereboullet) in a mark and recapture study. *Freshwater Crayfish*, **4**, 159–64.

Brown, M. J., Brown, P. B., Bryant, S. J., et al. (1993). Buttongrass moorland ecosystems. In: S. J. Smith & M. R. Banks (eds) *Tasmanian Wilderness: World Heritage Values*. Royal Society of Tasmania, Hobart, TAS: 101–8.

Brown, S., Hickey, C. & Harrington, B. (eds) (2000). *The U. S. Shorebird Conservation Plan*. Manomet Center for Conservation Sciences, Manomet, MA.

Brusconi, S., Bertocchi, S., Renai, B., et al. (2008). Conserving indigenous crayfish: stock assessment and habitat requirements in the threatened *Austropotamobius italicus*. *Aquatic Conservation: Marine and Freshwater Ecosystems*, **8**(7), 1227–39.

Bubb, D. H., Thom, T. J. & Lucas, M. C. (2007). Spatial ecology of the white-clawed crayfish in an upland stream and implications for the conservation of this endangered species. *Aquatic Conservation: Marine and Freshwater Ecosystems*, **18**, 647–57.

Buglife (2010). Selecting Ark sites for white-clawed crayfish. Buglife – The Invertebrate Conservation Trust [available at www.buglife.org.uk/conservation/currentprojects/Species+Action/Conserving+our+Crayfish/Crayfish+Ark+Site+Selection+Criteria].

Buhay, J. E. & Crandall, K. A. (2008). Taxonomic revision of cave crayfishes in the genus *Orconectes*, subgenus *Orconectes* (Decapoda: Cambaridae) along the Cumberland Plateau, including a description of a new species, *Orconectes barri*. *Journal of Crustacean Biology*, **28**, 57–67.

Buřič, M., Kozák, P. & Vích, P. (2008). Evaluation of different marking methods for spiny-cheek crayfish (*Orconectes limosus*). *Knowledge and Management of Aquatic Ecosystems*, **389**, article 02, doi:10.1051/kmae:2008004.

Burkenroad, M. D. (1963). The evolution of the Eucarida (Crustacea, Eumalacostraca), in relation to the fossil record. *Tulane Studies in Geology*, **2**, 1–18.

Burkenroad, M. D. (1981). The higher taxonomy and evolution of Decapoda (Crustacea). *Transactions of the San Diego Society of Natural History*, **19**, 251–68.

Butler, M. J. & Stein, R. A. (1985). An analysis of the mechanisms governing species replacement in crayfish. *Oecologia*, **66**, 168–77.

Büttiker, B. (1987). Concerning crayfish in Switzerland. *Freshwater Crayfish*, **7**, 2–5.

Byrne, C. F., Lynch, J. M. & Bracken, J. J. (1999). A sampling strategy for stream populations of white-clawed crayfish, *Austropotamobius pallipes* (Lereboullet) (Crustacea, Astacidae). *Biology and Environment: Proceedings of the Royal Irish Academy*, **99**, 89–94.

Byron, C. J. & Wilson, K. A. (2001). Rusty crayfish (*Orconectes rusticus*) movement within and between habitats in Trout Lake, Vilas County, Wisconsin. *Journal of the North American Benthological Society*, **20**, 606–14.

Cabantous, M. A. (1974). Introduction and rearing of *Pacifastacus* at the research centre of Les Clouzioux, 18450 Brinon s/Sauldre, France. *Freshwater Crayfish*, **2**, 49–55.

Cabral, J. A., Anastácio, P. M., Carvalho, R. & Marques, J. C. (1997). A non-harmful chemical method of red swamp crayfish, *Procambarus clarkii*, population control and non-target organism problematics in the lower Modego River valley, Portugal. *Freshwater Crayfish*, **11**, 286–92.

Calman, W. T. (1904). On the classification of the Crustacea Malacostraca. *Annals and Magazine of Natural History*, **13**(74), 144–58.

Calman, W. T. (1909). Crustacea. In: R. Lankester (ed.) *A Treatise on Zoology*. Adam and Black, London: 1–345.

Capelli, G. M. (1975). Distribution, life history and ecology of crayfish in northern Wisconsin, with emphasis on *Orconectes propinquus* (Girard). DPhil thesis, University of Wisconsin, Madison, WI.

Capelli, G. M. (1982). Displacement of northern Wisconsin crayfish by *Orconectes rusticus* (Girard). *Limnology & Oceanography*, **27**, 741–5.

Carapelli, A., Liò, P., Nardi, F., van der Wath, E. & Frati, F. (2007). Phylogenetic analysis of mitochondrial protein coding genes confirms the reciprocal paraphyly of Hexapoda and Crustacea. *BMC Evolutionary Biology*, **7**(Suppl. 2), S8.

Caro, T. M. & O'Doherty, G. (1999). On the use of surrogate species in conservation biology. *Conservation Biology*, **13**(4), 805–14.

Carral, J. M., Celada, J. D., González, J., et al. (1993). Wild freshwater crayfish populations in Spain: current status and perspectives. *Freshwater Crayfish*, **9**, 158–62.

Cerenius, L. & Söderhäll, K. (1992). Crayfish diseases and crayfish as vectors for important disease. *Finnish Fisheries Research*, **14**, 125–33.

Cerenius, L., Rufelt, S. & Söderhäll, K. (1992). Effects of Ampropylfos ((*RS*)-1-aminopropylphosphonic acid) on zoospore formation, repeated zoospore emergence and oospore formation in *Aphanomyces* spp. *Pesticide Science*, **36**(3), 189–94.

Cerenius, L., Bangyeekhun, E., Keyser P. & Söderhäll, K. (2003). Host prophenoloxidase expression in freshwater crayfish is linked to increased resistance to the crayfish plague fungus, *Aphanomyces astaci*. *Cellular Microbiology*, **5**, 353–7.

Cerenius, L., Andersson, G. & Söderhäll, K. (2009). *Aphanomyces astaci* and crustaceans. In: K. Lamour & S. Kamoun (eds) *Oomycete Genetics and Genomics: Diversity, Interactions, and Research Tools*. John Wiley & Sons, Hoboken, NJ.

Changeux, T. (2003). Changes in crayfish distribution in metropolitan France according to the national surveys performed by the Conseil Supérieur de la Pêche from 1977 to 2001. *Bulletin Français de la Pêche et de la Pisciculture*, **370**–1, 17–42.

Chappuis, P. A. (1927). *Die Tierwelt der unterirdischen Gewässer*. Die Binengewässer, Vol. 3, Schweizerbart, Stuttgart: 176 pp.

Christoffersen, M. L. (1988). Phylogenetic systematics of the Eucarida (Crustacea, Malacostraca). *Revista Brasiliera de Zoologia*, **5**, 325–51.

Clark, E. (1936). Notes on the habits of land crayfishes. *Victorian Naturalist*, **53**, 65–8.

Collas, M., Julien, C. & Monnier, D. (2007). La situation des écrevisses en France: résultats des enquêtes nationales réalisées entre 1977 et 2006 par le Conseil Supérieur de la pêche. *Bulletin Français de la Pêche et de la Pisciculture*, **386**, 1–38.

Collins, V. (2006). £100,000 battle against alien crayfish ends in defeat. *Crayfish News: IAA Newsletter*, **28**(1), 10–11.

Comeaux, M. L. (1972). *Atchafalaya Swamp Life: Settlement and Food Occupations*. In: R. F. Perkins (ed.) *Geoscience and Man*, Vol. II. Louisiana State University, Baton Rouge, LA.

Commission of the European Communities (2008). Communication from the Commission to the Council, the European Parliament, the European Economic and Social Committee and the Committee of the Regions Towards an EU Strategy on Invasive Species [SEC(2008) 2887 & SEC(2008) 2886]: 10 pp.

Cook, E. J., Ashton, G., Campbell, M., et al. (2008). Non-native aquaculture species releases: implications for aquatic ecosystems. In: M. Holmer, K. Black, C. M. Duarte, N. Marbà & I. Karakassis (eds) *Aquaculture in the Ecosystem*. Springer: 155–84.

Cooper J. E. (1975). Ecological and behavioural studies in Shelta Cave, Alabama, with emphasis on the decapod crustaceans. PhD thesis, University of Kentucky, Lexington, KY.

Cope, E. D. (1872). On the Wyandotte Cave and its fauna. *American Naturalist*, **6**(7), 406–22.

Corey, S. (1987). Comparative fecundity of four species of crayfish in southwestern Ontario, Canada (Decapoda, Astacidea). *Crustaceana*, **52**, 276–86.

Correia, A. M. & Ferreira, Ó. (1995). Burrowing behavior of the introduced red swamp crayfish *Procambarus clarkii* (Decapoda: Cambaridae) in Portugal. *Journal of Crustacean Biology*, **15**, 248–57.

Coughran, J. (2006). Biology of the freshwater crayfishes of northeastern New South Wales, Australia. PhD Thesis, School of Environmental Science & Management, Southern Cross University, Australia.

Coughran, J., Leckie, S. & Gartside, D. (2008). Distribution, habitat and conservation status of the freshwater crayfishes, *Cherax cuspidatus* Riek and *Cherax leckii* Coughran (Decapoda: Parastacidae). *Freshwater Crayfish*, **16**, 19–26.

Cowan, D. F. (1991). The role of olfaction in courtship behavior of the American lobster *Homarus americanus*. *Biological Bulletin*, **181**, 402–7.

Cox, P. A., Banack, S. A., Murch, S. J., et al. (2005). Diverse taxa of cyanobacteria produce β-*N*-methylamino-L-alanine, a neurotoxic amino acid. *PNAS*, **102**, 5074–8.

Crandall, K. (2003). Parastacidae, Astacoides, freshwater crayfishes. In: S. M. Goodman & J. P. Benstead (eds) *The Natural History of Madagascar*. The University of Chicago Press, Chicago, IL: 608–612.

Crandall, K. A. & Buhay, J. E. (2008). Global diversity of crayfish (Astacidae, Cambaridae, and Parastacidae – Decapoda) in freshwater. *Hydrobiologia*, **595**, 295–301.

Crandall, K. A., Harris, J. D. & Fetzner, J. W. (2000a). The monophyletic origin of freshwater crayfish estimated from nuclear and mitochondrial DNA sequences. *Proceedings of the Royal Society of London*, **B 267**, 1679–86.

Crandall, K. A., Fetzner, J. W., Jr, Jara, G. G. & Buckup, L. (2000b). On the phylogenetic positioning of the South American freshwater crayfish genera (Decapoda: Parastacidae). *Journal of Crustacean Biology*, **20**, 530–40.

Creed, R. P. (1994). Direct and indirect effects of crayfish grazing in a stream community. *Ecology*, **75**, 2091–103.

Creed, R. P., Jr & Reed, J. M. (2004). Ecosystem engineering by crayfish in a headwater stream community. *Journal of the North American Benthological Society*, **23**, 224–36.

Crocker, D. W. & Barr, D. W. (1968). *Handbook of the Crayfishes of Ontario*. University of Toronto Press, Toronto.

Cuellar, L. & Coll, M. (1983). Epizootiology of the crayfish plague (Aphanomycosis) in Spain. *Freshwater Crayfish*, **5**, 545–7.

Cukerzis, J. M. (1988). *Astacus astacus* in Europe. *Freshwater Crayfish*, **7**, 309–40.

Cumberlidge, N. & Sternberg, R. V. (2002). The freshwater crabs of Madagascar (Crustacea, Decapoda, Potamoidea). *Zoosystema*, **24**, 41–79.

Cumberlidge, N., Ng, P. K. L., Yeo, D. C. J., et al. (2009). Freshwater crabs and the biodiversity crisis: importance, threats, status and conservation challenges. *Biological Conservation*, **142**, 1665–73.

Curtis, C. F. (1985). Theoretical models of the use of insecticide mixtures for the management of resistance. *Bulletin of Entomological Research*, **75**, 259–65.

D'Agaro, E., De Luise, G. & Lanari, D. (1999). The current status of crayfish farming in Italy. *Freshwater Crayfish*, **12**, 506–17.

DAISIE (2009). *Handbook of Alien Species in Europe*. Invading Nature: Springer Series in Invasion Ecology 3. Springer, Dordrecht, The Netherlands.

Darwall, W., Smith, K., Allen, D., et al. (2009). Freshwater biodiversity: a hidden resource under threat. In: J.-C. Vié, C. Hilton-Taylor & S. N. Stuart (eds) *Wildlife in a Changing World: An Analysis of the 2008 IUCN Red List of Threatened Species*. IUCN, Gland, Switzerland: 43–54.

Da Silva-Castiglioni, D., López Greco, L., Turcato Oliveira, G. & Bond-Buckup, G. (2008). Characterization of the sexual pattern of *Parastacus varicosus* (Crustacea: Decapoda: Parastacidae). *Invertebrate Zoology*, **127**, 426–32.

Davic, R. D. (2003). Linking keystone species and functional groups: a new operational definition of the keystone species concept. *Conservation Ecology (online)*, **7**, r11.

Davies, P. E., Cook, L. S. J., Munks, S. A. & Meggs, J. (2005). *Astacopsis gouldi* Clark: habitat characteristics and relative abundance of juveniles. *Tasforests*, **16**, 1–17.

Davies, P. E., Munks, S. A., Cook, L. S. J., Von Minden, P. & Wilson, D. (2007). *Mapping Suitability of Habitat for the Giant Freshwater Crayfish*, Astacopsis gouldi*: Background Document to GIS Mapping Layer*. Forest Practices Authority Scientific Report 4. Forest Practices Authority, Hobart, TAS.

Davis, J., Sim, L. & Chambers, J. (2010). Multiple stressors and regime shifts in shallow aquatic ecosystems in antipodean landscapes. *Freshwater Biology*, **55**(Suppl. 1), 5–18.

Degerman, E., Anders Nilsson, P., Nystrom, P., Nilsson, E. & Olsson, K. (2006). Are fish populations in temperate streams affected by crayfish? A field survey and prospects. *Environmental Biology of Fishes*, **78**, 231–9.

De Grave, S., Pentcheff, N. D., Ahyong, S. T., et al. (2009). A classification of living and fossil genera of decapod crustaceans. *Raffles Bulletin of Zoology*, Supplement **21**, 1–109.

Dehus, P., Dussling, U. & Hoffmann, C. (1999). Notes on the occurrence of the calico crayfish (*Orconectes immunis*) in Germany. *Freshwater Crayfish*, **12**, 786–90.

Delibes, M. & Adrian, I. (1987). Effects of crayfish introduction on otter *Lutra lutra* food in the Doñana National Park, SW Spain. *Biological Conservation*, **42**, 153–9.

Demers, A. & Reynolds, J. D. (2002). A survey of the white-clawed crayfish *Austropotamobius pallipes* (Lereboullet), and of water quality in two catchments in eastern Ireland. *Bulletin Français de la Pêche et de la Pisciculture*, **367**, 729–40.

Demers, A. & Reynolds, J. D. (2003). The distribution of the white-clawed crayfish, *Austropotamobius pallipes*, in eight catchments in Ireland in relation to water quality. In: D. M. Holdich & P. J. Sibley (eds) *Management and Conservation of Crayfish: Proceedings of a Conference held on 7th November, 2002*. Environment Agency, Bristol, UK: 94–103.

Demers. A., Reynolds, J. D. & Cioni, A. (2003). Habitat preferences of different size classes of *Austropotamobius pallipes* in an Irish river. *Bulletin Français de la Pêche et de la Pisciculture*, **370–1**, 127–38.

Demers, A., Lucey, J., McGarrigle, M. L. & Reynolds, J. D. (2005). The distribution of the white-clawed crayfish *Austropotamobius pallipes* in Ireland. *Biology and Environment: Proceedings of the Royal Irish Academy*, **105B**, 65–9.

Demers, A., Souty-Grosset, C., Trouilhé, M. C., et al. (2006). Tolerance of three European native species of crayfish to hypoxia. *Hydrobiologia*, **560**, 425–32.

DEWHA (Department of the Environment, Water, Heritage and the Arts) (2008). *Engaeus granulatus*. In: *Species Profile and Threats Database*. Department of the Environment, Water, Heritage and the Arts, Canberra.

Diamond, J. M., Bressler, D. W. & Serveiss, V. B. (2002). Assessing relationships between human land uses and the decline of native mussels, fish, and macroinvertebrates in the Clinch and Powell River watershed, USA. *Environmental Toxicology and Chemistry*, **21**, 1147–55.

Diéguez-Uribeondo, J. (2006). The dispersion of the *Aphanomyces astaci*-carrier, *Pacifastacus leniusculus* by humans represents the main cause of disappearance of the indigenous crayfish *Austropotamobius pallipes* in Navarra. *Bulletin Français de la Pêche et de la Pisciculture*, **380–1**, 1303–12.

Diéguez-Uribeondo, J. (2009). Current techniques, approaches and knowledge in diagnosis of crayfish plague and other crayfish diseases. *Knowledge and Management of Aquatic Ecosystems*, 394–5, article 02.

Diéguez-Uribeondo, J. & Cerenius, L. (1998). The inhibition of extracellular proteinases from *Aphanomyces* spp by three different proteinase inhibitors from crayfish blood. *Mycological Research*, **102**, 820–4.

Diéguez-Uribeondo, J. & Muzquiz, J. L. (2005). The use of the fungus *Aphanomyces astaci* for biological control of the invasive species *Cherax destructor*. Poster presentation at International Workshop: Biological Invasions in Inland Waters, Florence, Italy.

Diéguez-Uribeondo, J. & Söderhäll, K. (1993). *Procambarus clarkii* Girard as a vector for the crayfish plague fungus, *Aphanomyces astaci* Schikora. *Aquaculture Research*, **24**, 761–5.

Diéguez-Uribeondo, J., Cerenius, L. & Söderhäll, K. (1994). Repeated zoospore emergence in *Saprolegnia parasitica*. *Mycological Research*, **98**, 810–15.

Diéguez-Uribeondo, J., Huang, T. S., Cerenius, L. & Söderhäll, K. (1995). Physiological adaptation of an *Aphanomyces astaci* strain isolated from the freshwater crayfish *Procambarus clarkii*. *Mycological Research*, **99**, 574–8.

Diéguez-Uribeondo, J., Rueda-Diez, A., Castién, E. & Bascones, J. C. (1997a). A plan of restoration for the native freshwater crayfish, *Austropotamobius pallipes* in Navarra. *Bulletin Français de la Pêche et de la Pisciculture*, **347**, 625–37.

Diéguez-Uribeondo, J., Temino, C., & Muzquiz J. L. (1997b). The crayfish plague fungus (*Aphanomyces astaci*) in Spain. *Bulletin Français de la Pêche et de la Pisciculture*, **347**, 753–63.

Diéguez-Uribeondo, J., Cerenius, L., Dykova, I., et al. (2006). Pathogens, parasites and ectocommensals. In: C. Souty-Grosset, D. M. Holdich, P. Y. Noël, J. D. Reynolds & P. Haffner (eds) *Atlas of Crayfish in Europe*. Patrimoines naturels 64. Muséum National d'Histoire naturelle, Paris: 133–49.

Diéguez-Uribeondo, J., García, M. A., Cerenius, L., et al. (2009). Phylogenetic relationships among plant and animal parasites, and saprotrophs in *Aphanomyces* (Oomycetes). *Fungal Genetics and Biology*, **46**, 365–76.

DiStefano, R. J., Gale, C. M., Wagner, B. A. & Zweifel, R. D. (2003). A sampling method to assess lotic crayfish communities. *Journal of Crustacean Biology*, **23**, 678–90.

DiStefano, R. J., Litvan, M. E. & Horner, P. T. (2009). The bait industry as a potential vector for alien crayfish introductions: problem recognition by fisheries agencies and a Missouri evaluation. *Fisheries*, **34**(12), 586–97.

Dixon, C. J., Ahyong, S. & Schram, F. R. (2003). A new hypothesis of decapod phylogeny. *Crustaceana*, **76**, 935–75.

Doran, N. (1999). *Burrowing Crayfish* (Engaeus) *Group Recovery Plan 2001–2005*. Parks and Wildlife Service, TAS DPIWE [available at www.environment.gov.au/biodiversity/threatened/publications/recovery/burrowing-crayfish/index.html].

Doran, N. E. & Richards, K. (1996). *Management Requirements for Rare and Threatened Burrowing Crayfish in Tasmania*. Report to the Tasmanian RFA Environment and Heritage Technical Committee, Hobart, TAS.

Dorn, N. J., Urgelles, R. & Trexler, J. C. (2005). Evaluating active and passive sampling methods to quantify crayfish density in a freshwater wetland. *Journal of the North American Benthological Society*, **24**, 346–56.

DPIW (2007). *Tasmania's Freshwater Burrowing Crayfish*. Department of Primary Industries and Water, Hobart, Tasmania [available at www.dpiw.tas.gov.au/inter.nsf/WebPages/LJEM-73J92W?open].

Dudgeon, D., Arthington, A. H., Gessner, M. P., et al. (2006). Freshwater biodiversity: importance, threats, status and conservation challenges. *Biological Reviews of the Cambridge Philosophical Society*, **81**, 163–82.

Dunham, D. W. & Oh, J. W. (1996). Sex discrimination by female *Procambarus clarkii* (Girard, 1852) (Decapoda, Cambaridae): use of chemical and visual stimuli. *Crustaceana*, **69**, 534–42.

Dunham, P. J. (1979). Mating in the American lobster: stage of molt cycle and sex pheromone. *Journal of Marine Behaviour & Physiology*, **6**, 1–11.

Dunn, J. C., McClymont, H. E., Christmas, M. & Dunn, A. M. (2009). Competition and parasitism in the native white clawed crayfish *Austropotamobius pallipes* and the invasive signal crayfish *Pacifastacus leniusculus* in the UK. *Biological Invasions*, **11**, 315–24.

Eberly, W. R. (1960). Competition and evolution in cave crayfish of southern Indiana. *Systematic Zoology*, **9**, 29–32.

Edgerton, B. F., Henttonen, P., Jussila, J., et al. (2004). Understanding the causes of disease in European freshwater crayfish. *Conservation Biology*, **18**(6), 1466–74.

Edsman, L. (2004). The Swedish story about import of live crayfish. *Bulletin Français de la Pêche et de la Pisciculture*, **372**–3, 281–8.

Edsman, L. & Schröder, S. (2009). *Åtgärdsprogram för Flodkräfta 2008–2013* (Astacus astacus). Fiskeriverket och Naturvårdsverket, Report 5955.

Edsman, L. & Śmietana, P. (2004). Roundtable 2. Exploitation, conservation and legislation. *Bulletin Français de la Pêche et de la Pisciculture*, **372**–3, 457–64.

Edsman, L., Farris J. S., Källersjö, M. & Prestegaard, T. (2002). Genetic differentiation between noble crayfish, *Astacus astacus* (L.) populations detected by microsatellite length variation in the rDNA ITS1 region. *Bulletin Français de la Pêche et de la Pisciculture*, **367**, 691–706.

EIFAC (1992). *Report of the Seventeenth Session of the European Inland Fisheries Advisory Commission, Lugano, Switzerland, 19–26 May 1992*. FAO Fisheries Report 333099-E.

Ellis, B. A. & Morris, S. (1995). Effects of extreme pH on the physiology of the Australian 'yabby' *Cherax destructor*: acute and chronic changes in haemolymph carbon dioxide, acid-base and ionic status. *Journal of Experimental Biology*, **198**, 395–407.

Elvey, W., Richardson, A. M. M. & Barmuta, L. (1996). Interactions between the introduced yabby, *Cherax destructor*, and the endemic crayfish, *Astacopsis franklinii*, in Tasmanian streams. *Freshwater Crayfish*, **11**, 349–63.

Elvira, B., Gnicola, G. & Almodovari, A. (1996). Pike and red swamp crayfish: a new case on predator–prey relationships between aliens in central Spain. *Journal of Fish Biology*, **48**, 437–46.

Emery, A. R. (1975). Stunted bass: a result of competing cisco and limited crayfish stocks. In: R. H. Stroud & H. Clepper (eds) *Black Bass Biology and Management*. Sport Fishing Institute, Washington, DC: 154–64.

Environment Agency (1995). *Biodiversity: The UK Steering Group Report*, 2 volumes. HMSO, London.

Erencin, Z. & Köksal, G. (1977). On the crayfish, *Astacus leptodactylus*, in Anatolia. *Freshwater Crayfish*, **3**, 187–92.

Escosa, R. (1990). L'écrevisse rouge (*Procambarus clarkii*), problèmes dans le Delta de l'Ebro. *L'Astaciculteur de France*, **23**, 2–4.

European Commission (EC) (2008). *Towards an EU Strategy on Invasive Species.* (COM/2008) 789, European Commission, 68 pp.

European Economic and Social Committee (2009). *Opinion of the European Economic and Social Committee on the Communication from the Commission to the Council, the European Parliament, the European Economic and Social Committee and the Committee of the Regions – Towards an EU Strategy on Invasive Species COM* (2008*) 789 Final.* NAT/433 – CESE 1034/2009. European Economic and Social Committee, Brussels [available at http://eescopinions.eesc.europa.eu/EESCopinionDocument.aspx?identifier=ces\nat\nat433\ces1034–2009_ac.doc&language=EN].

Evans, L. H. & Edgerton, B. F. (2002). Pathogens, parasites and commensals. In: D. M. Holdich (ed.) *Biology of Freshwater Crayfish*. Blackwell Science, Oxford, UK: 377–438.

Everard, M., Gray, J., Wilkins-Kindemba, V. & Cowx, I. G. (2009). Impacts of invasive species on ecosystem services: the case of the signal crayfish (*Pacifastacus leniusculus*). *Environmental Law & Management*, **21**(5), 250–7.

Eversole, A. G. (2008). Crayfish culture along the east coast of the United States. *Freshwater Crayfish*, **16**, 1–5.

Eversole, A. G. & Folz, J. W. (1993). Habitat relationship of two crayfish species in a mountain stream. *Freshwater Crayfish*, **9**, 300–10.

Eversole, A. G. & Seller, B. C. (1996). Comparison of relative crayfish toxicity values. *Freshwater Crayfish*, **11**, 274–85.

Eversole, A. G., Whetstone J. M. & Sellers B. C. (1995). *Handbook of Relative Acute Toxicity Values for Crayfish.* South Carolina Sea Grant Consortium, Charleston, SC.

Fahrig, L. (2003). Effects of habitat fragmentation on biodiversity. *Annual Review of Ecology, Evolution & Systematics*, **34**, 487–515.

Fausch, K. D., Baxter, G. V. & Murakami, M. (2010). Multiple stressors in north temperate streams: lessons from linked forest–stream ecosystems in northern Japan. *Freshwater Biology*, **55**(Suppl. 1), 120–34.

FBMA (2007). *China Fisheries Statistical Yearbook* (in Chinese). Fisheries Bureau of Ministry of Agriculture, Beijing.

Feminella, J. W. & Resh, V. H. (1989). Submersed macrophytes and grazing crayfish: an experimental study of herbivory in a California freshwater marsh. *Holarctic Ecology*, **12**, 1–8.

Ferraro, P. J. (2002). The local costs of establishing protected areas in low-income nations: Ranomafana National Park, Madagascar. *Ecological Economics*, **43**, 261–75.

Fetzner, J. W., Jr (2006). *Global Crayfish Resources at the Carnegie Museum of Natural History* [available at http://iz.carnegiemnh.org/crayfish/].

Fitzpatrick, J. F., Jr (1975). The taxonomy and biology of the prairie crawfishes, *Procambarus hagenianus* (Faxon) and allies. *Freshwater Crayfish*, **2**, 381–9.

Fjälling, A. (1995). Crayfish traps in Swedish fisheries. *Freshwater Crayfish*, **8**, 201–14.

Fleury, B. & Sherry, T. (1995). Long-term population trends of colonial wading birds in the southern United States: the impact of crayfish aquaculture on Louisiana populations. *Auk*, **112**, 613–32.

Fleury, B., Sherry, T. & Huner, J. V. (1999). Agricultural wetlands and the conservation of coastal wading birds in Louisiana. In: A. Profitt, N. N. Rabalais, D. J. Reed & R. E. Turner (eds) *Recent Research in Coastal Louisiana: Natural System Function and Response to Human Influence*. Louisiana Sea Grant Program, Baton Rouge, LA: 287–94.

Foden, W., Mace, G. M., Vie, J.-C., et al. (2009). Species susceptibility to climate change impacts. In: J.-C. Vie, C. Hilton-Taylor & S. N. Stuart (eds) *Wildlife in a Changing World: An Analysis of the 2008 IUCN Red List of Threatened Species*. IUCN, Gland, Switzerland: 77–88.

Fonseca, J. C., Marques, J. C. & Madeira, V. M. C. (1997). Oxygen uptake inhibition in *Procambarus clarkii*, red swamp crayfish by biodegradable surfactants: an ecotechnological approach for population control in rice fields. *Freshwater Crayfish*, **11**, 235–42.

Foster, J. & Harper, D. (2007). Status and ecosystem interactions of the invasive Louisianan red swamp crayfish *Procambarus clarkii* in East Africa. In: F. Gherardi (ed.) *Biological Invaders in Inland Waters: Profiles, Distribution and Threats*. Invading Nature: Springer Series in Invasion Ecology. Springer, Dordrecht, The Netherlands: 91–101.

France, R. L. (1993). Effect of experimental lake acidification on the crayfish *Orconectes virilis* population recruitment and age composition in north-western Ontario, Canada. *Biological Conservation*, **63**, 53–9.

Fratini, S., Zaccara, S., Barbaresi, S., et al. (2005). Phylogeography of the threatened crayfish (genus *Austropotamobius*) in Italy: implications for its taxonomy and conservation. *Heredity*, **94**(1), 108–18.

Frederick, P. C. & Ogden. J. C. (2001). Pulsed breeding of long-legged wading birds and the importance of infrequent severe droughts in the Florida Everglades. *Wetlands*, **21**, 484–91.

Freeman, M. A., Turnbull, J. F., Yeomans, W. E. & Bean, C. W. (2010). Prospects for management strategies of invasive crayfish populations with an emphasis on biological control. *Aquatic Conservation: Marine and Freshwater Ecosystems*, **20**, 211–23.

Frutiger, A. & Müller, R. (2002). Controlling unwanted *Procambarus clarkii* populations by fish predation. *Freshwater Crayfish*, **13**, 309–15.

Frutiger, A., Borner, S., Büsser, T., et al. (1999). How to control unwanted populations of *Procambarus clarkii* in Central Europe? *Freshwater Crayfish*, **12**, 714–26.

Füreder, L. (ed.) (2009). *Flusskrebse Biologie – Ökologie – Gefährdung*. Veröffentlichungen des Naturmuseums Sudtirol. Nr. 6. Folio Verlag, Vienna.

Füreder, L. & Pöckl, M. (2007). Ecological traits of aquatic NIS invading Austrian freshwaters. In: F. Gherardi (ed.) *Biological Invaders in Inland Waters: Profiles, Distribution and Threats*. Invading Nature: Springer Series in Invasion Ecology. Springer, Dordrecht, The Netherlands: 233–57.

Füreder, L. & Reynolds, J. D. (2003). Is *Austropotamobius pallipes* a good bioindicator? *Bulletin Français de la Pêche et de la Pisciculture*, **370–1**, 157–63.

Füreder, L. & Souty-Grosset, C. (eds) (2005). *European Native Crayfish in Relation to Land-use and Habitat Deterioration, with a Special Focus on* Austropotamobius torrentium. Special Issue of *Bulletin Français de la Pêche et de la Pisciculture*, **376–7** (CRAYNET volume 3): 357 pp.

Füreder, L., Oberkofler, B., Hanel, R., Leiter, J. & Thaler, B. (2003). The freshwater crayfish *Austropotamobius pallipes* in South Tyrol: heritage species and bioindicator, *Bulletin Français de la Pêche et de la Pisciculture*, **370–1**, 79–95.

Füreder, L., Edsman, L., Holdich, D., et al. (2006). Indigenous crayfish habitat and threats. In: C. Souty-Grosset, D. M. Holdich, P. Y. Noel, J. D. Reynolds & P. Haffner (eds) *Atlas of Crayfish in Europe*. Patrimoines naturels 64. Muséum National d'Histoire naturelle, Paris: 25–47.

Furse, J. M., & Wild, C. H. (2002). Terrestrial activities of *Euastacus sulcatus*, the Lamington spiny crayfish (Decapoda: Parastacidae). *Freshwater Crayfish*, **13**, 604.

Fürst, M. (1977). Introduction of *Pacifastacus leniusculus* (Dana) in Sweden: methods, results and management. *Freshwater Crayfish*, **3**, 229–47.

Gallagher, M. B., Dick, J. T. A. & Elwood, R. W. (2006). Riverine habitat requirements of the white-clawed crayfish, *Austropotamobius pallipes*. *Biology & Environment: Proceedings of the Royal Irish Academy*, **106B**, 1–8.

Gamradt, S. C. & Kats, L. B. (1996). The effect of introduced crayfish and mosquitofish on California newts (*Taricha torosa*). *Conservation Biology*, **10**, 1155–62.

Garcia-Arberas, L. & Rallo, A. (2000). Survival of natural populations of *Austropotamobius pallipes* in rivers in Bizkaia, Basque Country (North Iberian Peninsula). *Bulletin Français de la Pêche et de la Pisciculture*, **356**(1) (Spécial écrevisses, volume 2), 17–30.

García-Llorente, M., Martín-López, B., González, J. A., Alcorlo, P. & Montes, C. (2008). Social perceptions of the impacts and benefits of invasive alien species: implications for management. *Biological Conservation*, **141**, 2969–83.

Garza de Yta, A. (2009). Hatchery, nursery, nutrition and stock evaluation of redclaw crayfish *Cherax quadricarinatus*. PhD thesis, Auburn University, AL: 115 pp.

Gaston, K. J. & Spicer, J. I. (1998). *Biodiversity: An Introduction*. Blackwell Science, Oxford, UK: 113 pp.

Genovesi, P. (2005). Eradications of invasive alien species in Europe: a review. *Biological Invasions*, **7**, 127–33.

Genovesi, P. (2007). Toward a European strategy to halt biological invasions in inland waters. In: F. Gherardi (ed.) *Biological Invaders in Inland Waters: Profiles, Distribution, and Threats*. Invading Nature: Springer Series in Invasion Ecology. Springer, Dordrecht, The Netherlands: 507–42.

Genovesi, P. & Shine, C. (2003). *European Strategy on Invasive Alien Species*. Convention on the Conservation of European Wildlife and Natural Habitats Report T-PVS/(2003) 7 revised 1 to Standing Committee 23rd meeting, Strasbourg, 1–5 December 2003. Council of Europe.

Gherardi, F. (2002). Behaviour. In: D. M. Holdich (ed.) *Biology of Freshwater Crayfish*. Blackwell Science, Oxford, UK: 258–90.

Gherardi, F. (2006). Crayfish invading Europe: the case study of *Procambarus clarkii*. *Marine and Freshwater Behaviour and Physiology*, **39**, 175–91.

Gherardi, F. (ed.) (2007a). *Biological Invaders in Inland Waters: Profiles, Distribution, and Threats*. Invading Nature: Springer Series in Invasion Ecology. Springer, Dordrecht, The Netherlands: 733 pp.

Gherardi, F. (2007b). The impact of freshwater NIS: what are we missing? In: F. Gherardi (ed.) *Biological Invaders in Inland Waters: Profiles, Distribution, and Threats*. Invading Nature: Springer Series in Invasion Ecology. Springer, Dordrecht, The Netherlands: 437–62.

Gherardi, F. (2007c). Understanding the impact of invasive crayfish. In: F. Gherardi (ed.) *Biological Invaders in Inland Waters: Profiles, Distribution, and Threats*. Invading Nature: Springer Series in Invasion Ecology. Springer, Dordrecht, The Netherlands: 507–42.

Gherardi, F. (2010). Invasive crayfish and freshwater fishes of the world. Invited review paper. *Revue Science et Technique*, **29**(2), 241–54.

Gherardi, F. & Acquistapace, P. (2007). Invasive crayfish in Europe: the impact of *Procambarus clarkii* on the littoral community of a Mediterranean lake. *Freshwater Biology*, **52**, 1249–59.

Gherardi, F. & Barbaresi, S. (2000). Invasive crayfish: activity patterns of *Procambarus clarkii* in the rice fields of the Lower Guadalquivir (Spain). *Archiv für Hydrobiologie*, **150**, 153–68.

Gherardi, F. & Barbaresi, S. (2008). Feeding opportunism of the red swamp crayfish, *Procambarus clarkii*, an invasive species. *Freshwater Crayfish*, **16**, 77–85.

Gherardi, F. & Cioni, A. (2004). Agonism and interference competition in freshwater decapods. *Behaviour*, **141**, 1297–324.

Gherardi, F. & Daniels, W. H. (2004). Agonism and shelter competition between invasive and indigenous crayfish species. *Canadian Journal of Zoology*, **82**, 1923–32.

Gherardi, F. & Holdich, D. M. (eds) (1999). *Crayfish in Europe as Alien Species: How to Make the Best of a Bad Situat*ion? Crustacean Issues 11. A. A. Balkema, Rotterdam: 299 pp.

Gherardi, F. & Lazzara L. (2006). Effects of the density of an invasive crayfish (*Procambarus clarkii*) on pelagic and surface microalgae in a Mediterranean wetland. *Archiv für Hydrobiologie*, **165**(3), 401–14.

Gherardi, F. & Panov, V.E. (2009). Alien species fact sheets: *Procambarus clarkii* (Girard, 1852), red swamp crayfish/crawfish (Cambaridae / Crustacea). In DAISIE (Delivering Alien Invasive Species Inventories for Europe (edn) *Handbook of alien species in Europe.* Springer, Dordrecht, The Netherlands: 316.) [available at www.europe-aliens.org/pdf/Procambarus_clarkii.pdf].

Gherardi, F. & Souty-Grosset, C. (eds) (2006). *European Crayfish as Heritage Species: Linking Research and Management Strategies to Conservation and Socio-economic Development.* Special Issue of *Bulletin Français de la Pêche et de la Pisciculture*, **380–1** (CRAYNET volume 4): 566 pp.

Gherardi, F., Tarducci, F. & Micheli, F. (1989). Energy maximization and foraging strategies in *Potamon fluviatile* (Decapoda, Brachyura). *Freshwater Biology*, **22**, 233–45.

Gherardi, F., Barbaresi, S. & Raddi, A. (1999a). The agonistic behaviour in the red swamp crayfish, *Procambarus clarkii*: functions of the chelae. *Freshwater Crayfish*, **12**, 233–43.

Gherardi, F., Baldaccini, G. N., Ercolini, P., et al. (1999b). The situation in Italy. In: F. Gherardi & D. M. Holdich (eds) *Crayfish in Europe as Alien Species: How to Make the Best of a Bad Situation?* Crustacean Issues 11. A. A. Balkema, Rotterdam : 107–28.

Gherardi, F., Acquistapace, P. & Barbaresi, S. (2000a). The significance of chelae in the agonistic behaviour of the white-clawed crayfish, *Austropotamobius pallipes*. *Marine and Freshwater Behaviour and Physiology*, **33**, 187–200.

Gherardi, F., Barbaresi, S. & Salvi, G. (2000b). Spatial and temporal patterns in the movement of *Procambarus clarkii*, an invasive crayfish. *Aquatic Sciences*, **62**, 179–93.

Gherardi, F., Raddi, A., Barbaresi, S. & Salvi, G. (2000c). Life history patterns of the red swamp crayfish, *Procambarus clarkii*, in an irrigation ditch in Tuscany, Italy. *Crustacean Issues*, **12**, 99–108.

Gherardi, F., Renai, B. & Corti, C. (2001). Crayfish predation on tadpoles: a comparison between a native (*Austropotamobius pallipes*) and an alien species (*Procambarus clarkii*). *Bulletin Français de la Pêche et de la Pisciculture*, **361**, 659–68.

Gherardi, F., Acquistapace, P., Tricarico, E. & Barbaresi, S. (2002a). Ranging behaviour of the red swamp crayfish in an invaded habitat: the onset of hibernation. *Freshwater Crayfish*, **14**, 330–7.

Gherardi, F., Barbaresi, S., Vaselli, O. & Bencini, A. (2002b). A comparison of trace metal accumulation in indigenous and alien freshwater macro-decapods. *Marine and Freshwater Behaviour and Physiology*, **35**, 179–88.

Gherardi, F., Tricarico, E. & Ilhéu, M. (2002c). Movement patterns of an invasive crayfish, *Procambarus clarkii*, in a temporary stream of southern Portugal. *Ethology, Ecology & Evolution*, **14**, 183–97.

Gherardi, F., Souty-Grosset, C. & Reynolds, J. D. (2003). Understanding and managing bio-diversity in relation to native crayfish populations in Europe. *Bulletin Français de la Pêche et de la Pisciculture*, **370**–1, 7–14.

Gherardi, F., Copp, G. H., Cowx, I. G. & Rosenthal, H. (2010). Foreword: Alien species in aquaculture and fisheries. *Journal of Applied Ichthyology*, **26** (Suppl. 2) Special Issue: *Alien Species in Aquaculture and Fisheries*: iii–iv.

Gibson, F. A. (1979). An international code of practice and the Irish regulations relating to certain aquatic organisms. In: R. P. Kernan, O. V. Mooney & A. E. J. Went (eds) *The Introduction of Exotic Species: Advantages and Problems*. Royal Irish Academy, Dublin: 69–72.

Gil-Sánchez, J. M. & Alba-Tercedor, J. (2002). Ecology of the native and introduced crayfishes *Austropotamobius pallipes* and *Procambarus clarkii* in southern Spain and implications for conservation of the native species. *Biological Conservation*, **105**, 75–80.

Giribet, G., Carranza, S., Baguna, J., Riutort, M. & Ribera, C. (1996). First molecular evidence for the existence of a Tardigrada plus Arthropoda clade. *Molecular Biology and Evolution*, **13**, 76–84.

Gleeson, R. A. (1980). Pheromone communication in the reproductive behaviour of the blue crab, *Callinectes sapidus*. *Marine Ecology Progress Series*, **244**, 179–89.

Goddard, S. (1979). Explore the native potential first. *Fish Farmer*, **2**, 47.

Goldman, C. R. (1973). Ecology and physiology of the California crayfish *Pacifastacus leniusculus* (Dana) in relation to its suitability for introduction into European waters. *Freshwater Crayfish*, **1**, 105–20.

Goldman, C. R. & Rundquist, J. C. (1977). A comparative ecological study of the Californian crayfish *Pacifastacus leniusculus* (Dana), from two sub-alpine lakes (Lake Tahoe and Lake Donner). *Freshwater Crayfish*, **3**, 57–80.

Good, J. A. (2009). Local and regional studies of Cryptobiota: esoteric stamp-collecting or essential ecology? *Bulletin of the Irish Biogeographical Society*, **33**, 115–63.

Gouin, N., Grandjean, F., Pain, S., Souty-Grosset, C. & Reynolds, J. (2003). Origin and colonization history of the white-clawed crayfish, *Austropotamobius pallipes* in Ireland. *Heredity*, **91**(1), 70–7.

Gouin, N., Grandjean, F. & Souty-Grosset, C. (2006). Population genetic structure of the endangered crayfish *Austropotamobius pallipes* in France based on microsatellite variation: biogeographical inferences and conservation implications. *Freshwater Biology*, **51**, 1369–87.

Gowing, H. & Momot, W. T. (1979). Impact of brook trout (*Salvelinus fontinalis*) predation on the crayfish *Orconectes virilis* in 3 Michigan lakes. *Journal of the Fisheries Research Board of Canada*, **36**, 1191–6.

Grandjean, F., Harris, D. J., Souty-Grosset, C. & Crandall, K. (2000). Systematics of the European endangered crayfish species *Austropotamobius pallipes* (Decapoda, Astacidae). *Journal of Crustacean Biology*, **20**(3), 522–9.

Grandjean, F., Bouchon, D. & Souty-Grosset, C. (2002a). Systematics of the European endangered crayfish species *Austropotamobius pallipes* (Decapoda: Astacidae) with a re-examination of the status of *Austropotamobius berndhauseri*. *Journal of Crustacean Biology*, **22**(3), 677–81.

Grandjean, F., Frelon-Raimond, M. & Souty-Grosset, C. (2002b). Compilation of molecular data for the phylogeny of the genus *Austropotamobius*: one species or several? *Bulletin Français de la Pêche et de la Pisciculture*, **367**(3), 671–80.

Grandjean, F., Jouteux, R., Ropiquet, A., Bachelier, E. & Bramard, M. (2002c). Biological water quality assessment in running-water sites harbouring the endangered crayfish *Austropotamobius pallipes*, based on macroinvertebrates and its potential in habitat selection for restocking. *Freshwater Crayfish*, **13**, 338–48.

Grandjean, F., Momon, J. & Bramard, M. (2004). Biological water quality assessment of the white-clawed crayfish habitat based on macroinvertebrate communities: usefulness for its conservation. *Bulletin Français de la Pêche et de la Pisciculture*, **370–1** (CRAYNET volume 1), 115–25.

Growns, I. O. & Richardson, A. M. M. (1988). The diet and burrowing habits of the freshwater crayfish *Parastacoides tasmanicus tasmanicus* Clark (Decapoda: Parastacidae). *Australian Journal of Marine and Freshwater Research*, **39**, 525–34.

Guan, R. Z. (1997). An improved method for marking crayfish. *Crustaceana*, **70**, 641–52.

Guan, R. Z. & Wiles, P. R. (1996). Growth, density and biomass of crayfish, *Pacifastacus leniusculus*, in a British lowland river. *Aquatic Living Resources*, **9**(3), 265–72.

Guan, R.-Z. & Wiles P. R. (1997). Ecological impact of introduced crayfish on benthic fishes in a British lowland river. *Conservation Biology*, **11**, 641–7.

Guiaşu, R. C. (2002). *Cambarus*. In: D. M. Holdich (ed.) *Biology of Freshwater Crayfish*. Blackwell Science, Oxford, UK: 609–34.

Guiaşu, R. C., Saleh, N. Mozel, E. and Dunham, D. W. (2005). Low aggression in juvenile burrowing crayfish, *Fallicambarus fodiens* (Cottle, 1863) (Decapoda, Cambaridae). *Crustaceana*, **78**, 421–8.

Gutiérrez-Yurrita, P. J., Sancho, G., Bravo, M. A., Baltanas, A. & Montes, C. (1998). Diet of the red swamp crayfish *Procambarus clarkii* in natural ecosystems of the Doñana National Park temporary fresh-water marsh (Spain). *Journal of Crustacean Biology*, **18**(1), 120–7.

Gutiérrez-Yurrita, P. J., Martinez, J. M., Ilhéu, M., et al. (1999). The status of crayfish populations in Spain and Portugal. In: F. Gherardi & D. M. Holdich (eds) *Crayfish in Europe as Alien Species: How to Make the Best of a Bad Situation?* Crustacean Issues 11. A. A. Balkema, Rotterdam: 161–92.

Habsburgo-Lorena, A. S. (1979). Present situation of exotic species of crayfish introduced into Spanish continental waters. *Freshwater Crayfish*, **4**, 175–84.

Habsburgo-Lorena, A. S. (1983). Some observations on crayfish farming in Spain. *Freshwater Crayfish*, **5**, 549–51.

Habsburgo-Lorena, A. S. (1986). The status of the *Procambarus clarkii* population in Spain. *Freshwater Crayfish*, **6**, 131–3.

Haertel-Borer, S. S., Zak, D., Eckmann, R., Baade, U. & Holker, F. (2005). Population density of the crayfish, *Orconectes limosus*, in relation to fish and macroinvertebrate densities in a small mesotrophic lake: implications for the lake's food web. *International Review of Hydrobiology*, **90**(5–6), 523–33.

Hall, D. J., Cooper, W. E. & Werner, E. E. (1970). An experimental approach to the production dynamics and structure of freshwater animal communities. *Limnology and Oceanography*, **15**, 839–928.

Hamr, P. (1997). A giant's tale: the life history of *Astacopsis gouldi* (Decapoda: Parastacidae) a freshwater crayfish from Tasmania. *Freshwater Crayfish*, **11**, 13–33.

Hamr, P. (2002). *Orconectes*. In: D. M. Holdich (ed.) *Biology of Freshwater Crayfish*. Blackwell Science, Oxford, UK: 585–608.

Hamr, P. & Richardson, A. M. M. (1994). The life history of *Parastacoides tasmanicus tasmanicus* Clark, a burrowing freshwater crayfish from south-west Tasmania. *Australian Journal of Marine and Freshwater Research*, **45**, 455–70.

Hamrin, S. F. (1987). Seasonal crayfish activity as influenced by fluctuating water levels and presence of a fish predator, *Holarctic Ecology*, **10**, 45–51.

Hansen, B. & Richardson, A. M. M. (2006). A revision of the Tasmanian endemic freshwater crayfish genus *Parastacoides* (Crustacea: Decapoda: Parastacidae). *Invertebrate Systematics*, **20**, 713–69.

Hanson, J. M., Chambers, P. A. & Prepas, E. E. (1990). Selective foraging by the crayfish *Orconectes virilis* and its impact on macroinvertebrates. *Freshwater Biology*, **24**, 69–80.

Hansson, L.-A., Bronmark, C., Anders Nilsson, P. & Anjornsson, K. (2005). Conflicting demands on wetland ecosystem services: nutrient retention, biodiversity or both? *Freshwater Biology*, **50**, 705–14.

Hardege, J. D., Jennings, A., Hayden, D., et al. (2002). Novel behavioural assay and partial purification of a female derived sex pheromone in *Carcinus maenas*. *Marine Ecology Progress Series*, **244**, 179–89.

Harding, J. S., Benfield, E. F., Bolstad, P. V., Helfman, G. S. & Jones, E. B. D., III (1998). Stream biodiversity: the ghost of land use past. *Proceedings of the National Academy of Sciences USA*, **95**, 14843–7.

Harper, D. M. & Mavuti, K. M. (2004). Lake Naivasha, Kenya: ecohydrology to guide the management of a tropical protected area. *Ecohydrology & Hydrobiology*, **4**, 287–305.

Harper, D. M., Smart, A. C., Coley, S., et al. (2002). Distribution and abundance of the Louisiana red swamp crayfish *Procambarus clarkii* Girard at Lake Naivasha, Kenya between 1987 and 1999. *Hydrobiologia*, **488** (*Developments in Hydrobiology* 168), 143–51.

Harper, D. M., Boar, R., Everard, M. & Hickley, P. (eds) (2003). *Lake Naivasha, Kenya*. Papers submitted to the Conference *Science and the Sustainable Management of Shallow Tropical Waters, Naivasha, 1999*. Kluwer Academic, Dordrecht, The Netherlands: 216 pp.

Harper, D. M., Smart, A. C., Coley, S., et al. (2007). Crayfish assemblage shifts in a large drought-prone wetland: the roles of hydrology and competition. *Freshwater Biology*, **52**(12), 2399–411.

Harsányi, T. & Rogovszky, Z. (1996). Fogadi örökbe egy patakot! 4. Rákfelmeres, Kutatástervezes és adatfeldolgozás. (Adopt a stream! 4. Crayfish monitoring, research plan and data processing). Fiatalok Természetismereti Klubja and Goncol Alapitvány, Budapest, Vác: 108 pp.

Hart, D. D. (1992). Community organization in streams; the importance of species interactions, physical factors and chance. *Oecologia*, **91**, 220–8.

Hart, K. M. (1958). Pyrethrum in the disinfection of public water mains. *Pyrethrum Post*, **4**(3), 8–12.

Harwood, J. & Stokes, K. (2003). Coping with uncertainty in ecological advice: lessons from fisheries. *Trends in Ecology and Evolution*, **18**(12), 617–22.

Hasiotis, S. T. (1999). The origin and evolution of freshwater crayfish based on crayfish body and trace fossils. *Freshwater Crayfish*, **12**, 49–70.

Hasiotis, S. T. & Mitchell, C. E. (1989). Lungfish burrows in the upper Triassic Chinle and Dolores formations, Colorado Plateau. Discussion: new evidence suggests origin by a burrowing decapod crustacean. *Journal of Sedimentary Petrology*, **59**, 871–5.

Håstein, T. & Gladhaug, O. (1973). The occurrence of the crayfish plague in Norway and attempts to prevent further spread of the disease. *Freshwater Crayfish*, **1**, 181–4.

Håstein, T. & Gladhaug, O. (1974). The present status of the crayfish plague in Norway. *Freshwater Crayfish*, **2**, 273–6.

Haya, K. (1989). Toxicity of pyrethroid insecticides to fish. *Environmental Toxicology and Chemistry*, **8**, 381–91.

Hazlett, B. A. (1985). Chemical detection of sex and condition in the crayfish *Orconectes virilis*. *Journal of Chemical Ecology*, **11**, 181–9.

Hazlett, B. A. (1999). Responses to multiple chemical cues by the crayfish *Orconectes virilis*. *Behaviour*, **136**, 161–77.

Heborg, L.-M., Rudwick, D. A., Siliang, Y., Lodge, D. M. & MacIsaac, H. J. (2007). Predicting the range of Chinese mitten crabs in Europe. *Conservation Biology*, **21**, 1316–23.

Hefti, D. & Stucki, P. (2006). Crayfish management for Swiss waters. *Bulletin Français de la Pêche et de la Pisciculture*, **380**–1, 937–50.

Hein, C. L., Roth, B. M., Ives, A. R. & Vander Zanden, M. J. (2006). Fish predation and trapping for rusty crayfish (*Orconectes rusticus*) control: a whole-lake experiment. *Canadian Journal of Fisheries and Aquatic Sciences*, **63**, 383–93.

Hein, C. L., Vander Zanden, M. J. & Magnuson, J. J. (2007). Intensive trapping and increased fish predation cause massive decline of an invasive crayfish. *Freshwater Biology*, **52**, 1134–46.

Helms, B. H. & Creed, R. P. (2005). The effects of 2 coexisting crayfish on an Appalachian river community. *Journal of the North American Benthological Society*, **24**, 113–22.

Henttonen, P. & Huner, J. V. (1999). The introduction of alien species of crayfish in Europe: a historical introduction. In: F. Gherardi & D. M. Holdich (eds) *Crayfish in Europe as Alien Species: How to Make the Best of a Bad Situation?* Crustacean Issues 11. A. A. Balkema, Rotterdam: 13–22.

Hill, A. M. & Lodge, D. M. (1999). Replacement of resident crayfishes by an exotic crayfish: the roles of competition and predation. *Ecological Applications*, **9**(2), 678–90.

Hiruta, S. (1999). The present status of crayfish in Britain and the conservation of the native species in Britain and Japan. *Journal of Environmental Education*, **2**, 119–32.

Hobbs, H. H., Jr (1942). *The Crayfishes of Florida*. University of Florida Publications in Biological Science Series, 3: 179 pp.

Hobbs, H. H., Jr (1972). The subgenera of the crayfish genus *Procambarus* (Decapoda: Astacidae). *Smithsonian Contributions to Zoology*, **117**, 1–22.

Hobbs, H. H., Jr (1987). A review of the crayfish genus *Astacoides* (Decapoda: Parastacidae). *Smithsonian Contributions to Zoology*, **443**, 1–50.

Hobbs, H. H., Jr (1988). Crayfish distribution, adaptive radiation and evolution. In: D. M. Holdich & R. S. Lowery (eds) *Freshwater Crayfish: Biology, Management and Evolution*. Croom Helm, London: 52–82.

Hobbs, H. H., Jr (1989). The nature and effects of disturbance relative to invasions. In: J. A. Drake, H. A. Mooney, F. diCastri, et al. (eds) *Biological Invasions: A Global Perspective*. SCOPE 37. John Wiley and Sons, New York: 389–405.

Hobbs, H. H., Jr & Hall, E. T., Jr (1975). Crayfishes (Decapoda: Astacidae). In: C. W. J. Hart & S. L. H. Fuller (eds) *Pollution Ecology of Freshwater Invertebrates*. Academic Press, New York: 195–214.

Hobbs, H. H., Jr & Whiteman, M. (1991). Notes on the burrows, behavior, and color of the crayfish *Fallicambarus (F.) devastator* (Decapoda, Cambaridae). *Southwestern Naturalist*, **36**, 127–35.

Hobbs, H. H., III (1974). Observations on the cave-dwelling crayfishes of Indiana. *Freshwater Crayfish*, **2**, 405–14.

Hochwimmer, G., Tober, R., Bibars-Reiter, R., Licek, E. & Steinborn, R. (2009). Identification of two GH18 chitinase family genes and their use as targets for detection of the crayfish-plague oomycete *Aphanomyces astaci*. *BMC Microbiology*, **9**, 184.

Hockley, N. J., Jones, J. P. G., Andriahajaina, F., et al. (2005). When should communities and conservationists monitor exploited resources? *Biodiversity and Conservation*, **14**, 2795–806.

Hofkin, B. V., Mkoji, G. M., Koech, D. K. & Loker, E. S. (1991). Control of schistosome-transmitting snails in Kenya by the North American crayfish *Procambarus clarkii*. *American Journal of Tropical Medicine and Hygiene*, **45**, 339–44.

Holdich, D. M. (1987). The dangers of introducing alien animals with particular reference to crayfish. *Freshwater Crayfish*, **7**, xv–xxx.

Holdich, D. M. (1999). The negative effects of established crayfish introductions. In: F. Gherardi & D. M. Holdich (eds) *Crayfish in Europe as Alien Species: How to Make the Best of a Bad Situation?* Crustacean Issues 11. A. A. Balkema, Rotterdam: 31–47.

Holdich, D. M. (2002a). *Biology of Freshwater Crayfish*. Blackwell Science, Oxford, UK: 702 pp.

Holdich, D. M. (2002b). Background and functional morphology. In: D. M. Holdich (ed.) *Biology of Freshwater Crayfish*. Blackwell Science, Oxford, UK: 3–29.

Holdich, D. M. (2002c). Present distribution of crayfish in Europe and some adjoining countries. *Bulletin Français de la Pêche et de la Pisciculture*, **367**, 611–50.

Holdich, D. M. (2003). Crayfish in Europe: an overview of taxonomy, legislation, distribution and crayfish plague outbreaks. In: D. M. Holdich & P. J. Sibley (eds) *Management and Conservation of Crayfish: Proceedings of a Conference held in Nottingham on 7th November, 2002*. Environment Agency, Bristol, UK: 15–34.

Holdich, D. M. & Domaniewski, J. C. J. (1995). Studies on a mixed population of the crayfish *Austropotamobius pallipes* and *Pacifastacus leniusculus* in England. *Freshwater Crayfish*, **10**, 37–45.

Holdich, D. M. & Pöckl, M. (2005). Does legislation work in protecting vulnerable species? *Bulletin Français de la Pêche et de la Pisciculture*, **376**–7, 809–27.

Holdich, D. M. & Pöckl, M. (2007). Invasive crustaceans in European inland waters. In: F. Gherardi (ed.) *Biological Invaders in Inland Waters: Profiles, Distribution and Threats*. Invading Nature: Springer Series in Invasion Ecology. Springer, Dordrecht, The Netherlands: 29–75.

Holdich, D. M. & Rogers, W. D. (1995). *Species Action Plan for the White-clawed Crayfish in Britain*. In: G. Wynne, M. Avery, L. Campbell, et al. (eds) *Biodiversity Challenge* (2nd edn). RSPB, Sandy, UK.

Holdich, D. M. & Rogers, W. D. (1997). The white-clawed crayfish, *Austropotamobius pallipes*, in Great Britain and Ireland with particular reference to its conservation in Great Britain. *Bulletin Français de la Pêche et de la Pisciculture*, **347**, 597–616.

Holdich, D. M. & Rogers, D. (2000). Habitat requirements of the white-clawed crayfish, *Austropotamobius pallipes*. In: D. Rogers & J. Brickland (eds) *Crayfish Conference Leeds*. Environment Agency, Leeds, UK: 109–21.

Holdich, D. M. & Sibley, P. J. (2009). ICS and NICS in Britain in the 2000s. In: J. Brickland, D. M. Holdich & E. M. Imhoff (eds) *Crayfish Conservation in the British Isles: Proceedings of a Conference held on 25th March 2009 in Leeds, UK*: 13–33.

Holdich, D. M., Rogers, W. D. & Reader, J. P. (1995a). *Crayfish Conservation*. Final Project Record for National Rivers Authority R&D Contract 378/N&Y. National Rivers Authority, Bristol, UK.

Holdich, D. M., Rogers, W. D., Reader J. P. & Harlioglu, M. M. (1995b). Interactions between three species of freshwater crayfish (*Austropotamobius pallipes*, *Astacus leptodactylus* and *Pacifastacus leniusculus*). *Freshwater Crayfish*, **10**, 46–56.

Holdich, D. M., Harlioglu, M. M. & Firkins, I. (1997). Salinity adaptations of crayfish in British waters, with particular reference to *Austropotamobius pallipes, Astacus leptodactylus* and *Pacifastacus leniusculus. Estuarine, Coastal & Shelf Science*, **44**, 147–54.

Holdich, D. M., Gydemo, R. & Rogers, W. D. (1999). A review of possible methods for controlling nuisance populations of alien crayfish. In: F. Gherardi & D. M. Holdich (eds) *Crayfish in Europe as Alien Species: How to Make the Best of a Bad Situation?* Crustacean Issues 11. A. A. Balkema, Rotterdam: 245–70.

Holdich, D., Reynolds, J. & Edsman, L. (2002). Monitoring in conservation and management of indigenous crayfish populations. *Bulletin Français de la Pêche et de la Pisciculture*, **367**, 875–80.

Holdich, D., Sibley, P. & Peay, S. (2004). The white-clawed crayfish: a decade on. *British Wildlife*, **15**(3), 153–64.

Holdich, D. M., Peay, S., Foster, J., Hiley, P. D. & Brickland, J. H. (2006). Studies on the white-clawed crayfish (*Austropotamobius pallipes*) associated with muddy habitats. *Bulletin Français de la Pêche et de la Pisciculture*, **380–1**, 1055–78.

Holdich, D. M., Palmer, M. & Sibley, P. J. (2009a). The indigenous status of *Austropotamobius pallipes* in Britain. In: J. Brickland, D. M. Holdich and E. M. Imhoff (eds) *Crayfish Conservation in the British Isles: Proceedings of a Conference held on 25th March 2009 in Leeds, UK*: 1–12.

Holdich, D. M., Reynolds, J. D., Souty-Grosset, C. & Sibley, P. J. (2009b). A review of the ever increasing threat to European crayfish from non-indigenous crayfish species. *Knowledge and Management of Aquatic Ecosystems*, **394**–5, article 11.

Holthuis, L. B. (1986). The freshwater crayfish of New Guinea. *Freshwater Crayfish*, **6**, 48–58.

Horn, A. C. M., Buckup, M., Noro, C. K. & Barcelos, D. F. (2008). Morfologia externa de *Parastacus brasiliensis* (Decapoda, Parastacidae). *Iheringia, Série Zoologia*, **98**, 148–55.

Horton, M. P. (2009). Establishing the island of Ireland's first ark site for the white-clawed crayfish *Austropotamobius pallipes* in the Ballinderry River System, Co. Tyrone. In: J. Brickland, D. M. Holdich & E. M. Imhoff (eds) *Crayfish Conservation in the British Isles: Proceedings of a Conference held on 25th March 2009 in Leeds, UK*: 87–94.

Horwitz, P. (1988). Secondary sexual characteristics of females of the freshwater crayfish genus *Engaeus* (Decapoda: Parastacidae). *Crustaceana*, **54**, 25–32.

Horwitz, P. (1990a). A taxonomic revision of species in the freshwater crayfish genus *Engaeus* Erichson (Decapoda: Parastacidae). *Invertebrate Taxonomy*, **4**, 427–614.

Horwitz, P. (1990b). The translocation of freshwater crayfish in Australia: potential impact, the need for control and global relevance. *Biological Conservation*, **54**, 291–305.

Horwitz, P. (1995). The conservation status of Australian freshwater crayfish: review and update. *Freshwater Crayfish*, **10**, 70–80.

Horwitz, P. H. J. & Knott, B. (1983). The burrowing habit of the koonac, *Cherax plebejus* (Decapoda: Parastacidae). *Western Australian Naturalist*, **15**, 113–17.

Horwitz, P. H. J. &. Knott, B. (1991). The faunal assemblage in freshwater crayfish burrows in sedgeland and forest at Lightning Plains, Western Tasmania. *Papers & Proceedings of the Royal Society of Tasmania*, **125**, 29–32.

Horwitz, P. H. J. & Knott, B. (1996). The distribution and spread of the yabby *Cherax destructor* complex in Australia: speculations, hypotheses and the need for research. *Freshwater Crayfish*, **10**, 81–91.

Horwitz, P. H. J. & Richardson, A. M. M. (1986). An ecological classification of the burrows of Australian freshwater crayfish. *Australian Journal of Marine and Freshwater Research*, **37**, 237–42.

Horwitz, P. H. J., Richardson, A. M. M. & Cramp, P. (1984). Aspects of the life history of the burrowing freshwater crayfish, *Engaeus leptorhynchus* at Rattrays Marshes, north-east Tasmania. *Tasmanian Naturalist*, **82**, 1–5.

Huang, T. S., Cerenius, L. & Söderhäll, K. (1994). Analysis of genetic diversity in the crayfish plague fungus, *Aphanomyces astaci*, by random amplification of polymorphic DNA. *Aquaculture*, **126**, 1–9.

Hudina, S. & Lucić, A. (2009). Distribution and dispersal of signal crayfish (*Pacifastacus leniusculus*) in river Mura. In: P. Kozák & A. Kouba (eds) *Abstract Book: Future of Native Crayfish in Europe, Regional European Crayfish Workshop, 7th–10th September 2009*. Písek, Czech Republic: 46.

Hulme, P. E., Pysek, P., Nentwig, W. & Vilà, M. (2009). Will threat of biological invasions unite the European Union? *Science*, **324**, 40–1.

Huner, J. V. (1977). Introductions of the Louisiana red swamp crayfish, *Procambarus clarkii* (Girard): an update. *Freshwater Crayfish*, **3**, 193–202.

Huner, J. V. (1997). The effect of flooding date on crayfish, *Procambarus* spp., production in southern Louisiana experimental ponds. *Freshwater Crayfish*, **11**, 524–32.

Huner, J. V. (1999). The relation between pond size and crayfish (*Procambarus* spp.) production. *Freshwater Crayfish*, **12**, 573–92.

Huner, J. V. (2000). Crawfish and waterbirds. *American Scientist*, **88**, 301–3.

Huner, J. V. (2002). *Procambarus*. In: D. M. Holdich (ed.) *Biology of Freshwater Crayfish*. Blackwell Science, Oxford, UK: 541–84.

Huner, J. V. & Barr, J. E. (1984). *Red Swamp Crawfish: Biology and Exploitation*. Louisiana Sea Grant Program, Louisiana State University, Baton Rouge, LA.

Huner, J. V. & Barr, J. E. (1991). *Red Swamp Crawfish: Biology and Exploitation*, 3rd edn. Louisiana State University, Baton Rouge, LA.

Huner, J. V., Jeske, C. W. & Norling, W. (2002). Managing agricultural wetlands for waterbirds in the coastal regions of Louisiana, USA. *Waterbirds* **25** (Special Publication 2), 66–78.

Huner, J. V., Jeske, C. W. & Musumeche, M. J. (2009). The importance of working wetlands as avian habitat in Louisiana. In: T. D. Rich, C. Arizmendi, D. W. Demares, & C. Thompson (eds) *Tundra to Tropics: Connecting Birds, Habitats and People*. Proceedings of the 4th International Partners in Flight Conference, 13–16 February 2008. Partners in Flight, McAllen, TX: 235–43.

Huxley, T. H. (1880). *The Crayfish: An Introduction to the Study of Zoology*. Kegan Paul, London.

Ilhéu, M. & Bernardo, J. M. (1997). Life history and population biology of red swamp crayfish, *Procambarus clarkii*, in a Mediterranean reservoir. *Freshwater Crayfish*, **11**, 54–9.

Ingle, R. W. & Thomas, W. (1974). Mating and spawning of the crayfish *Austropotamobius pallipes* (Crustacea: Astacidae). *Journal of Zoology*, **173**, 525–38.

IUCN (2000). *Guidelines for the Prevention of Biodiversity Loss Caused by Alien Invasive Species*. International Union for Conservation of Nature, Gland, Switzerland, February 2000 [available at http://iucn.org/].

IUCN (2003). *Guidelines for Application of IUCN Red List Criteria at Regional Levels. Version 3.0*. IUCN Species Survival Commission, Gland, Switzerland and Cambridge, UK.

IUCN (2004). *2004 IUCN Red List of Threatened Species* [available at www.iucnredlist.org/].

IUCN (2009). *IUCN Red List of Threatened Species*. Version 2009.1 [available at www.iucn-redlist.org/].

IUCN (2010). *IUCN Red List of Threatened Species*. Version 2010.4 [available at www.iucn-redlist.org/].

Jimenez, S. A. & Faulkes, Z. (2010). Establishment and care of a laboratory colony of partheno-genetic marbled crayfish, Marmorkrebs. *Invertebrate Rearing*, **1**(1), 10.

Johnsen, S. & Vralstad, T. (2009). Signalkreps og Krebsepest i Haldenvassdraget forslag til tiltaksplan. NINA Rapport 474: 23 pp.

Johnsen, S., Taugbøl, T., Andersen, O., Museth, J. & Vralstad, T. (2007). The first record of the non-indigenous signal crayfish *Pacifastacus leniusculus* in Norway. *Biological Invasions*, **9**, 939–41.

Jones, C. G., Lawton, J. H. & Shachak, M. (1994). Organisms as ecosystem engineers. *Oikos*, **69**, 373–86.

Jones, C. M. (1990). *The Biology and Aquaculture Potential of the Tropical Freshwater Crayfish*, Cherax quadricarinatus. Queensland Department of Primary Industries, Brisbane: 109 pp.

Jones, C. M. & Ruscoe, I. M. (2002). Biological and aquacultural characteristics of five stocks of redclaw, *Cherax quadricarinatus* (von Martens) (Decapoda: Parastacidae) from northern Queensland. *Freshwater Crayfish*, **13**, 115–36.

Jones, J. B. (1981). Growth of two species of crayfish (*Paranephrops* sp.) in New Zealand. *New Zealand Journal of Marine and Freshwater Research*, **15**, 15–20.

Jones, J. P. G. (2004). The sustainability of crayfish harvesting in Ranomafana National Park, Madagascar. PhD thesis, University of Cambridge, Cambridge, UK.

Jones, J. P. G. & Coulson, T. (2006). Population regulation and demography in a harvested fresh-water crayfish from Madagascar. *Oikos*, **112**, 602–11.

Jones, J. P. G., Andriahajaina, F. B., Hockley, N. J., Balmford, A. & Ravoahangimalala, O. R. (2005). A multidisciplinary approach to assessing the sustainability of freshwater crayfish harvesting in Madagascar. *Conservation Biology*, **19**, 1863–71.

Jones, J. P. G., Andeiahajaina, F. B., Ranambinintsoa, E. H., Hockley, N. J. & Ravoahangimalala, O. R. (2006). The economic importance of freshwater crayfish harvesting in Madagascar and the potential of community-based conservation to improve management. *Oryx*, **40**(2), 1–9.

Jones, J. P. G., Andriahajaina, F. B., Hockley, N. J., Crandall, K. A. & Ravoahangimalala, O. R. (2007). The ecology and conservation status of Madagascar's endemic freshwater crayfish (*Parastacidae; Astacoides*). *Freshwater Biology*, **52**, 1820–33.

Jones, J. P. G., Rasamy, J. R., Harvey, A., et al. (2009). The perfect invader: a parthenogenic crayfish poses a new threat to Madagascar's freshwater biodiversity. *Biological Invasions*, **11**, 1475–82.

Josefsson, M. & Andersson, B. (2001). The environmental consequences of alien species in the Swedish lakes Mälaren, Hjälmaren, Vänern and Vättern. *Ambio*, **30**(8), 514–21.

Jussila, J., Ojala, K. & Mannonen, A. (2008). Noble crayfish (*Astacus astacus*) reintroduction project in the river Pyhäjoki, western Finland: a case study. *Freshwater Crayfish*, **16**, 51–6.

Kapoor-Vijay, P. & Usher, M. B. (eds) (1993). *Identification of Key Species for Conservation and Socio-Economic Development: Proceedings of a Workshop*. Commonwealth Science Council, London: 145 pp.

Katz, L. C. (1980). Effects of burrowing by the fiddler crab, *Uca pugnax* (Smith). *Estuarine & Coastal Marine Science*, **11**, 233–7.

Kawai, T. (1996). Distribution of the Japanese crayfish, *Cambaroides japonicus* in Hokkaido, Japan, and its loss of habitat in eastern Hokkaido. *Memoirs of the Kushiro City Museum*, **20**, 5–12.

Keitt, T. H., Lewis, M. A. & Holt, R. D. (2001). Allee effects, invasion pinning, and species' borders. *American Naturalist*, **157**, 203–16.

Kettunen, M. & ten Brink, P. (2006). *Value of Biodiversity: Documenting EU Examples where Biodiversity Loss has led to the Loss of Ecosystem Services*. Final Report to the European Commission. Institute for European Environmental Policy (IEEP), Brussels: 131 pp.

Knipling, E. F. (1955). Possibilities of insect control or eradication through the use of sexually sterile males. *Journal of Economic Entomology*, **48**, 902–4.

Köksal, F. (1988). *Astacus leptodactylus* in Europe. In: D. M. Holdich & R. S. Lowery (eds) *Freshwater Crayfish: Biology, Management and Evolution*. Croom Helm, London: 365–400.

Kouba, A., Buřič, M. & Kozák, P. (2010). Bioaccumulation and effects of heavy metals in crayfish: a review. *Water, Air, and Soil Pollution*, **211**, 5–16.

Koutrakis, E. T., Machino, Y., Kallianiotis, A. & Holdich, D. M. (2005). *Austropotamobius torrentium* (Schrank, 1803) in the Aggitis cave (northern Greece). Is it a cave-dwelling species? *Bulletin Français de la Pêche et de la Pisciculture*, **376–7**, 529–37.

Koutrakis, E. T., Perdikaris, C., Machino, Y., Savvidis, G., & Margaris, N. (2007). Distribution, recent mortalities and conservation measures of crayfish in Hellenic fresh waters. *Bulletin Français de la Pêche et de la Pisciculture*, **385**, 25–44.

Kozák, P. & Policar, T. (2003). Practical elimination of signal crayfish *Pacifastacus leniusculus* (Dana) from a pond. In: D. M. Holdich & P. J. Sibley (eds) *Management and Conservation of Crayfish: Proceedings of a Conference held on 7th November, 2002*. Environment Agency, Bristol, UK: 200–8.

Kozák, P., Duris, Z. & Policar, T. (2002). The stone crayfish (*Austropotamobius torrentium*) in the Czech Republic. *Bulletin Français de la Pêche et de la Pisciculture*, **367**, 707–13.

Kozubíková, E., Filipová, L., Kozák, P., et al. (2009). Prevalence of the crayfish plague pathogen *Aphanomyces astaci* in invasive American crayfishes in the Czech Republic. *Conservation Biology*, **23**(5), 1204–13.

Kremen, C., Raymond, I. & Lances, K. (1998). An interdisciplinary tool for monitoring conservation impacts in Madagascar. *Conservation Biology*, **12**, 549–63.

Kusabs, I. A. & Quinn, J. M. (2009). Use of a traditional Maori harvesting method, the tau köura, for monitoring köura (freshwater crayfish, *Paranephrops planifrons*) in Lake Rotoiti, North Island, New Zealand. *New Zealand Journal of Marine & Freshwater Research*, **43**, 713–22.

Kushlan, J. A., Steinkamp, K. C., Parsons, K. C., et al. (2002). *Waterbird Conservation for the Americas: The North American Waterbird Conservation Plan, Version 1*. Waterbird Conservation for the Americas, Washington, DC: 78 pp.

Lake, P. S. (1977). Pholeteros: the faunal assemblage found in crayfish burrows. *Australian Society for Limnology Newsletter*, **15**, 57–60.

Lamontagne, S. & Rasmussen, J. B. (1993). Estimates of density in lakes using quadrats: maximizing precision and efficiency. *Canadian Journal of Fisheries and Aquatic Sciences*, **50**, 623–6.

Lance, D. R., McInnis, D. O., Rendon, P. & Jackson, C. G. (2000). Courtship among sterile and wild *Ceratitis capitata* (Diptera: Tephritidae) in field cages in Hawaii and Guatemala. *Annals of the Entomological Society of America*, **93**, 1179–85.

Laurent, P. J. (1979). Premiers résultats des introductions expérimentales en eaux closes de *Pacifastacus leniusculus*. *La Pisciculture Française*, **56**, 57.

Laurent, P. J. (1988). *Austropotamobius pallipes* and *A. torrentium* with observations on their interactions with other species in Europe. In: D. M. Holdich & R. S. Lowery (eds) *Freshwater Crayfish: Biology, Management and Evolution*. Croom Helm, London: 341–364 & 426–79.

Laurent, P. J. (1992). Introductions d'écrevisses en France et dans le monde, historique et conséquences. *Bulletin Français de la Pêche et de la Pisciculture*, **344**–5, 345–56.

Laurent, P. J. (1995). Eradication of unwanted crayfish species for astacological management purposes. *Freshwater Crayfish*, **8**, 121–33.

Laurent, P. J., Nicolas, J. & Parris, L. (1993). Five years of action in Lorraine and Morvan (France) to restore the noble crayfish, *Astacus astacus*. *Freshwater Crayfish*, **9**, 380–9.

Lawrence, C. & Jones, C. (2002). *Cherax*. In: D. M. Holdich (ed.) *Biology of Freshwater Crayfish*. Blackwell Science, Oxford, UK: 635–69.

Lawrence, C. S., Morrissy, N. M., Vercoe, P. E. & Williams, L. H. (2006). Harvesting freshwater crayfish (*Cherax albidus* Clark) by trapping contributes to high densities and stunted animals: a preliminary population model. *Freshwater Crayfish*, **15**, 24–35.

Lee, N. (2000). Effects of cobalt-60 gamma irradiation on the Malaysian prawn *Macrobrachium rosenbergii*. PhD thesis, Louisiana State University, LA.

Lewis, S. D. (2002). *Pacifastacus*. In: D. M. Holdich (ed.) *Biology of Freshwater Crayfish*. Blackwell Science, Oxford, UK: 511–40.

Lewis, S. D. & Horton, H. F. (1997). Life history and population dynamics of the signal crayfish, *Pacifastacus leniusculus*, in Lake Billy Chinook, Oregon. *Freshwater Crayfish*, **11**, 34–53.

Light, T., Erman, D. C., Myrick, C. & Clarke, J. (1995). Decline of the Shasta crayfish (*Pacifastacus fortis* Faxon) of northeastern California. *Conservation Biology*, **9**, 1567–77.

Liras, V., Lindberg, M., Nystrom, P., et al. (2002). Can ingested cyanobacteria be harmful to the signal crayfish (*Pacifastacus leniusculus*)? *Freshwater Biology*, **39**(2), 233–42.

Little, E. E. (1976). Ontogeny of maternal behavior and brood pheromone in crayfish. *Journal of Comparative Physiology*, **112**, 133–42.

Little, E. E. (1979). Chemical communication in maternal behaviour of crayfish. *Nature*, **255**, 400–1.

Lodge, D. M. (1993). Biological invasions: lessons for ecology. *Trends in Ecology & Evolution*, **8**, 133–7.

Lodge, D. M. (2001). Responses of lake biodiversity to global changes. In: O. E. Sala, F. S. Chapin & E. Huber-Sannwald (eds) *Future Scenarios of Global Biodiversity*. Springer-Verlag, New York: 277–313.

Lodge, D. M. & Hill, A. H. (1994). Factors governing species composition, population size, and productivity of cool-water crayfishes. *Nordic Journal of Freshwater Research*, **69**, 111–36.

Lodge, D. M. & Lorman, J. G. (1987). Reduction of submerged macrophyte biomass and species richness by the crayfish *Orconectes rusticus*. *Canadian Journal of Fisheries and Aquatic Sciences*, **44**, 591–7.

Lodge, D. M., Bekel, A. L. & Magnuson, J. J. (1985). Lake bottom tyrant. *Journal of Natural History*, **94**, 32–7.

Lodge, D. M., Stein, R. A., Brown, K. M., et al. (1998). Predicting impact of freshwater exotic species on native biodiversity: challenges in spatial scaling. *Australian Journal of Ecology*, **23**, 53–67.

Lodge, D. M., Taylor, C. A., Holdich, D. M. & Skurdal, J. (2000a). Nonindigenous crayfishes threaten North American freshwater biodiversity: lessons from Europe. *Fisheries*, **25**(8), 7–20.

Lodge, D. M., Taylor, C. A., Holdich, D. M. & Skurdal, J. (2000b) Reducing impacts of exotic crayfish introductions: new policies needed. *Fisheries*, **25**(8), 21–3.

Lorman, J. G. (1980). Ecology of the crayfish *Orconectes rusticus* in northern Wisconsin. *Crustaceana*, **38**, 82–86.

Loughman, Z. T. (2010). Ecology of *Cambarus dubius* (upland burrowing crayfish) in north-central West Virginia. *Southeastern Naturalist*, **9** (Special Issue 3), 217–30.

Lowe, S. J., Browne, M. & Boudjelas, S. (2000). *100 of the World's Worst Invasive Alien Species.* IUCN/SSC Invasive Species Specialist Group (ISSG), Auckland, New Zealand.

Lowery, R. S. (1988). Growth, moulting and reproduction. In: D. M. Holdich & R. S. Lowery (eds) *Freshwater Crayfish: Biology, Management and Exploitation.* Croom Helm, London: 88–113.

Lozano, J. & Martín, J. (1988). Trabajos de investigación sobre aculcultura y gestión en la provincia de Cuenca. In: JCCM & Diputatión de Cuenca (eds) *I Jomadas de Acuicultura en Castilla-La-Mancha, Cuenca*: 155–97.

Lucey, J. (1999). A chronological account of the crayfish *Austropotamobius pallipes* (Lereboullet) in Ireland. *Bulletin of the Irish Biogeographical Society*, **23**, 143–61.

Lukowicz, M. von (1999). Freshwater crayfish in the fisheries legislation of federal states (Bundesländer) of Germany. *Freshwater Crayfish*, **12**, 890–9.

Lux, S. A., Vilardi, J. C., Liedo, P., et al. (2002). Effects of irradiation on the courtship behavior of medfly (Diptera: Tephritidae) mass reared for the sterile insect technique. *Florida Entomologist*, **85**, 102–12.

Lynas, J., Lindhjem, P., Storey, A. & Knott, B. (2004). Is the yabby, *Cherax destructor* (Parastacidae) in Western Australia an ecological threat? *Freshwater Crayfish*, **14**, 37–44.

Lynas, J., Storey, A. W. & Knott, B. (2007). Introduction and spread of crayfish (Parastacidae) in Western Australia and their potential to displace indigenous species. In: F. Gherardi (ed.) *Biological Invaders in Inland Waters: Profiles, Distribution and Threats.* Invading Nature: Springer Series in Invasion Ecology. Springer, Dordrecht, The Netherlands: 577–96.

Lyons, R. & Kelly-Quinn, M. (2003). An investigation into the disappearance of *Austropotamobius pallipes* (Lereboullet) populations in the headwaters of the Nore River, Ireland, and the correlation to water quality. *Bulletin Français de la Pêche et de la Pisciculture*, **370–1**, 139–50.

MacArthur, R. H. & Wilson, E. O. (1967). *The Theory of Island Biogeography.* Princeton University Press, Princeton, NJ.

Mace, G. M. & Baillie, J. E. M. (2007). The 2010 Biodiversity Indicators: challenges for science and policy. *Conservation Biology*, **21**(6), 1406–13.

Mace, G. M., Cramer, W., Diaz, S., et al. (2010). Biodiversity targets after 2010. *Current Opinion in Environmental Stability*, **2**, 3–8.

Machino, Y. & Diéguez-Uribeondo, J. (1998). Un cas de peste de l'écrevisse en France dans le bassin de la Seine. *L'Astaciculteur de France*, **54**, 2–11.

Machino, Y. & Füreder, L. (2005). How to find a stone crayfish *Austropotamobius torrentium* (Schrank, 1803): a biogeographic study in Europe. *Bulletin Français de la Pêche et de la Pisciculture*, **376–7**, 507–17.

Mack, R. N., Simberloff, D., Lonsdale, W. M., et al. (2000). Biotic invasions: causes, epidemiology, global consequences, and control. *Ecological Applications* **10**(3), 689–710.

Maguire, I., Klobucar, G. I. V., Gottstein Matocek, S. & Erben, R. (2003). Distribution of *Austropotamobius pallipes* (Lereboullet) in Croatia: past and present. *Bulletin Français de la Pêche et de la Pisciculture*, **370–1**, 57–71.

Manchester, S. J. & Bullock, J. (2000). The impacts of non-native species on UK biodiversity and the effectiveness of control. *Journal of Applied Ecology*, **37**, 845–64.

Mande, S. H. & Williams, D. D. (1963). Behaviour of crayfish in water currents: hydrodynamics of eight species in reference to their distribution patterns in southern Ontario. *Canadian Journal of Fisheries and Aquatic Science*, **40**, 68–77.

Mannonen, A. & Halonen, T. (2000). *The Crayfish Strategy of the Fisheries Administration* (in Finnish).

Mantelatto, F. L. M., Robles, R., Biagi, R. & Felder, D. L. (2006). Molecular analysis of the taxonomic and distributional status for the hermit crab genera *Loxopagurus* Forest, 1964 and *Isocheles* Stimpson, 1858 (Decapoda, Anomura, Diogenidae). *Zoosystema*, **28**, 495–506.

Mantelatto, F .L. M., Robles, R. & Felder, D. L. (2007). Molecular phylogeny of the western Atlantic species of the genus *Portunus* (Crustacea, Brachyura, Portunidae). *Zoological Journal of the Linnean Society*, **150**, 211–20.

Martin, J. W. & Davis, G. E. (2001). *An Updated Classification of the Recent Crustacea*. Science Series No. 39. Natural History Museum of Los Angeles County, CA: 132 pp.

Martin, P., Kohlmann, K. & Scholtz, G. (2007). The parthenogenetic Marmorkrebs (marbled crayfish) produces genetically uniform offspring. *Naturwissenschaften*, **94**, 843–6.

Martinez, R., Rico, E. & Alonso, F. (2003). Characterisation of *Austropotamobius italicus* (Faxon, 1914) in a central Spain area. *Bulletin Français de la Pêche et de la Pisciculture*, **370–1**, 43–56.

Marzano, F. N., Scalici, M., Chiesa, S., et al. (2009). The first record of the marbled crayfish adds further threats to fresh waters in Italy. *Aquatic Invasions*, **4**(2), 401–4.

Mason, J. C. (1970). Copulatory behaviour of the crayfish, *Pacifastacus trowbridgii* (Stimpson). *Canadian Journal of Zoology*, **48**, 969–76.

Mason, J. C. (1974). *Aquaculture Potential of the Freshwater Crayfish* (Pacifastacus*). 1. Studies During 1970*. Fisheries Research Board Canada Technical Report 440: 43 pp.

Mason, J. C. (1975). Crayfish production in a small woodland stream. *Freshwater Crayfish*, **2**, 449–79.

Master, L. L, Flack, S. R & Stein, B. A. (eds) (1998). *Rivers of Life: Critical Watersheds for Protecting Freshwater Biodiversity*. The Nature Conservancy, Arlington, VA.

Mathews, L. M., Adams, L., Anderson, E., et al. (2008). Genetic and morphological evidence for substantial hidden biodiversity in a freshwater crayfish species complex. *Molecular Phylogenetics and Evolution*, **48**, 126–35.

Matthews, M. A. & Reynolds, J. D. (1992). Ecological impact of crayfish plague in Ireland. *Hydrobiologia*, **234**, 1–6.

Matthews, M. A. & Reynolds, J. D. (1995). A population study of the white-clawed crayfish *Austropotamobius pallipes* (Lereboullet) in an Irish reservoir. *Journal of the Royal Irish Academy*, **95B**, 99–109.

Matthews, M. A., Reynolds, J. D. & Keatinge, M. J. (1993). Macrophyte reduction and benthic community alteration by the crayfish *Austropotamobius pallipes* (Lereboullet). *Freshwater Crayfish*, **9**, 289–99.

McAllister, D. E., Hamilton, A. L. & Harvey, B. (1997). Global freshwater biodiversity: striving for the integrity of freshwater ecosystems. *Sea Wind*, **11**(3): 140 pp.

McClain, W. R., Romaire, R. P., Lutz, C. G. & Shirley, M. G. (2007). *Louisiana Crawfish Production Manual*. Publication No. 2637. Louisiana State University Agricultural Center, Baton Rouge, LA.

McGeogh, M. A., Chown, S. L. & Kalwij, J. M. (2006). A global indicator for biological invasion. *Conservation Biology*, **20**, 1635–46.

McGeogh, M. A., Butchart, S. H. M., Spear, D., et al. (2010). Global indicators of biological invasion: species numbers, biodiversity impact and policy responses. *Diversity & Distributions*, **16**, 95–108.

McGriff, D. (1983). Growth, maturity and fecundity of the crayfish, *Pacifastacus leniusculus*, from the Sacramento-San Joaquin Delta. *California Fish & Game*, **69**, 227–42.

McLeese, D. W. (1970). Detection of dissolved substances by the American lobster (*Homarus americanus*) and olfactory attraction between lobsters. *Journal of Fisheries Research Board Canada*, **27**, 1371–8.

McMahon, B. R. (2002). Physiological adaptation to environment. In: D. M. Holdich (ed.) *Biology of Freshwater Crayfish*. Blackwell Science, Oxford, UK: 327–76.

McMahon, B. R. & J. J. Hankinson (1993). Respiratory adaptations of burrowing crayfish. *Freshwater Crayfish*, **9**, 174–82.

Meadows, P. S. & Meadows, A. (1991). *The Environmental Impact of Burrowing Animals and Animal Burrows*. Clarendon Press, Oxford, UK.

Medgyesi, N., Lackner, R. & Pelser, B. (2009). The resettlement of brown trout in alpine streams of the Hohe Tauern National Park. In: *Proceedings of the 4th Symposium of the Hohe Tauern National Park for Research in Protected Areas, September 17–19, 2009, Kaprun Castle, Salzburg.* Hohe Tauern National Park, Mittersill, Austria.

Mickasch, T. M. (1999). Distribution of *Austropotamobius pallipes* and *Orconectes limosus* in the Swiss Midlands. *Freshwater Crayfish*, **12**, 796–800.

Mikkola, H. (1996). Alien freshwater crustacean and indigenous mollusc species with aquaculture potential in eastern and southern Africa. *Southern African Journal of Aquatic Sciences*, **22**, 90–9.

Millennium Ecosystem Assessment (2005). *Ecosystems and Human Well-being: Biodiversity Synthesis*. World Resources Institute. Island Press, Washington, DC [available at www.millenniumassessment.org/en/index.html].

Miller, A. D. & Austin, C. M. (2006). The complete mitochondrial genome of the mantid shrimp *Harpiosquilla harpax*, and a phylogenetic investigation of the Decapoda using mitochondrial sequences. *Molecular Phylogenetics and Evolution*, **38**, 565–74.

Miller, G. C. & Van Hyning, J. M. (1970). The commercial fishery for fresh-water crawfish, *Pacifastacus leniusculus* (Astacidae), in Oregon, 1893–1956. *Research Reports Fishery Commission of Oregon*, **2**(1), 77–89.

Mills, B. J., Morrissy, N. M. & Huner, J. V. (1994). Cultivation of freshwater crayfish in Australia. In: J. V. Huner (ed.) *Freshwater Crayfish Aquaculture in North America, Europe and Australia*. Food Product Press, Norwood, Australia: 217–89.

Mills, J. S., Soule, M. E. & Doak, D. F. (1993). The keystone-species concept in ecology and conservation. *BioSciences*, **43**, 219–24.

Mito, T. & Uesugi, T. (2004). Invasive alien species in Japan: the status quo and the new legislation for the prevention of their adverse effects. *Global Environmental Research*, **8**, 171–91.

Molony, B. W., Morrissy, N. M. & Bird, C. (2002). The West Australian recreational marron fishery (*Cherax tenuimanus* (Smith): history and future challenges. *Freshwater Crayfish*, **13**, 207–20.

Momot, W. T. (1984). Crayfish production: a reflection of community energetics. *Journal of Crustacean Biol*ogy, **4**, 35–54.

Momot, W. T. (1986). Production and exploitation of the crayfish, *Orconectes virilis*, in northern climates. In: G. S. Jamieson & N. Bourne (eds) *North Pacific Workshop on Stock Assessment and Management of Invertebrates*. Canadian Special Publication of Fisheries & Aquatic Sciences 92: 154–67.

Momot, W. T. (1991). Potential for exploitation of freshwater crayfish in coolwater systems: management guidelines and issues. *Fisheries*, **16**, 14–21.

Momot, W. T. (1993). The role of exploitation in altering the processes regulating crayfish populations. *Freshwater Crayfish*, **9**, 101–17.

Momot, W. T. (1995). Redefining the role of crayfish in aquatic systems. *Review of Fisheries Science*, **3**, 33–63.

Momot, W. T. (1997). History of the range extension of *Orconectes rusticus* into northwestern Ontario and Lake Superior. *Freshwater Crayfish*, **11**, 61–72.

Momot, W. T. & Romaire, R. P. (1982). Use of a seine to detect stunted crawfish populations in ponds, a preliminary report. *Journal of the World Mariculture Society*, **13**(2), 384–90.

Momot, W. T., Gowing, H. & Jones, P. D. (1978). The dynamics of crayfish and their role in ecosystems. *American Midland Naturalist*, **99**, 10–35.

Montague, C. L. (1982). The influence of fiddler crab burrows and burrowing on metabolic processes in salt marsh sediments. In: V. S. Kennedy (ed.) *Estuarine Comparisons*. Academic Press, New York: 283–301.

Montes, C., Bravo-Utrera, M. A., Baltanas, A., Duarte C. & Gutiérrez-Yurrita P. J. (1993). *Bases ecológicas para la gestion del Cangrejo Rojo de las Marismas en el Parque Nacional de Doñana*. ICONA, Ministerio de Agricultura y Pesca, Madrid.

Moore, J. W. (2006). Animal ecosystem engineers in streams. *BioScience*, **56**, 237–46.

Morgan, G. E. (1988). *An Evaluation of Management Strategies and Tactics for Harvesting Orconectes rusticus in Ontario*. Ontario Ministry of Natural Resources Policy Paper 2.

Morgan, G. E. & Momot, W. T. (1988). Exploitation of *Orconectes virilis* in northern climates: complementarity of management options with self-regulatory life history strategies. *Freshwater Crayfish*, **7**, 69–80.

Moritz, C. (1994). Defining "Evolutionarily Significant Units" for conservation. *Trends in Ecology and Evolution*, **9**, 373–5.

Morrissy, N. M. (1976). Aquaculture of marron, *Cherax tenuimanus* (Smith). Part 2. Breeding and early rearing. *Fisheries Research Bulletin of Western Australia*, **17**(2), 1–32.

Morrissy, N. M. (1978). The past and present distribution of marron in Western Australia. *Fisheries Research Bulletin of Western Australia*, **22**, 1–38.

Morrissy, N. M. (1990). Optimum and favourable temperatures for growth of *Cherax tenuimanus* (Smith, 1912) (Decapoda: Parastacidae). *Australian Journal of Marine and Freshwater Research*, **41**, 735–46.

Morrissy, N. M. (2002). Culturing the marvellous marron in Western Australia: 1967–1997. *Freshwater Crayfish*, **13**, 13–38.

Morrissy, N. M. & Cassells, G. (1992). *Spread of the Introduced Yabby Cherax albidus Clark, 1936 in Western Australia*. Fisheries Western Australia Fisheries Research Report 92: 27 pp.

Moyle, P. B. & Light, T. (1996). Fish invasions in California: do abiotic factors determine success? *Ecology*, **77**, 1666–70.

Müller, R. & Frutiger, A. (2001). Effects of intensive trapping and fish predation on an (unwanted) population of *Procambarus clarkii*. In: *Abstracts of the Annual Meeting of the North American Benthological Society*. NABS, LaCrosse, WI: 3–8.

Mundahl, N. D. & Benton, M. J. (1990). Aspects of the thermal ecology of the rusty crayfish *Orconectes rusticus* (Girard). *Oecologia*, **82**(2), 210–16.

Musumeche, M. J., Huner, J. V., Mikuska, T., Richard, G. & Leonard, B. (2002). The avifauna of an agricultural wetland complex in the western Gulf Coastal Plain of Louisiana, USA. *Proceedings of the Louisiana Academy of Sciences*, **64**, 22–37.

Naiman, R. J. & Dudgeon, D. (2010). Global alteration of freshwaters: influences on human and environmental well-being. *Ecological Research*, **10**, doi:10.1007/s11284–010–0693–3.

Naiman, R. J., Prieur-Richard, A. H., Arthington, A., et al. (2006). *Freshwater Biodiversity: Challenges for Freshwater Biodiversity Research*. Diversitas Report No. 5: 48 pp.

Nardi, P. A., Bernini, F., Bo, T., et al. (2005). Status of *Austropotamobius pallipes* complex in the watercourses of the Alessandria province (N-W Italy). *Bulletin Français de la Pêche et de la Pisciculture*, **376–7**, 585–98.

National Audubon Society (2007). Waterbird conservation files and common birds in decline files [available at http://audubon.org/].

Naura, M. & Robinson, M. (1998). Principles of using river habitat survey to predict the distribution of aquatic species: an example applied to the native white-clawed crayfish, *Austropotamobius pallipes*. *Aquatic Conservation: Marine and Freshwater Ecosystems*, **8**, 515–27.

Nelson, J. (2003). *Unpublished Report to the Burrowing Crayfish Recovery Team on* Engaeus granulatus *Survey Work as of July 2003*. Threatened Species Unit, Department of Primary Industries, Water and Environment, Tasmania.

Neveu, A. (2001a). Can resident carnivorous fish slow down introduced alien crayfish spread? Efficacity of 3 fish species versus 2 crayfish species in experimental design. *Bulletin Français de la Pêche et de la Pisciculture*, **361**, 683–704.

Neveu, A. (2001b). Experimental confrontation between resident omnivorous fish (11 species) and introduced alien crayfish (2 species). *Bulletin Français de la Pêche et de la Pisciculture*, **361**, 705–35.

Newcombe, K. J. (1975). The pH tolerance of the crayfish *Parastacoides tasmanicus* (Erichson) (Decapoda, Parastacidae). *Crustaceana*, **29**, 231–4.

Ng, P. K. L., Guinot, D. & Davi, P. J. (2008). Systema Brachyurorum. Part I. An annotated checklist of extant brachyuran crabs of the world. *Raffles Bulletin of Zoology*, **17**, 1–286.

Nguyen, T. T. T. (2005). A genetic investigation on translocation of Australian commercial freshwater crayfish, *Cherax destructor*. *Aquatic Living Resources*, **18**, 319–23.

Nguyen, T. T. T., Meewan, M., Ryan, S. & Austin, C. M. (2002). Genetic diversity and translocation in the marron, *Cherax tenuimanus* (Smith): implications for management and conservation. *Fisheries Management & Ecology*, **9**, 163–73.

Nguyen, T. T. T., Austin, C. M., Meewan, M. M., Schultz, M. B. & Jerry, D. R. (2004). Phylogeography of the freshwater crayfish *Cherax destructor* Clark (Parastacidae) in inland Australia: historical fragmentation and recent range expansion. *Biological Journal of the Linnean Society*, **83**(4), 539–50.

Nolfi, J. R. (1977). Preliminary studies in closed-system crayfish culture. *Freshwater Crayfish*, **3**, 181–6.

Nolfi, J. R. & Miltner, M. (1978). Preliminary studies on a potential crayfish fishery in Vermont. *Freshwater Crayfish*, **4**, 313–21.

Non-Native Species Secretariat (NNSS) (2008). GB non-native species secretariat [available at https://secure.fera.defra.gov.uk/nonnativespecies/home/index.cfm].

Noro, C., López-Greco, L. S. & Buckup, L. (2008). Gonad morphology and type of sexuality in *Parastacus defossus* Faxon 1898, a burrowing, intersexed crayfish from southern Brazil (Decapoda: Parastacidae). *Acta Zoologia*, **8**, 59–67.

Norrocky, M. J. (1984). Burrowing crayfish trap. *Ohio Journal of Science*, **84**, 65–6.

Norrocky, M. J. (1991). Observations on the ecology, reproduction and growth of the burrowing crayfish *Fallicambarus* (*Creaserinus*) *fodiens* (Decapoda, Cambaridae) in north-central Ohio. *American Midland Naturalist*, **125**, 75–86.

Nowicki, P., Tirelli, T., Mussat Sartor, R., Bona, F. & Pessani, D. (2008). Monitoring crayfish using a mark–recapture method: potentials, recommendations and limitations. *Biodiversity & Conservation*, **17**, 3513–30.

Nyström, P. (1999). Ecological impact of introduced and native crayfish on freshwater communities: European perspectives. In: F. Gherardi & D. M. Holdich (eds) *Crayfish in Europe* as *Alien Species: How to Make the Best of a Bad Situation?* Crustacean Issues 11. A. A. Balkema, Rotterdam: 63–85.

Nyström, P. (2002). Ecology. In: D. M. Holdich (ed.) *Biology of Freshwater Crayfish*. Blackwell Science, Oxford, UK: 192–235.

Nyström, P. & Strand, J. A. (1996). Grazing by a native and an exotic crayfish on aquatic macrophytes. *Freshwater Biology*, **36**(3), 673–82.

Nyström, P., Bronmark, C. & Graneli, W. (1999). Influence of an exotic and a native crayfish species on a littoral benthic community. *Oikos*, **85**(3), 545–53.

Obande, R. A. & Kusemiju, K. (2008). Food and feeding habits of *Atya gabonensis* from lower River Benue in Northern Nigeria. *West African Journal of Applied Ecology*, **13**, 77–82.

O'Brien, B. G. (1998). The natural diet of the freshwater crayfish *Cherax tenuimanus* (Smith, 1912) (Decapoda: Parastacidae) as determined by gut content analysis. *Freshwater Crayfish*, **10**, 151–62.

O'Connor, W., Hayes, G., Reynolds, J. D., O'Keeffe, C. & Lynn, D. (2009). *Monitoring of White-clawed Crayfish* Austropotamobius pallipes *in Irish Lakes: A Technical Manual*. Irish Wildlife Manuals. National Parks & Wildlife Service, Department of the Environment, Heritage and Local Government, Dublin.

Oidtmann, B., Cerenius, L., Schmid, I., Hoffmann, R. & Söderhäll, K. (1999). Crayfish plague epizootics in Germany: classification of two German isolates of the crayfish plague fungus *Aphanomyces astaci* by random amplification of polymorphic DNA. *Diseases of Aquatic Organisms*, **35**, 235–8.

Oidtmann, B., Heitz, E., Rogers D. & Hoffmann, R. W. (2002). Transmission of crayfish plague. *Diseases of Aquatic Organisms*, **52**, 159–67.

Oidtmann, B., Geiger, S., Steinbauer, P., Culas, A. & Hoffmann, R. W. (2006). Detection of *Aphanomyces astaci* in North American crayfish by polymerase chain reaction. *Diseases of Aquatic Organisms*, **72**, 53–64.

Olden, J. D., McCarthy, J. M., Maxted, J. T., Fetzer, W. W. & Vander Zanden, M. J. (2006). The rapid spread of rusty crayfish (*Orconectes rusticus*) with observations on native crayfish declines in Wisconsin (USA) over the past 130 years. *Biological Invasions*, **8**, 1621–8.

Ormerod, S. J., Dobson, M., Hildrew, A. G. & Townsend, C. R. (2010). Multiple stressors in freshwater ecosystems. *Freshwater Biology*, **55** (Suppl. 1), 1–4.

Owen, S. F. (2001). Meeting energy budgets by modulation of behaviour and physiology in the eel (*Anguilla anguilla* L.). *Comparative Biochemistry and Physiology A*, **128**, 631–44.

Page, T. J., Cook, B. D., von Rintelen, T., von Rintelen, K. & Hughes, J. M. (2007). Evolutionary relationships of atyid shrimps imply both ancient Caribbean radiations and common marine dispersals. *Journal of the North American Benthological Society*, **27**, 68–83.

Paine, R. T. (1969). The Pisaster–Tegula interaction: prey patches, predator food preference, and intertidal community structure. *Ecology*, **50**, 950–61.

Palmer, M. A. (1994). *Action Plan for the Conservation of the Native Crayfish* Austropotamobius pallipes *in the United Kingdom*. JNCC Report No. 193.

Palmer, M. A., Menninger, H. L. & Bernhardt, E. (2010). River restoration, habitat heterogeneity and biodiversity: a failure of theory or practice? *Freshwater Biology*, **55** (Suppl. 1), 205–22.

Panov, V. E. & Gollasch, S. (2006). *Aquatic Invasions*: The new European journal of applied research on biological invasions in aquatic ecosystems. *Aquatic Invasions*, **1**, 1–3.

Parkyn, S. M., Collier, K. J. & Hicks, B. J. (2002). Growth and population dynamics of crayfish *Paranephrops planifrons* in streams with semi-native forest and pastoral land uses. *New Zealand Journal of Marine and Freshwater Research*, **36**, 847–61.

Pârvulescu, L., Paloş, C. & Molnar, P. (2009). First record of the spiny-cheek crayfish *Orconectes limosus* (Rafinesque, 1817) (Crustacea: Decapoda: Cambaridae) in Romania. *North-Western Journal of Zoology*, **5**(2), 424–8.

Peay, S. (2000). *Guidance on Works Affecting White-Clawed Crayfish*. Report to English Nature and the Environment Agency.

Peay, S. (2003a). *Guidance on Habitat for White-clawed Crayfish and How to Restore It*. R&D Technical Report WI-067/TR. Environment Agency, Bristol, UK: 66 pp.

Peay, S. (2003b). *Monitoring the White-clawed Crayfish* Austropotamobius pallipes. Conserving Natura 2000 Rivers Monitoring series No. 1. English Nature, Peterborough, UK.

Peay, S. (2004). A cost-led evaluation of survey methods and monitoring for white-clawed crayfish: lessons from the UK. *Bulletin Français de la Pêche et de la Pisciculture*, 372–3, 335–52.

Peay, S. (2006). Latest crayfish biocide treatment in Scotland. *Crayfish News*, **28**(4), 5–7.

Peay, S. (2009a). Selection criteria for 'ark sites' for white-clawed crayfish. In: J. Brickland, D. M. Holdich & E. M. Imhoff (eds) *Crayfish Conservation in the British Isles: Proceedings of Conference held on 25th March 2009 in Leeds, UK*: 63–70.

Peay, S. (2009b). Invasive non-indigenous crayfish species in Europe: recommendations on managing them. *Knowledge and Management of Aquatic Ecosystems*, 394–5, article 9.

Peay, S. & Hiley, P. D. (2004). *A Review of Angling and Crayfish*. Report to the Environment Agency, Thames Region, March 2004.

Peay, S., Hiley, P. D., Collen, P. & Martin, I. (2006a). Biocide treatment of ponds in Scotland to eradicate signal crayfish. *Bulletin Français de la Pêche et de la Pisciculture*, 380–1, 1363–79.

Peay, S., Proud, A. & Ward, D. (2006b). White-clawed crayfish in muddy habitats: monitoring the populations in the River Ivel, Bedfordshire, UK. *Bulletin Français de la Pêche et de la Pisciculture*, **380–1**, 1079–94.

Peay, S., Holdich, D. M. & Brickland, J. (2010). Risk assessments of non-indigenous crayfish in Great Britain. *Freshwater Crayfish*, **17**, 109–22.

Penn, G. H. & Fitzpatrick, J. F. (1963), Interspecific competition between two sympatric species of dwarf crayfishes. *Ecology*, **44**, 793–97.

Perry, W. L., Feder, J. L., Dwyer, G. & Lodge, D. M. (2001a). Hybrid zone dynamics and species replacement between *Orconectes* crayfishes in a northern Wisconsin lake. *Evolution*, **55**, 1153–66.

Perry, W. L., Feder, J. L. & Lodge, D. M. (2001b). Implications of hybridization between introduced and resident *Orconectes* crayfishes. *Conservation Biology*, **15**, 1656–66.

Perry, W. L., Lodge, D. M., & Feder, J. L. (2002). Importance of hybridization between indigenous and nonindigenous freshwater species: an overlooked threat to North American biodiversity. *Systematic Biology*, **51**(2), 255–75.

Persic, A. (2006). Loss of ecosystem services due to the decline/disappearance of three European native crayfish species from Atlantic area (France and Ireland), Scandinavia (Sweden) and circum-Alpine region (Austria). In: M. Kettunen & P. ten Brink (eds) *Value of Biodiversity: Documenting EU Examples where Biodiversity Loss has led to the Loss of Ecosystem Services*. ENV.G.1/FRA/2004/0081. Final Report for the European Commission. Institute for European Environmental Policy (IEEP), Brussels: Annex 1, 12 pp.

Persson, M. & Söderhäll, K. (1983). *Pacifastacus leniusculus* Dana and its resistance to the parasitic fungus *Aphanomyces astaci* Schikora. *Freshwater Crayfish*, **5**, 292–8.

Persson, M., Cerenius, L. & Söderhäll, K. (1987). The influence of haemocyte number on the resistance of the freshwater crayfish, *Pacifastacus leniusculus* Dana, to the parasitic fungus *Aphanomyces astaci*. *Journal of Fish Diseases*, **10**, 471–7.

Peters, J. A., Kreps, T. & Lodge, D. M. (2008). Assessing the impacts of rusty crayfish (*Orconectes rusticus*) on submergent macrophytes in a north-temperate U.S. lake using electric fences. *American Midland Naturalist*, **159**, 287–97.

Phillips, I. D., Vinebrooke, R. D. & Turner, M. A. (2009). Experimental reintroduction of the crayfish species *Orconectes virilis* into recovering acidified Lake 302S (Experimental Lakes Area, Canada). *Canadian Journal of Fisheries and Aquatic Sciences*, **66**(11), 1892–1902.

Pianka, E. R. (1970). On *r*- and *K*-selection. *American Naturalist*, **104**, 592–7.

Piper, L. (2000). *Potential for Expansion of the Freshwater Crayfish Industry in Australia: A Report for the Rural Industries Research and Development Corporation*. Rural Industries Research and Development Corporation, Canberra: 32 pp.

Pixell-Goodrich, H. P. (1956). Crayfish epidemics. *Parasitology*, **46**, 830–3.

Pöckl, M. (1999). Freshwater crayfish in the legislation of Austria: federal, national and international laws. *Freshwater Crayfish*, **12**, 899–914.

Pöckl, M. (2002). Draft programme for the conservation of native crayfish species in Austria. *Freshwater Crayfish*, **13**, 221–32.

Pöckl, M. & Pekny, R. (2002). Interaction between native and alien species of crayfish in Austria: case studies. *Bulletin Français de la Pêche et de la Pisciculture*, **367**, 763–76.

Policar, T. & Kozák, P. (2005). Comparison of trap and baited stick catch efficiency for noble crayfish (*Astacus astacus* L.) in the course of the growing season. *Bulletin Français de la Pêche et de la Pisciculture*, **376–7**, 675–86.

Policar, T., Smyth, J., Flanigan, M., Kozák, P. & Kouba, A. (2010). Optimum water temperature for intensive production of *Austropotamobius pallipes* (Lereboullet) juveniles. *Freshwater Crayfish*, **17**, 51–5.

Portelance, B. (1987). *Avis scientifique sur l'exploitation des populations d'écrevisses du lac Saint Pierre et du fleuve Saint Laurent*. Avis scientifique 87/4. Ministère du Loisir, de la Chasse et de la Pêche. Ministère de l'Agriculture, des Pêcheries et de l'Alimentation, Quebec.

Porter, M. L., Perez-Losada, M. & Crandall, K. A. (2005). Model-based multi-locus estimation of decapod phylogeny and divergence times. *Molecular Phylogenetics and Evolution*, **37**, 355–69.

Price, J. E. & Welch, S. M. (2009). Semi-quantitative methods for crayfish sampling: sex, size and habitat bias. *Journal of Crustacean Biology*, **29**(2), 208–16.

Prigioni, C., Balestrieri, A. & Remonti, L. (2007). Decline and recovery in otter *Lutra lutra* populations in Italy. *Mammal Review*, **37**(1), 71–9.

Puky, M., Poboljsaj, K., Janev, B., et al. (1999). The educational aspects of the International Salamander Year, a twelve country project in Europe. In: *Annual Conference of the Canadian Amphibian and Reptile Conservation Network, Québec, 14–18 October, 1999.*

Puky, M., Reynolds, J. D. & Grandjean, F. (2002). Education as a key to decapod conservation. *Bulletin Français de la Pêche et de la Pisciculture*, **367**, 911–16.

Puky, M., Reynolds, J. D. & Schad, P. (2005). Native and alien Decapoda species in Hungary, distribution, status, conservation importance. *Bulletin Français de la Pêche et de la Pisciculture*, **376–7**, 553–68.

Punzalan, D., Guiaşu, R. C., Belchior, D. & Dunham, D. W. (2001). Discrimination of conspecific-built chimneys from human-built ones by the burrowing crayfish, *Fallicambarus fodiens* (Decapoda, Cambaridae). *Invertebrate Biology*, **120**, 58–66.

Pyšek, P., Jarošík, V., Hulme, P. E., et al. (2010). Disentangling the role of environmental and human pressures on biological invasions across Europe. **PNAS** (online), doi:10.1073/pnas.1002314107.

Qvenild, T., Skurdal, J. & Dehli, E. (1982). *Fangst og bestandsdynamikk for kreps i Steinsfjorden.* Tyrifjordutvalget, fagrapport nr. 16: 45 pp.

Rabeni, C. F., Collier, K. J., Parkyn, S. M. & Hicks, B. J. (1997). Evaluating methods of sampling stream crayfish. *New Zealand Journal of Marine & Freshwater Research,* **31,** 693–700.

Rach, J. J. & Bills, T. D. (1989). Crayfish control with traps and largemouth bass. *Progressive Fish-Culturist,* **51,** 157–60.

Rantamäki, J., Cerenius, L. & Söderhäll, K. (1992). Prevention of transmission of the crayfish plague fungus (*Aphanomyces astaci*) to the freshwater crayfish *Astacus astacas* by treatment with $MgCl^2$. *Aquaculture,* **104,** 11–18.

Rees, G. H. (1962). Effects of gamma radiation on two decapod crustaceans, *Palaemonetes pugio* and *Uca pugnax. Chesapeake Science,* **3,** 29–34.

Reid, W. V. & Miller, K. R. (1989). *Keeping Options Alive: The Scientific Basis for Conserving Biodiversity.* World Resources Institute, Washington, DC.

Reid, W. V., McNeely, J. A., Tunstall, D. B., Bryant, D. A. & Winograd, M. (1993). *Biodiversity Indicators for Policy-Makers.* World Resources Institute, Washington, DC.

Renai, B. & Gherardi, F. (2004). Predatory efficiency of crayfish: comparison between indigenous and non-indigenous species. *Biological Invasions,* **6,** 89–99.

Renai, B., Bertocchi, S., Brusconi, S., et al. (2006). Ecological characterisation of streams in Tuscany for the management of the threatened crayfish *Austropotamobius italicus. Bulletin Français de la Pêche et de la Pisciculture,* **380–1,** 1095–114.

Renai, B, Trouilhé, M. C., Bourdon, B., et al. (2008). Impact of heat wave on streams harbouring the white-clawed crayfish (*Austropotamobius pallipes*) in western France (Deux-Sèvres). *Freshwater Crayfish,* **16,** 57–69.

Revenga, C. & Kura, Y. (2003). *Status and Trends of Biodiversity of Inland Water Ecosystems.* Technical Series No. 11. Secretariat of the Convention on Biological Diversity, Montreal, Canada.

Reyjol, Y. & Roqueplo, C. (2002). Preferential habitat analysis of the white-clawed crayfish, notably juveniles, in three brooks of Corrèze – France. In: C. Souty-Grosset & F. Grandjean (eds) *Knowledge-based Management of European Native Crayfish* (Crayfish Special Issue, Vol. 4), *Bulletin Français de la Pêche et de la Pisciculture,* **367,** 741–62.

Reynolds, J. D. (1988a). Crayfish extinctions and crayfish plague in Ireland. *Biological Conservation,* **45,** 279–85.

Reynolds, J. D. (1988b). Options for crayfish culture and exploitation in Ireland. *Freshwater Crayfish,* **7,** 327–31.

Reynolds, J. D. (1989). Phenotypic variability in freshwater crayfish and its implications for aquaculture. In: J. C. Aldrich (ed.) *Phenotypic Responses and Individuality in Aquatic Ectotherms.* Japaga, Ashford, Ireland: 197–201.

Reynolds, J. D. (1997). The present status of freshwater crayfish in Ireland. *Bulletin Français de la Pêche et de la Pisciculture,* **347,** 693–700.

Reynolds, J. D. (1998). *Conservation Management of the White-clawed Crayfish* Austropotamobius pallipes. *Part 1.* Irish Wildlife Manuals No. 1. Duchas – The Heritage Service, Department of Arts, Heritage, Gaeltacht and the Islands, Dublin: 28 pp.

Reynolds, J. D. (2002). Growth and reproduction. In: D. M. Holdich (ed.) *Biology of Freshwater Crayfish.* Blackwell Science, Oxford, UK: 152–91.

Reynolds, J. D. (2006). Man-handled? How and when did freshwater invertebrates cross the sea to Ireland? A review with particular reference to crustaceans. Post-glacial Colonization Conference: Mind the Gap 2006. Special Supplement to *The Irish Naturalists' Journal* 2008, 83–95.

Reynolds, J. D. (2009a). Monitoring and capture methods for freshwater crayfish stocks (Metody monitoringu vyskytu a odchytu sladkovodnich raku). *Bulletin vurh Vodnany*, **45**(2–3), 82–90.

Reynolds, J. D. (2009b). The current status of white-clawed crayfish in Ireland. In: J. Brickland, D. M. Holdich & E. M. Imhoff (eds) *Crayfish Conservation in the British Isles: Proceedings of a Conference held on 25th March 2009, Leeds, UK*: 35–41.

Reynolds, J. D. & Demers, A. (2006). Comparison of white-clawed crayfish populations in Irish and French streams, with comments on its future survival in Europe. *Bulletin Français de la Pêche et de la Pisciculture*, **380**–1, 1115–20.

Reynolds, J. D. & Matthews, M. A. (1993). Experimental fishery of *Austropotamobius pallipes* (Lereboullet) stocks in an Irish midlands lake. *Freshwater Crayfish*, **9**, 147–53.

Reynolds, J. D. & Matthews, M. A. (1996). Conservation strategies for the Irish freshwater crayfish. In: J. D. Reynolds (ed.) *The Conservation of Aquatic Systems*. Royal Irish Academy, Dublin: 151–5.

Reynolds, J. D. & O'Keeffe, C. (2005). Dietary patterns in stream- and lake-dwelling populations of *Austropotamobius pallipes*. *Bulletin Français de la Pêche et de la Pisciculture*, **376**–7, 715–30.

Reynolds, J. D. & Puky, M. (2005). The importance of public education for the effective conservation of European native crayfish. *Bulletin Français de la Pêche et de la Pisciculture*, **376**–7, 837–45.

Reynolds, J. D. & Souty-Grosset, C. (2003a). CRAYNET: Programme and potential. In: D. M. Holdich & P. J. Sibley (eds) *Management & Conservation of Crayfish: Proceedings of a Conference held on 7th November 2002*. Environment Agency, Bristol, UK: 2–14.

Reynolds, J. D. & Souty-Grosset, C. (eds) (2003b). *The Endangered Native Crayfish* Austropotamobius pallipes, *Bioindicator and Heritage Species*. Special Issue of *Bulletin Français de la Pêche et de la Pisciculture*, **370**–1 (CRAYNET volume 1): 230 pp.

Reynolds, J. D., Celada, J. C., Carral, J. M. & Matthews, M. A. (1992). Reproduction of astacid crayfishes in captivity: current developments and implications for culture, with special reference to Ireland and Spain. *Invertebrate Reproduction & Development*, **22**, 253–66.

Reynolds, J. D., Demers, A. & Marnell, F. (2002a). Managing an abundant crayfish source for conservation: *A. pallipes* in Ireland. *Bulletin Français de la Pêche et de la Pisciculture*, **367**, 823–32.

Reynolds, J., Gouin, N., Pain, S., et al. (2002b). Irish crayfish populations: ecological survey and preliminary genetical findings. *Freshwater Crayfish*, **13**, 551–61.

Reynolds, J. D., Demers, A., Peay, S., et al. (2006). Crayfish conservation and management. In: C. Souty-Grosset, D. M. Holdich, P. Y. Noel, J. D. Reynolds & P. Haffner (eds) *Atlas of Crayfish in Europe*. Muséum national d'Histoire naturelle, Paris: 152–7.

Reynolds, J. D., O'Connor, W., O'Keeffe, C. & Lynn, D. (2009). *A Technical Manual for Monitoring White-clawed Crayfish Austropotamobius pallipes (Lereboullet) in Irish Lakes*. Irish Wildlife Manuals No. 45. National Parks and Wildlife Service, Dublin.

Reynolds, J. D., Lynn, D., O'Keeffe, C., et al. (2010). Conservation assessment and current status of protected white-clawed crayfish, *Austropotamobius pallipes* (Lereboullet), in Ireland. *Freshwater Crayfish*, **17**, 123–7.

Ricciardi, A. & Rasmussen, J. B. (1999). Extinction rates of North American freshwater fauna. *Conservation Biology*, **13**, 1220–2.

Richards, C., Kutka, F. J., McDonald, M. E., Merrick, G. W. & Devore, P. W. (1996). Life history and temperature effects on catch of northern orconectid crayfish. *Hydrobiologia*, **319**, 111–18.

Richards, K. & Fuke, P. (1977). Freshwater crayfish: the first centre in Britain. *Fish Farming International*, **4**, 5–7.

Richardson, A. M. M. (1983). The effect of the burrows of a crayfish on the respiration of the surrounding soil. *Soil Biology and Biochemistry*, **15**, 239–42.

Richardson, A. M. M. (2007). Behavioral ecology of semi terrestrial crayfish. In: J. E. Duffy & M. Thiel (eds) *Evolutionary Ecology of Social and Sexual Systems: Crustaceans as Model Organisms*. Oxford University Press, New York: 319–38.

Richardson, A. M. M. & Doran, N. E. (2008). The role of burrowing crayfish in Tasmanian sedgelands. *Australasian Plant Conservation*, **16**(3), 22–4.

Richardson, A. M. M. & Swain, R. (1990). Pattern and persistence in the burrows of two species of the freshwater crayfish *Parastacoides* (Decapoda: Parastacidae) in south-west Tasmania. *Memoirs of the Queensland Museum*, **31**, 283.

Richardson, A. M. M. & Swain, R. (2002). The sting in the tail: spination of the tail fan in freshwater crayfish. *Freshwater Crayfish*, **13**, 515–24.

Richardson, A. M. M. & Wong, V. (1995). The effect of the burrowing crayfish *Parastacoides* on the vegetation of Tasmanian wet heathlands. *Freshwater Crayfish*, **10**, 174–82.

Richardson, A. M. M., Doran, N. & Hansen, B. (1999). The conservation status of Tasmanian freshwater crayfish. *Freshwater Crayfish*, **12**, 863–77.

Richardson, A. M. M., Doran, N. & Hansen, B. (2006). The geographic ranges of Tasmanian crayfish: extent and pattern. *Freshwater Crayfish*, **15**, 347–64.

Ridge, J., Simon, T. P., Karns, D. & Robb, J. (2008). Comparison of three burrowing crayfish capture methods based on relationships with species morphology, seasonality and habitat quality. *Journal of Crustacean Biology*, **28**, 466–72.

Riek, E. F. (1972). The phylogeny of the Parastacidae (Crustacea: Astacoidea) and descriptions of a new genus of Australian freshwater crayfishes. *Australian Journal of Zoology*, **20**, 369–89.

Robles, R., Schubart, C. D., Conde, J. E., et al. (2007). Molecular phylogeny of the American *Callinectes* Stimpson, 1860 (Brachyura: Portunidae), based on two partial mitochondrial genes. *Marine Biology*, **150**, 1265–74.

Robles, R., Tudge, C. C., Dworschak, P. C., Poore, G. C. B. & Felder, D. L. (2009). Molecular phylogeny of the Thalassinidea based on nuclear and mitochondrial genes. In: J. W. Martin, D. L. Felder & K. A. Crandall (eds) *Decapod Crustacean Phylogenetics*. Crustacean Issues 18. CRC Press, Boca Raton, FL: 301–18.

Rode, A. L. & Babcock, L. E. (2003). Phylogeny of fossil and extant freshwater crayfish and some closely related nephropid lobsters. *Journal of Crustacean Biology*, **23**, 418–35.

Rodrigues, A. S. L., Pilgrim, J. D., Lamoreux, J. F., Hoffmann, M. & Brooks, T. M. (2006). The value of the IUCN Red List for conservation. *Trends in Ecology and Evolution*, **21**, 71–6.

Rodríguez, C. F., Bécares, E. B. & Fernández-Aláez, M. (2003). Shift from clear to turbid phase in Lake Chozas (NW Spain) due to the introduction of American red swamp crayfish (*Procambarus clarkii*). *Hydrobiologia*, **506–9**, 421–6.

Rogers, W. D. & Holdich, D. M. (1995). Crayfish production in Britain. *Freshwater Crayfish*, **10**, 583–96.

Rogers, W. D. & Holdich, D. M. (1997). *Crayfish Surveys on the Rivers Wensum, Bure, and Gipping Catchments, Sections of the River Yare, and the Rivers Stiffkey and Glaven*. Report to Environment Agency and English Nature.

Rogers, W. D., Roqueplo, C., Bramard, M. & Demers, A. (2002). Crayfish management: habitat restoration. *Bulletin Français de la Pêche et de la Pisciculture*, **367**, 923–8.

Romaire, R. P. (1990). *Crawpop: Red Swamp Crawfish Aquaculture Simulation Model*. School of Forestry, Wildlife & Fisheries, Louisiana State University, Baton Rouge, LA.

Romaire, R. P. (1995). Harvesting methods and strategies used in commercial procambarid crawfish aquaculture. *Journal of Shellfish Research*, **14**, 545–51.

Romero, X. M. (1997). Production of red claw crayfish in Ecuador. *World Aquaculture*, **28**, 5–10.

Rosensweig, M. L. (2003). Reconciliation ecology and the future of species diversity. *Oryx*, **37**, 194–205.

Ross, M. (2004). What do we know about natural resources and civil war? *Journal of Peace Research*, **41**, 337–56.

Roussel, J. M., Bardonnet, A. & Claude, A. (1999). Microhabitat of brown trout when feeding on drift and when resting in a lowland salmonid brook: effects on weighted usable area. *Archiv für Hydrobiologie*, **146**, 413–29.

Rudolph, E. H. (1990). Caracteres sexuales externos del camarón excavador, *Parastacus nicoleti* (Philippi, 1882). *Biota (Osorno, Chile)*, **8**, 19–34.

Rudolph, E. H. (2002). New records of intersexuality in the freshwater crayfish species *Samastacus spinifrons* (Decapoda, Parastacidae). *Journal of Crustacean Biology*, **22**, 377–89.

Rudolph, E. H. & Crandall, K. A. (2005). A new species of burrowing crayfish *Virilastacus rucapihuelensis* (Crustacea: Decapoda: Parastacidae) from southern Chile. *Proceedings of the Biological Society of Washington*, **118**, 765–76.

Rudolph, E. H. & Crandall, K. A. (2007). A new species of burrowing crayfish *Virilastacus retamali* (Decapoda: Parastacidae) from the southern Chilean peatland. *Journal of Crustacean Biology*, **27**, 502–12.

Rudolph, E. H., Verdi, A. & Tapia, J. (2001). Intersexuality in the burrowing crayfish *Parastacus varicosus* Faxon, 1898 (Decapoda, Parastacidae). *Crustaceana*, **74**, 27–37.

Saiki, M. K. & Tash, J. C. (1979). Use of cover and dispersal by crayfish to reduce predation by largemouth bass. In: D. L. Johnson & R. A. Stein (eds) *Response of Fish to Habitat Structure in Standing Water*. American Fisheries Society, North Central Division, Bethesda, MD: 44–8.

Sala, O. E., Chapin, F. S., Armesto, J. J., et al. (2000). Biodiversity: global biodiversity scenarios for the year 2100. *Science*, **287**, 1770–4.

Sandodden, R. & Johnsen, S.I. (2010). Eradication of introduced signal crayfish *Pacifastacus leniusculus* using the pharmaceutical BETAMAX VET®. *Aquatic Invasions*, **5**(1), 75–81.

Saunders, D. L., Hobbs, R. J. & Margules, C. R. (1991). Biological consequences of ecosystem fragmentation. *Conservation Biology*, **5**, 18–32.

Savini, D., Occhipinti-Ambrogi, A., Marchini, A., et al. (2010). The top 27 animal alien species introduced into Europe for aquaculture and related activities. *Journal of Applied Ichthyology*, **26**, 1–7.

Scalera, R. (2008). *EU Funding for Management and Research of Invasive Alien Species in Europe*. Support for a Pilot Project on 'Streamlining European 2010 Biodiversity Indicators (SEBI2010)': 42 pp.

Scalici, M. & Gibertini, G. (2005). Can *Austropotamobius italicus meridionalis* be used as a monitoring instrument in Central Italy? Preliminary observations. *Bulletin Français de la Pêche et de la Pisciculture*, **376**–7, 613–25.

Scalici, M., Chiesa, S., Gherardi, F., et al. (2009). The new threat to Italian inland waters from the alien crayfish 'gang': the Australian *Cherax destructor* Clark, 1936. *Hydrobiologia*, **632**, 341–5.

Schilderman, P. A. E. L., Moonen, E. J. C., Maas, L. M., Welle, I. & Kleinjans, J. C. S. (1999). Use of crayfish in biomonitoring studies of environmental pollution of the River Meuse. *Ecotoxicology & Environmental Safety*, **44**(3), 241–52.

Scholtz, G. (2002). Phylogeny and evolution. In: D. M. Holdich (ed.) *Biology of Freshwater Crayfish*. Blackwell Science, Oxford, UK: 30–52.

Scholtz, G. & McLay, C. L. (2009). Is the Brachyura Podotremata a monophyletic group? In: J. W. Martin, D. L. Felder & K. A. Crandall (eds) *Decapod Crustacean Phylogenetics*. Crustacean Issues 18. CRC Press, Boca Raton, FL: 409–27.

Scholtz, G. & Richter, S. (1995). Phylogenetic systematics of the reptantian Decapoda (Crustacea, Malacostraca). *Zoological Journal of the Linnean Society*, **113**, 289–328.

Scholtz, G., Braband, A., Tolly, L., et al. (2003). Parthenogenesis in an outsider crayfish. *Nature*, **421**, 806.

Schram, F. R. (2001). Phylogeny of decapods: moving towards a consensus. *Hydrobiologia*, **449**, 1–20.

Schubart, C. D., Neigel, J. E. & Felder, D. L. (2000). Use of the mitochondrial 16S rRNA gene for phylogenetic and population studies of Crustacea. *Crustacean Issues*, **12**, 817–30.

Schulz, H. K., Stucki, T. & Souty-Grosset, C. (2002). Management: reintroductions and restocking. *Bulletin Français de la Pêche et de la Pisciculture*, **367**, 917–22.

Schulz, R. (2000). Status of the noble crayfish *Astacus astacus* (L.) in Germany: monitoring protocol and the use of RAPD markers to assess the genetic structure of populations. *Bulletin Français de la Pêche et de la Pisciculture*, **356**, 123–38.

Schulz, R. (2004). Field studies on exposure, effects and risk mitigation of aquatic nonpoint-source insecticide pollution: a review. *Journal of Environmental Quality*, **33**, 419–48.

Schuster, G. A., Taylor, C. A. & Johansen, J. (2008). An annotated checklist and preliminary designation of drainage distributions of the crayfishes of Alabama. *Southeastern Naturalist*, **7**(3), 493–504.

Sellars, M. J. & Preston, N. P. (2005). The effects of ionizing radiation on the reproductive capacity of adult *Penaeus (Maruspenaeus) japonicus* (Bate). *Aquaculture Research*, **36**(11), 1144–7.

Sheil, D. (2001). Conservation and biodiversity monitoring in the tropics: realities, priorities, and distractions. *Conservation Biology*, **15**, 1179–82.

Shore, R.F., Malcolm, H.M., Wienburg, C.L., et al. (2005). *Wildlife and Pollution: 2001/02 Annual Report*. JNCC Report No. 352. Centre for Ecology and Hydrology Project No. C00554. Centre for Ecology and Hydrology, Monks Wood, UK.

Shyamsundar, P. & Kramer, R. (1997). Biodiversity conservation – at what cost? A study of households in the vicinity of Madagascar's Mantadia National Park. *Ambio*, **26**, 180–4.

Sibley, P. J. (2003a). Conservation, management and legislation: the UK experience. *Bulletin Français de la Pêche et de la Pisciculture*, **370**–1, 209–17.

Sibley, P. J. (2003b). The distribution of crayfish in Britain. In: D. M. Holdich & P. J. Sibley (eds) *Management and Conservation of Crayfish*. Environment Agency, Bristol, UK: 64–72.

Sibley, P., Clarkson, M., Frayling, M. & Stenson, C. (2007). Translocating the white-clawed crayfish *Austropotamobius pallipes*. In: P. Hickley & S. Axford (eds) *Fisheries & Conservation Successes & Failures*. Institute of Fisheries Management Conference Proceedings: 42–51.

Sibley, P. J., Holdich, D. M. & Lane, M.-R. (2009). Invasive crayfish in Britain: management and mitigation. *International Urban Ecology Review*, **4**, 105–18.

Sibree, J. (1915). *A Naturalist in Madagascar*. Seeley, Service & Co, London.

Simberloff, D. (2002). Today Tiritiri Matangi, tomorrow the World! Are we aiming too low in invasives control? In: C. R. Veitch & M. N. Clout (eds) *Turning the Tide: The Eradication of Invasive Species*. IUCN, Gland, Switzerland: 4–13.

Simberloff, D. (2009). We can eliminate invasions or live with them: successful management projects. *Biological Invasions*, **11**, 149–57.

Sinclair, E. A., Fetzner, J. W., Jr, Buhay, J. E. & Crandall, K. A. (2004). Proposal to complete a phylogenetic taxonomy and systematic revision for freshwater crayfish (Astacidea). *Freshwater Crayfish*, **14**, 21–9.

Skurdal, J. (1995). Human impact on natural populations of European crayfish. *Fauna (Oslo)*, **48**, 134–43.

Skurdal, J. & Qvenild T. (1986). Growth, maturity, and fecundity of *Astacus astacus* in Lake Steinsfjorden, S.E. Norway. *Freshwater Crayfish*, **6**, 182–86.

Skurdal, J. & Taugbøl, T. (1994). Minimum size regulation as a tool in crayfish management. *Nordic Journal of Freshwater Research*, **69**, 144–8.

Skurdal, J. & Taugbøl, T. (2002). *Astacus*. In: D. M. Holdich (ed.) *Biology of Freshwater Crayfish*. Blackwell Science, Oxford, UK: 467–510.

Skurdal, J., Qvenild, T., Taugbøl, T. & Gamas, E. (1993). A long term study of exploitation, yield and stock structure of noble crayfish *Astacus astacus* in Lake Steinsfjorden, S.E. Norway. *Freshwater Crayfish*, **9**, 118–33.

Skurdal, J., Qvenild, T., Taugbøl, T. & Gamas, E. (1995). Size and sex composition of noble crayfish *Astacus astacus* in trap catches in Lake Steinsfjorden, S.E. Norway: effect of exploitation. *Freshwater Crayfish*, **8**, 249–56.

Skurdal, J., Gamas, T. & Taugbøl, T. (2002). Management strategies, yield and population development of the noble crayfish *Astacus astacus* in Lake Steinsfjorden. *Bulletin Français de la Pêche et de la Pisciculture*, **367**, 845–60.

Smith, D. G. (1981). Evidence for hybridization between two crayfish species (Decapoda: Cambaridae: *Orconectes*) with a comment on the phenomenon in cambarid crayfish. *American Midland Naturalist*, **105**(2), 405–7.

Söderbäck, B. & Edsman, L. (1998). *Åtgärdsprogram för bevarande av flodkräftan (Action Plan for the Restoration of Noble Crayfish)* (in Swedish). Fiskeriverket and Naturvårdsverket, Stockholm.

Söderhäll, K. & Axajon, R. (1982). Effect of quinones and melanin on mycelial growth of *Aphanomyces* spp. and extracellular protease of *Aphanomyces astaci*, a parasite on crayfish. *Journal of Invertebrate Pathology*, **39**, 105–9.

Söderhäll, K. & Cerenius L. (1992). Crustacean immunity. *Annual Review of Fish Diseases*, **2**, 3–23.

Söderhäll, K. & Cerenius, L. (1999). The crayfish plague fungus: history and recent advances. *Freshwater Crayfish*, **12**, 11–35.

Söderhäll, L. & Söderhäll, K. (2002). Immune reactions. In: D. M. Holdich (ed.) *Biology of Freshwater Crayfish*. Blackwell Science, Oxford, UK: 439–64.

Somers, K. M. & Stechey, D. M. (1986). Variable trappability of crayfish associated with bait type, water temperature and moon phase. *American Midland Naturalist*, **116**, 36–44.

Sommer, T. (1984). The biological response of the crayfish *Procambarus clarkii* to transplantation into Californian ricefields. *Aquaculture*, **41**, 373–84.

Southwood, T. R. E. (1972). The insect/plant relationship: an evolutionary perspective. In: H. F. van Enden (ed.) *Insect/Plant Relationships: Symposium of the Royal Entomological Society of London*, **6**, 3–30.

Southwood, T. R. E. (1977). Habitat, the template for ecological strategies. *Journal of Animal Ecology*, **46**, 337–65.

Souty-Grosset, C. (2005). The EU-network CRAYNET: impacts on fundamental questions. *Bulletin Français de la Pêche et de la Pisciculture*, **376**-7, 495–503.

Souty-Grosset, C. (2009). Ochrana původních-evropských sladkovodních raků: recentní příklady z Evropy. In: *Odborný seminář Ochrana raků v kontextu s rybářským hospodařením* (OP Rybářství, CZ.1.25/3.1.00/08.00.00287): 5–12.

Souty-Grosset, C. & Grandjean, F. (eds) (2002). *Knowledge-based Management of European Native Crayfish: Exchanges Between Researchers and Managers*. IAA European Meeting, Poitiers, France, September 13–15, 2001. Special Issue of *Bulletin Français de la Pêche et de la Pisciculture*, **367** (Spécial écrevisses, volume. 4): 402 pp.

Souty-Grosset, C. & Reynolds, J. D. (2010). Current ideas on methodological approaches in European crayfish conservation and restocking procedure. Published online in *Knowledge and Management of Aquatic Ecosystems*, **394**-5, article 01.

Souty-Grosset, C., Schulz, R. & Madec, J. (2005). Crayfish protection programmes in Europe. *Bulletin Français de la Pêche et de la Pisciculture*, **376**-7, 797–807.

Souty-Grosset, C., Holdich, D. M., Noël, P. Y., Reynolds, J. D. & Haffner, P. (eds) (2006). *Atlas of Crayfish in Europe*. Patrimoines naturels 64. Muséum National d'Histoire naturelle, Paris: 187 pp.

Spears, T., Abele, L. G. & Kim, W. (1992). The monophyly of brachyuran crabs: a phylogenetic study based on 18S rRNA. *Systematic Biology*, **41**, 446–61.

Spears, T., Abele, L. G. & Applegate, M. A. (1994). Phylogenetic study of cirripedes and selected relatives (Thecostraca) based on 18S rDNA sequence analysis. *Journal of Crustacean Biology*, **14**, 641–56.

Spink, J. & Frayling, M. (2000). An assessment of post-plague reintroduced native white-clawed crayfish *Austropotamobius pallipes* in the Sherston Avon and Tetbury Avon, Wiltshire. *Freshwater Forum*, **14**, 59–69.

Stammer, H. J. (1932). Die Fauna des Timavo: ein Beitrag zur Kenntniss der Höhlengewässer, des Süss- und Brackwassers im Karst. *Zoologische Jahrbücher: Abteilung für Systematik, Ökologie und Geographie der Tiere*, **63**(5/6), 521–656.

Starobogatov, Y. I. (1995). Taxonomy and geographical distribution of crayfishes of Asia and East Europe (Crustacea, Decapoda, Astacoidei). *Arthropoda Selecta*, **4**(3), 3–25.

Statzner, B. & Bêche, L. A. (2010). Can biological invertebrate traits resolve effects of multiple stressors on running-water ecosystems? *Freshwater Biology*, **55** (Suppl. 1), 80–119.

Statzner, B. & Sagnes, P. (2008). Crayfish and fish as bioturbators of streambed sediments: assessing joint effects of species with different mechanistic abilities. *Geomorphology*, **93**, 267–87.

Statzner, B., Fiever, E., Champagne, J.-Y., Morel, R. & Hervain, E. (2000). Crayfish as geomorphic agents and ecosystem engineers: biological behaviour affects sand and gravel erosion in experimental streams. *Limnology and Oceanography*, **45**, 1030–40.

Statzner, B., Peltret, O. & Tomanova, S. (2003). Crayfish as geomorphic agents and ecosystem engineers: effect of a biomass gradient on baseflow and flood-induced transport of gravel and sand in experimental streams. *Freshwater Biology*, **48**, 147–63.

Stebbing, P. D., Watson, G. J., Bentley, M. G., et al. (2003). Reducing the threat: the potential use of pheromones to control invasive signal crayfish. *Bulletin Français de la Pêche et de la Pisciculture*, **370**–1, 219–24.

Stebbing, P. D., Watson, G. J., Bentley, M. G., et al. (2004). *Evaluation of the Capacity of Pheromones for Control of Invasive Non-native Crayfish*. English Nature Research Reports, Peterborough, UK: 38 pp.

Stechey, D. M. & Somers, K. M. (1983). An analysis of four Ontario species of crayfish for aquaculture. In: *Proceedings of the First International Conference on Warm Water Aquaculture – Crustacea*: 221–30.

Stein, R. A. (1976). Polymorphism in crayfish chelae: functional significance linked to reproductive activities. *Canadian Journal of Zoology*, **54**, 220–7.

Stein, R. A. (1977). Selective predation, optimal foraging, and the predator–prey interaction between fish and crayfish. *Ecology*, **58**, 1237–53.

Stein, R. A. & Magnuson, J. J. (1976). Behavioral response of crayfish to a fish predator. *Ecology*, **57**, 751–61.

Stewart, P. M., Miller, J. M., Heath, W. H. & Simon, T. P. (2010). Microhabitat partitioning of crayfish assemblages in wadeable streams in the coastal plains of southeastern Alabama. *Southeastern Naturalist*, **9** (Special Issue 3), 245–56.

Stillman, J. H. & Reeb, C. A. (2001). Molecular phylogeny of eastern Pacific porcelain crabs, genera *Petrolisthes* and *Pachycheles*, based on the mtDNA 16S rDNA sequence: phylogeographic and systematic implications. *Molecular Phylogenetics and Evolution*, **19**, 236–45.

Strayer, D. L. (2010). Alien species in fresh waters: ecological effects, interactions with other stressors, and prospects for the future. *Freshwater Biology*, **55** (Suppl. 1), 152–74.

Strayer, D. L. & Dudgeon, D. (2010). Freshwater biodiversity conservation: recent progress and future challenges. *Journal of the North American Benthological Society*, **29**(1), 344–58.

Stucki, P., Zaugg, B., Büttiker, B., et al. (2005). *Plan d'action national pour les écrevisses*. Rapport OFEV: 41 pp.

Suter, P. J. (1977). The biology of two species of *Engaeus* (Decapoda: Parastacidae) in Tasmania. II. Life history and larval development, with particular reference to *E. cisternarius*. *Australian Journal of Marine and Freshwater Research*, **28**, 85–93.

Suter, P. J. & Richardson, A. M. M. (1977). The biology of two species of *Engaeus* (Decapoda: Parastacidae) in Tasmania. III. Habitat, food, associated fauna and distribution. *Australian Journal of Marine and Freshwater Research*, **28**, 95–103.

Swahn, J.-Ö. (2004). The cultural history of crayfish. *Bulletin Français de la Pêche et de la Pisciculture*, **372**–3, 243–61.

Swecker, C. D., Jones, T. G., Donahue, K., II, McKinney, D. & Smith, G. D. (2010). The extirpation of *Orconectes limosus* (spinycheek crayfish) populations in West Virginia. *Southeastern Naturalist*, **9**, 155–64.

Tack, P. I. (1941). The life history and ecology of the crayfish *Cambarus immunis* Hagen. *American Midland Naturalist*, **25**, 420–45.

Taugbøl, T. (2004a) Reintroduction of noble crayfish *Astacus astacus* after crayfish plague event in Norway. *Bulletin Français de la Pêche et de la Pisciculture*, **372**–3, 315–28.

Taugbøl, T. (2004b). Exploitation is a prerequisite for conservation of *Astacus astacus*. *Bulletin Français de la Pêche et de la Pisciculture*, **372**–3, 275–9.

Taugbøl, T. & Peay, S. (2004). Reintroduction of native crayfish and habitat restoration. *Bulletin Français de la Pêche et de la Pisciculture*, **372**–3, 465–71.

Taugbøl, T. & Skurdal, J. (1998). *Forslag til Forvaltningsplan for Kreps: Utredning for DN 1998–1*. Direktoratet for Naturforvaltning, Trondheim, Norway.

Taugbøl, T. & Skurdal, J. (1999). The future of native crayfish in Europe: how to make the best of a bad situation? In: F. Gherardi & D. M. Holdich (eds) *Crayfish in Europe as Alien Species: How to Make the Best of a Bad Situation?* Crustacean Issues 11. A. A. Balkema, Rotterdam: 271–9.

Taugbøl, M. C. & Souty-Grosset, C. (eds) (2004). *European Native Crayfish with a Special Focus on* Astacus astacus*: Linking Socioeconomics and Conservation*. Special Issue of *Bulletin Français de la Pêche et de la Pisciculture*, **372–3** (CRAYNET volume 2): 254 pp.

Taugbøl, T., Skurdal, J. & Håstein, T. (1993). Crayfish plague and management strategies in Norway. *Biological Conservation*, **63**, 75–82.

Taugbøl, T., Skurdal, J. & Burba, A. (1998). *Freshwater Crayfish in Lithuania. I: Action Plan for Management. II: Crayfish Status Report*. Østlandsforskning, Rapport 12/1998, 83 s.

Taylor, C. A. (2002). Taxonomy and conservation of native crayfish stocks. In: D. M. Holdich (ed.) *Biology of Freshwater Crayfish*. Blackwell Science, Oxford, UK: 236–57.

Taylor, C. A. & Schuster, G. A. (2004). *The Crayfishes of Kentucky*. Illinois Natural History Survey Special Publication, No. 28. Champaign, IL: 219 pp.

Taylor, C. A., Warren, M. L., Jr, Fitzpatrick, J. F., Jr, et al. (1996). Conservation status of crayfishes of the United States and Canada. *Fisheries*, **21**, 25–38.

Taylor, C. A., Schuster, G. A., Cooper, J. E., et al. (2007). A reassessment of the conservation status of crayfishes of the United States and Canada: the effects of 10+ years of increased awareness. *Fisheries*, **32**(8), 372–89.

Tews, J., Brose, U., Grimm, V., et al. (2004). Animal species diversity driven by habitat heterogeneity/diversity: the importance of keystone structures. *Journal of Biogeography*, **31**, 79–92.

Thompson, A. G. (1989). UK crayfish sales rise. *Fish Farming International*, December 1989.

Thompson, A. G. (1990). Demand stays high for this choice of the gourmets. *Fish Farmer*, Jan–Feb 1990, 105–8.

Thörnqvist, P. O. & Söderhäll, K. (1993). *Psorospermium haeckeli* and its interaction with the crayfish defence system. *Aquaculture*, **117**, 205–13.

Tockner, K. & Stanford, J. A. (2002). Riverine floodplains: present state and future trends. *Environmental Conservation*, **29**: 308–30.

Tockner, K., Fusch, M., Borchardt, D. & Lorang, M. S. (2010). Multiple stressors in coupled river–floodplain ecosystems. *Freshwater Biology*, **55** (Suppl. 1), 135–51.

Toon, A., Finley, M., Staples, J. & Crandall, K. A. (2009). Decapod phylogenetics and molecular evolution. In: J. W. Martin, D. L. Felder & K. A. Crandall (eds) *Decapod Crustacean Phylogenetics*. Crustacean Issues 18. CRC Press, Boca Raton, FL: 348–59.

Torre, M. & Rodriquez, P. (1964). *El cangrejo de río en España*. Servicio national de pesca fluvial y caza, Ministeria de Agricultura, Madrid: 107 pp.

Tricarico, E., Bertocchi, S., Brusconi, S., et al. (2008). Depuration of microcystin-LR from the red swamp crayfish *Procambarus clarkii* with assessment of food quality. *Aquaculture*, **285**, 90–5.

Tricarico, E., Vilizzi, L., Gherardi, F. & Copp, G. H. (2010). Calibration of FI-ISK, an invasiveness screening tool for nonnative freshwater invertebrates. *Risk Analysis*, **30**(2), 285–92.

Trombulak, S. C. & Frissell, C. A. (2000). Review of ecological effects of roads on terrestrial and aquatic communities. *Conservation Biology*, **56**, 107–27.

Trouilhé, M. C., Ricard, F., Parinet, B., Grandjean, F. & Souty-Grosset, C. (2004). Management of the white-clawed crayfish (*Austropotamobius pallipes*) in western France: abiotic and biotic factors study. *Bulletin Français de la Pêche et de la Pisciculture*, **370–1** (CRAYNET volume 1): 97–114.

Trouilhé, M. C., Souty-Grosset, C., Grandjean, F. & Parinet, B. (2008). Physical and chemical water requirements of the white-clawed crayfish (*Austropotamobius pallipes*) in western France. *Aquatic Conservation: Marine and Freshwater Ecosystems*, **17**(5), 520–38.

Tsang, L. M., Ma, K. Y., Ahyong, S. T., Chan, T. Y. & Chu, K. H. (2008). Phylogeny of Decapoda using two nuclear protein-coding genes: origin and evolution of the Reptantia. *Molecular Phylogenetics and Evolution*, **48**, 359–68.

Tudge, C. C. & Cunningham, C. W. (2002). Molecular phylogeny of the mud lobsters and mud shrimps (Crustacea: Decapoda: Thalassinidea) using nuclear 18S rDNA and mitochondrial 16S rDNA. *Invertebrate Systematics*, **16**, 839–47.

Tulonen, J., Erkamo, E., Jussila, J. & Mannonen, A. (2008). The effects of minimum size regulations and exploitation on population dynamics of the noble crayfish (*Astacus astacus* (Linnaeus)) in a small lake in central Finland: a seven-year study. *Freshwater Crayfish*, **16**, 7–14.

Tuusti, J., Taugbøl, T., Skurdal, J. and Kukk, L. (1998). *Freshwater Crayfish in Estonia. I: Action Plan for Management. II: Crayfish Status Report.* Østlandsforskning, Rapport 2/1998, 92 s.

Twohey, M. B., Sorensen, P. W. & Li, W. (2003). Possible applications of pheromones in an integrated sea lamprey management program. *Journal of Great Lakes Research*, **29**, 794–800.

Unestam, T. (1969). On the physiology of zoospore production in *Aphanomyces astaci*. *Physiologia Plantarum*, **22**, 236–45.

Unestam, T. (1972). On the host range and origin of the crayfish plague fungus. *Report of the Institute of Fresh-water Research, Drottningholm*, **52**, 192–8.

Unestam, T. (1974). The dangers of introducing new crayfish species. *Freshwater Crayfish*, **2**, 557–61.

Unestam, T. (1975). Defense reactions in and susceptibility of Australian and New Guinean freshwater crayfish to European-crayfish-plague fungus. *Australian Journal of Experimental Biology and Medical Science*, **53**, 349–59.

Unestam, T. & Weiss, D. W. (1970). The host–parasite relationship between freshwater crayfish and the crayfish disease fungus *Aphanomyces astaci*: responses to infection by a susceptible and a resistant species. *Journal of General Microbiology*, **60**, 77–90.

Usio, N. (2007). Endangered crayfish in Northern Japan: distribution, abundance and microhabitat specificity in relation to stream and riparian environment. *Biological Conservation*, **134**, 517–26.

Usio, N., Nakata, K., Kawai, T. & Kitano, T. (2007). Distribution and control status of the invasive signal crayfish (*Pacifastacus leniusculus*) in Japan. *Japanese Journal of Limnology*, **68**, 471–82.

Usio, N., Kamiyama, R., Saji, A. & Takamura, N. (2009). Size-dependent engineering impacts of invasive alien crayfish on a littoral marsh community. *Biological Conservation*, **142**, 1480–90.

Vennerström, P, Söderhäll, K. & Cerenius, L. (1998). The origin of two crayfish plague (*Aphanomyces astaci*) epizootics in Finland on noble crayfish, *Astacus astacus*. *Annales Zoologici Fennici*, **35**(1), 43–6.

Vey, A., Söderhäll, K. & Ajaxon, R. (1983). Susceptibility of *Orconectes limosus* Raff. to the crayfish plague, *Aphanomyces astaci*. *Freshwater Crayfish*, **5**, 284–91.

Vié, J.-C., Hilton-Taylor, C., Pollock, C., et al. (2008). The IUCN Red List: a key conservation tool. In: J.-C. Vié, C. Hilton-Taylor and S. N. Stuart (eds). *The 2008 Review of the IUCN Red List of Threatened Species*. IUCN, Gland, Switzerland.

Vié, J.-C., Hilton-Taylor, C. & Stuart, S. N. (eds) (2009). *Wildlife in a Changing World: An Analysis of the 2008 IUCN Red List of Threatened Species*. IUCN, Gland, Switzerland.

Vigneux, E. (ed.) (1997). *Le genre Austropotamobius*. Special Issue, Volume 1. *Bulletin Français de la Pêche et de la Pisciculture*, **347**(4), 589–763.

Vigneux, E. (ed.) (2000). *Les espèces natives d'Europe*. Special Issue, Volume 2. *Bulletin Français de la Pêche et de la Pisciculture*, **356**(1), 1–155.

Vigneux, E. (ed.) (2001). *Interactions entre les écrevisses natives et d'autres espèces*. Special Issue, Volume 3. *Bulletin Français de la Pêche et de la Pisciculture*, **361**, 611–735.

Vigneux, E., Thibault, M., Marnell, F. & Souty-Grosset, C. (2002). National legislation, EU directives and conservation. *Bulletin Français de la Pêche et de la Pisciculture*, **367**, 887–98.

Vilà, M., Basnou, C., Pyšek, P., et al. (2009). How well do we understand the impacts of alien species on ecosystem services? A pan-European cross-taxa assessment. *Frontiers in Ecology and the Environment (online)*, **8**, 135–44.

Viljamaa-Dirks, S. Heinikainen, S., Nieminen, M., Vennerström, P., & Pelkonen, S. (2011). Persistent infection by crayfish plague *Aphanomyces astaci* in a noble crayfish population – a case report. *Bulletin of the European Association of Fish Pathologists*, **31** (5), in press.

Vitousek, P. M., Ehrlich, P., Ehrlich, A. & Matson, P. M. (1986). Human appropriation of the products of photosynthesis. *BioScience*, **36**(6), 368–73.

Vogt, G. (2008). Investigation of hatching and early post-embryonic life of freshwater crayfish by in vitro culture, behavioural analysis and light and electron microscopy. *Journal of Morphology*, **269**, 790–811.

Vörösmarty, C., Lettenmaier, D., Leveque, C., et al. (2004). Humans transforming the global water system. *EOS, American Geophysical Union Transactions*, **85**, 509–14.

Vörösmarty, C., Lévêque, C. & Revenga, C. (2005). Fresh water. In: *Millennium Assessment Working Group 2 Report: Conditions and Trends*. Island Press, Washington, DC.

Vrålstad, T., Knutsen, A. K., Tengs, T. & Holst-Jensen, A. (2009). A quantitative TaqMan MGB real-time polymerase chain reaction-based assay for detection of the causative agent of crayfish plague *Aphanomyces astaci*. *Veterinary Microbiology*, **137**, 146–55.

Walther, G. R., Roques, A., Hulme, P. E., et al. (2009). Alien species in a warmer world: risks and opportunities. *Trends in Ecology and Evolution*, **24**, 686–93.

Warren, M. L., Jr & Burr, B. M. (1994). Status of freshwater fishes of the United States: overview of an imperiled fauna. *Fisheries*, **19**(1), 6–8.

Weagle, K. V. & Ozburn, G. W. (1970). Sexual dimorphism in the chela of *Orconectes virilis* (Hagen). *Canadian Journal of Zoology*, **48**, 1041–2.

Welch, S. M. & Eversole, A. G. (2006). Comparison of two burrowing crayfish trapping methods. *Southeastern Naturalist*, **5**, 27–30.

Weller, C. (1973). *The Commercial Potential of Crayfish in Oregon and Washington*. Report to the Small Tribes Organization of Western Washington, prepared for Bureau of Indian Affairs, Washington DC, Contract No. 14–20–0500–3517: 9 pp.

Welsh, S. A., Loughman, Z. J. & Simon, T. P. (2010). Concluding remarks: A symposium on the conservation, biology and natural history of crayfishes from the southern United States. *Southeastern Naturalist*, **9** (Special Issue 3), 267–9.

Wenger, S. J. (2008). Use of surrogates to predict the stressor response of imperiled species. *Conservation Biology*, **22**(6), 1564–71.

Westman, K. (1973). Cultivation of the American crayfish *Pacifastacus leniusculus*. *Freshwater Crayfish*, **1**, 211–20.

Westman, K. (1991). The crayfish fishery in Finland: its past, present and future. *Finnish Fisheries Research*, **12**, 187–216.

Westman, K. (1992). Management of the noble crayfish *Astacus astacus* (L.) and the signal crayfish *Pacifastacus leniusculus* (Dana) in Finland. *Finnish Fisheries Research*, **14**, 39–51.

Westman, K. (1999). Review of historical and recent crayfish fishery, catch, trade and utilization in Finland. *Freshwater Crayfish*, **12**, 495–505.

Westman, K & Westman, P. (1992). Present status of crayfish management in Europe. *Finnish Fisheries Research*, **14**, 1–22.

Westman, K., Suman, O. & Pursiainen, M. (1978). Electric fishing in sampling crayfish. *Freshwater Crayfish*, **4**, 251–5.

Westman, K., Pursiainen, M. & Vilkman, R. (1979). A new folding trap model which prevents crayfish from escaping. *Freshwater Crayfish*, **4**, 235–42.

Westman, K., Pursiainen, M. & Westman, P. (1990). *Status of Crayfish Stocks: Fisheries, Diseases and Culture in Europe.* Report No. 3. Finnish Game & Fisheries Research Institute, Helsinki, Finland.

Westman, K., Savolainen, R. & Pursiainen, M. (1993). A comparative study on the growth and moulting of the noble crayfish *Astacus astacus* (L.) and the signal crayfish *Pacifastacus leniusculus* (Dana) populations in a small forest lake in southern Finland. *Freshwater Crayfish*, **9**, 451–65.

Wetzel, J. E., II & Brown, P. B. (1993). Growth and survival of juvenile *Orconectes virilis* and *Orconectes immunis* at different temperatures. *Journal of the World Aquaculture Society*, **24**, 330–43.

Whiting, A. S., Lawler, S. H., Horwitz, P. & Crandall, K. A. (2000). Biogeographic regionalization of Australia: assigning conservation priorities based on endemic freshwater crayfish phylogenetics. *Animal Conservation*, **3**, 155–63.

Wilcox, B. A. (1984). In situ conservation of genetic resources: determinants of minimum area requirements. In: J. A. McNeely & K. R. Miller (eds) *National Parks, Conservation and Development: Proceedings of the World Congress on National Parks.* Smithsonian Institution Press, Washington, DC: 18–20.

Williams, A. B. & Leonard, A. B. (1952). The crayfishes of Kansas. *University of Kansas Science Bulletin*, **34**, 961–1012.

Williams, D. D., Williams, N. E. and Hynes, H. B. N. (1974). Observations on the life history and burrow construction of the crayfish *Cambarus fodiens* (Cottle) in temporary streams in southern Ontario. *Canadian Journal of Zoology*, **52**, 365–70.

Williams, J. D., Warren, M. L., Jr, Cummings, K. S., Harris, J. L. & Neves, R. J. (1993). Conservation status of freshwater mussels of the United States and Canada. *Fisheries*, **18**(9), 6–22.

Williams, T. (1997). Killer weeds. *Audubon*, **99**, 24–31.

Williamson, M. & Fitter, A. (1996). The varying success of invaders. *Ecology*, **77**, 1661–6.

Wilson, E. O. (1988). *Biodiversity.* National Academic Press, Washington, DC.

Wilson, K. A., Magnuson, J. J., Kratz, T. K. & Willis, T. V. (2004). A longterm rusty crayfish (*Orconectes rusticus*) invasion: dispersal patterns and community changes in a north temperate lake. *Canadian Journal of Fisheries and Aquatic Sciences*, **61**, 2255–66.

Wilson, M. A. & Carpenter, S. R. (1999). Economic valuation of freshwater ecosystem services in the United States: 1971–1997. *Ecological Applications*, **9**, 772–83.

Wiltshire, E. & Reynolds, J. D. (2006). Bird predation on Turkish crayfish in central London. *London Naturalist*, **85**, 121–4.

Wingfield, M. J. (2002). An overview of the Australian freshwater crayfish industry. *Freshwater Crayfish*, **13**, 177–84.

Wright, R. & Williams, M. (2000). Long term trapping of signal crayfish at Wixoe on the River Stour, Essex. In: W. D. Rogers & J. Brickland (eds) *Proceedings of the Crayfish Conference held on 26th/27th April 2000 in Leeds*. Environment Agency, Bristol, UK: 81–8.

Wu, T. & Gao, P. (2008). Status and development prospects of the freshwater red swamp crayfish (in Chinese). *Inland Fisheries*, **2**, 15–17.

Xenopoulos, M. A., Lodge, D. M., Alcamo, J., et al. (2005). Scenarios of freshwater fish extinctions from climate change and water withdrawal. *Global Change Biology*, **11**, 1557–64.

Yildiz, H. Y., Koksal, G. & Benli, A. C. K. (2004). Physiological responses of the crayfish, *Astacus leptodactylus*, to saline water. *Crustaceana*, **77**, 1271–6.

Yue, G. H., Wang, G. L., Zhu, B. Q., et al. (2008). Discovery of four natural clones in a crayfish species *Procambarus clarkii*. *International Journal of Biological Sciences*, **4**, 279–82.

Zaccara, S., Stefani, F., Galli, P., Nardi, P. A. & Crosa, G. (2004). Taxonomic implications in conservation management of white-clawed crayfish (*Austropotamobius pallipes*) (Decapoda, Astacidae) in Northern Italy. *Biological Conservation*, **120**(1), 1–10.

Glossary

abdomen	the segmented hindmost part of the body. In decapods it is composed of six segments and a telson.
adaptation	a genetically determined characteristic that enhances an organism's ability to cope with its environment.
Allee threshold	critical population size or density below which the per capita population growth rate becomes negative.
allele	one of several forms of the same gene.
allochthonous	not indigenous.
allometric growth	phenomenon whereby parts of the same organism grow at different rates. The opposite of isometric growth.
allopatry	the occurrence of related organisms in separate geographical areas with no overlap.
Annulus ventralis	sperm storage structure found between the rear pereiopods on female cambarid crayfish.
antennae	the second pair of cephalic appendages.
antennules	first pair of cephalic appendages.
antibody	any of a large variety of proteins normally present in the body or produced in response to an antigen, which it neutralizes, thus producing an immune response.
Aphanomyces astaci	oomycetous pathogen responsible for the crayfish plague.
apomictic	without sexual reproduction.
appendage	any part of the body that is attached at one point but moves freely (e.g. antennae, walking legs, swimmerets).
ark sites	sites with suitable habitat for native crayfish, which are completely isolated from both non-native crayfish and crayfish plague.
asexual	type of reproduction involving formation of new individuals from one parent without DNA exchange.
autochthonous	within its natural area of distribution.
autocidal	interfering with reproduction: a method of pest control in which sterile or genetically altered crayfish are released to reduce the breeding success of the local crayfish population.

BAP	Biodiversity Action Plan.
BCMA	British Crayfish Marketing Association.
benthic invertebrates	aquatic invertebrates such as crustaceans and larval insects that inhabit the bottom of a stream or lake.
berried	term used to describe a female crayfish carrying eggs or a brood of young attached to her abdomen (ventral).
biogeography	the biological study of the geographical distribution of living organisms, e.g. crayfish.
bioindicator	an organism which requires specific ecological conditions.
biological diversity	the variability among living organisms from all sources, including terrestrial, marine and other aquatic ecosystems and the ecological complexes of which they are part, including diversity within and between species and between ecosystems.
biomagnification	sequence of processes in an ecosystem through which higher concentrations of a particular chemical, such as the pesticide DDT, are found in organisms higher up the food chain, generally through a series of prey–predator relationships.
bioturbation	disturbance of the soil or sediment by living things. It may include displacing soil by plant roots, digging by burrowing animals, pushing sediment aside, or eating and excreting sediment.
BMP	Best Management Practices, a term used in the USA and Canada to describe a type of water pollution control.
branchiobdellids	leech-like worms that are obligate ectosymbionts of crayfish.
buffer zone	the region near the border of a protected area; a transition zone between areas managed for different objectives.
burrow	the home of hypogean species; subterranean tunnel(s), usually having a circular or oval opening (on the ground in floodplains, in banks, or stream bottoms), and sometimes having a chimney.
burrower	crayfish that spends some of its life history confined in excavated burrows: Primary – crayfish that spend almost their entire lives in subterranean galleries; Secondary – crayfish that spend much of their lives in burrows but frequently move into open water during rainy seasons; Tertiary – crayfish that live in open water and retreat to burrows in response to several factors: (a) to remain below frost line during winter, (b) to find protective cover and to avoid desiccation as waterbodies disappear, (c) females enter as period of ovulation approaches and remain in burrows to lay and brood eggs.
Cambrian	major division of the geological timescale that began about 542 million years before the present (BP) at the end of the Proterozoic eon and

ended about 490 million years BP with the beginning of the Ordovician period. It is the first period of the Paleozoic era of the Phanerozoic eon. The Cambrian is the earliest period in whose rocks are found numerous large, distinctly fossilizable multicellular organisms that are more complex than sponges or medusoids. During this time, roughly 50 separate major groups of organisms or 'phyla', including almost all the basic body plans of modern animals, emerged suddenly, in most cases without evident precursors. This radiation of animal phyla is referred to as the Cambrian explosion.

carapace length (CL)	in crayfish, the distance from tip of rostrum to mid-caudodorsal margin of carapace.
carapace or dorsal shield	a shield (exoskeleton) overlying cephalothoracic somites of body; a shield-like, grooved but unjointed structure covering the cephalon (head) and thorax dorsally and forming the covering (branchiostegite) of the gill chamber laterally.
Carboniferous	period from about 355 million years to about 295 million years ago. The rocks formed during this time interval include a wide variety of sedimentary, igneous, and metamorphic rocks. Sedimentary rocks in the lower portion of the Carboniferous are typically carbonates, such as limestones and dolostones, and locally some evaporites.
carcinization	hypothesized process whereby a crustacean evolves into a crab-like form from a non-crab-like form.
caridoid facies	basic group of characters distinguishing Eumalacostracan crustaceans: enclosure of thorax by carapace, movable stalked eye, biramous antennules, antennae with scaphocerites, thoracopods with natatory exopods, ventrally flexed abdomen, and tail fan.
catchment	hydrographic basin, drainage basin.
caudal	posterior (rear, tail) end of organism.
CBD	United Nations Convention on Biological Diversity, which was opened for signature at the Rio de Janeiro 'Earth Summit' in 1992.
cephalic	pertaining to the head.
cephalothorax	term sometimes applied to the unjointed carapace, but more properly to the fusion of the five anterior cephalic segments and their appendages (antennae and mouthparts) with that of the thorax and its appendages (maxillipeds and pereiopods); portion of body bearing eyes and all appendages through fifth pereiopod (fused head and thorax), anterior to the abdomen.
cervical groove	groove dividing the carapace into cephalon and thorax.
cervical spine	spine on lateral surface of carapace immediately posterior to cervical groove of crayfish.
charophytes	group of submerged aquatic plants of ancient origin, ranging in height from a few cms to a metre, living entirely submerged in water.

chela (pl. chelae)	forceps-like structure (claw or pincer), consisting of two opposed distal podomeres, the dactyl (moveable finger) and propodus, of first, second, and third pereiopods of crayfish; (entire first walking leg is called the cheliped).
cheliped	the first pair of pereiopods. Pereiopods bearing chelae; in crayfish literature applied almost exclusively to first pereiopod.
chemotaxis	phenomenon in which organisms direct their movements according to certain chemicals in their environment.
chimney	evidence of a subterranean burrow (not all burrows have chimneys) indicated by a cylindrical pile of mudballs elevated above the surface.
chitinase	enzyme that breaks chitin and enables pathogens such as *Aphanomyces astaci* to penetrate and colonize the crayfish cuticle.
CITES	Convention of International Trade in Endangered Species of wild fauna and flora (www.cites.org).
clade	a branch of a diagram (tree) assumed to be an estimate of a phylogeny.
cladoceran	small crustaceans commonly called water fleas, part of the class Branchiopoda. They form a monophyletic group, which is currently divided into four suborders.
conservation	a discipline that embraces preservation, maintenance, sustainable utilization, restoration and enhancement of the natural environment.
constructed wetland	a system of artificially created marshy areas of vegetation with frequent flooding, designed to treat wastewater through natural biological processes.
COP-VI	Sixth Ordinary Meeting of the Conference of the Parties (COP) to the Convention on Biological Diversity, The Hague, 2002.
CPUE	catch per unit (of) effort.
crayfish	a small, lobster-like freshwater crustacean decapod.
crayfish plague	a crayfish disease caused by the fungus-like oomycete *Aphanomyces astaci* that has devastated the native European populations of crayfish.
CRAYNET	European thematic network: 'European crayfish as keystone species – linking science, management and economics with sustainable environmental quality'.
Cretaceous	third and last period of the Mesozoic era, between 145 and 65 million years ago (MYA), characterized by the development of flowering plants and ending with the sudden extinction of the dinosaurs and many other forms of life.
cryptobiota	small organisms, both eukaryotes and prokaryotes, lacking vernacular names.
cyclic dimorphism	form alteration in adult male American Cambaridae (Asian Cambaridae do not exhibit this phenomenon): **Form I** (breeding) occurs in the autumn, winter and spring, and **Form II** (non-breeding) occurs in summer.

cyanobacteria (blue-green algae, blue-green bacteria, Cyanophyta)	phylum of bacteria that obtain their energy through photosynthesis. Significant component of the marine nitrogen cycle and important primary producer in ocean, but also found on land.
DAISIE	Delivering Alien Invasive Species Inventories for Europe.
dimorphic	systematic difference in form between individuals of different sex.
DNA sequence	the relative order of base pairs, whether in a fragment of DNA (deoxyribonucleic acid) composition, e.g. of the molecule bringing the genetic information: a gene, a chromosome, or an entire genome.
dorsal	top or back of the crayfish. Directional term indicating the back or top of an animal or object.
DPIW	Department of Primary Industries and Water (Tasmania).
EC, EU	The European Commission (EC) is the executive body of the European Union of States (EU). The initials EC also stood for 'European Community' before the Treaty of Lisbon was adopted in 2009.
ecdysis	shedding of an outer integument or layer of skin, as by insects, crustaceans, and snakes; moulting.
ECISM	Proposed European Centre for Invasive Species Management.
ecological niche	milieu where an organism finds favourable living conditions (*syn.* habitat); term describing the relational position of a species or population in its ecosystem.
ecosystem engineer	any organism that creates or modifies habitats. Jones *et al.* (1994) identified two different types of ecosystem engineer: **Allogenic** engineers, modifying the environment by mechanically changing materials from one form to another; **Autogenic** engineers, modifying the environment by modifying themselves (particularly plants).
ecosystem service	fundamental life-support services upon which human civilization depends. The services provided by ecosystems that are of value to humans, e.g. food, water, shore protection, cultural values, regulation of climate.
ecosystem functions	ecological processes e.g. nutrient retention, succession, productivity, decomposition.
ecosystem health	an ecosystem is considered healthy if it is stable, resilient to stress and continuously provides a particular set of services.
ectocommensal	an ectosymbiont that feeds on the food particles liberated by the host during its feeding process.
ectosymbiont	a smaller species in an ecological association with a larger, host species where the smaller lives on the external surface of the host.
EIA	Environmental Impact Assessment.
EIFAC	European Inland Fisheries Advisory Commission.
Endangered (EN) species	*see* species / Endangered species.

endemic	organism native to a particular area (e.g. a peninsula, an island, a water drainage).
Eocene	pertaining to an epoch of the Tertiary period, lasting from about 56 to 34 MYA.
EPBC	Environmental Protection and Biodiversity Conservation Act 1999 (Australia).
epigean	an organism's activity above the substrate or soil surface.
epizootic	epidemic outbreak of disease in an animal population, often with the implication that it may extend to humans.
ESU (evolutionary significant unit)	the meaning has changed over the years. Originally ESUs were defined as separate population segments that contained distinct suites of adaptive variation. Moritz (1994) defined ESUs according to whether population segments were reciprocally monophyletic for mitochondrial DNA markers, and significantly different in one or more nuclear markers. ESUs are historically isolated lineages defined by molecular studies. For example, an ESU could be a population that is reproductively isolated from other populations of the same species, which therefore represents an important part of the evolutionary history and potential of the species.
eutrophication	high nutrient enrichment of waters; in aquatic systems, associated with wide swings in dissolved oxygen concentrations and frequent algal blooms.
exoskeleton	calcified covering of the body, which is shed at every moult.
exuvium/exuvia, moult cast	the cast-off exoskeleton after an animal has moulted.
fecundity	number of eggs laid by a female at one time (relative fecundity), or throughout its life (absolute fecundity).
flagship species	*see* species / flagship species.
Form I and Form II	alternative stages of life cycle in male American cambarid crayfish.
fyke-net	a fish trap consisting of a cylindrical net suspended over a series of hoops, laid horizontally in the water.
gene	the basic functional unit of heredity. A gene is typically transcribed into an RNA molecule; transcribed RNA can either be a functional endpoint itself (e.g. ribosomal RNA) or a messenger RNA that will be translated into a protein.
gene flow	the movement of genes between populations. This involves the migration of individuals from one population to another and subsequent successful mating.
genetic diversity	the variation in the genetic composition of individuals within or between species; the heritable genetic variation within and between populations.

genetic drift	a process driven by random sampling of gametes within each generation that can produce changes in allele frequencies over time. Genetic drift is more pronounced in small than in large populations.
genotype	often the complete suite of genes of a particular individual or group of individuals. Alternatively, the allelic composition of a locus or set of loci under study.
GIS (geographical information system)	computer mapping which links various databases to geographically scalable maps.
gonads	organs in males (testes) and in females (ovaries) which produce gametes, haploid germ cells.
gonado-somatic index (GSI)	calculation of gonad mass as a proportion of total body mass = [gonad weight / total tissue weight] × 100.
gonopods	modified first and second pairs of pleopods in male astacid crayfish.
habitat	milieu where an organism finds favourable living conditions (*syn*. biotope).
haemocyte	blood cells of invertebrates.
haemolymph	circulating and tissue-bathing fluid of arthropods; composed of cells and plasma, often loosely termed as 'blood'.
HAP	in the UK, a Habitat Action Plan, related to Biodiversity Action Plans.
haplotype	alternate form of a particular DNA sequence or gene. In conservation genetics, often used in reference to variants of genes of the haploid genomes of organelles (e.g. mitochondrial haplotypes).
harpacticoid copepods	order of the Copepoda, with about 1700 species known; most are benthic copepods found throughout the world in the marine environment and in fresh water. A few are planktonic or live in association with other organisms. Harpacticoida represents the second-largest meiofaunal group in marine sediment milieu.
heritage species	*see* species / heritage species.
hermaphrodite	animal or plant that normally possesses both male and female reproductive systems, producing both eggs and sperm.
heterozygous	having two different alleles in a locus. When used to refer to the whole genotype, indicates that the individual has different alleles at most loci. When used to refer to a species as having low or high heterozygosity relative to other species, this indicates that the species has a relatively high number of variable loci.
holarctic distribution	distribution of organisms found in both Eurasia and North America.

homotopic	organism spending its entire life cycle in one habitat; solely aquatic.
hybridization	crossing of individuals from genetically different strains, populations or species.
hyphae	cellular tubes characteristic of fungi.
hypogean	located under the Earth's surface; underground.
hyporheic	referring to the region of water exchange between groundwater and surface water; often inhabited by numerous invertebrates; interstices formed in substrate of streams (between coarse sand, gravel and cobble).
IAA	International Association of Astacology.
ICS	indigenous crayfish species.
IEEP	Institute for European Environmental Policy.
indicator species	*see* species / indicator species.
indigenous	a species native to a given geographical zone; original inhabitants.
intentional introduction	an introduction made deliberately by humans, involving the purposeful movement of a species outside its natural range and dispersal potential (with authorization or not).
introduction	human-assisted movement of species into an area where they did not formerly exist. Such introductions are made because of hunting, fishing, economic development, and as biological control agents.
introgression	the introduction of genes through hybridization with a distinct race or species.
invasive species	non-native (or alien) to the ecosystem under consideration and whose introduction or spread causes, or is likely to cause, economic or environmental harm or harm to human health.
IPCC	Intergovernmental Panel on Climate Change.
iteroparous	capable of breeding or reproducing multiple times.
IUCN	The International Union for Conservation of Nature (www.iucn.org) is the oldest and largest global conservation body. It brings together 78 states, 112 governmental agencies, 735 NGOs, 35 affiliates, and 10 000 scientists and other experts from 181 states. Its mission is to influence, encourage and assist societies throughout the world to conserve the integrity and diversity of nature and to ensure that any use of natural resources is equitable and ecologically sustainable.
JNCC	Joint Nature Conservation Committee. Adviser to the UK government on nature conservation issues.
Jurassic	geological period that extends from the end of the Triassic to the beginning of the Cretaceous (middle period of the Mesozoic era), about 200 to 145 MYA. During this time, the supercontinent Pangaea broke up into the northern supercontinent Laurasia and the southern supercontinent Gondwana.

keystone species	*see* species / keystone species.
K-selected species	selection favours organisms with a low rate of reproduction but whose populations expand to the maximum number of individuals that the habitat can support. Therefore, *K*-selected species tend to be highly adapted to their environment and are able to compete successfully for food and other resources. They also tend to inhabit stable environments and have relatively long life spans.
land use	the way that land is developed and used with reference to human activities such as agricultural, residential or commercial uses.
lentic	standing water environments (e.g. lakes, ponds, bogs, backwaters, swamps, temporary pools).
littoral zone	the area of water shallow enough to allow rooted macrophytes (aquatic plants) to grow; generally indicates waterbody edges, lake shores and peripheral shallows.
lotic	flowing waters (e.g. springs, brooks, streams, rivers).
MAFF	UK Ministry of Agriculture, Fisheries and Food, now replaced by DEFRA (Department for Environment, Food and Rural Affairs).
management units (MU)	populations/segments of a species that are functionally independent and have low current levels of gene flow among them. Management units are typically delineated based on statistically significant differences in allele frequencies for at least one locus.
mangrove	area of tropical evergreen trees or shrubs of the genus *Rhizophora*, having stilt-like intertwining aerial roots and growing below the highest tide levels in estuaries and along coasts, forming dense thickets.
mark–recapture method	method using marked animals, commonly used in ecology to estimate population size.
markers	*see* molecular markers.
MEA	Millennium Ecosystem Assessment, called for by UN Secretary-General Kofi Annan in 2000 and initiated in 2001. More than 1360 experts worldwide have collaborated to produce five technical volumes and six synthesis reports providing a state-of-the-art scientific appraisal of the conditions and trends in the world's ecosystems.
melanin	pigments largely of animal origin that are high-molecular-weight polymers of indole quinone. Colours include black/brown, yellow, red and violet. Found in feathers, cuttle ink, human skin, hair and eyes, and in cellular immune responses and wound healing in arthropods and crustaceans.
meiosis	cell division that produces reproductive cells in sexually reproducing organisms; the nucleus divides into four nuclei each containing half the chromosome number, leading to gametes in animals.

mesocosm	experimental closed and medium-sized design for ecological studies.
metapopulation	a group of spatially separated populations of the same species connected by dispersing individuals.
microcystins	cyclic non-ribosomal peptides produced by cyanobacteria: they are cyanotoxins and can be very toxic to animals, including humans.
microsatellite markers	microsatellites, also known as simple sequence repeats (SSRs) or short tandem repeats (STRs) are short, noncoding DNA sequences that are repeated many times within the genome of an organism. Many repeats tend to be concatenated at the same locus.
microsporidia	obligate intracellular parasites that appear to be phylogenetically closely related to fungi.
Miocene	pertaining to an epoch of the Tertiary period, the period from 25 to 10 MYA when grazing mammals became widespread.
mitigation	minimization of the potential impact of a threat or warning.
mitochondrial DNA (mtDNA)	a circular segment of DNA residing in the cell's mitochondria. In mammals, mtDNA makes up less than 1% of the total cellular DNA. It codes for some 30 proteins.
mitochondrial DNA RFLP (restriction fragment length polymorphism)	variation between individuals in mtDNA fragment sizes cut by specific restriction enzymes; polymorphic sequences that result in RFLPs are used as markers on both physical maps and genetic linkage maps. RFLPs are usually caused by mutation at a cutting site.
molecular markers	any Mendelian-inherited, usually variable, protein or nucleotide sequence used in molecular biology, evolutionary and ecological genetics, and conservation genetics.
monitoring	process of continually checking, observing, recording or testing the operation of some procedure (for example, after reintroducing a population).
moulting	the process of growing by shedding the exoskeleton and regrowing a new one (initially soft, hardening over time).
monophyly (monophyletic)	a term for a grouping of evolutionary lineages that includes a common ancestor and ALL descendant lineages.
MYA	million years ago.
native species	*see* species / native species.
nauplius	free-swimming first stage of the larva of some crustaceans, having an unsegmented body with three pairs of appendages and a single median eye.

Natura 2000	ecological network of protected areas in the territory of the European Union.
natural resources	environmental assets that include habitats such as land and water and the species of flora and fauna that are sustained by them.
NGO	non-governmental organization.
niche	in ecology, status of a species within its environment and community, and affecting its survival.
non-indigenous (exotic, introduced) species	plants and animals that originate elsewhere and migrate or are brought into an area.
NICS	non-indigenous crayfish species.
no-go areas	in the UK, areas where unlicensed keeping of non-indigenous crayfish is not permitted, in order to protect indigenous crayfish and their habitats.
obligate	an organism that requires a certain factor for a system to continue, e.g. life cycle of a branchiobdellidan requires the presence of a live crayfish.
OECD	Organisation for Economic Cooperation and Development.
OIE	Office International des Epizooties, the former name of the World Organization for Animal Health.
oligotrophic	for example a pond or a lake low in plant nutrients and having a large amount of dissolved oxygen throughout.
ontogeny	origin and development of an organism from the fertilized egg to its mature form.
oomycetes	group of filamentous protist organisms, traditionally considered fungi but of different phylogenetic origin.
ostracod	tiny marine and freshwater crustacean with a shrimp-like body enclosed in a bivalve shell (called seed shrimp).
overexploitation	excessive capture of specimens which does not permit integral restoration of stocks of reproducers.
ovigerous	carrying eggs.
ovotestis	hermaphroditic gonad that contains both testicular and ovarian tissue.
paraphyly (paraphyletic)	a phylogenetic term that refers to a group of organisms that includes a common ancestor and some, but not all, of its descendant lineages.
parasite	an organism that lives in or on the living tissue of a host organism at its expense.

parasitism	biological interaction between the host and the parasite. It is a type of symbiosis, by one definition, although another definition of symbiosis excludes parasitism, since it requires that the host benefit from the interaction as well as the parasite.
parthenogenetic	animal reproduction in which an unfertilized egg develops into a new individual.
pathogen	any disease-producing microorganism.
pathology	the anatomical or functional manifestations of disease.
PCA	principal component analysis.
pelagic	living or occurring in the waters of lakes or the open sea.
pereiopod	in decapods, one of five pairs of appendages (legs) supporting the cephalothorax; walking and chelate legs (as opposed to the five swimmerets).
Permian	the seventh and last period of the Paleozoic era, about 299 to 251 MYA, characterized by the formation of the supercontinent Pangaea, the rise of conifers, and the diversification of reptiles and ending with the largest known mass extinction in the history of life.
pheromone	chemical agent secreted by an animal that produces a change in the sexual or social behaviour of another individual of the same species; a volatile hormone that acts as a behaviour-altering agent.
phylogenetics	the study of the evolutionary affinities of groups of organisms.
phylogeny	the evolutionary history of a group of organisms, typically represented by a bifurcating tree.
phylogeography	the study of the geographical distribution of genetic variation emphasizing the evolutionary (phylogenetic) relationships between populations.
PIT tags	PIT stands for 'passive integrated transponder'. PIT tags are injected internally under the skin or into muscle of crayfish for studying their dispersal capability.
plague (crayfish)	disease lethal to crayfish caused by the pathogenic oomycete *Aphanomyces astaci*.
Pleistocene	pertaining to an epoch of the Tertiary period, from 2.6 MYA to about 12 000 years ago and including the last Ice Ages.
pleopods	appendages on the underside of the abdomen (tail) in malacostracans; in male astacid crayfish the first two pairs are modified into copulatory stylets.
pleura	lateral extensions of the abdominal segments in crayfish.
Pliocene	pertaining to an epoch of the Tertiary period, which occurred from 10 to 2 MYA, and was characterized by increased size and numbers of mammals, the growth of mountains and global climatic cooling.
poaching	taking fish illegally.

polymorphism	for a locus or suite of loci, the presence of two or more genotypes, alleles, or haplotypes within a population or species.
polyphyly (polyphyletic)	a phylogenetic term that refers to a group of lineages that are unrelated and have different recent common ancestors.
polytrophic	obtaining food from several different organic sources.
polysaccharide	any of a class of carbohydrates, such as starch and cellulose, consisting of a number of monosaccharides joined by glycosidic bonds.
population	a group of individuals with common ancestry that are much more likely to mate with one another than with individuals from another group.
population bottleneck	a severe, temporary reduction in effective population size.
porcelain disease	a crayfish disease caused by the microsporidian organism *Thelohania contejeani.*
postorbital carapace length	in crayfish, distance from orbit to mid-caudodorsal (posterior) margin of carapace.
pre-introduction	release of a species into an area where it was indigenous before it was exterminated by a natural event or by humans (e.g. overharvesting or habitat destruction).
precautionary principle	one of the primary foundations of the precautionary principle, and globally accepted definitions, results from the work of the Rio Conference, or 'Earth Summit' in 1992:
	'In order to protect the environment, the precautionary approach shall be widely applied by States according to their capabilities. Where there are threats of serious or irreversible damage, lack of full scientific certainty shall not be used as a reason for postponing cost-effective measures to prevent environmental degradation.'
	This definition is important for several reasons. First, it explains the idea that scientific uncertainty should not preclude preventative measures to protect the environment. Second, the use of 'cost-effective' measures indicates that costs can be considered. This is different from a 'no-regrets' approach, which ignores the costs of preventative action.
primary producer	organism producing biomass from inorganic compounds (autotrophs). In almost all cases it is a photosynthetically active organism.
prophenoloxidase	a melanin-synthesizing enzyme.
protected area	a legally established land or water area under either public or private ownership, that is regulated and managed to achieve specific conservation objectives.

Psorospermum	parasite of freshwater crayfish belonging to the protoctistan Mesomycetozoa clade that is phylogenetically located near the fungal animal divergence.
pyknosis	a degenerative state of the cell nucleus.
Ramsar Convention	The Convention on Wetlands of International Importance, especially as waterfowl habitat, is an international treaty for the conservation and sustainable utilization of wetlands.
recruitment (population)	the process of adding new individuals to a population or subpopulation (as of breeding or legally catchable individuals) by growth, reproduction, immigration, and stocking.
Red List (IUCN)	this list classifies species at high risk of global extinction in order to set priorities for conservation measures for protection of these species.
reintroduction	release of an organism to an area where it was formerly present, *see* restocking.
remediation	clean-up of a polluted site.
resilience	property of an ecosystem which characterizes ecosystem behaviour in relation to a perturbation.
restocking, reinforcement, supplementation	release of a species into an area where it is already present in order to increase its population size.
riparian	of, on, or relating to the banks of a natural body of water.
rostrum	the pointed, anterior extension of the crayfish carapace, partly covering the eyestalks and bases of antennae and antennules.
r-selected	species tending to be small in size, having large broods with high fatalities, and living in unpredictable environments where the probability of long-term survival is minimal. They may not live longer than is required to mate and reproduce.
SAC	Special Area of Conservation, corresponds exactly to Natura 2000 site.
Saprolegnia	genus of oomycetes that comprises saprophytic species often encountered on freshwater animals, as well as pathogenic species, e.g. *S. parasitica*.
saprophytic	an organism whose nutrition involves uptake of dissolved organic material from decaying plant or animal matter.
SCUBA	self-contained underwater breathing apparatus: portable apparatus containing compressed air used for breathing under water.
semelparous	reproducing only once during its lifetime.
semi-natural habitat	a habitat which has been detectably changed by human actions, or one which is managed by humans but still resembles a natural

	habitat in the diversity of its species and the complexity of their interrelationships.
sexual reproduction	a biological process by which organisms create descendants through the combination of genetic material.
sexually dimorphic	indicating that females and males of a taxon can be distinguished visually.
SMRT	sterile male release technique.
species	no single definition is agreed upon. A biological species is comprised of sets of organisms capable of producing viable, fertile offspring (i.e. an emphasis on reproductive compatibility). Phylogenetic species concepts emphasize the evolutionary history of groups of organisms, typically emphasizing monophyletic clusters of lineages that are diagnosably distinct from other such clusters, irrespective of such attributes as reproductive compatibility.
species / Endangered species	a species present in such small numbers that it is at risk of extinction. A species is considered as Endangered when it is not Critically Endangered but is facing a very high risk of extinction in the wild in the near future.
species / flagship species	a species that appeals to the public and has other features that make it suitable for communicating conservation concerns.
species / heritage species	an iconic species which is rare or very restricted in its distribution.
species / indicator species	a species whose presence indicates the presence of a set of other species and whose absence indicates the lack of that entire set of species, or a species believed to reflect the effects of a disturbance regime or the efficacy of efforts to mitigate disturbance effects.
species / keystone species	a species whose loss from an ecosystem would cause a greater than average change in other species' populations or ecosystem processes; whose continued well-being is vital for the functioning of a whole community.
species / native species	A species that occurs naturally in a particular geographical area, *syn.* indigenous species.
species / sibling	species very similar in appearance, behaviour and other characteristics although they are reproductively isolated.
species / species complex	a group of sibling species.
species / surrogate species	a species that is tested or examined to estimate responses of other species for which direct testing is impractical.
species / umbrella species	the protection of an umbrella species protects a wide range of coexisting species in the same habitat, which may be lesser known and difficult to protect otherwise.

species / vulnerable species	a species facing a high risk of extinction in the wild in the medium-term future.
spermatophore	capsule or compact mass of spermatozoa extruded by the males of crayfish and directly transferred to the reproductive parts of the female.
stakeholder	person who has an interest (stake) in a project or organization, such as a business.
subspecies	a subdivision of a species – a population or series of populations occupying a discrete range or differing genetically from other subspecies of the same species.
surber	sampler used for quantitative analysis of benthic stream organisms.
surrogate species	*see* species / surrogate species.
sustainable development	the strategy through which uses of natural resources are assured for short- and long-term production with minimal environmental destruction and loss to biological diversity.
sympatric / syntopic	organisms of different species living in a defined space in harmony.
systematics	the study of the historical evolutionary and genetic relationships between organisms and of their phenotypic similarities and differences.
taxonomy	the theory and practice of describing, naming and classifying plants and animals.
telson	terminal segment of the abdomen, divided by a transverse groove in crayfish.
Thelohania contejeani	microsporidian crayfish parasite that causes porcelain disease.
translocation	deliberate and mediated movement of an organism from one place with free release in another. It can be divided into three main classes: introduction, reintroduction, and restocking.
Triassic	geological period of the Mesozoic era, about 250–200 MYA, characterized by the diversification of land life, the rise of dinosaurs, and the appearance of the earliest mammals.
troglobyte, ite	animal living entirely in the dark parts of caves. Such animals are specifically adapted to life in total darkness, and may have no functioning eyes or have no pigmentation. Examples include some cambarid crayfish.
trophic niche	a group of independent traits characterizing consumer–resource links for a species.
tularemia	bacterial disease of northern regions transmitted by various Arthropoda, characterized by an ulcer at the site of inoculation that may develop into septicaemia.
umbrella species	see species / umbrella species.

UN	United Nations.
uropods	last paired appendages on the crayfish abdomen, forming tail fan with telson.
vaulted	used to describe the carapace of burrowing crayfish; raised rather than dorso-ventrally compressed, presumably to allow more room for gill respiration; vaulted carapaces often have very narrow or linear areolas.
ventral	underside of a crayfish or of its appendages.
virus	a small particle that can infect other biological organisms. Viruses are obligate intracellular parasites, meaning that they can only reproduce by invading and taking over other cells, because they lack the cellular machinery for self-reproduction.
Vulnerable (VU) species	see species / Vulnerable species.
watercourse	the bed or channel of a waterway.
WFD	European Commission (EC) or European Union (EU) Water Framework Directive (2000/60/EC).
zoospore	a motile flagellated asexual spore, as of certain algae, oomycetes and fungi.

Index

Note: It is advisable to check species entries under both common and scientific names (see end papers)